The
Random
House
Basic Dictionary

German-English
English-German

From the **Ballantine Reference Library**
Published by Ballantine Books:

The Random House Basic Dictionary

German-English
English-German

by Jenni Karding Moulton

Under the General Editorship of
Professor William G. Moulton
Princeton University

The Ballantine Reference Library
Ballantine Books · New York

Copyright © 1981, 1967, 1959 by Random House, Inc.

All rights reserved under International and Pan-American Copyright Conventions. Published in the United States by Ballantine Books, a division of Random House, Inc., New York, and simultaneously in Canada by Random House of Canada Limited, Toronto.

Library of Congress Catalog Card Number: 67-20647

ISBN 0-345-34600-9

This edition published by arrangement with Random House, Inc.

Previously published as *The German Vest Pocket Dictionary* and *The Random House German Dictionary*.

Manufactured in the United States of America

First Ballantine Books Edition: August 1981

22 21 20 19 18 17 16 15 14 13

Concise Pronunciation Guide

Consonants

b Usually like English *b:* **Bett, graben.** But when final or before *s* or *t*, like English *p:* **das Grab, des Grabs, er gräbt.**

c In foreign words only. Before *a, o, u,* like English *k:* **Café'.** Before *ä, e, i* in words borrowed from Latin, like English *ts:* **Cicero;** otherwise usually with the foreign pronunciation.

ch After *a, o, u, au,* a scraping sound like Scottish *ch* in *loch,* made between the back of the tongue and the roof of the mouth: **Dach, Loch, Buch, auch.** In other positions, much like English *h* in *hue:* **Dächer, Löcher, Bücher, ich, manch, welch, durch.** In words borrowed from Greek or Latin, initial *ch* before *a, o, u, l, r* is like English *k:* **Charak'ter, Chor, Christ.** In words borrowed from French it is like German *sch:* **Chance.**

chs As a fixed combination, like English *ks:* **der Dachs,** *the badger.* But when the *s* is an ending, like German *ch* plus *s:* **des Dachs,** genitive of **das Dach,** *the roof.*

ck As in English: **backen, Stock.**

d Usually like English *d:* **Ding, Rede.** But when final or before *s,* like English *t:* **das Band, des Bands.**

dt Like English *tt:* **Stadt** just like **statt.**

f As in English: **Feuer, Ofen, Schaf.**

g Usually like English *g* in *get:* **Geld, schlagen, Könige, reinigen.** But when final or before *s* or *t,* like English *k:* **der Schlag, des Schlags, er schlägt.** However, *ig* when final or before *s* or *t* is like German *ich:* **der König, des Königs, er reinigt.** In words borrowed from French, *g* before *e* is like English *z* in *azure:* **Loge.**

h As in English: **hier.** But after vowels it is only a sign of vowel length, and is not pronounced: **gehen, Bahn, Kuh.**

j Like English *y:* **Jahr.** In a few words borrowed from French, like English *z* in *azure:* **Journal'.**

k As in English: **kennen, Haken, buk.**

l Not the "dark *l*" of English *mill, bill,* but the "bright *l*" of English *million, billion:* **lang, fallen, hell.**

m As in English: **mehr, kommen, dumm.**

n As in English: **neu, kennen, kann.**

ng Always like English *ng* in *singer,* never like English *ng + g* in *finger.* German **Finger, Hunger.**

p As in English: **Post, Rippe, Tip.**

pf Like English *pf* in *cupful:* **Kopf, Apfel, Pfund.**

ph	As in English: **Philosophie'**.	
qu	Like English *kv:* **Quelle, Aqua'rium**.	
r	When followed by a vowel, either a gargled sound made between the back of the tongue and the roof of the mouth, or (less commonly) a quick flip of the tongue tip against the gum ridge: **Ring, Haare, bessere.** When not followed by a vowel, a sound much like the *ah* of English *yeah,* or the *a* of *sofa:* **Haar, besser.**	

Consonants

s	Usually like English *z* in *zebra,* or *s* in *rose:* **sie, Rose.** But when final or before a consonant, like English *s* in *this:* **das, Wespe, Liste, Maske.**
sch	Like English *sh* in *ship,* but with the lips rounded: **Schiff, waschen, Tisch.**
sp st	At the beginning of a word, like *sch* + *p, sch* + *t:* **Spiel, Stahl.**
ss ß	Like English *ss* in *miss. ss* is written only after a short vowel when another vowel follows: **müssen.** Otherwise ß is written: finally **muß,** before a consonant **mußte,** or after a long vowel **Muße.**
t	As in English: **tun, bitter, Blatt.**
th	Always like *t:* **Thea'ter;** never like English *th.*
tion	Pronounced *tsyohn:* **Nation', Aktion'.**
tsch	Like *t* + *sch:* **deutsch.**
tz	Like English *ts:* **sitzen, Platz.**
v	In German words, like English *f:* **Vater, Frevel.** In foreign words, like English *v:* **Novem'ber, Moti've;** but finally and before *s,* like *f*

	again: **das Motiv', des Motivs'.**	
w	Like English *v:* **Wagen, Löwe.**	
x	As in English: **Hexe.**	
z	Always like English *ts:* **zehn, Kreuz, Salz.**	

Short vowels

a	Satz	Between English *o* in *hot* and *u* in *hut.*
ä e	Sätze setze	Like English *e* in *set.*
i	sitze	Like English *i* in *sit.*
o	Stock	Like English *o* in *gonna,* or the "New England short *o*" in *coat, road;* shorter than English *o* in *cost.*
ö	Stöcke	Tongue position as for short *e,* lips rounded as for short *o.*
u	Busch	Like English *u* in *bush.*
ü y	Büsche mystisch	Tongue position as for short *i,* lips rounded as for short *u.*

Unaccented short e

e	beginne	Like English *e* in *begin, pocket.*

Long vowels

a ah aa	Tal Zahl Saal	Like English *a* in *father.*
ä äh	Täler zählen	In elevated speech, like English *ai* in *fair;* otherwise just like German long *e.*
e eh ee	wer mehr Meer	Like English *ey* in *they,* but with no glide toward a *y* sound.

i	mir	Like English *i* in *machine*, but with no glide toward a *y* sound.	ü	Hüte	Tongue position as for long *i*, lips rounded as for long *u*.
ih	ihr		üh	Kühe	
ie	Bier		y	Typ	

long vowels

Diphthongs

o	Ton	Like English *ow* in *slow*, but with no glide toward a *w* sound.	ei	Seite	Like English *i* in *side*. Also spelled *ey*, *ay* in names: *Meyer, Bayern*.
oh	Sohn		ai	Saite	
oo	Boot				
ö	Töne	Tongue position as for long *e*, lips rounded as for long *o*.	au	Haut	Like English *ou* in *out*.
öh	Sohne				
			eu	heute	Like English *oi* in *oil*.
			äu	Häute	
u	Hut	Like English *u* in *rule*, but with no glide toward a *w* sound.			
uh	Kuh				

The Spelling of vowel length

	Short	Long
An accented vowel is always short when followed by a doubled consonant letter, but nearly always long when followed by a single consonant letter.	schlaff	Schlaf
	wenn	wen
	still	Stil
	offen	Ofen
	öffnen	Öfen
Note that	Butter	Puter
	dünne	Düne
ck counts as the doubled form of k:	hacken	Haken
tz counts as the doubled form of z:	putzen	duzen
ss counts as the doubled form of ß:	Masse	Maße
Vowels are always long when followed by (unpronounced) h:	wann	Wahn
	stelle	stehle
	irre	ihre
	Wonne	wohne
	gönne	Söhne
	Rum	Ruhm
	dünn	kühn
Vowels are always long when they are written double:	Stadt	Staat
	Bett	Beet
	Gott	Boot
In this respect, ie counts as the doubled form of i:	bitte	biete

German Accentuation

Most German words are accented on the first syllable: **Mo'nate, ar'beitete, Düsenkampfflugzeuge.** However, the prefixes **be-, emp-, ent-, er-, ge-, ver-, zer-** are never accented: **befeh'len, der Befehl', empfan'gen, der Empfang'**, etc. Other prefixes are usually accented in nouns: **der Un'terricht,** but unaccented in verbs: **unterrich'ten.** Foreign words are often accented on a syllable other than the first: **Hotel'. Muse'um, Photographie'.**

Note particularly the accentuation of such forms as **übertre'ten, ich übertre'te** *I overstep,* where **über** is a prefix; but **ü'bertreten, ich trete... über** *I step over* where **über** is a separate word, despite the fact that **ü'bertreten** is spelled without a space. These two types will be distinguished in this dictionary by writing **übertre'ten** but **über•treten.**

German spelling does not indicate the place of the accent. In this dictionary, accent will be marked when it falls on a syllable other than the first: **Befehl', unterrich'ten, Photographie'.** Where it is not marked, the accent is on the first syllable: **Monate, arbeitete, Düsenkampfflugzeuge, Unterricht, über•treten.**

Nouns

This listing	means this
Wagen,-	plural is **Wagen**.
Vater,-	plural is **Väter**.
Tisch,-e	plural is **Tische**.
Sohn,-e	plural is **Söhne**.
Bild,-er	plural is **Bilder**.
Haus,-er	plural is **Häuser**.
Auge,-n	plural is **Augen**.
Ohr,-en	plural is **Ohren**.
Hotel',-s	plural is **Hotels'**.
Muse'um,-e'en	plural is **Muse'en**.
Doktor,-o'ren	plural is **Dokto'ren**.
Kopie',-i'en	plural is **Kopi'en**, with three syllables.
Kuß,-sse	final ß changes to medial **ss** because the **u** is short.
Fuß,-e	final ß kept in all forms because the **u** is long.
Junge,-n,-n	nominative singular is **Junge**, all other forms are **Jungen**.
Name(n),-	declined like **Wagen** (above), except that nominative singular is **Name**.
Beamt'-	takes adjective endings: **ein Beamter, der Beamte, zwei Beamte, die zwei Beamten.**
Milch	has no plural.
Leute, *n.pl.*	has no singular.

From almost any German noun meaning some kind of man or boy, a noun meaning the corresponding woman or girl can be formed by adding **-in**: **der Arbeiter** *worker (man or boy)*, **die Arbeiterin** *worker (woman or girl)*; **der Russe** *Russian (man or boy)*, **die Russin** *Russian (woman or girl)*. Such feminine nouns will not usually be listed in this dictionary, unless they involve some sort of irregularity: **der Franzo'se**, *Frenchman*, **die Franzö'sin** *Frenchwoman* (irregular because of the umlaut).

Adjectives

Most German adjectives can also be used, without ending, as adverbs: **schlecht** *bad, badly*. The few which never occur without ending as adverbs are listed with a following hyphen: **link-** *left*, **ober-** *upper*, **zweit-** *second*. (The corresponding adverbs are **links** *to the left*, **oben** *above*, **zweitens** *secondly*.)

Adjectives which take umlaut in the comparative and superlative are listed as follows: **lang (⁻)**, i.e., the comparative and superlative are **länger**, **längst-**.

Limiting or determining adjectives are listed in the nominative singular masculine, with an indication of the nominative singular neuter and feminine: **der, das, die, dieser,-es,-e; ein,-,-e.**

Descriptive adjectives take the following endings:

| | Strong endings | | | | Weak endings | | | |
	masc.	neut.	fem.	pl.	masc.	neut.	fem.	pl.
nom.	-er	-es	-e	-e	-e	-e	-e	-en
acc.	-en	-es	-e	-e	-en	-e	-e	-en
dat.	-em	-em	-er	-en	-en	-en	-en	-en
gen.	-en	-en	-er	**-er**	-en	-en	-en	-en

Weak endings are used if the adjective is preceded by an inflected form of a limiting (determining) adjective; strong endings are used otherwise.

Verbs

Regular weak verbs are listed simply in the infinitive: **machen**. If a verb is used with a separable prefix (accented adverb), this is indicated by a raised dot: **auf·machen** (i.e., the infinitive is **aufmachen**, the present **ich mache... auf**, the past **ich machte... auf**, the past participle **aufgemacht**). An asterisk after a verb refers to the following lists of irregular weak and strong verbs. The sign † means that a verb takes the auxiliary verb **sein**; the sign ‡ means that a verb can take either **sein** or **haben**.

Irregular weak verbs

Infinitive	3rd sg. present	Past	Subjunctive	Past participle
haben	hat	hatte	hätte	gehabt
bringen	bringt	brachte	brächte	gebrach
denken	denkt	dachte	dächte	gedacht
dünken	dünkt, deucht	dünkte, deuchte	dünkte, deuchte	gedünkt, gedeucht
brennen	brennt	brannte	brennte	gebrannt
kennen	kennt	kannte	kennte	gekannt
nennen	nennt	nannte	nennte	genannt
†rennen	rennt	rannte	rennte	gerannt
senden	sendet	sandte	sendete	gesandt
wenden	wendet	wandte	wendete	gewandt
dürfen	darf	durfte	dürfte	gedurft

Infinitive	3rd sg. present	Past	Subjunctive	Past participle
können	kann	konnte	könnte	gekonnt
mögen	mag	mochte	mohe	gemocht
müssen	muß	mußte	müßte	gemußt
sollen	soll	sollte	sollte	gesollt
wollen	will	wollte	wollte	gewollt
wissen	weiß	wußte	wüßte	gewußt

Strong verbs

If a derived or compound verb is not listed, its forms may be found by consulting the simple verb. The sign + means that a regular weak form is also used.

Infinitive	3rd sg. present	Past	Subjunctive	Past participle
backen	bäckt	+buk	+büke	gebacken
befehlen	befiehlt	befahl	beföhle	befohlen
beginnen	beginnt	begann	begönne, begänne	begonnen
beißen	beißt	biß	bisse	gebissen
bergen	birgt	barg	bärge	geborgen
†bersten	birst	barst	bärste	geborsten
bewegen	bewegt	bewog	bewöge	bewogen
‡beigen	biegt	bog	böge	gebogen
bieten	bietet	bot	böte	geboten
binden	bindet	band	bände	gebunden
bitten	bittet	bat	bäte	gebeten
blasen	bläst	blies	bliese	gablasen
†bleiben	bleibt	blieb	bliebe	geblieben
braten	brät	briet	briete	gebraten
brechen	bricht	brach	bräch	gebrochen
dingen	dingt	+dang	+dänge	+gedungen
dreschen	drischt	drosch, drasch	drösche, dräsche	gedroschen
†dringen	dringt	drang	dränge	gedrungen
†erbleichen	erbleicht	+erblich	+erbliche	+erblichen
erlöschen	erlischt	erlosch	erlösche	erloschen
essen	ißt	aß	äße	gegessen
‡fahren	fährt	fuhr	führe	gefahren
†fallen	fällt	fiel	fiele	gefallen
fangen	fängt	fing	finge	gefangen
fechten	ficht	focht	föchte	gefochten
finden	findet	fand	fände	gefunden
flechten	flicht	flocht	flöchte	geflochten
‡fliegen	fliegt	flog	flöge	geflogen
†fliehen	flieht	floh	flöhe	geflohen
†fließen	fließt	floß	flösse	geflossen
fressen	frißt	fraß	fräße	gefressen
frieren	friert	fror	fröre	gefroren
gären	gärt	+gor	+göre	+gegoren
gebären	gebiert	gebar	gebäre	geboren
geben	gibt	gab	gäbe	gegeben
†gedeihen	gedeiht	gedieh	gediehe	gediehen
†gehen	geht	ging	ginge	gegangen
†gelingen	gelingt	gelang	gelänge	gelungen

Infinitive	3rd sg. present	Past	Subjunctive	Past participle
gelten	gilt	galt	gölte, gälte	gegolten
†genesen	genest	genas	genäse	genesen
genießen	genießt	genoß	genösse	genossen
†geschehen	geschieht	geschah	geschähe	geschehen
gewinnen	gewinnt	gewann	gewönne gewänne	gewonnen
gießen	gießt	goß	gösse	gegossen
gleichen	gleicht	glich	gliche	geglichen
†gleiten	gleitet	glitt	glitte	geglitten
glimmen	glimmt	+glomm	+glömme	+geglommen
graben	gräbt	grub	grübe	gegraben
greifen	greift	griff	griffe	gegriffen
halten	hält	hielt	hielte	gehalten
hängen	hängt	hing	hinge	gehangen
hauen	haut	+hieb	+hiebe	gehauen
heben	hebt	hob, hub	höbe, hübe	gehoben
heißen	heißt	hieß	heiße	geheißen
helfen	hilft	half	hülfe, hälfe	geholfen
klimmen	klimmt	+klomm	+klömme	+geklommen
klingen	klingt	klang	klänge	geklungen
kneifen	kneift	kniff	kniffe	gekniffen
†kommen	kommt	kam	käme	gekommen
†kriechen	kriecht	kroch	kröche	gekrochen
laden	lädst	lud	lüde	geladen
lassen	läßt	ließ	leiße	gelassen
†laufen	läuft	lief	liefe	gelaufen
leiden	leidet	litt	litte	gelitten
leihen	leiht	lieh	liehe	geliehen
lesen	liest	las	läse	gelesen
liegen	liegt	lag	läge	gelegen
lügen	lügt	log	löge	gelogen
meiden	meidet	mied	miede	gemieden
melken	+milkt	+molk	+mölke	+gemolken
messen	mißt	maß	mäße	gemessen
mißlingen	mißlingt	mißlang	mißlänge	mißlungen
nehmen	nimmt	nahm	näme	genommen
pfeifen	pfeift	pfiff	pfiffe	gepfiffen
preisen	preist	pries	priese	gepriesen
quellen	quillt	quoll	quölle	gequollen
raten	rät	riet	riete	geraten
reiben	reibt	rieb	riebe	gerieben
†reißen	reißt	riß	risse	gerissen
†reiten	reitet	ritt	ritte	geritten
riechen	riecht	roch	röche	gerochen

Infinitive	3rd sg. present	Past	Subjunctive	Past participle
ringen	ringt	rang	ränge	gerungen
rinnen	rinnt	rann	ränne, rönne	geronnen
rufen	ruft	rief	riefe	gerufen
saufen	säuft	soff	söffe	gesoffen
saugen	saugt	+sog	+söge	+gesogen
schaffen	schafft	schuf	schüfe	geschaffen
schallen	schallt	+scholl	+schölle	geschallt
‡scheiden	scheidet	schied	schiede	geschieden
scheinen	scheint	schien	schiene	geschienen
schelten	schilt	schalt	schölte	gescholten
scheren	schert	+schor	+schöre	+geschoren
schieben	schiebt	schob	schöbe	geschoben
schießen	schießt	schoß	schösse	geschossen
schinden	schindet	schund	schünde	geschunden
schlafen	schläft	schlief	schliefe	geschlafen
schlagen	schlägt	schlug	schlüge	geschlagen
†schleichen	schleicht	schlich	schliche	geschlichen
schleifen	schleift	schliff	schliffe	geschliffen
schließen	schließt	schloß	schlösse	geschlossen
schlingen	schlingt	schlang	schlänge	geschlungen
schmeißen	schmeißt	schmiß	schmisse	geschmissen
schmeizen	schmilzt	schmolz	schmölze	geschmolzen
schnauben	schnaubt	+schnob	+schnöbe	+geschnoben
schneiden	schneidet	schnitt	schnitte	geschnitten
schrecken	schrickt	schrak	schräke	geschrocken
schreiben	schreibt	schrieb	schriebe	geschrieben
schreien	schreit	schrie	schriee	geschrie(e)n
†schreiten	schreitet	schritt	schritte	geschritten
schweigen	schweigt	schwieg	schwiege	geschwiegen
schwellen	schwillt	schwoll	schwölle	geschwollen
‡schwimmen	schwimmt	schwamm	schwömme, schwämme	geschwommen
†schwinden	schwindet	schwand	schwände	geschwunden
schwingen	schwingt	schwang	schwänge	geschwungen
schwören	schwört	+schwur, schwor	+schwüre	+geschworen
sehen	sieht	sah	sähe	gesehen
sein	ist	war	wäre	gewesen
sieden	siedet	+sott	+sötte	+gesotten
singen	singt	sang	sänge	gesungen
†sinken	sinkt	sank	sänke	gesunken
sinnen	sinnt	sann	sänne, sönne	gesonnen
sitzen	sitzt	saß	säße	gesessen
speien	speit	spie	spiee	gespie(e)n

Infinitive	3rd sg. present	Past	Subjunctive	Past participle
spinnen	spinnt	spann	spönne, spänne	gesponnen
spleißen	spleißt	spliß	splisse	gesplissen
sprechen	spricht	sprach	spräche	gesprochen
sprießen	sprießt	sproß	sprösse	gesprossen
†springen	springt	sprang	spränge	gesprungen
stechen	sticht	stach	stäche	gestochen
stecken	steckt	+stak	+stäke	gesteck
stehen	steht	stand	stände, stünde	gestanden
stehlen	stiehlt	stahl	stähle, stöhle	gestohlen
†steigen	steigt	stieg	stiege	gestiegen
†sterben	stirbt	starb	stürbe	gestorben
‡stieben	stiebt	+stob	+stöbe	+gestoben
stinken	stinkt	stank	stänke	gestunken
‡stoßen	stößt	stieß	stieße	gestoßen
streichen	streicht	strich	striche	gestrichen
streiten	streitet	stritt	stritte	gestritten
tragen	trägt	trug	trüge	getragen
treffen	trifft	traf	träfe	getroffen
‡treiben	treibt	trieb	triebe	getrieben
‡treten	tritt	trat	träte	getreten
trinken	trinkt	trank	tränke	getrunken
trügen	trügt	trog	tröge	getrogen
tun	tut	tat	täte	getan
verbleichen	verbleicht	verblich	verbliche	verblichen
verderben	verdirbt	verdarb	verdürbe	verdorben
verdrießen	verdrießt	verdroß	verdrösse	verdrossen
vergessen	vergißt	vergaß	vergäße	vergessen
verlieren	verliert	verlor	verlöre	verloren
†wachsen	wächst	wuchs	wüchse	gewachsen
wägen	wägt	wog	wöge	gewogen
waschen	wäscht	wusch	wüsche	gewaschen
weben	webt	+wob	+wöbe	+gewoben
weichen	weicht	wich	wiche	gewichen
weisen	weist	wies	wiese	gewiesen
werben	wirbt	warb	würbe	geworben
†werden	wird	wurde, (ward)	würde	geworden
werfen	wirft	warf	würfe	geworfen
wiegen	wiegt	wog	wöge	gewogen
winden	windet	wand	wände	gewunden
wringen	wringt	wrang	wränge	gewrungen
zeihen	zeiht	zieh	ziehe	geziehen
‡ziehen	zieht	zog	zöge	gezogen
zwingen	zwingt	zwang	zwänge	gezwungen

Abbreviations

abbr.	abbreviation	*intr.*	intransitive
adj.	adjective	*jur.*	juridical
adv.	adverb	*m.*	masculine
arch.	architecture	*math.*	mathematics
art.	article	*med.*	medicine
bot.	botany	*mil.*	military
chem.	chemistry	*n.*	noun
comm.	commercial	*naut.*	nautical
conj.	conjunction	*nt.*	neuter
cpds.	compounds	*num.*	number
eccles.	ecclesiastical	*pl.*	plural
econ.	economics	*pol.*	politics
elec.	electricity	*pred.*	predicate
f.	feminine	*prep.*	preposition
fam.	familiar	*pron.*	pronoun
fig.	figuratively	*sg.*	singular
geogr.	geography	*tech.*	technical
geom.	geometry	*tr.*	transitive
gov't.	government	*typogr.*	typography
gram.	grammar	*vb.*	verb
interj.	interjection	*zool.*	zoology

Useful Phrases

Hello *(or)* How do you do?   Guten Tag.
Good morning.   Guten Morgen.
Good evening.   Guten Abend.
How are you?   Wie geht es Ihnen?
Fine, thanks, and you?   Gut, danke, und Ihnen?
I'm fine, too, thanks.   Auch gut, danke.
Please.   Bitte.
Thank you.   Danke schön.
You're welcome.   Bitte schön.
Good luck.   Alles Gute.
Good night.   Gute Nacht.
Good-bye.   Auf Wiedersehen.

Can you please help me?   Können Sie mir bitte helfen?
Do you understand me?   Verste'hen Sie mich?
I don't understand you.   Ich verste'he Sie nicht.
Please speak slowly.   Sprechen Sie bitte langsam.
Please say it again.   Sagen Sie es bitte noch einmal.
I don't speak German very well.   Ich spreche nicht sehr gut Deutsch.
Do you speak English?   Sprechen Sie Englisch?
What do you call that in German?   Wie heißt das auf deutsch?
How do you say…in German?   Wie sagt man…auf deutsch?
What's your name, please?   Wie heiß en Sie bitte?
My name is…   Ich heiße…

What time is it?   Wieviel Uhr ist es?
How much does that cost?   Wieviel kostet das?
I'd like to buy…   Ich möchte gern…kaufen.
I'd like to eat.   Ich möchte gernessen.
Where is there a good restaurant?   Wo ist hier ein gutes Restaurant?
I'm hungry (thirsty).   Ich habe Hunger (Durst).

Waiter, the check, please.   Herr Ober, bitte zahlen.
Where is there a good hotel?   Wo ist hier ein gutes Hotel'?

How do I get to the station?   Wie komme ich zum Bahnhof?
I'm sick.   Ich bin krank.
I need a doctor.   Ich brauche einen Arzt.
I want to send a telegram.   Ich möchte gern ein Telegramm' schicken.

Where can I change money?   Wo kann ich hier Geld wechseln?
Do you accept travelers checks?   Nehmen Sie Reiseschecks?
Right away.   Sofort'.
Help!   Hilfe!
Come in.   Herein'.
Hello (*on telephone*).   Hier... (*say your name*).
Stop.   Halt.
Hurry.   Schnell.
To the right.   Rechts.
To the left.   Links.
Straight ahead.   Gera'de aus.

Signs

Vorsicht	Caution
Achtung	Watch out
Ausgang	Exit
Eingang	Entrance
Halt	Stop
Geschlossen	Closed
Geöffnet	Open
Langsam	Slow
Verboten	Prohibited
Gesperrt	Road closed
Einbahnstraße	One way street
Raucher	For smokers
Nichtraucher	For non-smokers
Rauchen verboten	No smoking
Kein Zutritt	No admittance
Damen (*or*) **Frauen**	Women
Herren (*or*) **Männer**	Men
Abort	Toilet

Weights and Measures

The Germans use the *Metric System* of weights and measures, which is a decimal system in which multiples are shown by the prefixes: Dezi- (one tenth); Zenti- (one hundredth); Milli- (one thousandth); Deka- (ten); Hekto- (hundred); Kilo- (thousand).

1 Zentimeter	=	.3937 inches
1 Meter	=	39.37 inches
1 Kilometer	=	.621 mile
1 Zentigramm	=	.1543 grain
1 Gramm	=	15.432 grains
1 Pfund (½ Kilogramm)	=	1.1023 pounds
1 Kilogramm	=	2.2046 pounds
1 Tonne	=	2,204 pounds
1 Zentiliter	=	.338 ounces
1 Liter	=	1.0567 quart (liquid); .908 quart (dry)
1 Kiloliter	=	264.18 gallons

Numerals

Cardinal

1	eins	32	zweiunddreißig
2	zwei	40	vierzig
3	drei	43	dreiundvierzig
4	vier		
5	fünf	50	fünfzig
6	sechs	54	vierundfünfzig
7	sieben	60	sechzig
8	acht	65	fünfundsechzig
9	neun	70	siebzig
10	zehn	76	sechsundsiebzig
11	elf		
12	zwölf	80	achtzig
13	dreizehn	87	siebenundachtzig
14	vierzehn		
15	fünfzehn	90	neunzig
16	sechzehn	98	achtundneunzig
17	siebzehn		
18	achtzehn	100	hundert
19	neunzehn	101	hunderteins
20	zwanzig	202	zweihundertzwei
21	einundzwanzig	1,000	tausend
30	dreißig	1,000,000	eine Million'

Ordinal

1st	erst	14th	vierzehnt-
2nd	zweit-	15th	fünfzehnt-
3rd	dritt-	16th	sechzehnt-
4th	viert-	17th	siebzehnt-
5th	fünft-	18th	achtzehnt-
6th	sechst-	19th	neunzehnt-
7th	sieb(en)t-	20th	zwanzigst-
8th	acht-	21st	einundzwanzigst-
9th	neunt-	30th	dreißigst-
10th	zehnt-	32nd	zweiunddreißigst-
11th	elft-	40th	vierzigst-
12th	zwölft-	43rd	dreiundvierzigst-
13th	dreizehnt-	50th	fünfzigst-

54th	vierundfünfzigst-	90th	neunzigst-
60th	sechzigst-	98th	achtundneunzigst-
65th	fünfundsechzigst-	100th	hundertst-
70th	siebzigst-	101st	hunderterst-
76th	sechsundsiebzigst-	202nd	zweinhundertzweit-
80th	achtzigst-	1,000th	tausendst-
87th	siebenundachtzigst-	1,000,000	millionst'-

Decimals

Instead of a decimal point, a comma is used:

English: 3.82 "three point eight two"
German: 3,82 „drei Komma acht zwei"

Fractions

the half; half a pound	die Hälfte; ein halbes Pfund
one and a half	anderthalb, eineinhalb
the third; two-thirds	das Drittel; zweidrittel
the fourth; three-fourths	das Viertel; dreiviertel
the fifth; four-fifths	das Fünftel; vierfünftel

Days of the Week

Sunday	der Sonntag
Monday	der Montag
Tuesday	der Dienstag
Wednesday	der Mittwoch
Thursday	der Donnerstag
Friday	der Freitag
Saturday	der Sonnabend
	or der Samstag

Months

January	der Januar	July	der Juli
February	der Februar	August	der August'
March	der März	September	der Septem'ber
April	der April'	October	der Okto'ber
May	der Mai	November	der Novem'ber
June	der Juni	December	der Dezem'ber

German-English

A

Aachen, n.nt. Aachen, Aix-la-Chapelle.

Aal, -e, n.m. eel.

ab, adv. down; off; **(ab Berlin)** leaving Berlin; **(ab heute)** from today on.

ab-ändern, vb. revise.

Abänderung, -en, n.f. variation, revision.

Abart, -en, n.f. variety, species.

Abbau, n.m. working; reduction, razing.

ab-bauen, vb. raze; mine.

Abbild, -er, n.nt. image, effigy.

ab-blenden, vb. dim (headlights).

ab-brechen*, vb. break off; cease, stop.

Abbruch, -e, n.m. breaking off; cessation; damage.

ab-danken, vb. abdicate.

Abdankung, -en, n.f. abdication.

Abdruck, -e, n.m. (printed) impression, copy.

Abdruck, -e, n.m. impress, mark, cast.

Abend, -e, n.m. evening; **(zu A. essen*)** dine, have dinner.

Abendbrot, -e, n.nt. supper.

Abenddämmerung, -en, n.f. dusk.

Abendessen, -, n.nt. dinner, supper.

Abendland, n.nt. Occident.

abendländisch, adj. occidental.

abendlich, adj. evening.

Abendmahl, -e, n.nt. Holy Communion, Lord's Supper.

abends, adv. in the evening.

Abenteuer, -, n.nt. adventure.

abenteuerlich, adj. adventurous.

Abenteurer, -, n.m. adventurer.

aber, conj. but.

Aberglaube(n), -, n.m. superstition.

abergläubisch, adj. superstitious.

abermals, adv. once again.

Abessi'nien, n.nt. Abyssinia.

ab-fahren*, vb. leave, depart.

Abfahrt, -en, n.f. departure.

Abfall, -e, n.m. slope; decrease; defection; rubbish.

ab-fallen*, vb. fall off; decrease; revolt.

abfällig, adj. precipitous; derogatory.

ab-fangen*, vb. intercept.

ab-fassen, vb. draw up, compose.

ab-fertigen, vb. take care of, expedite.

ab-feuern, vb. discharge (gun).

ab-finden*, vb. **(sich a. mit)** put up with.

Abfluß, -sse, n.m. drain(age), outlet.

ab-führen, vb. lead off.

Abführmittel, -, n.nt. laxative.

Abgabe, -n, n.f. levy.

Abgasbestimmungen, n.f.pl. emission controls.

ab-geben*, vb. hand over; check (baggage); cast (vote).

abgebrüht, adj. hard-boiled.

abgedroschen, adj. trite.

abgelegen, adj. remote.

abgemacht, adj. settled, agreed.

abgeneigt, adj. averse, disinclined.

abgenutzt, adj. worn-out.

Abgeordnet-, n.m.&f. representative, deputy.

abgeschieden, adj. separated, secluded; departed.

abgesehen von, prep. aside from.

ab-gewinnen*, vb. gain from.

Abgott, -er, n.m. idol.

Abgötterei, -en, n.f. idolatry.

Abgrenzung, -en, n.f. demarcation.

Abgrund, -e, n.m. abyss, precipice.

ab-halten*, vb. hold off, restrain, deter.

abhan'den, adv. missing; **(a. kommen*)** get lost.

Abhandlung, -en, n.f. treatise.

Abhang, -e, n.m. slope.

ab-hängen*, vb. depend.

abhängig, adj. dependent.

Abhängigkeit, n.f. dependence.

ab-härten, vb. harden.

ab-helfen*, vb. remedy.

Abhilfe, -n, n.f. remedy, relief.

abhold, adj. averse, disinclined.

ab-holen, vb. go and get, pick up, call for.

ab-hören, vb. listen to, monitor.

Abitur', -e, n.nt. final examination at end of secondary school; high school degree.

Abkehr, n.f. turning away.

Abkomme, -n, -n, n.m. descendant, offspring.

Abkommen, -, n.nt. convention; agreement.

Abkömmling, -e, n.m. offspring, descendant; derivative.

ab-kühlen, vb. cool off.

ab-kürzen, vb. abbreviate, abridge.

Abkürzung, -en, n.f. abbreviation; abridgment.

ab-laden*, vb. unload.

Ablage, -n, n.f. depot, place of deposit.

Ablaß, -sse, n.m. letting off, drainage; (eccles.) indulgence.

ab-lassen*, vb. let off, drain; desist.

Ablativ, -e, n.m. ablative.

Ablauf, n.m. running off, expiration.

ab-laufen*, vb. run off, expire.

Ablaut, -e, n.m. ablaut (vowel alteration, as in singen, sang, gesungen).

ab-legen, vb. discard, take off.

ab-lehnen, vb. decline, reject.

Ablehnung, -en, n.f. rejection.

ab-leiten, vb. derive.

Ableitung, -en, n.f. derivation.

ab-lenken, vb. divert, distract.

Ablenkung, -en, n.f. diversion, distraction.

ab-leugnen, vb. deny, disavow.

Ableugnung, -en, n.f. denial, disavowal.

Ablichtung, -en, n.f. photocopy.

ab-liefern, vb. deliver.

Ablieferung, -en, n.f. delivery.

ab-lösen, vb. relieve.

Ablösung, -en, n.f. relief.

Abmarsch, -e, n.m. marching off, departure.

ab-melden, vb. report the departure of.

ab-mühen, vb. (sich a.) toil.

Abnahme, -n, n.f. decrease.

abnehmbar, adj. removable.

ab-nehmen*, vb. (tr.) take off, remove; (intr.) decrease, lose weight.

Abnehmer, -, n.m. purchaser.

Abneigung, -en, n.f. antipathy, dislike, aversion.

abnorm', adj. abnormal.

ab-nötigen, vb. force from.

ab-nutzen, vb. wear (something) out.

Abnutzung, n.f. wearing out.

Abonnement', -s, n.nt. subscription.

abonnie'ren, vb. subscribe.

Abordnung, -en, n.f. delegation.

Abort, -e, n.m. toilet.

Abort', -e, n.m. abortion.

ab-rackern, vb. (sich a.) drudge.

ab-raten*, vb. dissuade.

ab-räumen, vb. clear off.

ab-rechnen, vb. settle accounts.

Abrechnung, -en, n.f. settlement of accounts.

Abrede, -n, n.f. (in A. stellen) deny.

Abreise, -n, n.f. departure.

ab-reisen, vb. depart.

ab-reißen*, vb. tear off; demolish.

Abriß, -sse, n.m. outline, summary.

ab-rüsten, vb. disarm.

Abrüstung, -en, n.f. disarmament.

Absage, -n, n.f. refusal (of an invitation), calling off.

ab-sagen, vb. decline, revoke.

Absatz, -e, n.m. paragraph; heel; landing; sale, market.

ab-schaben, vb. scrape off, abrade.

ab-schaffen*, vb. abolish.

Abschaffung, -en, n.f. abolition.

ab-schätzen, vb. appraise, estimate.

Abschätzung, -en, n.f. appraisal, estimate.

Abschaum, n.m. dregs.

Abscheu, n.m. abhorrence, loathing.

abscheu'lich, adj. abominable, detestable.

Abschied, -e, n.m. departure, leave, farewell.

Abschlag, -e, n.m. chips; repulse; refusal.

ab-schlagen*, vb. chip off; repel; refuse.

abschlägig, adj. negative, refusing.

ab-schleifen*, vb. grind off, abrade.

ab-schließen*, vb. lock up, close off; conclude.

Abschluß, -sse, n.m. conclusion.

ab-schneiden*, vb. cut off.

Abschnitt, -e, n.m. section.

ab-schrecken, vb. frighten off.

abschreckend, adj. forbidding.

Abschreckung, n.f. deterrence.

Abschreckungsmittel, -, n.nt. deterrent.

ab-schreiben*, vb. copy.

Abschrift, -en, n.f. copy.

abschüssig, adj. precipitous.

ab-schweifen, vb. digress.

ab-schwören*, vb. abjure.

Abschwörung, -en, n.f. abjuration.

absehbar, adj. foreseeable.

ab-sehen*, vb. look away; see from; (a. von) give up; (auf mich abgesehen) aimed at me; (ist abzusehen) can be seen.

abseits, adv. aside, apart.

ab-senden*, vb. send off, mail.

Absender, -, n.m. sender.

Absendung, -en, n.f. dispatch.

ab-setzen, vb. set off, set down, depose.

Absicht, -en, n.f. intent, purpose; (mit A.) on purpose.

absichtlich, adj. intentional.

absolut', adj. absolute.

absolvie'ren, vb. absolve; complete; finish (school); pass (an examination).

abson'derlich, adj. peculiar.

ab-sondern, vb. separate, detach; secrete.

absorbie'ren, vb. absorb.

Absorbie'rungsmittel, -, n.nt. absorbent.

Absorption', -en, n.f. absorption.

ab-spannen, vb. loosen (tension), relax.

ab-spielen, vb. (sich a.) occur, take place.

ab-splittern, vb. chip.

Absprache, -n, n.f. agreement.

ab-sprechen*, vb. deny.

ab-springen*, vb. jump down, bail out (of a plane).

Absprung, -e, n.m. jump down, parachute jump; digression.

ab-stammen, vb. be descended.

Abstammung, -en, n.f. descent, ancestry; derivation.

Abstand, -e, n.m. distance, interval; (von etwas A. nehmen*) renounce.

ab-statten, vb. grant; (einen Besuch a.) pay a visit.

ab-stauben, vb. dust.

Abstecher, -, n.m. digression, side trip.

ab-stehen*, vb. stand off, stick out.

ab-steigen*, vb. descend, dismount; put up at (an inn).

ab-stellen, vb. put away; turn off.

ab-stempeln, vb. stamp, cancel.

ab-sterben*, vb. die out.

Abstieg, -e, n.m. descent.

ab-stimmen, vb. vote.

Abstimmung, -en, n.f. vote, plebiscite.

abstinent', adj. abstinent.

Abstinenz', n.f. abstinence.

ab-stoßen*, vb. knock off, repel, repulse.

abstoßend, adj. repulsive.

abstrahie'ren, vb. abstract.

abstrakt', adj. abstract.

Abstraktion', -en, n.f. abstraction.

ab-streifen, vb. strip.

Abstufung, -en, n.f. gradation.

ab-stumpfen, vb. become dull, blunt; make dull, blunt.

Absturz, -e, n.m. fall, crash.

ab-stürzen, vb. fall, crash.

absurd', adj. absurd.

Abszeß', -sse, n.m. abscess.

Abtei', -en, n.f. abbey.

Abteil, -e, n.nt. compartment.

Abtei'lung, -en, n.f. division, section.

ab-tragen*, vb. wear out.

ab-treiben*, vb. drive off; cause an abortion.

Abtreibung, -en, n.f. abortion.

ab-trennen, vb. detach.

ab-treten*, vb. cede.

Abtretung, -en, n.f. withdrawal, cession, surrender.

Abtritt, -e, n.nt. departure, exit; latrine.

ab-tun*, vb. put aside, settle.

ab-wägen*, vb. weigh out, consider.

ab-wandeln, vb. change, inflect.

ab-wandern, vb. depart, migrate.

ab-warten, vb. wait (to see what will happen), bide one's time.

abwärts, adv. downwards.

ab-waschen*, vb. wash off.

Abwaschung, -en, n.f. ablution.

ab-wechseln, vb. alternate, take turns.

abwechselnd, adj. alternate.

Abwechs(e)lung, -en, n.f. change, alternation.

Abweg, -e, n.m. wrong way,

devious path; (auf A.e geraten*) go astray.

abwegig, adj. errant.

Abwehr, n.f. warding off, defense.

Abwehrdienst, -e, n.m. counterintelligence service.

ab-wehren, vb. ward off, prevent.

ab-weichen*, vb. deviate, depart.

Abweichung, -en, n.f. deviation, departure.

ab-weisen*, vb. send away, repulse.

ab-wenden*, vb. turn away, deflect, avert.

ab-werfen*, vb. throw down, shed.

ab-werten, vb. devaluate.

Abwertung, -en, n.f. devaluation.

abwesend, adj. absent.

Abwesende-, n.m.&f. absent person, absentee.

Abwesenheit, -en, n.f. absence.

ab-wickeln, vb. unwind.

ab-winken, vb. gesture "no".

Abwurf, -e, n.m. throwing down; thing thrown down.

ab-zahlen, vb. pay off.

ab-zählen, vb. count off.

ab-zapfen, vb. draw off, tap.

ab-zehren, vb. waste away, consume.

Abzeichen, -, n.nt. badge, medal, insignia.

ab-ziehen*, vb. (tr.) draw off, subtract, deduct; (intr.) march off.

Abzug, -e, n.m. marching off, departure; drawing off, subtraction, drain; print; trigger.

ab-zwingen*, vb. force away from, extort.

Acetylen', n.nt. acetylene.

ach, interj. oh.

Achat', -e, n.m. agate.

Achse, -n, n.f. axis, axle.

Achsel, -n, n.f. shoulder.

acht, num. eight.

acht-, adj. eighth.

Acht, n.f. attention, care; (sich in A. nehmen*) watch out, be on one's guard; (außer A. lassen*) pay no attention to, neglect.

Achtel, -, n.nt. eighth part; (ein a.) one-eighth.

achten, vb. respect; (a. auf) pay attention to.

ächten, vb. outlaw, ostracise.

achtern, adv. aft.

acht-geben*, vb. watch out, pay attention.

acht-haben*, vb. watch out, pay attention.

achtlos, adj. heedless.

achtsam, adj. attentive.

Achtung, n.f. attention, regard, esteem; (A.!) watch out! attention!

achtzehn, num. eighteen.

achtzehnt-, adj. eighteenth.

achtzig, num. eighty.

achtzigst-, *adj.* eightieth.

Achtzigstel, -, *n.nt.* eightieth part; **(ein a.)** one-eightieth.

ächzen, *vb.* groan, moan.

Acker, ∷, *n.m.* field.

Ackerbau, *n.m.* farming.

addie'ren, *vb.* add.

ade', *interj.* adieu.

Adel, *n.m.* nobility.

Ader, -n, *n.f.* vein.

adieu, *interj.* adieu.

Adjektiv, -e, *n.nt.* adjective.

adjekti'visch, *adj.* adjectival.

Adjutant', -en, -en, *n.m.* adjutant, aide, aide-de-camp.

Adler, -, *n.m.* eagle.

Adler-, *cpds.* aquiline.

Adlig, *adj.* noble.

Adlig-, *n.m.&f.* nobleman, -woman.

Admiral', -e, *n.m.* admiral.

Admiralität', -en, *n.f.* admiralty.

adoptie'ren, *vb.* adopt.

Adoption', -en, *n.f.* adoption.

Adres'se, -n, *n.f.* address.

adressie'ren, *vb.* address.

adrett', *adj.* trim, smart.

Advent', *n.m.* Advent, each of the four Sundays before Christmas.

Adverb', -ien, *n.nt.* adverb.

adverbial', *adj.* adverbial.

Advokat', -en, -en, *n.m.* lawyer.

Aeronau'tik, *n.f.* aeronautics.

Affä're, -n, *n.f.* affair, love affair.

Affe, -n, -n, *n.m.* ape, monkey.

Affekt', -e, *n.m.* affect.

affektiert', *adj.* affected.

Affektiert'heit, -en, *n.f.* affectation.

äffen, *vb.* ape, mock.

Affix, -e, *n.nt.* affix.

Affront', -s, *n.m.* affront, snub.

Afrika, *n.nt.* Africa.

Afrika'ner-, -, *n.m.* African.

afrika'nisch, *adj.* African.

AG, *abbr.* (= Aktiengesellschaft) company.

Agent', -en, -en, *n.m.* agent.

Agentur', -en, *n.f.* agency.

Aggression', -en, *n.f.* aggression.

aggressiv', *adj.* aggressive.

agie'ren, *vb.* act.

Agno'stiker, -, *n.m.* agnostic.

agno'stisch, *adj.* agnostic.

Ägyp'ten, *n.nt.* Egypt.

Ägyp'ter, -, *n.m.* Egyptian.

ägyp'tisch, *adj.* Egyptian.

Ahn, -en, *n.m.* ancestor.

Ahne, -n, *n.f.* ancestress.

ähneln, *vb.* resemble.

ahnen, *vb.* have any idea (that something will happen); forebode.

ähnlich, *adj.* similar.

Ähnlichkeit, -en, *n.f.* similarity.

Ahnung, -en, *n.f.* foreboding; hunch; **(ich habe keine A.)** I have no idea.

ahnungslos, *adj.* unsuspecting.

ahnungsvoll, *adj.* ominous.

Ahorn, -e, *n.m.* maple tree.

Ähre, -n, *n.f.* ear (of grain).

Ajatol'lah, -s, *n.m.* ayatollah.

Akade'mie, -'ien, *n.f.* academy.

akade'misch, *adj.* academic.

Aka'zie, -n, *n.f.* acacia.

Akkord', -e, *n.m.* chord.

akkreditie'ren, *vb.* accredit.

Akku'mula'tor, -to'ren, *n.m.* battery.

Akkusativ, -e, *n.m.* accusative.

Akne, -n, *n.f.* acne.

Akrobat', -en, -en, *n.m.* acrobat.

Akt, -e, *n.m.* act; nude (drawing).

Akte, -n, *n.f.* document, dossier, file.

Aktenmappe, -n, *n.f.* brief case.

Aktie, -n, *n.f.* share (of stock).

Aktiengesellschaft, -en, *n.f.* corporation, stock company.

Aktion', -en, *n.f.* action, undertaking.

Aktionär', -e, *n.m.* stockholder.

aktiv', *adj.* active.

aktivie'ren, *vb.* activate.

Aktivie'rung, -en, *n.f.* activation.

aktuell', *adj.* topical.

Akupunktur', -en, *n.f.* acupuncture.

Aku'stik, *n.f.* acoustics.

aku'stisch, *adj.* acoustic.

akut', *adj.* acute.

Akzent', -e, *n.m.* accent.

akzentuie'ren, *vb.* accentuate.

Alarm', -e, *n.m.* alarm, alert.

alarmie'ren, *vb.* alarm, alert.

Alaun', -e, *n.m.* alum.

albern, *adj.* silly.

Albi'no, -s, *n.m.* albino.

Album, -ten, *n.nt.* album.

Alchimie', *n.f.* alchemy.

Alchimist', -en, -en, *n.m.* alchemist.

Alge, -n, *n.f.* alga.

Algebra, *n.f.* algebra.

algebra'isch, *adj.* algebraic.

alias, *adv.* alias.

Alibi, -s, *n.nt.* alibi.

Aliment', -e, *n.nt.* alimony.

Alka'li, -en, *n.nt.* alkali.

alka'lisch, *adj.* alkaline.

Alkohol, -e, *n.m.* alcohol.

Alkoho'liker, -, *n.m.* alcoholic.

alkoho'lisch, *adj.* alcoholic.

Alko'ven, -, *n.m.* alcove.

All, *n.nt.* universe.

all; aller, -es, -e, *pron.&adj.* all.

Allee', -'e'en, *n.f.* avenue.

Allegorie', -'ien, *n.f.* allegory.

allein', **1.** *adv.* alone. **2.** *conj.* but.

allei'nig, *adj.* sole, only.

allemal, *adv.* always; **(ein für a.)** once and for all.

allenfalls, *adv.* in any case.

allenthal'ben, *adv.* everywhere.

aller-, *cpds.* of all; **allerbest'**, best of all; etc.

allerart, *adv.* all sorts of.

allerdings', *adv.* certainly, to be sure, indeed.

Allergie', -'l'en, *n.f.* allergy.

allerhand, *adv.* all sorts of; **(das ist ja a.)** that's tremendous, that's the limit.

allerlei, *adv.* all sorts of.

alles, *pron.* everything.

allesamt, *adv.* altogether.

allgemein, *adj.* general, common; **(im a. en)** generally, in general.

Allgemein'heit, -en, *n.f.* generality, general public.

Allianz', -en, *n.f.* alliance.

Alliga'tor, -o'ren, *n.m.* alligator.

alliie'ren, *vb.* ally.

Alliiert'-, *n.m.&f.* ally.

alljähr'lich, *adj.* annual.

allmäch'tig, *adj.* almighty, omnipotent.

allmäh'lich, *adj.* gradual.

allmo'natlich, *adj.* monthly.

allnächt'lich, *adj.* nightly.

Alltag, -e, *n.m.* weekday, tedium.

alltäg'lich, *adj.* daily, routine.

allzu, *adv.* all too.

Almanach, -e, *n.m.* almanac.

Almosen, -, *n.nt.* alms.

Alpdruck, ∷e, *n.m.* nightmare.

Alpen, *n.pl.* Alps.

Alphabet', -e, *n.nt.* alphabet.

alphabe'tisch, *adj.* alphabetical.

alphabetisie'ren, *vb.* alphabetize.

als, *conj.* as, when; than.

alsbald', *adv.* immediately.

alsdann', *adv.* thereupon.

also, *adv.* so, thus, and so, hence, therefore.

alt, *adj.* old.

Alt, -e, *n.m.* alto.

Altar', ∷e, *n.m.* altar.

Altar'diener, -, *n.m.* acolyte.

Alter, -, *n.nt.* age.

altern, *vb.* age.

alternativ', *adj.* alternative.

Alternati've, -n, *n.f.* alternative.

Altertum, -ümer, *n.nt.* antiquity.

altertüm'lich, *adj.* archaic.

Altertumskunde, *n.f.* archaeology.

Ältest-, *n.m.* elder.

alther'gebracht, *adj.* traditional.

Altjahrsa'bend, -e, *n.m.* New Year's Eve.

altklug, ∷, *adj.* precocious.

ältlich, *adj.* elderly.

altmodisch, *adj.* old-fashioned.

Altruis'mus, *n.m.* altruism.

Altstimme, -n, *n.f.* alto.

Alumi'nium, *n.nt.* aluminum.

Amal'gam', -e, *n.nt.* amalgam.

amalgamie'ren, *vb.* amalgamate.

Amateur', -e, *n.m.* amateur.

Amboß, -sse, *n.m.* anvil.

ambulant', *adj.* ambulatory.

Ameise, -n, *n.f.* ant.

Ame'rika, *n.nt.* America.

Amerika'ner, -, *n.m.* American.

amerika'nisch, *adj.* American.

Amethyst', -e, n.m. amethyst.

Ammoniak, n.nt. ammonia.

Amnestie', -i'en, n.f. amnesty.

Amö'be, -n, n.f. amoeba.

amoralisch, adj. amoral.

amortisie'ren, vb. amortize.

Ampere, -, (pron. Ampär') n.nt. ampere.

amphi'bisch, adj. amphibious.

amputie'ren, vb. amputate.

Amputiert'-, n.m.&f. amputee.

Amt, "er, n.nt. office.

amtie'ren, vb. officiate.

amtlich, adj. official.

Amtseinführung, -en, n.f. inauguration.

Amtsschimmel, n.m. red tape.

Amtstratsch, n.m. grapevine, gossip.

amüsie'ren, vb. amuse; (sich a.) have a good time.

an, prep. at, on, to.

Anachronis'mus, -men, n.m. anachronism.

analog', adj. analogous.

Analogie', -i'en, n.f. analogy.

analo'gisch, adj. analogical.

Analphabet', -en, -en, n.m. illiterate.

Analphabe'tentum, n.nt. illiteracy.

Analy'se, -n, n.f. analysis.

analysie'ren, vb. analyze.

Analy'tiker, -, n.m. analyst.

analy'tisch, adj. analytic(al).

Anarchie', -i'en, n.f. anarchy.

Anästhesie', n.f. anesthesia.

Anatomie', -i'en, n.f. anatomy.

Anbau, -ten, n.m. cultivation; addition (to a house).

Anbeginn, n.m. origin.

anbei', adv. inclosed, herewith.

an-beten, vb. worship, adore.

Anbetracht, n.m. (in A.) in view of.

Anbetung, -en, n.f. adoration.

an-bieten*, vb. offer.

Anblick, -e, n.m. sight, view, appearance.

an-brechen*, vb. begin; break; (der Tag bricht an) day breaks, dawns.

Anbruch, "e, n.m. beginning, (day)break, (night)fall.

Andacht, -en, n.f. devotion.

andächtig, adj. devout.

andauernd, adj. continual.

Andenken, -, n.nt. memory, memorial, souvenir.

ander-, adj. other, different.

and(e)rerseits, adv. on the other hand.

ändern, vb. change, alter.

anders, adv. otherwise, else.

anderswie, adv. otherwise.

anderswo, adv. elsewhere.

anderthalb, num. one and a half.

Änderung, -en, n.f. change, alteration.

an-deuten, vb. indicate, imply.

Andeutung, -en, n.f. indication, implication.

Andrang, n.m. rush, crowd.

an-drehen, vb. turn on.

an-eignen, vb. seize, appropriate.

Aneignung, -en, n.f. seizure, appropriation.

aneinan'der, adv. to one another, together.

Anekdo'te, -n, n.f. anecdote.

an-ekeln, vb. disgust.

an-erkennen* (or anerken'nen*), vb. acknowledge.

anerkennenswert, adj. creditable.

Anerkennung, -en, n.f. acknowledgment, recognition.

an-fahren*, vb. drive up against, collide with; hit; speak sharply to.

Anfall, "e, n.m. attack.

an-fallen*, vb. fall upon, attack.

Anfang, "e, n.m. beginning.

an-fangen*, vb. begin.

Anfänger, -, n.m. beginner.

anfänglich, adj. initial.

anfangs, adv. in the beginning.

an-fassen, vb. take hold of, grasp.

an-fechten*, vb. assail.

an-fertigen, vb. prepare, manufacture.

an-feuchten, vb. moisten.

an-feuern, vb. fire, incite, inspire.

an-flehen, vb. beseech.

an-fliegen*, vb. fly at.

Anflug, "e, n.m. approach flight, slight attack, touch.

an-fordern, vb. claim, demand.

Anfrage, -n, n.f. inquiry, application.

an-freunden, vb. (sich a. mit) befriend.

an-führen, vb. lead on; allege; cite; dupe.

Anführung, -en, n.f. leadership; quotation, allegation.

Anführungsstrich, -e, n.m. quotation mark.

Anführungszeichen, n.nt. quotation mark.

Angabe, -n, n.f. fact cited, statement, assertion; (pl.) data.

an-geben*, vb. cite as a fact, state, assert; brag, boast.

Angeber, -, n.m. boaster.

Angeberei', -en, n.f. boast, boastfulness.

angeberisch, adj. boastful.

angeblich, adj. as stated, alleged.

angeboren, adj. innate, congenital.

Angebot, -e, n.nt. bid, offer.

angebracht, adj. proper.

angeheiratet, adj. related by marriage.

an-gehen*, vb. concern.

angehend, adj. beginning, incipient.

an-gehören, vb. belong to.

angehörig, adj. belonging to.

Angehörig-, n.m.&f. dependent.

Angeklagt-, n.m.&f. accused, defendant.

Angel, -n, n.f. hinge, axis; fishing tackle.

angelegen, adj. important, of concern.

Angelegenheit, -en, n.f. matter, concern, affair.

angelehnt, adj. leaned against, ajar.

angeln, vb. fish, angle.

angemessen, adj. adequate, appropriate, suitable.

angenehm, adj. pleasant, agreeable.

angesehen, adj. respected, respectable.

Angesicht, -er, n.nt. face.

Angestellt-, n.m.&f. employee.

angewandt, adj. applied.

an-gewöhnen, vb. accustom to.

Angewohnheit, -en, n.f. habit, custom.

an-gleichen*, vb. assimilate, adjust.

Angleichung, -en, n.f. assimilation.

Angler, -, n.m. fisherman.

an-gliedern, vb. affiliate.

Angliederung, -en, n.f. affiliation.

angreifbar, adj. assailable.

an-greifen*, vb. attack, assault.

Angreifer, -, n.m. attacker, aggressor.

an-grenzen, vb. abut, border on.

angrenzend, adj. contiguous.

Angriff, -e, n.m. attack, aggression.

Angriffslust, n.f. aggressiveness.

Angst, "e, n.f. fear; (A. haben*, A. sein*) be afraid.

ängstigen, vb. frighten.

ängstlich, adj. timid, anxious.

an-haben*, vb. have on, wear.

Anhalt, -e, n.m. hold; basis.

an-halten*, vb. (tr.) stop, arrest; (intr.) last, continue.

anhaltend, adj. lasting.

Anhaltspunkt, -e, n.m. point of reference, basis, clue.

Anhang, "e, n.m. appendix; adherents.

Anhänger, -, n.m. follower; pendant; trailer.

an-häufen, vb. amass, accumulate.

Anhäufung, -en, n.f. accumulation.

an-heften, vb. affix, attach.

anheim'stellen, vb. submit.

Anhieb, -e, n.m. first stroke; (auf A.) right away, right off the bat.

an-hören, vb. listen to.

Anilin', n.nt. aniline.

Ankauf, "e, n.m. purchase.

an-kaufen, vb. buy.

Anker, -, n.m. anchor.

Ankerplatz, "e, n.m. anchorage.

an-ketten, vb. chain.

Anklage, -n, *n.f.* accusation, indictment, impeachment.

an-klagen, *vb.* accuse, indict, impeach.

Ankläger, -, *n.m.* accuser, plaintiff.

an-klammern, *vb.* fasten (with a clamp); (**sich a.**) cling.

an-kommen*, *vb.* arrive; (**a. auf**) depend upon.

an-kündigen, *vb.* announce.

Ankunft, ⁻e, *n.f.* arrival.

an-kurbeln, *vb.* crank up, get started.

Anlage, -n, *n.f.* arrangement, disposition, investment; enclosure; (*pl.*) grounds.

an-langen, *vb.* (*tr.*) concern; (*intr.*) arrive.

Anlaß, ⁻sse, *n.m.* cause, motivating factor.

an-lassen*, *vb.* leave on; start.

Anlasser, -, *n.m.* starter.

anläßlich, *prep.* on the occasion of.

Anlauf, ⁻e, *n.m.* start, warmup; attack.

an-laufen*, *vb.* run at, make for; swell, rise.

an-legen, *vb.* put on; invest; land.

an-lehnen, *vb.* lean against, leave ajar.

Anleihe, -n, *n.f.* loan.

an-leiten, *vb.* lead to, instruct.

Anleitung, -en, *n.f.* instruction.

an-lernen, *vb.* train.

an-machen, *vb.* fix, attach, turn on.

an-maßen, *vb.* assume, presume.

anmaßend, *adj.* arrogant, presumptuous.

Anmaßung, -en, *n.f.* arrogance, presumption.

an-melden, *vb.* announce.

Anmeldung, -en, *n.f.* announcement, report, registration.

an-merken, *vb.* note.

Anmerkung, -en, *n.f.* (foot)note.

an-messen*, *vb.* measure for, fit.

Anmut, *n.f.* grace, charm.

anmutig, *adj.* graceful.

an-nähern, *vb.* approach.

annähernd, *adj.* approximate.

Annäherung, -en, *n.f.* approach, approximation.

Annahme, -n, *n.f.* acceptance, adoption; assumption, supposition.

annehmbar, *adj.* acceptable.

an-nehmen*, *vb.* accept, assume, suppose, infer.

Annehmlichkeit, -en, *n.f.* pleasure, agreeableness.

Annonce, -n, *n.f.* advertisement.

annonci'ren, *vb.* advertise.

annulli'ren, *vb.* annul.

Anomalie, -l'en, *n.f.* anomaly.

anonym', *adj.* anonymous.

an-ordnen, *vb.* order, arrange.

Anordnung, -en, *n.f.* order, arrangement.

an-packen, *vb.* grab hold of, get started with.

an-passen, *vb.* adapt, fit, try on; (**sich a.**) conform.

Anpassung, -en, *n.f.* adaptation.

anpassungsfähig, *adj.* adaptable, adaptive.

Anprall, *n.m.* collision, impact.

an-preisen*, *vb.* praise, recommend.

Anprobe, -n, *n.f.* fitting.

Anrecht, -e, *n.nt.* right, claim.

Anrede, -n, *n.f.* address, speech.

an-reden, *vb.* speak to, accost.

an-regen, *vb.* stimulate, incite.

Anregung, -en, *n.f.* stimulation; suggestion.

Anreiz, -e, *n.m.* stimulus, incentive.

an-reizen, *vb.* incite.

Anruf, -e, *n.m.* appeal, (telephone) call.

an-rufen*, *vb.* appeal to, invoke; call up.

Anrufung, *n.f.* invocation.

an-rühren, *vb.* touch; (cooking) mix.

an-sagen, *vb.* announce.

Ansager, -, *n.m.* announcer.

an-sammeln, *vb.* amass; (**sich a.**) congregate, gather.

Ansammlung, -en, *n.f.* collection, backlog.

ansässig, *adj.* resident.

Ansatz, ⁻e, *n.m.* start; estimate; charge; added piece.

an-schaffen*, *vb.* get, obtain.

Anschaffung, -en, *n.f.* acquisition.

an-schauen, *vb.* look at.

anschaulich, *adj.* graphic, clear.

Anschauung, -en, *n.f.* view, opinion.

Anschein, -e, *n.m.* appearance.

anscheinend, *adj.* apparent.

Anschlag, ⁻e, *n.m.* stroke; poster; estimate; plot.

an-schlagen*, *vb.* (*tr.*) strike; affix, fasten, post; estimate; (*intr.*) work, start to function.

an-schließen*, *vb.* fasten with a lock, adjoin; (**sich a.**) join; fit tight.

Anschluß, -sse, *n.m.* connection, annexation.

an-schnallen, *vb.* buckle on.

an-schneiden*, *vb.* start cutting.

an-schreiben*, *vb.* write down, score, charge.

Anschrift, -en, *n.f.* address.

an-sehen*, *vb.* look at.

Ansehen, *n.nt.* reputation, repute.

ansehnlich, *adj.* handsome; considerable, notable.

an-setzen, *vb.* fix, affix; set, schedule; estimate.

Ansicht, -en, *n.f.* view, opinion.

an-siedeln, *vb.* settle, colonize.

an-spannen, *vb.* stretch, strain; harness.

Anspannung, -en, *n.f.* strain, tension.

an-spielen, *vb.* start to play; allude.

Anspielung, -en, *n.f.* allusion.

an-spornen, *vb.* spur on.

Ansprache, -n, *n.f.* pronunciation; talk.

an-sprechen*, *vb.* address, accost.

ansprechend, *adj.* attractive.

Anspruch, ⁻e, *n.m.* claim; (**A. machen auf**) lay claim to; (**in A. nehmen***) require, take up.

anspruchslos, *adj.* unassuming.

anspruchsvoll, *adj.* pretentious.

an-stacheln, *vb.* goad, incite.

Anstalt, -en, *n.f.* arrangement, institution.

Anstand, *n.m.* propriety; objection.

anständig, *adj.* decent.

Anständigkeit, -en, *n.f.* decency.

anstatt', *adv.* instead of.

an-stecken, *vb.* pin on, put on; light, set fire to; infect.

ansteckend, *adj.* contagious.

Ansteckung, -en, *n.f.* contagion.

an-stehen*, *vb.* line up, stand in line.

an-steigen*, *vb.* rise.

an-stellen, *vb.* place; hire, employ.

Anstellung, -en, *n.f.* employment.

Anstieg, -e, *n.m.* rise.

an-stiften, *vb.* incite, instigate.

an-stimmen, *vb.* intone, tune up.

Anstoß, ⁻e, *n.m.* shock; impetus; offense.

an-stoßen*, *vb.* knock, bump against, nudge; offend; clink glasses.

anstoßend, *adj.* adjoining.

anstößig, *adj.* offensive.

an-streben, *vb.* strive for.

an-streichen*, *vb.* paint; underline; mark.

an-strengen, *vb.* strain; (**sich a.**) exert oneself, try hard.

anstrengend, *adj.* strenuous.

Anstrengung, -en, *n.f.* effort, exertion.

Anstrich, -e, *n.m.* coat of paint; appearance; touch.

Ansturm, ⁻e, *n.m.* assault, run (on a bank).

Antark'tis, *n.f.* Antarctic.

antark'tisch, *adj.* antarctic.

Anteil, -e, *n.m.* share.

Anten'ne, -n, *n.f.* antenna.

antik', *adj.* antique.

Antl'ke, *n.f.* antiquity, classical times.

Antilo'pe, -n, *n.f.* antelope.

Antimon', *n.nt.* antimony.

antinuklear', *adj.* antinuclear.

Antipathie', -l'en, *n.f.* antipathy.

Antiquar', -e, *n.m.* second-hand bookdealer, antique dealer.

Antiquariat', -e, *n.nt.* second-hand bookstore.

antiqua'risch, *adj.* second-hand.

antisep'tisch, *adj.* antiseptic.

antisozial', *adj.* antisocial.

Antlitz, -e, *n.nt.* countenance.

Antrag, ⁓e, *n.m.* offer, proposal, motion.

an-treffen*, *vb.* meet up with.

an-treiben*, *vb.* drive on, propel, incite.

an-treten*, *vb.* enter into (office), start out on, step forward.

Antrieb, -e, *n.m.* impulse, impetus, force.

Antritt, -e, *n.m.* entrance into, start.

an-tun*, *vb.* put on, inflict, cause.

Antwort, -en, *n.f.* answer.

antworten, *vb.* answer.

an-vertrauen, *vb.* entrust; (sich a.) confide.

an-wachsen*, *vb.* grow, increase.

Anwalt, ⁓e, *n.m.* attorney, advocate.

Anwärter, -, *n.m.* applicant, aspirant.

an-weisen*, *vb.* instruct, direct; assign.

Anweisung, -en, *n.f.* instruction, assignment; money order.

anwendbar, *adj.* applicable.

an-wenden*, *vb.* apply, use.

Anwendung, -en, *n.f.* application, use.

anwesend, *adj.* present.

Anwesenheit, -en, *n.f.* presence.

Anwurf, ⁓e, *n.m.* slur.

Anzahl, *n.f.* quantity, number.

an-zahlen, *vb.* make a down payment.

Anzahlung, -en, *n.f.* down payment.

an-zapfen, *vb.* tap.

Anzeichen, -, *n.nt.* sign, symptom.

an-zeichnen, *vb.* mark, note.

Anzeige, -n, *n.f.* notice, advertisement; denunciation.

an-zeigen, *vb.* announce, advertise; denounce.

Anzeiger, -, *n.m.* advertiser; informer.

an-ziehen*, *vb.* draw along, attract; put on, dress; rise.

anziehend, *adj.* attractive.

Anziehungskraft, ⁓e, *n.f.* attraction; (A. der Erde) gravity.

Anzug, ⁓e, *n.m.* suit; approach.

an-zünden, *vb.* ignite, light.

an-zweifeln, *vb.* doubt, question.

apart, *adj.* out of the ordinary.

Apart'heid, *n.f.* apartheid.

Apathie', -i'en, *n.f.* apathy.

apa'thisch, *adj.* apathetic.

Apfel, ⁓, *n.m.* apple.

Apfelmus, *n.nt.* applesauce.

Apfelsi'ne, -'n, *n.f.* orange.

apoplek'tisch, *adj.* apoplectic.

Apos'tel, -, *n.m.* apostle.

aposto'lisch, *adj.* apostolic.

Apothe'ke, -n, *n.f.* pharmacy.

Apothe'ker, -, *n.m.* pharmacist.

Apparat', -e, *n.m.* apparatus.

Appetit', *n.m.* appetite.

appetit'lich, *adj.* appetizing, inviting.

applaudie'ren, *vb.* applaud.

Applaus', *n.m.* applause.

Apriko'se, -n, *n.f.* apricot.

April', *n.m.* April.

Aquarell', -e, *n.nt.* watercolor.

Aqua'rium, -ien, *n.nt.* aquarium.

Äqua'tor, *n.m.* equator.

äquatorial', *adj.* equatorial.

Araber, -, *n.m.* Arab.

ara'bisch, *adj.* Arabic, Arabian.

Arbeit, -en, *n.f.* work.

arbeiten, *vb.* work.

Arbeiter, -, *n.m.* worker, workman, laborer.

Arbeiterschaft, *n.f.* labor.

Arbeitge'ber, -, *n.m.* employer.

arbeitslos, *adj.* unemployed.

Arbeitslosigkeit, *n.f.* unemployment.

Arbeitszimmer, -, *n.nt.* study.

Archäologie', *n.f.* archaeology.

Archipel', -e, *n.m.* archipelago.

Architekt', -en, -en, *n.m.* architect.

architekto'nisch, *adj.* architectural.

Architektur', -en, *n.f.* architecture.

Archiv', -e, *n.nt.* archives.

Are'na, -nen, *n.f.* arena.

arg, *adj.* bad.

Argenti'nien, *n.nt.* Argentina.

Ärger, *n.m.* anger, annoyance, bother.

ärgerlich, *adj.* angry, annoying.

ärgern, *vb.* annoy, make angry, bother; (sich ä.) be angry.

Ärgernis, -se, *n.nt.* nuisance.

Arglist, *n.f.* guile.

arglos, *adj.* harmless, unsuspecting.

Argument', -e, *n.nt.* argument.

argumentie'ren, *vb.* argue.

Argwohn, *n.m.* suspicion.

argwöhnisch, *adj.* suspicious.

Arie, -n, *n.f.* aria.

Aristokrat', -en, -en, *n.m.* aristocrat.

Aristokratie', -i'en, *n.f.* aristocracy.

aristokra'tisch, *adj.* aristocratic.

Arithmetik', *n.f.* arithmetic.

Arka'de, -n, *n.f.* arcade.

arktisch, *adj.* arctic.

arm (⁓), *adj.* poor.

Arm, -e, *n.m.* arm.

Arm-, *n.m.&f.* pauper.

Armband, ⁓er, *n.nt.* bracelet.

Armbanduhr, -en, *n.f.* wristwatch.

Armee', -me'en, *n.f.* army.

Ärmel, -, *n.m.* sleeve.

Armleuchter, -, *n.m.* candelabrum.

armselig, *adj.* beggarly, miserable.

Armut, *n.f.* poverty, destitution.

Aro'ma, -s, *n.nt.* aroma.

arrangie'ren, *vb.* arrange.

arrogant', *adj.* arrogant.

Arroganz', -en, *n.f.* arrogance.

Arsen', *n.nt.* arsenic.

Art, -en, *n.f.* kind, sort, species; way, manner; (A. und Weise) way.

Arte'rie, -i'en, *n.f.* artery.

Arthri'tis, *n.f.* arthritis.

artig, *adj.* good, well-behaved.

Arti'kel, -, *n.m.* item, article.

artikulie'ren, *vb.* articulate.

Artillerie', -i'en, *n.f.* artillery.

Artischo'cke, -n, *n.f.* artichoke.

Arzt, ⁓e, *n.m.* physician, doctor; (praktischer A.) general practitioner.

ärztlich, *adj.* medical.

As, -se, *n.nt.* ace.

Asbest', -e, *n.m.* asbestos.

Asche, -n, *n.f.* ash; (glühende A.) embers.

Asch(en)becher, -, *n.m.* ashtray.

aschgrau, *adj.* ashen.

Asiat', -en, -en, *n.m.* Asian.

asia'tisch, *adj.* Asian.

Asien, *n.nt.* Asia.

Asket', -en, -en, *n.m.* ascetic.

aske'tisch, *adj.* ascetic.

Asphalt', -e, *n.m.* asphalt.

Aspirin', *n.nt.* aspirin.

assimilie'ren, *vb.* assimilate.

Assistent', -en, -en, *n.m.* assistant.

assoziie'ren, *vb.* associate.

Ast, ⁓e, *n.m.* branch.

ästhe'tisch, *adj.* aesthetic.

Asthma, *n.nt.* asthma.

Astigmatis'mus, -men, *n.m.* astigmatism.

Astrologie', -i'en, *n.f.* astrology.

Astronaut', -en, -en, *n.m.* astronaut.

Astronomie', -i'en, *n.f.* astronomy.

Asyl', -e, *n.nt.* asylum.

Atelier', -s, *n.nt.* studio.

Atem, -, *n.m.* breath.

atemlos, *adj.* breathless.

Atempause, -n, *n.f.* respite.

Atheist', -en, -en, *n.m.* atheist.

Äther, *n.m.* ether.

äthe'risch, *adj.* ethereal.

Athlet', -en, -en, *n.m.* athlete.

athle'tisch, *adj.* athletic.

Atlan'tik, *n.m.* Atlantic Ocean.

atlan'tisch, *adj.* Atlantic.

Atlas, -lan'ten, *n.m.* atlas.

atmen, *vb.* breathe.

Atmen, *n.nt.* breathing.

Atmosphäre, -n, *n.f.* atmosphere.

atmosphä'risch, *adj.* atmospheric.

Atmung, *n.f.* respiration.

Atom', -e, *n.nt.* atom.

atomar', *adj.* atomic.

atomisie'ren, *vb.* atomize.

Atom'müll, *n.m.* nuclear waste.

Atomsperr'vertrag, ²e, *n.m.* non-proliferation treaty.

Attaché', -s, *n.m.* attaché.

Attentat', -e, *n.nt.* attempt on someone's life.

Attentä'ter, -, *n.m.* assassin.

Attest', -e, *n.nt.* certificate.

ätzen, *vb.* etch; *(med.)* cauterize.

au, *interj.* ouch.

auch, *adv.* also, too; **(a. nicht)** not … either; **(a. jetzt)** even now.

Audienz', -en, *n.f.* audience.

audiovisuell', *adj.* audiovisual.

Audito'rium, -rien, *n.nt.* auditorium.

auf, *prep.* on, onto.

auf·atmen, *vb.* breathe a sigh of relief.

Aufbau, *n.m.* erection, construction; structure.

auf·bauen, *vb.* erect.

auf·blasen*, *vb.* inflate.

auf·brechen*, *vb.* break open; start out.

auf·decken, *vb.* uncover, unearth.

auf·dringen, *vb.* obtrude; **(sich a.)** obtrude.

aufdringlich, *adj.* obtrusive, importunate.

aufeinan'derfolgend, *adj.* successive, consecutive.

Aufenthalt, *n.m.* stay.

auf·erlegen, *vb.* impose.

Auferstehung, *n.f.* resurrection.

auf·fallen*, *vb.* be conspicuous.

auffällig, *adj.* noticeable, conspicuous, flashy.

Auffälligkeit, -en, *n.f.* conspicuousness, flashiness.

auf·fangen*, *vb.* catch; intercept.

auf·fassen, *vb.* conceive, interpret.

Auffassung, -en, *n.f.* conception, interpretation.

auf·flammen, *vb.* flash, flare up.

auf·fordern, *vb.* ask, invite, summon.

Aufforderung, -en, *n.f.* invitation, summons.

auf·frischen, *vb.* refresh.

auf·führen, *vb.* list; (theater) perform.

Aufführung, -en, *n.f.* performance.

Aufgabe, -n, *n.f.* task, assignment; (school) lesson.

Aufgang, ²e, *n.m.* rise.

auf·geben*, *vb.* give up, abandon; (luggage) check

through; (food) serve; *(jur.)* waive.

Aufgebot, -e, *n.nt.* banns.

aufgebracht, *adj.* angry, provoked.

auf·gehen*, *vb.* (sun etc.) rise; *(math.)* leave no remainder; *(fig.)* be absorbed in.

auf·halten*, *vb.* hold open; stop, detain; (sich a.) stay.

auf·hängen*, *vb.* suspend; hang.

auf·heben*, *vb.* revoke, nullify; (zeitweilig a.) suspend.

Aufheben, *n.nt.* ado, fuss.

Aufhebung, -en, *n.f.* revocation, abolition.

auf·heitern, *vb.* cheer up.

auf·hören, *vb.* stop, quit.

Aufhören, *n.nt.* cessation.

auf·klären, *vb.* enlighten; (sich a.) clear.

Aufklärung, *n.f.* enlightenment.

auf·kommen*, *vb.* come into use; **(a. für)** be responsible for.

Auflage, -n, *n.f.* printing, circulation.

Auflauf, ²e, *n.m.* crowd, mob; soufflé.

auf·lösen, *vb.* dissolve.

Auflösung, -en, *n.f.* dissolution.

auf·machen, *vb.* open; (sich a.) set out for.

Aufmachung, -en, *n.f.* make-up.

aufmerksam, *adj.* attentive, polite; alert.

Aufmerksamkeit, -en, *n.f.* attention, attentiveness.

auf·muntern, *vb.* cheer up.

Aufnahme, -n, *n.f.* reception; (photo) shot; (phonograph, tape) recording.

auf·nehmen*, *vb.* take in; (phonograph, tape) record; film, photograph.

auf·opfern, *vb.* (sich a.) sacrifice oneself.

auf·passen, *vb.* pay attention, look out for.

auf·raffen, *vb.* (sich a.) bestir oneself.

auf·räumen, *vb.* put in order; (mit etwas a.) debunk.

aufrecht, *adj.* upright.

aufrecht·erhalten*, *vb.* maintain, uphold.

Aufrechterhaltung, *n.f.* maintenance.

auf·regen, *vb.* excite, agitate; (sich a.) get excited.

Aufregung, -en, *n.f.* excitement.

aufreibend, *adj.* exhausting.

auf·reihen, *vb.* string.

auf·reißen*, *vb.* tear open.

auf·richten, *vb.* erect.

aufrichtig, *adj.* sincere, heartfelt.

Aufruf, -e, *n.m.* proclamation.

Aufruhr, *n.m.* riot; (in A. geraten*) riot.

aufrührerisch, *adj.* insurgent; inflammatory.

auf·sagen, *vb.* recite.

aufsässig, *adj.* rebellious.

Aufsatz, ²e, *n.m.* essay.

auf·saugen, *vb.* suck up, absorb.

auf·schieben*, *vb.* postpone, delay, procrastinate.

Aufschlag, ²e, *n.m.* surtax; (trousers, sleeve) cuff.

auf·schlagen*, *vb.* open; hit the ground.

auf·schließen*, *vb.* unlock.

Aufschluß, -sse, *n.m.* information.

aufschlußreich, *adj.* informative.

Aufschnitt, *n.m.* cut; **(kalter A.)** cold cuts.

Aufschrift, -en, *n.f.* inscription; address.

Aufschub, *n.m.* postponement, stay.

Aufschwung, *n.m.* upward swing, boost.

auf·sehen*, *vb.* look up.

Aufsehen, *n.nt.* sensation.

aufsehenerregend, *adj.* spectacular.

auf·setzen, *vb.* put on.

Aufsicht, *n.f.* supervision.

auf·speichern, *vb.* store up.

auf·springen*, *vb.* leap up; fly open; (skin) chap.

Aufstand, ²e, *n.m.* uprising, insurrection.

aufständisch, *adj.* insurgent.

Aufständisch-, *n.m.* insurgent.

auf·stapeln, *vb.* stack.

auf·stehen*, *vb.* get up, rise, arise.

auf·steigen*, *vb.* mount, ascend, rise.

auf·stellen, *vb.* put up; nominate.

Aufstieg, -e, *n.m.* ascent, advancement.

auf·suchen, *vb.* look up; seek.

auf·tauchen, *vb.* emerge.

Auftrag, ²e, *n.m.* instruction, order.

auf·tragen*, *vb.* instruct, assign; lay on; wear out; (food) serve up.

auf·treiben*, *vb.* raise.

auf·trennen, *vb.* rip.

auf·treten*, *vb.* appear; act.

Auftreten, *n.nt.* appearance; (sicheres A.) poise.

auf·wachen, *vb.* awake.

Aufwand, *n.m.* expenditure, display.

auf·warten, *vb.* wait upon; wait up.

aufwärts, *adv.* upward(s).

auf·wecken, *vb.* wake up.

auf·wenden*, *vb.* expend.

auf·wiegen*, *vb.* balance.

auf·zählen, *vb.* enumerate; itemize.

auf·zeichnen, *vb.* record.

auf·ziehen*, *vb.* draw open; (watch) wind; (knitting) unravel; (child) rear.

Aufzug, ¨e, *n.m.* lift, hoist, elevator; procession; (theater) act.

auf·zwingen*, *vb.* force upon.

Auge, -n, *n.nt.* eye; **(blaues A.)** black eye.

Augenarzt, ¨e, *n.m.* oculist.

Augenblick, -e, *n.m.* moment, instant.

augenblicklich, *adj.* momentary, instant.

Augenbraue, -n, *n.f.* eyebrow.

Augenglas, -er, *n.nt.* eyeglass.

Augenhöhle, -n, *n.f.* eye socket.

Augenlid, -er, *n.nt.* eyelid.

Augenschein, *n.m.* evidence.

augenscheinlich, *adj.* ostensible.

Augensicht, *n.f.* eyesight.

Augenwimper, -n, *n.f.* eyelash.

August, *n.m.* August.

aus, *prep.* out of, from.

aus·arbeiten, *vb.* elaborate.

aus·arten, *vb.* degenerate.

aus·atmen, *vb.* exhale.

aus·bessern, *vb.* repair, mend.

aus·beuten, *vb.* exploit.

aus·bilden, *vb.* educate, train.

aus·bleiben*, *vb.* stay out; fail to materialize.

Ausblick, -e, *n.m.* outlook; view.

aus·brechen*, *vb.* erupt.

aus·breiten, *vb.* spread, expand.

aus·brennen*, *vb.* burn out; *(med.)* cauterize.

Ausbruch, ¨e, *n.m.* outbreak, outburst, eruption.

aus·brüten, *vb.* hatch.

aus·buchten, *vb.* **(sich a.)** bulge.

Ausdauer, *n.f.* endurance, stamina.

ausdauernd, *adj.* enduring.

aus·dehnen, *vb.* expand, extend; prolong; **(sich a.)** distend, dilate.

Ausdehnung, -en, *n.f.* expanse, expansion.

aus·denken*, *vb.* think up, invent.

aus·drehen, *vb.* turn out.

Ausdruck, ¨e, *n.m.* expression, term.

aus·drücken, *vb.* express, phrase.

ausdrücklich, *adj.* explicit.

ausdrucksvoll, *adj.* expressive.

auseinan'der, *adv.* apart, asunder.

auseinan'der·gehen*, *vb.* part; diverge.

auseinan'der·nehmen*, *vb.* take apart.

auseinan'der·reißen*, *vb.* tear apart, disrupt.

auserlesen, *adj.* choice.

aus·fallen*, *vb.* fall out, not take place.

Ausflug, ¨e, *n.m.* excursion, outing.

aus·fragen, *vb.* interrogate, quiz.

Ausfuhr, *n.f.* export.

aus·führen, *vb.* carry out, execute; export.

ausführend, *adj.* executive.

ausführlich, *adj.* detailed, explicit.

Ausführung, -en, *n.f.* execution; statement.

Ausgabe, -n, *n.f.* expense, expenditure; issuance; edition; (computer) output.

Ausgang, ¨e, *n.m.* exit; end.

aus·geben*, *vb.* give out; spend, expend; issue; **(sich a. für)** pose as.

ausgefallen, *adj.* rare; odd.

aus·gehen*, *vb.* go out; date.

ausgelassen, *adj.* hilarious.

ausgenommen, *adj.* except for.

ausgestorben, *adj.* extinct.

ausgesucht, *adj.* select.

ausgezeichnet, *adj.* excellent.

aus·gleichen*, *vb.* balance, adjust.

aus·gleiten*, *vb.* slip.

Ausguß, ¨sse, *n.m.* sink.

aus·halten*, *vb.* hold out; bear.

aus·händigen, *vb.* hand out, over.

Aushilfe, -n, *n.f.* assistance; stopgap.

aus·hungern, *vb.* starve out.

aus·kleiden, *vb.* undress.

aus·kommen*, *vb.* get along (with).

Auskommen, *n.nt.* livelihood.

Auskunft, ¨e, *n.f.* information.

aus·lachen, *vb.* laugh at.

aus·laden*, *vb.* unload.

Auslage, -n, *n.f.* outlay; display.

Ausland, *n.nt.* foreign country; **(im A.)** abroad.

Ausländer, -, *n.m.* foreigner, alien.

ausländisch, *adj.* foreign, alien.

aus·lassen*, *vb.* leave out; let out.

aus·legen, *vb.* lay out; interpret; (money) advance.

Auslegung, -en, *n.f.* interpretation.

Auslese, -n, *n.f.* selection.

aus·liefern, *vb.* extradite.

aus·löschen, *vb.* extinguish, efface.

aus·lösen, *vb.* release, unleash.

Ausmaß, -e, *n.nt.* dimension.

Ausnahme, -n, *n.f.* exception.

aus·nutzen, *vb.* utilize; exploit.

aus·packen *vb.* unpack.

aus·pressen, *vb.* squeeze.

Auspuff, -e, *n.m.* exhaust.

aus·radieren, *vb.* erase, obliterate.

aus·rangieren, *vb.* scrap.

aus·rechnen, *vb.* figure out.

aus·reichen, *vb.* suffice.

aus·reißen*, *vb.* run away, bolt.

aus·renken, *vb.* dislocate.

aus·richten, *vb.* align; execute; deliver (a message).

aus·rotten, *vb.* exterminate, eradicate.

Ausruf, -e, *n.m.* exclamation.

aus·rufen*, *vb.* proclaim, exclaim.

Ausrufungszeichen, -, *n.nt.* exclamation point.

aus·ruhen, *vb.* rest.

ausruhsam, *adj.* restful.

aus·rüsten, *vb.* equip.

Aussage, -n, *n.f.* statement; testimony.

aus·sagen, *vb.* testify.

Aussatz, *n.m.* leprosy.

aus·schalten, *vb.* eliminate; *(elec.)* disconnect.

Ausschalter, -, *n.m.* *(elec.)* cutout.

aus·scheiden*, *vb.* eliminate; *(med.)* secrete; retire, withdraw.

Ausscheidung, -en, *n.f.* elimination.

aus·schelten*, *vb.* berate.

aus·schimpfen, *vb.* scold, bawl out.

aus·schlafen*, *vb.* sleep as long as one wants to.

Ausschlag, ¨e, *n.m. (med.)* rash; **(den A. geben*)** clinch the matter.

aus·schließen*, *vb.* shut out, exclude.

ausschließlich, *adj.* exclusive.

Ausschluß, *n.m.* exclusion.

aus·schmücken, *vb.* embellish.

Ausschnitt, -e, *n.m.* section; clipping; neck (of dress).

aus·schöpfen, *vb.* bail out (water), exhaust.

Ausschuß, ¨sse, *n.m.* committee, board.

aus·schweifen, *vb.* go far afield; dissipate.

aus·sehen*, *vb.* look, appear.

außen, *adv.* outside; **(nach a.)** outward.

Außenbezirk, -e, *n.m.* outskirts.

Außenseite, -n, *n.f.* outside.

Außenwelt, *n.f.* outside.

außer, *prep.* beside(s), except; out of; **(a. sich)** beside oneself.

äußer-, *adj.* exterior, external.

außerdem, *adv.* besides.

außergewöhnlich, *adj.* extraordinary.

äußerlich, *adj.* outward.

äußern, *vb.* utter.

außerordentlich, *adj.* exceedingly.

äußerst-, *adj.* extreme.

äußerst, *adv.* extremely.

Äußerst-, *n.nt.* extremity.

außerstan'de, *adv.* unable.

Äußerung, -en, *n.f.* utterance.

aus·setzen, *vb.* set out; expose, subject.

Aussetzung, -en, *n.f.* exposure.

Aussicht, -en, *n.f.* view; prospect.

aus·speien*, *vb.* disgorge.

Aussprache, -n, *n.f.* pronunciation.

aus·sprechen*, *vb.* enunciate,

pronounce; (falsch a.) mis-pronounce.

aus·spucken, vb. spit (out).

aus·spülen, vb. rinse.

Ausstand, ⁻e, n.m. strike.

aus·statten, vb. equip, endow.

Ausstattung, -en, n.f. equipment, décor.

aus·stehen*, vb. bear, stand.

aus·steigen*, vb. get out.

aus·stellen, vb. show, exhibit; issue.

Ausstellung, -en, n.f. exhibit, exhibition.

aus·sterben*, vb. die out.

Aussterben, n.nt. extinction.

aus·stoßen*, vb. expel.

aus·strahlen, vb. radiate.

Ausstrahlung, -en, n.f. radiation.

aus·streichen*, vb. delete.

aus·strömen, vb. emanate.

aus·suchen, vb. choose, select.

Austausch, n.m. exchange.

austauschbar, adj. exchangeable.

aus·tauschen, vb. exchange.

aus·teilen, vb. distribute.

Auster, -n, n.f. oyster.

aus·tilgen, vb. expunge.

aus·tragen*, vb. deliver.

aus·treiben*, vb. drive out, exorcise.

aus·treten*, vb. step out; resign; secede.

aus·üben, vb. exercise, practice.

Ausübung, -en, n.f. exercise, practice.

Ausverkauf, n.m. sale.

Auswahl, -en, n.f. choice, selection, assortment.

aus·wählen, vb. select, pick.

aus·walzen, vb. roll out, laminate.

Auswanderer, -, n.m. emigrant.

aus·wandern, vb. emigrate.

auswärtig, adj. external.

Ausweg, -e, n.m. way out, escape.

aus·weichen*, vb. evade, dodge.

ausweichend, adj. evasive.

Ausweis, -e, n.m. pass, identification.

aus·weisen*, vb. evict; (sich a.) identify oneself.

Ausweisung, -en, n.f. eviction.

auswendig, adj. by heart; (a. lernen) memorize.

aus·werten, vb. evaluate; reclaim.

Auswertung, -en, n.f. evaluation; reclamation.

aus·wickeln, vb. unwrap.

aus·wirken, vb. work out; (sich a.) have an effect.

Auswirkung, -en, n.f. effect, impact.

aus·wischen, vb. wipe out.

Auswuchs, ⁻e, n.m. protuberance, excrescence.

aus·zahlen, vb. pay out.

aus·zeichnen, vb. distinguish; (sich a.) excel.

aus·ziehen*, vb. move out; (clothes) take off; (sich a.) undress.

Auszug, ⁻e, n.m. exodus; excerpt, extract.

authentisch, adj. authentic.

Auto, -s, n.nt. auto.

Autobahn, -en, n.f. superhighway.

Autobus, -se, n.m. bus.

Autogramm', -e, n.nt. autograph.

Automat', -en, -en, n.m. automat; automaton.

Automation', n.f. automation.

automa'tisch, adj. automatic.

autonom', adj. autonomous.

autoritär, adj. authoritarian.

Autorität', -en, n.f. authority.

Axt, ⁻e, n.f. axe.

azur'blau, adj. azure.

B

Baby, -s, n.nt. baby.

Bach, ⁻e, n.m. brook.

Backe, -n, n.f. cheek, jowl.

backen*, vb. bake.

Bäcker, -, n.m. baker.

Bäckerei', -en, n.f. bakery, pastry shop.

Backpflaume, -n, n.f. prune.

Backstein, -e, n.m. brick.

Bad, ⁻er, n.nt. bath.

Badeanstalt, -en, n.f. public bath.

Badeanzug, ⁻e, n.m. bathing suit.

Bademantel, -⁻, n.m. bathrobe.

baden, vb. bathe.

Badeort, -e, n.m. bathing resort.

Badewanne, -n, n.f. bathtub.

Badezimmer, -, n.nt. bathroom.

Bahn, -en, n.f. path, course.

Bahnhof, ⁻e, n.m. station.

Bahnsteig, -e, n.m. platform.

Bahre, -n, n.f. bier.

Bajonett', -e, n.nt. bayonet.

Bakte'rie, -n, n.f. germ.

Bakte'rium, -rien, n.nt. bacterium.

balance'ren, vb. balance.

bald, adv. soon, shortly.

Balken, -, n.m. beam.

Balkon', -s or -e, n.m. balcony.

Ball, ⁻e, n.m. ball.

ballen, vb. (fist) clench.

Balleri'na, -nen, n.f. ballerina.

Ballon', -s, n.m. balloon.

Balsam, -e, n.m. balsam, balm.

balsamie'ren, vb. embalm.

Bambus, -se, n.m. bamboo.

banal', adj. banal.

Bana'ne, -n, n.f. banana.

Band, -e, n.nt. bond, tie.

Band, ⁻e, n.m. (book) volume.

Band, ⁻er, n.nt. band, ribbon, tape.

Bande, -n, n.f. band, gang.

bändigen, vb. tame.

Bandit', -en, -en, n.m. bandit, desperado.

bange(n), adj. afraid.

Bank, ⁻e, n.f. bench.

Bank, -en, n.f. bank.

Bankgeschäft, -e, n.nt. banking; banking firm.

Bankier', -s, n.m. banker.

bankrott', adj. bankrupt.

Bankrott', n.m. bankruptcy.

Bann, -e, n.m. ban; (eccles.) excommunication.

bannen, vb. banish, outlaw.

Banner, -, n.nt. banner.

bar, adj. cash.

Bar, -s, n.f. bar.

Bär, -en, -en, n.m. bear; (Große B.) Big Dipper.

Barbar', -en, -en, n.m. barbarian.

Barbarei', -en, n.f. barbarism.

barba'risch, adj. barbarian, barbarous.

barfuß, adj. barefoot.

Bargeld, -er, n.nt. cash.

Bariton, -e, n.m. baritone.

Barium, n.nt. barium.

Barke, -n, n.f. bark.

barmher'zig, adj. merciful.

Barmixer, -, n.m. bartender.

barock', adj. baroque.

Barome'ter, -, n.nt. barometer.

barome'trisch, adj. barometric.

Baron', -e, n.m. baron.

Baroness'e, -n, n.f. baroness.

Barrika'de, -n, n.f. barricade.

Bart, ⁻e, n.m. beard.

Barthaar, -e, n.nt. whisker.

bärtig, adj. bearded.

bartlos, adj. beardless.

Barzahlung, -en, n.f. cash payment.

Baseball-Spiel, -e, n.nt. baseball.

basie'ren, vb. base.

Basis, -sen, n.f. basis.

Baß, ⁻sse, n.m. bass.

Bastard, -e, n.m. bastard.

Bataillon', -e, n.nt. battalion.

Batist', -e, n.m. cambric; batiste.

Batterie', -i'en, n.f. battery.

Bau, -ten, n.m. construction; building; structure.

Bauch, ⁻e, n.m. belly.

bauen, vb. build, construct.

Bauer, -n, n.m. farmer, peasant; (chess) pawn.

Bauernhaus, ⁻er, n.nt. farmhouse.

Bauernhof, -e, n.m. farmyard.

baufällig, adj. dilapidated.

Baukunst, n.f. architecture.

Baum, -e, n.m. tree.

Baumeister, -, n.m. builder.

baumeln, vb. dangle; (b. lassen*) dangle.

bäumen, vb. (sich b.) rear.

Baumstamm, -e, n.m. log.

Baumwolle, n.f. cotton.

bauschig, adj. baggy.

Bauunternehmer, -, n.m. contractor.

Bazar', -e, n.m. bazaar.

Bazil'lus, -len, n.m. bacillus.

beab'sichtigen, *vb.* intend.

beach'ten, *vb.* notice, pay attention to.

beach'tenswert, *adj.* noteworthy.

beacht'lich, *adj.* remarkable.

Beach'tung, -en, *n.f.* notice, consideration.

Beamt'-, *n.m.* official.

bean'spruchen, *vb.* lay claim to.

bean'standen, *vb.* object to.

bean'tragen, *vb.* propose, move.

beant'worten, *vb.* answer.

bear'beiten, *vb.* work; adapt; handle, process.

beauf'sichtigen, *vb.* supervise.

beauf'tragen, *vb.* commission.

Beauf'tragt-, *n.m.* commissioner.

bebau'en, *vb.* till; build on.

beben, *vb.* quake, tremble.

Becher, -, *n.m.* beaker, goblet.

Becken, -, *n.nt.* basin; pelvis.

Bedacht', *n.m.* deliberation, care.

bedäch'tig, *adj.* cautious, deliberate.

bedan'ken, *vb.* **(sich bei jemandem für etwas b.)** thank someone for something.

Bedarf', *n.m.* need, demand.

bedau'erlich, *adj.* regrettable.

bedau'ern, *vb.* regret.

Bedau'ern, *n.nt.* regret.

bede'cken, *vb.* cover over.

beden'ken*, *vb.* bear in mind.

Beden'ken, -, *n.nt.* compunction, misgiving.

bedeu'ten, *vb.* mean, signify.

bedeu'tend, *adj.* significant, important.

Bedeu'tung, -en, *n.f.* significance, meaning.

bedeu'tungslos, *adj.* insignificant.

bedie'nen, *vb.* serve, wait on; operate (machine); follow suit (cards); **(sich b.)** help oneself.

Bedie'ner, -, *n.m.* operator (of a machine).

Bedient'-, *n.m.&f.* servant, attendant.

Bedie'nung, *n.f.* service.

bedingt', *adj.* conditional, qualified.

Bedin'gung, -en, *n.f.* condition.

bedin'gungslos, *adj.* unconditional.

bedrän'gen, *vb.* beset.

bedro'hen, *vb.* menace, threaten.

bedrü'cken, *vb.* oppress.

bedrü'ckend, *adj.* oppressive.

bedür'fen*, *vb.* have need of.

Bedürf'nis, -se, *n.nt.* need, requirement.

Bedürf'nisanstalt, -en, *n.f.* comfort station.

bedürf'tig, *adj.* indigent, needy; in need of.

Beefsteak, -s, *n.nt.* beefsteak.

beeh'ren, *vb.* honor.

beei'len, *vb.* **(sich b.)** hurry.

beein'drucken, *vb.* impress.

beein'flussen, *vb.* influence.

beein'trächtigen, *vb.* impair.

been'den, *vb.* end, finish.

been'digen, *vb.* end, finish.

Beer'digung, -en, *n.f.* funeral.

beer'digen, *vb.* inter, bury.

Beere, -n, *n.f.* berry.

befä'higen, *vb.* enable, qualify.

befahr'bar, *adj.* passable.

befal'len*, *vb.* fall upon, attack.

befan'gen, *adj.* embarrassed.

befas'sen, *vb.* touch; **(sich b. mit)** take up, attend to, deal with.

Befehl', -e, *n.m.* command, order.

befeh'len*, *vb.* command, order.

Befehls'haber, -, *n.m.* commander.

befes'tigen, *vb.* fasten, fortify, confirm.

befeuch'ten, *vb.* moisten.

befin'den*, *vb.* find, deem; **(sich b.)** be located, feel.

befle'cken, *vb.* stain.

beflei'ßigen, *vb.* **(sich b.)** endeavor, take pains.

befol'gen, *vb.* follow, observe, obey.

beför'dern, *vb.* advance, promote, transport.

Beför'derungsmittel, *n.nt.* conveyance.

befra'gen, *vb.* question, interrogate.

befrei'en, *vb.* liberate, exempt.

Befrei'ung, -en, *n.f.* liberation, release.

befrem'den, *vb.* appear strange to, alienate.

befreun'den, *vb.* befriend; **(sich b. mit)** make friends with.

befrie'digen, *vb.* satisfy.

befrie'digend, *adj.* satisfactory.

Befrie'digung, -en, *n.f.* satisfaction.

befruch'ten, *vb.* fertilize, fructify.

Befug'nis, -se, *n.f.* authority.

befugt', *adj.* authorized.

befüh'len, *vb.* feel, finger.

Befund', *n.m.* finding(s).

befürch'ten, *vb.* fear.

befür'worten, *vb.* advocate, recommend.

begabt', *adj.* gifted.

Bega'bung, -en, *n.f.* talent.

bege'ben*, *vb.* **(sich b.)** betake oneself; occur.

begeg'nen, *vb.* meet, encounter.

Begeg'nung, -en, *n.f.* meeting, encounter.

bege'hen*, *vb.* commit.

begeh'ren, *vb.* desire, covet.

begeis'tern, *vb.* inspire.

begeis'tert, *adj.* enthusiastic.

Begeis'terung, *n.f.* enthusiasm.

Begier'de, -n, *n.f.* desire, lust.

begie'rig, *adj.* eager, desirous.

begie'ßen*, *vb.* water.

Beginn', *n.m.* beginning.

begin'nen*, *vb.* begin.

Begin'nen, *n.nt.* inception.

beglau'bigen, *vb.* certify, accredit.

Beglau'bigungsschreiben, *n.nt.* credentials.

beglei'chen*, *vb.* settle.

beglei'ten, *vb.* accompany.

beglei'tend, *adj.* concomitant.

Beglei'ter, -, *n.m.* companion, escort; accompanist.

Beglei'tung, -en, *n.f.* accompaniment.

beglück'wünschen, *vb.* congratulate.

begna'digen, *vb.* pardon.

begnü'gen, *vb.* **(sich b. mit)** content oneself with.

begra'ben*, *vb.* bury.

Begräb'nis, -se, *n.nt.* burial, funeral.

begrei'fen*, *vb.* comprehend.

begreif'lich, *adj.* understandable.

begren'zen, *vb.* limit.

Begren'zung, -en, *n.f.* limitation.

Begriff', -e, *n.m.* concept; **(im B. sein*)** be about to.

begrün'den, *vb.* establish; justify.

begrü'ßen, *vb.* greet.

Begrü'ßung, -en, *n.f.* greeting, salutation.

begüns'tigen, *vb.* favor, support.

Begüns'tigung, -en, *n.f.* favoritism, encouragement.

behä'big, *adj.* portly.

beha'gen, *vb.* please.

Beha'gen, *n.nt.* comfort, pleasure.

behag'lich, *adj.* comfortable, pleasant.

behal'ten*, *vb.* keep.

Behäl'ter, -, *n.m.* container.

behan'deln, *vb.* treat.

Behand'lung, -en, *n.f.* treatment.

Behang', -¨e, *n.m.* drapery.

behar'ren, *vb.* persevere, insist.

beharr'lich, *adj.* constant, persistent.

Beharr'lichkeit, *n.f.* perseverance.

behaup'ten, *vb.* assert, maintain; allege.

Behaup'tung, -en, *n.f.* assertion.

behe'ben*, *vb.* remove.

Behelf', -e, *n.m.* expedient, makeshift.

behel'fen*, *vb.* **(sich b. mit)** make do with.

behel'ligen, *vb.* bother.

behen'd(e), *adj.* nimble, agile.

beher'bergen, *vb.* shelter, lodge.

beher'schen, *vb.* rule, govern; control, master; dominate.

Beherr'schung, *n.f.* rule, mastery.

beher'zigen, *vb.* take to heart.

beherzt, *adj.* courageous, game.

behilf'lich, *adj.* helpful.

behin'dern, *vb.* impede.

Behin'derung, -en, *n.f.* impediment.

Behör'de, -n, *n.f.* governing office, authority.

Behuf', **-e**, *n.m.* purpose; benefit.

behufs', *prep.* for the purpose of.

behü'ten, *vb.* guard, protect, keep from; **(Gott behüte)** God forbid.

behut'sam, *adj.* cautious.

bei, *prep.* at, near, by; in connection with; **(b. mir)** at my house, on my person.

bei-behalten*, *vb.* retain.

Beibehaltung, -en, *n.f.* retention.

Beiblatt, **-er**, *n.nt.* supplement.

bei-bringen*, *vb.* bring forward; **(jemandem etwas b.)** make something clear to someone, teach someone something.

Beichte, -n, *n.f.* confession.

beichten, *vb.* confess.

Beichtstuhl, **-e**, *n.m.* confessional.

Beichtvater, **-**, *n.m.* confessor.

beide, *adj.&pron.* both.

Beifall, **-e**, *n.m.* applause.

Beifallsruf, -e, *n.m.* cheer.

bei-fügen, *vb.* add, enclose, attach, include.

Beifügung, -en, *n.f.* attachment.

Beihilfe, -n, *n.f.* assistance.

bei-kommen*, *vb.* get at.

Beil, -e, *n.nt.* hatchet.

Beilage, -n, *n.f.* enclosure; supplement.

beiläufig, *adj.* incidental.

bei-legen, *vb.* add, attach to, enclose.

Beileid, -e, *n.nt.* condolence.

bei-messen*, *vb.* attribute.

Beimessung, -en, *n.f.* attribution.

Beimischung, -en, *n.f.* admixture.

Bein, -e, *n.nt.* leg.

beinahe, *adv.* almost.

bei-ordnen, *vb.* adjoin, coordinate.

bei-pflichten, *vb.* agree with.

beirren, *vb.* confuse.

beisammen, *adv.* together.

Beisein, *n.nt.* presence.

beiseite, *adv.* aside, apart.

Beispiel, -e, *n.nt.* example.

beispiellos, *adj.* unheard of.

beißen*, *vb.* bite.

beißend, *adj.* biting, acrid.

Beistand, **-e**, *n.m.* assistance.

bei-stehen*, *vb.* assist.

bei-stimmen, *vb.* agree.

Beitrag, **-e**, *n.m.* contribution.

bei-tragen*, *vb.* contribute.

Beiträger, -, -, *n.m.* contributor.

bei-treten*, *vb.* join.

Beitritt, -e, *n.m.* joining.

bei-wohnen, *vb.* attend, witness.

Beiwort, -e, *n.nt.* epithet.

Beize, -n *n.f.* corrosion, stain.

beizeiten, *adv.* in good time.

beizen, *vb.* corrode, stain.

bejah'en, *vb.* affirm, say yes to.

bejah'end, *adj.* affirmative.

bejahrt', *adj.* aged.

bejam'mern, *vb.* deplore.

bejam'mernswert, *adj.* deplorable.

bekäm'pfen, *vb.* combat.

bekannt', *adj.* well-known; acquainted.

Bekannt'-, *n.m.&f.* acquaintance.

bekannt'-geben*, *vb.* make known, announce.

bekannt'lich, *adv.* as is well known.

bekannt'-machen*, *vb.* acquaint, make known.

Bekannt'machung, -en, *n.f.* proclamation.

Bekannt'schaft, -en, *n.f.* acquaintance.

bekeh'ren, *vb.* convert.

beken'nen*, *vb.* confess.

Bekennt'nis, -se, *n.nt.* confession.

bekla'gen, *vb.* deplore, lament; **(sich b. über)** complain about.

bekla'genswert, *adj.* deplorable, lamentable.

Beklagt'-, *n.m.&f.* accused, defendant.

beklei'den, *vb.* clothe, cover; fill (a position).

Beklei'dung, -en, *n.f.* clothing, covering.

beklem'men*, *vb.* oppress.

Beklom'menheit, *n.f.* anxiety.

bekom'men*, *vb.* get, obtain, receive; agree with, suit.

bekös'tigen, *vb.* feed, board.

bekräf'tigen, *vb.* confirm, corroborate.

beküm'mern, *vb.* grieve, distress.

Beküm'mernis, -se, *n.f.* grief, distress.

bekun'den, *vb.* manifest.

bela'den*, *vb.* load, burden.

Belag', **-e**, *n.m.* covering, surface; (food) spread.

bela'gern, *vb.* besiege.

Bela'gerung, -en, *n.f.* siege.

Belang', **-e**, *n.m.* importance.

belan'gen, *vb.* concern; sue.

belang'los, *adj.* unimportant, irrelevant.

belang'reich, *adj.* important, relevant.

belas'ten, *vb.* load, burden, strain; incriminate.

beläs'tigen, *vb.* annoy, bother, molest.

Belas'tung, -en, *n.f.* strain; inconvenience; incrimination.

belau'fen*, *vb.* **(sich b. auf)** amount to.

bele'ben, *vb.* animate, enliven.

Beleg', **-e**, *n.m.* proof, evidence, documentation.

bele'gen, *vb.* attest; reserve (seat); sign up for (academic subject).

belegt', *adj.* **(b. es Brot)** sandwich.

beleh'ren, *vb.* teach.

belei'digen, *vb.* insult.

Belei'digung, -en, *n.f.* insult.

beleuch'ten, *vb.* illuminate.

Beleuch'tung, -en, *n.f.* illumination.

Belgien, *n.nt.* Belgium.

Belgier, **-, -**, *n.m.* Belgian.

belgisch, *adj.* Belgian.

belich'ten, *vb.* expose.

Belich'tung, -en, *n.f.* exposure.

belie'ben, *vb.* please; **(wie beliebt?)** I beg your pardon?

Belie'ben, *n.nt.* pleasure, discretion; **(nach B.)** as you please.

belie'big, *adj.* any (you wish); **(eine b.e Zahl)** any number you want.

beliebt', *adj.* popular.

Beliebt'heit, *n.f.* popularity.

bellen, *vb.* bark.

beloh'nen, *vb.* reward.

Beloh'nung, -en, *n.f.* reward.

belü'gen*, *vb.* lie to.

belus'tigen, *vb.* amuse, entertain.

bema'len, *vb.* paint up.

beman'nen, *vb.* man.

bemerk'bar, *adj.* noticeable, perceptible.

bemer'ken, *vb.* notice; remark.

bemer'kenswert, *adj.* notable.

Bemer'kung, -en, *n.f.* remark.

bemü'hen, *vb.* trouble; **(sich b.)** take pains, try hard.

benach'bart, *adj.* neighboring.

benach'richtigen, *vb.* notify.

Benach'richtigung, -en, *n.f.* notification.

benach'teiligen, *vb.* put at a disadvantage, handicap.

beneh'men*, *vb.* take away; **(sich b.)** behave.

Beneh'men, *n.nt.* behavior.

benei'den, *vb.* envy.

benei'denswert, *adj.* enviable.

benom'men, *adj.* groggy, confused.

benö'tigen, *vb.* need.

benut'zen, *vb.* use.

Benut'zung, -en, *n.f.* use.

Benzin', *n.nt.* gas, gasoline.

beob'achten, *vb.* observe.

Beob'achtung, -en, *n.f.* observation.

bequem', *adj.* comfortable, convenient.

Bequem'lichkeit, -en, *n.f.* comfort.

bera'ten*, *vb.* advise; **(sich b.)** deliberate.

Bera'ter, -, *n.m.* adviser, consultant.

berau'ben, *vb.* rob, deprive of.

Berau'bung, -en, *n.f.* deprivation.

berau'schen, *vb.* intoxicate.

bere'chenbar, *adj.* calculable.

berech'nen, *vb.* calculate, compute.

berech'nend, *vb.* calculating.

Berech'nung, -en, *n.f.* calculation, computation.

berech'tigen, *vb.* justify, entitle.

Berech'tigung, -en, *n.f.* justification.

bere'den, *vb.* persuade.

Bered'samkeit, *n.f.* eloquence.

beredt', *adj.* eloquent.

Bereich', -e, *n.m.* domain, scope.

berei'chern, *vb.* enrich.

berei'sen, *vb.* tour.

bereit', *adj.* ready, prepared.

berei'ten, *vb.* make ready, prepare.

bereits', *adv.* already.

bereit'willig, *adj.* willing (to oblige).

bereu'en, *vb.* repent, regret.

Berg, -e, *n.m.* mountain.

bergab', *adv.* downhill.

bergan', *adv.* uphill.

Bergarbeiter, -, *n.m.* .miner.

bergauf', *adv.* uphill.

Bergbau, *n.m.* mining.

Bergkette, -n, *n.f.* mountain range.

Bergsteiger, -, *n.m.* mountain climber.

Bergung, *n.f.* salvage.

Bergwerk, -e, *n.nt.* mine.

Bericht', -e, *n.m.* report.

berich'ten, *vb.* report.

Bericht'erstatter, -, *n.m.* reporter.

berich'tigen, *vb.* report.

Berich'tigung, -en, *n.f.* correction.

bersten*, *vb.* burst.

berüch'tigt, *adj.* notorious.

berück'sichtigen, *vb.* consider, take into consideration; allow for.

Beruf', -e, *n.m.* profession.

beru'fen*, *vb.* call, appoint; (sich b. auf) refer to, appeal to.

berufs'mäßig, *adj.* professional.

Beru'fung, -en, *n.f.* summons, appointment; appeal.

beru'hen, *vb.* rest, be based.

beru'higen, *vb.* quiet, calm.

Beru'higungsmittel, -, *n.nt.* sedative.

berühmt', *adj.* famous.

Berühmt'heit, -en, *n.f.* celebrity.

berüh'ren, *vb.* touch.

Berüh'rung, -en, *n.f.* touch.

besa'gen, *vb.* say, indicate, mean.

besagt', *adj.* (afore)said.

besänf'tigen, *vb.* soften, soothe.

Besatz', -e, *n.m.* border, trimming, facing.

Besat'zung, -en, *n.f.* occupying forces; crew.

beschä'digen, *vb.* damage.

Beschä'digung, -en, *n.f.* damage.

beschaf'fen, *vb.* get, obtain, procure; provide.

beschaf'fen, *adj.* constituted; (so b.) of such a nature.

Beschaf'fenheit, -en, *n.f.* nature, quality.

beschäf'tigen, *vb.* employ, occupy, keep busy.

beschäf'tigt, *adj.* busy, engaged.

Beschäf'tigung, -en, *n.f.* occupation, employment.

beschä'men, *vb.* shame.

beschämt', *adj.* ashamed.

beschat'ten, *vb.* shade.

beschau'en, *vb.* look at, contemplate.

beschau'lich, *adj.* contemplative.

Bescheid', -e, *n.m.* answer, decision; information; (B. geben*) let know; (B. wissen* über) know all about.

beschei'den*, *vb.* allot, apportion; inform.

beschei'den, *adj.* modest.

Beschei'denheit, *n.f.* modesty.

beschei'nigen, *vb.* certify.

Beschei'nigung, -en, *n.f.* certificate, certification.

beschen'ken, *vb.* (b. mit) make a present of.

beschie'ßen*, *vb.* shoot at, shell, bombard.

Beschie'ßung, -en, *n.f.* bombardment.

beschimp'fen, *vb.* abuse, insult.

Beschim'pfung, -en, *n.f.* abuse, insult.

beschir'men, *vb.* protect.

Beschlag', -e, *n.m.* metal fitting, coating, condensation; (in B. nehmen*) confiscate.

beschla'gen*, *vb.* cover with, coat, mount; (sich b.) become coated, tarnish.

beschla'gen, *adj.* experienced, proficient.

Beschlag'nahme, -n, *n.f.* seizure, confiscation.

beschlag'nahmen, *vb.* seize, confiscate.

beschleu'nigen, *vb.* quicken, accelerate.

beschlie'ßen*, *vb.* finish, conclude, decide, make up one's mind.

Beschluß', -sse, *n.m.* decision, conclusion.

beschmie'ren, *vb.* smear, spread on.

beschmut'zen, *vb.* make dirty, soil.

beschnei'den*, *vb.* cut off, clip, circumcise.

beschö'nigen, *vb.* make pretty, gloss over, excuse.

beschrän'ken, *vb.* limit.

beschränkt', *adj.* limited, of limited abilities.

Beschrän'kung, -en, *n.f.* limitation.

beschrei'ben*, *vb.* describe.

Beschrei'bung, -en, *n.f.* description.

beschul'digen, *vb.* blame, accuse, incriminate.

Beschul'digung, -en, *n.f.* incrimination.

beschüt'zen, *vb.* protect.

Beschwer'de, -n, *n.f.* complaint, burden, trouble.

beschwe'ren, *vb.* burden; (sich bei jemandem über etwas b.) complain to someone about something.

beschwer'lich, *adj.* burdensome.

beschwich'tigen, *vb.* appease, soothe.

Beschwich'tigung, -en, *n.f.* appeasement.

beschwipst', *adj.* tight.

beschwö'ren*, *vb.* swear to; implore.

Beschwö'rung, -en, *n.f.* swearing by oath; entreaty; exorcism.

besei'tigen, *vb.* remove.

Besei'tigung, -en, *n.f.* removal.

Besen, -, *n.m.* broom.

beses'sen, *adj.* mad, possessed.

beset'zen, *vb.* occupy, fill; trim.

Beset'zung, *n.f.* occupation.

besich'tigen, *vb.* view, inspect, look around in.

Besich'tigung, -en, *n.f.* view, inspection, sight-seeing.

besie'deln, *vb.* settle, colonize.

Besie'd(e)lung, -en, *n.f.* settlement, colonization.

besie'geln, *vb.* steal.

besie'gen, *vb.* defeat.

besin'nen*, *vb.* (sich b.) remember, think over; (sich anders b.) change one's mind.

Besin'nung, -en, *n.f.* consideration, recollection; senses, consciousness.

besin'nungslos, *adj.* senseless, unconscious.

Besitz', -e, *n.m.* possession, property.

besit'zen*, *vb.* possess, own.

Besit'zer, -, *n.m.* proprietor.

besitz'gierig, *adj.* possessive.

Besit'zung, -en, *n.f.* possession.

besof'fen, *adj.* drunk.

besoh'len, *vb.* sole.

beson'der-, *adj.* special.

Beson'derheit, -en, *n.f.* peculiarity.

beson'ders, *adv.* especially.

beson'nen, *adj.* thoughtful, cautious.

besor'gen, *vb.* take care of, get.

Besorg'nis, -se, *n.f.* apprehension, anxiety.

besorgt', *adj.* anxious, worried.

Besor'gung, -en, *n.f.* management, care; errand.

bespöt'teln, *vb.* ridicule.

bespre'chen*, *vb.* discuss, talk over.

Bespre'chung, -en, *n.f.* discussion, review, conference.

besprit'zen, *vb.* spatter.

besser, *adj.* better.

bessern, *vb.* make better, improve.

Besserung, -en, *n.f.* amelioration, improvement; (gute B.!) I hope you get well soon.

best-, *adj.* best.

Bestand', -e, *n.m.* duration, stability; supply, stock.

bestän'dig, *adj.* steady, stable, constant.

Bestand'teil, -e, *n.m.* constituent, ingredient.

bestär'ken, *vb.* strengthen.

bestä'tigen, *vb.* confirm, acknowledge, verify.

Bestä'tigung, -en, *n.f.* confirmation, verification.

bestat'ten, *vb.* bury.

Bestat'tung, -en, *n.f.* burial.

beste'chen*, *vb.* bribe.

beste'chend, *adj.* attractive, tempting.

Beste'chung, -en, *n.f.* bribery, graft, corruption.

Besteck', -e, *n.nt.* set of implements; knife, fork, and spoon.

beste'hen*, *vb.* exist; (test) undergo, pass; (b. auf) insist on; (b. aus) consist of.

Beste'hen, *n.nt.* existence; insistence.

besteh'len*, *vb.* steal from, rob.

bestei'gen*, *vb.* climb up, ascend; mount; go on board.

bestel'len, *vb.* order; send for; give a message; appoint; till.

Bestel'lung, -en, *n.f.* order; message; appointment; cultivation.

bestens, *adv.* very well.

besteu'ern, *vb.* tax.

Besteu'erung, -en, *n.f.* taxation.

Bestie, -n, *n.f.* beast.

bestimm'bar, *adj.* definable, ascertainable, assignable.

bestim'men, *vb.* determine, decide, specify, designate, destine, dispose.

bestimmt', *adj.* definite.

Bestim'mungsort, -e, *n.m.* destination.

bestra'fen, *vb.* punish.

bestrah'len, *vb.* irradiate, treat with rays.

bestre'ben, *vb.* (sich b.) strive.

Bestre'bung, -en, *n.f.* effort.

bestreit'bar, *adj.* disputable.

bestrei'ten*, *vb.* contest, dispute, deny.

bestri'cken, *vb.* entangle, ensnare, captivate, charm.

bestür'men, *vb.* storm, attack, implore.

bestürzt', *adj.* dismayed.

Bestür'zung, -en, *n.f.* dismay.

Besuch', -e, *n.m.* visit, call; visitor, company; attendance.

besu'chen, *vb.* visit, attend.

Besu'cher, -, *n.m.* visitor.

betagt', *adj.* aged.

betä'tigen, *vb.* operate; show; (sich b.) be active.

betäu'ben, *vb.* stun, deafen, stupefy.

betäu'bend, *adj.* stupefying, narcotic, anesthetic.

Bete, -n, *n.f.* beet.

betei'ligen, *vb.* cause to share in; (sich b.) take part.

Betei'ligung, -en, *n.f.* participation.

beten, *vb.* pray.

beteu'ern, *vb.* assert, swear.

Beteu'erung, -en, *n.f.* assertion.

beti'teln, *vb.* entitle.

Beton', -s, *n.m.* concrete.

beto'nen, *vb.* stress.

Beto'nung, -en, *n.f.* stress.

betö'ren, *vb.* infatuate.

Betracht', *n.m.* consideration.

betrach'ten, *vb.* look at, consider, observe, contemplate.

beträcht'lich, *adj.* considerable.

Betrach'tung, -en, *n.f.* consideration, contemplation.

Betrag', -e, *n.m.* amount, sum.

betra'gen*, *vb.* amount to; (sich b.) behave.

Betra'gen, *n.nt.* behavior.

betrau'ern, *vb.* mourn for, deplore.

Betreff', *n.m.* (in B.) in regard to.

betref'fen*, *vb.* affect, concern.

betreffs', *prep.* in regard to.

betrei'ben*, *vb.* carry on.

betre'ten*, *vb.* step upon, enter.

betreu'en, *vb.* take care of.

Betrieb', -e, *n.m.* works, management, activity; (in B.) running.

betrin'ken*, *vb.* (sich b.) get drunk.

betrof'fen, *adj.* taken aback; affected.

betrü'ben, *vb.* grieve.

Betrüb'nis, -se, *n.f.* grief.

Betrug', *n.m.* deceit, deception, fraud.

betrü'gen*, *vb.* deceive, cheat.

betrü'gerisch, *adj.* deceitful, crooked.

betrun'ken, *adj.* drunk, drunken.

Bett, -en, *n.nt.* bed.

Bettdecke, -n, *n.f.* bedspread.

betteln, *vb.* beg.

Bettler, -, *n.m.* beggar.

Bettplatz, -e, *n.m.* berth.

Bettzeug, *n.nt.* bedding, bedclothes.

beugen, *vb.* bend.

Beugung, -en, *n.f.* bend; inflection.

Beule, -n, *n.f.* swelling, bump, lump.

beun'ruhigen, *vb.* disturb, agitate.

Beun'ruhigung, -en, *n.f.* alarm, agitation.

beur'kunden, *vb.* authenticate.

beur'lauben, *vb.* give leave (of absence) to.

beur'teilen, *vb.* judge.

Beute, -n, *n.f.* booty, loot.

Beutel, -, *n.m.* bag, purse, pouch.

Bevöl'kerung, -en, *n.f.* population.

bevoll'mächtigen, *vb.* authorize, give full power to.

Bevoll'mächtigung, -en, *n.f.* authorization.

bevor', *conj.* before.

bevor'stehen*, *vb.* be about to happen, be in store for.

bevor'stehend, *adj.* imminent.

bevor'zugen, *vb.* favor.

bewa'chen, *vb.* guard, watch.

bewaff'nen, *vb.* arm.

Bewaff'nung, -en, *n.f.* armament.

bewah'ren, *vb.* keep, preserve.

bewäh'ren, *vb.* (sich b.) prove itself.

Bewah'rung, -en, *n.f.* conservation.

bewäl'tigen, *vb.* overcome, master.

bewan'dert, *adj.* (b. in) experienced in, conversant with.

bewe'gen*, *vb.* induce.

bewe'gen, *vb.* move.

Beweg'grund, -e, *n.m.* motive.

beweg'lich, *adj.* movable, active.

Bewe'gung, -en, *n.f.* movement, motion, exercise.

bewe'gungslos, *adj.* motionless.

bewei'nen, *vb.* bewail, deplore.

Beweis', -e, *n.m.* proof, evidence.

bewei'sen*, *vb.* prove, demonstrate.

bewer'ben*, *vb.* (sich b. um) apply for.

Bewer'ber, -, *n.m.* applicant, contestant, suitor.

Bewer'bung, -en, *n.f.* application.

bewer'ten, *vb.* evaluate, grade.

bewil'ligen, *vb.* approve, appropriate.

Bewil'ligung, -en, *n.f.* approval, appropriation.

bewir'ken, *vb.* cause, effect.

bewir'ten, *vb.* be host to, entertain.

bewohn'bar, *adj.* habitable.

bewoh'nen, *vb.* inhabit.

Bewoh'ner, -, *n.m.* inhabitant, occupant.

bewölkt', *adj.* cloudy.

bewun'dern, *vb.* admire.

bewun'dernswert, *adj.* admirable.

Bewun'derung, -en, *n.f.* admiration.

bewußt', *adj.* conscious, aware.

bewußt'los, *adj.* unconscious.

Bewußt'sein, *n.nt.* consciousness; (bei B.) conscious.

bezah'len, *vb.* pay.

Bezah'lung, -en, *n.f.* pay, payment.

bezau'bern, vb. bewitch, enchant.

bezeich'nen, vb. mark, designate, signify.

bezeich'nend, adj. characteristic.

Bezeich'nung, -en, n.f. designation.

bezeu'gen, vb. testify, attest.

bezie'hen*, vb. cover with, upholster, put on clean sheets; move into; draw (pay); **(sich b.)** cloud over; **(sich b. auf)** refer to.

Bezie'hung, -en, n.f. reference, relation; pull, drag.

Bezirk', -e, n.m. district.

Bezug', -̈e, n.m. cover(ing), case; supply; reference.

Bezug'nahme, n.f. reference.

bezwe'cken, vb. have as one's purpose, aim at.

bezwei'feln, vb. doubt.

Bibel, -n, n.f. Bible.

Biber, -, n.m. beaver.

Bibliothek', -en, n.f. library.

Bibliothekar', -e, n.m. librarian.

Bibliotheka'rin, -nen, n.f. librarian.

biblisch, adj. Biblical.

bieder, adj. upright, bourgeois.

biegen*, vb. bend; **(sich b.)** buckle.

biegsam, adj. flexible, pliable.

Biegung, -en, n.f. bend.

Biene, -n, n.f. bee.

Bier, -e, n.nt. beer.

Bierlokal, -e, n.nt. tavern, pub.

Biest, -er, n.m. beast; brute.

bieten*, vb. bid, offer.

Bieter, -, n.m. bidder.

bifokal', adj. bifocal.

Bigamie', n.f. bigamy.

bigott', adj. bigoted.

Bild, -er, n.nt. picture, painting.

bilden, vb. form.

bildend, adj. educational, formative.

Bildhauer, -, n.m. sculptor.

bildhauern, vb. sculpture.

bildlich, adj. figurative.

Bildung, n.f. learning, education, refinement.

Billard, n.nt. billiards.

Billett', -e, n.nt. ticket.

billig, adj. cheap; equitable.

billigen, vb. approve.

Billigkeit, -en, n.f. cheapness, justness.

Billion', -en, n.f. billion.

Binde, -n, n.f. bandage; **(Damenbinde)** sanitary napkin.

binden*, vb. tie; bind.

bindend, adj. binding.

Bindestrich, -e, n.m. hyphen.

Bindfaden, -̈, n.m. string.

Bindung, -en, n.f. tie, bond; **(ski)** binding; **(fig.)** obligation.

binnen, prep. within.

Binnenland, -̈er, n.nt. inland.

Biographie', -i'en, n.f. biography.

biogra'phisch, adj. biographical.

Biologie', -i'en, n.f. biology.

biolo'gisch, adj. biological.

Biosignalrück'gabe, -n, n.f. biofeedback.

Birke, -n, n.f. birch.

Birne, -n, n.f. pear.

bis, adv.&prep. till, until.

Bischof, -̈e, n.m. bishop.

bisher', adv. hitherto.

Biskuit', -e, n.nt. biscuit.

Bißchen, -, n.nt. bit; **(ein b.)** a bit, a little.

Bissen, -, n.m. bite, mouthful.

Bit, -, n.nt. (computer) bit.

bitte, interj. please; you are welcome.

Bitte, -n, n.f. request, plea.

bitten*, vb. ask, request; beg.

bitter, adj. bitter.

bizarr', adj. bizarre, freak.

Bizeps, -e, n.m. biceps.

blähen, vb. bloat, puff up.

Blama'ge, -n, n.f. disgrace.

blamie'ren, vb. disgrace.

blank, adj. bright, shining; (without money) broke.

Blase, -n, n.f. bubble; bladder; blister.

Blasebalg, -̈e, n.m. bellows.

blasen*, vb. blow.

blaß, adj. pale.

Blässe, -n, n.f. paleness.

Blatt, -̈er, n.nt. leaf.

Blattern, n.pl. smallpox.

blau, adj. blue.

Blaubeere, -n, n.f. blueberry.

Blech, n.nt. tin.

Blei, n.nt. lead.

bleiben*, vb. stay, remain.

bleich, adj. pale; **(b. werden)** blanch.

bleichen, vb. bleach.

bleiern, adj. leaden.

bleifrei, adj. unleaded.

Bleistift, -e, n.m. pencil.

blenden, vb. blind, dazzle.

Blick, -e, n.m. look, glance.

blicken, vb. look, glance.

blind, adj. blind.

Blinddarm, -̈e, n.m. appendix.

Blinddarmentzündung, -en, n.f. appendicitis.

Blindheit, -en, n.f. blindness.

blinken, vb. blink.

Blinklicht, -er, n.nt. blinker.

blinzeln, vb. blink; wink.

Blitz, -e, n.m. lightning.

blitzen, vb. flash, emit lightening.

blitzsauber, adj. immaculate.

Block, -s, n.m. bloc; block; (paper) pad.

Blocka'de, -n, n.f. blockade.

blockfrei, adj. non-aligned.

blockie'ren, vb. block; (account) freeze.

blöde, adj. stupid, dumb.

Blödsinn, n.m. idiocy, nonsense.

blödsinnig, adj. idiotic.

blond, adj. blond.

bloß, 1. adj. bare. **2.** adv. only, merely.

Blöße, -n, n.f. nakedness; (fig.) weak spot.

Bloßstellung, -en, n.f. exposure.

Bluejeans, n.pl. blue jeans.

Bluff, -s, n.m. bluff.

bluffen, vb. bluff.

blühen, vb. bloom; flourish.

blühend, adj. prosperous.

Blume, -n, n.f. flower.

Blumengeschäft, -e, n.nt. flower shop.

Blumenhändler, -, n.m. florist.

Blumenkohl, -e, n.m. cauliflower.

Blumenstrauß, -̈e, n.m. bouquet.

blumig, adj. flowery.

Bluse, -n, n.f. blouse.

Blut, n.nt. blood.

blutarm, adj. anemic; (fig.) penniless.

Blutarmut, n.f. anemia.

Blutdruck, -e, n.m. blood pressure.

Blüte, -n, n.f. bloom, blossom; (fig.) prime.

bluten, vb. bleed.

blütenreich, adj. florid.

Bluterguß, -̈sse, n.m. hemorrhage.

Bluterkrankheit, n.f. hemophilia.

Bluthund, -e, n.m. bloodhound.

blutig, adj. bloody.

blutlos, adj. bloodless.

blutunterlaufen, adj. bloodshot.

Blutvergießen, n.nt. bloodshed.

Blutvergiftung, -en, n.f. blood poisoning.

Bö, -en, n.f. squall.

Bock, -̈e, n.m. buck.

bockig, adj. obstinate.

Bockwurst, -̈e, n.f. sausage.

Boden, -̈, n.m. ground, soil, bottom; floor; attic; **(Grund und B.)** real estate.

bodenlos, adj. bottomless.

Bodensatz, n.m. dregs.

Bogen, -, n.m. arch; bow; (paper) sheet.

Bogenschießen, n.nt. archery.

Bogenschütze, -n, -n, n.m. archer.

Böhme, -n, -n, n.m. Bohemian.

Böhmen, n.nt. Bohemia.

böhmisch, adj. Bohemian.

Bohne, -n, n.f. bean; **(grüne B.)** string bean.

bohren, vb. bore, drill.

Bohrer, -, n.m. drill.

Boli'vien, n.nt. Bolivia.

Bollwerk, -e, n.nt. bulwark.

bombardie'ren, vb. bombard.

Bombe, -n, n.f. bomb, bombshell.

bomben, vb. bomb.

Bombenflugzeug, -e, n.nt. bomber.

bombensicher, adj. bomb-proof.

Boot, -e, n.nt. boat.

Bord, -e, n.nt. shelf; board; **(an B.) aboard; (an B. gehen)** board.

Bordell, -e, n.nt. brothel.

Bordstein, -e, n.m. curb, curbstone.

borgen, vb. borrow.

borniert, adj. stupid.

Börse, -n, n.f. purse; stock exchange.

Borste, -n, n.f. bristle.

Borte, -n, n.f. trimming, braid.

Bös-, n.nt. evil.

bösartig, adj. malicious; (med.) malignant.

Böschung, -en, n.f. bank, embankment.

böse, adj. bad, evil; angry, mad.

Bösewicht, -e, n.m. scoundrel.

boshaft, adj. malicious.

Bosheit, -en, n.f. malice.

böswillig, adj. malevolent.

Bota'nik, n.f. botany.

bota'nisch, adj. botanical.

Bote, -n, -n, n.m. messenger.

Botschaft, -en, n.f. message; embassy.

Botschafter, -, n.m. ambassador.

Bouillon, -s, n.f. consommé.

boxen, vb. box, spar.

Boxen, n.nt. boxing.

Boxkampf, -e, n.m. boxing match.

Boykott, -e, n.m. boycott.

boykottie'ren, vb. boycott.

Brand, -e, n.m. conflagration; blight.

branden, vb. surge.

brandmarken, vb. brand.

Brandstifter, -, n.m. arsonist.

Brandstiftung, -en, n.f. arson.

Brandung, -en, n.f. surf, breakers.

Branntwein, -e, n.m. brandy.

Brasi'lien, n.nt. Brazil.

braten*, vb. roast, fry.

Braten, -, n.m. roast.

Bratpfanne, -n, n.f. frying pan, griddle.

Bratrost, -e, n.m. oven rack; broiler.

Bratsche, -n, n.f. viola.

Bräu, n.nt. brew.

Brauch, -e, n.m. custom, usage.

brauchbar, adj. useful.

brauchen, vb. need, require; use.

brauen, vb. brew.

Brauer, -, n.m. brewer.

Brauerei', -en, n.f. brewery.

braun, adj. brown.

bräunen, vb. brown; tan.

brausen, vb. roar.

Braut, -e, n.f. bride.

Brautführer, -, n.m. usher (at a wedding).

Bräutigam, -e, n.m. bridegroom.

Brautjungfer, -n, n.f. bridesmaid.

brav, adj. upright; (of children) good.

Bravour', n.f. bravado.

brechen*, vb. break; (med.) fracture.

Brechmittel, -, n.nt. emetic.

Brei, -e, n.m. pap; (fig.) pulp.

breit, adj. broad, wide.

Breite, -n, n.f. breadth, width; latitude.

Bremse, -n, n.f. brake; gadfly.

bremsen, vb. brake, put on the brake.

brennbar, adj. combustible.

brennen*, vb. burn, scorch.

brennend, adj. burning; fervid.

Brenner, -, n.m. burner.

Brennholz, n.nt. firewood.

Brennpunkt, -e, n.m. focus.

Brennstoff, -e, n.m. fuel.

brenzlich, adj. risky, precarious.

Brett, -er, n.nt. board, plank.

Bretterbude, -n, n.f. shack.

Brezel, -n, n.f. pretzel.

Brief, -e, n.m. letter.

Briefkasten, -, n.m. mailbox.

Briefmarke, -n, n.f. stamp.

Briefpapier, n.nt. stationery.

Brieftasche, -n, n.f. wallet, billfold.

Briefträger, -, n.m. postman.

Briefumschlag, -e, n.m. envelope.

Briefwechsel, n.m. correspondence.

Briga'de, -n, n.f. brigade.

Brille, -n, n.f. spectacles, glasses.

bringen*, vb. bring; take.

Brise, -n, n.f. breeze.

Britan'nien, n.nt. Britain.

Brite, -n, -n, n.m. Briton.

britisch, adj. British.

Brocken, -, n.m. crumb.

Brombeere, -n, n.f. blackberry.

bronchial', adj. bronchial.

Bronchi'tis, n.f. bronchitis.

Bronze, -n, n.f. brooch.

Broschü're, -n, n.f. pamphlet, booklet.

Brot, -e, n.nt. bread; **(beleg'tes B.)** sandwich.

Brötchen, -, n.nt. roll, bun.

Bruch, -e, n.m. break, breach, fracture; hernia; (fig.) violation.

brüchig, adj. brittle.

Bruchrechnung, n.f. fractions.

Bruchstück, -e, n.nt. fragment.

Bruchteil, -e, n.m. fraction.

Brücke, -n, n.f. bridge.

Bruder, -, n.m. brother.

brüderlich, adj. brotherly, fraternal.

Brüderschaft, -en, n.f. fraternity.

Brühe, -n, n.f. broth.

brühen, vb. scald.

brüllen, vb. yell, bellow, howl.

brummen, vb. hum, buzz; grumble.

Brünet'te, -n, n.f. brunette.

Brunnen, -, n.m. well, fountain.

brünstig, adj. fervent.

brüsk, adj. brusque.

Brust, -e, n.f. breast, chest.

brüsten (sich b.) boast.

Brut, -en, n.f. brood.

brutal', adj. brutal.

Brutalität', -en, n.f. brutality.

brüten, vb. brood.

brutto, adj. gross.

Bube, -n, -n, n.m. boy; (cards) jack.

Buch, -er, n.nt. book.

Buchbinder, -, n.m. bookbinder.

Buchbinderei', -ei'en, n.f. bookbindery.

Buche, -n, n.f. beech.

buchen, vb. book, reserve (plane seat, hotel).

Bücherei', -en, n.f. library.

Bücherschrank, -e, n.m. bookcase.

Buchführung, -en, n.f. accounting, bookkeeping.

Buchhalter, -, n.m. accountant, bookkeeper.

Buchhändler, -, n.m. bookseller.

Buchhandlung, -en, n.f. bookstore.

Büchse, -n, n.f. can.

Büchsenöffner, -, n.m. can opener.

Buchstabe(n), -, (or -n, -n), n.m. letter (of the alphabet).

buchstabie'ren, vb. spell; **(falsch b.)** misspell.

buchstäblich, adj. literal.

Bucht, -en, n.f. bay.

Buchweizen, n.m. buckwheat.

Buckel, -, n.m. hump, protuberance; hunchback.

buckelig, adj. hunchbacked.

bücken, vb. **(sich b.)** bend down, stoop.

Bude, -n, n.f. booth, stall, stand.

Büfett', -s, n.nt. buffet.

Büffel, -, n.m. buffalo.

Bug, -e, n.m. bow.

Bügeleisen, -, n.nt. flatiron.

bügeln, vb. iron, press.

Bühne, -n, n.f. stage.

Bühnenausstattung, -en, n.f. scenery.

Bulldogge, -n, n.f. bulldog.

Bulle, -n, -n, n.m. bull.

Bummel, -n, n.m. spree.

bummeln, vb. gallivant.

Bund, -e, n.m. league, federation.

Bund, -e, n.nt. bunch, bundle.

Bündel, -, n.nt. bundle.

Bundes, cpds. federal.

Bundesbahn, n.f. West German Federal Railway.

Bundeskanzler, n.m. chancellor of West Germany.

Bundesrat, n.m. upper house of West German parliament.

bundesstaatlich, adj. federal.

Bundestag, n.m. lower house of West German parliament.

Bündnis, -se, n.nt. alliance.

bunt, *adj.* colorful; varicolored, motley.

Bürde, -n, *n.f.* burden.

Bürge, -n, -n, *n.m.* sponsor, guarantor.

Bürger, -, *n.m.* citizen.

bürgerlich, *adj.* civil; bourgeois.

Bürgermeister, -, *n.m.* mayor.

Bürgerschaft, *n.f.* citizenry.

Bürgersteig, -e, *n.m.* sidewalk.

Burgfriede(n), -n, *n.m.* truce.

Bürgschaft, -en, *n.f.* guaranty, bond, bail.

Burgun'der, -, -, *n.m.* burgundy (wine).

Büro', -s, *n.nt.* office, bureau.

Bursche, -n, -n, *n.m.* chap, fellow.

Bürste, -n, *n.f.* brush.

bürsten, *vb.* brush.

Bus, -se, *n.m.* bus.

Busch, -e, *n.m.* bush, shrub.

Büschel, -, *n.nt.* bunch.

buschig, *adj.* bushy.

Busen, -, *n.m.* bosom.

Buße, -n, *n.f.* atonement, penitence; fine, penalty.

büßen, *vb.* do penance, atone for.

Büste, -n, *n.f.* bust.

Büstenhalter, -, *n.m.* brassiere.

Butter, *n.f.* butter.

Butterblume, -n, *n.f.* buttercup.

Butterbrot, -e, *n.nt.* slice of bread and butter.

Buttermilch, *n.f.* buttermilk.

buttern, *vb.* churn.

C

Café', -s, *n.nt.* café.

Cellist', -en, -en, *n.m.* cellist.

Cello, -s, *n.nt.* cello.

Chance, -n, *n.f.* opportunity, odds.

chao'tisch, *adj.* chaotic.

Charak'ter, -e're, *n.m.* character.

charakterisie'ren, *vb.* characterize.

charakteris'tisch, *adj.* characteristic.

Charis'ma, *n.nt.* charisma.

Charme, *n.m.* charm.

Charterflug, -e, *n.m.* charter flight.

Chauffeur', -e, *n.m.* chauffeur.

Chaussee', -e'en, *n.f.* highway.

Chef, -s, *n.m.* chef; boss.

Chemie', *n.f.* chemistry.

Chemika'lien, *n.pl.* chemicals.

Chemiker, -, *n.m.* chemist.

chemisch, *adj.* chemical.

Chemotherapie', *n.f.* chemotherapy.

Chiffre, -n, *n.f.* cipher.

China, *n.nt.* China.

Chine'se, -n, -n, *n.m.* Chinese.

chine'sisch, *adj.* Chinese.

Chinin', *n.nt.* quinine.

Chiroprak'tiker, -, *n.m.* chiropractor.

Chirurg', -en, -en, *n.m.* surgeon.

Chirurgie', *n.f.* surgery.

Chlor, -s, *n.nt.* chlorine.

Chloroform', -, *n.nt.* chloroform.

Cholera, *n.f.* cholera.

chole'risch, *adj.* choleric.

Chor, -s, *n.m.* choir; chorus.

Chorgang, -e, *n.m.* aisle.

Chorsänger, -, *n.m.* chorister.

Christ, -en, -en, *n.m.* Christian.

Christenheit, *n.f.* Christendom.

Christentum, -, *n.nt.* Christianity.

christlich, *adj.* Christian.

Christus, *n.m.* Christ.

Chrom, *n.nt.* chrome, chromium.

Chronik, -en, *n.f.* chronicle.

chronisch, *adj.* chronic.

Chronologie', -i'en, *n.f.* chronology.

chronolo'gisch, *adj.* chronological.

Chrysanthe'me, -en, *n.f.* chrysanthemum.

Clown, -s, *n.m.* clown.

Cocktail, -s, *n.m.* cocktail.

College, -s, *n.nt.* college.

Couch, -es, *n.f.* couch.

Coupon', -s, *n.m.* coupon.

Cousin', -s, *n.m.* (male) cousin.

Cousi'ne, -en, *n.f.* (female) cousin.

Cowboy, -s, *n.m.* cowboy.

Crème, -s, *n.f.* cream.

D

da, 1. *conj.* because, since, as. 2. *adv.* there; here; then.

dabei', *adv.* near it; present; in so doing, at the same time.

Dach, -er, *n.nt.* roof.

Dachrinne, -n, *n.f.* eaves.

Dachstube, -n, *n.f.* garret.

Dachtraufe, -n, *n.f.* gutter.

dadurch', *adv.* thereby.

dafür', *adv.* for that; instead.

dage'gen, *adv.* against it; on the other hand.

daher', *adv.* therefore, hence.

dahin', *adv.* (to) there.

dahin'ter, *adv.* behind it.

damals, *adv.* then, at that time.

Dame, -n, *n.f.* lady.

Damebrett, -er, *n.nt.* checkerboard.

Damenhut, -e, *n.m.* lady's hat.

Damenunterwäsche, *n.f.* lingerie.

Damespiel, *n.nt.* checkers.

damit', 1. *conj.* in order that. 2. *adv.* with it, with them, at that.

Damm, -e, *n.m.* dam, causeway, levee.

dämmern, *vb.* dawn.

Dämmerung, -en, *n.f.* twilight.

Dämon, -o'nen, *n.m.* demon.

Dampf, -e, *n.m.* steam, vapor fume.

Dampfboot, -e, *n.nt.* steamboat.

dampfen, *vb.* steam.

dämpfen, *vb.* muffle; (cooking) steam.

Dampfer, -, *n.m.* steamship.

Däne, -n, -n, *n.m.* Dane.

Dänemark, *n.nt.* Denmark.

dänisch, *adj.* Danish.

dank, *prep.* owing to.

Dank, -, *n.m.* thanks.

dankbar, *adj.* thankful, grateful.

Dankbarkeit, -en, *n.f.* gratitude.

danken, *vb.* thank.

dann, *adv.* then, after that.

darauf, *adv.* on it, on them; after that, thereupon.

dar-bieten°, *vb.* present.

Darbietung, -en, *n.f.* presentation; entertainment.

dar-legen, *vb.* state.

Darlegung, -en, *n.f.* exposé, exposition.

Darlehen, -, *n.nt.* loan.

Darm, -e, *n.m.* intestine.

dar-stellen, *vb.* represent, constitute; present; portray.

Darstellung, -en, *n.f.* presentation; representation, depiction; (graphische D.) diagram.

Dasein, *n.nt.* existence.

daß, *conj.* that.

Datenverarbeitung, -en, *n.f.* data processing.

datie'ren, *vb.* date.

Dattel, -n, *n.f.* date.

Datum, -ten, *n.nt.* date.

Dauer, *n.f.* duration, length.

dauerhaft, *adj.* durable, lasting.

Dauerhaftigkeit, *n.f.* durability.

dauern, *vb.* last, continue; take (a while).

dauernd, *adj.* lasting, continual.

Dauerwelle, -n, *n.f.* permanent wave.

Daumen, -, *n.m.* thumb.

Daune, -n, *n.f.* down.

dazu', *adv.* in addition.

dazwi'schen-kommen°, *vb.* intervene.

dazwi'schen-treten°, *vb.* intercede.

Dazwi'schentreten, *n.nt.* intervention.

DDR (Deutsche Demokrat'ische Republik) East Germany (German Democratic Republic).

Deba'kel, -, *n.nt.* debacle.

Debat'te, -n, *n.f.* debate.

Debet, -s, *n.nt.* debit.

Debüt', -s, *n.nt.* debut.

Debütan'tin, -nen, *n.f.* debutante.

Deck, -s, *n.nt.* deck.

Decke, -n, *n.f.* cover; blanket; ceiling.

Deckel', -n, *n.m.* lid.

decken, *vb.* cover; **(sich d.)** coincide, jibe.

Deckung', -en, *n.f.* cover(ing); collateral.

defekt', *adj.* defective.

Defekt', -e, *n.m.* defect.

Defensi've, -n, *n.f.* defensive.

Definition', -en, *n.f.* definition.

definitiv', *adj.* definite; definitive.

Defizit, -e, *n.nt.* deficit.

Deflation', -en, *n.f.* deflation.

Degen, -, *n.m.* sword; epée.

Degeneration', *n.f.* degeneration.

degeneriert', *adj.* degenerate.

degradie'ren, *vb.* demote.

dehnen, *vb.* stretch, expand; drawl.

Dehnung, -en, *n.f.* stretch(ing), expansion.

Deich, -e, *n.m.* dike.

Dekan', -e, *n.m.* dean.

Deklamation', -en, *n.f.* declamation.

deklamie'ren, *vb.* declaim.

deklarie'ren, *vb.* declare.

Deklination', -en, *n.f.* declension.

deklinie'ren, *vb.* decline.

Dekorateur', -e, *n.m.* decorator.

dekorativ', *adj.* decorative, ornamental.

dekorie'ren, *vb.* decorate.

Dekret', -e, *n.nt.* decree.

Delegation', -en, *n.f.* delegation.

delegie'ren, *vb.* delegate.

Delegiert', -, *n.m.&f.* delegate.

delikat', *adj.* delicate, dainty.

Delikates'se, -n, *n.f.* delicacy.

Deli'rium, -rien, *n.nt.* delirium.

Demago'ge, -n, -n, *n.m.* demagogue.

demgemäß, *adv.* accordingly.

demnächst', *adv.* shortly, soon.

demobilisie'ren, *vb.* demobilize.

Demobilisie'rung, -en, *n.f.* demobilization.

Demokrat', -en, -en, *n.m.* democrat.

Demokratie', -n, *n.f.* democracy.

demokra'tisch, *adj.* democratic.

demolie'ren, *vb.* wreck.

demonstrativ', *adj.* demonstrative.

demonstrie'ren, *vb.* demonstrate.

demoralisie'ren, *vb.* demoralize.

Demut, *n.f.* humility.

demütig, *adj.* humble.

demütigen, *vb.* humiliate.

Demütigung, -en, *n.f.* humiliation.

demzufolge, *adv.* accordingly; consequently.

denkbar, *adj.* imaginable.

denken*, *vb.* think, reason.

Denker, -, *n.m.* thinker.

Denkmal, "er, *n.nt.* monument, memorial.

Denkungsart, *n.f.* mode of thinking, mentality.

denkwürdig, *adj.* memorable.

denn, **1.** *conj.* for. **2.** *adv.* do tell me; I wonder.

dennoch, *adv.* still, yet, nevertheless.

denunzie'ren, *vb.* denounce, inform.

Deportation', -en *n.f.* deportation.

deportie'ren, *vb.* deport.

Depot', -s, *n.nt.* depot.

Depression', -en, *n.f.* depression.

deprimie'ren, *vb.* depress.

der, das, die, 1. *art.&adj.* the, that. **2.** *pron.* he, she, it, they; that one. **3.** *rel. pron.* who, which, that.

derart, 1. *adj.* such, of such a kind. **2.** *adv.* in such a way.

derb, *adj.* coarse; stout; earthy.

dermaßen, *adv.* to such a degree, in such a manner.

Deserteur', -e, *n.m.* deserter.

Desertion', -en, *n.f.* desertion.

deshalb, *adv.* therefore, hence.

desinfizie'ren, *vb.* disinfect.

desodorisie'ren, *vb.* deodorize.

Despot', -en, -en, *n.m.* despot.

despo'tisch, *adj.* despotic.

Destillation', -en, *n.f.* distillation.

destillie'ren, *vb.* distill.

desto, *adv.* **(d. besser)** so much the better; **(je mehr, d. besser)** the more the better.

deswegen, *adv.* therefore, that's why.

Detail', -s, *n.nt.* detail.

Detektiv', -e, *n.m.* detective.

deuten, *vb.* interpret; point.

deutlich, *adj.* clear, distinct.

deutsch, *adj.* German.

Deutsch-, *n.m.&f.* German.

Deutschland, *n.nt.* Germany.

Deutung, -en, *n.f.* interpretation.

Dezem'ber, -, *n.m.* December.

dezentralisie'ren, *vb.* decentralize.

Dezi'bel, -n, *n.f.* decibel.

Dezimal'-, *cpds.* decimal.

dezime'ren, *vb.* decimate.

Diagno'se, -n, *n.f.* diagnosis.

diagnostizie'ren, *vb.* diagnose.

diagonal', *adj.* diagonal.

Diagramm', -e, *n.nt.* graph.

Dialekt', -e, *n.m.* dialect.

Dialog', -e, *n.m.* dialogue.

Diamant', -en, *n.m.* diamond.

diametral', *adj.* diametrical.

Diät, -en, *n.f.* diet.

diät'gemäß, *adj.* dietary.

dicht, *adj.* dense, thick; tight.

Dichte, *n.f.* density.

Dichter, -, *n.m.* poet.

dichterisch, *adj.* poetic.

Dichtheit, *n.f.* thickness.

Dichtung, -en, *n.f.* poetry; *(tech.)* packing, gasket.

dick, *adj.* thick, fat, stout.

Dicke, *n.f.* thickness.

dicken, *vb.* thicken.

Dickicht, *n.nt.* thicket, brush.

dicklich, *adj.* chubby.

Dieb, -e, *n.m.* thief, robber.

Diebstahl, "e, *n.m.* theft, larceny.

Diele, -n, *n.f.* hall, hallway.

dienen, *vb.* serve.

Diener, -, *n.m.* valet, butler.

Dienerschaft, -en, *n.f.* servant.

Dienst, -e, *n.m.* service.

Dienstag, -e, *n.m.* Tuesday.

dienstbeflissen, *adj.* assiduous; officious.

Dienstmädchen, -, *n.nt.* maid.

Dienstpflicht, *n.f.* compulsory military service, draft.

Dienstvorschrift, -en, *n.f.* regulation.

Dieselmotor, -en, *n.m.* diesel engine.

dieser, -es, -e, *pron.&adj.* this.

differential', *adj.* differential.

differenzie'ren, *vb.* differentiate.

Diktat', -e, *n.nt.* dictation.

Dikta'tor, -o'ren, *n.m.* dictator.

diktato'risch, *adj.* dictatorial.

Diktatur', -en, *n.f.* dictatorship.

diktie'ren, *vb.* dictate.

Dilem'ma, -s, *n.nt.* dilemma, predicament.

Dilettant', -en, -en, *n.m.* dilettante.

Dill, *n.m.* dill.

Ding, -e, *n.nt.* thing.

dingen*, *vb.* hire.

Diphtherie', *n.f.* diphtheria.

Diplom', -e, *n.nt.* diploma.

Diplomat', -en, -en, *n.m.* diplomat.

Diplomatie', *n.f.* diplomacy.

diploma'tisch, *adj.* diplomatic.

direkt', *adj.* direct; downright.

Direkti've, -n, *n.f.* directive.

Direk'tor, -o'ren, *n.m.* director.

Direkto'rium, -ien, *n.nt.* directorate, directory.

Dirigent', -en, -en, *n.m.* conductor.

dirigie'ren, *vb.* conduct.

Diskont', -e, *n.m.* discount.

Diskont'satz, "e, *n.m.* interest rate.

Diskothek', -en, *n.f.* discotheque.

diskret', *adj.* discreet.

Diskretion', *n.f.* discretion.

diskriminie'ren, *vb.* discriminate.

Diskriminie'rung, -en, *n.f.* discrimination.

Diskussion', -en, *n.f.* discussion.

diskutie'ren, *vb.* discuss.

disqualifizie'ren, *vb.* disqualify.

Dissertation', -en, *n.f.* dissertation.

Disziplin', *n.f.* discipline.

diszipline'ren, *vb.* discipline.

Diva, -s, *n.f.* diva.

divers', *adj.* miscellaneous.

Division', -en, *n.f.* division.

D-Mark, -, *n.f.* (= deutsche Mark) mark, West German unit of currency.

doch, 1. *conj.* yet. 2. *adv.* yet; indeed; oh yes.

Docht, -e, *n.m.* wick.

Dock, -s, *n.nt.* dock.

docken, *vb.* dock.

Dogma, -men, *n.nt.* dogma.

dogma'tisch, *adj.* dogmatic.

Doktor, -o'ren, *n.m.* doctor.

Doktorat', -e, *n.nt.* doctorate.

doktrinär', *adj.* doctrinaire.

Dokument', -e, *n.nt.* document.

dokumenta'risch, *adj.* documentary.

dokumentie'ren, *vb.* document, authenticate.

Dolch, -e, *n.m.* dagger.

Dollar, -s, *n.m.* dollar.

dolmetschen, *vb.* interpret.

Dolmetscher, -, *n.m.* interpreter.

Dom, -e, *n.m.* cathedral, dome.

Domi'nion, -s, *n.nt.* dominion.

Donau, *n.f.* Danube.

Donner, -, *n.m.* thunder.

donnern, *vb.* thunder.

Donnerstag, -e, *n.m.* Thursday.

Donnerwetter, *n.nt.* (zum D.) confound it!; (what) in thunder.

Doppel-, *cpds.* double, dual.

Doppelgänger, -, *n.m.* double.

doppelkohlensaur, *adj.* (d. es Natron) bicarbonate of soda.

Doppelpunkt, -e, *n.m.* colon.

doppelt, *adj.* double.

Dorf, -̈er, *n.nt.* village.

Dorn, -en, *n.m.* thorn.

dörren, *vb.* dry, parch.

dort, *adv.* there.

Dose, -n, *n.f.* (small) box, can.

dösen, *vb.* doze.

Dosie'rung, -en, *n.f.* dosage.

Dosis, -sen, *n.f.* dose.

Drache, -n, -n, *n.m.* dragon.

Draht, -̈e, *n.m.* wire.

Drahtaufnahmegerät, -e, *n.nt.* wire recorder.

drahtlos, *adj.* wireless.

drall, *adj.* buxom.

Drama, -men, *n.nt.* drama.

Drama'tiker, -, *n.m.* dramatist.

drama'tisch, *adj.* dramatic.

dramatisie'ren, *vb.* dramatize.

Drang, -̈e, *n.m.* urge.

drängeln, *vb.* crowd.

drängen, *vb.* urge, press.

Drangsal, -e, *n.f.* distress.

drapie'ren, *vb.* drape.

drastisch, *adj.* drastic.

draußen, *adv.* outside.

Dreck, *n.m.* dirt, mud.

dreckig, *adj.* filthy.

Drehbuch, -̈er, *n.nt.* scenario (film).

drehen, *vb.* turn; make (a movie).

Drehpunkt, -e, *n.m.* pivot, fulcrum.

Drehung, -en, *n.f.* turning.

drei, *num.* three.

Dreieck, -e, *n.nt.* triangle.

dreifach, *adj.* triple.

dreifältig, *adj.* threefold.

dreimal, *adv.* thrice, three times.

dreißig, *num.* thirty.

dreißigst-, *adj.* thirtieth.

Dreißigstel, -, *n.nt.* thirtieth part; (ein d.) one-thirtieth.

dreist, *adj.* bold; fresh, nervy.

dreizehn, *num.* thirteen.

dreschen*, *vb.* thresh, thrash.

Drill, *n.m.* drill.

Drillbohrer, -, *n.m.* drill.

dringen*, *vb.* force one's way, penetrate; insist.

dringend, *adj.* urgent.

dringlich, *adj.* pressing.

Dringlichkeit, *n.f.* urgency.

drinnen, *adv.* inside.

dritt-, *adj.* third.

Drittel, -, *n.nt.* third part; (ein d.) one-third.

drittens, *adv.* in the third place, thirdly.

Dritte Welt, *n.f.* Third World.

drittletzt, *adj.* third from last.

Droge, -n, *n.f.* drug.

Drogerie', -'en, *n.f.* drug store.

Drogist', -en, *n.m.* druggist.

drohen, *vb.* threaten.

dröhnen, *vb.* sound, boom, roar.

Drohung, -en, *n.f.* threat.

drollig, *adj.* droll, funny.

Droschke, -n, *n.f.* hack, cab.

Drossel, -n, *n.f.* thrush.

drosseln, *vb.* throttle, cut down.

drüben, *adv.* over there.

Druck, -e, *n.m.* print(ing), impression.

Druck, -̈e, *n.m.* pressure.

drucken, *vb.* print.

Drucken, *n.nt.* printing.

drücken, *vb.* press, squeeze; oppress; (sich d.) get out of work, shirk.

drückend, *adj.* pressing, oppressive.

Druckerpresse, -n, *n.f.* printing-press.

drunter, *adv.* underneath.

Drüse, -n, *n.f.* gland.

Dschungel, -, *n.m. or nt.* (-n f.), jungle.

du, *pron.* you (familiar); thou.

ducken, *vb.* (sich d.) duck.

Duell', -e, *n.nt.* duel.

Duett', -e, *n.nt.* duet.

Duft, -̈e, *n.m.* fragrance.

duftig, *adj.* fragrant.

dulden, *vb.* tolerate.

duldsam, *adj.* tolerant.

Duldsamkeit, *n.f.* tolerance.

dumm(-), *adj.* stupid, dumb.

Dummheit, -en, *n.f.* stupidity.

Dummkopf, -̈e, *n.m.* dullard, idiot.

dumpf, *adj.* dull, musty.

Düne, -n, *n.f.* dune.

Dung, *n.m.* dung.

düngen, *vb.* fertilize.

Dünger, *n.m.* fertilizer, manure.

dunkel, *adj.* dark; obscure.

Dunkel, *n.nt.* dark(ness).

Dünkel, *n.m.* pretension.

dünken*, *vb.* seem; (mich dünkt) methinks.

dünn, *adj.* thin.

Dunst, -̈e, *n.m.* haze, vapor.

dunsten, *vb.* steam, fume.

dünsten, *vb.* steam, stew.

dunstig, *adj.* hazy.

Duplikat', -e, *n.nt.* duplicate.

Dur, *n.nt.* major; (A-Dur) A-major.

durch, *prep.* through; by means of.

durchaus', *adv.* entirely, by all means.

durchblät'tern, *vb.* leaf through.

Durchblick, -e, *n.m.* view (through something).

durch-blicken, *vb.* look through; be visible.

durchbli'cken, *vb.* see through, discern.

durchboh'ren, *vb.* pierce.

Durchbruch, -̈e, *n.m.* breakthrough.

durchdacht', *adj.* thought out.

durch-drehen, *vb.* panic.

durch-dringen*, *vb.* force one's way through, penetrate.

durchdrin'gen*, *vb.* permeate, impregnate.

durcheinan'der, *adv.* through one another; all mixed up.

Durcheinan'der, *n.nt.* confusion, turmoil, mess.

Durchfahrt, -en, *n.f.* passage, transit.

Durchfall, *n.m.* diarrhea.

durch-fallen*, *vb.* fail (a test).

durchführbar, *adj.* practicable.

durch-führen, *vb.* carry out.

Durchgang, -̈e, *n.m.* passage through; passageway; (D. gesperrt!) closed to traffic.

durch-gehen*, *vb.* go through; bolt, run away.

durchgehend, *adj.* nonstop.

durch-helfen*, *vb.* help through; (sich d.) get along somehow.

durch-kreuzen, *vb.* cross out.

durchkreu'zen, *vb.* cross, intersect; thwart.

durch-leuchten, *vb.* shine through.

durchleuch'ten, *vb.* illuminate, irradiate, X-ray.

durchlö'chern, *vb.* perforate, puncture.

Durchlö'cherung, -en, *n.f.* perforation.

Durchmesser, -, *n.m.* diameter.

durchnäs'sen, *vb.* drench, soak.

Durchreise, -n, *n.f.* journey through; (auf der D.) passing through.

durch-schauen, *vb.* look through.

durchschau'en, *vb.* see through, understand.

durch-schneiden*, vb. cut in two.

durchschnei'den*, vb. cut, bisect, intersect.

Durchschnitt, -e, n.m. average.

durchschnittlich, adj. average.

durch-sehen*, vb. see through.

durchse'hen*, vb. look over, scrutinize; revise.

durch-setzen, vb. put through, get accepted.

durchset'zen, vb. intersperse, permeate.

Durchsicht, n.f. view; perusal.

durchsichtig, adj. transparent.

durch-sickern, vb. leak through, seep through.

durch-stechen*, vb. stick through.

durchste'chen*, vb. puncture, pierce.

durchsu'chen, vb. search.

Durchsu'chung, -en, n.f. search.

durchwüh'len, vb. ransack.

dürfen*, vb. be permitted, may.

dürftig, adj. meager.

dürr, adj. dry, barren.

Dürre, -n, n.f. drought, barrenness.

Durst, n.m. thirst.

dürsten, vb. thirst.

durstig, adj. thirsty.

Dusche, -n, n.f. shower.

Düse, -n, n.f. nozzle, jet.

Dusel, n.m. good luck.

duselig, adj. fizzy; stupid.

Düsenflugzeug, -e, n.nt. jet plane.

Düsenkampfflugzeug, n.nt. jet fighter plane.

düster, adj. gloomy.

Düsterheit, n.f. gloom.

Dutzend, -e, n.nt. dozen.

duzen, vb. call a person du.

Dyna'mik, n.f. dynamics.

dyna'misch, adj. dynamic.

Dynamit', n.nt. dynamite.

Dyna'mo, -s, n.m. dynamo.

Dynastie', -i'en, n.f. dynasty.

Dyslexie', n.f. dyslexia.

D-Zug, -̈e, n.m. (= Durchgangszug) train with corridors in the cars; express train.

E

Ebbe, n.f. low tide.

ebben, vb. ebb.

eben, adj. even, level.

eben, adv. just; exactly.

Ebene, -n, n.f. plain, level ground; plane.

ebenfalls, adv. likewise.

ebenso, adv. likewise; (e. groß) just as big.

ebnen, vb. level, make smooth.

Echo, -s, n.nt. echo.

echt, adj. genuine.

Echtheit, -en, n.f. authenticity, genuineness.

Ecke, -n, n.f. corner.

eckig, adj. angular.

edel, adj. noble.

Edelstein, -e, n.m. jewel.

Efeu, n.m. ivy.

EG (Europäische Gemeinschaft), n.f. Common Market.

egal', adj. equal; (es ist mir e.) I don't care, it makes no difference to me.

Egois'mus, n.m. egoism.

Egoist', -en, -en, n.m. egotist.

Egotis'mus, n.m. egotism.

ehe, conj. before.

Ehe, -n, n.f. marriage, matrimony.

Ehebrecher, -, n.m. adulterer.

Ehebrecherin, -nen, n.f. adulteress.

Ehebruch, -̈e, n.m. adultery.

ehedem, adv. formerly.

Ehefrau, -en, n.f. wife.

Ehegatte, -n, -n, n.m. spouse; husband.

Ehegattin, -nen, n.f. wife.

ehelich, adj. marital; legitimate.

ehelos, adj. celibate.

Ehelosigkeit, n.f. celibacy.

ehemalig, adj. former.

ehemals, adv. formerly.

Ehemann, -̈er, n.m. husband.

Ehepaar, -e, n.nt. married couple.

eher, adv. sooner, earlier; rather.

ehern, adj. brazen, brass.

Ehescheidung, -en, n.f. divorce.

Ehestand, n.m. matrimony.

ehrbar, adj. honorable.

Ehre, -n, n.f. honor.

ehren, vb. honor.

ehrenamtlich, adj. honorary, unpaid.

Ehrengast, -̈e, n.m. guest of honor.

Ehrenplatz, -̈e, n.m. place of honor.

ehrenvoll, adj. honorable.

ehrenwert, adj. worthy.

ehrerbietig, adj. respectful.

Ehrerbietung, -en, n.f. reverence, obeisance.

Ehrfurcht, n.f. awe, respect, reverence.

Ehrgeiz, n.m. ambition.

ehrgeizig, adj. ambitious.

ehrlich, adj. honest, sincere.

Ehrlichkeit, -en, n.f. honesty.

ehrlos, adj. dishonorable.

Ehrlosigkeit, n.f. dishonor.

ehrsam, adj. honest, respectable.

Ehrsamkeit, n.f. respectability.

Ehrung, -en, n.f. tribute.

ehrwürdig, adj. reverend, venerable.

Ei, -er, n.nt. egg.

Eiche, -n, n.f. oak.

Eichhörnchen, -, n.nt. squirrel.

Eid, -e, n.m. oath.

Eidam, -e, n.m. son-in-law.

eidesstattlich, adj. under oath; (e.e Erklä'rung) affidavit.

Eidgenosse, -n, -n, n.m. confederate.

Eidgenossenschaft, -en, n.f. confederation; (Schweizerische E.) Swiss Confederation.

eidgenössisch, adj. federal; Swiss.

Eifer, n.m. zeal, eagerness.

Eifersucht, n.f. jealousy.

eifersüchtig, adj. jealous.

eifrig, adj. zealous, eager, ardent.

Eigelb, n.nt. yolk.

eigen, adj. own; typical of.

Eigenart, -en, n.f. peculiarity, inherent nature.

eigenartig, adj. peculiar.

Eigenheit, -en, n.f. peculiarity.

eigenmächtig, adj. arbitrary.

Eigenname(n), -, n.m. proper name.

Eigennutz, n.m. selfishness.

eigennützig, adj. selfish.

Eigenschaft, -en, n.f. quality.

Eigenschaftswort, -̈er, n.nt. adjective.

Eigensinn, n.m. obstinacy, willfulness.

eigensinnig, adj. obstinate, willful.

eigentlich, 1. adj. actual. 2. adv. as a matter of fact.

Eigentum, n.nt. property.

Eigentümer, -, n.m. owner.

Eigentumswohnung, -en, n.f. condominium.

eignen, vb. (sich e.) be suited.

Eilbote, -n, -n, n.m. special delivery messenger; (per E.n) by special delivery.

Eilbrief, -e, n.m. special delivery letter.

Eile, n.f. haste, hurry.

eilen, vb. hurry.

eilig, adj. hasty, urgent.

Eilpost, n.f. special delivery.

Eimer, -, n.m. pail.

ein, -, -e, art. & adj. a, an; (stressed) one.

einan'der, pron. one another, each other.

ein-äschern, vb. cremate.

Einäscherung, -en, n.f. cremation.

ein-atmen, vb. inhale.

Einbahn-, cpds. one-way.

Einband, -̈e, n.m. binding.

ein-bauen, vb. install.

ein-behalten*, vb. withhold.

ein-berufen*, vb. summon, convoke.

ein-bilden, vb. (sich e.) imagine.

Einbildung, -en, n.f. imagination; conceit.

ein-binden*, vb. bind.

Einblick, -e, n.m. insight.

Einbrecher, -, n.m. burglar.

ein-bringen*, vb. yield.

Einbruch, -̈e, n.m. burglary.

Einbuchtung, -en, n.f. dent; bay.

ein-bürgern, vb. naturalize.
Einbuße, n.f. forfeiture.
ein-büßen, vb. forfeit.
ein-dämmen, vb. dam.
eindeutig, adj. clear, unequivocal.
ein-dringen, vb. (sich e.) encroach upon.
ein-dringen*, vb. penetrate, intrude, invade.
Eindringling, -e, n.m. intruder.
Eindruck, -̈e, n.m. impression.
eindrucksvoll, adj. impressive.
ein-engen, vb. hem in.
einer, -es, -e, pron. one, a person; one thing.
einerlei*, adj. of one kind; (es ist mir e.) it's all the same to me.
einerseits, adv. on the one hand.
einfach, adj. simple, plain.
Einfachheit, n.f. simplicity.
Einfahrt, -en, n.f. gateway, entrance.
Einfall, -e, n.m. collapse; bright idea.
ein-fallen*, vb. fall in; invade; occur to.
einfältig, adj. simple.
ein-fassen, vb. edge, trim.
ein-finden*, vb. (sich e.) present oneself, show up.
ein-flößen, vb. instill with.
Einfluß, -̈sse, n.m. influence.
einflußreich, adj. influential.
ein-fordern, vb. demand, reclaim.
einförmig, adj. uniform.
ein-fügen, vb. insert; (sich e.) adapt oneself.
Einfuhr, n.f. import, importation.
ein-führen, vb. import, induct.
Einführung, -en, n.f. induction; introduction.
Eingabe, -n, n.f. petition; (computer) input.
Eingang, -̈e, n.m. entrance.
ein-geben*, vb. give; inspire.
eingebildet, adj. conceited.
eingeboren, adj. native, indigenous.
Eingeborenen-, n.m.&f. native.
Eingebung, -en, n.f. inspiration.
eingedenk, adj. mindful.
eingefleischt, adj. inveterate.
ein-gehen*, vb. enter; shrink; cease, perish.
eingehend, adj. detailed, thorough.
Eingemachte-, n.nt. preserves.
eingenommen, adj. partial, prejudiced.
Eingesessen-, n.m.&f. inhabitant.
Eingeständnis, -sse, n.nt. confession, admission.
ein-gestehen*, vb. confess, admit.
Eingeweide, n.pl. intestines.
ein-gewöhnen, vb. acclimate.
ein-graben*, vb. bury.
ein-greifen*, vb. interfere.

Eingriff, -e, n.m. intervention.
ein-halten*, vb. check, stop; observe, keep.
ein-händigen, vb. hand in.
einheimisch, adj. native.
Einheimisch-, n.m.&f. native.
Einheit, -en, n.f. unit.
einheitlich, adj. uniform.
einher', adv. along.
ein-holen, vb. gather; overtake.
ein-hüllen, vb. wrap up, enfold.
einig, adj. united, agreed.
einige, pron.&adj. some, several.
einigen, vb. unite; (sich e.) agree.
einigermaßen, adv. to some extent.
Einigkeit, n.f. unity.
ein-impfen, vb. inoculate.
ein-kassieren, vb. collect.
Einkauf, -̈e, n.m. purchase.
ein-kaufen, vb. purchase.
ein-kehren, vb. put up (at an inn).
ein-kerkern, vb. incarcerate.
ein-klammern, vb. bracket; put in parentheses.
Einklang, -̈e, n.m. harmony.
ein-kleiden, vb. clothe.
ein-klemmen, vb. wedge in.
Einkommen, -, n.nt. income.
Einkommensteuer, -n, n.f. income tax.
ein-kreisen, vb. encircle.
Einkünfte, n.pl. revenue.
ein-laden*, vb. invite.
Einladung, -en, n.f. invitation.
Einlage, -n, n.f. enclosure, filling; deposit.
Einlaß, -̈sse, n.m. admission, entrance.
ein-laufen*, vb. enter; shrink.
ein-legen, vb. insert; deposit; pickle.
ein-leiten, vb. introduce.
einleitend, adj. introductory.
Einleitung, -en, n.f. introduction.
ein-leuchten, vb. make sense.
einleuchtend, adj. plausible.
ein-lösen, vb. redeem.
Einlösung, -en, n.f. redemption.
ein-machen, vb. preserve, can.
einmal, adv. once; (auf e.) all of a sudden; (noch e.) once again; (nicht e.) not even.
einmalig, adj. occurring only once, single, unique.
Einmarsch, -̈e, n.m. marching into, entry.
ein-mauern, vb. wall in.
ein-mengen, vb. mix in; (sich e.) interfere.
ein-mischen, vb. mix in; (sich e.) intervene, meddle.
Einmischung, -en, n.f. intervention.
Einnahme, -n, n.f. receipt; capture.
ein-nehmen*, vb. take; captivate.
Einöde, n.f. desolate place, solitude.

ein-ordnen, vb. arrange, file.
ein-packen, vb. pack up, wrap up.
ein-pflanzen, vb. plant.
ein-prägen, vb. impress.
ein-rahmen, vb. frame.
ein-räumen, vb. concede.
ein-rechnen, vb. include, allow for.
Einrede, -n, n.f. objection.
ein-reden, vb. talk into, persuade.
ein-reihen, vb. arrange.
ein-reißen*, vb. tear down.
ein-richten, vb. furnish, arrange, establish.
Einrichtung, -en, n.f. arrangement, institution.
ein-rücken, vb. move in; indent.
eins, num. one.
einsam, adj. lone(ly), lonesome.
Einsamkeit, n.f. loneliness, solitude.
ein-sammeln, vb. gather in.
Einsatz, -̈e, n.m. inset; stake (in betting); (mil.) sortie.
ein-schalten, vb. switch on, shift into, tune in.
ein-schärfen, vb. inculcate.
ein-schätzen, vb. assess, estimate.
ein-schiffen, vb. embark.
ein-schlafen*, vb. go to sleep.
Einschlag, -̈e, n.m. impact; envelope.
ein-schlagen*, vb. drive in; strike, break; take.
einschlägig, adj. pertinent, relevant.
ein-schließen*, vb. lock up, in; enclose, include, involve.
einschliesslich, adj. inclusive.
ein-schmeicheln, vb. (sich e.) insinuate oneself.
ein-schnappen, vb. snap shut; get annoyed.
Einschnitt, -e, n.m. cut, notch, segment.
ein-schränken, vb. limit, restrict.
Einschränkung, -en, n.f. restriction.
Einschreibebrief, -e, n.m. registered letter.
ein-schreiben*, vb. inscribe; register.
ein-schüchtern, vb. intimidate.
Einschüchterung, -en, n.f. intimidation.
ein-segnen, vb. consecrate, confirm.
ein-sehen*, vb. look into, realize.
ein-seifen, vb. soap, lather.
einseitig, adj. one-sided.
ein-setzen, vb. set in; appoint; install.
Einsicht, -en, n.f. insight; inspection.
Einsiedler, -, n.m. hermit.
ein-spannen, vb. stretch; harness, enlist.

ein·sperren, *vb.* lock up, imprison.

ein·spritzen, *vb.* inject.

Einspritzung, -en, *n.f.* injection.

Einspruch, ⁀e, *n.m.* protest; (E. erhe'ben*) to protest.

einst, *adv.* once, one day.

ein·stecken, *vb.* put in one's pocket.

ein·stehen*, *vb.* (e. für) stand up for, take the place of.

ein·steigen*, *vb.* get in; (e.!) allaboard!

ein·stellen, *vb.* put in, tune in, engage; stop, suspend.

Einstellung, -en, *n.f.* attitude; adjustment; suspension.

ein·stimmen, *vb.* chime in, join in, agree.

einstimmig, *adj.* unanimous.

Einstimmigkeit, -en *n.f.* unanimity.

ein·studieren, *vb.* practice, rehearse.

Einsturz, ⁀e, *n.m.* collapse.

einstweilen, *adv.* in the meantime.

ein·tauchen, *vb.* dip.

ein·tauschen, *vb.* exchange, swap.

ein·teilen, *vb.* divide, arrange, classify.

Einteilung, -en, *n.f.* classification.

eintönig, *adj.* monotonous.

Eintracht, *n.f.* harmony, concord.

ein·tragen*, *vb.* register, enter, record; bring in.

einträglich, *adj.* profitable.

Eintragung, -en, *n.f.* entry.

ein·treffen*, *vb.* arrive, happen.

ein·treten*, *vb.* enter.

Eintritt, -e, *n.m.* entry; beginning.

Eintrittskarte, -n, *n.f.* ticket of admission.

ein·üben, *vb.* practice.

ein·verleiben, *vb.* incorporate, annex.

Einvernehmen, -, *n.nt.* accord.

Einverständnis, -se, *n.nt.* agreement.

Einwand, ⁀e, *n.m.* objection.

Einwanderer, -, *n.m.* immigrant.

ein·wandern, *vb.* immigrate.

Einwanderung, -en, *n.f.* immigration.

einwandfrei, *adj.* sound, unobjectionable.

ein·wechseln, *vb.* change, cash.

ein·weichen, *vb.* soak.

ein·weihen, *vb.* consecrate, initiate.

Einweihung, -en, *n.f.* consecration, inauguration.

ein·wenden*, *vb.* wrap up.

ein·werfen*, *vb.* throw in; object, interject.

ein·wickeln, *vb.* wrap up.

ein·willigen, *vb.* consent.

Einwilligung, -en, *n.f.* consent, approval.

Einwirkung, -en, *n.f.* influence.

Einwohner, -, *n.m.* inhabitant, resident.

Einwurf, ⁀e, *n.m.* slot; objection.

ein·zahlen, *vb.* pay in, deposit.

Einzahlung, -en, *n.f.* deposit.

Einzäunung, -en, *n.f.* enclosure.

ein·zeichnen, *vb.* inscribe.

Einzelheit, -en, *n.f.* detail.

einzeln, *adj.* single, individual.

ein·ziehen*, *vb.* (tr.) pull in, furl, seize, draft; (intr.) move in, march in.

einzig, *adj.* only, sole, single.

einzigartig, *adj.* unique.

Einzug, ⁀e, *n.m.* entry.

ein·zwingen, *vb.* force in, squeeze in.

Eis, *n.nt.* ice.

Eisberg, -e, *n.m.* iceberg.

Eisen, *n.nt.* iron.

Eisenbahn, -en, *n.f.* railroad.

Eisenbahnwagen, -, *n.m.* railroad coach.

Eisenwaren, *n.pl.* hardware.

eisern, *adj.* iron.

eisig, *adj.* icy.

Eisregen, *n.m.* sleet.

Eisschrank, ⁀e, *n.m.* ice-box, refrigerator.

eitel, *adj.* vain.

Eitelkeit, -en *n.f.* vanity.

Eiter, *n.m.* pus.

Eiterbeule, -n, *n.f.* abscess.

Eitergeschwulst, ⁀e, *n.f.* abscess.

Eiweiß, *n.nt.* white of egg.

Ekel, *n.m.* disgust.

ekelerregend, *adj.* nauseating.

ekelhaft, *adj.* disgusting.

ekeln, *vb.* arouse disgust; (sich e. vor) be disgusted by.

EKG (**Elektrokardiogramm'**, -e), *n.nt.* electrocardiogram.

Ekstase, -n, *n.f.* ecstasy.

eksta'tisch, *adj.* ecstatic.

Ekzem', -e, *n.nt.* eczema.

elas'tisch, *adj.* elastic.

Elefant', -en, -en, *n.m.* elephant.

elegant', *adj.* elegant, chic, smart.

Eleganz', *n.f.* elegance.

elektrifizie'ren, *vb.* electrify.

Elek'triker, -, *n.m.* electrician.

elek'trisch, *adj.* electric.

Elektrizität', *n.f.* electricity.

Elek'tron, -o'nen, *n.nt.* electron.

Elektro'nenrechner, -, *n.m.* computer.

Elektro'nenwissenschaft, *n.f.* electronics.

Element', -e, *n.nt.* element.

elementar', *adj.* elemental, elementary.

Elend, *n.nt.* misery.

elend, *adj.* miserable, wretched; sick.

elf, *num.* eleven.

Elfenbein, *n.nt.* ivory.

elft-, *adj.* eleventh.

Elftel, -, *n.nt.* eleventh part; (ein e.) one-eleventh.

Eli'te, *n.f.* elite.

Elixier', -e, *n.nt.* elixir.

Ellbogen, -, *n.m.* elbow.

Elle, -, *n.f.* ell, yard.

Elsaß, *n.nt.* Alsace.

elterlich, *adj.* parental.

Eltern, *n.pl.* parents.

Email'le, *n.f.* enamel.

emanzipie'ren, *vb.* emancipate.

Embar'go, -s, *n.nt.* embargo.

Emblem', -e, *n.nt.* emblem.

Embryo, -s, *n.m.* embryo.

Empfang', ⁀e, *n.m.* reception.

empfan'gen*, *vb.* receive; conceive (child).

Empfäng'er, -, *n.m.* receiver, recipient, addressee.

empfäng'lich, *adj.* susceptible.

empfeh'len*, *vb.* recommend, commend.

empfeh'lenswert, *adj.* (re)commendable.

Empfeh'lung, -en, *n.f.* recommendation.

empfin'den*, *vb.* feel, sense.

empfind'lich, *adj.* sensitive.

empfind'sam, *adj.* sentimental.

Empfin'dung, -en, *n.f.* feeling, sensation.

empfin'dungslos, *adj.* insensitive.

empor', *adv.* upward, aloft.

empö'ren, *vb.* make indignant; (sich e.) be furious; rebel.

empor'ragen, *vb.* rise up, tower.

empor'schwingen*, *vb.* (sich e.) soar upward.

Empö'rung, -en, *n.f.* indignation; rebellion.

emsig, *adj.* busy, industrious.

Emulsion', -en, *n.f.* emulsion.

Ende, -n, *n.nt.* end.

enden, *vb.* end.

endgültig, *adj.* definitive, conclusive, final.

endigen, *vb.* end.

endlich, **1.** *adj.* final; finite. **2.** *adv.* at last.

endlos, *adj.* endless.

Endstation, -en, *n.f.* terminus.

Energie', -n, *n.f.* energy.

energie'los, *adj.* languid.

ener'gisch, *adj.* energetic.

eng, *adj.* narrow, tight.

engagie'ren, *vb.* engage, hire.

Enge, -n, *n.f.* narrowness; narrow place; (in die E. trei'ben*) drive into a corner.

Engel, -, *n.m.* angel.

England, *n.nt.* England.

Engländer, -, *n.m.* Englishman.

englisch, *adj.* English.

Enkel, -, *n.m.* grandson.

Enkelin, -nen, *n.f.* granddaughter.

Enkelkind, -er, *n.nt.* grandchild.

enorm', *adj.* enormous.

Ensem'ble, -s, *n.nt.* ensemble.

entar'ten, *vb.* degenerate.

entbeh'ren, *vb.* go without.

entbehr'lich, *adj.* dispensable.

Entbeh'rung, -en, *n.f.* privation.

entbin'den*, *vb.* set free; deliver.

Entbin'dung, -en, *n.f.* delivery.

entblö'ßen, *vb.* denude, uncover, bare.

entde'cken, *vb.* discover.

Entde'ckung, -en, *n.f.* discovery.

Ente, -n, *n.f.* duck.

enteh'ren, *vb.* dishonor.

entelg'nen, *vb.* dispossess.

entfa'chen, *vb.* kindle.

entfal'len*, *vb.* fall to; slip from (memory).

entfal'ten, *vb.* unfold.

entfer'nen, *vb.* remove.

entfernt', *adj.* removed; distant.

Entfer'nung, -en, *n.f.* removal; distance.

entfes'seln, *vb.* unchain, release.

entflam'men, *vb.* inflame.

entflie'hen*, *vb.* flee, escape.

entfrem'den, *vb.* estrange, alienate.

entfüh'ren*, *vb.* carry off, abduct, kidnap.

Entfüh'rung, -en, *n.f.* abduction.

entge'gen, *adv.&prep.* opposite, contrary to; towards.

entge'gengesetzt, *adj.* opposite.

entge'genkommen*, *vb.* come towards; be obliging.

entge'gensetzen, *vb.* oppose.

entgeg'nen, *vb.* reply, retort.

entge'hen*, *vb.* elude.

Entgelt', *n.nt.* remuneration.

entglei'sen*, *vb.* jump the track; make a slip.

Entglei'sung, -en, *n.f.* derailment; blunder.

enthal'ten*, *vb.* hold, contain; (sich e.) refrain.

enthalt'sam, *adj.* abstemious.

Enthalt'samkeit, -en, *n.f.* abstinence.

Enthal'tung, *n.f.* forbearance.

enthe'ben*, *vb.* oust.

Enthe'bung, -en, *n.f.* ouster.

enthül'len, *vb.* unveil, disclose.

Enthül'lung, -en, *n.f.* disclosure, exposé.

Enthusiast', -en, -en, *n.m.* enthusiast.

entklei'den, *vb.* undress, divest.

entkom'men*, *vb.* escape.

entkräf'ten, *vb.* debilitate.

entla'den*, *vb.* unload.

entlang', *adv.&prep.* along.

entlas'sen*, *vb.* dismiss, release.

Entlas'sung, -en, *n.f.* dismissal, release.

entlau'fen*, *vb.* run away.

entle'digen, *vb.* free from, exempt.

entle'gen, *adj.* remote.

entmilitarisie'ren, *vb.* demilitarize.

entmu'tigen, *vb.* discourage.

Entmu'tigung, -en, *n.f.* discouragement.

entneh'men*, *vb.* take from, infer from.

entner'ven, *vb.* enervate.

entrah'men, *vb.* skim.

enträt'seln, *vb.* decipher.

entrei'ßen*, *vb.* snatch from.

entrich'ten, *vb.* pay, settle.

entrin'nen*, *vb.* run away from.

entrüs'ten, *vb.* make indignant; (sich e.) become indignant.

entrüs'tet, *adj.* indignant.

Entrüs'tung, -en, *n.f.* indignation.

entsa'gen, *vb.* renounce, abjure.

entschä'digen, *vb.* compensate, indemnify.

Entschä'digung, -en, *n.f.* compensation, indemnification.

entschei'den*, *vb.* decide.

entschei'dend, *adj.* decisive.

Entschei'dung, -en, *n.f.* decision.

entschie'den, *adj.* decided, definite.

entschlie'ßen*, *vb.* (sich e.) decide.

entschlos'sen, *adj.* determined.

Entschlos'senheit, *n.f.* determination.

entschlüp'fen, *vb.* slip away from.

Entschluß', -sse, *n.m.* decision.

entschul'digen, *vb.* excuse; (sich e.) apologize.

Entschul'digung, -en, *n.f.* excuse, apology.

entset'zen, *vb.* dismiss; horrify; (sich e.) be horrified.

Entset'zen, *n.nt.* horror.

entsetz'lich, *adj.* horrible.

entsin'nen*, *vb.* (sich e.) recollect.

entspan'nen, *vb.* relax.

Entspan'nung, *n.f.* détente.

entspre'chen*, *vb.* correspond.

entspre'chend, *adj.* corresponding (to), respective.

entste'hen*, *vb.* arise, originate.

entstel'len, *vb.* disfigure, deform, distort, mutilate, garble.

enttäu'schen, *vb.* disappoint.

Enttäu'schung, -en, *n.f.* disappointment.

entthro'nen, *vb.* dethrone.

entwaff'nen, *vb.* disarm.

entwäs'sern, *vb.* drain.

entweder, *conj.* (e. . . . oder) either . . . or.

entwei'chen*, *vb.* escape.

entwen'den*, *vb.* steal.

entwer'fen*, *vb.* sketch, draft, plan.

entwer'ten, *vb.* depreciate, cancel.

entwi'ckeln, *vb.* develop.

Entwick'ler, -, *n.m.* developer.

Entwick'lung, -en, *n.f.* development.

Entwick'lungshilfe, *n.f.* foreign aid.

Entwick'lungsland, ¨-er, *n.nt.* developing nation.

entwir'ren, *vb.* disentangle.

entwi'schen*, *vb.* slip away from.

entwür'digen, *vb.* dishonor.

Entwurf', ¨-e, *n.m.* sketch, design, draft, plan.

entzie'hen*, *vb.* remove, extract.

entzü'cken, *vb.* delight.

Entzü'cken, -, *n.nt.* delight.

entzü'ckend, *adj.* delightful, charming.

Entzü'ckung, -en, *n.f.* rapture.

entzünd'bar, *adj.* inflammable.

entzün'den, *vb.* inflame.

entzün'det, *adj.* infected.

Entzün'dung, -en, *n.f.* inflammation, infection.

entzwei', *adv.* in two, apart.

Enzy'klika, -ken, *n.f.* encyclical.

Enzyklopädie', -'en, *n.f.* encyclopaedia.

Epidemie', -'en, *n.f.* epidemic.

epide'misch, *adj.* epidemic.

Epilepsie', *n.f.* epilepsy.

Epilog', -e, *n.m.* epilogue.

Episo'de, -n, *n.f.* episode.

Epo'che, -n, *n.f.* epoch.

Epos (*pl.* Epopen) *n.f.* epic poem.

er, *pron.* he, it.

erach'ten, *vb.* consider.

erbar'men, *vb.* have pity; (sich e.) pity.

Erbar'men, *n.nt.* pity.

erbärm'lich, *adj.* pitiful.

erbar'mungslos, *adj.* pitiless.

erbau'en, *vb.* construct; edify.

erbau'lich, *adj.* edifying.

Erbau'ung, -, *n.f.* edification.

Erbe, -n, -n, *n.m.* heir.

Erbe, *n.nt.* inheritance, heritage.

erben, *vb.* inherit.

Erbfolge, *n.f.* succession.

erbie'ten*, *vb.* (sich e.) offer, volunteer.

erbit'ten, *vb.* ask for.

erbit'tern, *vb.* embitter.

erblas'sen, *vb.* turn pale.

erblei'chen*, *vb.* turn pale.

erblich, *adj.* hereditary.

Erblichkeit, *n.f.* heredity.

erblicken, *vb.* catch sight of.

erbo'sen, *vb.* make angry; (sich e.) get angry.

erbre'chen*, *vb.* break open; (sich e.) vomit.

Erbschaft, -en, *n.f.* inheritance.

Erbse, -n, *n.f.* pea.

Erbstück, -e, *n.nt.* heirloom.

Erdbeben, -, *n.nt.* earthquake.

Erdbeere, -n, *n.f.* strawberry.

Erdboden, *n.m.* ground, soil.

Erde, *n.f.* earth.

erden, *vb.* ground.

erden'ken*, *vb.* think up.

erdenk'lich, *adj.* imaginable.

Erdgeschoß, n.nt. ground floor.

Erdhügel, -, n.m. mound.

erdich'ten, vb. invent, imagine.

erdich'tet, adj. fictional.

Erdich'tung, n.f. fiction.

erdig, adj. earthy.

Erdkreis, -e, n.m. sphere.

Erdkugel, -n, n.f. globe.

Erdkunde, n.f. geography.

Erdnuß, -sse, n.f. peanut.

Erdöl, -e, n.nt. petroleum.

erdrei'sten, vb. (sich e.) be so bold.

erdros'seln, vb. strangle.

erdrü'cken, vb. crush (to death), stifle.

Erdteil, -e, n.m. continent.

erdul'den, vb. endure.

ereig'nen, vb. (sich e.) happen.

Ereig'nis, -se, n.nt. event.

erig'nisreich, adj. eventful.

erfah'ren*, vb. come to know, learn, experience.

erfah'ren, adj. experienced, adept.

Erfah'rung, -en, n.f. experience.

erfas'sen, vb. grasp, realize; apprehend.

erfin'den*, vb. invent; contrive.

Erfin'der, -, n.m. inventor.

erfin'derisch, adj. inventive; ingenious.

Erfin'dung, -en, n.f. invention.

Erfolg, -e, n.m. success.

erfolglos, adj. unsuccessful.

erfolgreich, adj. successful; (e. sein*) to succeed.

erfor'derlich, adj. required.

erfor'dern, vb. require.

Erfor'dernis, -se, n.nt. requirement, requisite.

erfor'schen, vb. explore.

Erfor'schung, -en, n.f. exploration.

erfreu'en, vb. delight, gratify; (sich e.) enjoy.

erfreu'lich, adj. enjoyable.

erfrie'ren*, vb. freeze.

erfri'schen, vb. refresh, invigorate.

Erfri'schung, -en, n.f. refreshment.

erfül'len, vb. fill; fulfill.

Erfül'lung, -en, n.f. fulfillment.

ergän'zen, vb. supplement, amend.

Ergän'zung, -en, n.f. supplement, complement.

erge'ben*, vb. yield; result in; (sich e.) result, follow; surrender.

erge'ben, adj. devoted.

Ergeb'nis, -se, n.nt. result, outcome.

ergie'big, adj. productive.

ergöt'zen, vb. delight.

ergötz'lich, adj. delectable.

ergrei'fen*, vb. grasp, seize.

Ergrif'fenheit, n.f. emotion.

Erguß, -sse, n.m. effusion.

erha'ben, adj. elevated; lofty, sublime.

Erha'benheit, n.f. grandeur.

erhal'ten*, vb. maintain, preserve; get, obtain.

Erhal'tung, n.f. maintenance, preservation; acquisition.

erhär'ten, vb. harden.

erha'schen, vb. snatch.

erhe'ben*, vb. raise.

erheb'lich, adj. considerable.

erhei'tern, vb. brighten, cheer.

erhel'len, vb. illuminate.

erhitz'en, vb. heat.

erhö'hen, vb. raise, heighten; ennoble.

Erhö'hung, -en, n.f. elevation; rise; enhancement.

erho'len, vb. (sich e.) get better, recuperate.

Erho'lung, n.f. recuperation, recreation.

erhö'ren, vb. hear.

erin'nern, vb. remind; (sich e.) remember, recollect.

Erin'nerung, -en, n.f. remembrance, memory.

erkäl'ten, vb. (sich e.) catch cold.

Erkäl'tung, -en, n.f. cold.

erken'nen*, vb. recognize.

erkennt'lich, adj. recognizable; thankful.

Erkennt'nis, -se, n.f. realization, knowledge.

erklä'ren, vb. explain, declare.

erklä'rend, adj. explanatory.

Erklä'rung, -en, n.f. explanation; declaration.

erklet'tern, vb. climb up, scale.

erklin'gen*, vb. (re)sound.

erkran'ken, vb. be taken ill.

erkun'digen, vb. (sich e.) inquire.

Erkun'digung, -en, n.f. inquiry.

erlan'gen, vb. obtain, attain.

Erlaß', -sse, n.m. decree.

erlas'sen*, vb. decree; forgive.

erlau'ben, vb. allow, permit.

Erlaub'nis, n.f. permission, permit.

erläu'tern, vb. illustrate; elucidate.

Erläu'terung, -en, n.f. illustration; elucidation.

Erleb'nis, -se, n.nt. event, experience.

erle'digen, vb. take care of, settle.

erle'digt, adj. settled; exhausted.

erleich'tern, vb. lighten, facilitate; relieve.

Erleich'terung, -en, n.f. ease, relief.

erlei'den*, vb. suffer.

erle'sen, adj. chosen.

erleuch'ten, vb. illuminate.

erlie'gen*, vb. succumb.

Erlös, n.m. proceeds.

erlö'schen*, vb. go out, be extinguished; become extinct.

erlö'sen, vb. deliver, redeem.

Erlö'ser, n.m. redeemer.

Erlö'sung, -en, n.f. deliverance, redemption.

ermäch'tigen, vb. empower, enable.

Ermäch'tigung, -en, n.f. authorization.

ermah'nen, vb. admonish.

erman'geln, vb. lack.

ermä'ßigen, vb. reduce.

Ermä'ßigung, -en, n.f. reduction.

ermat'ten, vb. tire.

ermes'sen*, vb. calculate; comprehend.

ermit'teln, vb. ascertain.

Ermitt'lung, -en, n.f. detection.

ermög'lichen, vb. make possible, enable.

ermor'den, vb. murder.

Ermor'dung, -en, n.f. murder, assassination.

ermü'den, vb. tire.

ermun'tern, vb. rouse; cheer up.

ermu'tigen, vb. encourage.

Ermu'tigung, -en, n.f. encouragement.

ernäh'ren, vb. nourish, nurture.

Ernäh'rung, n.f. nourishment, nutrition.

erneu'ern*, vb. appoint, nominate.

Ernen'nung, -en, n.f. appointment, nomination.

erneu'ern, vb. renew.

Erneu'erung, -en, n.f. renewal.

ernie'drigen, vb. debase, degrade.

Ernie'drigung, -en, n.f. degradation.

ernst, adj. earnest; severe, serious.

Ernst, n.m. earnestness; gravity, seriousness.

Ernte, -n, n.f. harvest, crop.

ernten, vb. harvest, reap.

Ero'berer, -, n.m. conqueror.

ero'bern, vb. conquer.

Ero'berung, -en, n.f. conquest.

eröff'nen, vb. open.

Eröff'nung, -en, n.f. opening.

erör'tern, vb. discuss, debate.

Erör'terung, -en, n.f. discussion, debate.

Ero'tik, n.f. eroticism.

ero'tisch, adj. erotic.

erpicht', adj. intent.

erpres'sen, vb. blackmail.

Erpres'sung, -en, n.f. blackmail, extortion.

erqui'cken, vb. refresh.

erra'ten*, vb. guess.

erre'gen, vb. arouse, excite.

Erre'gung, -en, n.f. excitement; emotion.

errei'chen, vb. reach; achieve.

errich'ten, vb. erect, establish.

Errich'tung, -en, n.f. erection.

errin'gen*, vb. achieve; gain.

Errun'genschaft, -en, n.f. achievement, attainment.

Ersatz', n.m. compensation; substitute; cpds. spare.

erschaf'fen*, vb. create.

Erschaf'fung, -en, n.f. creation.

erschei'nen*, vb. appear.

Erschei'nung, -en, n.f. appearance; apparition; phenomenon.

erschie'ßen*, vb. shoot (dead).

erschla'gen*, vb. slay.

erschlie'ßen*, vb. open, unfold.

erschöp'fen, vb. exhaust.

erschöpft', adj. weary, exhausted.

Erschöp'fung, n.f. exhaustion.

erschre'cken, vb. scare, frighten, startle.

erschre'cken*, vb. become scared, become frightened, be startled.

erschüt'tern, vb. shake, shock.

Erschüt'terung, -en, n.f. shock; vibration.

erschwe'ren, vb. make more difficult, aggravate.

erschwing'lich, adj. within one's means.

erse'hen*, vb. see, learn.

erset'zen, vb. make good, replace; supersede.

ersicht'lich, adj. evident.

ersin'nen*, vb. devise.

erspa'ren, vb. save.

erst, 1. adj. first. 2. adv. not until, only.

erstar'ren, vb. get numb, stiffen; congeal.

erstat'ten, vb. refund, recompense.

erstau'nen, vb. astonish, amaze.

Erstau'nen, n.nt. amazement, astonishment.

erstaun'lich, adj. amazing.

erste'hen*, vb. arise; get, obtain.

erstei'gen*, vb. climb.

erstens, adv. in the first place, firstly.

erster-, adj. former.

ersti'cken, vb. stifle, suffocate, smother.

Ersti'ckung, -en, n.f. suffocation, asphyxiation, choking.

erstklassig, adj. first-class, first-rate.

erstre'ben, vb. aspire to.

erstreck'en, vb. (sich e.) extend, range.

ersu'chen, vb. request.

ertap'pen, vb. catch, surprise.

ertei'len, vb. give, administer.

Ertrag', -e, n.m. yield, return.

ertrag'bar, adj. bearable.

ertra'gen*, vb. bear, endure.

erträg'lich, adj. passable.

erträn'ken, vb. (tr.) drown.

ertrin'ken*, vb. (intr.) drown.

erü'brigen, vb. (sich e.) not be necessary.

erwa'chen, vb. wake.

erwach'sen*, vb. arise, grow.

erwach'sen, adj. grown, grown-up, adult.

Erwach'sen-, n.m.&f. adult.

erwä'gen, vb. deliberate, ponder.

Erwä'gung, -en, n.f. consideration.

erwäh'nen, vb. mention.

Erwäh'nung, -en, n.f. mention.

erwar'ten, vb. expect, await.

Erwar'tung, -en, n.f. expectation, anticipation.

erwe'cken, vb. awaken.

erwei'chen, vb. soften, mollify; (sich e. lassen*) relent.

erwei'sen*, vb. prove; render.

erwei'tern, vb. widen, extend.

erwer'ben*, vb. acquire.

Erwer'bung, -en, n.f. acquisition.

erwi'dern, vb. reply; return, reciprocate.

Erwi'derung, -en, n.f. reply; return.

erwir'ken, vb. bring about.

erwi'schen, vb. catch, get hold of.

erwünscht', adj. desired.

erwür'gen, vb. strangle.

erzäh'len, vb. tell, narrate, relate.

Erzäh'lung, -en, n.f. story, narrative, tale.

Erzbischof, -e, n.m. archbishop.

Erzdiözese, -n, n.f. archdiocese.

erzeu'gen, vb. create, produce; (elec.) generate.

Erzeug'nis, -se, n.nt. product.

Erzherzog, -e, n.m. archduke.

erzie'hen*, vb. educate.

Erzie'her, -, n.m. educator.

Erzie'herin, -nen, n.f. governess.

erzie'herisch, adj. education; breeding.

erzür'nen, vb. (sich e.) become angry.

erzwin'gen*, vb. force.

es, pron. it.

Esche, -n, n.f. ash (tree).

Esel, -, n.m. donkey, ass, jackass.

Eskalation', n.f. escalation.

eskalie'ren, vb. escalate.

eßbar, adj. edible.

essen*, vb. eat.

Essen, n.nt. food.

Essenz', -en, n.f. essence; flavoring.

Essig, n.m. vinegar.

Eßlöffel, -, n.m. tablespoon.

Eta'ge, -n, n.f. floor, story.

Etat', -s, n.m. budget.

ethnisch, adj. ethnic.

Etikett', -e, n.nt. tag, label, sticker.

Etiket'te, n.f. etiquette.

etliche, pron. several.

etwa, adv. about, approximately, more or less, maybe.

etwaig, adj. eventual.

etwas, 1. pron. something. 2. adv. somewhat.

Eule, -n, n.f. owl.

Euro'pa, n.nt. Europe.

Europä'er, -, n.m. European.

europä'isch, adj. European.

evakuie'ren, vb. evacuate.

evange'lisch, adj. evangelical, Protestant.

Evangelist', -en, -en, n.m. evangelist.

Evange'lium, n.nt. gospel.

Eventualität', -en, n.f. contingency.

eventuell', adj. possible, potential.

ewig, 1. adj. eternal, everlasting. 2. adv. forever.

Ewigkeit, -en, n.f. eternity.

Exa'men, -, n.nt. examination.

Exemplar', -e, n.nt. specimen, copy.

exerzie'ren, vb. drill.

Existenz', -en, n.f. existence.

existie'ren, vb. exist.

exo'tisch, adj. exotic.

Experiment', -e, n.nt. experiment.

experimentie'ren, vb. experiment.

explodie'ren, vb. explode, detonate.

Explosion', -en, n.f. explosion.

explosiv', adj. explosive.

Export', -e, n.m. export.

exportie'ren, vb. export.

Expreß', -sse, n.m. express train.

extra, adj. extra.

Extravaganz, -en, n.f. extravagance.

extrem', adj. extreme.

Exzellenz', -en, n.f. Excellency.

exzen'trisch, adj. eccentric.

Exzentrizität', -en, n.f. eccentricity.

F

Fabel, -n, n.f. fable.

fabelhaft, adj. fabulous, wonderful.

Fabrik', -en, n.f. factory, plant.

Fabrikant', -en, -en, n.m. manufacturer.

Fabrikat', -e, n.nt. manufactured article; (deutsches F.) made in Germany.

Fach, -er, n.nt. compartment; profession; (academic) subject.

fächern, vb. fan.

fachmännisch, adj. professional.

Fackel, -, n.f. torch.

fade, adj. flavorless, insipid.

Faden, -, n.m. thread, filament.

fadenscheinig, adj. threadbare.

fähig, adj. able, capable, competent.

Fähigkeit, -en, n.f. ability, capability, competence.

fahnden, vb. search.

Fahne, -n, n.f. flag.

Fahnenflucht, n.f. desertion.

Fahnenflüchtig-, n.m. deserter.

Fähnrich, -e, n.m. ensign.

Fahrbahn, -, n.f. lane.

Fähre, -n, n.f. ferry.

fahren*, vb. drive, ride, go.

Fahrer, -, *n.m.* driver.
Fahrgeld, -er, *n.nt.* fare.
Fahrkarte, -n, *n.f.* ticket.
fahrlässig, *adj.* negligent.
Fahrplan, ⁼e, *n.m.* timetable, schedule.
fahrplanmäßig, *adj.* scheduled.
Fahrpreis, -e, *n.m.* fare.
Fahrrad, ⁼er, *n.nt.* bicycle.
Fahrrinne, -n, *n.f.* lane.
Fahrstuhl, ⁼e, *n.m.* elevator.
Fahrt, -en, *n.f.* ride; trip.
Fährte, -n, *n.f.* track, trail.
Fahrzeug, -e, *n.nt.* vehicle, conveyance.
Faktor, -o'ren, *n.m.* factor.
Fakultät', -en, *n.f.* faculty.
fakultativ', *adj.* optional.
Fall, ⁼e, *n.m.* fall; case.
Falle, -n, *n.f.* trap; pitfall.
fallen*, (*f.* fall, drop; (f. lassen*) drop.
fällen, *vb.* fell.
fällig, *adj.* due; (f. werden*) become due, mature.
Fälligkeit, *n.f.* maturity.
falls, *conj.* in case, if.
falsch, *adj.* false, wrong; fake; deceitful.
fälschen, *vb.* forge, counterfeit.
Fälscher, -, *n.m.* forger.
Falschheit, -en, *n.f.* falseness, deceit.
Fälschung, -en, *n.f.* forgery.
Falte, -n, *n.f.* fold, crease, pleat; wrinkle.
falten, *vb.* fold, pleat, crease.
familiär, *adj.* familiar; intimate.
Fami'lie, -n, *n.f.* family.
Fami'lienname(n), -, *n.m.* surname.
famos', *adj.* splendid.
Fana'tiker, -n, *n.m.* fanatic.
fana'tisch, *adj.* fanatic, rabid.
Fanatis'mus, *n.m.* fanaticism.
Fanfa're, -n, *n.f.* fanfare.
Fang, ⁼e, *n.m.* catch.
fangen*, *vb.* catch, capture.
Fänger, -, *n.m.* catcher.
Farbe, -n, *n.f.* color; paint; dye; (cards) suit.
färben, *vb.* color, dye.
farbenreich, *adj.* colorful.
Färber, -, *n.m.* dyer.
farbig, *adj.* colored.
farblos, *adj.* colorless, drab.
Farbstoff, -e, *n.m.* dye (stuff).
Farbton, ⁼e, *n.m.* shade.
Farbtönung, -en, *n.f.* tint.
Färbung, -en, *n.f.* coloring, hue.
Farce, -n, *n.f.* farce.
Farmer, -, *n.m.* farmer.
Fasching, *n.m.* carnival, Mardi Gras.
Faschis'mus, *n.m.* fascism.
Faschist', -en, -en, *n.m.* fascist.
faschis'tisch, *adj.* fascist.
faseln, *vb.* talk nonsense.
Faser, -n, *n.f.* fiber.
Faß, ⁼sser, *n.nt.* barrel, keg, vat, cask.
Fassa'de, -n, *n.f.* façade.
fassen, *vb.* grasp; seize; (sich

f.) compose oneself; (fasse dich kurz!) make it short.
Fasson', -s, *n.f.* shape.
Fassung, -en, *n.f.* version; gem setting; *(fig.)* composure; (aus der F. bringen*) rattle.
fassungslos, *adj.* bewildered, staggered.
Fassungsvermögen, -, *n.nt.* capacity; comprehension.
fast, *adv.* almost, nearly.
fasten, *vb.* fast.
Fastenzeit, *n.f.* Lent.
faszinie'ren, *vb.* fascinate.
fauchen, *vb.* puff; (of cats) spit.
faul, *adj.* lazy; rotten.
faulenzen, *vb.* loaf.
Faulenzer, -n, *n.m.* loafer.
Fäulnis, *n.f.* decay, putrefaction.
Faultier, -e, *n.nt.* sloth.
Faust, ⁼e, *n.f.* fist.
Februar, -e, *n.m.* February.
fechten*, *vb.* fence.
Feder, -n, *n.f.* feather, plume; pen.
federleicht, *adj.* feathery.
federn, *vb.* feather; have good springs.
Fee, Fe'en, *n.f.* fairy.
Fegefeuer, *n.nt.* purgatory.
Fehde, -n, *n.f.* feud.
fehlbar, *adj.* fallible.
fehlen, *vb.* lack; be absent or missing.
Fehler, -, *n.m.* mistake; error; flaw, imperfection, defect; blunder.
fehlerfrei, *adj.* flawless.
fehlerhaft, *adj.* faulty, imperfect, defective.
fehlerlos, *adj.* faultless.
fehl·gebären*, *vb.* abort, have a miscarriage.
Fehlgeburt, -en, *n.f.* miscarriage, abortion.
fehl·gehen*, *vb.* err, go astray.
Fehlschlag, ⁼e, *n.m.* failure; setback.
Fehltritt, -e, *n.m.* slip.
Feier, -n, *n.f.* celebration.
feierlich, *adj.* ceremonious; solemn.
Feierlichkeit, -en, *n.f.* ceremony, solemnity.
feiern, *vb.* celebrate.
Feiertag, -e, *n.m.* holiday.
feige, *adj.* cowardly.
Feige, -n, *n.f.* fig.
Feigheit, -en, *n.f.* cowardice.
Feigling, -e, *n.m.* coward.
Feile, -n, *n.f.* file.
feilen, *vb.* file.
feilschen, *vb.* bargain, haggle.
fein, *adj.* fine, delicate; elegant; subtle.
Feind, -e, *n.m.* foe, enemy.
feindlich, *adj.* hostile.
Feindschaft, -en, *n.f.* enmity, feud.
Feindseligkeit, -en, *n.f.* purity; delicacy; elegance; subtlety.
Feingefühl, *n.nt.* sensitivity.

Feinheit, -en, *n.f.* purity; delicacy; elegance; subtlety.
feinsinnig, *adj.* ingenious.
feist, *adj.* fat, plump.
Feld, -er, *n.nt.* field.
Feldbett, -en, *n.nt.* cot.
Feldherr, -n, -en, *n.m.* commander.
Feldstecher, -, *n.m.* binoculars.
Feldzug, ⁼e, *n.m.* campaign.
Fell, -e, *n.nt.* skin, pelt, hide.
Fels(en), -, *n.m.* rock, boulder.
Felsblock, ⁼e, *n.m.* boulder.
felsig, *adj.* rocky, craggy.
Fenster, -, *n.nt.* window.
Fensterladen, ⁼, *n.m.* shutter.
Fensterscheibe, -n, *n.f.* windowpane.
Ferien, *n.pl.* vacation.
Ferienort, -e, *n.m.* resort.
fern, *adj.* far, distant, remote.
Fernanruf, -e, *n.m.* long-distance call.
ferner, *adv.* moreover, furthermore.
Ferngespräch, -e, *n.nt.* long-distance call.
Fernglas, ⁼er, *n.nt.* binocular(s).
Fernrohr, -e, *n.nt.* telescope.
Fernsehapparat, -e, *n.m.* television set.
Fernsehen, *n.nt.* television.
Fernsprecher, -, *n.m.* telephone.
Ferse, -n, *n.f.* heel.
fertig, *adj.* finished, complete, ready, done; (f. sein*) be through; (f. bringen*) complete, accomplish.
Fertigkeit, -en, *n.f.* dexterity, knack.
fesch, *adj.* chic.
Fessel, -n, *n.f.* fetter, irons, handcuffs; ankle.
Fesselgelenk, -e, *n.nt.* ankle.
fesseln, *vb.* chain; (fig.) captivate, fascinate.
fest, *adj.* firm, solid; fixed, steady; tight.
Fest, -e, *n.nt.* feast, celebration.
Feste, -n, *n.f.* fort, stronghold.
Festessen, -, *n.nt.* banquet, feast.
fest·fahren*, *vb.* run aground; (fig.) come to an impasse.
fest·halten*, *vb.* hold fast to, adhere to; detain.
festigen, *vb.* solidify, consolidate.
Festigkeit, *n.f.* firmness, solidity.
fest·klammern, *vb.* clamp; (sich f.) hold fast.
Festland, *n.nt.* mainland.
fest·legen, *vb.* fix, lay down.
festlich, *adj.* festive.
Festlichkeit, -en, *n.f.* festivity.
fest·machen, *vb.* fasten, make fast.
Festmahl, -e, *n.nt.* feast.
fest·nehmen*, *vb.* arrest.
fest·setzen*, *vb.* fix, establish; determine.

Festspiel, -e, *n.nt.* festival.

fest·stehen*, *vb.* be stable; be certain.

feststehend, *adj.* stationary.

fest·stellen, *vb.* determine, ascertain; state.

Festtag, -e, *n.m.* holiday.

Festung, -en, *n.f.* fortress.

fett, *adj.* fat, greasy.

Fett, -e, *n.nt.* fat, grease.

fetten, *vb.* grease.

fettig, *adj.* fatty, greasy, oily.

fettleibig, *adj.* obese.

Fetzen, -, *n.m.* rag; scrap.

feucht, *adj.* moist, damp, humid.

Feuchtigkeit, *n.f.* moisture, dampness, humidity.

feuchtkalt, *adj.* clammy.

Feuer, -, *n.nt.* fire, (*fig.*) verve.

Feueralarm, -e, *n.m.* fire alarm.

feuergefährlich, *adj.* inflammable.

Feuerleiter, -n, *n.f.* fire escape.

Feuermelder, -, *n.m.* fire alarm (box).

feuern, *vb.* fire.

Feuersbrunst, *n.f.* conflagration.

Feuerspritze, -n, *n.f.* fire engine.

Feuerstein, -e, *n.m.* flint.

Feuerwaffe, -n, *n.f.* firearm.

Feuerwechsel, -, *n.m.* skirmish.

Feuerwehrmann, ̈er, *n.m.* fireman.

Feuerwerk, -e, *n.nt.* fireworks.

Feuerzeug, -e, *n.nt.* cigarette lighter.

feurig, *adj.* fiery.

Fichte, -n, *n.f.* pine, fir.

fidel', *adj.* jolly.

Fieber, *n.nt.* fever.

fieberhaft, *adj.* feverish.

fiebern, *vb.* be feverish.

Fieberwahnsinn, -e, *n.m.* delirium.

Fiedel, -n, *n.f.* fiddle.

Figur', -en, *n.f.* figure.

figür'lich, *adj.* figurative.

Fiktion', -en, *n.f.* figment.

Filet', -s, *n.nt.* fillet.

Film, -e, *n.m.* film, movie, motion-picture.

filmen, *vb.* film.

Filmschauspieler, -, *n.m.* movie actor.

Filter, -, *n.m.* filter.

filtrie'ren, *vb.* filter.

Filz, -e, *n.m.* felt.

Fina'le, -s, *n.nt.* finale.

Finan'zen, *n.pl.* finances.

finanziell', *adj.* financial.

finanzie'ren, *vb.* finance.

Finanz'mann, ̈er, *n.m.* financier.

Finanz'wirtschaft, -en, *n.f.* finance.

finden*, *vb.* find, locate.

Finderlohn, *n.m.* reward (for returning lost articles).

findig, *adj.* ingenious, resourceful.

Findigkeit, *n.f.* ingenuity.

Findling, -e, *n.m.* foundling.

Finger, -, *n.m.* finger.

Fingerabdruck, ̈e, *n.m.* fingerprint.

Fingernagel, ̈, *n.m.* fingernail.

fingie'ren, *vb.* feign, simulate.

fingiert', *adj.* fictitious.

finster, *adj.* dark; saturnine.

Finsternis, -se, *n.f.* darkness; eclipse.

Firma (*pl.* **Firmen**), *n.f.* firm, company.

Firnis, -se, *n.m.* varnish.

firnissen, *vb.* varnish.

Fisch, -e, *n.m.* fish.

fischen, *vb.* fish.

Fischer, -, *n.m.* fisherman.

Fischgeschäft, -e, *n.nt.* fish-store.

Fixie'rung, -en, *n.f.* fixation.

flach, *adj.* flat, shallow.

Fläche, -n, *n.f.* plane, area.

Flachheit, -en, *n.f.* flatness.

Flachs, *n.m.* flax.

flackern, *vb.* flare, flicker.

Flagge, -n, *n.f.* flag.

Flak, -(s), *n.f.* (= **Fliegerabwehrkanone**) antiaircraft (fire, troops).

Flak-, *cpds.* antiaircraft.

Flame, -n, -n, *n.m.* Fleming.

Flamme, -n, *n.f.* flame, blaze.

flammend, *adj.* flaming; (*fig.*) enthusiastic.

Flanell', -e, *n.m.* flannel.

Flanke, -n, *n.f.* flank.

flankie'ren, *vb.* flank.

Flasche, -n, *n.f.* bottle, flask.

flattern, *vb.* flutter, flap.

flau, *adj.* slack, dull.

Flaum, *n.m.* down, fuzz.

flaumig, *adj.* downy, fuzzy, fluffy.

Flechte, -n, *n.f.* braid.

Fleck, -e, *n.m.* spot, stain, blotch.

Fledermaus, ̈e, *n.f.* bat.

Flegel, -, *n.m.* rowdy, boor.

flehen, *vb.* implore, beseech.

flehentlich, *adj.* beseeching.

Fleisch, *n.nt.* flesh, meat.

fleischig, *adj.* fleshy.

fleischlich, *adj.* carnal.

Fleiß, *n.m.* diligence, hard work.

fleißig, *adj.* industrious, hard working.

flicken, *vb.* patch.

Flicken, -, *n.m.* patch.

Flickwerk, *n.nt.* patchwork.

Flieder, *n.m.* lilac.

Fliege, -n, *n.f.* fly.

fliegen*, *vb.* fly.

Flieger, -, *n.m.* flier, aviator.

fliehen*, *vb.* flee.

Fliese, -n, *n.f.* tile, flagstone.

fließen*, *vb.* flow.

fließend, *adj.* fluent.

flimmern, *vb.* flicker.

flink, *adj.* nimble, spry.

Flirt, -s, *n.m.* flirt, flirtation.

flirten, *vb.* flirt.

Flitterwochen, *n.pl.* honeymoon.

Flocke, -n, *n.f.* flake.

Floh, ̈e, *n.m.* flea.

Floß, ̈e, *n.nt.* float, raft.

Flosse, -n, *n.f.* fin.

Flöte, -n, *n.f.* whistle; flute.

flott, *adj.* afloat; smart, dashing.

Flotte, -n, *n.f.* fleet, navy.

Fluch, ̈e, *n.m.* curse.

fluchen, *vb.* swear, curse.

Fluchen, *n.nt.* profanity.

Flucht, *n.f.* escape, flight, getaway; (**in die F. schlagen***) rout.

flüchten, *vb.* flee.

flüchtig, *adj.* fleeting, cursory; superficial.

Flüchtling, -en, *n.m.* refugee, fugitive.

Flug, ̈e, *n.m.* flight.

Flugblatt, ̈er, *n.nt.* leaflet.

Flügel, -, *n.m.* wing.

Flughafen, ̈, *n.m.* airport.

Flugpersonal, *n.nt.* flight attendants.

Flugzeug, -e, *n.nt.* airplane.

Flunder, -n, *n.f.* flounder.

flunkern, *vb.* fib.

fluoreszie'rend, *adj.* fluorescent.

Fluß, ̈sse, *n.m.* river; flux.

flüssig, *adj.* liquid, fluid; (**f. machen**) liquefy.

Flüssigkeit, -en, *n.f.* fluid, liquid.

flüstern, *vb.* whisper.

Flut, -en, *n.f.* flood, high tide.

fluten, *vb.* flood.

Folge, -n, *n.f.* consequence, outgrowth; succession; (**zur F. haben***) result in.

folgen, *vb.* follow; succeed.

folgend, *adj.* subsequent.

folgenreich, *adj.* consequential.

folgenschwer, *adj.* momentous.

folgerichtig, *adj.* consistent.

folgern, *vb.* infer, deduce.

Folgerung, -en, *n.f.* inference, deduction.

folglich, *adv.* consequently.

Folter, -n, *n.f.* torture.

Fond, -s, *n.m.* fund.

Fondant', -s, *n.m.* bonbon.

Förderer, -, *n.m.* sponsor.

förderlich, *adj.* helpful, conducive.

fordern, *vb.* demand.

fördern, *vb.* promote, further; (mining) mine, haul.

Forderung, -en, *n.f.* demand, claim.

Förderung, -en, *n.f.* furtherance, advancement.

Forel'le, -n, *n.f.* trout.

Form, -en, *n.f.* form, shape; mold; (**in F. sein***) be fit, be in fine shape.

Formalität', -en, *n.f.* formality.

Format', -e, *n.nt.* format; (*fig.*) stature.

Formation', -en, *n.f.* formation.

Formel, -n, *n.f.* formula.

formell', *adj.* formal.

formen, *vb.* form, shape, mold.

Förmlichkeit, -en, n.f. formality.

formlos, adj. formless.

Formular', -e, n.nt. form, blank.

formulie'ren, vb. formulate.

forschen, vb. explore, search.

Forscher, -, n.m. explorer.

Forschung, -en, n.f. research.

fort, adv. away, gone; forward.

Fortdauer, n.f. continuity.

fortdauernd, adj. continuous.

fort·fahren*, vb. drive away; proceed, continue.

fort·gehen*, vb. leave; continue.

fortgeschritten, adj. advanced.

fort·pflanzen, vb. propagate.

fort·schreiten*, vb. progress.

Fortschritt, -e, n.m. progress, advance.

fortschrittlich, adj. progressive.

fort·setzen, vb. continue.

Fortsetzung, -en, n.f. continuation.

fortwährend, adj. continuous.

Foyer, -s, n.nt. foyer.

Fracht, -en, n.f. freight, cargo.

Frachtbrief, -e, n.m. bill of lading.

Frachter, -, n.m. freighter.

Frachtschiff, -e, n.nt. freighter.

Frachtspesen, n.pl. freight charges.

Frage, -n, n.f. question.

Fragebogen, -, n.m. questionnaire.

fragen, vb. ask, inquire.

fragend, adj. interrogative.

Fragezeichen, -, n.nt. question mark.

fraglich, adj. questionable.

fragmenta'risch, adj. fragmentary.

fragwürdig, adj. questionable.

Fraktur', n.f. (med.) fracture; German type (print).

Frankreich, n.nt. France.

Franse, -n, n.f. fringe.

Franzo'se, -n, -n, n.m. Frenchman.

Franzö'sin, -nen, n.f. Frenchwoman.

französisch, adj. French.

frappant', adj. striking.

fraternisie'ren, vb. fraternize.

Fratze, -n, n.f. grimace; face, mug.

Frau, -en, n.f. woman, wife; Mrs.

Frauenarzt, -̈e, n.m. gynecologist.

Fräulein, -, n.nt. Miss.

fraulich, adj. womanly.

frech, adj. impudent; saucy.

Frechheit, -en, n.f. impertinence, effrontery.

frei, adj. free; frank; vacant.

Frei-, n.nt. outdoors.

Freier, -, n.m. suitor.

freigebig, adj. generous.

Freigebigkeit, n.f. liberality, generosity.

freigestellt, adj. optional.

frei·halten*, vb. keep free; treat.

Freiheit, -en, n.f. liberty, freedom.

Freiherr, -n, -en, n.m. baron.

frei·lassen*, vb. free; leave blank.

freilich, adv. to be sure.

Freimarke, -n, n.f. stamp.

Freimaurer, -, n.m. Mason.

freimütig, adj. candid, heart-to-heart.

freisinnig, adj. liberal.

frei·sprechen*, vb. acquit, absolve.

Freispruch, -̈e, n.m. acquittal.

Freitag, -e, n.m. Friday.

freiwillig, adj. voluntary; (sich f. melden) volunteer; enlist.

Freiwillig-, n.m.&f. volunteer.

Freizeit, n.f. leisure time.

fremd, adj. strange; foreign, alien.

Fremd-, n.m.&f. stranger.

Fremdenführer, -, n.m. guide.

Fremdenzimmer, -, n.nt. guest room, room to let.

frequentie'ren, vb. habituate.

Frequenz', -en, n.f. frequency.

Fresko, -ken, n.nt. fresco.

fressen*, vb. (of animals) eat; stuff oneself.

Freude, -n, n.f. joy, pleasure.

Freudenfeuer, -, n.nt. bonfire.

freudig, adj. joyful, joyous.

freudlos, adj. cheerless.

freuen, vb. make glad; (sich f.) be glad, rejoice.

Freund, -e, n.m. friend.

Freundin, -nen, n.f. friend (female).

freundlich, adj. friendly, kind.

freundlicherweise, adv. kindly.

Freundlichkeit, n.f. kindness, friendliness.

freundlos, adj. friendless.

Freundschaft, -en, n.f. friendship.

freundschaftlich, adj. amicable.

Frevel, -, n.m. outrage.

frevelhaft, adj. sacrilegious; flagrant.

Friede(n), n.m. peace.

Friedensvertrag, -̈e, n.m. peace treaty.

friedfertig, adj. peaceable.

Friedhof, -̈e, n.m. cemetery, graveyard.

friedlich, adj. peaceable, peaceful.

frieren*, vb. freeze.

Frikassee', -s, n.nt. fricassee.

frisch, adj. fresh, crisp.

Frische, n.f. freshness.

Friseur', -e, n.m. barber, hairdresser.

Friseu'se, -n, n.f. hairdresser (female).

frisie'ren, vb. dress the hair; (fig.) tamper with.

Frist, -en, n.f. limited period; respite.

Frisur', -en, n.f. coiffure, hairdo.

frivol', adj. frivolous.

froh, adj. glad.

fröhlich, adj. gay, cheerful.

Fröhlichkeit, n.f. cheerfulness, merriment.

frohlo'cken, vb. rejoice.

frohlo'ckend, adj. jubilant.

fromm (-̈, -) adj. pious, religious, devout.

Frömmelei', -en, n.f. bigotry.

Frömmigkeit, n.f. piety.

Frömmler, -, n.m. bigot.

frönen, vb. indulge.

Front, -en, n.f. front.

Frosch, -̈e, n.m. frog.

Frost, -̈e, n.m. frost, chill.

frösteln, vb. feel chilly.

frostig, adj. frosty.

Frucht, -̈e, n.f. fruit.

fruchtbar, adj. fruitful, fertile; prolific.

Fruchtbarkeit, n.f. fertility.

fruchtlos, adj. fruitless.

früh, adj. early.

früher, adj. earlier; former.

Frühjahr, -e, n.nt. spring.

Frühling, -e, n.m. spring.

frühreif, adj. precocious.

Frühstück, -e, n.nt. breakfast.

frühzeitig, adj. early.

Fuchs, -̈e, n.m. fox.

fügen, vb. join; (sich f.) comply, submit.

fügsam, adj. docile.

fühlbar, adj. tangible.

fühlen, vb. feel, sense.

führen, vb. lead, guide, direct.

Führer, -, n.m. leader, guide.

Führerschein, -e, n.m. driver's license.

Fülle, n.f. fullness, wealth; (in Hülle und F.) galore.

füllen, vb. fill.

Füllfederhalter, -, n.m. fountain pen.

Füllung, -en, n.f. filling.

Fund, -e, n.m. find, discovery.

Fundament', -e, n.nt. foundation.

fundie'ren, vb. base.

fünf, num. five.

fünft -, adj. fifth.

Fünftel, -, n.nt. fifth part; (ein f.) one-fifth.

fünfzig, num. fifty.

fünfzigst-, adj. fiftieth.

Fünfzigstel, -, n.nt. fiftieth part; (ein f.) one-fiftieth.

Funke(n), -, n.m. spark.

funkeln, vb. sparkle.

funkelnagelneu, adj. brand-new.

funken, vb. radio.

Funktion', -en, n.f. function.

Funktionär', -e, n.m. functionary.

funktionie'ren, vb. function.

für, prep. for.

Furche, -n, n.f. furrow.

Furcht, n.f. fright, fear, dread.

furchtbar, adj. terrible.

fürchten, vb. fear; (sich f. vor) be afraid of.

furchtlos, adj. fearless.

Furchtlosigkeit, n.f. fearlessness.

furchtsam, *adj.* fearful.

Fürst, -en, -en, *n.m.* prince, ruler.

fürstlich, *adj.* princely.

Furt, -en, *n.f.* ford.

Furun'kel, -n, *n.f.* boil.

Fürwort, -̈er, *n.nt.* pronoun.

Fusion', -en, *n.f.* fusion, merger.

Fuß, -̈e, *n.m.* foot.

Fußball, -̈e, *n.m.* football.

Fußboden, -̈, *n.m.* floor; flooring.

Fußgänger, -, *n.m.* pedestrian.

Fußnote, -n, *n.f.* footnote.

Fußpfleger, -, *n.m.* chiropodist.

Futter, -, *n.nt.* feed, fodder; lining.

füttern, *vb.* feed; (clothing) line.

Futurologie', *n.f.* futurology.

G

Gabardine, *n.m.* gabardine.

Gabe, -n, *n.f.* gift, donation; faculty.

Gabel, -n, *n.f.* fork.

gaffen, *vb.* gape.

gähnen, *vb.* yawn.

galant', *adj.* gallant.

Galanterie', -en, *n.f.* gallantry.

Gala-Uniform, *n.f.* full dress.

Galerie', -'en, *n.f.* gallery.

Galgen, -, *n.m.* gallows.

Galle, -n, *n.f.* gall, bile.

Gallenblase, -n, *n.f.* gall bladder.

gallertartig, *adj.* gelatinous.

gallig, *adj.* bilious.

Galopp', -s, *n.m.* gallop; (leichter G.) canter.

galoppie'ren, *vb.* gallop.

galvanisie'ren, *vb.* galvanize.

Gama'sche, -n, *n.f.* gaiters, leggings.

Gang, -̈e, *n.m.* walk; corridor, aisle; course; (auto) gear.

Gangrän', -e, *n.nt.* gangrene.

Gangster, -, *n.m.* gangster.

Gans, -̈e, *n.f.* goose.

Gänsemarsch, *n.m.* single file.

ganz, 1. *adj.* whole, entire. 2. *adv.* quite, rather; (g. gut) pretty good; (g. und gar) completely.

Ganz-, *n.nt.* whole (thing).

Ganzheit, *f.* entirety.

gänzlich, *adj.* complete.

gar, 1. *adj.* cooked, done. 2. *adv.* (g. nicht) not at all; (g. nichts) nothing at all.

Gara'ge, -n, *n.f.* garage.

Garantie', -i'en, *n.f.* guarantee.

garantie'ren, *vb.* guarantee, warrant.

Garbe, -n, *n.f.* sheaf.

Gardero'be, -n, *n.f.* clothes; cloakroom.

gären*, *vb.* ferment.

Garn, -e, *n.nt.* yarn; thread.

Garne'le, -n, *n.f.* shrimp.

garnie'ren, *vb.* garnish.

Garnison', -en, *n.f.* garrison.

Garnitur', -en, *n.f.* set.

garstig, *adj.* nasty.

Garten, -̈, *n.m.* garden, yard.

Gartenbau, *n.m.* horticulture.

Gärtner, -, *n.m.* gardener.

Gas, -e, *n.nt.* gas.

Gashebel, -, *n.m.* accelerator.

gasig, *adj.* gassy.

Gasse, -n, *n.f.* narrow street, alley.

Gast, -̈e, *n.m.* guest.

Gastarbeiter, -, *n.m.* foreign worker.

gastfrei, *adj.* hospitable.

Gastfreiheit, *n.f.* hospitality.

gastfreundlich, *adj.* hospitable.

Gastfreundschaft, *n.f.* hospitality.

Gastgeber, -, *n.m.* host.

Gastgeberin, -nen, *n.f.* hostess.

Gasthaus, -̈er, *n.nt.* inn.

gastrono'misch, *adj.* gastronomical.

Gaststube, -n, *n.f.* taproom.

Gatte, -n, -n, *n.m.* husband.

Gattin, -nen, *n.f.* wife.

Gattung, -en, *n.f.* species, genus.

Gau, -e, *n.m.* district, province.

Gaul, -̈e, *n.m.* nag.

Gaumen, -, *n.m.* palate.

Gaze, -n, *n.f.* gauze.

Geäch'tet, *n.m.* outlaw.

Gebäck', *n.nt.* pastry.

Gebär'de, -n, *n.f.* gesticulation; gesture.

gebä'ren, *vb.* (sich g.) behave.

gebä'ren*, *vb.* bear.

Gebäu'de, -, *n.nt.* building.

geben*, *vb.* give; deal (cards); (es gibt) there is, there are.

Gebet', -e, *n.nt.* prayer.

Gebiet', -e, *n.nt.* territory, region, field.

gebie'ten*, *vb.* command.

Gebie'ter, -, *n.m.* master.

Gebil'de, -, *n.nt.* form, structure.

gebil'det, *adj.* educated, civilized, cultured.

Gebir'ge, -, *n.nt.* mountainous area, mountains; mountain range.

gebir'gig, *adj.* mountainous.

Gebiß', -sse, *n.nt.* teeth; denture; (horse) bit.

Geblüt', *n.nt.* descent, family.

gebo'ren, *adj.* born.

Gebor'genheit, *n.f.* safety.

Gebot', -e, *n.nt.* command(ment).

Gebräu', -e, *n.nt.* brew, concoction.

Gebrauch', -̈e, *n.m.* use; usage, custom.

gebrau'chen, *vb.* use.

gebräuch'lich, *adj.* customary.

Gebrauchs'anweisung, -en, *n.f.* directions (for use).

Gebre'chen, -, *n.nt.* infirmity.

gebrech'lich, *adj.* decrepit.

Gebrü'der, *n.pl.* brothers.

Gebrüll', *n.nt.* roar, howl.

gebückt', *adj.* stooped.

Gebühr', -en, *n.f.* charge, fee; (nach G.) duly; (über alle G.) excessively.

gebüh'ren, *vb.* be due; (sich g.) be proper.

gebüh'rend, *adj.* duly.

gebühr'lich, *adj.* proper.

Geburt', -en, *n.f.* birth; childbirth; (von G. an) congenital.

Gebur'tenkontrolle, *n.f.* birth control.

gebür'tig, *adj.* native.

Geburts'datum, -ten, *n.nt.* date of birth.

Geburts'helfer, -, *n.m.* obstetrician.

Geburts'ort, -e, *n.m.* birthplace.

Geburts'schein, -e, *n.m.* birth certificate.

Geburts'tag, -e, *n.m.* birthday.

Gebüsch', -e, *n.nt.* bushes, shrubbery.

Geck, -en, -en, *n.m.* dandy.

Gedächt'nis, -sse, *n.nt.* memory.

Gedächt'nisfeier, -n, *n.f.* commemoration.

Gedan'ke(n), -, *n.m.* thought, idea.

gedan'kenlos, *adj.* thoughtless, unthinking.

gedan'kenvoll, *adj.* thoughtful.

Gedeck', -e, *n.nt.* cover, table setting.

gedei'hen*, *vb.* thrive.

geden'ken*, *vb.* remember, commemorate.

Gedicht', -e, *n.nt.* poem.

gedie'gen, *adj.* solid.

Gedrän'ge, *n.nt.* crush.

gedrängt', *adj.* concise.

Geduld', *n.f.* patience.

gedul'den, *vb.* (sich g.) have patience, forbear.

gedul'dig, *adj.* patient.

geeig'net, *adj.* qualified; suitable.

Gefahr', -en, *n.f.* danger, jeopardy.

gefähr'den, *vb.* endanger, jeopardize.

gefähr'lich, *adj.* dangerous.

gefahr'los, *adj.* without danger.

Gefähr'te, -n, -n, *n.m.* companion.

gefal'len*, *vb.* please; (es gefällt mir) I like it.

Gefal'len, -, *n.m.* favor.

gefäl'lig, *adj.* obliging, pleasing.

Gefan'gen-, *n.m.&f.* prisoner, captive.

Gefan'gennahme, -n, *n.f.* capture.

Gefan'genschaft, -en, *n.f.* captivity.

Gefäng'nis, -sse, *n.nt.* prison, jail.

Gefäng'niswärter, -, *n.m.* jailer.

Gefäß', -e, *n.nt.* container.

gefaßt', *adj.* composed.

Gefecht', -e, *n.nt.* battle, engagement.

gefeit', adj. fortified against.

Gefie'der, n.nt. plumage.

gefleckt', adj. dappled.

geflis'sentlich, adj. intentional; studied.

Geflü'gel, n.nt. poultry.

Geflüs'ter, n.nt. whispering.

Gefol'ge, n.nt. retinue.

gefrä'ßig, adj. gluttonous.

Gefreit'-, n.m. corporal.

gefrie'ren*, vb. freeze.

Gefrier'fach, -er, n.nt. freezer (in refrigerator).

Gefro'ren -, n.nt. ice (cream).

gefü'gig, adj. compliant.

Gefühl', -e, n.nt. feeling, sensation; emotion, sentiment.

gefühl'los, adj. insensible, callous.

gefühls'mäßig, adj. emotional.

gefühl'voll, adj. sentimental.

gegen, prep. against; toward; about.

Gegenangriff', -e, n.m. counterattack.

Gegend, -en, n.f. region.

Gegengewicht, -e, n.nt. counterbalance.

Gegengift, -e, n.nt. antidote, antitoxin.

Gegenmaßnahme, -n, n.f. countermeasure.

Gegensatz, -e, n.m. contrast, opposite.

gegenseitig, adj. mutual.

Gegenstand, -e, n.m. object.

Gegenteil, n.nt. reverse, opposite.

gegenü'ber, prep.&adv. opposite.

gegenü'berstellen, vb. confront.

Gegenwart, n.f. present, presence.

gegenwärtig, adj. present.

Gegenwirkung, -en, n.f. counteraction.

Gegner, -, n.m. adversary, opponent.

Gehalt', -e, n.nt. content, substance.

Gehalt', -er, n.nt. salary, pay.

gehar'nischt, adj. armed; (fig.) vehement.

gehäs'sig, adj. malicious.

Gehäu'se, -, n.nt. casing.

geheim', adj. secret, cryptic.

Geheim'dienst, -e, n.m. secret service.

geheim'halten*, vb. keep secret.

Geheim'nis, -se, n.nt. secret, mystery.

geheim'nisvoll, adj. secretive, mysterious.

Geheiß', n.nt. command, behest.

gehen*, vb. go, walk; (wie geht es Ihnen?) how are you?

gehen-lassen*, vb. (sich g.) let oneself go.

Gehil'fe, -n, -n, n.m. helper, assistant.

Gehirn', -e, n.nt. brain.

Gehöft', -e, n.nt. farmstead.

Gehölz', -e, n.nt. woods.

Gehör', n.nt. hearing.

gehor'chen, vb. obey.

gehö'ren, vb. belong to.

gehö'rig, adj. belonging to; thorough, sound; appropriate.

gehor'sam, adj. obedient.

Gehor'sam, n.m. obedience, allegiance.

Geige, -n, n.f. violin.

Geisel, -n, n.m. hostage.

Geiser, -, n.m. geyser.

Geißel, -n, n.f. whip, scourge.

geißeln, vb. flagellate, scourge.

Geist, -er, n.m. mind, spirit; ghost; (Heiliger G.) Holy Spirit, Ghost.

geistesabwesend, adj. absent-minded.

Geistesgegenwart, n.f. presence of mind.

geistesgestört, adj. deranged.

Geisteswissenschaften, n.pl. arts.

geistig, adj. mental, spiritual.

geistlich, adj. ecclesiastic(al).

Geistlich -, n.m. minister, clergyman.

Geistlichkeit, n.f. clergy.

geistlos, adj. inane, vacuous.

geistreich, adj. bright, witty.

geiststötend, adj. dull.

Geiz, -e, n.m. avarice.

Geizhals, -e, n.m. miser.

geizig, adj. avaricious, miserly.

Geklap'per, n.nt. clatter.

Gekrit'zel, n.nt. scribbling.

gekün'stelt, adj. contrived.

Geläch'ter, n.nt. laughter.

Gela'ge, -, n.nt. banquet.

gelähmt', adj. crippled.

Gelän'de, -, n.nt. terrain.

Gelän'der, -, n.nt. railing, banister.

gelan'gen, vb. reach, get to.

gelas'sen, adj. placid, composed.

Gelati'ne, -n, n.f. gelatine.

geläu'fig, adj. familiar, fluent.

Geläu'figkeit, n.f. fluency.

gelaunt', adj. (gut g.) in good humor.

gelb, adj. yellow.

gelbbraun, adj. tan.

Geld, -er, n.nt. money.

Geldbeutel, -, n.m. purse.

geldlich, adj. monetary.

Geldschein, -e, n.m. bill.

Geldschrank, -e, n.m. safe.

Geldstrafe, -n, n.f. fine; (zu einer G. verurteilen) fine.

Geldwechsler, -, n.m. moneychanger.

Gelee', -s, n.nt. jelly.

gele'gen, adj. situated; opportune.

Gele'genheit, -en, n.f. occasion, chance.

gele'gentlich, adj. occasional.

Gelehr'samkeit, n.f. erudition, scholarship.

gelehrt', adj. learned, erudite.

Gelehr't-, n.m.&f. scholar.

Gelei'se, -, n.nt. track.

Geleit', n.nt. accompaniment; (freies G.) safe conduct.

gelei'ten, vb. escort.

Geleit'zug, -e, n.m. convoy.

Gelenk', -e, n.nt. joint.

gelen'kig, adj. supple.

gellebt', adj. beloved.

Gelieb'te, -n, n.f. beloved; mistress.

gelind', adj. mild, light.

gellen, vb. shriek.

gellend, adj. shrill.

gelo'ben, vb. vow, pledge.

gelten*, vb. be valid, apply, hold; be intended for; be considered; (das gilt nicht) that's not fair.

Geltung, n.f. standing, value.

Gelüb'de, -, n.nt. vow.

Gelüst', -e, n.nt. lust.

gemach', adv. slowly, gently.

Gemach', -er, n.nt. chamber.

gemäch'lich, adj. leisurely, slow and easy.

Gemahl', -e, n.m. husband; consort.

gemäß', prep. according to.

gemä'ßigt, adj. moderate.

gemein', 1. adj. mean, vile, vicious. 2. adv. in common.

Gemein'de, -n, n.f. community; municipality; congregation.

gemein'gültig, adj. generally accepted.

Gemein'platz, -e, n.m. platitude.

gemein'sam, adj. common, joint.

Gemein'schaft, n.f. community, fellowship.

Gemur'mel, -, n.nt. murmur.

Gemü'se, -, n.nt. vegetable.

Gemüt', -er, n.nt. mind, spirit, temper, heart.

gemüt'lich, adj. comfortable, homey, genial.

Gemüts'art, -en, n.f. temperament.

Gemüts'ruhe, n.f. placidity.

genau', adj. accurate, exact; fussy.

Genau'igkeit, -en, n.f. accuracy.

geneh'migen, vb. grant, approve.

Geneh'migung, -en, n.f. permission, license.

geneigt', adj. inclined.

General', -e, n.m. general.

Genera'tor, -o'ren, n.m. generator.

gene'sen*, vb. recover.

Gene'sung, n.f. convalescence, recovery.

genial', adj. ingenious, having genius.

Genialität', n.f. ingenuity, genius.

Genie', -s, n.nt. genius.

genie'ßen*, vb. enjoy, relish.

Genitiv, -e, n.m. genitive.

Genos'se, -n, n.m. companion; (derogatory) character.

Genos'senschaft, -en, n.f. association, co-operative society.

genug', *adj.* enough.

genü'gen, *vb.* be enough, suffice.

genü'gend, *adj.* satisfactory, sufficient.

genüg'sam, *adj.* modest.

Genüg'samkeit, *n.f.* frugality.

Genug'tuung, -en, *n.f.* satisfaction.

Genuß', -sse, *n.m.* enjoyment; relish.

Geograph', -en, -en, *n.m.* geographer.

Geographie', *n.f.* geography.

geogra'phisch, *adj.* geographical.

Geometrie', *n.f.* geometry.

geome'trisch, *adj.* geometric.

geord'net, *adj.* orderly.

Gepäck', *n.nt.* luggage, baggage.

Gepäck'träger, -, *n.m.* porter.

Gepäck'schein, -e, *n.m.* baggage check.

Geplau'der, *n.nt.* chat, small talk.

Geprä'ge, -, *n.nt.* stamp; character.

gera'de, 1. *adj.* straight, even. **2.** *adv.* just; (g. **aus**) straight ahead.

gera'de-stehen*, *vb.* stand straight; answer for.

geradezu', *adv.* downright.

Gerad'heit, *n.f.* erectness; directness.

Gerät', -e, *n.nt.* tool, appliance, utensil.

Geratewohl', *n.* (**aufs G.**) at random, haphazardly.

geraum', *adj.* considerable.

geräu'mig, *adj.* spacious.

Geräusch', -e, *n.nt.* noise.

geräusch'los, *adj.* noiseless.

gerben, *vb.* tan.

gerecht', *adj.* just, fair.

Gerech'tigkeit, *n.f.* justice.

Gere'de, *n.nt.* chatter; (**ins G.** **bringen**) make someone the talk of the town.

gereift', *adj.* mellow.

gereizt', *adj.* irritated, edgy.

Gereizt'heit, *n.f.* irritability.

gereu'en, *vb.* repent, regret.

Gericht', -e, *n.nt.* court, bar, tribunal; (food) course; (**Jüngstes G.**) doomsday, judgment day.

gericht'lich, *adj.* legal, judicial, forensic.

Gerichts'barkeit, *n.f.* jurisdiction.

Gerichts'gebäude, -, *n.nt.* courthouse.

Gerichts'saal, -säle, *n.m.* courtroom.

Gerichts'verhandlung, -en, *n.f.* court proceedings, trial.

gerie'ben, *adj.* cunning, sly.

gering', *adj.* slight, slim.

gering'achten, *vb.* look down upon.

gering'fügig, *adj.* negligible, petty.

gering'schätzen, *vb.* hold in low esteem.

gering'schätzig, *adj.* disparaging, derogatory.

gerin'nen*, *vb.* curdle, clot, coagulate.

Gerip'pe, -, *n.nt.* skeleton.

geris'sen, *adj.* shrewd.

Germa'ne, -n, -n, *n.m.* Teuton.

germa'nisch, *adj.* Germanic.

gern, *adv.* gladly, readily; (g. **haben***) like, be fond of; (g. **tun***) like to do.

Gerste, -n, *n.f.* barley.

Gerstenkorn, -er, *n.nt.* barleycorn; sty.

Geruch', -e, *n.m.* smell, odor, scent.

Gerücht', -e, *n.nt.* rumor.

geru'hen, *vb.* deign.

Gerüst', -e, *n.nt.* scaffold, scaffolding.

gesamt', *adj.* total.

Gesamt'heit, *n.f.* entirety.

Gesandt', -, *n.m.* ambassador, envoy.

Gesandt'schaft, -en, *n.f.* legation.

Gesang', -e, *n.m.* song, chant.

Gesang'buch, -er, *n.nt.* hymnal.

Geschäft', -e, *n.nt.* business, deal; shop, store.

geschäf'tig, *adj.* busy.

Geschäf'tigkeit, -en, *n.f.* bustle.

Geschäfts'mann, -er, *or* -leute, *n.m.* businessman.

geschäfts'mäßig, *adj.* businesslike.

Geschäfts'viertel, -, *n.nt.* downtown, business section.

gesche'hen*, *vb.* occur, happen.

Gesche'hnis, -se, *n.nt.* happening, occurrence.

gescheit', *adj.* bright, clever.

Geschenk', -e, *n.nt.* present.

Geschich'te, -n, *n.f.* story; history.

Geschick', *n.nt.* skill.

Geschick'lichkeit, -en, *n.f.* dexterity, facility.

geschickt', *adj.* skillful, clever, deft.

Geschirr', -e, *n.nt.* dishes; harness.

Geschlecht', -er, *n.nt.* genus, sex; gender; lineage, family.

geschlecht'lich, *adj.* sexual.

Geschmack', -e, *n.m.* taste, flavor.

geschmack'los, *adj.* tasteless; in bad taste.

geschmei'dig, *adj.* lithe.

Geschöpf', -e, *n.nt.* creature.

Geschoß', -sse, *n.nt.* missile, projectile.

Geschrei', *n.nt.* clamor.

Geschütz', -e, *n.nt.* gun.

Geschwa'der, -, *n.nt.* squadron.

Geschwätz', *n.nt.* idle talk, babble.

geschwät'zig, *adj.* talkative, gossipy.

geschwind', *adj.* swift.

Geschwin'digkeit, -en, *n.f.* speed, velocity.

Geschwin'digkeitsgrenze, -n, *n.f.* speed limit.

Geschwo'ren-, *n.m.&f.* juror; *(pl.)* jury.

Geschwulst', -e, *n.nt.* swelling, growth.

Geschwür', -e, *n.nt.* abscess, ulcer.

geseg'net, *adj.* blessed.

Gesel'le, -n, -n, *n.m.* journeyman; fellow.

gesel'len, *vb.* (**sich g.**) join.

gesel'lig, *adj.* sociable, gregarious.

Gesell'schaft, -en, *n.f.* society; company; party.

Gesell'schafterin, -nen, *n.f.* companion.

gesell'schaftlich, *adj.* social.

Gesell'schaftskleidung, -en, *n.f.* evening dress, dress clothes.

Gesell'schaftsreise, -n, *n.f.* group tour.

Gesetz', -e, *n.nt.* law, act.

Gesetz'antrag, -e, *n.m.* bill.

gesetz'gebend, *adj.* legislative.

Gesetz'geber, -, *n.m.* legislator.

Gesetz'gebung, *n.f.* legislation.

gesetz'lich, *adj.* lawful, legal.

gesetz'los, *adj.* lawless.

gesetz'mäßig, *adj.* legal.

Gesetz'mäßigkeit, *n.f.* legality.

gesetz'widrig, *adj.* illegal, unlawful.

Gesicht', -er, *n.nt.* face.

Gesichts'ausdruck, -e, *n.m.* facial expression, mien.

Gesichts'farbe, *n.f.* complexion.

Gesichts'kreis, *n.m.* horizon.

Gesichts'massage, -n, *n.f.* facial.

Gesichts'punkt, -e, *n.m.* point of view, aspect.

Gesichts'zug, -e, *n.m.* feature.

Gesin'del, *n.nt.* rabble.

gesinnt', *adj.* (g. **sein***) be of a mind, be disposed.

Gesin'nung, -en, *n.f.* attitude, way of thinking, views.

gesit'tet, *adj.* well-mannered, civilized.

gespannt', *adj.* tense; eager to know, curious.

Gespenst', -er, *n.nt.* ghost.

Gespie'le, -n, -n, *n.m.* playmate.

Gespräch', -e, *n.nt.* talk, conversation.

gesprä'chig, *adj.* talkative.

Gestalt', -en, *n.f.* figure, form, shape.

gestal'ten, *vb.* form, shape, fashion.

Gestal'tung, -en, *n.f.* formation, fashioning.

Gestam'mel, *n.nt.* stammering.

gestän'dig, *adj.* (g. **sein***) make a confession.

Geständ'nis, -se, *n.nt.* confession, avowal.

Gestank', *n.m.* stench.

gestat'ten, vb. permit.

Geste, -n, n.f. gesture.

geste'hen*, vb. confess, avow.

Gestein', n.nt. rock.

Gestell', -e, n.nt. stand, rack, frame.

gestern, adv. yesterday.

gestikulie'ren, vb. gesticulate.

Gestirn', -e, n.nt. star; constellation.

Gestirns'bahn, -en, n.f. orbit.

Gestrüpp', n.nt. scrub, brush.

Gesuch', -e, n.nt. application, petition, request.

gesucht', adj. far-fetched, contrived.

gesund', adj. healthy, sound, wholesome.

gesun'den, vb. recover.

Gesund'heit, n.f. health, fitness; (geistige G.) sanity.

Gesund'heitsattest, -e, n.nt. certificate of health.

gesund'heitsschädlich, adj. unhealthy.

Gesund'heitswesen, n.nt. sanitation.

Gesun'dung, n.f. recovery.

Getö'se, n.nt. uproar.

Getränk', -e, n.nt. drink, beverage; (alkoholfreies G.) soft drink.

getrau'en, vb. (sich g.) dare.

Getrei'de, n.nt. grain, cereal.

getrennt', adj. separate.

getreu', adj. faithful.

Getrie'be, -n, n.nt. gear.

getrost', adv. confidently.

Getu'e, n.nt. affectation, goings-on.

geübt', adj. experienced.

Gewächs', -e, n.nt. growth.

gewagt', adj. daring, hazardous.

Gewähr', n.f. guarantee.

gewäh'ren, vb. grant.

gewähr'leisten, vb. warrant, guarantee.

Gewahr'sam, n.m. custody.

Gewalt', -en, n.f. force, power.

Gewalt'herrschaft, n.f. despotism.

gewal'tig, adj. powerful, tremendous.

gewalt'sam, adj. forcible, violent.

gewalt'tätig, adj. violent.

Gewalt'tätigkeit, -en, n.f. violence.

Gewand', -er, n.nt. garb, garment.

gewandt', adj. facile, versatile.

Gewandt'heit, -en, n.f. deftness.

gewär'tig, adv. (g. sein*) be prepared.

Gewäs'ser, n.nt. waters.

Gewe'be, -, n.nt. tissue, texture.

Gewehr', -e, n.nt. rifle, gun.

Gewer'be, -, n.nt. trade, business.

Gewerk'schaft, -en, n.f. labor union.

Gewicht' -e, n.nt. weight.

gewiegt', adj. crafty.

gewillt', adj. willing.

Gewinn', -e, n.m. gain, profit.

gewinn'bringend, adj. lucrative.

gewin'nen*, vb. win, gain.

Gewin'ner, -, n.m. winner.

gewinn'süchtig, adj. mercenary, greedy.

Gewirr', n.nt. tangle, confusion.

gewiß', adj. certain.

Gewis'sen, -, n.nt. conscience.

gewis'senhaft, adj. conscientious.

gewis'senlos, adj. unprincipled.

Gewis'sensbiß, -sse, n.m. remorse, qualms.

gewisserma'ßen, adv. so to speak, as it were.

Gewiß'heit, -en, n.f. certainty.

Gewit'ter, -, n.nt. thunderstorm.

gewit'zigt, adj. clever.

gewo'gen, adj. (g. sein*) be disposed towards.

gewöh'nen, vb. accustom; (sich g. an) become accustomed to.

Gewohn'heit, -en, n.f. habit, custom, practice.

gewohn'heitsmäßig, adj. customary, habitual.

gewöhn'lich, adj. ordinary, usual, regular; common, vulgar.

gewohnt', adj. accustomed.

Gewöl'be, -, n.nt. vaulting, vault.

Gewühl', n.nt. shuffle, melee.

gewun'den, adj. coiled; sinuous.

Gewürz', -e, n.nt. spice, condiment, seasoning.

Gewürz'kraut -er, n.nt. herb.

Gezei'ten, n.pl. tide.

gezie'men, vb. be proper, befit.

Gicht, -en, n.f. gout, arthritis.

Giebel, -, n.m. gable.

Gier, n.f. greed(iness).

gierig, adj. greedy.

gießen*, vb. pour; cast (metal).

Gift, -e, n.nt. poison.

giftig, adj. poisonous.

Gilde, -n, n.f. guild.

Gin, -s, n.m. gin.

Gipfel, -, n.m. peak.

gipfeln, vb. culminate.

Gips, -e, n.m. gypsum, plaster.

Giraf'fe, -n, n.f. giraffe.

Girant', -en, -en, n.m. endorser.

Girat', -en, -en, n.m. endorsee.

girie'ren, vb. endorse (a check, note, etc.), put into circulation.

Giro, -s, n.nt. endorsement, circulation (of endorsed notes, etc.).

Gischt, -e, n.m. spray, foam.

Gitar're, -n, n.f. guitar.

Gitter, -, n.nt. grating; gate.

Gitterwerk, -e, n.nt. grating.

glaciert', adj. glacé.

Glanz, n.m. shine, sheen, gloss; brilliance, splendor.

glänzen, vb. shine.

glänzend, adj. shiny, brilliant.

Glas, -er, n.nt. glass.

Glaser, -, n.m. glazier.

gläsern, adj. made of glass.

glasie'ren, vb. glaze.

glasig, adj. glassy.

Glasscheibe, -n, n.f. pane.

Glasur, -en, n.f. glaze.

Glaswaare, -n, n.f. glassware.

glatt, adj. smooth, slippery; outright.

glätten, vb. smooth.

Glatzkopf, -e, n.m. bald head.

Glaube(n), -, n.m. belief, faith.

glauben, vb. believe.

Glaubensbekenntnis, -se, n.nt. confession of faith; creed.

glaubhaft, adj. believable.

gläubig, adj. believing, devout.

Gläubig-, n.m.&f. believer; creditor.

glaublich, adj. credible.

glaubwürdig, adj. credible.

Glaubwürdigkeit, n.f. credibility.

gleich, 1. adj. equal, same, even. 2. adv. right away.

gleichaltig, adj. of the same age.

gleichartig, adj. similar, homogeneous.

gleichberechtigt, adj. having equal rights.

Gleichberechtigung, -en, n.f. equality of rights.

gleichen*, vb. be like, equal, resemble.

gleichfalls, adv. likewise.

gleichförmig, adj. uniform.

gleichgesinnt, adj. likeminded.

gleichgestellt, adj. coordinate.

Gleichgewicht, n.nt. equilibrium.

gleichgültig, adj. indifferent.

Gleichgültigkeit, n.f. indifference.

Gleichheit, n.f. equality.

gleich-machen, vb. equalize.

Gleichmaß, n.nt. proportion, symmetry.

gleichmäßig, adj. even, regular.

Gleichmut, n.m. equanimity.

gleichmütig, adj. even-tempered.

Gleichnis, -se, n.nt. simile, parable.

gleichsam, adv. as it were.

gleichseitig, adj. equilateral.

gleich-setzen, vb. equate.

Gleichstrom, -e, n.m. direct current.

gleich-tun*, vb. do like, match up to.

Gleichung, -en, n.f. equation.

gleichwertig, adj. equivalent.

gleichwie, adv.&conj. just as.

gleichwohl, adv. nevertheless.

gleichzeitig, adj. simultaneous.

Gleis, -e, n.nt. track.

gleiten*, vb. glide, slide, slip.

Gletscher, -, n.m. glacier.

Gletscherspalte, -n, n.f. crevasse.

Glied, -er, n.nt. limb; link.

gliedern, vb. segment, classify.

Gliederung, -en, n.f. arrangement, structure.

Gliedmaßen, n.pl. limbs, extremities.

glitzern, vb. glitter.

Globus, -ben (-busse), n.m. globe.

Glocke, -n, n.f. bell.

Glockenschlag, ⸚e, n.m. stroke of the clock.

Glockenspiel, -e, n.nt. chimes, carillon.

Glockenturm, ⸚, n.m. belfry, bell-tower.

Glorie, -n, n.f. glory.

Glorienschein, -e, n.m. halo.

glorreich, adj. glorious.

glotzen, vb. stare.

Glück, n.nt. happiness, luck.

gluckern, vb. gurgle.

glücklich, adj. happy.

glücklicherweise, adv. fortunately.

glückselig, adj. blissful.

Glückseligkeit, -en, n.f. bliss.

glucksen, vb. gurgle.

Glücksfall, ⸚e, n.m. stroke of luck.

Glücksspiel, -e, n.nt. gamble; gambling.

Glücksspieler, -, n.m. gambler.

Glückwunsch, ⸚e, n.m. congratulation.

Glühbirne, -n, n.f. electric light bulb.

glühen, vb. glow.

glühend, adj. glowing, incandescent; ardent.

Glut, -en, n.f. heat, live coals; ardor, passion.

Glyzerin', n.nt. glycerine.

G.m.b.H.', abbr. (= Gesell'schaft mit beschränk'ter Haftung) incorporated, inc.

Gnade, n.f. grace, mercy.

gnadenreich, adj. merciful.

gnädig, adj. gracious, merciful; (g.e Frau) madam.

Gold, n.nt. gold.

Goldbarren, -, n.m. bullion.

golden, adj. golden.

Goldfisch, -e, n.m. goldfish.

goldig, adj. darling, cute.

Goldschmied, -e, n.m. goldsmith.

Golf, -e, n.m. gulf, bay.

Golf, n.nt. golf.

Golfplatz, ⸚e, n.m. golf course.

Gondel, -n, n.f. gondola.

gönnen, vb. grant, not begrudge; (sich g.) allow oneself; (das gönne ich ihm!) that serves him right!

Gör, -en, n.nt. brat, girl.

Goril'la, -s, n.m. gorilla.

Gosse, -n, n.f. gutter, drain.

Gotik, n.f. Gothic architecture.

gotisch, adj. Gothic.

Gott, ⸚er, n.m. god, deity.

gottähnlich, adj. godlike.

Götterdämmerung, n.f. twilight of the gods.

Gottesacker, ⸚, n.m. cemetery.

Gottesdienst, -e, n.m. (church) service.

Gottesgabe, -n.f. godsend.

Gotteshaus, ⸚er, n.nt. church.

Gotteslästerung, -en, n.f. blasphemy.

Gottheit, -en, n.f. deity, divinity.

Göttin, -nen, n.f. goddess.

göttlich, adj. godly, divine.

gottlob', interj. praise God.

gottlos, adj. godless.

Götze, -n, -n, n.m. idol, false god.

Götzenbild, -er, n.nt. idol.

Götzendienst, -e, n.m. idolatry.

Gouvernan'te, -n, n.f. governess.

Gouverneur', -e, n.m. governor.

Gouverneurs'amt, ⸚er, n.nt. governorship.

Grab, ⸚er, n.nt. grave.

graben*, vb. dig.

Graben, ⸚, n.m. trench, ditch.

Grablegung, -en, n.f. burial.

Grabmal, ⸚er, n.nt. tomb(stone).

Grabschrift, -en, n.f. epitaph.

Grabstein, -e, n.m. gravestone.

Grad, -e, n.m. degree.

Graf, -en, -en, n.m. count.

Gräfin, -nen, n.f. countess.

Grafschaft, -en, n.f. county.

Gram, n.m. grief, care.

grämen, vb. (sich g.) grieve, fret.

Gramm, -, n.nt. gram.

Gramma'tik, -en, n.f. grammar.

Gramma'tiker, -, n.m. grammarian.

gramma'tisch, adj. grammatical.

Grammophon', -e, n.nt. phonograph.

Grammophon'platte, -n, n.f. phonograph record.

Granat', -e, n.m. garnet.

Grana'te, -n, n.f. grenade.

Granit', n.m. granite.

granulie'ren, vb. granulate.

Graphiker, -, n.m. illustrator, commercial artist.

graphisch, adj. graphic.

Gras, ⸚er, n.nt. grass.

grasartig, adj. grasslike, grassy.

grasen, vb. graze.

grasig, adj. grassy.

gräßlich, adj. hideous.

Grat, -e, n.m. ridge.

Gräte, -n, n.f. bone (of a fish).

gratis, adj. gratis.

gratulie'ren, vb. congratulate.

grau, adj. gray.

Grauen, n.nt. horror.

grauenhaft, adj. ghastly.

grausam, adj. cruel.

grausig, adj. lurid.

Graveur', -e, n.m. engraver.

gravie'ren, vb. engrave.

gravitie'ren, vb. gravitate.

Grazie, -n, n.f. grace, charm.

graziös', adj. graceful.

greifbar, adj. tangible.

greifen*, vb. seize, grasp.

Greis, -e, n.m. old man.

Greisenalter, -, n.nt. old age.

Greisin, -nen, n.f. old woman.

grell, adj. garish, gaudy, shrill.

Grenze, -n, n.f. limit, border, boundary.

grenzen, vb. (g. an) border on.

grenzenlos, adj. boundless.

Greuel, -, n.m. horror, outrage.

greulich, adj. horrible.

Grieche, -n, -n, n.m. Greek.

Griechenland, n.nt. Greece.

griechisch, adj. Greek.

Griesgram, -e, n.m. grouch.

griesgrämig, adj. sullen.

Grieß, -e, n.m. semolina, coarse meal; gravel.

Griff, -e, n.m. grasp, grip, handle.

Grill, -s, n.m. grill; grillroom.

Grille, -n, n.f. cricket; whim.

grillen, vb. broil.

grillenhaft, adj. whimsical.

Grimas'se, -n, n.f. grimace.

Grimm, n.m. anger.

grimmig, adj. angry.

grinsen, vb. grin.

Grinsen, n.nt. grin.

Grippe, -n, n.f. grippe, influenza.

grob(-), adj. coarse, rough, crude.

Grobian, -e, n.m. boor, ruffian.

Grog, -s, n.m. grog.

Groll, n.m. anger, grudge.

grollen, vb. be angry, bear a grudge.

Gros, -se, n.nt. gross.

Groschen, -, n.m. ten pfennig piece; 1/100 of an Austrian schilling.

groß(-), adj. big, tall, great.

großartig, adj. grand, magnificent.

Großbritan'ien, n.nt. Great Britain.

Größe, -n, n.f. size, height, greatness.

Großeltern, n.pl. grandparents.

großenteils, adv. in large part, largely.

Großhandel, n.m. wholesale trade.

großherzig, adj. magnanimous.

großjährig, adj. of age.

Großmacht, ⸚e, n.f. major power.

Großmut, n.m. magnanimity, generosity.

großmütig, adj. magnanimous, generous.

Großmutter, ⸚, n.f. grandmother.

Grossrechenanlage, -n, n.f. (computer) mainframe.

großsprecherisch, adj. boastful.

Großstaat, -en, n.m. major power.

Großstadt, ⸚e, n.f. large city, metropolis.

Großstädter, -e, *n.m.* big city person.

größtenteils, *adv.* for the most part, mostly.

groß·tun*, *vb.* act big, boast.

Großvater, -̈, *n.m.* grandfather.

groß·ziehen*, *vb.* bring up, raise.

großzügig, *adj.* on a grand scale, generous, broad-minded.

grotesk', *adj.* grotesque.

Grotte, -n, *n.f.* grotto.

Grube, -n, *n.f.* pit; mine.

grübeln, *vb.* brood.

Grubenarbeiter, -, *n.m.* miner.

Gruft, -̈e, *n.f.* crypt, vault.

grün, *adj.* green.

Grund, -̈e, *n.m.* ground, bottom, basis, reason; (G. und Boden) land, real estate.

Grundbegriff, -e, *n.m.* basic concept.

Grundbesitz, -e, *n.m.* landed property.

Grundbesitzer, -, *n.m.* landholder.

gründen, *vb.* found.

Grundgesetz, -e, *n.nt.* basic law; constitution.

Grundlage, -n, *n.f.* basis.

grundlegend, *adj.* fundamental.

gründlich, *adj.* thorough.

Grundlinie, -n, *n.f.* base.

grundlos, *adj.* bottomless; unfounded.

Grundriß, -sse, *n.m.* outline, sketch.

Grundsatz, -̈e, *n.m.* principle.

grundsätzlich, *adj.* fundamental, on principle.

Grundschule, -n, *n.f.* elementary school.

Grundstoff, -e, *n.m.* basic material.

Grundstück, -e, *n.nt.* lot.

Gründung, -en, *n.f.* founding, establishment.

grunzen, *vb.* grunt.

Gruppe, -n, *n.f.* group.

gruppie'ren, *vb.* group.

gruselig, *adj.* uncanny, creepy.

Gruß, -̈e, *n.m.* greeting; salute.

grüßen, *vb.* greet; salute.

gucken, *vb.* look.

gültig, *adj.* valid.

Gültigkeit, *n.f.* validity.

Gummi, -s, *n.m.* rubber; eraser.

Gummi, -s, *n.nt.* gum.

gummiartig, *adj.* gummy.

Gummiband, -̈er, *n.nt.* elastic (band).

Gummischuhe, *n.pl.* overshoes, galoshes, rubbers.

Gunst, -̈e, *n.f.* favor.

günstig, *adj.* favorable.

Günstling, -e, *n.m.* favorite.

Gurgel, -n, *n.f.* throat, gullet.

gurgeln, *vb.* gargle.

Gurke, -n, *n.f.* cucumber; (saure G.) pickle.

Gurt, -e, *n.m.* girth, harness.

Gürtel, -, *n.m.* belt, girdle.

gürten, *vb.* gird.

Guru, -s, *n.m.* guru.

Guß, -̈sse, *n.m.* downpour; frosting; casting.

Gußstein, -e, *n.m.* sink, drain.

gut, 1. *adj.* good. 2. *adv.* well.

Gut, -̈er, *n.nt.* property; landed estate; (pl.) goods.

Gutachten, -, *n.nt.* (expert) opinion, (legal) advice.

gutaussehend, *adj.* good-looking.

Gutdünken, *n.nt.* opinion, discretion.

Güte, *n.f.* kindness; quality, purity.

gutgläubig, *adj.* credulous.

Guthaben, -, *n.nt.* credit; assets.

gut·heißen*, *vb.* approve.

gutherzig, *adj.* good-hearted.

gütig, *adj.* kind, friendly, gracious.

gütlich, *adj.* kind, friendly.

gut·machen, *vb.* make good; (wieder g.) make amends for.

gutmütig, *adj.* good-natured.

gut·schreiben*, *vb.* credit.

Gutschrift, -en, *n.f.* credit.

Gymna'sium, -ien, *n.nt.* secondary school preparing for university.

Gymnas'tik, *n.f.* gymnastics.

gymnas'tisch, *adj.* gymnastic.

H

ha, *abbr.* (= Hektar') hectare.

Haar, -e, *n.nt.* hair.

haarig, *adj.* hairy.

Haarklammer, -n, *n.f.* bobby pin.

Haarnadel, -n, *n.f.* hairpin.

haarscharf, *adj.* very sharp.

Haarschneiden, *n.nt.* haircut.

Haarschnitt, -e, *n.m.* (style of) haircut.

Haarspray, *n.m.* hairspray.

Habe, -n, *n.f.* property; (Hab und Gut) goods and chattels, all one's property.

haben*, *vb.* have.

Haben, -, *n.nt.* credit; (Soll und H.) debit and credit.

Habgier, *n.f.* greed.

habgierig, *adj.* greedy.

Habseligkeiten, *n.pl.* belongings.

Habsucht, *n.f.* greed.

habsüchtig, *adj.* greedy.

Hacke, -n, *n.f.* hoe, pick; heel.

hacken, *vb.* chip.

Hader, *n.m.* quarrel, strife.

hadern, *vb.* quarrel.

Hafen, -̈, *n.m.* harbor, port.

Hafenstadt, -̈e, *n.f.* seaport.

Hafer, *n.m.* oats.

Hafergrütze, *n.f.* oatmeal.

Haft, *n.f.* arrest, detention.

haftbar, *adj.* liable.

Haftbefehl, -e, *n.m.* warrant.

haften, *vb.* stick, adhere; be responsible.

Haftpflicht, -en, *n.f.* liability.

Hagel, *n.m.* hail.

Hagelwetter, -, *n.nt.* hailstorm.

hager, *adj.* gaunt.

Hahn, -̈e, *n.m.* rooster; faucet.

Haifisch, -e, *n.m.* shark.

Hain, -e, *n.m.* grove.

Haken, -, *n.m.* hook.

halb, *adj.* half.

halber, *prep.* because of, for the sake of.

halbie'ren, *vb.* halve.

Halbinsel, -n, *n.f.* peninsula.

halbjährlich, *adj.* semiannual.

Halbkreis, -e, *n.m.* semicircle.

Halbkugel, -n, *n.f.* hemisphere.

Halbmesser, -, *n.m.* radius.

Halbschuhe, *n.pl.* low shoes, oxfords.

halbwegs, *adv.* halfway.

Hälfte, -n, *n.f.* half.

Halfter, -, *n.nt.* halter.

Halle, -n, *n.f.* hall.

hallen, *vb.* sound, echo.

Halm, -e, *n.m.* blade, stalk.

hallo, *interj.* hello.

Hals, -̈e, *n.m.* neck.

Halsband, -̈er, *n.nt.* necklace.

halsbrecherisch, *adj.* breakneck.

Halskette, -n, *n.f.* necklace.

Halsschmerzen, *n.pl.* sore throat.

halsstarrig, *adj.* obstinate.

Halstuch, -̈er, *n.nt.* kerchief.

Halsweh, *n.nt.* sore throat.

halt, *interj.* halt.

halt, *adv.* after all, I think.

Halt, -e, *n.m.* halt; hold, support.

haltbar, *adj.* tenable.

halten*, *vb.* hold, keep, stop; (h. für) consider as.

Halter, -, *n.m.* holder.

Haltestelle, -n, *n.f.* stop.

halt·machen, *vb.* halt, stop.

Haltung, -en, *n.f.* attitude, posture.

Hammelbraten, -, *n.m.* roast mutton.

Hammelfleisch, *n.nt.* mutton.

Hammelkeule, -n, *n.f.* leg of mutton.

Hammer, -̈, *n.m.* hammer.

hämmern, *vb.* hammer.

Hämorrhoi'de, -n, *n.f.* hemorrhoid.

hamstern, *vb.* hoard.

Hand, -̈e, *n.f.* hand.

Handarbeit, -en, *n.f.* manual labor; needlework.

Handbremse, -n, *n.f.* hand brake, emergency brake.

Handbuch, -̈er, *n.nt.* handbook, manual.

Händedruck, *n.m.* clasp (of hands).

Handel, *n.m.* trade, commerce.

handeln, *vb.* act, trade, deal; (es handelt sich um . . .) it is a question of . . .

Handelsgeist, *n.m.* commercialism.

Handelsmarine, *n.f.* merchant marine.

Handelsreisend-, *n.m.* traveling salesman.

handfest, *adj.* sturdy.

Handfläche, **-n**, *n.f.* palm.

Handgelenk, **-e**, *n.nt.* wrist.

handhaben, *vb.* handle, manage.

Handikap, **-s**, *n.nt.* handicap.

Handlanger, **-**, *n.m.* handy man, general worker.

Händler, **-**, *n.m.* dealer, trader.

handlich, *adj.* handy.

Handlung, **-en**, *n.f.* action; plot.

Handschelle, **-n**, *n.f.* handcuff.

Handschrift, **-en**, *n.f.* handwriting.

Handschuh, **-e**, *n.m.* glove.

Handtasche, **-n**, *n.f.* pocketbook.

Handtuch, **ˉer**, *n.nt.* towel.

Handvoll, *n.f.* handful.

Handwerk, *n.nt.* handicraft, handiwork.

Handwerker, **-**, *n.m.* craftsman, artisan.

Hang, **ˉe**, *n.m.* slope; inclination.

Hängebrücke, **-n**, *n.f.* suspension bridge.

Hängematte, **-n**, *n.f.* hammock.

hängen*, *vb.* (*intr.*) hang, be suspended; (**an jemandem h.**) be attached to someone.

hängen(*), *vb.* (*tr.*) hang, suspend.

Hans, *n.m.* Hans; (**H. Dampf in allen Gassen**) jack-of-all-trades.

hänseln, *vb.* tease.

hantie'ren, *vb.* handle, manipulate.

hapern, *vb.* get stuck, be wrong.

Happen, **-**, *n.m.* morsel.

Harfe, **-n**, *n.f.* harp.

Harke, **-n**, *n.f.* rake.

harken, *vb.* rake.

Harm, *n.m.* grief.

harmlos, *adj.* harmless.

Harmonie', **-i'en**, *n.f.* harmony.

Harmo'nika, **-s**, *n.f.* harmonica.

harmo'nisch, *adj.* harmonious.

harmonisie'ren, *vb.* harmonize.

Harn, *n.m.* urine.

Harnblase, **-n**, *n.f.* (urinary) bladder.

harnen, *vb.* urinate.

Harnisch, **-e**, *n.m.* harness; armor.

Harpu'ne, **-n**, *n.f.* harpoon.

hart (**ˉ**), *adj.* hard, severe.

Härte, **-n**, *n.f.* hardness, severity.

härten, *vb.* harden, temper.

hartgekocht, *adj.* hard-boiled.

hartherzig, *adj.* hard-hearted.

hartnäckig, *adj.* stubborn.

Harz, **-e**, *n.nt.* resin, rosin.

Hasch, *n.m.* & *adj.* marijuana.

haschen, *vb.* catch, snatch.

Hase, **-n**, **-n**, *n.m.* hare.

Haselnuß, **ˉsse**, *n.f.* hazelnut.

Hasenbraten, **-**, *n.m.* roast hare.

Haspe, **-n**, *n.f.* hasp, hinge.

Haß, *n.m.* hatred.

hassen, *vb.* hate.

häßlich, *adj.* ugly.

Häßlichkeit, *n.f.* ugliness.

Hast, *n.f.* haste, hurry.

hasten, *vb.* hasten, hurry.

hastig, *adj.* hasty.

Haube, **-n**, *n.f.* hood.

Hauch, **-e**, *n.m.* breath.

hauchdünn, *adj.* extremely thin.

hauen*, *vb.* hew, chop, strike, spank; (**sich h.**) fight.

Haufen, **-**, *n.m.* pile, heap; crowd; large amount.

häufen, *vb.* heap.

häufig, *adj.* frequent.

Häufigkeit, **-en**, *n.f.* frequency.

Häufung, **-en**, *n.f.* accumulation.

Haupt, **ˉer**, *n.nt.* head.

Hauptamt, **ˉer**, *n.nt.* main office.

Hauptbahnhof, **ˉe**, *n.m.* main railroad station.

Häuptling, **-e**, *n.m.* chieftain.

Hauptmann, **-leute**, *n.m.* captain.

Hauptquartier, **-e**, *n.nt.* headquarters.

Hauptsache, **-n**, *n.f.* main, essential thing; principal matter.

hauptsächlich, *adj.* main, principal.

Hauptstadt, **ˉe**, *n.f.* capital.

Hauptwort, **ˉer**, *n.nt.* noun, substantive.

Haus, **ˉer**, *n.nt.* house.

Hausangestellt-, *n.m.&f.* servant.

Hausarbeit, **-en**, *n.f.* housework.

Hausaufgabe, **-n**, *n.f.* homework.

hausbacken, *adj.* homemade; plain.

hausen, *vb.* dwell, reside.

Häuserblock, **-s**, *n.m.* block.

Hausfrau, **-en**, *n.f.* housewife.

Haushalt, **-e**, *n.m.* household.

haus-halten*, *vb.* economize.

Haushälterin, **-nen**, *n.f.* housekeeper.

Haushaltung, *n.f.* housekeeping.

hausie'ren, *vb.* peddle.

hausie'ren, *vb.* peddle.

Hausie'rer, **-**, *n.m.* peddler.

häuslich, *adj.* domestic.

Hausmeister, **-**, *n.m.* janitor.

Hausrat, *n.m.* household goods.

Hausschuh, **-e**, *n.m.* slipper.

Haut, **ˉe**, *n.f.* skin, hide.

hautstraffend, *adj.* astringent.

Hebamme, **-n**, *n.f.* midwife.

Hebel, **-**, *n.m.* lever.

heben*, *vb.* raise, lift.

Hebrä'er, **-**, *n.m.* Hebrew.

hebrä'isch, *adj.* Hebrew.

hecheln, *vb.* heckle.

Hecht, **-e**, *n.m.* pike (fish).

Heck, **-e**, *n.nt.* stern, rear, tail.

Hecke, **-n**, *n.f.* hedge.

Heer, **-e**, *n.nt.* army.

Heft, **-e**, *n.nt.* notebook; handle, hilt.

heften, *vb.* fasten, pin, stitch, tack.

Hefter, **-**, *n.m.* folder.

heftig, *adj.* vehement.

Heftigkeit, *n.f.* vehemence.

hegen, *vb.* nurture.

Heide, **-n**, **-n**, *n.m.* heathen.

Heide, **-n**, *n.f.* heath.

Heidelbeere, **-n**, *n.f.* huckleberry.

heidnisch, *adj.* heathen.

heikel, *adj.* ticklish, tricky, delicate.

Heil, *n.nt.* welfare, safety, salvation.

heil, *adj.* whole; well, healed, unhurt.

Heiland, *n.m.* Savior.

Heilbad, **ˉer**, *n.nt.* spa.

heilbar, *adj.* curable.

Heilbutt, **-e**, *n.m.* halibut.

heilen, *vb.* heal, cure.

heilig, *adj.* holy, sacred.

Heilige, **-**, *n.m.&f.* saint.

heiligen, *vb.* hallow, sanctify.

Heiligenschein, **-e**, *n.m.* halo.

Heiligkeit, *n.f.* holiness, sanctity.

Heiligtum, **ˉer**, *n.nt.* sanctuary.

Heiligung, **-en**, *n.f.* sanctification, consecration.

Heilmittel, **-**, *n.nt.* remedy, cure.

Heilung, **-en**, *n.f.* healing, cure.

Heim, **-e**, *n.nt.* home.

heim, *adv.* home.

Heimat, *n.f.* home (town, country).

Heimatland, **ˉer**, *n.nt.* homeland.

heimatlich, *adj.* native.

heimatlos, *adj.* homeless.

Heimchen, **-**, *n.nt.* cricket.

heimisch, *adj.* domestic, homelike.

heimlich, *adj.* secret.

heim-suchen, *vb.* scourge.

Heimsuchung, **-en**, *n.f.* scourge.

heimtückisch, *adj.* malicious, treacherous.

heimwärts, *adv.* homeward.

Heimweh, *n.nt.* homesickness.

Heirat, **-en**, *n.f.* marriage.

heiraten, *vb.* marry.

Heiratsantrag, **ˉe**, *n.m.* proposal.

heiser, *adj.* hoarse.

heiß, *adj.* hot.

heissen*, *vb.* be called, be named; mean; call, order.

heiter, *adj.* cheerful; clear.

heizen, *vb.* heat, have the heat on.

Heizkörper, **-**, *n.m.* radiator.

Heizvorrichtung, **-en**, *n.f.* heater.

Hektar, **-e**, *n.m.* hectare.

hektisch, *adj.* hectic.

Hektogramm', -e, n.nt. hectogram.

Held, -en, -en, n.m. hero.

heldenhaft, adj. heroic.

Heldenmut, n.m. heroism.

Heldin, -nen, n.f. heroine.

helfen*, vb. help, aid, assist.

Helfer, -, n.m. helper.

Helfershelfer, -, n.m. confederate, accomplice.

hell, adj. bright, light.

Helligkeit, n.f. brightness.

Helm, -e, n.m. helmet.

Hemd, -en, n.nt. shirt.

hemmen, vb. stop, hinder.

Hemmnis, -se, n.nt. hindrance, obstacle.

Hemmschuh, -e, n.m. brake, drag, skid.

Hemmung, -en, n.f. restraint, inhibition.

Henkel, -, n.m. handle.

Henna, n.f. henna.

Henne, -n, n.f. hen.

her, adv. towards here; ago.

herab', adv. downwards.

herab'hängen, vb. droop.

herab'lassen*, vb. let down; (sich h.) condescend.

herab'lassend, adj. condescending.

Herab'lassung, -en, n.f. condescension.

herab'setzen, vb. set down, lower, reduce, disparage.

Herab'setzung, -en, n.f. reduction, disparagement.

heran', adv. up to, toward.

heran'gehen*, vb. walk up to, approach.

heran'nahen, vb. approach, draw near.

heran'wachsen*, vb. grow up.

herauf', adv. upwards.

heraus', adv. out.

heraus'bringen*, vb. bring out, publish.

Heraus'forderer, -, n.m. challenger.

heraus'fordern, vb. challenge.

heraus'fordernd, adj. defiant.

Heraus'forderung, -en, n.f. challenge, defiance.

heraus'geben*, vb. edit, publish.

Heraus'geber, -, n.m. editor, publisher.

heraus'kommen*, vb. come out, be published.

heraus'lassen*, vb. let out.

heraus'putzen, vb. dress up.

heraus'stellen, vb. put out; (sich h.) turn out to be.

heraus'ziehen*, vb. extract.

herb, adj. tart, bitter.

herbei', adv. toward here.

herbei'schaffen, vb. procure.

Herberge, -n, n.f. hostel.

herbergen, vb. shelter, lodge.

Herbheit, -en, n.f. tartness.

Herbst, -e, n.m. fall, autumn.

herbstlich, adj. autumnal.

Herd, -e, n.m. kitchen stove; hearth.

Herde, -n, n.f. herd.

herein', adv. in; (h.!) come in!

Hergang, ⁼e, n.m. course of events.

hergebracht, adj. customary.

hergelaufen, adj. of uncertain origin.

Hering, -e, n.m. herring.

Herkommen, -, n.nt. tradition; origin.

herkömmlich, adj. traditional.

Herkunft, ⁼e, n.f. origin, extraction.

her'leiten, vb. derive.

herme'tisch, adj. hermetic.

hernach', adv. afterwards.

hernie'der, adv. downwards, from above.

Herr, -n, -en, n.m. Mr., gentleman, lord, master.

Herrenbekleidung, n.f. menswear.

Herrenfriseur, -e, n.m. men's barber.

Herrenvolk, ⁼er, nt. master race.

her'richten, vb. set up, arrange.

Herrin, -nen, n.f. mistress.

herrisch, adj. imperious.

herrlich, adj. wonderful, splendid.

Herrlichkeit, n.f. glory, magnificence.

Herrschaft, n.f. rule; reign; estate.

Herrschaften, n.pl. master and mistress of the house; people of high rank; (meine H.) ladies and gentlemen.

herrschen, vb. rule, reign.

herrschend, adj. ruling, prevailing.

Herrscher, -, n.m. ruler.

herrschsüchtig, adj. imperious, tyrannical.

her'sagen, vb. recite.

her'stellen, vb. make, manufacture.

Herstellung, -n, n.f. manufacture.

Hertz, n.nt. hertz.

herü'ber, adv. over (towards here).

herum', adv. around, about.

herum'kriegen, vb. talk over, win over.

herum'lungern, vb. loaf around.

herum'nörgeln, vb. nag.

herum'pfuschen, vb. tamper.

herum'schnüffeln, vb. pry, snoop.

herum'stehen*, vb. stand around, loiter.

herun'ter, adv. down.

herun'tergekommen, adj. rundown, down at the heels.

herun'ter-lassen*, vb. lower.

herun'ter-machen, vb. dress down, tear apart, pan.

hervor', adv. forth, forward.

hervor'brechen*, vb. erupt.

hervor'bringen*, vb. bring forth, produce.

hervor'heben*, vb. emphasize.

hervor'quellen*, vb. gush; ooze.

hervor'ragend, adj. prominent, outstanding, superb.

hervor'rufen*, vb. evoke; provoke.

hervor'schießen*, vb. spurt.

hervor'stehen*, vb. protrude.

Herz(en), -, n.nt. heart.

her'zeigen, vb. show.

herzen, vb. hug, cuddle.

herzhaft, adj. hearty.

herzig, adj. lovable, darling.

Herzinfarkt, -e, n.m. heart attack.

herzlich, adj. cordial, affectionate.

Herzlichkeit, n.f. cordiality.

herzlos, adj. heartless.

Herzog, ⁼e, n.m. duke.

Herzogin, -nen, n.f. duchess.

Herzogtum, ⁼er, n.nt. dukedom, duchy.

heterosexuell', adj. heterosexual.

Hetze, -n, n.f. rush; agitation, inflammatory talk; hassle.

hetzen, vb. rush; hound, agitate, rabble-rouse.

Hetzerei', -en, n.f. rush; demagoguery.

hetzerisch, adj. inflammatory, demagogic.

Hetzredner, -, n.m. rabble rouser, demagogue.

Heu, n.nt. hay.

Heuchelei', -en, n.f. hypocrisy.

heucheln, vb. fake, feign; play the hypocrite.

Heuchler, -, n.m. hypocrite.

heuchlerisch, adj. hypocritical.

heuer, adv. this year.

Heugabel, -n, n.f. pitchfork.

Heuhaufen, -, n.m. haystack.

heulen, vb. howl; cry.

heurig, adj. of this year.

Heuschnupfen, -, n.m. hay fever.

heute, adv. today; (h. abend) tonight.

heutig, adj. today's.

Heuwiese, -n, n.f. hayfield.

Hexe, -n, n.f. witch.

hexen, vb. perform witchcraft; be a magician.

Hexenschuß, n.m. lumbago.

Hieb, -e, n.m. blow, stroke.

hienie'den, adv. here below.

hier, adv. here.

hierar'chisch, adj. hierarchical.

hierbei, adv. hereby.

hierher, adv. hither.

hiermit, adv. hereby, herewith.

Hifi, n.nt. high fidelity.

Hilfe, -n, n.f. help, aid.

hilfeflehend, adj. imploring.

Hilfeleistung, -en, n.f. assistance, aid.

hilflos, adj. helpless, defenseless.

Hilflosigkeit, n.f. helplessness.

hilfreich, adj. helpful.

hilfsbedürftig, adj. needy.

hilfsbereit, adj. cooperative.

Hilfsquelle, -n, n.f. resource.

Himbeere, -n, n.f. raspberry.

Himmel, -, n.m. heaven, sky.

Himmelfahrt, -en, n.f. ascension to heaven; (H. Christi) Ascension (Day) (40 days after Easter); (Mari'ä H.) Assumption (of the Blessed Virgin) (August 15).

himmelhochjauchzend, adj. jubilant.

himmelschreiend, adj. scandalous.

Himmelsrichtung, -en, n.f. point of the compass, direction.

himmlisch, adj. heavenly.

hin, adv. to there; gone; (h. und her) back and forth; (h. und wieder) now and then.

hinab', prep. down.

hinaus', adv. out.

hinaus'zögern, vb. procrastinate.

Hinblick, n.m. aspect. (In H. auf . . .) with regard to . . .

hinderlich, adj. hindering, inconvenient.

hindern, vb. hinder, deter.

Hindernis, -se, n.nt. hindrance, obstacle.

hin-deuten, vb. point to.

hinein', adv. in.

Hingabe, n.f. fervency.

hin-geben*, vb. give away, up; (sich h.) devote oneself; surrender.

Hingebung, n.f. devotion.

hingestreckt, adj. prostrate.

hin-halten*, vb. (fig.) delay.

hinken, vb. limp.

hin-legen, vb. lay down; (sich h.) lie down.

hin-purzeln, vb. tumble.

hin-reißen*, vb. (sich h. lassen) let oneself be carried away.

hinreißend, adj. captivating, ravishing.

hin-richten, vb. execute.

Hinrichtung, -en, n.f. execution.

Hinsicht, -en, n.f. respect, regard.

hinsichtlich, prep. in regard to, regarding, concerning.

hinten, adv. behind.

hintenherum', adv. from behind; (fig.) roundabout, through the back door.

hinter, prep. behind, beyond.

hinter-, adj. hind, back.

Hintergedanke(n), -, n.m. ulterior motive.

hinterge'hen*, vb. doublecross.

Hintergrund, -e, n.m. background.

Hinterhalt, -e, n.m. ambush.

hinterher', adv. afterward(s).

Hinterland, n.nt. hinterland.

hinterle'gen, vb. deposit.

Hinterlist, n.f. insidiousness, underhanded act.

hinterlistig, adj. insidious, designing, underhanded.

Hintertreffen, n.nt. (Ins H. geraten) fall behind.

Hintertür, -en, n.f. back door; (fig.) loophole.

hinterzie'hen*, vb. (fig.) defraud.

hinü'ber, adv. over, across.

hinun'ter, adv. down.

Hinweis, -e, n.m. reference; indication.

hin-weisen*, vb. point, refer, allude.

hinzu'-fügen, vb. add.

Hirn, -e, n.nt. brain.

Hirsch, -e, n.m. stag.

Hirschleder, -, n.nt. deerskin.

Hirt, -en, -en (Biblical Hirte, -n, -n), n.m. shepherd.

hissen, vb. hoist.

Histo'riker, -, n.m. historian.

histo'risch, adj. historic(al).

Hitze, n.m. heat.

hitzig, adj. heated, fiery, heady.

hitzköpfig, adj. hot-headed.

Hitzschlag, -e, n.m. heatstroke.

Hobel, -, n.m. plane.

hobeln, vb. plane.

hoch (boh-, böher, böchst), 1. adj. high, tall. 2. adv. up.

Hochebene, -n, n.f. plateau.

hocherfreut, adj. elated.

hochgradig, adj. intense, extreme.

Hochmut, n.m. haughtiness, pride.

hochmütig, adj. haughty, arrogant.

hoch-schätzen, vb. treasure.

Hochschule, -n, n.f. university.

Hochsommer, -, n.m. midsummer.

höchst, adv. highly, extremely.

Hochstapler, -, n.m. swindler, impersonator.

höchstenfalls, adv. at best, at the outside.

höchstens, adv. at best, at the outside.

Höchstgrenze, -n, n.f. top limit.

hochtrabend, adj. pompous, grandiloquent.

Hochverrat, n.m. high treason.

Hochzeit, -en, n.f. wedding.

Hochzeitsreise, -n, n.f. honeymoon.

hoch-ziehen*, vb. hoist.

hocken, vb. squat.

Hocker, -, n.m. stool.

Höcker, -, n.m. bump, hump.

Hockey, n.nt. hockey.

Hof, -e, n.m. court, courtyard; (den H. machen) court.

hoffen, vb. hope.

hoffentlich, adv. I hope.

Hoffnung, -en, n.f. hope.

hoffnungslos, adj. hopeless.

hoffnungsvoll, adj. hopeful.

höfisch, adj. courtly.

höflich, adj. polite, courteous, respectful, civil.

Höflichkeit, -en, n.f. courtesy.

Höhe, -n, n.f. height, altitude, elevation.

Hoheit, -en, n.f. Highness.

Höhepunkt, -e, n.m. high

point, highlight, climax, culmination.

höher, adj. higher.

hohl, adj. hollow.

Höhle, -n, n.f. cave, den.

Hohlraum, -e, n.m. hollow space, vacuum.

Hohn, n.m. mockery, derision.

höhnisch, adj. derisive, mocking.

höhnlächeln, vb. sneer, deride.

hold, adj. gracious, lovely.

holdselig, adj. gracious.

holen, vb. (go and) get, fetch.

Holland, n.m. Holland.

Holländer, -, n.m. Dutchman.

holländisch, adj. Dutch.

Hölle, n.f. inferno, hell.

höllisch, adj. infernal, hellish.

Hologramm', -e, n.nt. hologram.

Holographie', n.f. holography.

holprig, adj. bumpy.

Holz, -er, n.nt. wood, lumber, timber.

hölzern, adj. wooden.

Holzklotz, -e, n.m. block (of wood); log.

Holzkohle, -n, n.f. charcoal.

Holzschnitt, -e, n.m. woodcut.

Honig, n.m. honey.

Honorar', -e, n.nt. honorarium.

honorie'ren, vb. honor; remunerate.

Hopfen, -, n.m. hop(s).

hopsen, vb. hop, skip.

hops-gehen*, vb. go down the drain, go west.

hörbar, adj. audible.

horchen, vb. listen to; eavesdrop.

Horde, -n, n.f. horde.

hören, vb. hear.

Hörensagen, n.nt. hearsay.

Hörer, -, n.m. (telephone) receiver; (student) auditor.

hörig, adj. submissive; subservient.

Horizont', -e, n.m. horizon.

horizontal', adj. horizontal.

Hormon', -e, n.nt. hormone.

Horn, -er, n.nt. horn.

hörnern, adj. horny.

Hornhaut, -e, n.f. callous skin; cornea.

hornig, adj. horny.

Horoskop', -e, n.nt. horoscope.

Hort, -e, n.m. hoard; refuge, retreat.

Hörweite, n.f. earshot.

Hose, -n, n.f. trousers, pants.

Hosenband, -er, n.nt. garter.

Hostie, n.f. host.

Hotel', -s, n.nt. hotel.

Hotel'boy, -s, n.m. bellboy.

Hovercraft, n.nt. hovercraft.

hübsch, adj. pretty, handsome.

Hubschrauber, -, n.m. helicopter.

Huf, -e, n.nt. hoof.

Hüfte, -n, n.f. hip.

Hügel, -, n.m. hill.

Huhn, -er, n.nt. chicken, fowl.

Hühnerauge, -n, n.nt. corn (on the foot).

huldigen, vb. do homage to.

Hülle, -n, n.f. covering, casing; (in H. und Fülle) abundantly, in profusion.

hüllen, vb. clothe, wrap, envelop.

Hülse, -n, n.f. hull, husk; case.

human', adj. humane.

Humanis'mus, n.m. humanism.

Humanist', -en, -en, n.m. humanist.

humanitär'feier, adj. humanitarian.

Humanität', n.f. humanity.

Hummel, -n, n.f. bumblebee.

Hummer, -, n.m. lobster.

Humor', n.m. humor, wit.

Humorist', -en, -en, n.m. humorist.

humor'voll, adj. humorous.

humpeln, vb. hobble.

Hund, -e, n.m. dog, hound.

hundert, num. a hundred.

Hundert, -e, n.nt. hundred.

Hundertjahr'feier, -n, n.f. centenary, centennial.

hundertjährig, adj. centennial.

hundertst -, adj. hundredth.

Hundertstel, -, n.nt. hundredth part; (ein h.) one one-hundredth.

Hundezwinger, -, n.m. kennel.

Hündin, -nen, n.f. bitch.

hünenhaft, adj. gigantic.

Hunger, n.m. hunger.

hungern, vb. starve.

Hungersnot, ̈-e, n.f. famine.

Hungertod, n.m. starvation.

hungrig, adj. hungry.

Hupe, -n, n.f. auto horn.

hupen, vb. blow the horn.

hüpfen, vb. hop.

Hürde, -n, n.f. hurdle.

Hure, -n, n.f. whore.

husten, vb. cough.

Husten, n.m. cough.

Hut, ̈-e, n.m. hat.

Hut, n.f. care, protection; (auf der H. sein*) be on the alert.

hüten, vb. tend; (sich h.) beware, be careful not to do.

Hütte, -n, n.f. hut; shed, hovel; (tech.) foundry.

Hyazin'the, -n, n.f. hyacinth.

Hydrant', -en, -en, n.m. hydrant.

Hygie'ne, n.f. hygiene.

hygie'nisch, adj. hygienic, sanitary.

Hymne, -n, n.f. hymn, anthem.

Hypno'se, -n, n.f. hypnosis.

hypno'tisch, adj. hypnotic.

hypnotisie'ren, vb. hypnotize.

Hypothek', -en, n.f. mortgage.

Hypothe'se, -n, n.f. hypothesis.

hypothe'tisch, adj. hypothetical.

Hysterie', n.f. hysteria, hysterics.

hyste'risch, adj. hysterical.

I

ich, pron. I.

Ich, n.nt. ego.

ideal', adj. ideal.

Ideal', -e, n.nt. ideal.

idealisie'ren, vb. idealize.

Idealis'mus, n.m. idealism.

Idee', -e'en, n.f. idea, notion; (fixe I.) obsession.

identifizier'bar, adj. identifiable.

identifizie'ren, vb. identify.

iden'tisch, adj. identical.

Identität', -en, n.f. identity.

Idiot', -en, -en, n.m. idiot.

idio'tisch, adj. idiotic.

Idyll', -e, n.nt. idyl.

idyl'lisch, adj. idyllic.

ignorie'ren, vb. ignore.

illuminie'ren, vb. illuminate.

illuso'risch, adj. illusive, illusory.

Illustration', -en, n.f. illustration.

illustrie'ren, vb. illustrate.

imaginär', adj. imaginary.

Imam, -e, n.m. imam.

Imbiß, -sse, n.m. snack.

imita'tor, -o'ren, n.m. impersonator.

imitie'ren, vb. imitate.

immatrikulie'ren, vb. (sich i.) register in a university.

immer, adv. always.

immergrün, adj. evergreen.

immerhin', adv. after all, anyway.

Immobi'lien, n.pl. real estate.

immun', adj. immune.

Immunität', -en, n.f. immunity.

Imperfekt, -e, n.nt. imperfect tense.

Imperialis'mus, n.m. imperialism.

imperialis'tisch, adj. imperialist.

impfen, vb. vaccinate.

Impfstoff, -e, n.m. vaccine.

Impfung, -en, n.f. vaccination.

impli'cite, adv. by implication.

implizie'ren, vb. imply, implicate.

Import', -e, n.m. import.

importie'ren, vb. import.

imposant', adj. imposing.

impotent', adj. impotent.

Impotenz', n.f. impotence.

imprägnie'ren, vb. waterproof.

Impresa'rio, -s, n.m. impresario.

improvisie'ren, vb. improvise.

Impuls', -e, n.m. impulse.

impulsiv', adj. impulsive.

Impulsivität', n.f. spontaneity.

instan'de, adj. able, capable.

in, prep. in, into.

Inbegriff, -e, n.m. essence, embodiment.

inbegriffen, adj. included; implicit.

Inbrunst, n.f. ardor, fervor.

inbrünstig, adj. zealous, ardent.

Inder, -, n.m. Indian.

Index, -e or -dizes, n.m. index.

India'ner, -, n.m. (American) Indian.

india'nisch, adj. (American) Indian.

Indien, n.nt. India.

indikativ, -e, n.m. indicative.

indisch, adj. Indian.

indiskret, adj. indiscreet.

Individualität', -en, n.f. individuality.

individuell', adj. individual.

Individ'duum, -duen, n.nt. individual.

Indone'sien, n.nt. Indonesia.

Induktion', -en, n.f. induction.

induktiv', adj. inductive.

Industrie', -i'en, n.f. industry.

industriell', adj. industrial.

Industriell'e, -n, -n, n.m. industrialist.

induzie'ren, vb. induce.

infam', adj. infamous; beastly.

Infanterie', -n, n.f. infantry.

Infanterist', -en, -en, n.m. infantryman.

infiltrie'ren, vb. infiltrate.

Infinitiv, -e, n.m. infinitive.

infizie'ren, vb. infect.

Inflation', -en, n.f. inflation.

infolgedes'sen, adv. consequently.

informie'ren, vb. inform.

Ingenieur', -e, n.m. engineer.

Ingwer, n.m. ginger.

Inhaber, -, n.m. proprietor; (of an apartment) occupant.

Inhalt, n.m. content, volume, capacity.

Inhaltsangabe, -n, n.f. table of contents.

inhaltschwer, adj. momentous, weighty.

Inhaltsverzeichnis, -se, n.nt. table of contents, index.

Initiati've, -n, n.f. initiative.

inkog'nito, adv. incognito.

Inland, -n.nt. homeland; (im In- und Ausland) at home and abroad.

inländisch, adj. domestic.

inmit'ten, prep. amid, in the midst of.

innen, adv. inside.

Innen-, cpds. interior, inner; domestic.

Innenpolitik, n.f. domestic policy.

Innenseite, -n, n.f. inside.

inner-, adj. inner, interior, internal.

Inner-, n.nt. interior, inside; soul.

innerhalb, prep. within.

innerlich, adj. inward, intrinsic.

innerst-, adj. innermost.

innig, adj. intimate; fervent.

Innigkeit, n.f. fervor.

Innung, -en, n.f. guild.

Input, -s, n.m. input.

Insasse, -n, -n, *n.m.* occupant; inmate.

insbeson'dere, *adv.* especially.

Inschrift, -en, *n.f.* inscription.

Insekt', -en, *n.nt.* insect.

Insek'tenpulver, -, *n.nt.* insecticide.

Insel, -n, *n.f.* island.

Inserat', -e, *n.nt.* advertisement.

Inserent', -en, -en, *n.m.* advertiser.

insgeheim', *adv.* secretly.

insgesamt', *adv.* altogether.

Insig'nien, *n.pl.* insignia.

inso'fern, inso'weit, *adv.* to that extent, to this extent.

insofern', insoweit', *conj.* insofar as, to the extent that.

Inspek'tor, -o'ren, *n.m.* inspector.

inspizie'ren, *vb.* inspect.

Installation', -en, *n.f.* installation.

instand'halten', *vb.* keep up, keep in good repair.

Instand'haltung, *n.f.* maintenance.

instän'dig, *adj.* earnest.

instand'setzen', *vb.* repair, recondition; enable.

Instanz', -en, *n.f.* instance.

Instan'zenweg, -e, *n.m.* stages of appeal, channels.

Instinkt', -e, *n.m.* instinct.

instinktiv', *adj.* instinctive.

Institut', -e, *n.nt.* institute, institution.

Instrument', -e, *n.nt.* instrument.

Insulin', *n.nt.* insulin.

inszenie'ren, *vb.* stage.

Inszenie'rung, -en, *n.f.* scenario.

intakt', *adj.* intact.

integrie'ren, *vb.* integrate.

Intellekt', *n.m.* intellect.

intellektuell', *adj.* intellectual.

Intellektuell'-, *n.m. & f.* intellectual, highbrow, egghead.

intelligent', *adj.* intelligent.

Intelligenz', *n.f.* intelligence.

intensiv', *adj.* intense, intensive.

interessant', *adj.* interesting.

Interes'se, -n, *n.nt.* interest, concern.

interessie'ren, *vb.* interest.

Interjektion', -en, *n.f.* interjection.

international', *adj.* international.

internie'ren, *vb.* intern.

Internist', -en, -en, *n.m.* specialist for internal medicine.

interpretie'ren, *vb.* interpret.

interpunktie'ren, *vb.* punctuate.

Interpunktion', *n.f.* punctuation.

Interview', -s, *n.nt.* interview.

interview'en, *vb.* interview.

intim', *adj.* intimate.

Intoleranz', -n, *n.f.* intolerance.

intransitiv', *adj.* intransitive.

intravenös', *adj.* intravenous.

Intri'ge, -n, *n.f.* intrigue.

intrigie'ren, *vb.* plot, scheme.

Intuition', -en, *n.f.* intuition.

intuitiv', *adj.* intuitive.

Invali'de, -n, -n, *n.m.* invalid.

Invasion', -en, *n.f.* invasion.

Inventar', -e, *n.nt.* inventory.

Inventur', -en, *n.f.* inventory.

investie'ren, *vb.* invest.

inwendig, *adj.* inward, inner.

inzwi'schen, *adv.* in the meantime.

Irak', *n.nt.* Iraq.

Iran', *n.nt.* Iran.

irdisch, *adj.* earthly.

Ire, -n, -n, *n.m.* Irishman.

irgendein, -, -e, *adj.* any (at all), any old.

irgendeiner, -, -e, *pron.* anyone, anybody.

irgendetwas, *pron.* something or other, anything at all.

irgendjemand, *pron.* somebody or other.

irgendwann', *adv.* sometime.

irgendwelcher, -es, -e, *adj.* any.

irgendwie', *adv.* somehow.

irgendwo', *adv.* somewhere, anywhere.

irgendwohin', *adv.* (to) somewhere, anywhere.

irisch, *adj.* Irish.

Irland, *n.nt.* Ireland.

Irländer, -, *n.m.* Irishman.

**Ironie', n.f.* irony.

iro'nisch, *adj.* ironical.

irre, *adj.* astray, wrong; wandering, lost; insane.

irreführen, *vb.* mislead.

irreführend, *adj.* misleading.

irren, *vb.* err, go astray; **(sich i.)** err, be mistaken.

irrig, *adj.* mistaken.

irritie'ren, *vb.* irritate, annoy.

Irrsinn, *n.m.* nonsense, lunacy.

irrsinnig, *adj.* lunatic.

Irrtum, "er, *n.m.* error.

irrtümlich, *adj.* erroneous.

Isolationist', -en, -en, *n.m.* isolationist.

Isola'tor, -o'ren, *n.m.* insulator.

isolie'ren, *vb.* isolate; insulate.

Isolie'rung, -en, *n.f.* isolation; insulation.

Israel, *n.nt.* Israel.

Israe'li, -s, *n.m.* Israeli.

Israe'lisch, *adj.* Israeli.

Israelit', -en, -en, *n.m.* Israelite.

Ita'lien, *n.nt.* Italy.

Italie'ner, -, *n.m.* Italian.

italie'nisch, *adj.* Italian.

J

ja, 1. *interj.* yes. **2.** *adv.* as is well known, to be sure.

Jacht, -en, *n.f.* yacht.

Jacke, -n, *n.f.* jacket.

Jade, *n.m.* jade.

Jagd, -en, *n.f.* hunt; chase, pursuit.

jagen, *vb.* hunt; chase.

Jäger, -, *n.m.* hunter.

jäh, *adj.* sudden.

Jahr, -e, *n.nt.* year.

jahraus', jahrein', *adv.* year in, year out.

Jahrbuch, "er, *n.nt.* yearbook, almanac, annual; *(pl.)* annals.

Jahrestag, -e, *n.m.* anniversary.

Jahreszeit, -en, *n.f.* season.

Jahrgang, "e, *n.m.* (school) class; (wine) vintage.

Jahrhun'dert, -e, *n.nt.* century.

jährlich, *adj.* yearly, annual.

Jahrmarkt, "e, *n.m.* fair.

Jahrzehnt', -e, *n.nt.* decade.

Jähzorn, *n.m.* quick temper.

jähzornig, *adj.* quick-tempered.

Jammer, *n.m.* misery.

jämmerlich, *adj.* miserable; dismal.

Januar, -e, *n.m.* January.

Japan, *n.nt.* Japan.

Japa'ner, -, *n.m.* Japanese.

japa'nisch, *adj.* Japanese.

Jargon', -s, *n.m.* jargon, slang.

jäten, *vb.* weed.

jauchzen, *vb.* jubilate, cheer.

jawohl', *interj.* yes, sir.

Jazz, *n.m.* jazz.

je, *adv.* ever; apiece, each; **(j. nach)** in each case according to; **(j. nachdem)** according to whether, as the case may be; **(je mehr, je [desto, umso] besser)** the more the better.

Jeans, *n.pl.* jeans.

Jeansstoff, -e, *n.m.* denim.

jeder, -es, -e, *pron. & adj.* each, every.

jedoch', *conj.* yet; nevertheless.

jemals, *adv.* ever.

jemand, *pron.* someone, somebody; anyone, anybody.

jener, -es, -e, *pron & adj.* that, yonder; the former.

jenseits, *adv. & prep.* beyond, on the other side.

Jenseits, *n.nt.* beyond, life after death.

Jeru'salem, *n.nt.* Jerusalem.

Jesuit', -en, -en, *n.m.* Jesuit.

jetzig, *adj.* present.

jetzt, *adv.* now.

jeweilig, *adj.* in question, under consideration.

Joch, -e, *n.nt.* yoke.

Jockei, -s, *n.m.* jockey.

Jod, *n.nt.* iodine.

jodeln, *vb.* yodel.

Joghurt, *n.m. or nt.* yogurt.

johlen, *vb.* howl.

Joker, -, *n.m.* joker.

jonglie'ren, *vb.* juggle.

Jota, -s, *n.nt.* iota.

Journalist', -en, -en, *n.m.* journalist.

Jubel, *n.m.* jubilation, rejoicing.

jubeln, *vb.* shout with joy, rejoice.

Jubilä'um, -en, n.nt. jubilee.

jucken, vb. itch.

Jude, -n, -n, n.m. Jew.

Judentum, n.nt. Judaism, Jewry.

Judenverfolgung, -en, n.f. pogrom.

jüdisch, adj. Jewish.

Jugend, n.f. youth.

jugendlich, adj. youthful; adolescent, juvenile.

Jugendverbrecher, -, n.m. juvenile delinquent.

Jugendzeit, -en, n.f. youth, adolescence.

Jugosla'we, -n, -n, n.m. Yugoslav.

Jugosla'wien, n.nt. Yugoslavia.

jugosla'wisch, adj. Yugoslavian.

Juli, n.m. July.

jung (-), adj. young.

Jung-, n.nt. young (of an animal).

Junge, -n, -n, n.m. boy.

jungenhaft, adj. boyish.

Jünger, -, n.m. disciple.

Jungfer, -n, n.f. (alte J.) old maid, spinster.

Jungfrau, -en, n.f. virgin.

Junggeselle, -n, -n, n.m. bachelor.

Jüngling, -e, n.m. young man.

Juni, n.m. June.

Junker, -, n.m. aristocratic landowner (especially in Prussia).

Jurist', -en, -en, n.m. jurist; law student.

juris'tisch, adj. juridical, legal.

Justiz', n.f. justice.

Juwel', -en, n.nt. jewel.

Juwelier', -e, n.m. jeweler.

Jux, n.m. fun.

K

Kabarett', -e, n.nt. cabaret.

Kabel, -, n.nt. cable; cablegram.

Kabeljau, -e, n.m. cod.

kabeln, vb. cable.

Kabi'ne, -n, n.f. cabin, stateroom.

Kabinett', -e, n.nt. cabinet.

Kabriolett', -s, n.nt. convertible.

Kachel, -n, n.f. tile.

Kada'ver, -, n.m. carcass.

Kadett', -en, -en, n.m. cadet.

Käfer, -, n.m. beetle, bug.

Kaffee, n.m. coffee.

Kaffein', n.nt. caffeine.

Käfig, -e, n.m. cage.

kahl, adj. bald; bare.

Kahn, -e, n.m. boat, barge.

Kaiser, -, n.m. emperor.

Kaju'te, -n, n.f. cabin (on a boat).

Kaka'o, -s, n.m. cocoa.

Kalb, -er, n.nt. calf.

Kalbfleisch, n.nt. veal.

Kalbleder, -, n.nt. calfskin.

Kalen'der, -, n.m. calendar.

Kali, n.nt. potash, potassium.

Kali'ber, -, n.nt. caliber.

Kalium, n.nt. potassium.

Kalk, n.m. lime, chalk, calcium.

Kalkstein, n.m. limestone.

Kalorie', -i'en, n.f. calorie.

kalt(-), adj. cold.

kaltblütig, adj. cold-blooded.

Kälte, -n, n.f. cold(ness).

Kalzium, n.nt. calcium.

Kame'e, -n, n.f. cameo.

Kamel', -e, n.nt. camel.

Kamera, -s, n.f. camera.

Kamerad', -en, n.m. comrade.

Kamerad'schaft, -en, n.f. comradeship, camaraderie.

Kamil'le, -n, n.f. camomile.

Kamin', -e, n.m. fireplace, hearth; fireside.

Kamm, -e, n.m. comb; (mountain) crest.

kämmen, vb. comb.

Kammer, -n, n.f. room; chamber.

Kammermusik, n.f. chamber music.

Kampag'ne, -n, n.f. campaign.

Kampf, -e, n.m. fight, fighting, combat.

kämpfen, vb. fight.

Kampfer, n.m. camphor.

Kämpfer, -, n.m. fighter, combatant; champion.

kampfunfähig, adj. disabled.

Kanada, n.nt. Canada.

Kana'dier, -, n.m. Canadian.

kana'disch, adj. Canadian.

Kanal', -e, n.m. canal, channel; duct.

Kanalisation', n.f. canalization; sewer.

kanalisie'ren, vb. canalize; drain by sewer.

Kana'rienvogel, -, n.m. canary.

Kanda're, -n, n.f. curb (of a horse); (an die K. nehmen) take a person in hand.

Kandidat', -en, -en, n.m. candidate, nominee.

Kandidatur', -en, n.f. candidacy, nomination.

kandiert', adj. candied.

Känguruh', -s, n.nt. kangaroo.

Kanin'chen, -, n.nt. rabbit, bunny.

Kanne, -n, n.f. can, jug, pitcher.

Kanniba'le, -n, -n, n.m. cannibal.

Kanon, -s, n.m. canon.

Kanona'de, -n, n.f. cannonade.

Kano'ne, -n, n.f. cannon.

Kano'nenboot, -e, n.nt. gunboat.

Kanonier', -e, n.m. cannoneer.

kano'nisch, adj. canonical.

kanonisie'ren, vb. cannonize.

Kanta'te, -n, n.f. cantata.

Kante, -n, n.f. edge, border.

Kanti'ne, -n, n.f. canteen.

Kanu', -s, n.nt. canoe.

Kanzel, -n, n.f. pulpit.

Kanzlei', -en, n.f. chancellery.

Kanzler, -, n.m. chancellor.

Kap, -s, n.nt. cape.

Kapaun', -e, n.m. capon.

Kapel'le, -n, n.f. chapel; orchestra, band.

Kapell'meister, -, n.m. conductor, bandmaster.

kapern, vb. capture.

kapie'ren, vb. understand.

kapital', adj. capital.

Kapital', -ien, n.nt. capital.

kapitalisie'ren, vb. capitalize.

Kapitalis'mus, n.m. capitalism.

kapitalis'tisch, adj. capitalistic.

Kapitän', -e, n.m. captain.

Kapi'tel, -, n.nt. chapter.

kapitulie'ren, vb. capitulate.

Kappe, -n, n.f. cap, hood.

Kapsel, -n, n.f. capsule.

kaputt', adj. broken, busted; (k. machen) bust, wreck.

Kapu'ze, -n, n.f. hood.

Karabi'ner, -, n.m. carbine.

Karaf'fe, -n, n.f. decanter, carafe.

Karamel', n.nt. caramel.

Kara'te, n.nt. karate.

Karawa'ne, -n, n.f. caravan.

Karbid', n.nt. carbide.

Karbun'kel, -, n.m. carbuncle.

Kardinal', -e, n.m. cardinal.

Karfrei'tag, n.m. Good Friday.

Karies, n.f. caries.

Karikatur', -en, n.f. caricature; cartoon.

karikie'ren, vb. caricature.

karmin'rot(-), adj. crimson.

Karneval, -s, n.m. carnival.

Karo, -, n.nt. (cards) diamond(s).

Karpfen, -, n.m. carp.

Karre, -n, n.f. cart.

Karree', -s, n.nt. square.

Karren, -, n.m. cart.

Karrie're, -n, n.f. career; (K. machen) be successful, get far in one's profession.

Karte, -n, n.f. card; chart, map.

Kartei', -en, n.f. card index, file.

Kartell', -e, n.nt. cartel.

Kartenspiel, -e, n.nt. card game; deck of cards.

Kartof'fel, -n, n.f. potato.

Karton', -s, n.m. carton.

Karussell', -s, n.nt. merry-go-round.

Karwoche, n.f. Holy Week.

Kaschmir, -e, n.m. cashmere.

Käse, -, n.m. cheese.

Kaser'ne, -n, n.f. barracks.

Kasi'no, -s, n.nt. casino.

Kasse, -n, n.f. cash box; cash register; box-office; (bei K. sein*) be flush; (an der K. bezahlen) pay the cashier.

Kassenzettel, -, n.m. sales slip.

Kasset'te, -n, n.f. cassette.

kassie'ren, vb. collect (money due); dismiss.

Kassie'rer, -, n.m. teller, cashier.

Kaste, -n, n.f. caste.

kastei'en, *vb.* chastise, mortify.

Kasten, -, *n.m.* box, case.

Katalog', -e, *n.m.* catalogue.

Katapult', -e, *n.m.* catapult.

Katarrh', -e, *n.m.* catarrh.

Katas'ter, -, *n.nt.* register.

katastrophal', *adj.* disastrous, ruinous.

Katechis'mus, -men, *n.m.* catechism.

Kategorie', -i'en, *n.f.* category.

katego'risch, *adj.* categorical.

Kater, -, *n.m.* tomcat; hangover.

Kathedra'le, -n, *n.f.* cathedral.

Katho'de, -n, *n.f.* cathode.

Katholik', -en, -en, *n.m.* Catholic.

katho'lisch, *adj.* Catholic.

Katholizis'mus, -men, *n.m.* Catholicism.

Kattun', -e, *n.m.* gingham, calico.

Kätzchen, -, *n.nt.* kitten.

Katze, -n, *n.f.* cat.

katzenartig, *adj.* feline.

Katzenjammer, *n.m.* hangover.

kauen, *vb.* chew.

kauern, *vb.* crouch, cower.

Kauf, -e, *n.m.* purchase.

kaufen, *vb.* purchase, buy.

Käufer, -, *n.m.* buyer.

Kaufkontrakt, -e, *n.m.* bill of sale.

Kaufmann, -leute, *n.m.* businessman, merchant.

kaufmännisch, *adj.* commercial.

Kaugummi, -s, *n.nt.* chewing gum.

kaum, *adv.* scarcely, hardly, barely.

Kausalität', -en, *n.f.* causation.

Kaution', -en, *n.f.* surety; security; bail.

Kavalier', -e, *n.m.* cavalier.

Kavallerie, -n, *n.f.* cavalry.

Kaviar, *n.m.* caviar.

keck, *adj.* saucy.

Kegel, -, *n.m.* cone.

kegelförmig, *adj.* conic.

kegeln, *vb.* bowl.

Kehle, -n, *n.f.* throat.

Kehlkopfentzündung, -en, *n.f.* laryngitis.

kehren, *vb.* turn; brush, sweep.

Kehricht, *n.m.* sweepings; garbage.

Kehrseite, -n, *n.f.* reverse side; other side of the picture.

kehrt-machen, *vb.* turn around, about-face.

Kehrtwendung, *n.f.* about face.

keifen, *vb.* nag, scold.

Keil, -e, *n.m.* wedge.

Keilerei', -en, *n.f.* fracas, brawl.

Keim, -e, *n.m.* germ, bud.

keimen, *vb.* germinate.

keimfrei, *adj.* germ free, sterile.

keimtötend, *adj.* germicidal.

kein, -, -e, *adj.* not a, not any, no.

keiner, -es, -e, *pron.* no one, not any, none.

keinerlei, *adj.* not of any sort.

keineswegs, *adv.* by no means.

Keks, -e, *n.m.* biscuit, cookie.

Kelch, -e, *n.m.* cup, goblet, chalice; calyx.

Kelchglas, -er, *n.nt.* goblet.

Kelle, -n, *n.f.* ladle, scoop.

Keller, -, *n.m.* cellar.

Kellner, -, *n.m.* waiter.

Kellnerin, -nen, *n.f.* waitress.

kennen°, *vb.* know, be acquainted with.

kennen-lernen, *vb.* meet, become acquainted with.

Kenner, -, *n.m.* connoisseur.

Kennkarte, -n, *n.f.* identity card.

kenntlich, *adj.* recognizable.

Kenntnis, -se, *n.f.* knowledge, notice.

Kennzeichen, -, *n.nt.* sign, distinguishing mark, feature.

kennzeichnen, *vb.* mark, stamp, distinguish, characterize.

kentern, *vb.* capsize.

Kera'mik, -en, *n.f.* ceramics.

kera'misch, *adj.* ceramic.

Kerbe, -n, *n.f.* notch.

kerben, *vb.* notch.

Kerker, -, *n.m.* jail, prison.

Kerl, -e, *n.m.* fellow, guy.

Kern, -e, *n.m.* kernel, pit, core; nucleus; gist.

Kernenergie, *n.f.* nuclear energy.

Kerngehäuse, -, *n.nt.* core.

Kernhaus, -er, *n.nt.* core.

Kernphysik, *n.f.* nuclear physics.

Kernspaltung, -en, *n.f.* nuclear fission.

Kerosin', *n.nt.* kerosene.

Kerze, -n, *n.f.* candle.

Kessel, -, *n.m.* kettle, boiler.

Kette, -n, *n.f.* chain.

ketten, *vb.* chain, link.

Kettenreaktion, -en, *n.f.* chain reaction.

Ketzer, -, *n.m.* heretic.

Ketzerei', *n.f.* heresy.

keuchen, *vb.* gasp.

Keuchhusten, *n.m.* whooping-cough.

Keule, -n, *n.f.* club, cudgel; (meat) leg, joint.

keusch, *adj.* chaste.

Keuschheit, *n.f.* chastity.

kichern, *vb.* giggle.

Kiefer, -, *n.m.* jaw.

Kiefer, -n, *n.f.* pine.

Kiel, -e, *n.m.* keel.

Kielwasser, *n.nt.* wake.

Kieme, -n, *n.f.* gill.

Kiepe, -n, *n.f.* basket (carried on the back).

Kies, -e, *n.m.* gravel.

Kilo, -, *n.nt.* kilogram.

Kilohertz, *n.nt.* kilohertz.

Kilome'ter, *n.m. or nt.* kilometer.

Kilowatt', -, *n.nt.* kilowatt.

Kind, -er, *n.nt.* child.

Kinderarzt, -e, *n.m.* pediatrician.

Kinderbett, -en, *n.nt.* crib.

Kindergarten, -, *n.m.* kindergarten.

Kinderlähmung, -en, *n.f.* infantile paralysis, polio.

kinderlos, *adj.* childless.

Kinderraub, *n.m.* kidnapping.

Kinderräuber, -, *n.m.* kidnapper.

Kindersportwagen, -, *n.m.* stroller.

Kinderwagen, -, *n.m.* baby carriage.

Kinderzimmer, -, *n.nt.* nursery.

Kindheit, -en, *n.f.* childhood.

kindisch, *adj.* childish.

kindlich, *adj.* childlike.

Kinn, -e, *n.nt.* chin.

Kino, -s, *n.nt.* movie theater.

Kiosk', -e, *n.m.* kiosk, newsstand.

kippen, *vb.* tip, tilt.

Kirche, -n, *n.f.* church.

Kirchenlied, -er, *n.nt.* hymn.

Kirchenschiff, -e, *n.nt.* nave.

Kirchenstuhl, -e, *n.m.* pew.

Kirchhof, -e, *n.m.* churchyard.

kirchlich, *adj.* ecclesiastical.

Kirchspiel, -e, *n.nt.* parish.

Kirchturm, -e, *n.m.* steeple.

Kirsche, -n, *n.f.* cherry.

Kissen, -, *n.nt.* cushion, pillow.

Kissenbezug, -e, *n.m.* pillowcase.

Kiste, -n, *n.f.* crate, chest.

Kitsch, *n.m.* trash.

Kittel, -, *n.m.* smock.

kitzeln, *vb.* tickle.

kitzlig, *adj.* ticklish.

klaffen, *vb.* gape, yawn.

Klage, -n, *n.f.* complaint; suit.

Kläger, -, *n.m.* plaintiff.

kläglich, *adj.* miserable.

Klammer, -n, *n.f.* clamp, clasp; parenthesis.

Klamot'ten, *n.pl.* duds, rags, stuff.

Klampe, -n, *n.f.* cleat.

Klang, -e, *n.m.* sound, ring(-ing).

Klappbett, -en, *n.nt.* folding bed.

Klappe, -n, *n.f.* flap, lid, valve.

klappen, *vb.* flap, fold; come out right.

klappern, *vb.* clatter, chatter, rattle.

Klaps, -e, *n.m.* slap.

klar, *adj.* clear.

klären, *vb.* clear.

Klarheit, -en, *n.f.* clarity.

Klarinet'te, -n, *n.f.* clarinet.

klar-legen, *vb.* clarify.

klar-stellen, *vb.* clarify.

Klasse, -n, *n.f.* class.

Klassenkamerad, -en, -en, *n.m.* classmate.

Klassenzimmer, -, *n.nt.* classroom.

klassifizie'ren, *vb.* classify.

Klassifizie'rung, -en, *n.f.* classification.

klassisch, *adj.* classic(al).

Klatsch, *n.m.* gossip.

klatschen, *vb.* clap; gossip.

Klaue, -n, *n.f.* claw.

klauen, *vb.* snitch.

Klausel, -n, *n.f.* clause, proviso.

Klavier', -e, *n.nt.* piano.

Klebemittel, -, *n.nt.* glue, adhesive.

kleben, *vb.* paste; stick.

Klebgummi, -en, *n.m.* mucilage.

klebrig, *adj.* sticky.

Klebstoff, -e, *n.m.* paste.

kleckern, *vb.* spill, make a spot.

Klecks, -e, *n.m.* spot, stain.

Klee, *n.m.* clover.

Kleid, -er, *n.nt.* dress; *(pl.)* clothes.

kleiden, *vb.* clothe, dress.

Kleiderbügel, -, *n.m.* hanger.

Kleiderhändler, -, *n.m.* clothier.

Kleiderschrank, -̈e, *n.m.* clothes closet, wardrobe.

kleidsam, *adj.* becoming.

Kleidung, -en, *n.f.* clothing.

Kleidungsstück, -e, *n.nt.* garment.

klein, *adj.* little, small.

Kleingeld, -er, *n.nt.* change.

Kleinheit, -en, *n.f.* smallness.

Kleinigkeit, -en, *n.f.* trifle.

kleinlaut, *adj.* meek, subdued.

kleinlich, *adj.* petty.

Kleinod, -ien, *n.nt.* jewel, gem.

Kleister, -, *n.m.* paste.

Klemme, -n, *n.f.* clamp; dilemma, jam, tight spot.

klemmen, *vb.* pinch, jam.

Klempner, -, *n.m.* plumber.

Klepper, -, *n.m.* hack.

klerikal', *adj.* clerical.

Kleriker, -, *n.m.* clergyman.

Klerus, *n.m.* clergy.

klettern, *vb.* climb.

Klient, -en, -en, *n.m.* client.

Klima, -a'te, *n.nt.* climate.

Klimaanlage, -n, *n.f.* air conditioning (system).

klima'tisch, *adj.* climatic.

klimatisie'ren, *vb.* air-condition.

klimmen*, *vb.* climb.

Klinge, -n, *n.f.* blade.

Klingel, -n, *n.f.* (small) bell; buzzer.

klingeln, *vb.* ring.

klingen*, *vb.* ring, sound.

Klinik, -en, *n.f.* clinic, hospital.

klinisch, *adj.* clinical.

Klippe, -n, *n.f.* cliff, crag.

Klistier', -e, *n.nt.* enema.

Klo, -s, *n.nt.* (short for Klosett') bathroom, toilet.

Kloa'ke, -n, *n.f.* sewer, drain.

klobig, *adj.* clumsy.

klopfen, *vb.* knock, beat.

Klops, -e, *n.m.* meatball.

Klosett', -e, *n.nt.* water closet.

Kloß, -̈e, *n.m.* clump; dumpling.

Kloster, -̈, *n.nt.* monastery, nunnery.

Klosterbruder, -̈, *n.m.* friar.

Klostergang, -̈e, *n.m.* cloister(s).

Klotz, -̈e, *n.m.* block.

Klub, -s, *n.m.* club (social).

Kluft, -̈e, *n.f.* gap, cleft, fissure.

klug(-), *adj.* clever.

Klugheit, -en, *n.f.* cleverness.

Klumpen, -, *n.m.* lump.

klumpig, *adj.* lumpy.

knabbern, *vb.* nibble.

Knabe, -n, -n, *n.m.* lad, youth.

knacken, *vb.* click.

Knall, -e, *n.m.* bang, crack, pop.

knallen, *vb.* bang, pop.

knapp, *adj.* scarce, scant, tight, terse.

Knappheit, -en, *n.f.* scarcity, shortage, terseness.

knarren, *vb.* creak, rattle.

Knäuel, -, *n.m. or nt.* clew, ball; throng, crowd.

knauserig, *adj.* niggardly.

Knebel, -, *n.m.* cudgel; gag.

knebeln, *vb.* bind, gag.

Knecht, -e, *n.m.* servant, farm hand.

Knechtschaft, -en, *n.f.* bondage, servitude.

kneifen*, *vb.* pinch.

Kneifzange, -n, *n.f.* pliers.

Kneipe, -n, *n.f.* tavern, pub, joint.

kneten, *vb.* knead.

Knick, -e, *n.m.* bend, crack.

knicken, *vb.* bend, fold, crack.

Knicks, -e, *n.m.* curtsy.

Knie, -i'e, *n.nt.* knee.

kni'en, *vb.* kneel.

Kniff, -e, *n.m.* pinch; trick.

kniffig, *adj.* tricky.

knipsen, *vb.* snap, punch (ticket), take a snapshot, snap one's fingers.

knirschen, *vb.* grate, crunch; gnash (teeth).

knistern, *vb.* crackle.

knittern, *vb.* wrinkle.

Knöchel, -, *n.m.* knuckle.

Knochen, -, *n.m.* bone.

knochenlos, *adj.* boneless.

knochig, *adj.* bony.

Knödel, -, *n.m.* dumpling.

Knopf, -̈e, *n.m.* button.

Knopfloch, -̈er, *n.nt.* buttonhole.

Knorpel, -, *n.m.* cartilage.

Knorren, -, *n.m.* knot, gnarl.

knorrig, *adj.* knotty, gnarled.

Knospe, -n, *n.f.* bud.

knospen, *vb.* bud.

Knoten, -, *n.m.* knot.

knoten, *vb.* knot.

Knotenpunkt, -e, *n.m.* junction.

knüpfen, *vb.* tie, knot.

Knüppel, -, *n.m.* cudgel, club.

knurren, *vb.* growl.

knusp(e)rig, *adj.* crisp, crusty.

Kobalt, *n.m.* cobalt.

Koch, -̈e, *n.m.* cook.

Kochbuch, -̈er, *n.nt.* cookbook.

kochen, *vb.* cook, boil.

Köchin, -nen, *n.f.* cook.

Kode, -s, *n.m.* code.

Kodein', *n.nt.* codein.

ködern, *vb.* decoy.

Kodex, -dizes, *n.m.* code.

kodifizie'ren, *vb.* codify.

Koffein', -e, *n.nt.* caffeine.

koffein'frei, *adj.* decaffeinated.

Koffer, -, *n.m.* suitcase, trunk.

Kofferkuli, -s, *n.m.* baggage cart (airport).

Kognak, -s, *n.m.* brandy, cognac.

Kohl, -e, *n.m.* cabbage.

Kohle, -n, *n.f.* coal.

kohlen, *vb.* char.

Kohlenoxyd', *n.nt.* carbon monoxide.

Kohlenstoff, -e, *n.m.* carbon.

Koje, -n, *n.f.* bunk.

Kokain', *n.nt.* cocaine.

kokett', *adj.* coquettish.

Kokette, -n, *n.f.* coquette.

kokettie'ren, *vb.* flirt.

Kokon', -s, *n.m.* cocoon.

Koks, -e, *n.m.* coke.

Kolben, -, *n.m.* butt; piston.

Kolle'ge, -n, -n, *n.m.* colleague.

kollektiv', *adj.* collective.

Koller, -, *n.m.* rage, frenzy.

kölnisch Wasser, *n.nt.* eau-de-cologne.

kolonial', *adj.* colonial.

Kolonial'waren, *n.pl.* groceries.

Kolonial'warenhändler, -, *n.m.* grocer.

Kolonie', -i'en, *n.f.* colony.

Kolonisation', *n.f.* colonization.

kolonisie'ren, *vb.* colonize.

Kolon'ne, -n, *n.f.* column.

Kolorit', -e, *n.nt.* color(ing).

kolossal', *adj.* colossal.

Koma, *n.nt.* coma.

kombinie'ren, *vb.* combine.

Komet', -en, -en, *n.m.* comet.

Komiker, -, *n.m.* comedian.

Komikerin, -nen, *n.f.* comedienne.

komisch, *adj.* funny.

Komitee', -s, *n.nt.* committee.

Komma, -s, *(or* **-ta),** *n.nt.* comma.

Kommandant', -en, -en, *n.m.* commander, commanding officer.

Kommandantur', -en, *n.f.* commander's office.

kommen*, *vb.* come.

Kommentar', -e, *n.m.* commentary.

Kommenta'tor, -o'ren, *n.m.* commentator.

kommentie'ren, *vb.* comment on.

Kommissar', -e, *n.m.* commissary, commissioner.

Kommission', -en, *n.f.* commission.

Kommo'de, -n, *n.f.* bureau.

kommunal', *adj.* communal, municipal.

Kommunikant', -en, -en, *n.m.* communicant.

Kommunion', -en, *n.f.* communion.

Kommuniqué, -s, *n.nt.* communiqué.

Kommunis'mus, *n.m.* communism.

Kommunist', -en, -en, *n.m.* communist.

kommunis'tisch, *adj.* communistic.

kommunizie'ren, *vb.* commune; communicate.

Komödiant', -en, -en, *n.m.* comedian.

Komö'die, -n, *n.f.* comedy.

Kompagnon, -s, *n.m.* (business) partner.

kompakt', *adj.* compact.

Komparative, -e, -en *n.m.* comparative (degree).

Kompaß, -sse, *n.m.* compass.

kompensie'rend, *adj.* compensatory.

kompetent', *adj.* competent, authoritative.

Kompetenz', -en, *n.f.* competence, authority, jurisdiction.

komplex', *adj.* complex.

Komplex', -e, *n.m.* complex.

Komplikation', -en, *n.f.* complication.

Kompliment', -e, *n.nt.* compliment.

Kompli'ze, -n, -n, *n.m.* accomplice.

komplizie'ren, *vb.* complicate.

kompliziert', *adj.* complicated.

Komplott', -e, *n.nt.* plot.

komponie'ren, *vb.* compose.

Komponist', -en, -en, *n.m.* composer.

Komposition', -en, *n.f.* composition.

Kompott', -e, *n.nt.* compote.

Kompres'se, -n, *n.f.* compress.

Kompression', -en, *n.f.* compression.

Kompres'sor, -o'ren, *n.m.* compressor.

Kompromiß', -sse, *n.m.* compromise.

kompromittie'ren, *vb.* compromise.

Kompu'ter, -, *n.m.* computer.

Kondensation', -en, *n.f.* condensation.

Kondensa'tor, -o'ren, *n.m.* condenser.

kondensie'ren, *vb.* condense.

Kondi'tor, -o'ren, *n.m.* confectioner, pastry baker.

Konditorei', -el'en, *n.f.* café and pastry shop.

Konfekt', -e, *n.nt.* candy.

Konfektion', *n.f.* ready-made clothing.

Konferenz', -en, *n.f.* conference.

Konfirmation', -en, *n.f.* confirmation.

konfisze'ren, *vb.* confiscate.

Konfitü're, -n, *n.f.* jam.

Konflikt', -e, *n.m.* conflict.

konform', *adj.* in conformity.

konfrontie'ren, *vb.* confront.

konfus', *adj.* confused.

Kongreß', -sse, *n.m.* congress.

König, -e, *n.m.* king.

Königin, -nen, *n.f.* queen.

königlich, *adj.* royal.

Königreich, -e, *n.nt.* kingdom.

Königtum, *n.nt.* kingship, royalty.

Konjugation', -en, *n.f.* conjugation.

konjugie'ren, *vb.* conjugate.

Konjunktion', -en, *n.f.* conjunction.

Konjunktiv, -e, *n.m.* subjunctive.

konkav', *adj.* concave.

konkret', *adj.* concrete.

Konkurrent', -en, -en, *n.m.* competitor.

Konkurrenz', -en, *n.f.* competition.

konkurrie'ren, *vb.* compete.

Konkurs', -e, *n.m.* bankruptcy.

können*, *vb.* can, be able.

konsequent', *adj.* consistent.

Konservatis'mus, *n.m.* conservatism.

konservativ', *adj.* conservative.

Konservato'rium, -en, *n.nt.* conservatory.

Konser'venfabrik, -en, *n.f.* cannery.

konservie'ren, *vb.* preserve.

Konservie'rung, -en, *n.f.* conservation.

Konsistenz', *n.f.* consistency.

konsolidie'ren, *vb.* consolidate.

Konsonant', -en, -en, *n.m.* consonant.

konstant', *adj.* constant.

Konstellation', -en, *n.f.* constellation.

konstituie'ren, *vb.* constitute.

Konstitution', -en, *f.* constitution.

konstitutionell', *adj.* constitutional.

konstruie'ren, *vb.* construct.

Konstrukteur', -e, *n.m.* constructor, designer.

Konstruktion', -en, *n.f.* construction.

Konsul, -n, *n.m.* consul.

konsula'risch, *adj.* consular.

Konsulat', -e, *n.nt.* consulate.

Konsum', -s, *n.m.* consumption; (short for Konsum'laden, -, *n.m.*) cooperative store, co-op.

Konsument', -en, -en, *n.m.* consumer.

Konsum'verein, -e, *n.m.* cooperative (society).

Kontakt', -e, *n.m.* contact.

Kontinent, -e, *n.m.* continent.

kontinental', *adj.* continental.

Konto, -s *or* -ten *or* -ti, *n.nt.* account.

Kontobuch, -er, *n.nt.* bankbook, account book.

Kontor', -e, *n.nt.* office.

Kontorist', -en, -en, *n.m.* clerk.

Kontroll'abschnitt, -e, *n.m.* stub.

Kontrol'le, -n, *n.f.* control, check.

kontrollier'bar, *adj.* controllable.

kontrollie'ren, *vb.* control, check.

Kontroll'marke, -n, *n.f.* check.

Kontur', -en, *n.f.* contour, outline.

Konvaleszenz', *n.f.* convalescence.

Konvention', -en, *n.f.* convention.

konventionell', *adj.* conventional.

konvergie'ren, *vb.* converge.

konvertie'ren, *vb.* convert.

konvex', *adj.* convex.

Konvulsion', -en, *n.f.* convulsion.

konvulsiv', *adj.* convulsive.

Konzentration', -en, *n.f.* concentration.

Konzentrations'lager, -, *n.nt.* concentration camp.

konzentrie'ren, *vb.* concentrate.

konzen'trisch, *adj.* concentric.

Konzept', -e, *n.nt.* plan, draft; (aus dem K. bringen*) confuse.

Konzern', -e, *n.m.* (business) trust, pool.

Konzert', -e, *n.nt.* concert.

Konzession', -en, *n.f.* concession.

koordinie'ren, *vb.* coordinate.

Kopf, -e, *n.m.* head.

Kopfhaut, -e, *n.f.* scalp.

Kopfhörer, -, *n.m.* earphone.

Kopfkissen, -, *n.nt.* pillow.

Kopfsalat, -e, *n.m.* lettuce.

Kopfschmerzen, *n.pl.* headache.

Kopfsprung, -e, *n.m.* dive.

Kopftuch, -er, *n.nt.* kerchief.

Kopie', -i'en, *n.f.* copy.

kopie'ren, *vb.* copy, duplicate.

Kopier'maschine, -n, *n.f.* photocopier; copying machine.

koppeln, *vb.* couple.

Koral'le, -n, *n.f.* coral.

Korb, -e, *n.m.* basket.

Korbball, -e, *n.m.* basketball.

Korbwiege, -n, *n.f.* bassinet.

Korduanleder, -, *n.m.* cordovan.

Kore'a, *n.nt.* Korea.

Korin'the, -n, *n.f.* currant.

Kork, -e, *n.m.* cork (material).

Korken, -, *n.m.* cork (stopper).

Korkenzieher, -, *n.m.* corkscrew.

Korn, -, *n.m.* grain whiskey.

Korn, -e, *n.nt.* (type of) grain.

Korn, -er, *n.nt.* (individual) grain.

Körnchen, -, *n.nt.* granule.

Kornett', -e, *n.nt.* cornet.

körnig, *adj.* granular.

Kornkammer, -n, *n.f.* granary.

Kornspeicher, -, *n.m.* granary.

Körper, -, *n.m.* body.

Körperbau, *n.m.* physique.

Körperbehinderung, -en, *n.f.* physical disability.

Körperchen, -, n.nt. corpuscle.

Körperkraft, n.f. physical strength.

körperlich, adj. physical, corporeal.

Körperschaft, -en, n.f. corporation.

Korps, -, n.nt. corps.

korpulent', adj. corpulent.

korrekt', adj. correct.

Korrekt'heit, -en, n.f. correctness.

korrektiv', adj. corrective. dent.

Korrespondent', -en, -en, n.m. correspondent.

Korrespondenz', -en, n.f. correspondence.

korrespondie'ren, vb. correspond.

Korridor, -e, n.m. corridor.

korrigie'ren, vb. correct.

korrumpie'ren, vb. corrupt.

korrupt', adj. corrupt.

Korruption', -en, n.f. corruption.

Korsett', -s, n.nt. corset.

kosen, vb. fondle, caress.

Kosename(n), -, n.m. pet name.

kosme'tisch, adj. cosmetic.

kosmisch, adj. cosmic.

kosmopoli'tisch, adj. cosmopolitan.

Kosmos, -, n.m. cosmos.

Kost, n.f. food, fare, board.

kostbar, adj. costly, precious.

kosten, vb. cost; taste.

Kosten, n.pl. cost, charges, expenses.

Kostenanschlag, ̈e, n.m. estimate.

kostenfrei, adj. free of charge.

kostenlos, adj. free, without cost.

Kostgänger, -, n.m. boarder.

köstlich, adj. delicious.

kostspielig, adj. expensive.

Kostspieligkeit, -en, n.f. costliness.

Kostüm', -e, n.nt. costume; matching coat and skirt.

Kot, n.m. dirt, mud, filth.

Kotelett', -s, n.nt. cutlet, chop.

Köter, -, n.m. cur.

kotzen, vb. vomit.

Krabbe, -n, n.f. shrimp, crab.

Krach, -e, or -s, n.m. bang, crash, racket; row, fight.

krachen, vb. crash.

Kraft, ̈e, n.f. strength, force, power.

kraft, prep. by virtue of.

Kraftbrühe, -, n.f. bouillon.

Kraftfahrer, -, n.m. motorist.

Kraftfahrzeug, -e, n.nt. motor vehicle.

kräftig, adj. strong.

kraftlos, adj. powerless.

kraftstrotzend, adj. vigorous.

kraftvoll, adj. powerful.

Kraftwagen, -, n.m. automobile.

Kragen, -, n.m. collar.

Krähe, -n, n.f. crow.

Kralle, -n, n.f. claw.

Kram, ̈e, n.m. stuff, junk; business, affairs; retail trade, goods.

kramen, vb. rummage.

Krämer, -, n.m. small tradesman.

Krampf, ̈e, n.m. cramp, spasm.

krampfhaft, adj. spasmodic.

Kran, ̈e, n.m. crane, derrick.

Kranich, -e, n.m. crane.

krank(̈), adj. sick.

kranken, vb. suffer from, ail.

kränken, vb. offend.

Krankenauto, -s, n.nt. ambulance.

Krankenhaus, ̈er, n.nt. hospital.

Krankenschwester, -n, n.f. nurse.

Krankenwagen -, n.m. ambulance.

krankhaft, adj. morbid.

Krankheit, -en, n.f. sickness, disease.

kränklich, adj. sickly.

Kränkung, -en, n.f. offense.

Kranz, ̈e, n.m. wreath.

kraß, adj. crass, gross.

Kraßheit, -en, n.f. grossness.

kratzen, vb. scrape, scratch.

kraulen, vb. crawl.

kraus, adj. curly, crisp.

Krause, -n, n.f. frill.

kräuseln, vb. curl, ruffle.

Kraut, ̈er, n.nt. herb, plant.

Krawat'te, -n, n.f. necktie.

Krebs, -e, n.m. crayfish; (med.) cancer.

krebserregend, adj. carcinogenic.

kreden'zen, vb. serve, offer.

Kredit', -e, n.m. credit.

Kredit'karte, -n, n.f. credit card.

Kreide, -n, n.f. chalk.

kreidig, adj. chalky.

Kreis, -e, n.m. circle; district.

Kreisbahn, -en, n.f. orbit.

kreischen, vb. shriek.

Kreisel, -, n.m. top.

kreiseln, vb. spin like a top, gyrate.

kreisen, vb. circle, revolve.

kreisförmig, adj. circular.

Kreislauf, ̈e, n.m. circulation, circuit.

Krema'to'rium, -ien, n.nt. crematorium.

Krempe, -n, n.f. brim.

Krepp, n.m. crepe.

Kretonn'e, -s, n.m. cretonne.

Kreuz, -e, n.nt. cross; back; (music) sharp.

kreuzen, vb. cross; cruise, tack.

Kreuzer, -, n.m. cruiser.

Kreuzgang, -e, n.m. cloister.

kreuzigen, vb. crucify.

Kreuzigung, -en, n.f. crucifixion.

kreuz und quer, adv. crisscross.

Kreuzung, -en, n.f. cross(-breed); crossing, intersection.

Kreuzverhör, -e, n.nt. cross-examination.

Kreuzzug, ̈e, n.m. crusade.

Kreuzzügler, -, n.m. crusader.

kribbelig, adj. jittery.

kriechen*, vb. crawl, creep; grovel.

Krieg, -e, n.m. war.

kriegen, vb. get.

Krieger, -, n.m. warrior.

kriegerisch, adj. warlike. ◀

Kriegsdienst, -e, n.m. military service.

Kriegsdienstverweigerer, -, n.m. conscientious objector.

Kriegsgefangen-, n.m. prisoner of war.

Kriegsgericht, -e, n.nt. courtmartial.

Kriegslist, -en, n.f. stratagem.

Kriegslust, ̈e, n.f. belligerence.

kriegslustig, adj. bellicose.

Kriegsmacht, ̈e, n.f. military forces.

Kriegsschiff, -e, n.nt. warship.

kriegsversehrt, adj. disabled (by war).

Kriegszug, ̈e, n.m. military expedition.

Kriegszustand, ̈e, n.m. state of war.

kriminal', adj. criminal.

Krippe, -n, n.f. crib.

Krise, -n, n.f. crisis.

Kristall' -e, n.nt. crystal.

kristal'len, adj. crystal, crystalline.

kristallisie'ren, vb. crystallize.

Kritik', -en, n.f. criticism, critique, review.

Kritiker, -, n.m. critic.

kritisch, adj. critical.

kritisie'ren, vb. criticize.

kritzeln, vb. scribble.

Krocket'spiel, -e, n.nt. croquet.

Krokodil', -e, n.nt. crocodile.

Krone, -n, n.f. crown.

krönen, vb. crown.

Kronleuchter, -, n.m. chandelier.

Kronprinz, -en, -en, n.m. crown prince.

Krönung, -en, n.f. coronation.

Kropf, -e, n.m. crop; goiter.

Krücke, -n, n.f. crutch.

Krug, ̈e, n.m. pitcher.

Krümel, -, n.m. crumb.

krümeln, vb. crumble.

krumm (̈, -), adj. crooked.

krümmen, vb. bend; (sich k.) warp, buckle, double up (with pain or laughter).

Krümmung, -en, n.f. bend, curve; curvature.

Krüppel, -, n.m. cripple.

Kruste, -n, n.f. crust.

Kruzifix, -e, n.nt. crucifix.

Kübel, -, n.m. bucket.

Kubik'-, cpds. cubic.

kubisch, adj. cubic.

Küche, -n, n.f. kitchen.

Kuchen, -, n.m. cake.

Küchenchef, -s, n.m. chef.

Kugel, -n, *n.f.* sphere, ball, bullet.

kugelförmig, *adj.* spherical; globular.

Kuh, -e, *n.f.* cow.

kühl, *adj.* cool.

Kühle, *n.f.* coolness.

kühlen, *vb.* cool.

Kühler, -, *n.m.* auto radiator.

Kühlschrank, -e, *n.m.* refrigerator.

kühn, *adj.* bold.

Kühnheit, -en, *n.f.* boldness.

Küken, -, *n.nt.* chick.

kulinarisch, *adj.* culinary.

Kult, -e, *n.m.* cult.

kultivieren, *vb.* cultivate.

kultiviert, *adj.* cultured.

Kultivierung, *n.f.* cultivation.

Kultur, -en, *n.f.* culture.

kulturell, *adj.* cultural.

Kümmel, *n.m.* caraway.

Kummer, -, *n.m.* sorrow, grief.

kümmerlich, *adj.* miserable.

kümmern, *vb.* grieve, trouble, concern; (**sich k. um**) care about, look out for.

kummervoll, *adj.* sorrowful.

kund, *adj.* known.

Kunde, -n, -n, *n.m.* customer, client.

Kunde, -n, *n.f.* knowledge, information.

kund-geben*, *vb.* make known.

Kundgebung, -en, *n.f.* demonstration.

kundig, *adj.* well informed, knowing.

kündigen, *vb.* give notice; cancel.

Kündigung, -en, *n.f.* cancellation.

Kundschaft, -en, *n.f.* clientele.

künftig, *adj.* future.

Kunst, -e, *n.f.* art.

künsteln, *vb.* contrive.

kunstfertig, *adj.* skillful.

Künstler, -, *n.m.* artist.

künstlerisch, *adj.* artistic.

Künstlertum, *n.nt.* artistry.

künstlich, *adj.* artificial.

kunstlos, *adj.* artless.

Kunstseide, -n, *n.f.* rayon.

Kunststoff, -e, *n.m.* plastic.

Kunststück, -e, *n.nt.* feat, stunt.

kunstvoll, *adj.* artistic.

Kunstwerk, -e, *n.nt.* work of art.

Kunstwissenschaft, *n.f.* fine arts.

Kupfer, *n.nt.* copper.

kuppeln, *vb.* couple, join; pander.

Kuppelung, -en, *n.f.* clutch.

Kur, -en, *n.f.* cure.

Kurbel, -n, *n.f.* crank.

Kürbis, -se, *n.m.* pumpkin, gourd.

Kurier, -e, *n.m.* courier.

kurieren, *vb.* cure.

kurios', *adj.* odd, strange.

Kuriosität', -en, *n.f.* curio.

Kurio'sum, -sa, *n.nt.* freak.

Kurort, -e, *n.m.* resort.

Kurs, -e, *n.m.* course; rate of exchange.

Kursbuch, -er, *n.nt.* timetable.

kursie'ren, *vb.* circulate.

kursiv', *adj.* italic.

Kursus, Kurse, *n.m.* course.

Kurve, -n, *n.f.* curve.

kurz(-), *adj.* short; (**k. und bündig**) short and to the point.

Kürze, -n, *n.f.* shortness, brevity.

kürzen, *vb.* shorten.

kürzlich, *adj.* recently.

kurzsichtig, *adj.* near-sighted.

kurzum', *adv.* in short.

Kürzung, -en, *n.f.* shortening, cut.

Kurzwaren, *n.pl.* notions.

Kuß, -sse, *n.m.* kiss.

küssen, *vb.* kiss.

Küste, -n, *n.f.* coast, shore.

Küster, -, *n.m.* sexton.

Kutsche, -n, *n.f.* coach.

Kuvert', -s, *n.nt.* envelope.

L

Labe, -n, *n.f.* refreshment, comfort.

laben, *vb.* refresh, comfort.

Laborato'rium, -rien, *n.nt.* laboratory.

Labsal, -e, *n.nt.* refreshment, comfort.

Labyrinth', -e, *n.nt.* labyrinth.

Lache, -n, *n.f.* puddle.

lächeln, *vb.* smile.

Lächeln, *n.nt.* smile.

lachen, *vb.* laugh.

Lachen, *n.nt.* laugh(ing).

lächerlich, *adj.* ridiculous.

Lachs, *n.m.* salmon.

Lack, -e, *n.m.* lacquer.

Lackleder, *n.nt.* patent leather.

Lade, -n, *n.f.* box, chest, drawer.

laden*, *vb.* load, charge; summon.

Laden, -, *n.m.* shop; shutter.

Ladenkasse, -n, *n.f.* till.

Ladentisch, -e, *n.m.* counter.

Ladung, -en, *n.f.* load, cargo, shipment; charge.

Lage, -n, *n.f.* location, situation, condition.

Lager, -, *n.nt.* camp, lair, bed; deposit, depot, supply; bearing.

Lagerhaus, -er, *n.nt.* storehouse.

lagern, *vb.* lay down, store, deposit; (**sich l.**) camp; be deposited.

Lagerung, -en, *n.f.* storage, bearing; stratification, grain.

Lagu'ne, -n, *n.f.* lagoon.

lahm, *adj.* lame.

lähmen, *vb.* lame, cripple, paralyze.

Lähmung, -en, *n.f.* paralysis.

Laib, -e, *n.m.* loaf.

Laie, -n, *n.m.* layman.

Laienstand, *n.m.* laity.

Laken, -, *n.nt.* sheet.

Lamm, -er, *n.nt.* lamb.

Lampe, -n, *n.f.* lamp.

lancie'ren, *vb.* launch.

Land, -er, *n.nt.* land, country.

Landbau, *n.m.* agriculture.

Landebahn, -en, *n.f.* flight strip, runway.

landen, *vb.* land.

Landesverrat, *n.m.* high treason.

Landkarte, -n, *n.f.* map.

landläufig, *adj.* usual, ordinary.

ländlich, *adj.* rural.

Landschaft, -en, *n.f.* landscape, countryside.

Landser, -, *n.m.* common soldier, GI.

Landsmann, -leute, *n.m.* compatriot.

Landstraße, -e, *n.f.* highway.

Landstrich, -e, *n.m.* region.

Landung, -en, *n.f.* landing.

Landwirt, -e, *n.m.* farmer.

Landwirtschaft, *n.f.* agriculture.

landwirtschaftlich, *adj.* agricultural.

lang (-), *adj.* long, tall.

lange, *adv.* for a long time.

Länge, -n, *n.f.* length; longitude.

langen, *vb.* hand; suffice.

Langeweile, *n.f.* boredom.

langlebig, *adj.* long-lived.

länglich, *adj.* oblong.

Langmut, *n.m.* patience.

langmütig, *adj.* long-suffering.

längs, *adv. & prep.* along.

langsam, *adj.* slow.

Langsamkeit, *n.f.* slowness.

längst, *adv.* long since.

langweilen, *vb.* bore.

langweilig, *adj.* boring.

langwierig, *adj.* lengthy.

Lanze, -n, *n.f.* lance.

Lappa'lie, -n, *n.f.* trifle.

Lappen, -, *n.m.* rag; lobe.

Lärm, *n.m.* noise.

Larve, -n, *n.f.* mask; larva.

Laserstrahl, -en, *n.m.* laser beam.

lassen*, *vb.* let, permit; cause to, have (someone do something, something done); leave; leave off, stop.

lässig, *adj.* indolent, careless.

Last, -en, *n.f.* burden, encumbrance; load, weight, cargo.

Lastauto, -s, *n.nt.* truck.

lasten, *vb.* weigh heavily, be a burden.

Laster, -, *n.nt.* vice.

lasterhaft, *adj.* vicious, wicked.

lästern, *vb.* slander, blaspheme.

lästig, *adj.* troublesome, disagreeable.

Lastkraftwagen, -, *n.m.* (motor) truck.

Lastwagen, -n, *n.m.* (motor) truck.

Latein', *n.nt.* Latin.

latei'nisch, *adj.* Latin.

Later'ne, -n, n.f. lantern.

Latri'ne, -n, n.f. latrine.

latschen, vb. shuffle, slouch.

Latz, ¨-e, n.m. bib, flap.

lau, adj. tepid, lukewarm.

Laub, n.nt. foliage.

Lauer, n.f. ambush.

lauern, vb. lurk, lie in wait for.

Lauf, ¨-e, n.m. course, race, run; (gun) barrel.

Laufbahn, -en, n.f. career; runway, race track.

laufen*, vb. run, walk.

laufend, adj. running, current.

Läufer, -, n.m. runner; stair carpet; (chess) bishop.

Lauge, -n, n.f. lye.

Laune, -n, n.f. whim, caprice, fancy; mood, humor.

launenhaft, adj. capricious.

launig, adj. humorous.

launisch, adj. moody.

Laus, ¨-e, n.f. louse.

lauschen, vb. listen.

lausig, adj. lousy.

laut, adj. loud, aloud.

laut, prep. according to.

Laut, -e, n.m. sound.

Laute, -n, n.f. lute.

lauten, vb. read, say.

läuten, vb. ring, peal, sound.

lauter, adj. pure, sheer, nothing but.

Lauterkeit, -en, n.f. purity.

läutern, vb. purify.

lautlos, adj. soundless, silent.

Lautsprecher, -, n.m. loudspeaker.

lauwarm, adj. lukewarm; halfhearted.

Lava, n.f. lava.

Laven'del, n.m. lavender.

lax, adj. lax.

Laxheit, n.f. laxity.

leben, vb. live, be alive.

Leben, -, n.nt. life.

lebend, adj. living.

leben'dig, adj. living, alive; lively.

Leben'digkeit, n.f. liveliness, vivacity.

lebenserfahren, adj. experienced, sophisticated.

Lebensgefahr, -en, n.f. danger (to life).

lebensgefährlich, adj. highly dangerous.

Lebenskraft, n.f. vitality.

lebenslänglich, adj. lifelong, for life.

Lebensmittel, n.pl. provisions, groceries.

Lebensmittelgeschäft, -e, n.nt. grocery store.

Lebensstil, n.m. life style.

Lebensunterhalt, n.m. livelihood.

Leber, n.f. liver.

Lebewesen, -, n.nt. living being, organism.

lebewohl', interj. farewell, adieu.

lebhaft, adj. lively.

leblos, adj. lifeless.

Lebzeiten, n.pl. lifetime.

lechzen, vb. thirst, languish.

leck, adj. leaky, having a leak.

Leck, -e, n.nt. leak.

lecken, vb. leak; lick.

lecker, adj. tasty, appetizing.

Leder, -, n.nt. leather.

ledern, adj. leather(y).

ledig, adj. unmarried, single; vacant; exempt.

lediglich, adv. merely.

leer, adj. empty, vacant, blank.

Leere, -, n.f. emptiness.

leeren, vb. empty.

Leerlauf, n.m. neutral (gear).

legal', adj. legal.

legalisie'ren, vb. legalize.

Legat', -e, n.nt. bequest.

legen, vb. lay, place, put; (sich l.) lie down, subside.

legendär', adj. legendary.

Legen'de, -n, n.f. legend.

Legie'rung, -en, n.f. alloy.

Legion', -en, n.f. legion.

legitim', adj. legitimate.

legitimie'ren, vb. legitimize; (sich l.) prove one's identity.

Lehm, n.m. loam, clay.

Lehne, -n, n.f. back, arm (of a chair), support.

lehnen, vb. lean.

Lehnstuhl, ¨-e, n.m. armchair.

Lehrbuch, ¨-er, n.nt. textbook.

Lehre, -n, n.f. doctrine, teaching, lesson; apprenticeship.

lehren, vb. teach.

Lehrer, -, n.m. teacher.

Lehrgang, ¨-e, n.m. course of instruction.

Lehrplan, ¨-e, n.m. curriculum.

lehrreich, adj. instructive.

Lehrsatz, ¨-e, n.m. proposition.

Lehrstunde, -n, n.f. lesson.

Leib, -er, n.m. body; abdomen; womb.

leibhaft(ig), adj. incarnate, personified.

leiblich, adj. bodily.

Leiche, -n, n.f. corpse.

leicht, adj. light; easy.

Leichter, -, n.m. barge.

leichtfertig, adj. frivolous.

Leichtfertigkeit, n.f. frivolity.

leichtgläubig, adj. gullible, credulous.

Leichtigkeit, -en, n.f. ease.

Leichtsinn, n.m. frivolity.

leichtsinnig, adj. frivolous, reckless.

leid, adj. (es tut* mir l.) I'm sorry.

Leid, n.nt. suffering, sorrow, harm.

leiden*, vb. suffer; stand, endure; (gern l. mögen*) like.

Leiden, -, n.nt. suffering; illness.

Leidenschaft, -en, n.f. passion.

leidenschaftlich, adj. passionate.

leidenschaftslos, adj. dispassionate.

leider, adv. unfortunately.

leidig, adj. unpleasant.

leidlich, adj. tolerable.

Leier, -n, n.f. lyre.

leihen*, vb. lend; borrow.

leihweise, adv. on loan.

Leim, n.m. glue.

leimen, vb. glue.

Leine, -n, n.f. line, leash.

leinen, adj. linen.

Leinen, -, n.nt. linen.

Leinsamen, n.m. linseed.

Leinwand, n.f. canvas; (movie) screen.

leise, adj. soft, quiet, gentle.

leisten, vb. perform, accomplish; (sich l.) afford.

Leisten, -, n.m. last.

Leistung, -en, n.f. performance, accomplishment, achievement, output.

leistungsfähig, adj. efficient.

Leitartikel, -, n.m. editorial.

leiten, vb. lead, direct, conduct, manage.

Leiter, -, n.m. leader, director, manager.

Leiter, -n, n.f. ladder.

Leitfaden, ¨-, n.m. key, guide.

Leitsatz, ¨-e, n.m. guiding principle.

Leitung, -en, n.f. guidance, direction, management; wire, line, duct, tube; conduction.

Leitungsrohr, -e, n.nt. conduit.

Lektion', -en, n.f. lesson.

Lektor, -o'ren, n.m. university instructor.

Lektü're, -n, n.f. reading.

Lende, -n, n.f. loin.

Lendenstück, -e, n.nt. sirloin.

lenkbar, adj. steerable, dirigible, manageable.

lenken, vb. direct, steer, guide.

Lenkung, -en, n.f. guidance, steering, control.

Lenz, -e, n.m. spring.

Leopard', -en, -en, n.m. leopard.

Lerche, -n, n.f. lark.

lernen, vb. learn.

Lesart, -en, n.f. reading, version.

lesbar, adj. legible; worth reading.

lesbisch, adj. lesbian.

Lese, -n, n.f. vintage.

Lesebuch, ¨-er, n.nt. reader.

lesen*, vb. read; lecture; gather.

Leser, -, n.m. reader.

leserlich, adj. legible.

Lethargie', n.f. lethargy.

lethar'gisch, adj. lethargic.

Lettland, n.nt. Latvia.

letzt-, adj. last.

letzter-, adj. latter.

leuchten, vb. give forth light, shine.

Leuchter, -, n.m. candlestick.

Leuchtschirm, -e, n.m. fluorescent screen, television screen.

Leuchtsignal, -e, n.nt. flare.

Leuchtturm, ¨-e, n.m. lighthouse.

leugnen, vb. deny.

Leukoplast', n.nt. adhesive tape, band-aid.

Leumund, -e, *n.m.* reputation.
Leute, *n.pl.* people.
Leutnant, -s *or* -e, *n.m.* lieutenant.
leutselig, *adj.* affable.
Lexikon, -ka, *n.nt.* dictionary.
Liaison', -s, *n.f.* liaison.
liberal', *adj.* liberal.
Liberalis'mus, *n.m.* liberalism.
Libret'to, -s, *n.nt.* libretto.
Licht, -er, *n.nt.* light.
Lichtbild, -er, *n.nt.* photograph.
Lichtschimmer, -, *n.m.* glint.
Lichtspiel, -e, *n.nt.* moving picture.
Lid, -er, *n.nt.* eyelid.
lieb, *adj.* dear.
liebäugeln, *vb.* make eyes at.
Liebchen, -, *n.nt.* dearest, darling.
Liebe, -n, *n.f.* love.
Liebelei, -en, *n.f.* flirtation.
liebeln, *vb.* flirt, make love.
lieben, *vb.* love.
liebenswert, *adj.* lovable.
liebenswürdig, *adj.* amiable, kind.
lieber, *adv.* rather.
Liebesaffäre, -n, *n.f.* love affair.
liebevoll, *adj.* loving, affectionate.
lieb-haben*, *vb.* love.
Liebhaber, -, *n.m.* lover.
Liebhaberei', -en, *n.f.* hobby.
liebkosen, *vb.* fondle, caress.
Liebkosung, -en, *n.f.* caress.
lieblich, *adj.* lovely.
Liebling, -e, *n.m.* darling.
Lieblings-, *cpds.* favorite.
lieblos, *adj.* loveless.
Liebreiz, -e, *n.m.* charm.
Liebschaft, -en, *n.f.* love affair.
Liebst-, *n.m. & f.* dearest, sweetheart.
Lied, -er, *n.nt.* song.
liederlich, *adj.* slovenly; dissolute.
Lieferant', -en, -en, *n.m.* supplier.
liefern, *vb.* supply, deliver.
Lieferung, -en, *n.f.* delivery.
Lieferwagen, -, *n.m.* delivery van.
liegen*, *vb.* lie, be located.
Lift, -e, *n.m.* elevator.
Likör', -e, *n.m.* liqueur.
lila, *adj.* lilac, purple.
Lilie, -n, *n.f.* lily.
Limona'de, -n, *n.f.* lemonade.
Limo'ne, -n, *n.f.* lime.
Limousi'ne, -n, *n.f.* limousine, sedan.
lind, *adj.* mild, gentle.
lindern, *vb.* alleviate, ease, soothe.
Lineal', -e, *n.nt.* ruler.
linear', *adj.* linear.
Linguist', -en, -en, *n.m.* linguist.
linguis'tisch, *adj.* linguistic.
Linie, -n, *n.f.* line.
link-, *adj.* left.
Link-, *n.f.* left.

linkisch, *adj.* awkward, clumsy.
links, *adv.* to the left.
Linse, -n, *n.f.* lens; lentil.
Lippe, -n, *n.f.* lip.
Lippenstift, -e, *n.m.* lipstick.
liquidie'ren, *vb.* liquidate.
lispeln, *vb.* lisp, whisper.
List, -en, *n.f.* cunning, trick, ruse.
Liste, -n, *n.f.* list.
listig, *adj.* cunning, crafty.
Litanei', *n.f.* litany.
Litauen, *n.nt.* Lithuania.
Liter, -, *n.m. or nt.* liter.
litera'risch, *adj.* literary.
Literatur', -en, *n.f.* literature.
Lithographie', -l'en, *n.f.* lithograph(y).
Liturgie', -l'en, *n.f.* liturgy.
litur'gisch, *adj.* liturgical.
Livree', -e'en, *n.f.* livery.
Lizenz', -en, *n.f.* license.
Lob, -e, *n.nt.* praise.
loben, *vb.* praise.
lobenswert, *adj.* praiseworthy.
löblich, *adj.* praiseworthy.
lobpreisen, *vb.* praise, extol.
Lobrede, -n, *n.f.* eulogy.
Loch, -er, *n.nt.* hole.
lochen, *vb.* put a hole in, punch.
Locke, -n, *n.f.* lock, curl.
locken, *vb.* curl; lure.
locker, *adj.* loose.
lockern, *vb.* loosen.
lockig, *adj.* curly.
lodern, *vb.* blaze.
Löffel, -, *n.m.* spoon.
Logbuch, -er, *n.nt.* log.
Loge, -n, *n.f.* loge, box; (fraternal) lodge.
Logik, *n.f.* logic.
logisch, *adj.* logical.
Lohn, -e, *n.m.* reward; wages.
lohnen, *vb.* reward, pay, be of value; (sich l.) be worth the trouble.
lokal', *adj.* local.
Lokal', -e, *n.nt.* night club, bar, place of amusement; premises.
Lokomoti've, -n, *n.f.* locomotive.
Lokus, -se, *n.m.* toilet.
los, *adj.* loose; wrong; (was ist l.?) what's the matter?
Los, -e, *n.nt.* lot.
lösbar, *adj.* soluble.
los-binden*, *vb.* untie.
Löschblatt, -er, *n.nt.* blotter.
löschen, *vb.* extinguish, quench; unload.
lose, *adj.* loose, slack, lax, dissolute.
Lösegeld, -er *n.nt.* ransom.
lösen, *vb.* undo, solve, dissolve; buy (a ticket).
los-fahren*, *vb.* start out.
los-gehen*, *vb.* start out, go off, begin.
los-kommen*, *vb.* get loose.
los-lassen*, *vb.* get loose, let go.
los-lösen, *vb.* disconnect.

los-machen, *vb.* unfasten, free.
Lösung, -en, *n.f.* solution.
Lösungsmittel, -, *n.nt.* solvent.
los-werden*, *vb.* get rid of.
Lot, -e, *n.nt.* lead, plumbline.
löten, *vb.* solder.
lotrecht, *adj.* perpendicular.
Lotse, -n, -n, *n.m.* pilot.
lotsen, *vb.* pilot.
Lotterie', -l'en, *n.f.* lottery.
Löwe, -n, -n, *n.m.* lion.
Lücke, -n, *n.f.* gap.
lückenhaft, *adj.* with gaps, incomplete.
lückenlos, *adj.* without gaps, complete.
Luder, -, *n.nt.* scoundrel; slut; carrion.
Luft, -e, *n.f.* air.
Luftabwehr, -, *n.f.* anti-aircraft, air defense.
Luftangriff, -e, *n.m.* air raid.
Luftballon, -s, *n.m.* balloon.
Luftblase, -n, *n.f.* bubble.
Luftbrücke, -n, *n.f.* air lift.
luftdicht, *adj.* airtight.
Luftdruck, -e, *n.m.* air pressure.
lüften, *vb.* air, ventilate.
Luftfahrt, *n.nt.* aviation.
Luftflotte, -n, *n.f.* air fleet.
luftig, *adj.* airy.
luftkrank, -, *adj.* air-sick.
Luftlinie, -n, *n.f.* air line.
Luftpirat, -en, -en, *n.m.* hijacker.
Luftpost, *n.f.* airmail.
Luftsack, -e, *n.m.* airbag (automobile).
Luftschiff, -e, *n.nt.* airship, dirigible.
Luftsprung, -e, *n.m.* caper.
Luftstützpunkt, -e, *n.m.* air base.
Lüftung, *n.f.* ventilation.
Luftverpestung, *n.f.* air pollution.
Luftwaffe, -n, *n.f.* air force.
Luftzug, -e, *n.m.* draft.
Lüge, -n, *n.f.* lie.
lugen, *vb.* peep.
lügen*, *vb.* lie.
Lügner, -, *n.m.* liar.
Lümmel, -, *n.m.* lout.
Lump, -en, -en, *n.m.* bum.
Lumpen, -, *n.m.* rag.
Lunge, -n, *n.f.* lung.
Lungenentzündung, -en, *n.f.* pneumonia.
Lust, -e, *n.f.* pleasure; desire; (L. haben*) feel like (doing something).
lüstern, *adj.* lecherous.
lustig, *adj.* merry, gay.
Lüstling, -e, *n.m.* libertine.
lustlos, *adj.* listless.
Lustspiel, -e, *n.nt.* comedy.
Lutheraner, -, *n.m.* Lutheran.
lutherisch, *adj.* Lutheran.
lutschen, *vb.* suck.
Luxus, *n.m.* luxury.
Luxus-, *cpds.* de luxe.
Lymphe, -n, *n.f.* lymph.
lynchen, *vb.* lynch.
Lyrik, *n.f.* lyric poetry.

lyrisch, *adj.* lyric.

Lyze'um, -e'en, *n.nt.* girls' high school.

M

Maat, -e, *n.m.* mate.

machen, *vb.* make, do.

Macht, ¨e, *n.f.* power.

Machterweiterung, -en, *n.f.* aggrandizement.

mächtig, *adj.* powerful.

machtlos, *adj.* powerless.

Mädchen, -, *n.nt.* girl.

mädchenhaft, *adj.* girlish.

Mädel, -, *n.nt.* girl.

Mafia, *n.f.* mafia.

Magazin', -e, *n.nt.* magazine, storeroom, store.

Magd, ¨e, *n.f.* hired girl.

Magen, - *or* ¨, *n.m.* stomach.

Magenbeschwerden, *n.pl.* indigestion.

Magengeschwür, -e, *n.nt.* stomach ulcer.

Magenschmerzen, *n.pl.* stomach ache.

Magenverstimmung, -en, *n.f.* stomach upset.

mager, *adj.* lean.

Magermilch, *n.f.* skim milk.

Magie', *n.f.* magic.

magisch, *adj.* magic.

Magnat', -en, -en, *n.m.* magnate, tycoon.

Magne'sium, *n.nt.* magnesium.

Magnet', -e, *or* -en, -en, *n.m.* magnet.

magne'tisch, *adj.* magnetic.

Magnetophon', -e, *n.nt.* tape recorder.

Mahago'ni, *n.nt.* mahogany.

mähen, *vb.* mow.

Mahl, -e, *or* ¨er, *n.nt.* meal, repast.

mahlen, *vb.* grind.

Mahlzeit, -en, *n.f.* meal.

mahnen, *vb.* remind, urge, warn, dun.

Mahnung, -en, *n.f.* admonition, warning.

Mähre, -n, *n.f.* mare.

Mai, *n.m.* May.

Mais, *n.m.* corn, maize.

Maiskolben, -, *n.m.* corncob.

Majestät', -en, *n.f.* majesty.

majestä'tisch, *adj.* majestic.

Major', -e, *n.m.* major.

Majorität', -en, *n.f.* majority.

Majus'kel, -n, *n.f.* capital letter.

Makel, -, *n.m.* stain, blemish, flaw.

makellos, *adj.* spotless, flawless, immaculate.

Makkaro'ni, *n.pl.* macaroni.

Makler, -, *n.m.* broker.

Makre'le, -n, *n.f.* mackerel.

Makro'ne, -n, *n.f.* macaroon.

¹**Mal**, -e, *n.nt.* mark, sign, spot, mole.

²**Mal**, -e, *n.nt.* time; (**das erste M.**) the first time; (**2 mal 2**) 2 times 2.

mal, *adv.* (= **einmal**) once, just; (**nicht m.**) not even.

Mala'ria, *n.f.* malaria.

malen, *vb.* paint.

Maler, -, *n.m.* painter.

Malerei', -en, *n.f.* painting.

malerisch, *adj.* picturesque.

Malz, *n.nt.* malt.

man, *pron.* one, a person.

Manager, -, *n.m.* manager.

mancher, -es, -e, *pron. & adj.* many, many a.

mancherlei, *adj.* various.

manchmal, *adv.* sometimes.

Mandat', -e, *n.nt.* mandate.

Mandel, -n, *n.f.* almond; tonsil.

Mandoli'ne, -n, *n.f.* mandolin.

Mangel, ¨, *n.m.* lack, dearth, defect.

Mangel, -n, *n.f.* mangle.

mangelhaft, *adj.* faulty.

mangeln, *vb.* be lacking, deficient; (**es mangelt mir an . . .**) I lack . . .

mangels, *prep.* for lack of.

Manie', -i'en, *n.f.* mania.

Manier', -en, *n.f.* manner.

manier'lich, *adj.* mannerly, polite.

manikü'ren, *vb.* manicure.

manipulie'ren, *vb.* manipulate.

Manko, -s, *n.nt.* defect, deficiency.

Mann, ¨er, *n.m.* man, husband.

Männchen, -, *n.nt.* male (animal).

Mannesalter, *n.nt.* manhood.

mannhaft, *adj.* manly.

mannigfach, *adj.* manifold.

mannigfaltig, *adj.* manifold.

Mannigfaltigkeit, -en, *n.f.* diversity.

männlich, *adj.* male, masculine.

Männlichkeit, *n.f.* manliness.

Mannschaft, -en, *n.f.* crew, team, squad; (*pl.*) enlisted men.

Manö'ver, -, *n.nt.* maneuver.

manövrie'ren, *vb.* maneuver.

Manschet'te, -n, *n.f.* cuff.

Mantel, ¨, *n.m.* overcoat.

Manufaktur', -en, *n.f.* manufacture, factory.

Manuskript', -e, *n.nt.* manuscript.

Mappe, -n, *n.f.* portfolio, briefcase, folder.

Märchen, -, *n.nt.* fairy tale.

märchenhaft, *adj.* fabulous.

Märchenland, ¨er, *n.nt.* fairyland.

Margari'ne, *n.f.* margarine.

Marihua'na, *n.nt.* marijuana.

Mari'ne, -n, *n.f.* navy.

marinie'ren, *vb.* marinate.

Marionet'te, -n, *n.f.* marionette, puppet.

Mark, -, *n.f.* mark (unit of money); (**deutsche M.**) West German mark.

Mark, -en, *n.f.* border(land).

Marke, -n, *n.f.* mark; brand, sort; postage stamp, check, ticket.

markie'ren, *vb.* mark.

Marki'se, -n, *n.f.* awning.

Markstein, -e, *n.m.* boundary stone, landmark.

Markt, ¨e, *n.m.* market.

Marktplatz, ¨e, *n.m.* market place.

Marmela'de, -n, *n.f.* jam.

Marmor, -e, *n.m.* marble.

Maro'ne, -n, *n.f.* chestnut.

Marot'te, -n, *n.f.* whim, fad.

Marsch, ¨e, *n.m.* march.

Marsch, -en, *n.f.* marsh.

Marschall, ¨e, *n.m.* marshal.

marschie'ren, *vb.* march.

Marter, -n, *n.f.* torture.

martern, *vb.* torture.

Märtyrer, -, *n.m.* martyr.

Märtyrertum, *n.nt.* martyrdom.

März, *n.m.* March.

Marzipan', -e, *n.nt. or nt.* marzipan, almond paste.

Masche, -n, *n.f.* stitch, mesh.

Maschi'ne, -n, *n.f.* machine.

Maschi'nenbau, *n.m.* engineering.

Maschi'nengewehr, -e, *n.nt.* machine gun.

Maschinist', -en, -en, *n.m.* machinist.

Masern, *n.pl.* measles.

Maske, -n, *n.f.* mask.

Maskera'de, -n, *n.f.* masquerade.

maskie'ren, *vb.* mask.

Maskot'te, -n, *n.f.* mascot.

maskulin', *adj.* masculine.

Maß, -e, *n.nt.* measure(ment), dimension, extent, rate, proportion.

Massa'ge, -n, *n.f.* massage.

Masse, -n, *n.f.* mass.

massenhaft, *adj.* in large quantity.

Massenversammlung, -en, *n.f.* mass meeting.

massenweise, *adv.* in large numbers.

Masseur', -e, *n.m.* masseur.

maßgebend, *adj.* authoritative, standard.

maßgeblich, *adj.* authoritative, standard.

massie'ren, *vb.* massage.

massig, *adj.* bulky, solid.

mäßig, *adj.* moderate.

mäßigen, *vb.* moderate.

Mäßigkeit, *n.f.* temperance.

Mäßigung, *n.f.* moderation.

massiv', *adj.* massive.

maßlos, *adj.* immoderate, excessive.

Maßnahme, -n, *n.f.* measure, step.

Maßregel, -n, *n.f.* measure, step.

maßregelnd, *adj.* disciplinary.

Maßstab, ¨e, *n.m.* scale, rate, gauge, standard.

maßvoll, *adj.* moderate.

Mast, -e *or* -en, *n.m.* mast.

misten, vb. fatten.

Material', **-ien**, n.nt. material.

Materialis'mus, n.m. materialism.

Mate'rie, **-n**, n.f. matter, stuff.

materiell', adj. material.

Mathematik', n.f. mathematics.

Mathema'tiker, **-**, n.m. mathematician.

mathema'tisch, adj. mathematical.

Matrat'ze, **-n**, n.f. mattress.

Mätres'se, **-n**, n.f. mistress.

Matro'se, **-n**, **-n**, n.m. sailor.

matschig, adj. muddy, slushy; pulpy.

matt, adj. dull, tired.

Matte, **-n**, n.f. mat.

Mattigkeit, n.f. lassitude.

Mätzchen, **-**, n.nt. antic, foolish trick.

Mauer, **-n**, n.f. (outside) wall.

Maul, **:er**, n.nt. mouth, snout.

Maulkorb, **:e**, n.m. muzzle.

Maultier, **-e**, n.nt. mule.

Maulwurf, **:e**, n.m. mole.

Maure, **-n**, n.m. Moor.

Maurer, **-**, n.m. mason, bricklayer.

Maus, **:e**, n.f. mouse.

Mausole'um, **-le'en**, n.nt. mausoleum.

maximal', adj. maximum.

Maximum, **-ma**, n.nt. maximum.

Mayonnai'se, **-n**, n.f. mayonnaise.

m. E., abbr. (= meines Erach'tens) in my opinion.

Mecha'nik, n.f. mechanics, mechanism.

Mecha'niker, **-**, n.m. mechanic.

mecha'nisch, adj. mechanical.

mechanisie'ren, vb. mechanize.

Mechanis'mus, **-men**, n.m. mechanism.

Medail'le, **-n**, n.f. medal.

Medikament', **-e**, n.nt. drug, medicine.

Medium, **-ien**, n.nt. medium.

Medizin', **-en**, n.f. medicine.

Medizi'ner, **-**, n.m. medical man, medical student.

medizi'nisch, adj. medical.

Meer, **-e**, n.nt. sea.

Meerbusen, **-**, n.m. bay.

Meerenge, **-n**, n.f. strait.

Meeresboden, n.m. seabed.

Meeresbucht, **-en**, n.f. bay.

Meerrettich, **-e**, n.m. horseradish.

Megahertz, n.nt. megahertz.

Mehl, n.nt. flour, meal.

mehr, adj. more.

mehren, vb. increase.

mehrere, adj. several.

mehrfach, adj. multiple.

Mehrheit, **-en**, n.f. majority.

mehrmalig, adj. repeated.

mehrmals, adv. repeatedly.

Mehrwertsteuer, **-n**, n.f. value-added tax.

Mehrzahl, **-en**, n.f. majority; plural.

---

meiden*, vb. avoid.

Meile, **-n**, n.f. mile.

Meilenstein, **-e**, n.m. milestone.

mein, **-**, **-e**, adj. my.

meinen, vb. mean, think.

meiner, **-es**, **-e**, pron. mine.

meinetwegen, adv. for my sake; for all I care.

Meinung, **-en**, n.f. opinion.

Meinungsumfrage, **-n**, n.f. poll.

Meißel, **-**, n.m. chisel.

meist, **1.** adj. most (of). **2.** adv. mostly, usually.

meistens, adv. mostly, usually.

Meister, **-**, n.m. master; champion.

meisterhaft, adj. masterly.

Meisterschaft, **-en**, n.f. championship.

Meisterstück, **-e**, n.nt. masterpiece.

Melancholie, n.f. melancholy.

melancho'lisch, adj. melancholy.

Melas'se, n.f. molasses.

melden, vb. announce, notify, report.

Meldung, **-en**, n.f. announcement, notification, report.

melken*, vb. milk.

Melodie', **-l'en**, n.f. melody, tune.

melo'disch, adj. melodious.

Melo'ne, **-n**, n.f. melon; derby.

Membra'ne, **-n**, n.f. membrane.

Memoi'ren, n.pl. memoirs.

Memoran'dum, **-den**, n.nt. memorandum.

Menagerie', **-i'en**, n.f. menagerie.

Menge, **-n**, n.f. quantity; crowd, multitude; (eine M.) a lot.

Mensch, **-en**, **-en**, n.m. human being, person; man.

Menschenfeind, **-e**, n.m. misanthrope.

Menschenfreund, **-e**, n.m. humanitarian.

Menschenliebe, n.f. philanthropy.

Menschenmenge, **-n**, n.f. mob.

Menschenrechte, n.pl. human rights.

Menschenverstand, n.m. (gesunder M.) common sense.

Menschheit, n.f. mankind, humanity.

menschlich, adj. human; humane.

Menschlichkeit, n.f. humanity.

Menstruation', n.f. menstruation.

Mentalität', n.f. mentality.

Menthol', n.nt. menthol.

Menü, **-s**, n.nt. menu.

merken, vb. realize, notice; (sich m.) keep in mind; (sich nichts m. lassen*) not give oneself away.

Merkmal, **-e**, n.nt. mark, characteristic.

---

merkwürdig, adj. peculiar, odd, queer.

Messe, **-n**, n.f. fair; (eccles.) mass.

messen*, vb. measure; gauge; (sich m.) match.

Messer, **-**, n.nt. knife.

Messi'as, n.m. Messiah.

Messing, n.nt. brass.

Metall', **-e**, n.nt. metal.

metal'len, adj. metallic.

metal'lisch, adj. metallic.

Metall'waren, n.pl. hardware.

Meteor', **-e**, n.m. or nt. meteor.

Meteorologie', n.f. meteorology.

Meter, **-**, n.m. or nt. meter.

Metho'de, **-n**, n.f. method.

metrisch, adj. metric.

Metzger, **-**, n.m. butcher.

Metzgerei', **-en**, n.f. butcher shop.

Meuterei', **-en**, n.f. mutiny.

meutern, vb. mutiny.

Mexika'ner, **-**, n.m. Mexican.

mexika'nisch, adj. Mexican.

Mexiko, n.nt. Mexico.

Mieder, **-**, n.nt. bodice.

Miene, **-n**, n.f. mien.

Mienenspiel, **-e**, n.nt. pantomime.

Miete, **-n**, n.f. rent, rental.

mieten, vb. rent, lease, hire.

Mieter, **-**, n.m. tenant.

Mietvertrag, **:e**, n.m. lease.

Mietwohnung, **-en**, n.f. flat, apartment.

Migrä'ne, n.f. migraine.

Mikro'be, **-n**, n.f. microbe.

Mikrofilm, **-e**, n.m. microfilm.

Mikrophon', **-e**, n.nt. microphone.

Mikroskop', **-e**, n.nt. microscope.

Milbe, **-n**, n.f. mite.

Milch, n.f. milk.

Milchhändler, **-**, n.m. dairyman.

milchig, adj. milky.

Milchmann, **:er**, n.m. milkman.

Milchwirtschaft, **-en**, n.f. dairy.

mild, adj. mild, gentle, lenient.

Milde, n.f. mildness, leniency, clemency.

mildern, vb. mitigate, alleviate, soften; (mildernde Umstände) extenuating circumstances.

Milderung, **-en**, n.f. alleviation.

Militär', **-s**, n.nt. military.

Militär'dienstpflicht, **-en**, n.f. conscription.

militä'risch, adj. military.

Militaris'mus, n.m. militarism.

militaris'tisch, adj. militaristic.

Miliz', **-en**, n.f. militia.

Millime'ter, **-**, n.nt. millimeter.

Million', **-en**, n.f. million.

Millionär', **-e**, n.m. millionaire.

Milz, **-en**, n.f. spleen.

Minderheit, **-en**, n.f. minority.

minderjährig, adj. minor, not of age.

Minderjährigkeit, n.f. minority.

mindern, vb. reduce.

minderwertig, adj. inferior.

mindestens, adv. at least.

Mine, -n, n.f. mine.

Mineral', -e or ien, n.nt. mineral.

minera'lisch, adj. mineral.

Miniatur', -en, n.f. miniature.

minimal', adj. minimum, minute.

Minimum, -ma, n.nt. minimum.

Mini'ster, -, n.m. (cabinet) minister.

Ministe'rium, -rien, n.nt. ministry, department.

Mini'sterpräsident, -en, -en, n.m. prime minister.

minus, adv. minus.

Minu'te, -n, n.f. minute.

Minz'e, -n, n.f. mint.

mischen, vb. mix, mingle, blend.

Mischmasch, -e, n.m. hodgepodge.

Mischung, -en, n.f. mixture, blend.

mißachten, vb. disregard; slight.

Mißachtung, -en, n.f. disdain.

Mißbildung, -en, n.f. abnormality, deformity.

mißbilligen, vb. disapprove.

Mißbrauch, ˙e, n.m. abuse, misuse.

mißbrau'chen, vb. abuse.

mißdeu'ten, vb. misconstrue.

missen, vb. do without.

Mißerfolg, -e, n.m. failure.

Missetat, -en, n.f. misdeed, crime.

Missetäter, -, n.m. offender.

mißfal'len°, vb. displease.

Mißfallen, n.nt. displeasure.

Mißgeburt, -en, n.f. freak.

Mißgeschick, -e, n.nt. adversity, misfortune.

mißglü'cken, vb. fail.

mißglückt', adj. unsuccessful, abortive.

mißgön'nen, vb. begrudge.

mißhan'deln, vb. mistreat, maltreat.

Mission', -en, n.f. mission.

Missionar', -e, n.m. missionary.

Mißklang, ˙e, n.m. discord.

mißlin'gen°, vb. miscarry, fail.

mißra'ten, adj. ill-bred, low.

mißtrau'en, vb. distrust.

Mißtrauen, n.nt. distrust.

mißtrauisch, adj. suspicious, distrustful.

mißvergnügt, adj. cranky.

Mißverhältnis, -se, n.nt. disproportion.

Mißverständnis, -se, n.nt. misunderstanding.

mißverstechen°, vb. misunderstand.

Mist, n.m. manure, muck.

mistig, adj. misty.

mit, prep. with.

Mitarbeit, n.f. cooperation, collaboration.

mit·arbeiten, vb. collaborate.

Mitarbeiter, -, n.m. collaborator; (anonymer M.) ghost writer.

Mitbewerber, -, n.m. competitor.

mit·bringen°, vb. bring along; bring a present.

Mitbürger, -, n.m. fellow citizen.

miteinan'der, adv. together, jointly.

miteinbegriffen, adj. included; implied.

mitempfunden, adj. sympathizing; vicarious.

mit·fühlen, vb. sympathize.

mitfühlend, adj. sympathetic.

Mitgefühl, n.nt. sympathy.

mitgenommen, adj. the worse for wear.

Mitgift, -en, n.f. dowry.

Mitglied, -er, n.nt. member, fellow.

Mitgliedschaft, n.f. membership.

Mithelfer, -, n.m. accessory.

Mitleid, n.nt. pity, compassion; mercy.

mitleidig, adj. compassionate.

mit·machen, vb. string along, join, conform.

Mitmacher, -, n.m. conformer.

Mitmensch, -en, -en, n.m. fellow-man.

Mitschuld, n.f. complicity.

mitschuldig, adj. being an accessory.

Mitschüler, -, n.m. classmate.

Mitspieler, -, n.m. player.

Mittag, n.m. midday, noon.

Mittagessen, -, n.nt. noon meal, lunch, dinner.

Mittäter, -, n.m. accomplice.

Mitte, -n, n.f. middle, midst, center.

mit·teilbar, adj. communicable.

mit·teilen, vb. inform, communicate.

Mitteilung, -en, n.f. information, communication.

Mittel, -, n.nt. means, measure, expedient; medium.

mittel, adj. mean.

Mittelalter, n.nt. Middle Ages.

mittelalterlich, adj. medieval.

mittellos, adj. penniless, destitute.

mittelmäßig, adj. mediocre.

Mittelmeer, n.nt. Mediterranean Sea.

Mittelpunkt, -e, n.m. center, focus.

mittels, prep. by means of.

Mittelstand, n.m. middle class.

Mitternacht, n.f. midnight.

mittler-, adj. medium, middle.

Mittler-Osten, n.m. Middle East.

mittschiffs, adv. amidships.

Mittwoch, -e, n.m. Wednesday.

mit·wirken, vb. cooperate, assist, contribute.

mitwirkend, adj. contributory.

Möbel, -, n.nt. piece of furniture; (pl.) furniture.

Möbelwagen, -, n.m. moving van.

mobil', adj. mobile; (fig.) hale and hearty.

mobilisie'ren, vb. mobilize.

mobilisiert', adj. mobile.

möblie'ren, vb. furnish.

Mode, -n, n.f. mode, fashion.

Modell', -e, n.nt. model.

modellie'ren, vb. model.

Modenschau, n.f. fashion show.

modern, vb. rot.

modern', adj. modern, fashionable.

modernisie'ren, vb. modernize.

Modeschöpfer, -, n.m. designer.

modifizie'ren, vb. modify.

modisch, adj. modish, fashionable.

Mofa, -s, n.nt. moped.

mögen°, vb. like; may.

möglich, adj. possible; potential.

möglicherweise, adv. possibly.

Möglichkeit, -en, n.f. possibility; potential; facility.

Mohr, -en, -en, n.m. Moor.

Mehrrübe, -n, n.f. carrot.

Mole, -n, n.f. mole, jetty, breakwater.

Molkerei', -en, n.f. dairy.

Moll, n.nt. minor.

mollig, adj. plump; snug.

Moment', -e, n.m. moment, instant.

Moment', -e, n.nt. factor, impulse, motive.

momentan', adj. momentary.

Monarch', -en, -en, n.m. monarch.

Monarchie', -i'en, n.f. monarchy.

Monat, -e, n.m. month.

monatlich, adj. monthly.

Monatschrift, -en, n.f. monthly.

Mönch, -e, n.m. monk.

Mond, -e, n.m. moon.

Mondschein, n.m. moonlight.

Mondsichel, -n, n.f. crescent moon.

Monolog', -e, n.m. monologue.

Monopol', -e, n.nt. monopoly.

monopolisie'ren, vb. monopolize.

monoton', adj. monotonous.

Monotonie', n.f. monotony.

monströs', adj. monstrous, freak.

Montag, -e, n.m. Monday.

Montan'union, n.f. European Coal and Steel Community.

montie'ren, vb. assemble, mount.

monumental', adj. monumental.

Moor, -e, n.nt. moor.

Moos, -e, n.nt. moss.

Mop, -s, n.m. mop.

Moral', n.f. morals; morality; morale.

mora'lisch, adj. moral, ethical.

Moralist', -e, -en, n.m. moralist.

Morast', -e, n.m. morass, bog.

Mord, -e, n.m. murder, assassination.

morden, vb. murder.

Mörder, -, n.m. murderer.

Mords-, cpds. mortal; heck of a . . . .

morgen, adv. tomorrow.

Morgen, -, n.m. morning; acre.

Morgendämmerung, -en, n.f. dawn.

Morgenrock, ⁀e, n.m. dressing gown.

morgens, adv. in the morning.

Morphium, n.nt. morphine.

morsch, adj. rotten.

Mörser, -, n.m. mortar.

Mörtel, -, n.m. mortar.

Mosaik', -e, n.nt. mosaic.

Most, -e, n.m. grape juice, new wine; (Apfelmost) cider.

Mostrich, n.m. mustard.

Motiv', -e, n.nt. motif.

motivie'ren, vb. motivate.

Motivie'rung, -en, n.f. motivation.

Motor('), -o'ren, n.m. motor, engine.

motorisie'ren, vb. motorize, mechanize.

Motor'rad, ⁀er, n.nt. motorcycle.

Motte, -n, n.f. moth.

Motto, -s, n.nt. motto.

Mücke, -n, n.f. mosquito.

mucksen, vb. stir.

müde, adj. tired, sleepy; weary.

Müdigkeit, n.f. fatigue.

Muff, -e, n.m. muff.

muffig, adj. musty.

Mühe, -n, n.f. trouble, inconvenience; effort; (machen Sie sich keine M.) don't bother.

mühelos, adj. effortless.

mühen, vb. (sich m.) try, take the trouble.

Mühle, -n, n.f. mill.

Muhme, -n, n.f. aunt.

Mühsal, -e, n.f. trouble, hardship.

mühsam, adj. difficult, tedious, inconvenient.

mühselig, adj. laborious.

Mull, n.m. gauze.

Müll, n.m. garbage.

Mullah, -s, n.m. mullah.

Müller, -, n.m. miller.

multinational', adj. multinational.

Multiplikation', -en, n.f. multiplication.

multiplizie'ren, vb. multiply.

Mumie, -n, n.f. mummy.

Mund, ⁀er, n.m. mouth.

Mundart, -en, n.f. dialect.

Mündel, -, n.nt. ward.

münden, vb. run, flow into, end.

mündlich, adj. oral, verbal.

Mündung, -en, n.f. (river) mouth; (gun) muzzle.

Munition', -en, n.f. ammunition, munition.

munkeln, vb. rumor.

munter, adj. awake; sprightly, lusty.

Münze, -n, n.f. coin; mint.

mürbe, adj. mellow; (meat) tender; (cake) crisp; (fig.) weary.

murmeln, vb. murmur, mutter.

murren, vb. grumble.

mürrisch, adj. disgruntled, petulant, glum.

Mürrischkeit, n.f. glumness.

Muschel, -n, n.f. shell; mussel, clam.

Muse, -n, n.f. muse.

Muse'um, -e'en, n.nt. museum.

Musik', n.f. music.

musika'lisch, adj. musical.

Musikant', -en, -en, n.m. musician.

Musiker, -, n.m. musician.

Musik'kapelle, -n, n.f. band, orchestra.

Musik'pavillon, -s, n.m. bandstand.

Muskat', -n, n.m. nutmeg.

Muskel, -n, n.m. muscle.

Muskelkraft, ⁀e, n.f. muscular strength, brawn.

muskulös, adj. muscular.

Muße, n.f. leisure.

Musselin', -e, n.m. muslin.

müssen*, vb. must, have to.

müßig, adj. idle.

Müßigkeit, n.f. idleness.

Muster, -, n.nt. model; sample; pattern, design.

Musterbeispiel, -e, n.nt. paragon, perfect example.

mustergültig, adj. exemplary, model.

musterhaft, adj. exemplary.

mustern, vb. examine; (mil.) muster.

Musterung, -en, n.f. examination; (mil.) muster; (pattern) figuring.

Mut, n.m. courage, fortitude.

Mutation', -en, n.f. mutation.

mutig, adj. courageous.

Mutigkeit, n.f. pluck.

mutmaßen, vb. conjecture.

mutmaßlich, adj. presumable.

Mutmaßung, -en, n.f. conjecture.

Mutter, ⁀, n.f. mother.

Mutterleib, n.m. womb.

mütterlich, adj. maternal.

Mutterschaft, n.f. maternity.

mutterseelenallein', adj. all alone.

Muttersprache, -n, n.f. native language.

mutwillig, adj. deliberate, wilful.

Mütze, -n, n.f. cap, bonnet.

Myrte, -n, n.f. myrtle.

mysteriös', adj. mysterious.

Mystik, n.f. mysticism.

mystisch, adj. mystic.

Mythe, -n, n.f. myth.

N

na, interj. well; (n. also) there you are; (n. und ob) I should say so.

Nabe, -n, n.f. hub.

nach, prep. towards, to; after; according to; (n. und n.) by and by, gradually.

nach-affen, vb. ape, imitate.

nach-ahmen, vb. imitate, simulate.

Nachahmung, -en, n.f. imitation.

Nachbar, (-n,) -n, n.m. neighbor.

Nachbarschaft, -en, n.f. neighborhood.

nachdem', conj. after.

nach-denken*, vb. think, meditate, reflect.

nachdenklich, adj. contemplative, pensive.

Nachdruck, n.m. emphasis.

nachdrücklich, adj. emphatic.

nach-eifern, vb. emulate.

Nachfolger, -, n.m. successor.

Nachforschung, -en, n.f. investigation; research.

Nachfrage, -n, n.f. inquiry; (Angebot und N.) supply and demand.

nach-fühlen, vb. understand, appreciate.

nach-füllen, vb. refill.

nach-geben*, vb. give in, yield.

nach-gehen*, vb. follow; seek; (clock) be slow.

nachgiebig, adj. compliant.

nachhaltig, adj. lasting.

nach-helfen*, vb. assist, boost.

nachher, adv. afterward(s).

Nachhilfe, n.f. assistance.

Nachhilfelehrer, -, n.m. tutor.

nach-holen, vb. make up for.

Nachkomme, -n, -n, n.m. descendant.

Nachlaß, ⁀sse, n.m. estate.

nach-lassen*, vb. abate, subside.

nachlässig, adj. negligent, careless, derelict.

Nachlässigkeit, -en, n.f. negligence, carelessness.

nach-machen, vb. imitate.

Nachmittag, -e, n.m. afternoon.

Nachmittagsvorstellung, -en, n.f. matinee.

Nachnahme, -n, n.f. (per N.) C.O.D.

nach-prüfen, vb. check up, verify.

Nachricht, -en, n.f. information, message, notice; (pl.) news.

Nachrichtensendung, n.f. newscast.

nach-schlagen*, vb. look up, refer to.

Nachschrift, -en, n.f. postscript.

nach-sehen*, vb. look after;

look up; examine, check; *(fig.)* excuse, indulge.

Nachsehen, *n.nt.* **(das N. haben*)** be the loser.

Nachsicht, -en, *n.f.* indulgence, forbearance.

nachsichtig, *adj.* lenient, indulgent.

Nachspiel, -e, *n.nt.* postlude.

nach-spüren, *vb.* track down.

nächst-, *adj.* next nearest.

nach-stehen*, *vb.* be inferior.

nach-stellen, *vb.* pursue; (clock) put back.

Nächstenliebe, *n.f.* charity.

nächstens, *adv.* soon.

Nacht, -̈e, *n.f.* night.

Nachteil, -e, *n.m.* disadvantage, drawback.

nachteilig, *adj.* disadvantageous, adverse.

Nachthemd, -en, *n.nt.* nightgown.

Nachtigall, -en, *n.f.* nightingale.

Nachtisch, -e, *n.m.* dessert.

nächtlich, *adj.* nocturnal.

Nachtlokal, -e, *n.nt.* night club.

Nachtrag, -̈e, *n.m.* supplement.

nach-tragen*, *vb.* carry behind; *(fig.)* resent, bear a grudge.

Nachtwache, -n, *n.f.* vigil.

Nachweis, -e, *n.m.* proof, certificate.

nachweisbar, *adj.* demonstrable.

nach-weisen*, *vb.* demonstrate, prove.

Nachwelt, *n.f.* posterity.

Nachwirkung, -en, *n.f.* aftereffect.

nach-zählen, *vb.* count over again, count up.

nach-zeichnen, *vb.* trace.

nackt, *adj.* naked, nude; bare.

Nacktheit, *n.f.* nakedness, bareness.

Nadel, -n, *n.f.* needle, pin.

Nagel, -̈, *n.m.* nail.

nagen, *vb.* gnaw.

Nagetier, -e, *n.nt.* rodent.

nah(e) (näher, nächst-), *adj.* near.

Nähe, *n.f.* vicinity, proximity.

nähen, *vb.* sew.

Näherin, -nen, *n.f.* seamstress.

nähern, *vb.* (**sich n.**) approach.

nähren, *vb.* nourish; nurture.

nahrhaft, *adj.* nutritious, nourishing.

Nahrung, -en, *n.f.* nourishment, food.

Nahrungsmittel, *n.pl.* foodstuffs.

Naht, -̈e, *n.f.* seam.

naiv', *adj.* naïve.

Name(n), -, *n.m.* name.

namentlich, *adv.* by name, namely; considerable.

namhaft, *adj.* renowned.

nämlich, *adv.* that is to say, namely.

nanu', *interj.* well, what do you know?

Naphtha, *n.nt.* naphtha.

Narbe, -n, *n.f.* scar.

Narko'se, -n, *n.f.* anesthetic.

narko'tisch, *adj.* narcotic, anesthetic.

Narr, -en, -en, *n.m.* fool; (**zum N. halten***) fool, make a fool of.

narrensicher, *adj.* foolproof.

närrisch, *adj.* foolish, daffy.

Narzis'se, -n, *n.f.* narcissus; (**gelbe N.**) daffodil.

nasal', *adj.* nasal.

naschen, *vb.* nibble (secretly) on sweets.

Nase, -n, *n.f.* nose.

Nasenbluten, *n.nt.* nosebleed.

Nasenloch, -̈er, *n.nt.* nostril.

Nasenschleim, *n.m.* mucus.

naseweis, *adj.* fresh, know-it-all.

naß(-), *adj.* wet.

Nässe, *n.f.* wetness, moisture.

nässen, *vb.* wet.

Nation', -en, *n.f.* nation.

national', *adj.* national.

Nationalis'mus, *n.m.* nationalism.

Nationalität', -en, *n.f.* nationality.

National'ökonomie, *n.f.* political economics.

Natrium, *n.nt.* sodium.

Natron, *n.nt.* sodium.

Natur', -en, *n.f.* nature.

Natura'lien, *n.pl.* food produce.

naturalisie'ren, *vb.* naturalize.

Naturalist', -en, -en, *n.m.* naturalist.

Natur'forscher, -, *n.m.* naturalist.

Natur'kunde, *n.f.* nature study.

natür'lich, 1. *adj.* natural. **2.** *adv.* of course.

Natür'lichkeit, *n.f.* naturalness.

Natur'wissenschaftler, *n.m.* scientist.

nautisch, *adj.* nautical.

Navigation', *n.f.* navigation.

Nebel, -, *n.m.* fog, mist.

Nebelfleck, -e, *n.m.* nebula.

nebelhaft, *adj.* nebulous.

neb(e)lig, *adj.* foggy.

neben, *prep.* beside.

Nebenanschluß, -̈sse, *n.m.* (telephone) extension.

nebenbei', *adv.* besides; by the way, incidentally.

Nebenbuhler, -, *n.m.* rival.

nebeneinan'der, *adv.* beside one another, abreast.

Nebengebäude, -, *n.nt.* annex.

Nebenprodukt, -e, *n.nt.* byproduct.

Nebensache, -n, *n.f.* incidental matter.

nebensächlich, *adj.* incidental, irrelevant.

Nebenweg, -e, *n.m.* byway.

nebst, *prep.* with, including.

necken, *vb.* tease, kid.

neckisch, *adj.* playful, cute.

Neffe, -n, -n, *n.m.* nephew.

negativ', *adj.* negative.

Negativ', -e, *n.nt.* negative.

Neger, -, *n.m.* Negro.

Negligé, -s, *n.nt.* negligee.

nehmen*, *vb.* take.

Neid, *n.m.* envy.

neidisch, *adj.* envious.

neigen, *vb. (tr.)* incline, bow, bend; *(intr.)* lean, slant; *(fig.)* tend.

Neigung, -en, *n.f.* inclination; slant; tendency, trend; affection.

nein, *interj.* no.

Nelke, -n, *n.f.* carnation.

nennen*, *vb.* name, call.

nennenswert, *adj.* considerable, worth mentioning.

Nenner, -, *n.m.* denominator.

Nennwert, -e, *n.m.* denomination; face value.

Neon, *n.nt.* neon.

Nerv, -en, *n.m.* nerve.

Nervenkitzel, -, *n.m.* thrill.

nervös', *adj.* nervous, jittery; high-strung.

Nervosität', *n.f.* nervousness.

Nerz, -e, *n.m.* mink.

Nessel, -n, *n.f.* nettle.

Nest, -er, *n.nt.* nest.

nett, *adj.* nice, enjoyable.

netto, *adj.* net.

Netz, -e, *n.nt.* net, web; network.

Netzhaut, -̈e, *n.f.* retina.

neu, *adj.* new; (**aufs neue, von neuem**) anew.

Neubelebung, -en, *n.f.* revival.

Neuerung, -en, *n.f.* innovation.

Neugierde, *n.f.* curiosity.

neugierig, *adj.* curious, inquisitive.

Neuheit, -en, *n.f.* novelty.

Neuigkeit, -en, *n.f.* news; novelty.

Neujahr, *n.nt.* New Year; (**Fröhliches N.**) Happy New Year.

neulich, *adv.* the other day, recently.

Neuling, -e, *n.m.* novice.

neun, *num.* nine.

neunt-, *adj.* ninth.

Neuntel, -, *n.nt.* ninth part; (**ein n.**) one-ninth.

neunzig, *num.* ninety.

neunzigst-, *adj.* ninetieth.

Neunzigstel, -, *n.nt.* ninetieth part; (**ein n.**) one-ninetieth.

Neuralgie', *n.f.* neuralgia.

neuro'tisch, *adj.* neurotic.

neutral', *adj.* neutral.

Neutralität', *n.f.* neutrality.

Neutron, -o'nen, *n.nt.* neutron.

Neutro'nenbombe, -n, *n.f.* neutron bomb.

nicht, *adv.* not; (**n. wahr**) isn't that so, don't you, aren't we, won't they, etc.

Nichtachtung, *n.f.* disregard, disrespect.

Nichtanerkennung, -en, *n.f.* nonrecognition; repudiation.

Nichtbeachtung, *n.f.* disregard.

Nichte, -n, *n.f.* niece.

nichtig, *adj.* null, void.

nichts, *pron.* nothing.

Nichts, *n.nt.* nothingness, non-entity.

nichtsdestoweniger, *adv.* notwithstanding, nevertheless.

Nichtswisser, -, *n.m.* ignoramus.

nichtswürdig, *adj.* worthless, condemnable.

Nickel, *n.nt.* nickel.

nicken, *vb.* nod.

nie, *adv.* never.

nieder, *adv.* down.

Niedergang, *n.m.* decline.

niedergedrückt, *adj.* depressed.

niedergeschlagen, *adj.* dejected.

Niederkunft, *n.f.* childbirth.

Niederlage, -n, *n.f.* defeat; branch office.

Niederlande, *n.pl.* Netherlands.

Niederländer, -, *n.m.* Netherlander, Dutchman.

niederländisch, *adj.* Netherlandic, Dutch.

nieder-lassen*, *vb.* (**sich n.**) settle.

Niederlassung, -en, *n.f.* settlement.

nieder-metzeln, *vb.* massacre.

Niederschlag, ̈e, *n.m.* precipitation; sediment.

Niedertracht, *n.f.* meanness, infamy.

niederträchtig, *adj.* mean, vile, infamous.

niedlich, *adj.* pretty, cute.

niedrig, *adj.* low; base, menial.

niemals, *adv.* never.

niemand, *pron.* no one, nobody.

Niere, -n, *n.f.* kidney.

nieseln, *vb.* drizzle.

niesen, *vb.* sneeze.

Niete, -n, *n.f.* rivet; (lottery) blank; failure, washout.

Nihilismus, *n.m.* nihilism.

Nikotin', *n.nt.* nicotine.

nimmer, *adv.* never.

nimmermehr, *adv.* never again.

nirgends, nirgendwo, *adv.* nowhere.

Nische, -n, *n.f.* recess, niche.

nisten, *vb.* nestle.

Niveau', -s, *n.nt.* level.

nobel, *adj.* noble; liberal.

noch, *adv.* still, yet; (**n. einmal**) once more; (**n. ein**) another, an additional; (**weder . . . n.**) neither . . . nor.

nochmalig, *adj.* additional, repeated.

nochmal(s), *adv.* once more.

Noma'de, -n, -n, *n.m.* nomad.

nominal', *adj.* nominal.

Nonne, -n, *n.f.* nun.

Nonnenkloster, ̈e, *n.nt.* convent.

Nord, Norden, *n.m.* north.

nördlich, *adj.* northern; to the north.

Nordos'ten, *n.m.* northeast.

nordöst'lich, *adj.* northeastern; to the northeast.

Nordpol, *n.m.* North Pole.

Nordwes'ten, *n.m.* northwest.

nordwest'lich, *adj.* northwestern; to the northwest.

nörgeln, *vb.* gripe.

Norm, -en, *n.f.* norm, standard.

normal', *adj.* normal.

Norwegen, *n.nt.* Norway.

Norweger, -, *n.m.* Norwegian.

norwegisch, *adj.* Norwegian.

Not, ̈e, *n.f.* need, necessity; hardship; distress.

Notar', -e, *n.m.* notary.

Notbehelf, *n.m.* makeshift, stop-gap.

Notdurft, *n.f.* want; need.

notdürftig, *adj.* scanty, bare.

Note, -n, *n.f.* note.

Notfall, ̈e, *n.m.* emergency.

notgedrungen, *adv.* perforce.

notie'ren, *vb.* note, make a note.

Notie'rung, -en, *n.f.* quotation.

nötig, *adj.* necessary.

nötigen, *vb.* urge.

Notiz', -en, *n.f.* note.

Notiz'block, ̈e, *n.m.* notepaper pad.

Notiz'buch, ̈er, *n.nt.* notebook.

notleidend, *adj.* needy.

notwendig, *adj.* necessary.

Notwendigkeit, -en, *n.f.* necessity.

Novel'le, -n, *n.f.* short story.

Novem'ber, *n.m.* November.

Nu, *n.m.* jiffy.

nüchtern, *adj.* sober; (**auf nüchternen Magen**) on an empty stomach.

Nüchternheit, *n.f.* sobriety; unimaginativeness.

Nudeln, *n.pl.* noodles.

nuklear', *adj.* nuclear.

Null, -en, *n.f.* cipher; zero.

numerie'ren, *vb.* number.

nun, *adv.* now; (**von n. an**) henceforth.

nur, *adv.* only

Nuß, ̈sse, *n.f.* nut.

Nußschale, -n, *n.f.* nutshell.

Nüster, -n, *n.f.* nostril.

Nutzbarkeit, *n.f.* utility.

Nutzen, -, *n.m.* benefit.

nützen, *vb.* use, utilize; (*intr.*) be of use, help, benefit.

nützlich, *adj.* useful, beneficial.

nutzlos, *adj.* useless, futile.

Nutzlosigkeit, *n.f.* futility.

Nylon, *n.nt.* nylon.

Nymphe, -n, *n.f.* nymph.

O

Oa'se, -n, *n.f.* oasis.

ob, *conj.* whether; (**als o.**) as if.

Obdach, *n.nt.* shelter.

obdachlos, *adj.* homeless.

oben, *adv.* above; upstairs.

ober-, *adj.* upper.

Ober, -, *n.m.* (= Oberkellner) headwaiter, waiter; (**Herr O.!**) waiter!

Oberbefehlshaber, -, *n.m.* commander-in-chief.

Oberfläche, -n, *n.f.* surface.

oberflächlich, *adj.* superficial.

Oberhaupt, ̈er, *n.nt.* chief.

Oberherrschaft, *n.f.* sovereignty.

Oberschicht, *n.f.* upper stratum; upper classes; (geistige O.) intelligentsia.

oberst-, *adj.* supreme, paramount.

Oberst, -en, -en, *n.m.* colonel.

Oberstleut'nant, -s, *n.m.* lieutenant colonel.

obgleich', *conj.* although.

Obhut, *n.f.* keeping, charge.

obig, *adj.* above, aforesaid.

Objekt' -e, *n.nt.* object.

objektiv', *adj.* objective.

Objektiv', -e, *n.nt.* objective; lens.

Objektivität', *n.f.* objectivity, detachment.

Obliegenheit, -en, *n.f.* duty, obligation.

Obligation', -en, *n.f.* bond; obligation.

obligato'risch, *adj.* obligatory.

Obrigkeit, -en, *n.f.* authorities, government.

obschon', *conj.* although.

ob-siegen, *vb.* be victorious over.

Obst, *n.nt.* fruit.

Obstgarten, ̈, *n.m.* orchard.

obszön', *adj.* obscene.

Obus, -se, *n.m.* (= Oberleitungsomnibus) trolley bus.

ob-walten, *vb.* prevail, exist.

obwohl', *conj.* although.

Ochse, -n, -n *or* Ochs, -en, -en, *n.m.* ox.

öde, *adj.* bleak, desolate.

Öde, -n, *n.f.* bleakness, waste place.

oder, *conj.* or.

Ofen, ̈, *n.m.* stove, oven, furnace.

offen, *adj.* open, frank.

offenbar, *adj.* evident.

offenba'ren, *vb.* reveal.

Offenba'rung, -en, *n.f.* revelation.

Offenba'rungsschrift, -en, *n.f.* scripture.

Offenheit, *n.f.* frankness.

offenkundig, *adj.* manifest.

offensichtlich, *adj.* obvious.

Offensi've, -n, *n.f.* offense, offensive.

öffentlich, *adj.* public.

Öffentlichkeit, *n.f.* public.

offiziell', *adj.* official.

Offizier', -e, *n.m.* officer.

öffnen, *vb.* open.

Öffnung, -en, *n.f.* opening, aperture.

oft (̈), *adv.* often.

öfters, *adv.* quite often.

oftmals, *adv.* often (times).

Oheim, -e, *n.m.* uncle.

ohne, *prep.* without.

ohneglei'chen, *adv.* unequalled.

ohnehin, adv. in any case.

Ohnmacht, n.f. faint, unconsciousness; (in O. fallen*) faint.

ohnmächtig, adj. in a faint, powerless.

Ohr, -en, n.nt. ear.

Ohr, -e, n.nt. eye (of a needle, etc.).

Ohrenschmerzen, n.pl. earache.

Ohrring, -e, n.m. earring.

okay, pred. adv. okay.

okkult', adj. occult.

Ökologie', n.f. ecology.

ökologisch, adj. ecological.

Ökonom', -en, -en, n.m. farmer, manager.

Ökonomie', -i'en, n.f. economy; agriculture.

ökono'misch, adj. economical.

Okta've, -n, n.f. octave.

Okto'ber, n.m. October.

öku'me'nisch, adj. ecumenical.

Okzident, n.m. occident.

Öl, -e, n.nt. oil.

ölen, vb. oil.

ölig, adj. oily.

Oli've, -e, n.f. olive.

Ölung, -en, n.f. oiling; anointment; (letzt Ö.) extreme unction.

Oma, -s, n.f. granny, grandma.

Ombudsmann, ⸗er, n.m. ombudsman.

Omelett', -e, n.nt. omelet.

Omnibus, -se, n.m. (omni)bus.

ondulie'ren, vb. wave (hair).

Onkel, -, n.m. uncle.

Opa, -s, n.m. grandpa.

Opal', -e, n.m. opal.

Oper, -n, n.f. opera.

Operation', -en, n.f. operation.

operativ', adj. operative.

Operet'te, -n, n.f. operetta.

operie'ren, vb. operate.

Operngias, ⸗er, n.nt. opera glasses.

Opfer, -, n.nt. offering, sacrifice; victim, casualty.

opfern, adv. sacrifice.

Opium, n.nt. opium.

opponie'ren, vb. oppose.

Opposition', -en, n.f. opposition.

Optik, n.f. optics.

Optiker, -, n.m. optician.

Optimis'mus, n.m. optimism.

optimis'tisch, adj. optimistic.

optisch, adj. optic.

Oran'ge, -e, n.f. orange.

Orches'ter, -, n.nt. orchestra.

Orchide'e, -n, n.f. orchid.

Orden, -, n.m. order, medal, decoration.

ordentlich, adj. orderly, decent, regular.

ordinär', adj. vulgar.

ordnen, vb. put in order, sort, arrange.

Ordnung, -en, n.f. order.

Organ', -e, n.nt. organ.

Organisation', -en, n.f. organization.

orga'nisch, adj. organic.

organisie'ren, vb. organize; scrounge.

Organis'mus, -men, n.m. organism.

Organist', -en, -en, n.m. organist.

Orgel, -n, n.f. organ.

Orgie, -n, n.f. orgy.

Orient, n.m. Orient.

orienta'lisch, adj. oriental.

orientie'ren, vb. orient(ate).

Orientie'rung, -en, n.f. orientation.

Original', -e, n.nt. original.

Originalität', -en, n.f. originality.

originell', adj. original.

Ort, -e, n.m. place, locality, town.

Orter, -, n.m. navigator.

orthodox', adj. orthodox.

örtlich, adj. local.

ortsansässig, adj. resident, indigenous.

Ortschaft, -en, n.f. town, village.

Ost, Osten, n.m. east.

Ostblockstaaten, n.m.pl. Eastern European Nations.

Ostern, n.nt. Easter.

Österreich, n.nt. Austria.

Österreicher, -, n.m. Austrian.

österreichisch, adj. Austrian.

östlich, adj. eastern, easterly.

Ostsee, n.f. Baltic Sea.

ostwärts, adv. eastward.

Otter, -, n.m. otter.

Otter, -n, n.f. adder.

Ouvertü're, -n, n.f. overture.

oval', adj. oval.

Ozean, -e, n.m. ocean.

Ozeandampfer, -, n.m. ocean liner.

Ozon', -e, n.nt. ozone.

P

Paar, -e, n.nt. pair, couple; (ein paar) a few.

paaren, vb. mate.

Pacht, -en, n.f. lease, tenure.

Pachtbrief, -e, n.m. lease (document).

pachten, vb. lease (from).

Pächter, -, n.m. tenant.

Pachtzins, n.m. rent (money).

Pack, ⸗e, n.m. pack; rabble.

packen, vb. pack, seize, thrill.

Packen, -, n.m. pack.

Packung, -en, n.f. packing, wrapper, pack(age).

Pädago'ge, -n, -n, n.m. pedagogue.

Pädago'gik, n.f. pedagogy.

Paddel, -, n.nt. paddle.

paff, interj. bang.

Page, -n, -n, n.m. page.

Paket', -e, n.nt. package.

Pakt, -e, n.m. pact.

Palast', ⸗e, n.m. palace.

Palet'te, -n, n.f. palette.

Palme, -n, n.f. palm.

Pampelmu'se, -n, n.f. grapefruit.

Panik, n.f. panic.

Panne, -n, n.f. breakdown; flat tire.

Panora'ma, -men, n.nt. panorama.

Panther, -, n.m. panther.

Pantof'fel, -n, n.f. slipper.

Pantomi'me, -n, n.f. pantomime.

Panzer, -, n.m. armor; tank.

Panzer-, cpds. armored.

Papagei', -en, -en, n.m. parrot.

Papier', -e, n.nt. paper.

Papier'bogen, ⸗, n.m. sheet of paper.

Papier'korb, ⸗e, n.m. wastebasket.

Papier'krieg, -e, n.m. red tape, paperwork.

Papier'waren, n.pl. stationery.

Papp, -e, n.m. pap, paste.

Pappe, -n, n.f. cardboard.

Papst, ⸗e, n.m. pope.

päpstlich, adj. papal.

Papsttum, n.nt. papacy.

Para'de, -n, n.f. parade.

Paradies, n.nt. paradise.

paradox', adj. paradoxical.

Paradox', -e, n.nt. paradox.

Paraffin', -e, n.nt. paraffin.

Paragraph', -en, -en, n.m. paragraph.

parallel', adj. parallel.

Paralle'le, -n, n.f. parallel.

Paraly'se, -n, n.f. paralysis.

Parenthe'se, -n, n.f. parenthesis.

Parfüm', -e, n.nt. perfume.

pari, adv. at par.

Pari, n.nt. par.

Paris', n.nt. Paris.

Pari'ser, -, n.m. Parisian.

Park, -e or -s, n.m. park.

parken, vb. park.

Parkuhr, -en, n.f. parking meter.

Parkverbot, -e, n.nt. no parking.

Parlament', -e, n.nt. parliament.

parlamenta'risch, adj. parliamentary.

Parodie, -i'en, n.f. parody.

Paro'le, -n, n.f. password.

Partei', -en, n.f. party.

Partei'genosse, -n, -n, n.m. party comrade.

partei'isch, adj. partisan, biased.

partei'lich, adj. partisan, biased.

partei'los, adj. impartial.

Parter're, -s, n.nt. ground floor; orchestra (seats in theater).

Partie', -n, n.f. match.

Partisan', (-en,) -en, n.m. partisan; guerilla.

Partitur', -en, n.f. score.

Partizip', -ien, n.nt. participle.

Partner, -, n.m. partner, associate.

Parzel'le, -n, n.f. lot, plot.

Paß, -sse, *n.m.* pass; passport.

passn'bel, *adj.* passable.

Passagier', -e, *n.m.* passenger.

Passant', -en, -en, *n.m.* passer-by.

passen, *vb.* suit, fit; (p. zu) match.

passend, *adj.* fitting, suitable, proper.

passie'ren, *vb.* happen; pass.

Passion', *n.f.* passion.

passiv, *adj.* passive.

Passiv, -e, *n.nt.* passive.

Pasta, -sten, *n.f.* paste.

Paste, -n, *n.f.* paste.

Paste'te, -n, *n.f.* meat pie.

pasteurisie'ren, *vb.* pasteurize.

Pastil'le, -n, *n.f.* lozenge.

Pastor, -o'ren, *n.m.* minister.

Pate, -n, *n.m.* godfather.

Pate, -n, *n.f.* godmother.

Patenkind, -er, *n.nt.* godchild.

Patenonkel, -, *n.m.* godfather.

Patent', -e, *n.nt.* patent.

Patentante, -n, *n.f.* godmother.

Pathos, *n.nt.* pathos.

Patient', -en, -en, *n.m.* patient.

Patin, -nen, *n.f.* godmother.

Patriot', -en, -en, *n.m.* patriot.

patrio'tisch, *adj.* patriotic.

Patriotis'mus, *n.m.* patriotism.

Patro'ne, -n, *n.f.* cartridge; pattern.

Patrouil'le, -n, *n.f.* patrol.

Pauschal'preis, -e, *n.m.* total price.

Pause, -n, *n.f.* pause, intermission, recess.

Pavillon, -s, *n.m.* pavillion.

Pazifis'mus, *n.m.* pacifism.

Pazifist', -en, -en, *n.m.* pacifist.

Pech, *n.nt.* pitch, bad luck.

Pedal', -e, *n.nt.* pedal.

Pedant', -en, -en, *n.m.* pedant.

Pein, *n.f.* pain, agony.

peinigen, *vb.* torment.

peinlich, *adj.* embarrassing; meticulous.

Peitsche, -n, *n.f.* whip.

peitschen, *vb.* whip.

Pelz, -e, *n.m.* fur.

Pelzhändler, -, *n.m.* furrier.

Pendel, -, *n.m.* or *nt.* pendulum.

pendeln, *vb.* swing, oscillate.

Pendler, -, *n.m.* commuter.

Penicillin', *n.nt.* penicillin.

Pension', -en, *n.f.* pension; board, boarding house.

pensionie'ren, *vb.* pension; (sich p. lassen*) retire.

per, *prep.* per, by, with.

perfekt', *adj.* perfect.

Perfekt', -e, *n.nt.* perfect (tense).

Pergament', -e, *n.nt.* parchment.

Perio'de, -n, *n.f.* period, term.

perio'disch, *adj.* periodic.

Peripherie', -í'en, *n.f.* periphery.

Perle, -n, *n.f.* pearl.

Perlmutter, *n.f.* mother-of-pearl.

Persia'ner, *n.m.* Persian lamb.

Persien, *n.nt.* Persia.

Person', -en, *n.f.* person.

Personal', *n.pl.* personnel, staff.

Persona'lien, *n.pl.* personal data.

persön'lich, *adj.* personal.

Persön'lichkeit, -en, *n.f.* personage; personality.

Perspekti've, -n, *n.f.* perspective.

pervers', *adj.* perverse.

Pessimis'mus, *n.m.* pessimism.

pessimis'tisch, *adj.* pessimistic.

Pest, *n.f.* plague, pestilence.

Petersi'lie, *n.f.* parsley.

Petro'leum, *n.nt.* petroleum.

Petschaft, -en, *n.f.* seal.

Pfad, -e, *n.m.* path.

Pfadfinder, -, *n.m.* boy scout.

Pfahl, -ïe, *n.m.* pole, pile, post, stake.

Pfand, -ïer, *n.m.* pawn, pledge, security.

Pfandbrief, -e, *n.m.* bond, mortgage bond.

pfänden, *vb.* seize, attach, impound.

Pfandhaus, -ïer, *n.m.* pawnshop.

Pfanne, -n, *n.f.* pan.

Pfannkuchen, -, *n.m.* pancake.

Pfarrer, -, *n.m.* minister, priest.

Pfau, -e, *n.m.* peacock.

Pfeffer, -, *n.m.* pepper.

Pfefferkuchen, -, *n.m.* gingerbread.

Pfefferminze, *n.f.* peppermint.

Pfeife, -n, *n.f.* pipe, whistle.

pfeifen*, *vb.* whistle.

Pfeil, -e, *n.m.* arrow.

Pfeiler, -, *n.m.* pillar, pier.

Pfennig, -e, *n.m.* penny.

Pferd, -e, *n.nt.* horse.

Pferdestärke, -n, *n.f.* horsepower.

Pfiff, -e, *n.m.* whistle; trick.

pfiffig, *adj.* tricky, sly.

Pfingsten, *n.m.* Pentecost, Whitsuntide.

Pfirsich, -e, *n.m.* peach.

Pflanze, -n, *n.f.* plant.

pflanzen, *vb.* plant.

Pflaster, -, *n.nt.* plaster; pavement.

pflastern, *vb.* plaster, pave.

Pflaume, -n, *n.f.* plum.

Pflege, -n, *n.f.* care, nursing, cultivation.

Pflegeeltern, *n.pl.* foster parents.

pflegen, *vb.* take care of, nurse, cultivate; be accustomed.

Pflicht, -en, *n.f.* duty.

pflichtgemäß, *adj.* dutiful.

Pflock, -ïe, *n.m.* peg.

pflücken, *vb.* pick, gather.

Pflug, -ïe, *n.m.* plow.

pflügen, *vb.* plow.

Pforte, -n, *n.f.* gate, door, entrance.

Pförtner, -, *n.m.* janitor, doorman.

Pfosten, -, *n.m.* post, jamb.

Pfote, -n, *n.f.* paw.

Pfropf, -e, Pfropfen, -, *n.m.* stopper, plug.

pfropfen, *vb.* graft.

Pfund, -e, *n.nt.* pound.

pfuschen, *vb.* botch, bungle.

Pfütze, -n, *n.f.* puddle.

Phänomen', -e, *n.nt.* phenomenon.

Phantasie', -í'en, *n.f.* fantasy.

phantas'tisch, *adj.* fantastic.

Phase, -n, *n.f.* phase.

Philosoph', -en, -en, *n.m.* philosopher.

Philosophie', -í'en, *n.f.* philosophy.

philoso'phisch, *adj.* philosophical.

phlegma'tisch, *adj.* phlegmatic.

phone'tisch, *adj.* phonetic.

Phosphor, *n.m.* phosphorus.

Photoapparat, -e, *n.m.* camera.

photoelek'trisch, *adj.* photoelectric.

Photograph', -en, -en, *n.m.* photographer.

Photographie', -í'en, *n.f.* photograph(y).

Photokopie', -n, *n.f.* photocopy.

photokopie'ren, *vb.* photocopy.

Photokopier'maschine, -n, *n.f.* photocopier.

Physik', *n.f.* physics.

Physiker, -, *n.m.* physicist.

Physiologie', *n.f.* physiology.

physisch, *adj.* physical.

Pianist', -en, -en, *n.m.* pianist.

Pickel, -, *n.m.* pimple; ice axe.

picken, *vb.* peck.

Picknick, -s, *n.nt.* picnic.

piepsen, *vb.* peep.

Pier, -s, *n.m.* pier.

Pietät', *n.f.* piety.

Pigment', -e, *n.nt.* pigment.

pikant', *adj.* piquant.

Pilger, -, *n.m.* pilgrim.

Pille, -n, *n.f.* pill.

Pilot', -en, -en, *n.m.* pilot.

Pilz, -e, *n.m.* mushroom.

Pinsel, -, *n.m.* brush.

Pionier', -e, *n.m.* pioneer; (mil.) engineer.

Pisto'le, -n, *n.f.* pistol.

Pisto'lenhalter, -, *n.m.* holster.

Pizza, -s, *n.f.* pizza.

Plackerei', -en, *n.f.* drudgery.

plädie'ren, *vb.* plead.

Plädoyer', -s, *n.nt.* plea.

Plage, -n, *n.f.* trouble, affliction.

plagen, *vb.* plague, annoy, afflict.

Plagiat', *n.nt.* plagiarism.

Plakat', -e, *n.nt.* placard, poster.

Plan, -ïe, *n.m.* plan.

planen, *vb.* plan.

Planet', -en, -en, *n.m.* planet.

Planke, -n, *n.f.* plank.

planlos, *adj.* aimless.

planmäßig, *adj.* according to plan.

planschen, *vb.* splash.

Planta'ge, -n, *n.f.* plantation.

Plappermaul, ˵er, n.nt. chatterbox.

plappern, vb. babble.

Plasma, -men, n.nt. plasma.

Plastik, -en, n.f. sculpture.

plastisch, adj. plastic.

Plateau', -s, n.nt. plateau.

Platin, n.nt. platinum.

platt, adj. flat.

Plättbrett, ˵er, n.nt. ironing board.

Platte, -n, n.f. plate, slab, sheet, tray; (photographic) slide; (phonograph) record.

Plätteisen, -, n.nt. (flat) iron.

plätten, vb. iron.

Plattenspieler, -, n.m. record player.

Plattform, -en, n.f. platform.

Plattfuß, ˵e, n.m. flat foot.

plattie'ren, vb. plate.

Platz, ˵e, n.m. place, seat, square.

platzen, vb. burst.

Plauderei', -en, n.f. chat.

plaudern, vb. chat.

pleite, adj. broke.

Plombe, -n, n.f. (tooth) filling.

plötzlich, adj. sudden.

plump, adj. clumsy, tactless.

Plunder, n.m. old clothes, rubbish.

plündern, vb. plunder, pillage.

Plünderung, -en, n.f. pillage.

Plural, -e, n.m. plural.

plus, adv. plus.

Plüsch, -e, n.m. plush.

Plutokrat', -en, -en, n.m. plutocrat.

pneuma'tisch, adj. pneumatic.

Pöbel, n.m. mob, rabble.

pöbelhaft, adj. vulgar.

pochen, vb. knock, throb.

Pocke, -n, n.f. pock; (pl.) smallpox.

Podium, -ien, n.nt. rostrum.

Poesie', i'en, n.f. poetry.

Poet, -en, -en, n.m. poet.

poe'tisch, adj. poetic.

Poin'te, -n, n.f. point (of a joke), punch line.

Pokal', -e, n.m. goblet, cup.

Pol, -e, n.m. pole.

polar', adj. polar.

Polar'stern, n.m. North Star.

Pole, -n, -n, n.m. Pole.

Polen, n.nt. Poland.

Poli'ce, -n, n.f. (insurance) policy.

polie'ren, vb. polish.

Politik', n.f. politics, policy.

Poli'tiker, -, n.m. politician.

poli'tisch, adj. politic(al).

Politur', -en, n.f. polish.

Polizei', -en, n.f. police.

polizei'lich, adj. by the police.

Polizei'präsident, -en, -en, n.m. chief of police.

Polizei'präsidium, -ien, n.nt. police headquarters.

Polizei'revier, -e, n.nt. police station.

Polizei'richter, -, n.m. police state.

Polizei'staat, -en, n.m. police state.

Polizei'stunde, -n, n.f. curfew.

Polizei'wache, -n, n.f. police station.

Polizist', -en, -en, n.m. policeman.

pointsch, adj. Polish.

Polonä'se, -n, n.f. polonaise.

Polster, -, n.nt. pad, cushion.

polstern, vb. pad, upholster.

Polsterung, -en, n.f. padding, upholstery.

poltern, vb. rattle, bluster.

Polygamie', n.f. polygamy.

Poly'pen, n.pl. adenoids.

Polytech'nikum, -ken, n.nt. technical college.

Pomeran'ze, -n, n.f. orange.

Pony, -s, n.nt. pony; (pl.) bangs.

populär', adj. popular.

popularisie'ren, vb. popularize.

Popularität', n.f. popularity.

Pore, -n, n.f. pore.

porös', adj. porous.

Portal', -e, n.nt. portal.

Portefeuille', -s, n.nt. portfolio.

Portemonnaie', -s, n.nt. purse.

Portier', -s, n.m. doorman, concierge.

Portion', -en, n.f. portion, helping.

Porto, n.nt. postage.

Porträt', -s, n.nt. portrait.

Portugal, n.nt. Portugal.

Portugie'se, -n, -n, n.m. Portuguese.

portugie'sisch, adj. Portuguese.

Porzellan', -en, n.nt. porcelain, china.

Posau'ne, -n, n.f. trumpet.

Pose, -n, n.f. pose.

posie'ren, vb. strike a pose.

Position', -en, n.f. position.

positiv, adj. positive.

Posse, -n, n.f. prank, antic; farce.

Post, n.f. mail; post office.

Postamt, ˵er, n.nt. post office.

Postanweisung, -en, n.f. money order.

Postbote, -n, -n, n.m. postman.

Posten, -, n.m. post, station; item.

Postfach, ˵er, n.nt. post office box.

Postkarte, -n, n.f. post card.

postlagernd, adv. general delivery.

Postleitzahl, -en, n.f. zip code.

Poststempel, -, n.m. post mark.

Pracht, n.f. splendor.

prächtig, adj. splendid.

prachtvoll, adj. gorgeous.

Prädikat', -e, n.nt. predicate.

Präfix, -e, n.nt. prefix.

prägen, vb. stamp, coin, impress.

Prägung, -en, n.f. coinage.

prähistorisch, adj. prehistoric.

prahlen, vb. boast.

praktisch, adj. practical.

Prali'ne, -n, n.f. chocolate candy.

prallen, vb. bounce, be reflected.

Prämie, -n, n.f. premium, prize.

präparie'ren, vb. prepare.

Präposition', -en, n.f. preposition.

Präsens, n.nt. present.

präsentie'ren, vb. present.

Präsident', -en, -en, n.m. president.

prasseln, vb. patter, crackle.

Praxis, n.f. practice; doctor's office.

Präzedenz'fall, ˵e, n.m. precedent.

predigen, vb. preach.

Prediger, -, n.m. preacher.

Predigt, -en, n.f. sermon.

Preis, -e, n.m. price, cost; prize, praise.

Preiselbeere, -n, n.f. cranberry.

preisen*, vb. praise.

Preisgabe, -n, n.f. surrender, abandonment.

preis-ge'ben*, vb. surrender, abandon.

prellen, vb. toss; cheat.

Premie're, -n, n.f. première.

Premier'minister, -, n.m. prime minister.

Presse, n.f. press.

pressen, vb. press.

Prestige', n.nt. prestige.

Preuße, -n, -n, n.m. Prussian.

Preußen, n.nt. Prussia.

preußisch, adj. Prussian.

Priester, -, n.m. priest.

prima, adj. first class, swell.

primär', adj. primary.

Primel, -n, n.f. primrose.

primitiv', adj. primitive.

Prinz, -en, -en, n.m. prince.

Prinzes'sin, -nen, n.f. princess.

Prinzip', -ien, n.nt. principle.

Priorität', -en, n.f. priority.

Prise, -n, n.f. pinch.

Prisma, -men, n.nt. prism.

privat', adj. private.

Privileg', -ien, n.nt. privilege.

pro, prep. per.

Probe, -n, n.f. experiment, test; rehearsal; sample.

proben, vb. rehearse.

probeweise, adv. tentative.

Probezeit, -en, n.f. probation.

probie'ren, vb. try (out).

Problem', -e, n.nt. problem.

Produkt', -e, n.nt. product.

Produktion', n.f. production.

produktiv', adj. productive.

Produzent', -en, -en, n.m. producer.

produzie'ren, vb. produce.

profan', adj. profane.

Profes'sor, -o'ren, n.m. professor.

Profil', -e, n.nt. profile.

Profit', -e, n.m. profit.

profitie'ren, vb. profit.

Progno'se, -n, n.f. prognosis.

Programm', -e, n.nt. program.

Projekt', -e, n.nt. project.

Projektion', -en, *n.f.* projection.

Projek'tor, -o'ren, *n.m.* projector.

projizie'ren, *vb.* project.

Proklamation', -en, *n.f.* proclamation.

Prokurist', -en, -en, *n.m.* manager.

Proletariat', *n.nt.* proletariat.

Proleta'rier, -, *n.m.* proletarian.

proleta'risch, *adj.* proletarian.

Prolog', -e, *n.m.* prologue.

prominent', *adj.* prominent.

Prono'men, -mina, *n.nt.* pronoun.

Propagan'da, *n.f.* propaganda, publicity.

Propel'ler, -, *n.m.* propeller.

Prophet', -en, -en, *n.m.* prophet.

prophe'tisch, *adj.* prophetic.

prophezei'en, *vb.* prophesy.

Prophezei'ung, -en, *n.f.* prophecy.

Proportion', -en, *n.f.* proportion.

proppenvoll, *adj.* chock full.

Prosa, *n.f.* prose.

prosa'isch, *adj.* prosaic.

Prospekt', -e, *n.m.* prospectus.

Prostituiert'-, *n.f.* prostitute.

Protein', *n.nt.* protein.

Protest', -e, *n.m.* protest.

Protestant', -en, -en, *n.m.* Protestant.

protestie'ren, *vb.* protest.

Protokoll', -e, *n.nt.* minutes, record.

protzen, *vb.* show off.

protzig, *adj.* gaudy.

Proviant', *n.m.* food, supplies.

Provinz', -en, *n.f.* province.

provinziell', *adj.* provincial.

Provision', -en, *n.f.* commission.

proviso'risch, *adj.* temporary.

Provokation', -en, *n.f.* provocation.

provozie'ren, *vb.* provoke.

Prozent', -e, *n.nt.* per cent.

Prozent'satz, -e, *n.m.* percentage.

Prozeß', -sse, *n.m.* process; trial, lawsuit.

Prozession', -en, *n.f.* procession.

pride, *adj.* prudish.

prüfen, *vb.* test, examine, verify.

Prüfung, -en, *n.f.* test, examination, scrutiny.

Prügel, -, *n.m.* cudgel; (pl.) beating.

Prügelei', -en, *n.f.* brawl.

prügeln, *vb.* beat, thrash.

Prunk, *n.m.* pomp, show.

prunkvoll, *adj.* pompous, showy.

PS, *abbr.* (= Pferdestärke) horsepower.

Psalm, -en, *n.m.* psalm.

Pseudonym', -e, *n.nt.* pseudonym.

psychede'lisch, *adj.* psychedelic.

Psychia'ter, -, *n.m.* psychiatrist.

Psychiatrie', *n.f.* psychiatry.

Psychoanaly'se, -n, *n.f.* psychoanalysis.

Psycholo'ge, -n, -n, *n.m.* psychologist.

Psychologie', *n.f.* psychology.

psycholo'gisch, *adj.* psychological.

Psycho'se, -n, *n.f.* psychosis.

Publikation', -en, *n.f.* publication.

Publikum, *n.nt.* public, audience.

publizie'ren, *vb.* publish.

Pudding, -e, *n.m.* pudding.

Pudel, -, *n.m.* poodle.

Puder, -, *n.nt.* powder.

Puderdose, -n, *n.f.* compact.

pudern, *vb.* powder.

Puderquaste, -n, *n.f.* powder puff.

Puffer, -, *n.m.* buffer; potato pancake.

Pullo'ver, -, *n.m.* sweater.

Puls, -e, *n.m.* pulse.

Pulsader, -n, *n.f.* artery.

Pulsar, -s, *n.m.* pulsar.

pulsie'ren, *vb.* pulsate, throb.

Pult, -e, *n.nt.* desk, lectern.

Pulver, -, *n.nt.* powder.

Pumpe, -n, *n.f.* pump.

pumpen, *vb.* pump; borrow, lend.

Pumps, *n.pl.* pumps.

Punkt, -e, *n.m.* point, dot, period.

Punktgleichheit, *n.f.* tie.

Punktion', -en, *n.f.* puncture.

pünktlich, *adj.* punctual.

Punktzahl, -en, *n.f.* score.

Punsch, -e, *n.m.* punch.

Pupil'le, -n, *n.f.* pupil.

Puppe, -n, *n.f.* doll; chrysalis.

pur, *adj.* pure; (alcohol) straight.

Püree', -s, *n.nt.* purée.

Purpur, *n.m.* purple.

purpurn, *adj.* purple.

Puter, -, *n.m.* turkey.

Putsch, -e, *n.m.* attempt to overthrow the government.

Putz, *n.m.* finery.

putzen, *vb.* clean, polish.

Putzfrau, -en, *n.f.* cleaning woman.

putzig, *adj.* funny, droll, quaint.

Putzwaren, *n.pl.* millinery.

Puzzle, -s, *n.nt.* puzzle.

Pyja'ma, -s, *n.nt.* pajamas.

Pyrami'de, -n, *n.f.* pyramid.

Q

quadraphon', *adj.* quadraphonic.

Quadrat', -e, *n.nt.* square.

Quadrat'-, *cpds.* square.

quadra'tisch, *adj.* square.

quaken, *vb.* quack, croak.

Qual, -en, *n.f.* torment, agony, ordeal.

quälen, *vb.* torment, torture.

Qualifikation', -en, *n.f.* qualification.

qualifizie'ren, *vb.* qualify.

Qualität', -en, *n.f.* quality.

qualmen, *vb.* smoke.

qualvoll, *adj.* agonizing.

Quantität', -en, *n.f.* quantity.

Quarantä'ne, -n, *n.f.* quarantine.

Quark, *n.m.* curds.

Quarkkäse, *n.m.* cottage cheese.

Quartal', -e, *n.nt.* quarter of a year.

Quartett', -e, *n.nt.* quartet.

Quartier', -e, *n.nt.* lodging, billet.

Quarz, -e, *n.m.* quartz.

Quasar, *n.m.* quasar.

Quaste, -n, *n.f.* tuft.

Quatsch, *n.m.* nonsense, bunk, baloney.

Quecksilber, *n.nt.* mercury.

Quelle, -n, *n.f.* spring, source, well, fountain.

quellen*, *vb.* well, gush, flow.

quer, *adj.* cross(wise), diagonal.

Querschnitt, -, *n.m.* cross section.

Querstraße, -n, *n.f.* cross street.

Querverweis, -e, *n.m.* cross reference.

quetschen, *vb.* squeeze, bruise.

Quetschung, -en, *n.f.* contusion.

quietschen, *vb.* squeak.

Quintett', -e, *n.nt.* quintet.

quitt, *adj.* quits, even, square.

quittie'ren, *vb.* receipt.

Quittung, -en, *n.f.* receipt.

Quote, -n, *n.f.* quota.

R

Rabatt', -e, *n.m.* discount.

Rabau'ke, -n, -n, *n.m.* tough.

Rabbi'ner, -, *n.m.* rabbi.

Rabe, -n, -n, *n.m.* raven.

Rache, *n.f.* revenge.

rächen, *vb.* revenge, avenge.

Rachen, -, *n.m.* throat, jaws.

Rad, -er, *n.nt.* wheel.

Radar, *n.nt.* radar.

Radau', *n.m.* noise, racket.

radeln, *vb.* (bi)cycle.

rad-fahren*, *vb.* (bi)cycle.

Radfahrer, -, *n.m.* (bi)cyclist.

radie'ren, *vb.* erase; etch.

Radier'gummi, -s, *n.m.* (rubber) eraser.

Radie'rung, -en, *n.f.* etching.

Radies'chen, -, *n.nt.* radish.

radikal', *adj.* radical.

Radio, -s, *n.nt.* radio.

radioaktiv', *adj.* radioactive.

radioaktiv'-Niederschlag, *n.m.* fallout.

Radioapparat, -e, *n.m.* radio set.

Radioempfänger, -, *n.m.* radio receiver.

Radiosender, -, *n.m.* radio transmitter, broadcasting station.

Radiosendung, -en, *n.f.* radio broadcast.

Radium, *n.nt.* radium.

Radius, -ien, *n.m.* radius.

Radspur, -en, *n.f.* rut.

raffinie'ren, *vb.* refine.

raffiniert', *adj.* tricky, shrewd; sophisticated.

ragen, *vb.* extend, loom.

Rahm, *n.m.* cream.

rahmen, *vb.* frame.

Rahmen, -, *n.m.* frame.

Rake'te, -n, *n.f.* rocket.

Rake'tenwaffe, -n, *n.f.* missile.

rammen, *vb.* ram.

Rampe, -n, *n.f.* ramp.

Rand, -er, *n.m.* edge, brim, margin.

Rang, -e, *n.m.* rank.

rangie'ren, *vb.* switch, shunt.

Rangordnung, -en, *n.f.* hierarchy.

ranzig, *adj.* rancid.

Rapier', -en, *n.nt.* foil.

rasch, *adj.* quick.

rascheln, *vb.* rustle.

rasen, *vb.* rage.

Rasen, -n, *n.m.* lawn, turf.

rasend, *adj.* frenzied.

Raserei', -en, *n.f.* frenzy.

Rasierapparat, -e, *n.m.* safety razor.

rasie'ren, *vb.* shave.

Rasier'klinge, -n, *n.f.* razor blade.

Rasier'messer, -, *n.nt.* (straight) razor.

Rasse, -n, *n.f.* race; breed.

rasseln, *vb.* rattle.

Rast, -en, *n.f.* rest.

rasten, *vb.* rest.

rastlos, *adj.* restless.

Rasur', -en, *n.f.* erasure; shave.

Rat, -e, *n.m.* advice; councilor.

Rate, -n, *n.f.* payment, installment.

raten*, *vb.* guess, advise.

Ratenzahlung, *n.f.* payment by installments.

ratifizie'ren, *vb.* ratify.

Ration', -en, *n.f.* ration.

rationell', *adj.* rational, reasonable.

rationie'ren, *vb.* ration.

ratlos, *adj.* helpless, perplexed, at one's wit's end.

Ratlosigkeit, *n.f.* perplexity.

ratsam, *adj.* advisable.

Ratsamkeit, *n.f.* advisability.

Rätsel, -, *n.nt.* riddle, puzzle; enigma, mystery.

rätselhaft, *adj.* puzzling, mysterious.

Ratte, -n, *n.f.* rat.

rattern, *vb.* rattle.

Raub, *n.m.* robbery, plunder.

rauben, *vb.* rob.

Räuber, -, *n.m.* robber.

Rauch, *n.m.* smoke.

rauchen, *vb.* smoke.

Raucher, -, *n.m.* smoker.

räuchern, *vb.* smoke (fish, meat).

raufen, *vb.* pull, tear; (sich r.) fight, brawl.

Rauferei', -en, *n.f.* brawl.

rauh, *adj.* rough; harsh; rugged.

Rauheit, -en, *n.f.* roughness.

Raum, -e, *n.m.* room, space.

räumen, *vb.* vacate.

Raumfahrt, *n.f.* space travel.

Rauminhalt, *n.m.* volume, capacity, contents.

räumlich, *adj.* spatial.

Raumtransporter, *n.m.* space shuttle.

Räumung, *n.f.* (comm.) clearance; (mil.) evacuation.

raunen, *vb.* whisper.

Rausch, -e, *n.m.* intoxication.

rauschen, *vb.* roar, rustle.

Rauschgift, -e, *n.nt.* narcotic, dope.

Razzia, -ien, *n.f.* raid.

reagie'ren, *vb.* react, respond.

Reaktion', -en, *n.f.* reaction, response.

Reaktionär, -e, *n.m.* reactionary.

reaktionär', *adj.* reactionary.

reaktivie'ren, *vb.* recommission.

Reak'tor, -o'ren, *n.m.* reactor.

realisie'ren, *vb.* realize, put into effect.

Realisie'rung, -en, *n.f.* realization.

Realis'mus, *n.m.* realism.

Realist', -en, *n.f.* realist.

Realität', -en, *n.f.* reality.

Rebe, -n, *n.f.* vine; grape.

Rebstock, -e, *n.m.* vine.

Rechen, -, *n.m.* rake.

Rechenaufgabe, -n, *n.f.* arithmetic problem.

Rechenmaschine, -n, *n.f.* calculating machine.

Rechenschaft, *n.f.* account, responsibility; (R. ablegen) account for.

Rechenschieber, -, *n.m.* slide rule.

rechnen, *vb.* count, do sums, figure.

Rechnen, *n.nt.* arithmetic.

Rechnung, -en, *n.f.* figuring, computation; bill; (R. tragen*) take into account.

Rechnungsbuch, -er, *n.nt.* account book.

recht, *adj.* right; (r. haben*) be right.

Recht, -e, *n.nt.* right; (system of) law.

Rechteck, -e, *n.nt.* rectangle.

rechteckig, *adj.* rectangular, oblong.

rechtfertigen, *vb.* justify; vindicate.

Rechtfertigung, -en, *n.f.* justification.

rechtlich, *adj.* legal, judicial.

rechtmäßig, *adj.* lawful.

rechts, *adv.* (to the) right.

Rechtsanwalt, -e, *n.m.* lawyer.

rechtschaffen, *adj.* honest, righteous.

Rechtschaffenheit, *n.f.* honesty, righteousness.

Rechtschreibung, *n.f.* orthography, spelling.

Rechtsgelehrt-, *n.m.* jurist.

Rechtsprechung, *n.f.* jurisdiction.

Rechtsspruch, -e, *n.m.* judgment, sentence.

Rechtsstreit, -e, *n.m.* litigation.

Rechtswissenschaft, *n.f.* jurisprudence.

recken, *vb.* stretch.

Redakteur', -e, *n.m.* editor.

Redaktion', -en, *n.f.* editorial office; editor.

Rede, -n, *n.f.* speech, talk; (eine R. halten*) give a speech; (keine R. sein* von) be no question of; (jemanden zur R. stellen) confront a person with, take to task.

redegewandt, *adj.* eloquent.

Redekunst, *n.f.* rhetoric, oratory.

reden, *vb.* talk, speak; (vernünftig r. mit) reason with.

Redensart, -en, *n.f.* way of speaking; saying, idiom.

Redeteil, -e, *n.m.* part of speech.

Redewendung, -en, *n.f.* phrase, figure of speech.

redlich, *adj.* honest, upright.

Redner, -, *n.m.* speaker, orator.

redselig, *adj.* loquacious.

Reduktion', -en, *n.f.* reduction.

reduzie'ren, *vb.* reduce.

reell', *adj.* honest, sound.

reflektie'ren, *vb.* reflect.

Reflex', -e, *n.m.* reflex.

Reflexion', -en, *n.f.* reflection.

Reform', -en, *n.f.* reform.

reformie'ren, *vb.* reform.

Refrain', -s, *n.m.* refrain.

Regal', -e, *n.nt.* shelf.

rege, *adj.* alert; active.

Regel, -n, *n.f.* rule.

regelmäßig, *adj.* regular.

Regelmäßigkeit, *n.f.* regularity.

regeln, *vb.* regulate.

regelrecht, *adj.* regular, downright.

Regelung, -en, *n.f.* regulation.

regen, *vb.* stir, move.

Regen, -n, *n.m.* rain.

Regenbogen, -, *n.m.* rainbow.

Regenguß, -sse, *n.m.* downpour.

Regenmantel, -, *n.m.* raincoat.

Regenschirm, -e, *n.m.* umbrella.

Regie', *n.f.* direction.

regie'ren, *vb.* govern.

Regie'rung, -en, *n.f.* government.

Regi'me, -s, *n.nt.* regime.

Regiment', -er, *n.nt.* regiment.

Region', -en, *n.f.* region.

Regisseur', -e, n.m. director.

Regis'ter, -, n.nt. register, index.

Registrie'rung, -en, n.f. registration.

regnen, vb. rain.

regnerisch, adj. rainy.

regsam, adj. alert, quick.

regulie'ren, vb. regulate.

Reh, -e, n.nt. deer, roe.

rehabilitie'ren, vb. rehabilitate.

Rehleder, -, n.nt. deerskin.

Reibe, -n, n.f. grater.

reiben*, vb. rub; grate; chafe.

Reibung, -en, n.f. friction.

reich, adj. rich.

Reich, -e, n.nt. kingdom, empire, realm.

reichen, vb. (tr.) pass, hand, reach; (intr.) extend.

reichlich, adj. plentiful, ample, abundant.

Reichtum, ¨er, n.m. wealth, affluence.

Reichweite, n.m. reach, range.

reif, adj. ripe, mature.

Reife, n.f. maturity.

reifen, vb. ripen, mature.

Reifen, -, n.m. hoop; (auto, etc.) tire.

Reifenpanne, -n, n.f. puncture, blowout.

reiflich, adj. carefully considerate.

Reigen, -, n.m. (dance) round; (music) song.

Reihe, -n, n.f. row; series, succession.

reihen, vb. (sich r.) rank.

Reihenfolge, -n, n.f. sequence, succession.

Reim, -, n.m. rhyme.

rein, adj. clean, pure.

Reinfall, -¨e, n.m. flop.

rein·fallen*, vb. be taken in.

Reinheit, n.f. purity.

reinigen, vb. clean, cleanse.

Reinigung, -en, n.f. cleaning, cleansing; (chemische R.) dry-cleaner, dry-cleaning.

rein·legen, vb. trick, take in.

Reis, n.m. rice.

Reise, -n, n.f. trip, journey.

Reiseandenken, -, n.nt. souvenir.

Reisebüro, -s, n.nt. travel agency.

Reiseführer, -, n.m. guidebook.

reisen, vb. travel.

Reisend-, n.m.&f. traveler.

Reiseroute, -n, n.f. itinerary.

Reisescheck, -s, n.m. traveler's check.

reißen*, vb. rip, tear; (sich r. um) scramble for.

reißend, adj. rapid, racing.

Reißer, -, n.m. thriller, bestseller.

reiten*, vb. ride, horseback.

Reiter, -, n.m. rider.

Reiz, -e, n.m. charm, appeal; irritation.

reizbar, adj. sensitive, irritable.

reizen, vb. excite, tempt; irritate.

reizend, adj. adorable, lovely.

Reizfaktor, -en, n.m. irritant.

Reizmittel, -, n.nt. stimulant.

Reizung, -en, n.f. irritation.

rekeln, vb. (sich r.) stretch, sprawl.

Rekla'me, n.f. advertisement, advertising, publicity.

reklamie'ren, vb. reclaim; complain.

Rekord', -e, n.m. record.

Rekrut', -en, -en, n.m. draftee, recruit.

Rektor, -o'ren, n.m. headmaster; (university) president, chancellor.

relativ', adj. relative.

Religion', -en, n.f. religion.

religiös', adj. religious.

Rendezvous, -, n.nt. rendezvous, tryst.

Rennen, -, n.nt. race.

rennen*, vb. run, dash; race.

Renntier, -e, n.nt. reindeer.

renta'bel, adj. profitable.

Rente, -n, n.f. pension, income.

rentie'ren, vb. (sich r.) be profitable.

Reparation', -en, n.f. reparation.

Reparatur', -en, n.f. repair.

reparie'ren, vb. repair.

repatrile'ren, vb. repatriate.

Repertoire', -s, n.nt. repertoire.

Repor'ter, -, n.m. reporter.

Repräsentant', -en, -en, n.m. representative.

Repräsentation', -en, n.f. representation.

reproduzie'ren, vb. reproduce.

Reptil', -e or -ien, n.nt. reptile.

Republik', -en, n.f. republic.

republika'nisch, adj. republican.

requirie'ren, vb. requisition.

Requisition', -en, n.f. requisition.

Reservation', -en, n.f. reservation.

Reser've, -n, n.f. reserve.

reservie'ren, vb. reserve.

Reservoir', -s, n.nt. reservoir.

Residenz', -en, n.f. residence.

Resignation', -en, n.f. resignation.

resignie'ren, vb. resign.

resolut', adj. determined.

resonant', adj. resonant.

Resonanz', -en, n.f. resonance.

Respekt', n.m. respect, regard.

Rest, -e, n.m. rest, remnant.

Restaurant', -s, n.nt. restaurant.

restaurie'ren, vb. restore.

Restbestand, ¨e, n.m. residue.

restlos, adj. without remainder, entire.

Resultat', -e, n.nt. result.

Resümee', -s, n.nt. résumé.

retten, vb. rescue, save, salvage.

Retter, -, n.m. savior.

Rettung, -en, n.f. rescue; salvation.

Rettungsboot, -e, n.nt. lifeboat.

rettungslos, adj. irretrievable, hopeless.

Rettungsring, -e, n.m. life preserver.

Reue, n.f. repentance.

reuevoll, adj. repentant.

reuig, adj. penitent.

Revan'che, -n, n.f. revenge; return match.

Revers, -, n.m. lapel.

revidie'ren, vb. revise.

Revier', -e, n.nt. district.

Revision', -en, n.f. revision.

Revol'te, -n, n.f. revolt.

revoltie'ren, vb. revolt.

Revolution', -en, n.f. revolution.

revolutionär', adj. revolutionary.

Revol'ver, -, n.m. revolver, gun.

Rezept', -e, n.nt. receipt, recipe; prescription.

Rhabar'ber, n.m. rhubarb.

Rhapsodie', -i'en, n.f. rhapsody.

Rhein, n.m. Rhine.

rheto'risch, adj. rhetorical.

Rheuma, n.nt. rheumatism.

Rheumatis'mus, n.m. rheumatism.

rhythmisch, adj. rhythmical.

Rhythmus, -men, n.m. rhythm.

richten, vb. set right; (r. auf) turn to; (sich r. an) turn to; (sich r. nach) go by, be guided by, depend on; (jur.) judge.

Richter, -, n.m. judge.

richterlich, adj. judicial, judiciary.

Richterstand, n.m. judiciary.

richtig, adj. true, correct.

Richtigkeit, n.f. correctness.

Richtung, -en, n.f. direction; tendency.

riechen*, vb. smell.

Riecher, -, n.m. (fig.) hunch.

Riegel, -, n.m. bolt.

Riemen, -, n.m. strap; oar.

Riese, -n, -n, n.m. giant.

riesenhaft, adj. gigantic.

riesig, adj. tremendous, vast.

rigoros', adj. rigorous.

Rind, -er, n.nt. ox, cow, cattle.

Rinde, -n, n.f. bark.

Rindfleisch, n.nt. beef.

Rindsleder, -, n.nt. cowhide.

Ring, -e, n.m. ring.

ringeln, vb. curl.

ringen*, vb. struggle, wrestle.

Ringkampf, ¨e, n.m. wrestling match.

Rinne, -n, n.f. rut, groove.

Rinnstein, -e, n.m. curb, gutter.

Rippe, -n, n.f. rib.

Rippenfellentzündung, -en, n.f. pleurisy.

Risiko, -s, n.nt. risk, hazard, gamble.

riskie'ren, vb. risk, gamble.

Riß, -sse, n.m. tear, crack.

Ritt, -e, n.m. ride.

Ritter, -, *n.m.* knight.
ritterlich, *adj.* chivalrous.
rittlings, *adv.* astride.
Rituele', -e, *n.nt.* ritual.
rituell', *adj.* ritual.
Ritus, -en, *n.m.* rite.
Ritze, -n, *n.f.* crack.
Riva'le, -n, -n, *n.m.* rival.
rivalisie'ren, *vb.* rival.
Rivalität', -en, *n.f.* rivalry.
Rizinusöl, *n.nt.* castor oil.
Robbe, -n, *n.f.* seal.
Roboter, -, *n.m.* robot.
robust', *adj.* robust.
röcheln, *vb.* breathe heavily.
Rock, -e, *n.m.* (men) jacket; (women) skirt; (music) rock.
Rockmusik, *n.f.* rock music.
rodeln, *vb.* go sledding.
Rodelschlitten, -, *n.m.* sled.
Rogen, -, *n.m.* roe.
Roggen, *n.m.* rye.
roh, *adj.* raw, crude; *(fig.)* brutal.
Roheit, -en, *n.f.* crudeness, brutality.
Rohling, -e, *n.m.* rowdy.
Rohr, -e, *n.nt.* pipe; (gun) barrel; (bamboo, sugar) cane.
Röhre, -n, *n.f.* pipe, tube.
Rohrflöte, -n, *n.f.* reed pipe.
Rolle, -n, *n.f.* roll, coil; spool; role, part.
rollen, *vb.* roll.
Roller, -, *n.m.* scooter.
Rolltreppe, -n, *n.f.* escalator.
Rom, *n.nt.* Rome.
Roman', -e, *n.m.* novel.
roma'nisch, *adj.* Romance.
Roman'schriftsteller, -, *n.m.* novelist.
Roman'tik, *n.m.* romanticism, Romantic Movement.
roman'tisch, *adj.* romantic.
Roman'ze, -n, *n.f.* romance.
Römer, -, *n.m.* Roman.
römisch, *adj.* Roman.
röntgen, *vb.* x-ray.
Röntgenaufnahme, -n, *n.f.* x-ray.
Röntgenstrahlen, *n.pl.* x-rays.
rosa, *adj.* pink.
Rose, -n, *n.f.* rose.
Rosenkranz, :e, *n.m.* rosary.
rosig, *adj.* rosy.
Rosi'ne, -n, *n.f.* raisin.
Roß, -sse, *n.nt.* horse, steed.
Rost, *n.m.* rust; (oven) grate.
rosten, *vb.* rust.
rösten, *vb.* roast; toast.
rostig, *adj.* rusty.
rot (-), *adj.* red.
rotbraun, *adj.* red-brown, maroon.
Röteln, *n.pl.* German measles.
rotie'ren, *vb.* rotate.
Rotwein, -e, *n.m.* red wine, claret.
Roué', -s, *n.m.* roué, rake.
Rouge, *n.nt.* rouge.
Roula'de, -n, *n.f.* meat roll.
Route, -n, *n.f.* route.
Routi'ne, -n, *n.f.* routine.
routiniert', *adj.* experienced.
Rowdy, -s, *n.m.* hoodlum.

Rübe, -n, *n.f.* (gelbe R.) carrot; (rote R.) beet; (weisse R.) turnip.
Rubin', -e, *n.m.* ruby.
Rubrik', -en, *n.f.* category, heading.
ruchbar, *adj.* notorious.
ruchlos, *adj.* infamous, profligate.
Ruck, -e, *n.m.* jerk, wrench.
Rückantwort, -en, *n.f.* reply.
ruckartig, *adj.* jerky.
rückbezüglich, *adj.* reflexive.
Rückblick, *n.m.* retrospect.
rücken, *vb.* move, move over.
Rücken, -, *n.m.* back.
rückerstatten, *vb.* refund.
Rückfahrkarte, -n, *n.f.* return ticket.
Rückfahrt, -en, *n.f.* return trip.
Rückfall, :e, *n.m.* relapse.
Rückgabe, *n.f.* return, restitution.
Rückgang, :e, *n.m.* retrogression, decline.
rückgängig, *adj.* declining; (r. machen) cancel, revoke.
Rückgrat, -e, *n.nt.* spine, backbone.
Rückhalt, *n.m.* support, reserve.
rückhaltlos, *adj.* unreserved, frank.
Rückhand, :, *n.f.* backhand.
Rückkaufswert, -e, *n.m.* equity (mortgage, etc.).
Rückkehr, *n.f.* return; reversion.
Rückkopplung, -en, *n.f.* feedback.
Rückmarsch, :e, *n.m.* retreat.
Rucksack, :e, *n.m.* knapsack.
Rückschlag, :e, *n.m.* reverse, upset.
Rückschluß, :sse, *n.m.* conclusion.
Rückseite, -n, *n.f.* reverse, rear.
Rücksicht, -en, *n.f.* consideration.
Rücksichtnahme, *n.f.* consideration.
rücksichtslos, *adj.* inconsiderate; reckless, ruthless.
Rücksichtslosigkeit, -en, *n.f.* lack of consideration, illmannered behavior; ruthlessness.
rücksichtsvoll, *adj.* thoughtful, considerate.
Rückstand, :e, *n.m.* arrears; (in R. geraten*) fall behind, lag.
rückständig, *adj.* in arrears; backward, antiquated.
Rücktritt, -e, *n.m.* resignation.
rückwärts, *adv.* backward(s).
Rückwärtsgang, :e, *n.m.* reverse (gear).
ruckweise, *adv.* by fits and starts.
Rückzug, :e, *n.m.* retreat.
Rudel, -, *n.nt.* pack.
Ruder, -, *n.nt.* oar.
Ruderboot, -e, *n.nt.* rowboat.
rudern, *vb.* row.

Ruf, -e, *n.m.* call; reputation, standing.
rufen*, *vb.* call, shout.
Rufnummer, -n, *n.f.* (telephone) number.
Rüge, -n, *n.f.* reprimand.
rügen, *vb.* reprimand.
Ruhe, *n.f.* rest; calmness, tranquility; silence.
ruhelos, *adj.* restless.
ruhen, *vb.* rest, repose.
Ruhestand, *n.m.* retirement.
Ruhestätte, -n, *n.f.* resting place.
ruhig, *adj.* calm, composed; quiet; (das kannst du r. machen) go ahead and do it.
Ruhm, *n.m.* fame, glory.
rühmen, *vb.* praise, extol.
rühmenswert, *adj.* praiseworthy.
rühmlich, *adj.* laudable.
ruhmlos, *adj.* inglorious.
ruhmreich, *adj.* glorious.
Ruhr, *n.f.* dysentery.
Rührei, -er, *n.nt.* scrambled eggs.
rühren, *vb.* move, stir; (sich r.) stir.
rührend, *adj.* touching, pathetic.
rührig, *adj.* lively, bustling.
Rührung, *n.f.* emotion, compassion.
Rui'ne, -n, *n.f.* ruin.
ruinie'ren, *vb.* ruin.
Rum, *n.m.* rum.
Rummel, *n.m.* hubbub, racket.
rumpeln, *vb.* rumble.
Rumpf, :e, *n.m.* torso, fuselage, hull.
rund, *adj.* round, circular.
Runde, -n, *n.f.* round; (sports) lap.
Rundfunk, *n.m.* radio.
Rundfunksendung, -en, *n.f.* broadcast.
Rundfunksprecher, -, *n.m.* broadcaster.
Rundfunkübertragung, -en, *n.f.* broadcast.
rundlich, *adj.* plump.
Rundschreiben, -, *n.nt.* circular.
Runzel, -n, *n.f.* wrinkle.
runzeln, *vb.* wrinkle; (die Stirn r.) frown.
rupfen, *vb.* pluck.
Rüsche, -n, *n.f.* ruffle.
Ruß, *n.m.* soot, grime.
Russe, -n, *n.m.* Russian.
Rüssel, -n, *n.m.* trunk.
russisch, *adj.* Russian.
Rußland, *n.nt.* Russia.
rüsten, *vb.* prepare; *(mil.)* arm.
rüstig, *adj.* vigorous, spry.
Rüstung, -en, *n.f.* armament; armor.
rutschen, *vb.* slide, skid.
rütteln, *vb.* shake, jolt.

S

Saal, Säle, *n.m.* large room, hall.

Saat, -en, *n.f.* seed, sowing.

Sabbat, -en, *n.m.* Sabbath.

Säbel, -, *n.m.* saber.

Sabota'ge, *n.f.* sabotage.

Saboteur', -e, *n.m.* saboteur.

sabotie'ren, *vb.* sabotage.

Sacharin', *n.nt.* saccharine.

Sache, -n, *n.f.* thing, matter; cause.

Sachkundig-, *n.m.* expert.

sachlich, *adj.* objective, relevant, matter-of-fact; (art) functional.

Sachlichkeit, *n.f.* objectivity, detachment.

sacht, *adj.* soft.

sachte, *adv.* cautiously, gingerly.

Sachverständig-, *n.m.* expert.

Sack, -e, *n.m.* sack, bag.

Sadis'mus, *n.m.* sadism.

Sadist', -en, -en, *n.m.* sadist.

sadis'tisch, *adj.* sadistic.

säen, *vb.* sow.

Saft, -e, *n.m.* juice, sap.

saftig, *adj.* juicy, succulent.

Sage, -n, *n.f.* myth.

Säge, -n, *n.f.* saw.

sagen, *vb.* say, tell.

sägen, *vb.* saw.

sagenhaft, *adj.* mythical, fabulous.

Sago, *n.nt.* tapioca.

Sahne, *n.f.* cream.

Sahneeis, *n.nt.* ice cream.

Saison', -s, *n.f.* season.

Saite, -n, *n.f.* string, chord.

Sakrament', -e, *n.nt.* sacrament.

Sakrileg', -e, *n.nt.* sacrilege.

Sakristei, -en, *n.f.* sacristy, vestry.

Salat', -e, *n.m.* salad.

Salat'soße, -n, *n.f.* salad dressing.

Salbe, -n, *n.f.* salve, ointment.

salben, *vb.* anoint.

Saldo, -den, *n.m.* balance, remainder.

Salm, -e, *n.m.* salmon.

Salon', -s, *n.m.* salon.

salopp', *adj.* nonchalant.

salutie'ren, *vb.* salute.

Salve, -n, *n.f.* salvo.

Salz, -e, *n.nt.* salt.

salzen, *vb.* salt.

salzig, *adj.* salty.

Salzwasser, -, *n.nt.* brine.

Samen, -, *n.m.* seed.

sammeln, *vb.* collect, gather; (sich s.) (mil.) rally.

Sammler, -, *n.m.* collector.

Sammlung, -en, *n.f.* collection.

Samstag, -e, *n.m.* Saturday.

Samt, *n.m.* velvet.

samt, *adv.&prep.* together with.

sämtlich, *adj.* entire.

Sanato'rium, -rien, *n.nt.* sanatorium.

Sand, -e, *n.m.* sand.

Sanda'le, -n, *n.f.* sandal.

sandig, *adj.* sandy.

Sandtorte, -n, *n.f.* pound cake.

sanft, *adj.* gentle, meek.

Sanftmut, *n.m.* gentleness.

sanftmütig, *adj.* gentle, meek.

Sänger, -, *n.m.* singer.

sang- und klanglos, *adv.* quietly.

Sankt, *adj.* Saint.

Saphir', -e, *n.m.* sapphire.

Sardel'le, -n, *n.f.* anchovy.

Sardi'ne, -n, *n.f.* sardine.

Sarg, -e, *n.m.* coffin.

Sarkas'mus, *n.m.* sarcasm.

sarkas'tisch, *adj.* sarcastic.

Satan, *n.m.* Satan.

sata'nisch, *adj.* diabolical.

Satellit', -en, -en, *n.m.* satellite.

Satin', -s, *n.m.* satin.

Sati're, -n, *n.f.* satire.

sati'risch, *adj.* satirical.

satt, *adj.* satiated; (ich bin s.) I have had enough to eat; (ich habe es s.) I am sick of it; (sich s. essen*, sehen*) eat one's fill.

Sattel, -, *n.m.* saddle.

satteln, *vb.* saddle.

sättigen, *vb.* satiate, saturate.

Sättigung, *n.f.* satiation, saturation.

sattsam, *adv.* sufficiently.

Satz, -e, *n.m.* (gram.) sentence, clause; (music) movement; (dishes, tennis) set.

Satzlehre, *n.f.* syntax.

Satzung, -en, *n.f.* statute, bylaw.

Satzzeichen, -, *n.nt.* punctuation mark.

Sau, -e, *n.f.* sow.

sauber, *adj.* clean, neat.

Sauberkeit, *n.f.* cleanliness, neatness.

säuberlich, *adj.* clean, careful.

säubern, *vb.* cleanse, purge.

Säuberungsaktion, -en, *n.f.* purge.

sauer, *adj.* sour, acid.

Säuerlichkeit, -en, *n.f.* acidity.

Sauerstoff, *n.m.* oxygen.

saufen*, *vb.* drink heavily, guzzle.

Säufer, -, *n.m.* drunkard.

saugen*, *vb.* suck.

Saugen, *n.nt.* suction.

Sauger, -, *n.m.* nipple (baby's bottle).

Säugling, -e, *n.m.* infant, baby.

Säule, -n, *n.f.* pillar, column.

Saum, -e, *n.m.* seam, hem.

säumen, *vb.* hem; delay.

säumig, *adj.* tardy, delinquent.

Säure, -n, *n.f.* acid.

säuseln, *vb.* rustle.

sausen, *vb.* (wind) whistle; run, dash.

schaben, *vb.* scrape.

Schabernack, -e, *n.m.* hoax.

schäbig, *adj.* shabby.

Schach, *n.nt.* chess; (in S. halten*) keep at bay.

Schachbrett, -er, *n.nt.* chessboard.

Schachfigur, -en, *n.f.* chessman.

schachmatt', *adj.* checkmate; (fig.) exhausted.

Schachspiel, -e, *n.nt.* chess.

Schacht, -e, *n.m.* shaft.

Schachtel, -n, *n.f.* box.

schade, *adv.* too bad.

Schädel, -, *n.m.* skull.

schaden, *vb.* harm; be harmful.

Schaden, -, *n.m.* harm, damage.

Schadenersatz, *n.m.* indemnity, compensation, damages.

schadenfroh, *adj.* gloating; (s. sein*) gloat.

schadhaft, *adj.* defective.

schädigen, *vb.* wrong, damage.

schädlich, *adj.* harmful, injurious.

Schädling, -e, *n.m.* pest, destructive insect.

Schaf, -e, *n.nt.* sheep.

Schäfer, -, *n.m.* shepherd.

schaffen*, *vb.* make, create.

schaffen, *vb.* get done, achieve; (sich zu s. machen mit) to busy oneself with, tangle.

Schaffner, -, *n.m.* conductor.

Schafott', -e, *n.nt.* scaffold.

Schafskopf, -e, *n.m.* idiot.

Schaft, -e, *n.m.* shaft.

Schakal', -e, *n.m.* jackal.

Schal, -s, *n.m.* shawl, scarf.

schal, *adj.* stale.

Schale, -n, *n.f.* skin, rind; shell; dish, bowl.

schälen, *vb.* pare, peel.

Schalk, -e, *n.m.* rogue.

schalkhaft, *adj.* roguish.

Schall, -e, *n.m.* sound, ring.

Schalldämpfer, -, *n.m.* (auto) muffler; (gun) silencer.

Schallgrenze, -n, *n.f.* sound barrier.

Schallplatte, -n, *n.f.* phonograph record.

Schalot'te, -n, *n.f.* scallion.

Schaltanlage, -n, *n.f.* switchboard.

Schaltbrett, -er, *n.nt.* switchboard; control panel.

schalten, *vb.* shift; command; (s. und walten) do as one pleases.

Schalter, -, *n.m.* (elec.) switch; (ticket, etc.) window.

Schaltjahr, -e, *n.nt.* leap year.

Schaltung, -en, *n.f.* (elec.) connection; (auto) shift.

Scham, *n.f.* shame; chastity.

schämen, *vb.* shame; (sich s.) be ashamed.

Schamgefühl, -e, *n.nt.* sense of modesty.

schamhaft, *adj.* modest, chaste.

schamlos, *adj.* shameless, infamous.

Schamlosigkeit, *n.f.* shamelessness.

Schampun', -s, *n.nt.* shampoo.

schandbar, *adj.* shameful, disgraceful.

Schande, *n.f.* shame, dishonor.

schänden, *vb.* dishonor, ravish.

Schandfleck, -e, *n.m.* blemish, stigma.

schändlich, *adj.* infamous.

Schandtat, -en, *n.f.* crime.

Schindung, -en, *n.f.* desecration; rape.

Schankstube, -n, *n.f.* barroom.

Schanze, -n, *n.f.* entrenchment; (sein Leben in die S. schlagen*) risk one's life.

Schar, -en, *n.f.* flock, group, host.

scharf (-), *adj.* sharp, acute, keen.

Scharfblick, *n.m.* quick eye; acuteness.

Schärfe, -n, *n.f.* sharpness, acuteness.

schärfen, *vb.* sharpen.

Scharfrichter, -, *n.m.* executioner.

Scharfsinn, *n.m.* acumen, discernment.

scharfsinnig, *adj.* acute, shrewd.

Scharlach, *n.m.* scarlet fever.

scharlachrot, *adj.* scarlet.

Scharnier, -e, *n.nt.* hinge.

Schärpe, -n, *n.f.* sash.

Scharte, -n, *n.f.* crack.

Schatten, -, *n.m.* shade; shadow.

Schattenbild, -er, *n.nt.* silhouette.

Schattengestalt, -en, *n.f.* phantom, phantasm.

Schattenseite, -n, *n.f.* shady side; (fig.) disadvantage, drawback.

schattie'ren, *vb.* shade.

schattig, *adj.* shady.

Schatz, ¨e, *n.m.* treasure.

schätzen, *vb.* treasure, prize; estimate, gauge; esteem.

schätzenswert, *adj.* estimable.

Schatzmeister, -, *n.m.* treasurer.

Schätzung, -en, *n.f.* estimate.

schätzungsweise, *adv.* approximately.

Schau, *n.f.* show, exhibition; (zur S. tragen*) display.

Schauder, -, *n.m.* shudder, shiver.

schauderhaft, *adj.* horrible, ghastly.

schaudern, *vb.* shudder.

schauen, *vb.* see, look.

Schauer, -, *n.m.* shower; (fever) chill.

schauerlich, *adj.* gruesome.

Schaufel, -n, *n.f.* shovel; dustpan.

Schaufenster, -, *n.nt.* store window, display window.

Schaukel, -n, *n.f.* swing.

schaukeln, *vb.* swing, rock.

Schaukelstuhl, ¨e, *n.m.* rocking chair.

Schaum, *n.m.* froth, foam; lather.

schäumen, *vb.* froth, foam; lather.

Schaumgummi, *n.m.* foam rubber.

Schaumwein, -e, *n.m.* champagne.

Schauplatz, ¨e, *n.m.* scene, theater, locale.

schaurig, *adj.* horrible.

Schauspiel, -e, *n.nt.* drama; spectacle.

Schauspieler, -, *n.m.* actor.

Schauspielerin, -nen, *n.f.* actress.

Schaustellung, *n.f.* exhibition; ostentation.

Scheck, -s, *n.m.* check.

scheel, *adj.* (s. an-sehen*) look askance at.

Scheffel, -, *n.m.* bushel.

Scheibe, -n, *n.f.* disk; slice.

Scheide, -n, *n.f.* sheath; (water) divide; vagina.

scheiden*, *vb.* leave, part; (sich s. lassen*) get divorced.

Scheidewand, ¨e, *n.f.* partition.

Scheideweg, -e, *n.m.* crossroads.

Scheidung, -en, *n.f.* divorce.

Schein, *n.m.* shine, light, shimmer; brilliance.

scheinbar, *adj.* apparent; imaginary.

scheinen*, *vb.* shine; seem.

scheinheilig, *adj.* hypocritical.

Scheinwerfer, -, *n.m.* spotlight; headlight.

Scheinwerferlicht, *n.nt.* floodlight.

Scheitel, -, *n.m.* part (in the hair).

scheitern, *vb.* fail.

Schelle, -n, *n.f.* bell.

schellen, *vb.* ring.

Schelm, -e, *n.m.* rogue.

schelmisch, *adj.* roguish, mischievous.

Schelte, *n.f.* scolding.

schelten*, *vb.* scold.

Schema, -s, *n.nt.* scheme.

Schenke, -n, *n.f.* tavern, bar.

Schenkel, -, *n.m.* thigh.

schenken, *vb.* give (as a present).

Schenkstube, -n, *n.f.* taproom, bar.

Schenkung, -en, *nf.* donation.

Schere, -n, *n.f.* scissors, shears.

scheren*, *vb.* shear.

Schererei', -en, *n.f.* bother.

Scherz, -e, *n.m.* joke, jest.

scherzen, *vb.* joke, jest, kid.

scherzhaft, *adj.* jocular.

scheu, *adj.* shy.

Scheu, *n.f.* timidity.

scheuchen, *vb.* scare, shoo.

scheuen, *vb.* shy, shun.

Scheuer, -n, *n.f.* barn, shed.

scheuern, *vb.* scour.

Scheuklappe, -n, *n.f.* blinder.

Scheune, -n, *n.f.* barn, shed.

Scheusal, -e, *n.nt.* monster, fright.

scheußlich, *adj.* horrible.

Schi, -er, *n.m.* ski.

Schicht, -en, *n.f.* layer, stratum, class.

schick, *adj.* chic, stylish.

Schick, *n.m.* skill; stylishness.

schicken, *vb.* send; (sich s.) be proper.

Schickeria *n.f.* (slang) jet-set.

schicklich, *adj.* proper.

Schicksal, -e, *n.nt.* fate.

schicksalsschwer, *adj.* fateful.

Schickung, *n.f.* providence.

schieben*, *vb.* push, shove; engage in illegal transactions.

Schieber, -, *n.m.* profiteer.

Schiebung, -en, *n.f.* racketeering.

Schiedsrichter, -, *n.m.* umpire, referee.

schief, *adj.* crooked, askew.

Schiefer, *n.m.* slate.

schielen, *vb.* be cross-eyed, look cross-eyed.

Schienbein, -e, *n.nt.* shin.

Schiene, -n, *n.f.* rail; (med.) splint.

schier, 1. *adj.* sheer, pure. **2.** *adv.* almost.

Schierling, *n.m.* hemlock.

schießen*, *vb.* shoot.

Schießgewehr, -e, *n.nt.* gun.

Schiff, -e, *n.nt.* ship; nave (of a church).

Schiffahrt, *n.f.* navigation.

schiffbar, *adj.* navigable.

Schiffbau, *n.m.* ship building.

Schiffbruch, ¨e, *n.m.* shipwreck.

schiffen, *vb.* ship, navigate.

Schiffer, -, *n.m.* mariner.

Schiffsrumpf, ¨e, *n.m.* hull.

schikanie'ren, *vb.* annoy.

schi-laufen*, *vb.* ski.

Schild, -e, *n.m.* shield.

Schild, -er, *n.nt.* sign.

Schilddrüse, -n, *n.f.* thyroid gland.

schildern, *vb.* portray.

Schilderung, -en, *n.f.* portrayal.

Schildkröte, -n, *n.f.* turtle, tortoise.

Schilf, *n.nt.* reed.

Schilift, -s, *n.m.* ski lift.

schillern, *vb.* be iridescent.

Schilling, -e, *n.m.* shilling.

Schimmel, -, *n.m.* mold, mildew; white horse.

schimmelig, *adj.* moldy.

Schimmer, -, *n.m.* glimmer, gleam.

Schimpan'se, -n, -n, *n.m.* chimpanzee.

Schimpf, -e, *n.m.* insult, abuse, disgrace.

schimpfen, *vb.* insult, abuse; complain, gripe.

Schimpfwort, -e, *n.nt.* term of abuse.

schinden*, *vb.* flay; (fig.) torment; (sich s.) work hard, slave.

Schinken, -, *n.m.* ham.

Schirm, -e, *n.m.* screen; umbrella, parasol; shelter.

schirmen, *vb.* protect.

Schirmherr, -n, -en, *n.m.* patron.

Schlacht, -en, *n.f.* battle.

schlachten, *vb.* slaughter.

Schlächter, -, *n.m.* butcher.

Schlachtfeld, -er, *n.nt.* battlefield.

Schlachtschiff, -e, *n.nt.* battleship.

Schlacke, -n, *n.f.* slag, clinker, cinder.

Schlaf, *n.m.* sleep.

Schlafanzug, ̈-e, *n.m.* pajamas.

Schläfe, -n, *n.f.* temple.

schlafen*, *vb.* sleep, be asleep.

Schlafenszeit, -en, *n.f.* bedtime.

schlaff, *adj.* limp.

Schlaffheit, *n.f.* limpness, laxity.

Schlaflosigkeit, *n.f.* insomnia.

Schlafmittel, -, *n.nt.* sleeping pill.

schläfrig, *adj.* sleepy.

Schlafrock, ̈-e, *n.m.* dressing gown.

Schlafwagen, -, *n.m.* sleeping car.

Schlafzimmer, -, *n.nt.* bedroom.

Schlag, ̈-e, *n.m.* blow, stroke, shock.

Schlagader, -n, *n.f.* artery.

Schlaganfall, ̈-e, *n.m.* stroke; apoplexy.

Schlagbaum, ̈-e, *n.m.* wooden bar, (railroad customs) barrier.

schlagen*, *vb.* hit, strike, beat; fell (trees); coin (money).

Schlager, -, *n.m.* hit (song, play, book).

Schläger, -, *n.m.* hitter; bat, club.

Schlägerei', -en, *n.f.* brawl.

Schlagholz, ̈-er, *n.nt.* bat, club.

Schlagobers, *n.nt.* whipped cream.

Schlagsahne, *n.f.* whipped cream.

Schlagseite, *n.f.* list.

Schlagwort, -e, *n.nt.* slogan.

Schlagzeile, -n, *n.f.* headline.

Schlamm, *n.m.* muck, mud.

schlampig, *adj.* frowsy.

Schlange, -n, *n.f.* snake, serpent.

schlängeln, *vb.* **(sich s.)** wind, wriggle.

schlank, *adj.* slender, slim.

schlapp, *adj.* slack, flabby.

Schlappe, -n, *n.f.* rebuff, setback, defeat.

schlau, *adj.* sly, clever, astute.

Schlauch, ̈-e, *n.m.* hose, tube.

Schlaufe, -n, *n.f.* loop.

schlecht, *adj.* bad.

schlechterdings, *adv.* absolutely.

schlechthin, *adv.* quite, simply.

Schlegel, -, *n.m.* mallet, sledge hammer, drumstick.

schleichen*, *vb.* sneak, slink, crawl.

Schleier, -, *n.m.* veil.

schleierhaft, *adj.* veil-like; inexplicable, mysterious.

Schleife, -n, *n.f.* bow.

schleifen, *vb.* drag.

schleifen*, *vb.* grind, polish, sharpen.

Schleifmittel, -, *n.nt.* abrasive.

Schleifstein, -e, *n.m.* grindstone.

Schleim, *n.m.* slime; mucus.

Schleimhaut, ̈-e, *n.f.* mucous membrane.

schleimig, *adj.* slimy; mucous.

schlendern, *vb.* saunter, stroll.

schlenkern, *vb.* shamble, dangle, swing.

Schleppe, -n, *n.f.* train.

schleppen, *vb.* drag, lug, haul, tow.

Schlepper, -, *n.m.* tugboat, tractor.

Schleuder, -n, *n.f.* slingshot, catapult, centrifuge.

schleudern, *vb.* hurl, fling; skid.

schleunig, *adj.* speedy.

Schleuse, -n, *n.f.* sluice, lock.

Schlich, -e, *n.m.* trick.

schlicht, *adj.* plain, simple.

schlichten, *vb.* smooth; arbitrate.

Schlichter, -, *n.m.* arbitrator.

Schlichtung, -en, *n.f.* arbitration.

schließen*, *vb.* shut; close; conclude.

Schliessfach, ̈-er, *n.nt.* baggage locker.

schließlich, 1. *adj.* final. **2.** *adv.* at last.

Schliff, -e, *n.m.* cut, polish(ing), grind(ing); good manners, style; **(letzter S.)** final touch.

schlimm, *adj.* bad, serious.

Schlinge, -n, *n.f.* sling, noose.

schlingen*, *vb.* twist, wind; gulp.

schlingern, *vb.* roll.

Schlips, -e, *n.m.* necktie.

Schlitten, -, *n.m.* sled, sleigh.

Schlittschuh, -e, *n.m.* skate.

schlittschuh-laufen*, *vb.* skate.

Schlitz, -e, *n.m.* slit, slot, slash.

schlitzen, *vb.* slit, slash.

Schloß, ̈-sser, *n.nt.* lock; castle.

Schlot, -e, *n.m.* chimney, flue.

schlottern, *vb.* hang loosely, flop, shake.

Schlucht, -en, *n.f.* gorge, gulch.

schluchzen, *vb.* sob.

Schluck, -e, *n.m.* swallow.

Schluckauf, *n.m.* hiccup(s).

Schlückchen, -, *n.nt.* nip.

schlucken, *vb.* swallow.

Schlummer, *n.m.* slumber.

schlummern, *vb.* slumber.

Schlund, ̈-e, *n.m.* throat, gullet; chasm.

schlüpfen, *vb.* slip.

Schlüpfer, -, *n.m.* panties.

schlüpfrig, *adj.* slippery.

schlürfen, *vb.* sip.

Schluß, ̈-sse, *n.m.* end, close, conclusion.

Schlüssel, -, *n.m.* key.

Schlußfolgerung, -e, *n.f.* deduction, conclusion.

Schmach, *n.f.* disgrace, insult.

schmachten, *vb.* languish.

schmächtig, *adj.* slim, slight.

schmachvoll, *adj.* ignominious.

schmackhaft, *adj.* tasty.

schmähen, *vb.* abuse, revile.

schmal (-, ̈-), *adj.* narrow.

schmälern, *vb.* curtail, detract from.

Schmalz, *n.nt.* lard.

schmarotzen, *vb.* sponge (on).

Schmarot'zer, -, *n.m.* hanger-on; parasite.

schmatzen, *vb.* smack one's lips.

Schmaus, ̈-e, *n.m.* feast.

schmausen, *vb.* feast.

schmecken, *vb.* taste.

Schmeichelei', -en, *n.f.* flattery.

schmeichelhaft, *adj.* flattering.

schmeicheln, *vb.* flatter.

schmeißen*, *vb.* throw, hurl, chuck, hit.

schmelzen*, *vb.* melt.

Schmerz, -en, *n.m.* ache, pain.

schmerzen, *vb.* ache, pain, hurt.

schmerzhaft, *adj.* painful.

Schmetterling, -e, *n.m.* butterfly.

schmettern, *vb.* dash, smash; bray, blare.

Schmied, -e, *n.m.* blacksmith.

Schmiede, -n, *n.f.* forge.

schmieden, *vb.* forge.

schmiegen, *vb.* bend, press close, nestle, cling.

schmiegsam, *adj.* pliant, flexible.

Schmiere, -n, *n.f.* grease.

schmieren, *vb.* grease, smear, scribble; **(wie geschmiert')** like clockwork.

schmierig, *adj.* greasy, dirty, sordid.

Schmiermittel, -, *n.nt.* lubricant.

Schminke, -n, *n.f.* rouge, make-up, grease paint.

schminken, *vb.* put on make-up.

Schmiß, -sse, *n.m.* stroke, cut; dueling scar; verve.

schmökern, *vb.* browse.

schmollen, *vb.* pout, sulk.

schmoren, *vb.* stew.

schmuck, *adj.* smart, trim.

Schmuck, *n.m.* ornament, jewelry.

schmücken, *vb.* decorate.

Schmucknadel, -n, *n.f.* clip.

schmuggeln, *vb.* smuggle.

Schmuggel, -, *n.m.* smuggling.

Schmuggelware, -n, *n.f.* contraband.

Schmuggler, -, *n.m.* smuggler.

schmunzeln, *vb.* smirk, grin.

schmusen, *vb.* spoon, neck.

Schmutz, *n.m.* dirt, filth.

schmutzig, *adj.* dirty.

Schnabel, ̈-, *n.m.* beak.

Schnake, -n, *n.f.* gnat.

Schnalle, -n, *n.f.* buckle, clasp.

schnallen, *vb.* buckle.

schnalzen, *vb.* click (one's tongue), snap (one's fingers), crack (a whip).

schnappen, vb. snap, snatch, grab, catch, gasp (for breath).

Schnappschuß, -sse, n.m. snapshot.

Schnaps, :, n.m. hard liquor, whisky, brandy.

schnarchen, vb. snore.

schnarren, vb. buzz, whir, rattle, burr.

schnattern, vb. cackle.

schnauben, vb. pant, snort.

schnaufen, vb. breathe hard.

Schnauze, -, n.f. snout.

Schnecke, -n, n.f. snail.

Schnee, n.m. snow.

Schneesturm, -e, n.m. blizzard.

Schneid, n.m. bravado.

Schneide, -n, n.f. edge.

schneiden*, vb. cut.

schneidend, adj. cutting, scathing.

Schneider, -, n.m. tailor.

Schneiderin, -nen, n.f. dressmaker.

schneidig, adj. dashing.

schneien, vb. snow.

schnell, adj. quick.

schnellen, vb. flip, jerk.

Schnelligkeit, -en, n.f. swiftness.

Schnellzug, :e, n.m. express train.

schneuzen, vb. (sich s.) blow one's nose.

schnippisch, adj. saucy.

Schnitt, -e, n.m. cut, slice, incision.

Schnittbohne, -n, n.f. string bean.

Schnitte, -n, n.f. slice, sandwich.

Schnittlauch, n.m. chive(s).

Schnittmuster, -, n.nt. pattern.

Schnittpunkt, -e, n.m. intersection.

Schnittstelle, -n, f. (computer) interface.

Schnittwaren, n.pl. dry goods.

Schnittwunde, -n, n.f. cut.

Schnitzel, -, n.nt. chip; cutlet.

schnitzen, vb. carve, whittle.

Schnitzwerk, -e, n.nt. carving.

schnodd(e)rig, adj. insolent.

schnöde, adj. scornful, base.

Schnorchel, -, n.m. snorkel.

schnüffeln, vb. sniffle, snoop.

Schnuller, -, n.m. pacifier.

Schnupfen, -, n.m. cold (in the head).

Schnupftuch, :er, n.nt. handkerchief.

Schnuppe, -n, n.f. shooting star; (das ist mir S.) I don't care a hoot.

Schnur, :e, n.f. cord, string.

schnüren, vb. lace.

Schnurrbart, :e, n.m. mustache.

Schnürsenkel, -, n.m. shoelace.

Schock, -s, n.m. shock.

schockie'ren, vb. shock.

schofel(ig), adj. shabby, mean.

Schokola'de, -n, n.f. chocolate.

Scholle, -n, n.f. clod, soil.

schon, adv. already; even.

schön, adj. beautiful, nice.

schonen, vb. treat carefully, spare.

Schönheit, -en, n.f. beauty.

Schönheitssalon, -s, n.m. beauty parlor.

Schonung, -en, n.f. careful treatment, consideration.

schonungslos, adj. merciless.

Schopf, :e, n.m. forelock, crown.

schöpfen, vb. draw (water, breath); take from.

Schöpfer, -, n.m. creator.

schöpferisch, adj. creative.

Schöpfkelle, -n, n.f. scoop.

Schöpflöffel, -, n.m. ladle, dipper.

Schöpfung, -, n.f. creation.

Schoppen, -, n.m. glass of beer or wine; pint.

Schorf, n.m. scab.

Schornstein, -e, n.m. chimney, smokestack.

Schoß, :e, n.m. lap.

Schößling, -e, n.m. shoot.

Schote, -n, n.f. pod.

Schotte, -n, -n, n.m. Scotsman.

schottisch, adj. Scotch.

Schottland, n.nt. Scotland.

schräg, adj. oblique.

Schrägschrift, n.f. italics.

Schramme, -n, n.f. scratch.

Schrank, :e, n.m. wardrobe, locker, cupboard, cabinet.

Schranke, -n, n.f. barrier.

Schrapnell', -s, n.nt. shrapnel.

Schraube, -n, n.f. screw.

schrauben, vb. screw.

Schraubenschlüssel, -, n.m. wrench.

Schraubenzieher, -, n.m. screwdriver.

Schreck, -e, n.m. fright, scare.

Schrecken, -, n.m. terror, fear.

schreckhaft, adj. easily frightened.

schrecklich, adj. awful, terrible.

Schrei, -e, n.m. cry, scream, shout.

Schreibdame, -n, n.f. typist.

schreiben*, vb. write.

Schreiben, -, n.nt. letter.

Schreiber, -, n.m. clerk, scribe.

Schreibheft, -e, n.nt. notebook.

Schreibmaschine, -n, n.f. typewriter.

Schreibtisch, -e, n.m. desk.

Schreibung, -en, n.f. spelling.

Schreibwaren, n.pl. stationery.

schreien*, vb. cry, scream, shout.

schreiend, adj. flagrant.

Schrein, -e, n.m. shrine, casket, cabinet.

schreiten*, vb. stride, step.

Schrift, -en, n.f. writing, script; (Heilige S.) scripture(s).

Schriftführer, -, n.m. secretary (of an organization).

schriftlich, adj. written, in writing.

Schriftsatz, :e, n.m. type.

Schriftsteller, -, n.m. writer, author.

schrill, adj. shrill.

Schritt, -e, n.m. step, pace; crotch (of trousers).

schroff, adj. steep, abrupt, curt.

Schrotmehl, n.m. coarse meal, grits.

schrubbe(r)n, vb. scrub.

Schrulle, -n, n.f. whim.

schrumpfen, vb. shrink.

Schub, :e, n.m. shove, thrust; batch.

Schublade, -n, n.f. drawer.

schüchtern, adj. shy, bashful.

Schüchternheit, -en, nf. bashfulness, shyness.

Schuft, -e, n.m. cad, scoundrel.

schuften, vb. work hard, drudge.

Schuh, -e, n.m. shoe.

Schuhmacher, -, n.m. shoemaker.

Schuhputzer, -, n.m. bootblack.

Schuhwerk, -e, n.nt. footwear.

Schularbeiten, n.pl. homework.

Schulbeispiel, -e, n.nt. typical example.

Schuld, -en, n.f. fault, guilt, blame, debt.

schulden, vb. owe.

schuldhaft, adj. culpable.

schuldig, adj. guilty; due, owing.

Schuldigsprechung, -en, n.f. conviction.

Schuldirektor, -en, n.m. headmaster, principal.

schuldlos, adj. guiltless.

Schuldner, -, n.m. debtor.

Schule, -n, n.f. school.

schulen, vb. train, indoctrinate.

Schüler, -, n.m. (boy) pupil.

Schülerin, -nen, n.f. (girl) pupil.

Schulgeld, -er, n.nt. tuition.

Schulter, -n, n.f. shoulder.

schultern, vb. shoulder.

Schund, n.m. trash.

Schupo, -s, n.m. (= Schutzpolizist) cop.

Schuppe, -n, n.f. scale; (pl.) dandruff.

Schuppen, -, n.m. shed, hangar.

schüren, vb. poke, stir up, foment.

Schurke, -n, -n, n.m. villain, scoundrel.

Schürze, -n, n.f. apron.

Schuß, :sse, n.m. shot.

Schüssel, -n, n.f. dish, bowl.

Schuster, -, n.m. shoemaker.

Schutt, n.m. rubbish.

schütteln, vb. shake.

schütten, vb. shed, pour.

Schutz, n.m. protection.

Schütze, -n, -n, n.m. rifleman, marksman, shot.

schützen, vb. protect.

Schützengraben, :, n.m. trench, dugout.

Schutzhaft, n.f. protective custody.

Schutzheilig-, n.m.&f. patron saint.

Schutzherr, -n, -en, n.m. patron.

schutzlos, adj. unprotected, defenseless.

Schutzmann, ̈er, n.m. patrolman.

Schutzmarke, -n, n.f. trade mark.

schwach (̈), adj. weak.

Schwäche, -n, n.f. weakness.

schwächen, vb. weaken.

Schwachheit, -en, n.f. frailty.

schwächlich, adj. feeble.

Schwächling, -e, n.m. weakling.

Schwachsinn, n.m. feeble-mindedness.

schwachsinnig, adj. feeble-minded.

Schwachsinnig-, n.m.&f. moron.

Schwager, -̈r, n.m. brother-in-law.

Schwägerin, -nen, n.f. sister-in-law.

Schwalbe, -n, n.f. swallow.

Schwall, -e, n.m. flood.

Schwamm, ̈e, n.m. sponge.

Schwan, ̈e, n.m. swan.

schwanger, adj. pregnant.

Schwangerschaft, -en, n.f. pregnancy.

Schwangerschaftsverhütung, n.f. contraception.

schwankern, vb. totter, sway, vacillate, waver.

Schwankung, -en, n.f. fluctuation.

Schwanz, ̈e, n.m. tail.

schwänzen, vb. cut (a class).

Schwarm, ̈e, n.m. swarm.

schwärmen, vb. swarm; (s. für) be crazy about.

Schwärmer, -, n.m. enthusiast.

schwarz(-), adj. black; illegal.

Schwarz-, n. m. & f. Black (person).

Schwarzbrot, -e, n.nt. black bread.

schwärzen, vb. blacken.

Schwarzmarkt, ̈e, n.m. black market.

Schwarzseher, -, n.m. alarmist, pessimist.

schwatzen, schwätzen, vb. chatter, gab.

Schwebe, n.f. suspense, suspension; (in der S.) undecided.

schweben, vb. hover, be suspended, be pending.

Schwebezustand, -̈e, n.m. abeyance.

Schwede, -n, -n, n.m. Swede.

Schweden, n.nt. Sweden.

schwedisch, adj. Swedish.

Schwefel, n.m. sulphur.

Schweif, -e, n.m. tail, train.

schweifen, vb. roam, range.

schweigen*, vb. keep quiet, be silent.

Schweigen, n.nt. silence.

schweigsam, adj. silent.

Schwein, -e, n.nt. swine, hog, pig; good luck.

Schweinebraten, -, n.m. roast of pork.

Schweinefleisch, n.nt. pork.

Schweinerei', -en, n.f. awful mess, dirty business.

Schweinestall, ̈e, n.m. pigsty.

Schweinsleder, n.nt. pigskin.

Schweiß, n.m. sweat.

Schweiz, n.f. Switzerland.

Schweizer, -, n.m. Swiss.

schweizerisch, adj. Swiss.

schwelen, vb. smolder.

schwelgen, vb. revel.

Schwelgerei', -en, n.f. revelry.

Schwelle, -n, n.f. sill, threshold; (railroad) tie.

schwellen*, vb. swell.

schwenken, vb. wave, flourish, brandish.

schwer, adj. heavy; difficult.

Schwere, n.f. heaviness.

schwerfällig, adj. clumsy, ponderous, stolid.

Schwergewicht, n.nt. heavyweight.

schwerhörig, adj. hard of hearing.

Schwerkraft, n.f. gravity.

schwerlich, adj. with difficulty, hardly.

Schwermut, n.f. melancholy.

schwermütig, adj. moody, melancholy.

Schwert, -er, n.nt. sword; centerboard.

schwerwiegend, adj. grave.

Schwester, -n, n.f. sister; nurse.

Schwiegereltern, n.pl. parents-in-law.

Schwiegermutter, ̈, n.f. mother-in-law.

Schwiegersohn, ̈e, n.m. son-in-law.

Schwiegertochter, ̈, n.f. daughter-in-law.

Schwiegervater, ̈, n.m. father-in-law.

Schwiele, -n, n.f. callus.

schwielig, adj. callous.

schwierig, adj. difficult.

Schwierigkeit, -en, n.f. difficulty, trouble.

Schwimmbad, -̈er, n.nt. swimming pool.

schwimmen*, vb. swim.

Schwimmweste, -n, n.f. life-jacket.

Schwindel, -, n.m. dizziness; swindle, hoax; bunk.

Schwindelgefühl, n.nt. vertigo.

schwindeln, vb. swindle, cheat, fraud.

schwinden*, vb. disappear.

Schwindler, -, n.m. swindler, cheat, fraud.

schwindlig, adj. dizzy.

Schwindsucht, n.f. consumption.

schwindsüchtig, adj. consumptive.

schwingen*, vb. swing, brandish, oscillate.

Schwingung, -en, n.f. oscillation.

Schwips, -e, n.m. (einen S. haben*) be tipsy.

schwirren, vb. whir.

schwitzen, vb. sweat.

schwören, vb. swear.

schwul, adj. homosexual.

schwül, adj. sultry, muggy.

Schwulst, ̈e, n.m. bombast.

Schwund, n.m. disappearance, loss.

Schwung, ̈e, n.m. swing, verve, animation, motion.

Schwungkraft, n.f. drive.

schwunglos, adj. lackadaisical.

schwungvoll, adj. spirited.

Schwur, ̈e, n.m. oath.

sechs, num. six.

sechst-, adj. sixth.

Sechstel, -, n.nt. sixth part; (ein s.) one-sixth.

sechzig, num. sixty.

sechzigst-, adj. sixtieth.

Sechzigstel, -, n.nt. sixtieth part; (ein s.) one-sixtieth.

See, Se'en, n.m. lake.

See, Se'en, n.f. sea.

See-, cpds. naval, marine.

Seegang, n.m. (rough, calm) sea.

Seehund, -e, n.m. seal.

seekrank, adj. seasick.

Seekrankheit, n.f. seasickness.

Seele, -n, n.f. soul, spirit, mind.

Seeleute, n.pl. seamen.

seelisch, adj. spiritual.

Seelsorge, n.f. ministry.

Seemann, -leute, n.m. mariner.

Seemeile, -n, n.f. nautical mile.

Seeräuber, -, n.m. pirate.

Seereise, -n, n.f. cruise.

Seetang, n.m. seaweed.

seetüchtig, adj. seaworthy.

Seezunge, -n, n.f. sole.

Segel, -, n.nt. sail.

Segelboot, -e, n.nt. sailboat.

Segelflug, n.m. gliding.

Segelflugzeug, -e, n.nt. glider, sailplane.

segeln, vb. sail.

Segeltuch, n.nt. canvas, duck.

Segen, -, n.m. blessing.

Segment', -e, n.nt. segment.

segnen, vb. bless.

Segnung, -en, n.f. blessing, benediction.

sehen*, vb. see.

sehenswert, adj. worth seeing.

Sehenswürdigkeit, -en, n.f. sight(s).

Seher, -, n.m. seer, prophet.

Sehkraft, ̈e, n.f. (power of) sight, vision.

Sehne, -n, n.f. tendon, ligament, sinew.

sehnen, vb. (sich s.) long, yearn.

Sehnsucht, n.f. longing.

sehnsüchtig, adj. longing.

sehnsuchtsvoll, adj. longing.

sehr, adv. very, much, a lot.

Sehweite, -n, n.f. range of sight.

seicht, adj. shallow, insipid.

Seide, -n, n.f. silk.

Seidel, -, n.nt. beer mug.

seiden, adj. silk.

Seidenpapier, n.nt. tissue paper.

seidig, adj. silky.

Seife, -n, n.f. soap.

Seifenschaum, n.m. suds.

seihen, vb. strain.

Sell, -e, n.nt. rope, cable.

Seilbahn, -en, n.f. cableway.

sein°, vb. be.

sein, -, -e, adj. his, its.

Sein, n.nt. being.

seiner, -es, -e, pron. his, its.

seinerseits, adv. for his part.

seinerzeit, adv. at the time.

seinesgleichen, pron. equal to him, such as he.

seinetwegen, adv. for his sake; for all he cares.

seinetwillen, adv. (um s.) for his sake, because of him.

seit, 1. prep. since, for. 2. conj. since.

seitab', adv. aside.

seitdem, 1. conj. since. 2. adv. since then.

Seite, -n, n.f. side; page.

seitenlang, adj. going on for pages.

seitens, prep. on behalf of.

Seitensprung, -e, n.m. escapade.

Seitenstraße, -n, n.f. side street.

Seitenzahl, -en, n.f. number of pages.

seither, adv. since then.

seitlich, adj. lateral.

seitwärts, adv. sideways.

Sekretär', -e, n.m. secretary.

Sekretä'rin, -nen, n.f. secretary.

Sekt, -e, n.m. champagne.

Sekte, -n, n.f. sect, denomination.

Sekundant', -en, -en, n.m. second (at a duel).

sekundär', adj. secondary.

Sekun'de, -n, n.f. second.

selb-, adj. same.

selber, adv. (my-, your-, him-, etc.)self; (our-, your-, them-)selves.

selbst, adv. even; (my-, your-, him-, etc.)self; (our-, your-, them-)selves.

Selbstachtung, n.f. self-respect.

selbständig, adj. independent.

Selbständigkeit, n.f. independence.

Selbstbestimmung, n.f. self-determination.

selbstbewußt, adj. self-conscious.

Selbstbiographie, -n, autobiography.

selbstgefällig, adj. self-satisfied, smug.

selbstgefertigt, adj. homemade.

selbstgerecht, adj. self-righteous.

Selbstgespräch, -e, n.nt. monologue.

selbstlos, adj. unselfish.

Selbstmord, -e, n.m. suicide.

selbstredend, adj. self-evident.

selbstsicher, adj. self-confident.

Selbstsucht, n.f. selfishness.

selbstsüchtig, adj. selfish.

selbsttätig, adj. automatic.

selbstverständlich, adj. obvious.

Selbstverwaltung, n.f. home rule.

selbstzufrieden, adj. complacent.

Selbstzufriedenheit, n.f. complacency.

selig, adj. blessed; blissfully happy; deceased, late.

Seligkeit, -en, n.f. salvation; bliss.

selig-sprechen°, vb. beatify.

Sellerie, n.f. celery.

selten, 1. adj. rare, scarce. 2. adv. seldom.

Seltenheit, -en, n.f. rarity.

Selters, Selter(s)wasser, n.nt. soda water.

seltsam, adj. strange, queer, curious.

Seman'tik, n.f. semantics.

seman'tisch, adj. semantic.

Semes'ter, -, n.nt. semester, term.

Semiko'lon, -s, n.nt. semicolon.

Seminar', -e, n.nt. seminar(y).

Semit', -en, -en, n.m. Semite.

semi'tisch, adj. Semitic.

Semmel, -n, n.f. roll.

Senat', -e, n.m. senate.

Sena'tor, -o'ren, n.m. senator.

senden°, vb. send, ship.

senden, vb. broadcast.

Sender, -, n.m. sender, transmitter, broadcasting station.

Sendung, -en, n.f. shipment; broadcast, transmission.

Senf, n.m. mustard.

sengen, vb. scorch, singe.

Senior, -o'ren, n.m. senior citizen.

senken, vb. sink, lower, reduce.

senkrecht, adj. perpendicular.

Senkung, -en, n.f. depression, reduction.

Sensation', -en, n.f. sensation, thrill.

sensationell', adj. sensational.

Sense, -n, n.f. scythe.

sentimental', adj. sentimental.

Septem'ber, -, n.m. September.

Serbe, -n, -n, n.m. Serbian.

Serbien, n.nt. Serbia.

serbisch, adj. Serbian.

Serie, -n, n.f. series.

Serum, -a, n.nt. serum.

Servi'ce, n.nt. service, set.

servie'ren, vb. serve.

Servier'platte, -n, n.f. platter.

Serviet'te, -n, n.f. napkin.

Sessel, -, n.m. easy-chair.

seßhaft, adj. settled, established.

setzen, vb. set, put, place; (sich s.) sit down.

Seuche, -n, n.f. plague, epidemic.

seufzen, vb. sigh.

Seufzer, -, n.m. sigh.

sexuell', adj. sexual.

Siam, n.nt. Siam.

Siame'se, -n, -n, n.m. Siamese.

siame'sisch, adj. Siamese.

Sibi'rien, n.nt. Siberia.

sich, pron. (him-, her-, it-, your-)self, (him-, your-)selves; each other, one another.

Sichel, -n, n.f. sickle; crescent.

sicher, adj. sure, certain, safe, secure.

Sicherheit, -en, n.f. safety, security, certainty.

Sicherheitsnadel, -n, n.f. safety-pin.

sicherlich, adv. surely.

sichern, vb. secure, safeguard.

Sicherung, -en, n.f. fuse.

Sicht, n.f. sight.

sichtbar, adj. visible.

sichten, vb. sift; sight.

sickern, vb. seep.

sie, pron. she; they.

Sie, pron. you (normal polite).

Sieb, -e, n.nt. sieve, strainer.

sieben, vb. sift, strain.

sieben, num. seven.

sieb(en)t-, adj. seventh.

Sieb(en)tel,-, n.nt. seventh part; (ein s.) one-seventh.

siebzig, num. seventy.

siebzigst-, adj. seventieth.

Siebzigstel, -, n.nt. seventieth part; (ein s.) one-seventieth.

siedeln, vb. settle.

sieden°, vb. boil.

Siedler, -, n.m. settler.

Siedlung, -en, n.f. settlement.

Sieg, -e, n.m. victory.

Siegel, -, n.nt. seal.

siegeln, vb. seal.

siegen, vb. win, be victorious.

Sieger, -, n.m. winner, victor.

sieghaft, adj. triumphant.

siegreich, adj. victorious.

Signal', -e, n.nt. signal.

Signal'horn, -er, n.nt. bugle.

Silbe, -n, n.f. syllable.

Silber, n.nt. silver.

silbern, adj. silver.

Silberwaren, n.f. silverware.

silbisch, adj. syllabic.

silbrig, adj. silvery.

Silves'ter, n.nt. New Year's Eve.

Sims, -e, n.m. cornice; ledge, sill, mantelpiece.

singen°, vb. sing.

Singular, -e, n.m. singular.

sinken°, vb. sink, decline, fall.

Sinn, -e, n.m. sense, mind, meaning, taste.

Sinnbild, -er, n.nt. symbol.

sinnen*, *vb.* think, meditate, plot.

sinnig, *adj.* thoughtful, appropriate.

sinnlich, *adj.* sensual.

sinnlos, *adj.* senseless.

Sintflut, *n.f.* flood, deluge.

Sippe, -n, *n.f.* kin; clan, tribe.

Sire'ne, -n, *n.f.* siren.

Sirup, *n.m.* molasses; syrup.

Sitte, -n, *n.f.* custom; (*pl.*) mores, manners, morals.

Sittenlehre, *n.f.* ethics.

sittenlos, *adj.* immoral.

sittig, *adj.* chaste, well-bred.

sittlich, *adj.* moral.

Situation', -en, *n.f.* situation.

Sitz, -e, *n.m.* seat, residence.

sitzen*, *vb.* sit, be seated; fit; be in jail.

sitzen-bleiben*, *vb.* remain seated; get stuck (with); not be promoted.

sitzen-lassen*, *vb.* jilt.

Sitzplatz, -̈e, *n.m.* seat.

Sitzung, -en, *n.f.* session.

Sizilia'ner, -, *n.m.* Sicilian.

sizilia'nisch, *adj.* Sicilian.

Sizi'lien, *n.nt.* Sicily.

Skala, -len, *n.f.* scale.

Skandal', -e, *n.m.* scandal.

Skandina'vien, *n.nt.* Scandinavia.

Skandina'vier, -, *n.m.* Scandinavian.

skandina'visch, *adj.* Scandinavian.

Skelett', -e, *n.nt.* skeleton.

Skepsis, *n.f.* skepticism.

Skeptiker, -, *n.m.* skeptic.

skeptisch, *adj.* skeptic(al).

ski, -er, *n.m.* ski.

ski-laufen*, *vb.* ski.

skilehrer, -, *n.m.* ski instructor.

skilift, -s, *n.m.* ski lift.

Skizze, -n, *n.f.* sketch.

skizzie'ren, *vb.* sketch.

Sklave, -n, -n, *n.m.* slave.

Sklaverei', *n.f.* slavery.

Skrupel, -, *n.m.* scruple.

Slang, *n.m.* slang.

Slawe, -n, -n, *n.m.* Slav.

slawisch, *adj.* Slavic.

Slowa'ke, -n, -n, *n.m.* Slovak.

Slowakei', *n.f.* Slovakia.

slowa'kisch, *adj.* Slovakian.

Smaragd', -e, *n.m.* emerald.

Smoking, -s, *n.m.* dinner jacket, tuxedo.

Snob, -s, *n.m.* snob.

so, *adv.* so, thus; (**s. groß wie**) as big as.

Socke, -n, *n.f.* sock.

Sockenhalter, -, *n.m.* garter.

Soda, *n.nt.* soda.

Sodbrennen, *n.nt.* heartburn.

soe'ben, *adv.* just now.

Sofa, -s, *n.nt.* sofa.

sofort', *adv.* immediately.

sofor'tig, *adj.* instantaneous.

Sog, *n.m.* suction; undertow.

sogar', *adv.* yet, even.

sogenannt, *adj.* so-called.

Sohle, -n, *n.f.* sole.

Sohn, -̈e, *n.m.* son.

solch(er, -es, -e), *adj.* such.

solcherlei', *adj.* of such a kind.

solchermaßen, *adv.* in such a way.

Sold, -e, *n.m.* pay.

Soldat', -en, -en, *n.m.* soldier.

solid', *adj.* solid.

Solidarität', *n.f.* solidarity.

Solist', -en, -en, *n.m.* soloist.

Soll, *n.nt.* debit; quota.

sollen*, *vb.* be supposed to, be said to; shall; (**er sollte gehen***) he should, ought to go; (**er hätte gehen*sollen**) he should, ought to have gone.

Solo, -s, *n.nt.* solo.

Sommer, -, *n.m.* summer.

Sommersprosse, -n, *n.f.* freckle.

Sommerzeit, -en, *n.f.* summer time; daylight-saving time.

Sona'te, -n, *n.f.* sonata.

Sonde, -n, *n.f.* probe.

sonder, *prep.* without.

Sonder, *cpds.* special.

Sonderangebot, -e, *n.nt.* bargain, special sale.

sonderbar, *adj.* strange, queer.

sondergleichen, *adv.* without equal, unparalleled.

sonderlich, *adj.* peculiar.

sondern, *vb.* separate.

sondern, *conj.* but (on the contrary).

sondie'ren, *vb.* sound, probe.

Sonett', -e, *n.nt.* sonnet.

Sonnabend, -e, *n.m.* Saturday.

Sonne, -n, *n.f.* sun.

sonnen, *vb.* (**sich s.**) sun oneself, bask.

Sonnenbrand, -̈e, *n.m.* sunburn.

Sonnenbräune, *n.f.* sun tan.

sonnenklar, *adj.* clear as daylight.

Sonnenschein, *n.m.* sunshine.

Sonnenstich, -e, *n.m.* sun stroke.

sonnenverbrannt, *adj.* sunburned.

sonnig, *adj.* sunny.

Sonntag, -e, *n.m.* Sunday.

sonst, *adv.* otherwise, else; formerly.

sonstig, *adj.* other; former.

sonstwie, *adv.* in some other way.

sonstwo, *adv.* somewhere else.

sonstwoher, *adv.* from some other place.

sonstwohin, *adv.* to some other place.

Sopran', -e, *n.m.* soprano.

Sorbett, -e, *n.nt.* sherbet.

Sorge, -n, *n.f.* sorrow; worry, anxiety, apprehension; care.

sorgen, *vb.* (**s. für**) care for, provide; (**sich s.**) worry, concern oneself.

sorgenfrei, *adj.* carefree.

sorgenvoll, *adj.* worried, careworn.

Sorgfalt, *n.f.* care.

sorgfältig, *adj.* careful, meticulous.

sorglos, *adj.* carefree.

sorgsam, *adj.* careful, painstaking.

Sorte, -n, *n.f.* sort, kind.

sortie'ren, *vb.* sort, assort, classify.

Soße, -n, *n.f.* sauce, gravy.

souverän, *adj.* sovereign.

Souveränität', *n.f.* sovereignty.

soviel, *adv.* so much, as much.

sowie', *conj.* as well as; as soon as.

sowieso', *adv.* in any case.

Sowjet, -s, *n.m.* Soviet.

sowje'tisch, *adj.* Soviet.

Sowjetunion, *n.f.* Soviet Union.

sowohl', *adv.* as well; (**s. A als B, s. A wie B**) both A and B.

sozial', *adj.* social.

sozialisie'ren, *vb.* socialize, nationalize.

Sozialis'mus, *n.m.* socialism.

Sozialist', -en, -en, *n.m.* socialist.

sozialis'tisch, *adj.* socialistic.

Soziologie', *n.f.* sociology.

sozusagen, *adv.* as it were, so to speak.

Spaghet'ti, *n.pl.* spaghetti.

Spalt, -e, *n.m.* crack, chink.

spaltbar, *adj.* fissionable.

Spalte, -n, *n.f.* crevice, gap; (newspaper) column.

spalten, *vb.* split.

Spaltung, -en, *n.f.* cleavage, fission.

Spange, -n, *n.m.* clasp, buckle.

Spanien, *n.nt.* Spain.

Spanier, -, *n.m.* Spaniard.

spanisch, *adj.* Spanish.

Spann, -e, *n.m.* arch, instep.

Spanne, -n, *n.f.* span.

spannen, *vb.* stretch; tighten.

spannend, *adj.* exciting, gripping.

Spannkraft, *n.f.* elasticity; (*fig.*) energy.

Spannung, -en, *n.f.* tension; (*fig.*) close attention, suspense.

sparen, *vb.* save.

Spargel, -, *n.m.* asparagus.

Sparkasse, -n, *n.f.* savings bank.

spärlich, *adj.* sparse, meager.

sparsam, *adj.* thrifty, economical.

Sparsamkeit, *n.f.* thrift.

Spaß, -̈e, *n.m.* joke, fun.

spaßeshalber, *adv.* for the fun of it.

spaßig, *adj.* funny.

Spaßmacher, -, *n.m.* jester.

spät, *adj.* late.

Spaten, -, *n.m.* spade.

spätestens, *adv.* at the latest.

Spatz, -en, -en, *n.m.* sparrow.

spazie'ren-gehen*, *vb.* go for a walk, stroll.

Spazier'fahrt, -en, *n.f.* drive.

Spazier'gang, -̈, *n.m.* walk.

Specht, -e, n.m. woodpecker.

Speck, n.m. fat; bacon.

spedie'ren, vb. dispatch.

Spediteur', -e, n.m. shipping agent.

Speer, -e, n.m. spear; javelin.

Speiche, -n, n.f. spoke.

Speichel, n.m. saliva.

Speicher, -, n.m. loft, storage place.

speien*, vb. spit.

Speise, -n, n.f. food, nourishment.

Speisekammer, -n, n.f. pantry.

Speisekarte, -n, n.f. bill of fare, menu.

speisen, vb. (tr.) feed; (intr.) eat.

Speiseröhre, -n, n.f. esophagus.

Speisewagen, -, n.m. diner, dining-car.

Speisezettel, -, n.m. menu.

Speisung, -en, n.f. feeding.

Spekta'kel, n.m. noise, racket.

spekulie'ren, vb. speculate.

spenda'bel, adj. free and easy with money; (s. sein*) splurge.

Spende, -n, n.f. donation.

spenden, vb. give; donate.

Sperling, -e, n.m. sparrow.

Sperre, -n, n.f. barrier, blockade; gate.

sperren, vb. block, obstruct, blockade; (money) freeze.

Sperrfeuer, -, n.nt. barrage.

Sperrstunde, -n, n.f. curfew.

Spesen, n.pl. charges, expenses, (auf S.) on an expense account.

spezialisie'ren, vb. specialize.

Spezialist', -en, -en, n.m. specialist.

Spezialität', -en, n.f. specialty.

speziell', adj. special, specific.

spezi'fisch, adj. specific.

spezifizie'ren, vb. specify.

Sphäre, -n, n.f. sphere.

Sphinx, -en, n.f. sphinx.

spicken, vb. lard, interlard.

Spiegel, -, n.m. mirror.

spiegeln, vb. mirror, reflect.

Spiegelung, -en, n.f. reflection.

Spiel, -e, n.nt. play, game; gambling; pack (of cards).

Spielbank, -en, n.f. gambling casino.

spielen, vb. play, act; (um Geld s.) gamble.

spielerisch, adj. playful.

Spielgefährte, -n, -n, n.m. playmate.

Spielplatz, ⸚e, n.m. playground.

Spielraum, ⸚, n.m. room for action, range; elbow room; margin.

Spielwaren, n.pl. toys.

Spielzeug, -e, n.nt. toy.

Spieß, -e, n.m. spear; top sergeant.

Spinat', n.m. spinach.

Spindel, -n, n.f. spindle.

Spinett', -e, n.nt. spinet, harpsichord.

Spinne, -n, n.f. spider.

spinnen*, vb. spin; be crazy.

Spinngewebe, -, n.nt. cobweb.

Spion', -e, n.m. spy.

Spiona'ge, n.f. espionage.

spionie'ren, vb. spy.

Spira'le, -n, n.f. spiral.

spiral'förmig, adj. spiral.

Spiritis'mus, n.m. spiritism.

Spiritualis'mus, n.m. spiritualism.

Spirituo'sen, n.pl. liquor, spirits.

spitz, adj. pointed, acute.

Spitzbart, ⸚e, n.m. goatee.

Spitze, -n, n.f. point, tip, top; lace.

spitzenartig, adj. lacy.

spitzfindig, adj. shrewd; subtle.

Spitzhacke, -n, n.f. pick.

Spitzname(n), -, n.m. nickname.

Splitter, -, n.m. splinter, chip.

splittern, vb. splinter, shatter.

spontan', adj. spontaneous.

spora'disch, adj. sporadic.

Sporn, Sporen, n.m. spur.

Sport, -e, n.m. sport.

Sportler, -, n.m. sportsman, athlete.

sportlich, adj. athletic; sportsmanlike.

Sportplatz, ⸚e, n.m. athletic field, stadium.

Spott, n.m. mockery, ridicule.

spottbillig, adj. dirt cheap.

spotten, vb. mock, scoff.

Spötter, -, n.m. scoffer.

spöttisch, adj. derisive.

Sprache, -n, n.f. speech; language.

spracheigen, adj. idiomatic.

Sprachfehler, -, n.m. speech impediment.

Sprachführer, -, n.m. phrase book.

sprachgewandt, adj. fluent.

sprachlos, adj. speechless.

Sprachschatz, n.m. vocabulary.

Sprachwissenschaft, -en, n.f. linguistics, philology.

sprechen*, vb. speak, talk.

Sprecher, -, n.m. speaker, spokesman.

Sprechstunde, -n, n.f. office hour.

spreizen, vb. spread apart.

sprengen, vb. explode, break; sprinkle.

Sprengstoff, -e, n.m. explosive.

Sprichwort, ⸚er, n.nt. proverb, adage.

sprichwörtlich, adj. proverbial.

sprießen*, vb. sprout.

springen*, vb. jump; crack.

Springer, -, n.m. (chess) knight.

Springquell, -e, n.m. fountain.

sprinten, vb. sprint.

Spritze, -n, n.f. spray; injection; hypodermic.

spritzen, vb. spray, squirt, splash, inject.

spröde, adj. brittle; chapped; reserved, prim.

Sproß, -sse, n.m. sprout.

Sprößling, -e, n.m. shoot; offspring.

Sprotte, -n, n.f. sprat.

Spruch, ⸚e, n.m. saying.

Sprudel, -, n.m. bubbling water; soda water.

sprudeln, vb. bubble.

Sprudeln, n.nt. effervescence.

sprühen, vb. spark, sparkle.

Sprühregen, n.m. drizzle.

Sprung, ⸚e, n.m. jump; fissure, crack.

Sprungbrett, -er, n.nt. diving board; (fig.) stepping stone.

sprunghaft, adj. jumpy; erratic.

Sprungschanze, -n, n.f. ski-jump.

Spucke, n.f. spit, saliva.

spucken, vb. spit.

Spuk, -e, n.m. spook, ghost.

Spule, -n, n.f. spool, reel; (elec.) coil; bobbin.

spulen, vb. reel, wind.

spülen, vb. rinse, wash; (W.C.) flush.

Spülstein, -e, n.m. sink.

Spund, -e, n.m. spigot, tap.

Spur, -en, n.f. trace, track.

spuren, vb. follow the prescribed pattern.

spüren, vb. feel; trace.

spurlos, adj. without a trace.

Spurweite, -n, n.f. width of track, gauge.

sputen, vb. (sich s.) hurry up.

Staat, -en, n.m. state, government.

Staatenbund, ⸚e, n.m. federation.

staatlich, adj. national, governmental.

Staatsangehörig, n.m.&f. national citizen.

Staatsangehörigkeit, -en, n.f. citizenship, nationality.

staatsfeindlich, adj. subversive.

Staatskunst, n.f. statesmanship.

Staatsmann, ⸚er, n.m. statesman.

Staatssekretär, -e, n.m. undersecretary of a ministry.

Staatsstreich, -e, n.m. coup d'état.

Stab, ⸚e, n.m. staff, rod.

stabil', adj. stable.

stabilisie'ren, vb. stabilize.

Stabilität', n.f. stability.

Stachel, -n, n.m. sting, thorn, spike.

Stachelbeere, -n, n.f. gooseberry.

Stachelschwein, -e, n.nt. porcupine.

Stadion, -dien, n.nt. stadium.

Stadium, -dien, n.nt. stage.

Stadt, ⸚e, n.f. town, city.

stadtbekannt, adj. known all over town, notorious.

städtisch, *adj.* municipal; urban.

Stadtteil, -e, *n.m.* borough.

Staffel, -n, *n.f.* rung, step; *(mil.)* echelon, squadron.

staffeln, *vb.* graduate, stagger.

Stagflation', *n.f.* stagflation.

stagnie'ren, *vb.* stagnate.

stagnie'rend, *adj.* stagnant.

Stahl, -e, *n.m.* steel.

Stahlhelm, -e, *n.m.* steel helmet.

Stahlwaren, *n.pl.* cutlery; hardware.

Stall, -e, *n.m.* stall, stable, barn.

Stamm, -e, *n.m.* (tree) trunk; (word) stem; tribe, clan.

Stammbaum, -e, *n.m.* family tree; pedigree.

stammeln, *vb.* stammer.

stammen, *vb.* stem, originate, be descended.

Stammgast, -e, *n.m.* habitué.

stämmig, *adj.* sturdy, burly.

stampfen, *vb.* stamp, trample.

Stand, -e, *n.m.* stand(ing), position; level; status; class, estate.

Standard, -s, *n.m.* standard.

standardisie'ren, *vb.* standardize.

Ständchen, -, n.nt. serenade.

Ständer, -, *n.m.* rack, stand.

Standesamt, -er, *n.nt.* marriage bureau; registrar.

standesbewußt, *adj.* class-conscious.

standesgemäß, *adj.* according to one's rank.

standhaft, *adj.* steadfast.

Standhaftigkeit, *n.f.* constancy.

stand-halten*, *vb.* hold one's ground, withstand.

Standpunkt, -e, *n.m.* standpoint, point of view.

Stange, -n, *n.f.* rod, bar, pole; carton (of cigarettes).

Stapel, -, *n.m.* pile; stock; (ship) slip; (vom S. lassen*) launch.

stapeln, *vb.* pile up.

stapfen, *vb.* stamp, plod.

Star, -e, *n.m.* (eye) cataract; (bird) starling; (film) star.

stark (-), *adj.* strong.

Stärke, -n, *n.f.* strength; starch.

stärken, *vb.* strengthen; starch.

Stärkungsmittel, -, *n.nt.* tonic.

starr, *adj.* rigid.

starren, *vb.* stare.

Starrheit, *n.f.* rigidity.

starrköpfig, *adj.* stubborn, headstrong.

Starrsinn, *n.m.* obstinacy.

Start, -s, *n.m.* start.

Startbahn, -en, *n.f.* runway.

starten, *vb.* start.

Startklappe, -n, *n.f.* choke (auto).

Station', -en, *n.f.* station.

stationär', adj. stationary.

Stationsvorsteher, -, *n.m.* station master.

statisch, *adj.* static.

Statist', -en, -en, *n.m.* (theater) extra; *(fig.)* dummy.

Statis'tik, *n.f.* statistics.

Stativ', -e, *n.nt.* (photo) tripod.

statt, *prep.* instead of.

Stätte, -n, *n.f.* place.

statt-finden*, *vb.* take place.

stattlich, *adj.* imposing.

Statue, -n, *n.f.* statue.

Staub, *n.m.* dust.

staubig, *adj.* dusty.

Staudamm, -e, *n.m.* dam.

stauen, *vb.* dam up; **(sich s.)** be dammed up, get jammed up.

staunen, *vb.* be astonished, wonder.

Stauung, -en, *n.f.* congestion.

stechen*, *vb.* prick, sting, pierce, stab.

Stechschritt, *n.m.* goose step.

Steckdose, -n, *n.f.* (elec.) outlet, socket.

stecken(*), *vb. intr.* be located, be hidden; **(wo steckt er denn?)** where is he, anyhow?; **(s. bleiben*)** get stuck.

stecken, *vb. tr.* put, stick, pin, hide.

Steckenpferd, -e, *n.nt.* hobbyhorse; hobby.

Stecknadel, -n, *n.f.* pin.

Steckrübe, -n, *n.f.* turnip.

Steg, -e, *n.m.* path; footbridge.

stehen*, *vb.* stand, be located; be becoming; **(sich gut s.)** be on good terms; **(es steht dahin*)** it has yet to be shown.

stehen-bleiben*, *vb.* stop.

stehen-lassen*, *vb.* leave standing; leave behind, forget.

stehlen*, *vb.* steal.

Stehplatz, -e, *n.m.* standing room.

steif, *adj.* stiff, rigid.

Steifheit, -en, *n.f.* stiffness, rigidity.

Steig, -e, *n.m.* path.

steigen*, *vb.* climb, rise.

steigern, *vb.* increase, boost; **(sich s.)** increase, *(fig.)* work oneself up.

Steigung, -en, *n.f.* rise, slope, ascent.

steil, *adj.* steep.

Stein, -e, *n.m.* stone, rock.

Steingut, *n.nt.* earthenware, crockery.

steinigen, *vb.* stone.

Stelldichein, *n.nt.* rendezvous.

Stelle, -n, *n.f.* place, spot, point.

stellen, *vb.* place, put, set.

Stellenangebot, -e, *n.nt.* position offered.

Stellenvermittlung, -en, *n.f.* employment agency.

stellenweise, *adv.* in parts; in places.

Stellung, -en, *n.f.* position, place, stand; job; **(S. nehmen)** comment.

Stellungnahme, -n, *n.f.* comment, attitude.

stellvertretend, *adj.* assistant, deputy.

Stellvertreter, -, *n.m.* representative, deputy, alternate.

stemmen, *vb.* stem; **(sich s. gegen)** oppose, resist.

Stempel, -, *n.m.* stamp.

stempeln, *vb.* stamp; **(s. gehen)** be on the dole.

Stenographie', -i'en, *n.f.* shorthand.

stenographie'ren, *vb.* take shorthand, write shorthand.

Stenotypis'tin, -nen, *n.f.* stenographer.

Steppdecke, -n, *n.f.* quilt comforter.

Steppe, -n, *n.f.* steppe.

steppen, *vb.* stitch.

sterben*, *vb.* die.

sterblich, *adj.* mortal.

stereophon', *adj.* stereophonic, stereo.

steril', *adj.* sterile.

sterilisie'ren, *vb.* sterilize.

Sterilität', *n.f.* sterility.

Sterling, *n.m.* pound sterling.

Stern, -e, *n.m.* star.

Sternbild, -er, *n.nt.* constellation.

Sternchen, -, *n.nt.* asterisk.

Sternkunde, *n.f.* astronomy.

Sternwarte, -n, *n.f.* observatory.

stet(ig), *adj.* steady.

stets, *adv.* always.

Steuer, -, *n.nt.* rudder, helm.

Steuer, -n, *n.f.* tax.

steuern, *vb.* steer, pilot, navigate.

Steuerruder, -, *n.nt.* rudder.

Steuerzahler, -, *n.m.* taxpayer.

Steward, -s, *n.m.* steward.

Stewardeß, -ssen, *n.f.* stewardess.

Stich, -e, *n.m.* stab; bite, sting, stitch.

stichhaltig, *adj.* valid, sound.

Stichwort, -er, *n.nt.* cue.

sticken, *vb.* embroider.

Stickerei', -en, *n.f.* embroidery.

Stickstoff, *n.m.* nitrogen.

Stief-, *cpds.* step-; **(Stiefvater)** stepfather; etc.

Stiefel, -, *n.m.* boot.

Stiel, -e, *n.m.* handle; stalk, stem.

stier, *adj.* glassy (look).

Stier, -e, *n.m.* steer.

stieren, *vb.* stare.

Stift, -e, *n.m.* peg, pin, tack; crayon, pencil.

Stift, -e(r), *n.nt.* charitable institution.

stiften, *vb.* donate; found; endow.

Stiftung, -en, *n.f.* foundation; donation.

Stil, -e, *n.m.* style.

stilgerecht, *adj.* in good style, in good taste.

still, *adj.* still, quiet.

Stille, *n.f.* stillness, silence.

Stilleben, -, *n.nt.* still-life.

stillen, vb. still, quench; nurse (a baby).

stillos, adj. in bad taste.

stillschweigend, adj. silent; tacit, implicit.

Stillstand, n.m. halt.

Stimmabgabe, -n, n.f. vote; voting.

Stimmband, ⁻er, n.nt. vocal cord.

Stimme, -n, n.f. voice; vote.

stimmen, vb. tune; vote; be correct.

Stimmengleichheit, n.f. tie vote.

Stimmenprüfung, -en, n.f. canvass.

Stimmrecht, -e, n.nt. suffrage, franchise.

Stimmung, -en, n.f. mood; morale.

stimmungsvoll, adj. festive, moving; intimate.

Stimmzettel, -, n.m. ballot.

stinken*, vb. stink.

Stinktier, -e, n.nt. skunk.

Stint, -e, n.m. smelt.

Stipen'dium, -dien, n.nt. scholarship, grant.

Stirn, -en, n.f. forehead, brow.

Stirnhöhle, -n, n.f. sinus.

Stock, ⁻e, n.m. stick, cane.

stockdunkel, adj. pitch-dark.

stocken, vb. stop, come to a halt; falter.

Stockung, -en, n.f. stop, standstill; deadlock.

Stockwerk, -e, n.nt. floor, story.

Stoff, -e, n.m. matter, substance; material; cloth.

stofflich, adj. material.

stöhnen, vb. groan.

Stoiker, -, n.m. stoic.

stoisch, adj. stoical.

Stola, -len, n.f. stole.

stolpern, vb. stumble, trip.

stolz, adj. proud.

Stolz, n.m. pride.

stolzie'ren, vb. strut.

stopfen, vb. stuff; (socks, etc.) darn.

stoppen, vb. stop.

Stöpsel, -, n.m. stopper; (elec.) plug.

Stör, -e, n.m. sturgeon.

Storch, ⁻e, n.m. stork.

stören, vb. disturb, bother.

Störenfried, -e, n.m. intruder; troublemaker.

Störung, -en, n.f. disturbance; (radio) interference, static.

Stoß, ⁻e, n.m. blow, hit, thrust.

stoßen*, vb. push, kick, hit, thrust.

Stoßstange, -n, n.f. bumper.

stottern, vb. stutter.

Strafanstalt, -en, n.f. penal institution.

strafbar, adj. liable to punishment.

Strafe, -n, n.f. punishment; fine; sentence.

strafen, vb. punish.

straff, adj. taut, tight.

straffen, vb. tighten.

Strafgebühr, -en, n.f. fine.

Strafgericht, -e, n.nt. criminal court.

Strafkammer, -n, n.f. criminal court.

Sträfling, -e, n.m. convict.

Strafmandat, -e, n.nt. traffic ticket.

Strafporto, n.nt. postage due.

Strahl, -en, n.m. ray, beam; (water) spout.

strahlen, vb. beam, gleam, radiate.

Strahlen, n.nt. radiance.

strahlend, adj. radiant.

Strahlflugzeug, -e, n.nt. jet plane.

Strahlung, -en, n.f. radiation.

Strähne, -n, n.f. strand; streak.

stramm, adj. tight; (fig.) strapping.

strampeln, vb. kick.

Strand, -e, n.m. beach, shore.

stranden, vb. strand.

Strandgut, n.nt. jetsam.

Strang, ⁻e, n.m. rope; (über die Stränge schlagen*) run riot.

Strapa'ze, -n, n.f. exertion, drudgery.

Straße, -n, n.f. street, road.

Straßenbahn, -en, n.f. streetcar, trolley.

Strategie', n.f. strategy.

strate'gisch, adj. strategic.

Stratosphä're, n.f. stratosphere.

sträuben, vb. (sich s.) bristle; (fig.) struggle against, resist.

Strauch, ⁻er, n.m. shrub.

straucheln, vb. falter, stumble.

Strauß, ⁻e, n.m. bouquet; ostrich.

streben, vb. strive, endeavor, aspire.

Streben, n.nt. pursuit.

Strebepfeiler, -, n.m. flying buttress.

Streber, -, n.m. (school) grind; (society) social climber.

strebsam, adj. zealous.

Strecke, -n, n.f. stretch, distance.

strecken, vb. stretch; (die Waffen s.) lay down one's arms.

Streich, -e, n.m. stroke, blow; prank.

streicheln, vb. stroke, caress.

streichen*, vb. scratch; paint.

Streichholz, ⁻er, n.nt. match.

Streife, -n, n.f. patrol.

streifen, vb. touch lightly.

Streifen, -, n.m. strip.

Streik, -s, n.m. strike.

Streikposten, -, n.m. picket.

Streit, n.m. quarrel, dispute.

streiten*, vb. fight; (sich s.) quarrel.

Streitfrage, -n, n.f. controversy.

Streitpunkt, -e, n.m. point at issue.

streitsüchtig, adj. pugnacious.

streng, adj. strict, stern, severe.

strenggläubig, adj. orthodox.

streuen, vb. strew, scatter, sprinkle.

Strich, -e, n.m. stroke, line; (nach S. und Faden) thoroughly; (gegen den S.) against the grain.

Strick, -e, n.m. rope.

stricken, vb. knit.

strittig, adj. controversial.

Stroh, n.nt. straw.

Strolch, -e, n.m. vagabond.

Strom, ⁻e, n.m. stream; (elec.) current.

strömen, vb. stream, flow.

Stromkreis, -e, n.m. circuit.

stromlinienförmig, adj. streamlined.

Stromspannung, -en, n.f. voltage.

Strömung, -en, n.f. current; trend, drift.

Strudel, -, n.m. whirlpool.

Struktur', -en, n.f. structure.

Strumpf, ⁻e, n.m. stocking.

Strumpfband, ⁻er, n.nt. garter.

Strumpfbandgürtel, n.m. girdle.

Strumpfhose, -n, n.f. panty hose.

Strumpfwaren, n.pl. hosiery.

struppig, adj. shaggy.

Stube, -n, n.f. room.

Stuck, n.m. stucco.

Stück, -e, n.nt. piece; (theater) play.

stückeln, vb. patch, piece together.

stücken, vb. piece.

Student', -en, -en, n.m. student.

Studie, -n, n.f. study.

Studiengeld, -er, n.nt. tuition.

studie'ren, vb. study (at a university), be a student.

Studium, -dien, n.nt. study.

Stufe, -n, n.f. step.

stufenweise, adj. gradual, step by step.

Stuhl, ⁻e, n.m. chair.

stumm, adj. mute, silent.

Stummel, -, n.m. stub, butt.

Stümper, -, n.m. beginner, amateur.

stumpf, adj. blunt; stupid; (angle) obtuse.

Stumpf, ⁻e, n.m. stump.

Stunde, -n, n.f. hour; (school) class.

stündlich, adj. hourly.

stupsen, vb. joggle.

stur, adj. stubborn; obtuse.

Sturm, ⁻e, n.m. storm.

stürmen, vb. storm.

stürmisch, adj. stormy.

Sturz, ⁻e, n.m. fall; overthrow.

stürzen, vb. plunge, hurl, overthrow; rush, crash.

Stute, -n, n.f. mare.

Stütze, -n, n.f. support, prop, help.

stutzen, vb. trim.

stützen, vb. support.

Stützpunkt, -e, n.m. base.

Subjekt', -e, n.nt. subject.

sublimie'ren, vb. sublimate.

Substantiv, -e, *n.nt.* noun.
Substanz', -en, *n.f.* substance.
subtil', *adj.* subtle.
subtrahie'ren, *vb.* subtract.
Subvention', -en, *n.f.* subvention, subsidy.
Suche, *n.f.* search.
suchen, *vb.* search, seek, look for.
Sucht, *n.f.* addiction.
Süd, Süden, *n.m.* south.
südlich, *adj.* southern; to the south.
Südos'ten, *n.m.* southeast.
südöst'lich, *adj.* southeast.
Südpol, *n.m.* South Pole.
Südwe'sten, *n.m.* southwest.
südwest'lich, *adj.* southwest.
suggerie'ren, *vb.* suggest.
Sühne, -n, *n.f.* atonement, expiation.
sühnen, *vb.* atone for, expiate.
Sülze, *n.f.* jellied meat.
summa'risch, *adj.* summary.
Summe, -n, *n.f.* sum.
summen, *vb.* hum, buzz.
Sumpf, -e, *n.m.* swamp, mire.
Sünde, -n, *n.f.* sin.
Sündenvergebung, *n.f.* absolution.
Sünder, -, *n.m.* sinner.
Sündflut, *n.f.* the Flood; cataclysm.
sündhaft, *adj.* sinful.
sündigen, *vb.* sin.
super, *adj.* super.
Superstar, -s, *n.m.* superstar.
Suppe, -n, *n.f.* soup.
surren, *vb.* buzz.
suspendie'ren, *vb.* suspend.
süß, *adj.* sweet.
Süße, *n.f.* sweetness.
Sylve'ster, *n.nt.* New Year's Eve.
symbo'lisch, *adj.* symbolic.
Sympathie', -I'en, *n.f.* sympathy.
sympa'tisch, *adj.* likable, congenial; (med.) sympathetic.
Symphonie', -I'en, *n.f.* symphony.
sympho'nisch, *adj.* symphonic.
Symptom', -e, *n.nt.* symptom.
symptoma'tisch, *adj.* symptomatic.
Synago'ge, -n, *n.f.* synagogue.
synchronisie'ren, *vb.* synchronize.
Syndrom', -e, *n.nt.* syndrome.
Synonym', -e, *n.nt.* synonym.
Synthe'se, -n, *n.f.* synthesis.
synthe'tisch, *adj.* synthetic.
Syphilis, *n.f.* syphilis.
System', -e, *n.nt.* system.
systema'tisch, *adj.* systematic.
Szene, -n, *n.f.* scene.

T

Tabak, *n.m.* tobacco.
Tabel'le, -n, *n.f.* chart.
Tablett', -e, *n.nt.* tray.
Tablet'te, -n, *n.f.* tablet.

Tadel, -, *n.m.* reproof, reprimand; (school) demerit.
tadeln, *vb.* reprove, find fault with.
tadelnswert, *adj.* reprehensible.
Tafel, -n, *n.f.* tablet; table; chart; blackboard; bar (of chocolate).
täfeln, *vb.* panel.
Tag, -e, *n.m.* day; (guten T.) how do you do.
Tagebuch, -"er, *n.nt.* diary.
Tagesanbruch, *n.m.* daybreak.
Tageslicht, *n.nt.* daylight.
Tageszeitung, -en, *n.f.* daily newspaper.
täglich, *adj.* daily.
Tagung, -en, *n.f.* convention, meeting.
Taille, -n, *n.f.* waist.
Takt, *n.m.* tact; rhythm.
takttisch, *adj.* tactical.
Tal, -"er, *n.nt.* valley.
Talent', -e, *n.nt.* talent.
talentiert', *adj.* talented.
tändeln, *vb.* dally.
Tango, -s, *n.m.* tango.
Tank, -s, *n.m.* tank.
Tankstelle, -n, *n.f.* filling station.
Tanne, -n, *n.f.* fir, spruce.
Tante, -n, *n.f.* aunt.
Tantie'me, -n, *n.f.* bonus.
Tanz, -"e, *n.m.* dance.
tänzeln, *vb.* flounce, caper.
tanzen, *vb.* dance.
Tänzer, -, *n.m.* dancer.
Tanzsaal, -säle, *n.m.* dance hall, ballroom.
Tape'te, -n, *n.f.* wallpaper.
Tapezie'rer, -, *n.m.* upholsterer.
tapfer, *adj.* brave, valiant.
Tapisserie, -I'en, *n.f.* tapestry.
tappen, *vb.* grope.
tapsig, *adj.* gawky.
tarnen, *vb.* screen, camouflage.
Tarnung, -en, *n.f.* screen, camouflage.
Tasche, -n, *n.f.* pocket; handbag.
Taschenausgabe, -n, *n.f.* paperback.
Taschendieb, -e, *n.m.* pickpocket.
Taschenformat, *n.nt.* pocketsize.
Taschengeld, -er, *n.nt.* allowance, pocket money.
Taschenlampe, -n, *n.f.* flashlight.
Taschentuch, -"er, *n.nt.* handkerchief.
Tasse, -n, *n.f.* cup.
Tastatur', -en, *n.f.* keyboard.
Taste, -n, *n.f.* key.
tasten, *vb.* feel; grope.
Tastsinn, *n.m.* sense of touch.
Tat, -en, *n.f.* act, deed; (in der T.) indeed.
Tatbestand, *n.m.* facts, findings.
Täter, -, *n.m.* culprit.
tätig, *adj.* active.
Tätigkeit, -en, *n.f.* activity.

Tatkraft, -"e, *n.f.* energy.
tatkräftig, *adj.* energetic.
tätlich, *adj.* violent.
Tätlichkeit, -en, *n.f.* violence.
Tatsache, -n, *n.f.* fact.
tatsächlich, *adj.* actual, real.
Tatze, -n, *n.f.* paw, claw.
Tau, *n.m.* dew.
Tau, -e, *n.nt.* rope.
taub, *adj.* deaf.
Taube, -n, *n.f.* pigeon, dove.
tauchen, *vb.* dive, plunge, dip.
Taucher, -, *n.m.* diver.
Taufe, -n, *n.f.* baptism, christening.
taufen, *vb.* baptize, christen.
Taufkapelle, -n, *n.f.* baptistry.
taugen, *vb.* be worth; be of use.
Taugenichts, *n.m.* good-fornothing.
tauglich, *adj.* useful, qualified.
taumeln, *vb.* stagger.
taumelnd, *adj.* groggy.
Tausch, *n.m.* exchange, trade.
tauschen, *vb.* exchange.
täuschen, *vb.* deceive, delude, fool.
täuschend, *adj.* deceptive.
Tauschhandel, *n.m.* barter.
Täuschung, -en, *n.f.* deception, delusion, fallacy.
tausend, *num.* a thousand.
Tausend, -e, *n.nt.* thousand.
tausendst-, *adj.* thousandth.
Tausendstel, -, *n.nt.* thousandth part; (ein t.) one one-thousandth.
Taxe, -n, *n.f.* tax; taxi.
taxie'ren, *vb.* appraise, estimate.
Technik, *n.f.* technique; technology.
technisch, *adj.* technical.
Tee, -s, *n.m.* tea.
Teekanne, -n, *n.f.* tea-pot.
Teelöffel, -, *n.m.* teaspoon.
Teer, *n.m.* tar.
Teich, -e, *n.m.* pond, pool.
Teig, -e, *n.m.* dough, batter.
Teil, -e, *n.m.* part, portion, section.
teilbar, *adj.* divisible.
teilen, *vb.* divide, share.
teil-haben*, *vb.* share.
Teilhaber, -, *n.m.* partner.
Teilnahme, *n.f.* participation; sympathy.
teilnahmslos, *adj.* lethargic.
teil-nehmen*, *vb.* participate, partake.
Teilnehmer, -, *n.m.* participant, partner.
teils, *adv.* partly.
Teilung, -en, *n.f.* partition, division.
teilweise, *adv.* partly.
Teint, -s, *n.m.* complexion.
Telegramm', -e, *n.nt.* telegram.
Telegraph', -en, -en, *n.m.* telegraph.
telegraphie'ren, *vb.* telegraph.
Telephon', -e, *n.nt.* telephone.
Telephon'buch, -"er, *n.nt.* telephone directory.

Telephon'fräulein, -, *n.nt.* telephone operator.

telephonie'ren, *vb.* telephone.

Teller, -, *n.m.* plate.

Temperament', *n.nt.* temperament, disposition; vivacity.

temperament'voll, *adj.* temperamental; vivacious.

Temperatur', -en, *n.f.* temperature.

Tempo, -s, *n.nt.* speed; tempo.

Tendenz', -en, *n.f.* tendency, trend.

Tender, -, *n.m.* tender.

Tennis, *n.nt.* tennis.

Tennisschläger, -, *n.m.* tennis racket.

Tennisschuh, -e, *n.m.* sneaker.

Tenor', -e, *n.m.* tenor.

Teppich, -e, *n.m.* rug, carpet.

Termin', -e, *n.m.* fixed day, deadline.

Terpentin', *n.nt.* turpentine.

Terras'se, -n, *n.f.* terrace.

Testament', -e, *n.nt.* testament, will.

testamenta'risch, *adj.* testamentary, noted in the will.

teuer, *adj.* expensive, dear.

Teuerung, -en, *n.f.* rising cost of living.

Teufel, -, *n.m.* devil.

teuflisch, *adj.* diabolic.

Text, -e, *n.m.* text.

Texti'lien, *n.pl.* textiles.

Textil'ware, -n, *n.f.* textile.

Thea'ter, -, *n.nt.* theater; spectacle.

Thea'terkasse, -n, *n.f.* box office.

Thea'terstück, -e, *n.nt.* play.

Thea'terwissenschaft, -en, *n.f.* dramatics.

theatra'lisch, *adj.* theatrical.

Thema, -men, *n.nt.* theme, subject, topic.

Theolo'ge, -n, -n, *n.m.* theologian.

theore'tisch, *adj.* theoretical.

Theorie', -i'en, *n.f.* theory.

Therapie', *n.f.* therapy.

Thermome'ter, -, *n.nt.* thermometer.

These, -n, *n.f.* thesis.

Thron, -e, *n.m.* throne.

Thunfisch, -e, *n.m.* tuna.

tief, *adj.* deep, low; profound.

Tiefe, -n, *n.f.* depth.

Tiefebene, -n, *n.f.* plain, lowland.

tiefgründig, *adj.* profound.

Tiefkühler, -, *n.m.* freezer.

Tiefkühltruhe, -n, *n.f.* deep freeze.

tiefsinnig, *adj.* profound; pensive.

tieftraurig, *adj.* heartbroken.

Tier, -e, *n.nt.* animal.

Tierarzt, ⁻e, *n.m.* veterinary.

tierisch, *adj.* animal, bestial.

Tiger, -, *n.m.* tiger.

tilgen, *vb.* obliterate; delete; pay off, amortize.

Tilgung, -en, *n.f.* liquidation, amortization.

Tinte, -n, *n.f.* ink.

Tintenfisch, -e, *n.m.* octopus.

Tip, -s, *n.m.* hint, suggestion.

tippen, *vb.* type.

Tisch, -e, *n.m.* table.

Tischdecke, -n, *n.f.* tablecloth.

Tischler, -, *n.m.* carpenter.

Tischtuch, ⁻er, *n.nt.* tablecloth.

Titel, -, *n.m.* title.

Toast, *n.m.* toast.

toben, *vb.* rave, rage.

Tochter, ⁻, *n.f.* daughter.

Tod, *n.m.* death.

Todesfall, ⁻e, *n.m.* (case of) death.

Todesstrafe, -n, *n.f.* capital punishment.

tödlich, *adj.* deadly, mortal; lethal.

Toilet'te, -n, *n.f.* toilet.

Toilet'tenartikel, *n.pl.* toilet articles.

tolerant', *adj.* tolerant.

Toleranz', *n.f.* tolerance.

toll, *adj.* mad, crazy.

tollkühn, *adj.* foolhardy.

Tollwut, *n.f.* rabies.

tölpelhaft, *adj.* clumsy.

Toma'te, -n, *n.f.* tomato.

Ton, -e, *n.m.* tone, sound; clay.

tonangebend, *adj.* setting the style.

Tonart, -en, *n.f.* key.

Tonband, ⁻er, *n.nt.* magnetic tape.

Tonbandaufnehme, -n, *n.f.* tape recording.

Tonbandgerät, -e, *n.nt.* tape recorder.

tönen, *vb.* sound, resound, ring.

Tonfall, ⁻e, *n.m.* intonation, inflection.

Tonfilm, -e, *n.m.* sound movie.

Tonhöhe, -n, *n.f.* pitch.

Tonleiter, -n, *n.f.* scale.

Tonne, -n, *n.f.* ton; barrel.

Tonstufe, -n, *n.f.* (music) pitch.

Tonwaren, *n.pl.* earthenware.

Topf, ⁻e, *n.m.* pot.

Töpferware, -n, *n.f.* pottery.

Tor, -en, -en, *n.m.* fool.

Tor, -e, *n.nt.* gate, gateway; (sport) goal.

Torbogen, ⁻, *n.m.* archway.

Torheit, -en, *n.f.* folly.

töricht, *adj.* foolish.

torkeln, *vb.* lurch, stagger.

Torni'ster, -, *n.m.* knapsack, pack.

torpedie'ren, *vb.* torpedo.

Torpe'do, -s, *n.m.* torpedo.

Törtchen, -, *n.nt.* tart.

Torte, -n, *n.f.* tart, layer cake.

Tortur', -en, *n.f.* torture.

tosen, *vb.* rage, roar.

tot, *adj.* dead.

total', *adj.* total.

totalitär', *adj.* totalitarian.

töten, *vb.* kill.

Totenwache, -n, *n.f.* wake.

Toto, *n.m.* lottery.

Totschlag, ⁻e, *n.m.* (case of) manslaughter.

Tour, -en, *n.f.* tour, excursion, trip.

Tourist', -en, -en, *n.m.* tourist.

Trab, *n.m.* trot.

Trabant', -en, -en, *n.m.* henchman.

traben, *vb.* trot.

Tracht, -en, *n.f.* costume.

trachten, *vb.* seek, endeavor.

Tradition', -en, *n.f.* tradition.

traditionell', *adj.* traditional.

Tragbahre, -n, *n.f.* stretcher.

tragbar, *adj.* portable; bearable.

träge, *adj.* indolent, sluggish.

tragen*, *vb.* carry, bear; wear.

Träger, -, *n.m.* carrier; girder; (lingerie) straps.

Tragik, *n.f.* tragic art; calamity.

tragisch, *adj.* tragic.

Tragö'die, -n, *n.f.* tragedy.

Tragweite, -n, *n.f.* range; significance, consequence.

Trainer, -, *n.m.* coach.

trainie'ren, *vb.* train, work out; coach.

Trambahn, -en, *n.f.* trolley.

trampeln, *vb.* trample.

Tranchier'messer, -, *n.nt.* carving-knife.

Träne, -n, *n.f.* tear.

tränen, *vb.* water (eye).

Trank, ⁻e, *n.m.* potion.

tränken, *vb.* water (animals).

Transaktion', -en, *n.f.* transaction.

Transforma'tor, -o'ren, *n.m.* transformer, converter.

Transfusion', -en, *n.f.* transfusion.

transpirie'ren, *vb.* perspire.

transponie'ren, *vb.* transpose.

Transport', -e, *n.m.* transport.

transportie'ren, *vb.* transport.

transsexual', *adj.* transsexual.

Transvestit', -en, -en, *n.m.* transvestite.

Trapez', -e, *n.nt.* trapeze.

Traube, -n, *n.f.* grape.

trauen, *vb.* (*intr.*) trust; (*tr.*) marry, join in marriage.

Trauer, *n.f.* grief; mourning.

trauern, *vb.* grieve, mourn.

trauervoll, *adj.* mournful.

Traufe, -n, *n.f.* gutter; (vom Regen in die T.) out of the frying pan into the fire.

Traum, ⁻e, *n.m.* dream; (böser T.) nightmare.

träumen, *vb.* dream; (vor sich hin⁻.) daydream.

Träumer, -, *n.m.* dreamer.

Träumerei', -en, *n.f.* daydream, reverie.

träumerisch, *adj.* fanciful, faraway.

traumhaft, *adj.* dreamlike; dreamy.

traurig, *adj.* sad.

Trauring, -e, *n.m.* wedding ring.

Travelerscheck, -s, *n.m.* traveler's check.

Trecker, -, *n.m.* tractor.

Treff, *n.nt.* clubs (cards).

treffen*, *vb.* hit; meet; (sich t.) meet.

treffend, *adj.* pertinent.

Treffer, -, *n.m.* hit.

trefflich, *adj.* excellent.

treiben*, *vb. (tr.)* drive; be engaged in; *(intr.)* drift, float.

Trend, -s, *n.m.* trend.

trennen, *vb.* separate, divide; hyphenate; (sich t.) part.

Trennung, -en, *n.f.* separation, division.

treppab', *adv.* down the stairs.

treppauf', *adv.* up the stairs.

Treppe, -n, *n.f.* staircase, stairs.

Tresor', -e, *n.m.* vault.

treten*, *vb.* step, tread.

treu, *adj.* true, faithful, loyal.

Treue, *n.f.* faith, loyalty; allegiance.

Treueid, -e, *n.m.* oath of allegiance.

Treuhänder, -, *n.m.* trustee.

treuherzig, *adj.* trusting, guileless.

treulich, *adv.* faithfully.

treulos, *adj.* disloyal.

Treulosigkeit, -e, *n.f.* disloyalty.

Tribü'ne, -n, *n.f.* grandstand.

Trichter, -, *n.m.* funnel.

Trick, -s, *n.m.* trick.

Trickfilm, -e, *n.m.* animated cartoon.

Tricktrack, *n.nt.* backgammon.

Trieb, -e, *n.m.* sprout, shoot, urge.

Triebfeder, -n, *n.f.* mainspring.

triebhaft, *adj.* instinctive, unrestrained.

Triebwagen, -, *n.m.* railcar.

triefen*, *vb.* drip.

triftig, *adj.* weighty.

Trikot', *n.nt.* knitted cloth.

trimmen, *vb.* trim.

trinkbar, *adj.* drinkable.

trinken*, *vb.* drink.

Trinker, -, *n.m.* drunkard.

Trinkgeld, -er, *n.nt.* tip.

Trinkspruch, -e, *n.m.* toast.

Tripper, *n.m.* gonorrhea.

Tritt, -e, *n.m.* step; kick.

Trittleiter, -n, *n.f.* stepladder.

Triumph', -e, *n.m.* triumph.

triumphie'ren, *vb.* triumph.

trivial', *adj.* trivial.

trocken, *adj.* dry.

Trockenhaube, -n, *n.f.* hair drier.

trockenlegen, *vb.* (land) drain; (baby) change the diapers.

trocknen, *vb.* dry.

trödeln, *vb.* dawdle.

Trog, -e, *n.m.* trough.

trollen, *vb.* (sich t.) toddle off.

Trommel, -n, *n.f.* drum.

Trommelfell, -e, *n.nt.* eardrum.

Trompe'te, -n, *n.f.* trumpet.

Tropen, *n.pl.* tropics.

Tropfen, -, *n.m.* drop.

tropfen, *vb.* drip.

Tropfer, -, *n.m.* dropper.

Trophä'e, -n, *n.f.* trophy.

tropisch, *adj.* tropical.

Trost, *n.m.* consolation, solace, comfort.

trösten, *vb.* console, comfort.

trostlos, *adj.* desolate, dreary.

trostreich, *adj.* comforting.

Trott, *n.m.* trot.

Trottel, -, *n.m.* idiot, dope.

Trotz, *n.m.* defiance, spite.

trotz, *prep.* in spite of, despite, notwithstanding.

trotzdem, 1. *conj.* although, despite the fact that. 2. *adv.* nevertheless.

trotzen, *vb.* defy.

trotzig, *adj.* defiant.

trübe, *adj.* dim; muddy; cloudy.

Trubel, *n.m.* bustle, confusion.

trüben, *vb.* dim.

Trübsal, *n.f.* misery, sorrow.

trübselig, *adj.* sad, gloomy.

Trübsinn, *n.m.* dejection, gloom.

trübsinnig, *adj.* gloomy.

Trüffel, -n, *n.f.* truffle.

Trug, *n.m.* deceit; delusion.

trügen*, *vb. (tr.)* deceive; *(intr.)* be deceptive.

trügerisch, *adj.* deceptive; illusory; treacherous.

Trugschluß, -sse, *n.m.* fallacy.

Truhe, -n, *n.f.* chest.

Trümmer, *n.p.* ruins, debris.

Trunk, -e, *n.m.* drink; draught.

Trunkenbold, -e, *n.m.* drunkard.

Trunkenheit, *n.f.* drunkenness.

Trupp, -s, *n.m.* troop, squad.

Truppe, -n, *n.f.* troops.

Truppeneinheit, -en, *n.f.* unit, outfit.

Trust, -s, *n.m.* trust.

Truthahn, -e, *n.m.* turkey.

Tscheche, -n, -n, *n.m.* Czech.

tschechisch, *adj.* Czech.

Tschechoslowa'ke, -n, -n, *n.m.* Czechoslovakian.

Tschechoslowakei', *n.f.* Czechoslovakia.

tschechoslowa'kisch, *adj.* Czechoslovakian.

T-shirt, -s, *n.nt.* T-shirt.

Tube, -n, *n.f.* tube.

Tuberkulo'se, *n.f.* tuberculosis.

Tuch, -er, *n.nt.* cloth.

tüchtig, *adj.* able, efficient.

Tüchtigkeit, *n.f.* ability, efficiency.

Tücke, -n, *n.f.* malice, perfidy.

tückisch, *adj.* malicious, treacherous.

Tugend, -en, *n.f.* virtue.

tugendhaft, *adj.* virtuous.

tugendsam, *adj.* virtuous.

Tüll, *n.m.* tulle.

Tülle, -n, *n.f.* spout.

Tulpe, -n, *n.f.* tulip.

tummeln, *vb.* move about, romp.

Tummelplatz, -e, *n.m.* playground.

Tumor, -o'ren, *n.m.* tumor.

Tümpel, -, *n.m.* pool.

Tumult', -e, *n.m.* tumult, uproar; hubbub.

tun*, *vb.* do.

Tünche, -n, *n.f.* whitewash; *(fig.)* veneer.

Tunichtgut, -e, *n.m.* ne'er-do-well.

Tunke, -n, *n.f.* sauce, gravy.

tunken, *vb.* dunk.

Tunnel, -, *n.m.* tunnel.

tupfen, *vb.* dab.

Tür, -en, *n.f.* door; (mit der T. ins Haus fallen*) blurt out.

Turbi'nenjäger, -, *n.m.* turbojet plane.

Turbi'nenpropellertriebwerk, -e, *n.nt.* turbo-prop.

Türeingang, -e, *n.m.* doorway.

Türke, -n, -n, *n.m.* Turk.

Türkei', *n.f.* Turkey.

Türkis', -e, *n.m.* turquoise.

türkisch, *adj.* Turkish.

Turm, -e, *n.m.* tower, spire, steeple; (chess) castle, rook; (spitzer T.) spire.

türmen, *vb. (tr.)* pile up; *(intr.)* beat it; (sich t.) rise high.

turnen, *vb.* do gymnastics.

Turner, -, *n.m.* gymnast.

Turnhalle, -n, *n.f.* gym(nasium).

Turnier', -e, *n.nt.* tournament.

tuscheln, *vb.* whisper.

Tuschkasten, -, *n.m.* paint box.

Tüte, -n, *n.f.* (paper) bag, sack.

Tüttelchen, -, *n.nt.* dot.

Typ, -en, *n.m.* type.

Type, -n, *n.f.* (printing) type.

Typhus, *n.m.* typhus, typhoid fever.

typisch, *adj.* typical.

Typographie', *n.f.* typography.

Tyrann', -en, -en, *n.m.* tyrant.

Tyrannei', *n.f.* tyranny.

tyrannisie'ren, *vb.* tyrannize, oppress.

U

U-Bahn, -en, *n.f.* (= Untergrundbahn) subway.

übel, *adj.* evil; nasty; nauseated.

Übel, *n.nt.* evil; nuisance.

Übelkeit, *n.f.* nausea.

übelnehmen*, *vb.* hold against, resent.

Übeltat, -en, *n.f.* offence.

Übeltäter, -, *n.m.* offender.

üben, *vb.* practice.

über, *prep.* over, about, above, across, beyond.

überall, *adv.* everywhere.

überar'beiten, *vb.* work over; (sich ü.) overwork.

überaus, *adv.* exceedingly.

überbelichten, *vb.* overexpose.

überbie'ten*, *vb.* outbid; surpass.

Überbleibsel, -, *n.nt.* rest, leftover.

Überblick, -e, *n.m.* survey; general view.

überbli'cken, *vb.* survey.

überbrin'gen*, *vb.* deliver.

Überbrin'ger, -, *n.m.* bearer.

überbrü'cken, *vb.* bridge.

überdau'ern, *vb.* outlive, outlast.

überdies', *adv.* furthermore.

Überdruß, *n.m.* boredom; (bis zum Ü.) ad nauseam.

überdrüssig, *adj.* tired of, sick of.

übereilt', *adj.* rash, hasty.

übereinan'der, *adv.* one on top of the other.

überein'kommen*, *vb.* agree.

Überein'kommen, -, *n.nt.* agreement.

Überein'kunft, :e, *n.f.* agreement.

überein'stimmen, *vb.* agree.

Überein'stimmung, -en, *n.f.* agreement, accord.

überfah'ren*, *vb.* drive over, run over.

Überfahrt, -en, *n.f.* passage, crossing.

Überfall, :, *n.m.* raid; hold-up.

überfallen*, *vb.* attack suddenly, hold up.

überfällig, *adj.* overdue.

überflie'gen*, *vb.* fly over; (*fig.*) scan.

überfließen*, *vb.* overflow.

überflü'geln, *vb.* surpass.

Überfluß, :sse, *n.m.* abundance.

überflüssig, *adj.* superfluous.

überflu'ten, *vb.* overflow.

überfüh'ren, *vb.* transfer, transport; convict.

Überfüh'rung, -en, *n.f.* transport, transfer; (railroad) overpass.

überfüllt', *adj.* overcrowded, jammed.

Übergabe, *n.f.* delivery; surrender.

Übergang, :e, *n.m.* passage; transition.

überge'ben*, *vb.* hand over, deliver; (sich ü.) vomit.

über-gehen*, *vb.* go over to.

überge'hen*, *vb.* pass over, skip.

Übergewicht, *n.nt.* overweight; preponderance; (das Ü. bekommen*) get the upper hand.

über-greifen*, *vb.* spread; encroach.

Übergriff, -e, *n.m.* encroachment.

über-haben*, *vb.* be sick of, fed up with.

überhand'nehmen*, *vb.* spread, become dominant.

überhäu'fen, *vb.* overshadow.

überhaupt', *adv.* in general; altogether, at all.

überheb'lich, *adj.* overbearing.

überho'len, *vb.* overhaul; drive past, pass.

überholt', *adj.* out-of-date.

überhö'ren, *vb.* purposely not hear, ignore.

überla'den, *adj.* ornate.

überlas'sen*, *vb.* give to, yield, leave to.

überlau'fen*, *vb.* overrun; defect, desert.

überlau'fen, *adj.* overrun.

Überläufer, -, *n.m.* deserter.

überle'ben*, *vb.* outlive, survive.

Überle'ben, *n.nt.* survival.

überle'gen, *vb.* reflect on, think over.

überle'gen, *adj.* superior.

überlegt', *adj.* deliberate.

Überle'gung, -en, *n.f.* deliberation, consideration.

überlie'fern, *vb.* hand over.

Überlie'ferung, -en, *n.f.* tradition.

Übermacht, *n.f.* superiority.

überman'nen, *vb.* overpower.

Übermaß, *n.nt.* excess.

übermäßig, *adj.* excessive.

Übermensch, -en, -en, *n.m.* superman.

übermit'teln, *vb.* transmit, convey.

übermorgen, *adv.* the day after tomorrow.

Übermü'dung, *n.f.* overfatigue, exhaustion.

Übermut, *n.m.* high spirits; arrogance.

übernächst, *adj.* next but one.

übernach'ten, *vb.* spend the night, stay overnight.

übernatürlich, *adj.* supernatural.

überneh'men*, *vb.* take over.

überparteilich, *adj.* nonpartisan.

überprü'fen, *vb.* examine, check.

Überprü'fung, -en, *n.f.* checking, check-up.

überque'ren, *vb.* cross.

überra'gen, *vb.* surpass.

überra'gend, *adj.* superior.

überra'schen, *vb.* surprise.

Überra'schung, -en, *n.f.* surprise.

überre'den, *vb.* persuade.

Überre'dung, -en, *n.f.* persuasion.

überreich, *adj.* abundant, profuse.

überrei'chen, *vb.* hand over, present.

Überrest, -e, *n.m.* remains, relics.

überrum'peln, *vb.* take by surprise.

Überschallgeschwindigkeit, -en, *n.f.* supersonic speed.

überschat'ten, *vb.* overshadow.

überschät'zen, *vb.* overestimate.

überschau'en, *vb.* survey, get the whole view of.

überschla'fen*, *vb.* oversleep.

Überschlag, :e, *n.m.* estimate.

überschla'gen*, *vb.* pass over, skip; (sich ü.) turn over.

Überschrift, -en, *n.f.* title, heading, headline.

Überschuhe, *n.pl.* galoshes.

Überschuß, :sse, *n.m.* surplus.

überschüt'ten, *vb.* overwhelm.

überschwem'men, *vb.* inundate.

Überschwem'mung, -en, *n.f.* flood.

Übersee, *n.f.* oversea(s).

Überseedampfer, -, *n.m.* transoceanic liner.

überseh'bar, *adj.* capable of being taken in at a glance; foreseeable.

überse'hen*, *vb.* view; overlook, not notice, ignore.

Überse'hen, -, *n.nt.* oversight.

übersen'den*, *vb.* send, transmit; consign, remit.

überset'zen, *vb.* translate.

Überset'zung, -en, *n.f.* translation.

Übersicht, -en, *n.f.* overview; summary, outline.

übersichtlich, *adj.* clear; easily understandable.

überspannt', *adj.* eccentric.

übersprin'gen*, *vb.* skip.

übersprudelnd, *adj.* exuberant.

überste'hen*, *vb.* endure, survive.

überstei'gen*, *vb.* surpass.

überstim'men, *vb.* outvote, overrule.

Überstunde, -n, *n.f.* hour of overtime work; (*pl.*) overtime.

überstür'zen, *vb.* precipitate.

überstürzt', *adj.* headlong, precipitate.

übertrag'bar, *adj.* transferable.

übertra'gen*, *vb.* transfer, transmit; translate; (im Radio ü.) broadcast; (im Fernseh ü.) televise.

Übertra'gung, -en, *n.f.* transfer; translation; broadcast.

übertref'fen*, *vb.* surpass, excel.

übertrei'ben*, *vb.* exaggerate.

Übertrei'bung, -en, *n.f.* exaggeration.

über-treten*, *vb.* go over.

übertre'ten*, *vb.* trespass, violate, infringe.

Übertre'tung, -en, *n.f.* violation, infringement.

übertrie'ben, *adj.* exaggerated, extravagant.

übervor'teilen, *vb.* get the better of (someone).

überwa'chen, *vb.* watch over, keep under surveillance, control.

Überwa'chung, -en, *n.f.* surveillance, control.

überwäl'tigen, *vb.* overpower, overwhelm.

überwei'sen*, *vb.* transfer; remit.

Überwei'sung, -en, *n.f.* remittance.

überwer'fen*, *vb.* (sich ü.) have a falling-out with.

überwie'gen*, vb. outweigh; predominate.

überwie'gend, adj. preponderant.

überwin'den*, vb. conquer, overcome.

Überwin'dung, -en, n.f. conquest; effort, reluctance.

überwin'tern, vb. hibernate.

Überzahl, n.f. numerical superiority.

überzählig, adj. surplus.

überzeu'gen, vb. convince.

überzeu'gend, adj. convincing.

Überzeu'gung, -en, n.f. conviction.

Überzeu'gungskraft, n.f. forcefulness.

Überzieher, -, n.m. overcoat.

üblich, adj. customary, usual.

U-Boot, -e, n.nt. (= Unterseeboot) submarine.

übrig, adj. remaining, left over.

übrigbleiben*, vb. be left over; (es bleibt mir nichts anderes übrig) I have no other choice.

übrigens, adv. incidentally, by the way.

übrighaben*, vb. have left over; (nichts ü. für) have no use for.

Übung, -en, n.f. practice; exercise.

Übungsbeispiel, -e, n.nt. paradigm.

UdSSR, abbr. (= Union' der Soziali'stischen Sowjetrepubliken) Union of Soviet Socialist Republics.

Ufer, -, n.nt. shore, bank.

Ufereinfassung, -en, n.f. embankment.

uferlos, adj. limitless.

Uhr, -en, n.f. watch, clock; (wieviel U. ist es?) what time is it?; (sieben U.) seven o'clock.

Uhrmacher, -, n.m. watchmaker.

Uhu, -s, n.m. owl.

Ulk, -e, n.m. fun.

ulkig, adj. funny.

Ultra-, cpds. ultra.

um, prep. around; at (clock time); (um . . . zu) in order to; (je so mehr) the more, all the more so.

um-adressieren, vb. readdress.

um-arbeiten, vb. rework, revise.

umar'men, vb. embrace.

Umar'mung, -en, n.f. embrace.

um-bauen, vb. remodel.

um-biegen*, vb. turn, turn around.

um-bringen*, vb. kill.

um-drehen, vb. turn around, rotate, revolve.

Umdre'hung, -en, n.f. turn, revolution, rotation.

um-erziehen*, vb. reeducate.

umfah'ren*, vb. circumnavigate, circle.

um-fallen*, vb. fall over.

Umfang, ⸚e, n.m. circumference; extent; volume.

umfangreich, adj. extensive; comprehensive; voluminous.

umfas'sen, vb. enclose, surround; comprise.

umfas'send, adj. comprehensive.

um-formen, vb. remodel, transform, convert.

Umfrage, -n, n.f. inquiry, poll.

Umgang, n.m. intercourse, association.

Umgangssprache, n.f. colloquial speech, vernacular.

umge'ben*, vb. surround.

Umge'bung, -en, n.f. surroundings, environment; vicinity.

um-gehen*, vb. go around, circulate; (u. mit) deal with, handle; (mit dem Gedanken u.) contemplate, plan.

umge'hen*, vb. evade, circumvent.

Umge'hen, -, n.nt. evasion.

Umge'hung, -en, n.f. circumvention; (mil.) flanking movement.

Umge'hungsstraße, -n, n.f. bypass.

umgekehrt, 1. adj. reverse, inverse. 2. adv. the other way round.

um-gestalten, vb. transform, alter, modify.

umgren'zen, vb. enclose; circumscribe.

um-gucken, vb. (sich u.) look around.

um-haben*, vb. have on.

Umhang, ⸚e, n.m. wrap.

umher', adv. around, about.

umher'-gehen*, vb. walk around.

umher'-wandern, vb. wander.

Umkehr, n.f. return; reversal.

um-kehren, vb. turn (back, round, inside out, upside down).

Umkehrung, -en, n.f. reversal, reversing.

um-kippen, vb. turn over, tip over.

um-kleiden, vb. (sich u.) change one's clothes.

Umkleideraum, ⸚e, n.m. dressing-room.

um-kommen*, vb. perish.

Umkreis, -e, n.m. circumference; range, radius.

umkrei'sen, vb. circle around, rotate around.

Umlauf, n.m. circulation.

um-laufen*, vb. circulate.

um-legen, vb. put on; change the position, shift; change the date.

um-leiten, vb. divert.

Umleitung, -en, n.f. detour.

um-lernen, vb. learn anew, readjust one's views.

umliegend, adj. surrounding.

umrah'men, vb. frame.

umran'den, vb. edge.

um-rechnen, vb. convert.

umrei'ßen*, vb. outline.

umrin'gen, vb. surround.

Umriß, -sse, n.m. contour, outline.

um-rühren, vb. stir.

Umsatz, ⸚e, n.m. turnover, sales.

Umsatzsteuer, -n, n.f. sales tax.

um-schalten, vb. switch.

Umschau, n.f. (U. halten*) look around.

umschichtig, adv. in turns.

Umschlag, ⸚e, n.m. envelope; (book) cover; turnover; compress.

umschlie'ßen*, vb. encircle, encompass.

umschlin'gen*, vb. embrace.

um-schreiben*, vb. rewrite.

umschrei'ben*, vb. circumscribe, paraphrase.

Umschrei'bung, -en, n.f. paraphrase.

Umschrift, -en, n.f. transcription.

Umschwung, ⸚e, n.m. change, about-face.

um-sehen*, vb. (sich u.) look around.

um-setzen, vb. transpose; (goods) sell.

Umsicht, n.f. circumspection.

umsichtig, adj. circumspect, prudent.

umso, adv. (u. besser) so much the better; (je mehr, u. besser) the more the better.

umsonst', adv. in vain; gratis, free of charge.

Umstand, ⸚e, n.m. circumstance, condition; (pl.) formalities, fuss; (in anderen Umständen) pregnant.

umständlich, adj. complicated, fussy.

Umstandskleid, -er, n.nt. maternity dress.

Umstandswort, ⸚er, n.nt. adverb.

Umstehend-, n.m.&f. bystander.

um-steigen*, vb. transfer, change.

Umsteiger, -, n.m. transfer (ticket).

um-stellen, vb. change the position of; (sich u. auf) readjust, convert to; computerize.

umstel'len, vb. surround.

um-steuern, vb. reverse.

um-stimmen, vb. make someone change his mind.

um-stoßen*, vb. overturn, overthrow, upset.

umstri'cken, vb. ensnare.

Umsturz, ⸚e, n.m. overthrow, revolution.

um-stürzen, vb. overturn.

Umtausch, -e, n.m. exchange; (vom U. ausgeschlossen) no exchange.

umtauschbar, adj. exchangeable.

um-tauschen, vb. exchange.

trieb, -e, *n.m.* intrigue, machinations.

tun*, *vb.* (sich nach etwas look for, apply for.

wälzung, -en, *n.f.* upheaval, volution.

wandeln, *vb.* transform; ange; convert.

wechseln, *vb.* change, convert.

weg, -e, *n.m.* detour.

welt, *n.f.* environment.

weltschutz, *n.m.* environmental protection.

weltschutzler, -, *n.m.* environmentalist.

wer'ben*, *vb.* woo, court.

wer'bung, *n.f.* courtship.

werfen*, *vb.* overthrow; set.

ziehen*, *vb.* move; (sich u.) ange one's clothes.

ein'geln, *vb.* surround.

zug, -e, *n.m.* move; procession.

bhängig, *adj.* independent.

abhängigkeit, *n.f.* independence.

bömmlich, *adj.* indispensible.

blässig, *adj.* incessant.

bseh'bar, *adj.* unforeseeable.

bwendbar, *adj.* inevitable.

chtsam, *adj.* inattentive; reless.

hnlich, *adj.* dissimilar, unc.

ngebracht, *adj.* out of ace.

ngemessen, *adj.* unsuitable, mproper.

ngenehm, *adj.* unpleasant, tasteful.

annehmlichkeit, -en, *n.f.* uble.

asehnlich, *adj.* plain, inmspicuous.

nständig, *adj.* indecent, obene.

nwendbar, *adj.* inapplicae.

ppetitlich, *adj.* unappetizc; nasty.

art, -en, *n.f.* rudeness, bad anners.

rtig, *adj.* naughty.

uffällig, *adj.* inconicuous.

ufhörlich, *adj.* incessant.

ufmerksam, *adj.* inattenve.

aufmerksamkeit, -en, *n.f.* attentiveness; inadverance.

ufrichtig, *adj.* insincere.

aufrichtigkeit, -en, *n.f.* incerity; lie.

ausbleiblich, *adj.* inevitable.

usgeglichen, *adj.* unbalced, unstable.

usgesetzt, *adj.* continual.

ausstehlich, *adj.* insufferle.

unbändig, *adj.* unruly; excessive.

unbarmherzig, *adj.* merciless.

unbeabsichtigt, *adj.* unintentional.

unbeachtet, *adj.* unnoticed; (u. lassen*) ignore.

unbedacht, *adj.* thoughtless.

unbedenklich, *adj.* harmless.

unbedeutend, *adj.* insignificant.

unbedingt', *adj.* absolute, unconditional.

unbefangen, *adj.* natural, naïve.

unbefleckt, *adj.* immaculate; (u.e Empfängnis) Immaculate Conception.

unbefriedigend, *adj.* unsatisfactory.

unbefriedigt, *adj.* dissatisfied.

unbefugt, *adj.* unauthorized.

unbegabt, *adj.* untalented, dumb.

unbegreiflich, *adj.* incomprehensible.

unbegrenzt, *adj.* limitless.

Unbehagen, *n.nt.* discomfort.

unbehaglich, *adj.* uneasy.

unbeholfen, *adj.* awkward, clumsy.

unbekannt, *adj.* unknown, unfamiliar.

unbekümmert, *adj.* unconcerned.

unbeliebt, *adj.* unpopular.

unbemerkbar, *adj.* imperceptible.

unbemerkt, *adj.* unnoticed.

unbenommen, *adj.* (es bleibt* Ihnen u.) you are at liberty to.

unbequem, *adj.* inconvenient; uncomfortable.

unbere'chenbar, *adj.* incalculable; unreliable, erratic.

unberechtigt, *adj.* unauthorized; unjustified.

unberufen! *interj.* touch wood!

unbeschädigt, *adj.* undamaged.

unbescheiden, *adj.* immodest; selfish.

Unbescholtenheit, *n.f.* integrity.

unbeschreiblich, *adj.* indescribable.

unbeschrieben, *adj.* blank.

unbesehen, *adj.* unseen.

unbesieg'bar, *adj.* invincible.

unbesonnen, *adj.* thoughtless.

unbesorgt, *adj.* carefree, unconcerned.

unbeständig, *adj.* changeable.

unbestellbar, *adj.* undeliverable.

unbestimmt, *adj.* indefinite, vague.

unbestritten, *adj.* undisputed.

unbeträchtlich, *adj.* inconsiderable.

unbeugsam, *adj.* inflexible; obstinate.

unbewandert, *adj.* inexperienced.

unbewiesen, *adj.* not proved.

unbewohnbar, *adj.* uninhabitable.

unbewohnt, *adj.* uninhabited.

unbewußt, *adj.* unconscious; unknown.

unbezahl'bar, *adj.* priceless.

unbrauchbar, *adj.* useless.

und, *conj.* and.

Undank, *n.m.* ingratitude.

undankbar, *adj.* ungrateful.

undefinierbar, *adj.* indefinable.

undenklich, *adj.* inconceivable; (seit u. en Zeiten) since time out of mind.

undeutlich, *adj.* unclear, indistinct.

undicht, *adj.* leaky.

Unding, *n.nt.* absurdity, nonsense.

unduldsam, *adj.* intolerant.

undurchführbar, *adj.* not feasible.

undurchsichtig, *adj.* opaque.

uneben, *adj.* uneven.

unecht, *adj.* not genuine, false, counterfeit; artificial.

unehelich, *adj.* illegitimate.

unehrenhaft, *adj.* dishonorable.

unehrerbietig, *adj.* disrespectful.

unehrlich, *adj.* dishonest; insincere.

uneingeschränkt, *adj.* unlimited.

uneinig, *adj.* (u. sein*) disagree.

Uneinigkeit, -en, *n.f.* disagreement, dissension.

unempfindlich, *adj.* insensitive.

unend'lich, *adj.* infinite; (u. klein) infinitesimal.

Unend'lichkeit, -en, *n.f.* infinity.

unentbehrlich, *adj.* indispensable.

unentgeltlich, *adj.* gratuitous.

unentschieden, *adj.* undecided; (das Spiel ist u.) the game is a draw.

unentschlossen, *adj.* undecided.

unentwegt, *adj.* constant.

unerfahren, *adj.* inexperienced.

Unerfahrenheit, -en, *n.f.* inexperience.

unerfreulich, *adj.* unpleasant.

unerheblich, *adj.* insignificant, irrelevant.

unerhört', *adj.* unheard of, outrageous.

unerkannt, *adj.* unrecognized.

unerkennbar, *adj.* unrecognizable.

unerklärlich, *adj.* inexplicable.

unerläßlich, *adj.* indispensable.

unerlaubt, *adj.* unlawful, illegal, illicit.

unermeß'lich, *adj.* immeasurable.

unermüdlich, *adj.* unpleasant.

unerquicklich, *adj.* unpleasant.

unerschrocken, *adj.* intrepid.

unersetzlich, *adj.* irreplaceable.

unersprießlich, adj. unpleasant.

unerträglich, adj. unbearable, insufferable.

unerwartet, adj. unexpected.

unerwünscht, adj. unwelcome.

unerzogen, adj. ill-bred, ill-mannered.

unfähig, adj. unable, incapable, incompetent.

unfair, adj. unfair.

Unfall, "e, n.m. accident.

unfaß'bar, adj. incomprehensible.

unfaß'lich, adj. incomprehensible.

unfehl'bar, adj. infallible.

Unfeinheit, -en, n.f. crudeness, crudity.

unförmig, adj. shapeless.

unfreiwillig, adj. involuntary.

unfreundlich, adj. unkind, unfriendly; rude.

unfruchtbar, adj. barren, sterile.

Unfug, n.m. mischief.

unfügsam, adj. unmanageable.

Ungar, -n, -n, n.m. Hungarian.

ungarisch, adj. Hungarian.

Ungarn, n.nt. Hungary.

ungastlich, adj. inhospitable.

ungeachtet, prep. notwithstanding.

ungebildet, adj. uneducated.

ungebührlich, adj. improper.

ungebunden, adj. free.

Ungeduld, n.f. impatience.

ungeduldig, adj. impatient.

ungeeignet, adj. unqualified, unsuitable.

ungefähr, 1. adj. approximate. 2. adv. approximately, about.

ungefährlich, adj. harmless.

ungefällig, adj. unobliging, impolite.

ungeheuchelt, adj. sincere.

ungeheuer, adj. tremendous, huge.

Ungeheuer, -, n.nt. monster.

ungeheuerlich, adj. monstrous.

ungehobelt, adj. uncouth.

ungehörig, adj. improper, rude.

ungehorsam, adj. disobedient.

Ungehorsam, n.m. disobedience.

ungekünstelt, adj. unaffected, natural.

ungeläufig, adj. unfamiliar.

ungelegen, adj. inconvenient.

ungelenk, adj. clumsy.

ungelernt, adj. unskilled.

ungemein, adv. uncommonly.

ungemütlich, adj. uncomfortable.

ungeneigt, adj. disinclined.

ungeniert, adj. free and easy.

ungenießbar, adj. inedible; unbearable.

ungenügend, adj. insufficient; unsatisfactory.

ungerade, adj. uneven; (numbers) odd.

ungerecht, adj. unjust, unfair.

ungerechtfertigt, adj. unwarranted.

Ungerechtigkeit, -en, n.f. injustice.

ungeschehen, adj. (u. machen) to undo.

Ungeschicklichkeit, -en, n.f. clumsiness.

ungeschickt, adj. clumsy, awkward.

ungeschlacht, adj. uncouth.

ungesetzlich, adj. illegal.

ungesittet, adj. unmannerly.

ungestört, adj. undisturbed.

ungestraft, 1. adj. unpunished. 2. adv. with impunity.

ungestüm, adj. impetuous.

ungesund, adj. unhealthy; unsound.

Ungetüm, -e, n.nt. monster.

ungewandt, adj. awkward.

ungewiß, adj. uncertain.

Ungewißheit, -en, n.f. uncertainty.

Ungewitter, -, n.nt. thunderstorm.

ungewöhnlich, adj. unusual, abnormal.

ungewohnt, adj. unaccustomed, unfamiliar.

ungewollt, adj. unintentional.

ungezählt, adj. innumerable.

ungezügelt, adj. unrestrained.

ungezwungen, adj. easygoing.

Ungläubig-, n.m.&f. infidel.

unglaublich, adj. incredible.

unglaubwürdig, adj. unreliable.

ungleich, adj. unequal, uneven, unlike.

ungleichartig, adj. dissimilar.

Ungleichheit, -en, n.f. unequality, dissimilarity.

Unglück, -e, n.nt. misfortune, calamity, disaster, accident.

unglücklich, adj. unhappy; unfortunate.

unglücklicherweise, adv. unfortunately.

unglückselig, adj. disastrous; utterly miserable.

Ungnade, n.f. disfavor.

ungnädig, n.f. ungracious.

ungültig, adj. invalid, void; (für u. erklären) annul, declare null and void.

ungünstig, adj. unfavorable.

unhalt'bar, adj. untenable.

unhandlich, adj. unwieldy.

Unheil, n.nt. harm, disaster.

unheil'bar, adj. incurable.

unheilbringend, adj. fatal, ominous.

unheilvoll, adj. ominous.

unheimlich, adj. scary, sinister.

unhöflich, adj. impolite, rude.

unhygienisch, adj. unsanitary.

Uniform', -en, n.f. uniform.

uninteressant, adj. uninteresting.

unisex, adj. unisex.

universal', adj. universal.

Universität', -en, n.f. university.

unkenntlich, adj. unrecognizable.

unklar, adj. unclear, obscure.

unkleidsam, adj. unbecoming.

Unkosten, n.pl. expenses, overhead.

unlängst, adv. recently.

unlauter, adj. impure; unfair.

unleserlich, adj. illegible.

unlieb, adj. disagreeable.

unliebenswürdig, adj. unfriendly, impolite.

unlogisch, adj. illogical.

unlustig, adj. listless.

unmanierlich, adj. unmannered.

unmaßgeblich, adj. irrelevant; unauthoritative.

unmäßig, adj. immoderate.

Unmenge, -n, n.f. enormous quantity.

Unmensch, -en, -en, n.m. brute.

unmenschlich, adj. inhuman.

unmerklich, adj. imperceptible.

unmittelbar, adj. immediate.

unmodern, adj. old-fashioned, out of style.

unmöglich, adj. impossible.

unmoralisch, adj. immoral.

unnachahmlich, adj. inimitable.

unnah'bar, adj. inaccessible.

unnötig, adj. needless, unnecessary.

unnütz, adj. useless.

unordentlich, adj. disorderly, messy.

Unordnung, n.f. disorder.

unparteiisch, adj. impartial, neutral.

unpassend, adj. unsuitable; improper, off-color.

unpassier'bar, adj. impassable.

unpäßlich, adj. unwell, indisposed.

unpersönlich, adj. impersonal.

unpolitisch, adj. nonpolitical.

unpraktisch, adj. impractical.

unpünktlich, adj. not on time.

unrecht, adj. wrong; (u. haben°) be wrong.

Unrecht, n.nt. wrong, harm, injustice.

unreell, adj. dishonest.

unregelmäßig, adj. irregular.

unreif, adj. immature.

unrein, adj. unclean; impure.

unrichtig, adj. incorrect.

Unruhe, -n, n.f. unrest, trouble, disturbance.

unruhig, adj. restless, troubled, uneasy.

unschädlich, adj. harmless.

unscheinbar, adj. insignificant.

unschicklich, adj. improper.

unschlüssig, adj. undecided.

Unschuld, n.f. innocence.

unschuldig, adj. innocent.

unselig, adj. unhappy, fatal.

unser, -, -e, adj. our.

uns(e)rer, -es, -e, pron. ours.

unsicher, adj. uncertain; unsafe.

Unsicherheit, -en, n.f. uncertainty, insecurity.

unsichtbar, *adj.* invisible.
Unsinn, *n.m.* nonsense.
unsinnig, *adj.* absurd, nonsensical.
Unsitte, -n, *n.f.* bad habit.
unsittlich, *adj.* immoral.
unsterblich, *adj.* immortal.
unstet, *adj.* unsteady.
Unstimmigkeit, -en, *n.f.* discrepancy, disagreement.
untauglich, *adj.* unfit.
unteilbar, *adj.* indivisible.
unten, *adv.* below, down, downstairs.
unter, *prep.* under, beneath, below; among; (u. uns) just between you and me.
unter-, *adj.* under, lower.
Unterarm, -e, *n.m.* forearm.
unterbewußt, *adj.* subconscious.
Unterbewußtsein, *n.nt.* subconsciousness.
unterbie'ten°, *vb.* undercut; lower.
unterblei'ben°, *vb.* not get done.
unterbre'chen°, *vb.* interrupt.
Unterbre'chung, -en, *n.f.* interruption.
unterbrei'ten, *vb.* submit.
unter-bringen°, *vb.* lodge, accommodate.
unterdes'(sen), *adv.* meanwhile.
unterdrü'cken, *vb.* suppress, oppress, repress, stifle, subdue.
unterdrückt', *adj.* downtrodden.
Unterdrü'ckung, -en, *n.f.* suppression.
untereinan'der, *adv.* among them- (our-, your-)selves.
unterernährt, *adj.* undernourished.
Unterernährung, *n.f.* malnutrition.
Unterfüh'rung, -en, *n.f.* underpass.
Untergang, -e, *n.m.* downfall, decline.
untergeben, *adj.* subordinate.
Untergebene, *n.m.&f.* subordinate.
untergehen°, *vb.* perish; set (sun).
untergeordnet, *adj.* subordinate.
untergra'ben°, *vb.* undermine, subvert.
Untergrundbahn, -en, *n.f.* subway.
unterhalb, *prep.* below.
Unterhalt, *n.m.* maintenance, keep.
unterhal'ten°, *vb.* maintain, support; entertain; (sich u.) converse.
Unterhal'tung, -en, *n.f.* maintenance; entertainment, conversation.
Unterhand'lung, -en, *n.f.* negotiation.

Unterhaus, *n.nt.* lower house (of parliament, congress).
Unterhemd, -en, *n.nt.* undershirt.
Unterhose, -n, *n.f.* underpants.
unterjo'chen, *vb.* subjugate.
Unterkunft, -e, *n.f.* lodging.
Unterlage, -n, *n.f.* base, bed; evidence; bottom sheet.
unterlas'sen°, *vb.* omit, fail to do.
Unterlas'sung, -en, *n.f.* omission, default.
unterle'gen, *adj.* inferior.
Unterleib, -er, *n.m.* abdomen.
unterlie'gen°, *vb.* succumb to, be overcome by.
Untermieter, -, *n.m.* subtenant.
unterneh'men°, *vb.* undertake.
Unterneh'men, -, *n.nt.* enterprise.
unterneh'mend, *adj.* enterprising.
Unterneh'mer, -, *n.m.* entrepreneur, contractor.
Unterneh'mung, -en, *n.f.* undertaking.
Unteroffizier, -e, *n.m.* noncommissioned officer, sergeant.
Unterpfand, *n.nt.* pledge, security.
Unterre'dung, -en, *n.f.* discussion, parley.
Unterricht, *n.m.* instruction.
unterrich'ten, *vb.* instruct.
Unterrich'tung, *n.f.* guidance.
Unterrock, -e, *n.m.* slip, petticoat.
untersa'gen, *vb.* prohibit.
Untersatz, -e, *n.m.* base; saucer.
unterschät'zen, *vb.* underestimate.
unterschei'den, *vb.* distinguish, differentiate; (sich u.) differ.
Unterschied, -e, *n.m.* difference.
unterschiedslos, *adj.* indiscriminate.
unterschla'gen°, *vb.* embezzle, suppress.
unterschrei'ben°, *vb.* sign (one's name to).
Unterschrift, -en, *n.f.* signature.
Unterseeboot, -e, *n.nt.* submarine.
untersetzt', *adj.* chunky, thickset.
Unterstand, -e, *n.m.* dugout.
unterste'hen°, *vb.* (sich u.) dare.
Unterstel'lung, -en, *n.f.* innuendo, insinuation.
unterstrei'chen°, *vb.* underline, underscore.
unterstüt'zen, *vb.* support, back.
Unterstüt'zung, -en, *n.f.* support, backing.
untersu'chen, *vb.* investigate, examine.
Untersu'chung, -en, *n.f.* investigation, examination.

Untertan, (-en,) -en, *n.m.* subject.
Untertasse, -n, *n.f.* saucer.
unter-tauchen, *vb.* submerge.
Unterwäsche, *n.f.* underwear.
unterwegs', *adv.* on the way; bound for.
unterwei'sen°, *vb.* instruct.
Unterwei'sung, -en, *n.f.* instruction.
Unterwelt, *n.f.* underworld.
unterwer'fen°, *vb.* subjugate; subject to; (sich u.) submit (to).
Unterwer'fung, -en, *n.f.* submission.
unterwor'fen, *adj.* subject (to).
unterwür'fig, *adj.* subservient.
unterzeich'nen, *vb.* sign.
unterzie'hen°, *vb.* (sich u.) undergo.
untief, *adj.* shallow.
untreu, *adj.* unfaithful, disloyal.
Untreue, *n.f.* unfaithfulness, disloyalty.
untröstlich, *adj.* disconsolate.
unüberlegt, *adj.* inconsiderate, thoughtless.
unüberwindlich, *adj.* insuperable.
unumgänglich, *adj.* unavoidable.
unveränderlich, *adj.* invariable.
unverantwortlich, *adj.* irresponsible.
unverbesserlich, *adj.* incorrigible.
unverbindlich, *adj.* without obligation.
unverblümt, *adj.* blunt.
unvereinbar, *adj.* incompatible.
unvergeßlich, *adj.* unforgettable.
unvergleichlich, *adj.* incomparable.
unverheiratet, *adj.* unmarried.
unverhohlen, *adj.* frank, aboveboard.
unverkennbar, *adj.* unmistakable.
unvermeidlich, *adj.* inevitable.
unvermittelt, *adj.* abrupt.
unvermutet, *adj.* unexpected.
unverschämt, *adj.* shameless, impudent, nervy.
Unverschämtheit, -en, *n.f.* impertinence, gall.
unversehens, *adv.* unexpectedly.
unverständlich, *adj.* incomprehensible.
unverzüglich, *adj.* speedy, without delay.
unvollendet, *adj.* incomplete, unfinished.
unvollkommen, *adj.* incomplete, imperfect.
unvoreingenommen, *adj.* unbiased.
unvorhergesehen, *adj.* unforeseen.
unvorsichtig, *adj.* careless.
unwägbar, *adj.* imponderable.

unwahr(haftig), *adj.* untrue.

Unwahrheit, -en, *n.f.* untruth.

unwahrnehmbar, *adj.* imperceptible.

unwahrscheinlich, *adj.* improbable.

unweigerlich, *adj.* unhesitating; without fail.

unwesentlich, *adj.* immaterial, nonessential.

unwiderlegbar, *adj.* irrefutable.

unwiderstehlich, *adj.* irresistible.

unwillkürlich, *adj.* involuntary.

unwirksam, *adj.* ineffectual.

unwissend, *adj.* ignorant.

unwürdig, *adj.* unworthy.

Unzahl, *n.f.* tremendous number.

unzählig, *adj.* countless.

Unze, -n, *n.f.* ounce.

Unzucht, *n.f.* lewdness.

unzüchtig, *adj.* lewd.

unzufrieden, *adj.* dissatisfied.

Unzufriedenheit, -en, *n.f.* dissatisfaction.

unzulänglich, *adj.* insufficient, inadequate.

unzureichend, *adj.* insufficient.

unzuverlässig, *adj.* unreliable.

Ur-, *cpds.* original; very old; tremendously.

uralt, *adj.* very old, ancient.

Uraufführung, -en, *n.f.* première.

Urenkel, -, *n.m.* great-grandson.

Urenkelin, -nen, *n.f.* great-granddaughter.

Urgroßeltern, *n.pl.* great-grandparents.

Urgroßmutter, ⸚, *n.f.* great-grandmother.

Urgroßvater, ⸚, *n.m.* great-grandfather.

Urheber, -, *n.m.* author, originator.

Urheberrecht, -e, *n.nt.* copyright.

Urin, -e, *n.nt.* urine.

urinie'ren, *vb.* urinate.

Urkunde, -n, *n.f.* document.

Urlaub, -e, *n.m.* leave, furlough.

Urne, -n, *n.f.* urn; ballot box.

Urquell, -e, *n.m.* fountainhead.

Ursache, -n, *n.f.* cause; (keine U.) don't mention it.

Ursprung, ⸚e, *n.m.* origin.

ursprünglich, *adj.* original.

Urteil, -e, *n.nt.* judgment, sentence.

urteilen, *vb.* judge.

usurpie'ren, *vb.* usurp.

usw., *abbr.* (= und so weiter) etc., and so forth.

V

Vagabund', -en, -en, *n.m.* tramp.

vage, *adj.* vague.

Valu'ta, -ten, *n.f.* value; (foreign) currency.

Vanil'le, *n.f.* vanilla.

Variation', -en, *n.f.* variation.

Varieté', *n.nt.* variety show, vaudeville.

variie'ren, *vb.* vary.

Vase, -n, *n.f.* vase.

Vater, ⸚, *n.m.* father.

Vaterland, *n.nt.* fatherland.

väterlich, *adj.* fatherly, paternal.

vaterlos, *adj.* fatherless.

Vaterschaft, -en, *n.f.* fatherhood, paternity.

Vaterun'ser, *n.nt.* Lord's Prayer.

Veilchen, -, *n.nt.* violet.

Vene, -n, *n.f.* vein.

vene'risch, *adj.* venereal.

Venti'l, -e, *n.nt.* valve.

Ventilation', *n.f.* ventilation.

Ventila'tor, -o'ren, *n.m.* ventilator, fan.

ventilie'ren, *vb.* ventilate.

verab'reden, *vb.* agree upon; (sich v.) make an appointment, date.

Verab'redung, -en, *n.f.* appointment, engagement, date.

verab'scheuen, *vb.* abhor, detest.

verab'schieden, *vb.* dismiss; pass (a bill); (sich v.) take one's leave.

verach'ten, *vb.* scorn, despise.

verach'tenswert, *adj.* despicable.

veräcbt'lich, *adj.* contemptuous.

Verach'tung, -en, *n.f.* contempt.

verallgemei'nern, *vb.* generalize.

Verallgemei'nerung, -en, *n.f.* generalization.

veral'tet, *adj.* obsolete.

Veran'da, -den, *n.f.* porch.

verän'derlich, *adj.* changeable.

verän'dern, *vb.* change.

Verän'derung, -en, *n.f.* change.

veran'kern, *vb.* anchor, moor.

veran'lassen*, *vb.* cause, motivate.

Veran'lassung, -en, *n.f.* cause, motivation.

veran'schaulichen, *vb.* illustrate.

veran'stalten, *vb.* arrange, put on.

Veran'staltung, -en, *n.f.* arrangement, performance.

verant'wortlich, *adj.* responsible.

Verant'wortlichkeit, -en, *n.f.* responsibility.

Verant'wortung, -en, *n.f.* responsibility; accounting, justification.

verant'wortungslos, *adj.* irresponsible.

verant'wortungsvoll, *adj.* carrying responsibility.

verar'beiten, *vb.* process.

verär'gern, *vb.* exasperate.

verar'men, *vb.* become poor.

Verb, -en, *n.nt.* verb.

verbal', *adj.* verbal.

Verband', ⸚e, *n.m.* association; bandage, dressing.

verban'nen, *vb.* banish, exile.

Verban'nung, -en, *n.f.* banishment, exile.

verbau'en, *vb.* build badly; obstruct.

verber'gen*, *vb.* hide.

verbes'sern, *vb.* improve, correct.

Verbes'serung, -en, *n.f.* improvement, correction.

verbeu'gen, *vb.* (sich v.) bow.

Verbeu'gung, -en, *n.f.* bow.

verbeu'len, *vb.* dent, batter.

verbie'gen*, *vb.* bend (out of shape).

verbie'ten*, *vb.* forbid, prohibit, ban.

verbie'terisch, *adj.* prohibitive.

verbin'den*, *vb.* connect, join, combine; bandage.

verbind'lich, *adj.* binding, obligatory.

Verbin'dung, -en, *n.f.* connection, combination; (chemical) compound; (student) fraternity; (in V. stehen* mit) be in touch with; (sich in V. setzen mit) get in touch with.

verbis'sen, *adj.* suppressed; dogged.

verbit'ten*, *vb.* decline; not stand for.

verbit'tern, *vb.* embitter.

verblas'sen, *vb.* turn pale, fade.

Verbleib', *n.m.* whereabouts.

verblei'chen*, *vb.* grow pale, fade.

verblüf'fen, *vb.* dumbfound, flabbergast.

verbo'gen, *adj.* bent.

verbor'gen, *adj.* hidden.

Verbot', -e, *n.nt.* prohibition.

Verbrauch', *n.m.* consumption.

verbrau'chen, *vb.* consume, use up, wear out.

Verbrau'cher, -, *n.m.* consumer.

Verbrauchs'steuer, -n, *n.f.* excise tax.

Verbre'chen, -, *n.nt.* crime.

Verbre'cher, -, *n.m.* criminal.

verbre'cherisch, *adj.* criminal.

verbrei'ten, *vb.* disseminate, propagate, diffuse.

verbrenn'bar, *adj.* combustible.

verbren'nen*, *vb.* burn; cremate.

Verbren'nung, *n.f.* burning; cremation; combustion.

verbrin'gen*, *vb.* spend (time).

verbrü'hen, *vb.* scald.

verbun'den, *adj.* indebted, obliged.

verbün'den, *vb.* ally.

Verbün'det-, *n.m.* ally, confederate.

verbür'gen, *vb.* guarantee.

Verdacht', *n.m.* suspicion.

verdäch'tig, *adj.* suspicious, suspected.

verdam'men, *vb.* damn, condemn.

verdam'menswert, *adj.* damnable.

Verdamm'nis, *n.f.* (eternal) damnation.

verdammt', *adj.* damned; damn it!

Verdam'mung, -en, *n.f.* damnation.

verdam'pfen, *vb.* evaporate.

verdan'ken, *vb.* owe (something to someone), be indebted to.

verdau'en, *vb.* digest.

verdau'lich, *adj.* digestible.

Verdau'ung, *n.f.* digestion.

Verdau'ungsstörung, -en, *n.f.* indigestion.

Verdeck', -e, *n.nt.* deck covering; top (of an auto).

verden'ken*, *vb.* take amiss.

verder'ben*, *vb.* perish, spoil, ruin.

Verder'ben, *n.nt.* perdition, ruin, doom.

verderb'lich, *adj.* ruinous; perishable.

verderbt', *adj.* corrupt.

verdeut'lichen, *vb.* make clear.

verdich'ten, *vb.* thicken, solidify.

verdie'nen, *vb.* earn, deserve.

Verdienst', -e, *n.m.* earnings.

Verdienst', -e, *n.nt.* merit.

verdienst'lich, *adj.* meritorious.

verdient', *adj.* deserving, deserved.

verdol'metschen, *vb.* interpret, translate.

verdop'peln, *vb.* double.

Verdop'pelung, -en, *n.f.* doubling.

verdor'ren, *vb.* wither.

verdrängen, *vb.* push out, displace; suppress, inhibit.

Verdrän'gung, -en, *n.f.* displacement; repression, inhibition.

verdre'hen, *vb.* twist, distort, pervert.

verdrie'ßen*, *vb.* grieve, vex, annoy.

verdrieß'lich, *adj.* morose, sulky.

Verdruß, *n.m.* vexation, irritation.

verdun'keln, *vb.* darken.

Verdun'kelung, -en, *n.f.* blackout.

verdün'nen, *vb.* thin, dilute, rarefy.

verdut'zen, *vb.* bewilder.

vereh'ren, *vb.* adore, respect, revere.

Vereh'rer, -, *n.m.* admirer.

Vereh'rung, *n.f.* adoration, reverence.

verei'digen, *vb.* administer an oath to.

Verei'digung, -en, *n.f.* swearing-in.

Verein', -e, *n.m.* association.

verein'bar, *adj.* compatible.

verein'baren, *vb.* come to an agreement, reconcile.

Verein'barkeit, *n.f.* compatibility.

Verein'barung, -en, *n.f.* agreement.

verei'nen, *vb.* unify.

verein'fachen, *vb.* simplify.

verein'heitlichen, *vb.* standardize, make uniform.

verei'nigen, *vb.* unite.

Verei'nigte Staaten von Ame'rika, die, *n.pl.* United States of America.

Verei'nigung, -en, *n.f.* union, alliance, association, merger.

Verein'te Natio'nen, die, *n.pl.* United Nations.

verein'zelt, *adj.* isolated, individual; scattered, stray.

verei'teln, *vb.* thwart, foil.

verer'ben, *vb.* bequeath.

vererb'lich, *adj.* hereditary.

Verer'bung, -en, *n.f.* heredity.

verfah'ren*, *vb.* act, proceed, deal; (sich v.) lose one's way.

Verfah'ren, -, *n.nt.* procedure, process.

Verfall', *n.m.* decay, decline, disrepair.

verfal'len*, *vb.* decay, decline, deteriorate; fall due, lapse.

verfäl'schen, *vb.* falsify, adulterate.

Verfäl'schung, -en, *n.f.* falsification, adulteration.

verfäng'lich, *adj.* captious, insidious.

verfas'sen, *vb.* compose, write.

Verfas'ser, -, *n.m.* author.

Verfas'sung, -en, *n.f.* composition; state, condition; constitution.

verfas'sungsmäßig, *adj.* constitutional.

verfas'sungswidrig, *adj.* unconstitutional.

verfau'len, *vb.* rot.

verfault', *adj.* putrid.

verfecht'bar, *adj.* defensible.

verfeh'len, *vb.* miss.

verfei'nern, *vb.* refine.

Verfei'nerung, -en, *n.f.* refinement.

verfer'tigen, *vb.* manufacture.

verfil'men, *vb.* film, make a movie of.

verflie'ßen*, *vb.* flow away, lapse.

verflu'chen, *vb.* curse, damn.

verflucht', *adj.* cursed; damned; damn it!

verfol'gen, *vb.* pursue, haunt, persecute.

Verfol'gung, -en, *n.f.* pursuit, persecution.

Verfrach'ter, -, *n.m.* shipper.

verfrüht', *adj.* premature.

verfüg'bar, *adj.* available.

verfü'gen, *vb.* enact, order; (v. über) have at one's disposal.

Verfü'gung, -en, *n.f.* disposition, instruction, enactment; (mir zur V. stehen*) be at my

disposal; (mir zur V. stellen) place at my disposal.

verfüh'ren, *vb.* lead astray, entice, pervert, seduce.

verfüh'rerisch, *adj.* seductive.

vergan'gen, *adj.* past, last.

Vergan'genheit, *n.f.* past.

vergäng'lich, *adj.* ephemeral, transitory.

Verga'ser, -, *n.m.* carburetor.

verge'ben*, *vb.* forgive; (sich v.) misdeal (at cards); (sich etwas v.) compromise oneself.

verge'bens, *adv.* in vain.

vergeb'lich, *adj.* vain, futile.

Verge'bung, *n.f.* forgiveness.

vergegenwär'tigen, *vb.* envisage, picture to oneself.

verge'hen*, *vb.* pass, elapse; (sich v.) err, sin, commit a crime.

Verge'hen, -, *n.nt.* misdemeanor.

vergel'ten*, *vb.* repay; retaliate.

Vergel'tung, -en, *n.f.* recompense; retaliation.

Vergel'tungsmaßnahme, -n, *n.f.* reprisal.

verges'sen*, *vb.* forget.

Verges'senheit, *n.f.* oblivion.

vergeß'lich, *adj.* forgetful.

vergeu'den, *vb.* squander.

vergewal'tigen, *vb.* use force on, rape.

Vergewal'tigung, -en, *n.f.* rape.

vergewis'sern, *vb.* confirm; reassure.

vergie'ßen*, *vb.* shed.

vergif'ten, *vb.* poison.

Vergiß'meinnicht, -e, *n.nt.* forget-me-not.

Vergleich', -e, *n.m.* comparison.

vergleich'bar, *adj.* comparable.

verglei'chen*, *vb.* compare.

vergnü'gen, *vb.* amuse.

Vergnü'gen, *n.nt.* fun; (viel V.) have a good time.

vergnügt', *adj.* in good spirits, gay.

Vergnü'gung, -en, *n.f.* pleasure, amusement, diversion.

vergöt'tern, *vb.* idolize.

vergrei'fen*, *vb.* (sich v.) do the wrong thing; (sich an etwas v.) attack, misappropriate.

vergrö'ßern, *vb.* enlarge, magnify.

Vergrö'ßerung, -en, *n.f.* enlargement.

vergrö'ßerungsapparat, -e, *n.m.* enlarger.

Vergün'stigung, -en, *n.f.* favor; reduction.

vergü'ten, *vb.* pay back.

verhaf'ten, *vb.* arrest.

Verhaftung, -en, *n.f.* arrest.

verhal'ten*, *vb.* hold back; (sich v.) be, behave.

verhal'ten, *adj.* suppressed.

Verhal'ten, *n.nt.* behavior.

Verhält'nis, -se, *n.nt.* relation(ship), proportion, ratio; love affair; (pl.) circumstances, conditions.

verhält'nismäßig, adj. relative, comparative.

verhan'deln, vb. negotiate.

Verhand'lung, -en, n.f. negotiation.

Verhand'lungsweise, n.f. procedure.

Verhäng'nis, -se, n.nt. fate, destiny.

verhäng'nisvoll, adj. fatal, fateful.

verhar'ren, vb. remain, persist.

verhär'ten, vb. harden, stiffen.

verhaßt', adj. hateful, odious.

verhau'en*, vb. beat up; make a mess of.

verhed'dern, vb. (sich v.) get snarled, caught.

verhee'ren, vb. desolate.

verhee'rend, adj. disastrous.

verheim'lichen, vb. conceal.

verhei'raten, vb. marry off; (sich v.) get married.

verherr'lichen, vb. glorify.

verhin'dern, vb. prevent, hinder.

Verhin'derung, n.f. prevention, hindrance.

verhoh'len, adj. hidden, clandestine.

Verhör', -e, n.nt. interrogation, hearing.

verhö'ren, vb. interrogate.

verhun'gern, vb. starve to death.

verhü'ten, vb. prevent.

Verhü'tung, -en, n.f. prevention.

Verhü'tungsmittel, -, n.nt. contraceptive device.

verir'ren, vb. (sich v.) lose one's way, go astray.

Verkauf', -̈e, n.m. sale.

verkau'fen, vb. sell.

Verkäu'fer, -, n.m. clerk, salesman.

verkäuf'lich, adj. saleable.

Verkehr', n.m. trade, traffic; relations, intercourse.

verkeh'ren, vb. (tr.) change; (intr.) run, go; associate, consort, frequent.

Verkehrs'ampel, -n, n.f. traffic light.

Verkehrs'flugzeug, -e, n.nt. air liner.

Verkehrs'licht, -er, n.nt. traffic light.

verkehrt', adj. reversed, wrong, backwards.

verken'nen*, vb. mistake, misunderstand.

verket'ten, vb. link.

verkla'gen, vb. sue, accuse.

Verklagt'-, n.m.&f. defendant.

verklärt', adj. transfigured, radiant.

verklei'den, vb. disguise; panel.

verklei'nern, vb. make smaller; belittle.

Verklei'nerung, -en, n.f. diminution; disparagement.

verknüp'fen, vb. connect, relate.

verkom'men*, vb. decay, come down in the world, die.

verkom'men, adj. squalid, dissolute.

verkör'pern, vb. embody.

verkör'pert, adj. incarnate.

Verkör'perung, -en, n.f. embodiment, epitome.

verkrüp'pelt, adj. crippled.

verklim'mern, vb. wither.

verkün'd(ig)en, vb. announce, proclaim.

Verkün'd(ig)ung, -en, n.f. announcement, Annunciation.

verkür'zen, vb. shorten.

verla'den*, vb. load, ship.

Verla'der, -, n.m. shipper.

Verlag', -e, n.m. publishing house.

verla'gern, vb. shift, displace.

verlan'gen, vb. demand, require, ask; (v. nach) desire, long for.

Verlan'gen, n.nt. demand, request, craving.

verlän'gern, vb. lengthen, prolong, extend, renew.

Verlän'gerung, -en, n.f. prolongation, extension, renewal.

verlas'sen*, vb. leave, abandon, forsake; (sich v. auf) depend on, rely on.

verlas'sen, adj. abandoned, deserted, forlorn.

verläß'lich, adj. dependable.

Verlauf', n.m. course, lapse.

verlau'fen*, vb. pass, elapse; (sich v.) get lost.

verle'ben, vb. pass.

verliebt', adj. dissipated.

verle'gen, vb. move, shift; block; misplace; publish.

verle'gen, adj. embarrassed.

Verle'ger, -, n.m. publisher.

Verle'gung, -en, n.f. transfer, removal.

verlei'hen*, vb. lend; confer, bestow.

Verlei'hung, -en, n.f. bestowal.

verlei'ten, vb. lead astray, inveigle.

verler'nen, vb. forget.

verletz'bar, adj. vulnerable.

verlet'zen, vb. hurt, offend; violate, infringe.

Verlet'zung, -en, n.f. injury; violation.

verleug'nen, vb. deny, disown.

verleum'den, vb. slander.

verleum'derisch, adj. libelous.

Verleum'dung, -en, n.f. libel, slander.

verlie'ben, vb. (sich v.) fall in love.

verliebt', adj. in love.

verlie'ren*, vb. lose.

verlo'ben, vb. affiance, betroth; (sich v.) get engaged.

verlobt', adj. engaged.

Verlobt'-, n.m. fiancé.

Verlobt'-, n.f. fiancée.

Verlo'bung, -en, n.f. engagement.

verlo'cken, vb. entice, lure.

verlö'schen*, vb. go out, be extinguished.

Verlust', -e, n.m. loss; (pl.) casualties.

verma'chen, vb. bequeath.

Vermächt'nis, -se, n.nt. bequest, legacy.

vermäh'len, vb. espouse.

Vermäh'lung, -en, n.f. espousal.

vermeh'ren, vb. augment, multiply, increase.

vermeid'bar, adj. avoidable.

vermei'den*, vb. avoid.

vermeint'lich, adj. supposed.

vermen'gen, vb. blend; mix up.

Vermerk', -e, n.m. note; entry.

vermer'ken, vb. note down.

vermes'sen*, vb. measure, survey; (sich v.) have the audacity.

Vermes'senheit, n.f. presumptuousness.

Vermes'sung, -en, n.f. survey.

vermie'ten, vb. rent (to someone).

vermin'dern, vb. diminish.

vermis'sen, vb. miss.

vermit'teln, vb. mediate, negotiate, arrange.

Vermitt'ler, -, n.m. mediator.

vermö'ge, prep. by virtue of.

vermö'gen*, vb. be able.

Vermö'gen, -, n.nt. fortune, wealth, estate; ability, power.

vermö'gend, adj. wealthy, well-to-do.

vermuten, vb. presume.

vermut'lich, adj. presumable.

Vermu'tung, -en, n.f. surmise.

vernach'lässigen, vb. neglect.

Vernach'lässigung, -en, n.f. neglect.

verneh'men*, vb. perceive, hear, learn; examine.

vernehm'lich, adj. perceptible.

Verneh'mung, -en, n.f. hearing.

vernei'gen, vb. (sich v.) bow.

vernei'nen, vb. deny.

vernei'nend, adj. negative.

Vernei'nung, -en, n.f. denial.

vernich'ten, vb. annihilate, destroy.

vernich'tend, adj. devastating.

Vernich'tung, -en, n.f. annihilation, destruction.

Vernunft', n.f. reason.

vernunft'gemäß, adj. rational, according to reason.

vernünf'tig, adj. reasonable, sensible.

veröf'fentlichen, vb. publish.

Veröf'fentlichung, -en, n.f. publication.

verord'nen, vb. decree, order.

Verord'nung, -en, n.f. decree, ordinance, edict.

verpa'cken, vb. pack up, wrap up.

verpas'sen, vb. miss.

verpes'ten, vb. infect.

verpfän'den, vb. pawn, pledge.

verpfle'gen, vb. care for; feed.

Verpfle'gung, -en, n.f. food, board.

verpflich'ten, vb. oblige; (sich v.) commit oneself.

Verpflich'tung, -en, n.f. obligation.

Verrat', n.m. treason, betrayal.

verra'ten*, vb. betray.

Verräter, -, n.m. traitor.

verrä'terisch, adj. treacherous.

verrech'nen, vb. reckon up; (sich v.) make a mistake in figuring, miscalculate.

verrei'sen, vb. go away on a trip.

verreist', adj. away on a trip.

verren'ken, vb. sprain.

verrich'ten, vb. do, perform, carry out.

verrin'gern, vb. decrease.

verros'ten, vb. rust.

verrucht', adj. infamous, wicked.

verrückt', adj. mad, crazy.

Verruf', n.m. disrepute, notoriety.

verru'fen, adj. disreputable, notorious.

Vers, -e, n.m. verse.

versa'gen, vb. refuse; fail.

Versa'ger, -, n.m. failure, flop.

versam'meln, vb. assemble.

Versamm'lung, -en, n.f. assembly, gathering, meeting.

Versand', n.m. dispatch.

versäu'men, vb. neglect; miss.

Versäum'nis, -se, n.nt. omission.

verschaf'fen, vb. procure.

verschämt', adj. bashful, coy.

verschan'zen, vb. entrench.

verschär'fen, vb. intensify.

verschei'den, vb. expire.

verschen'ken, vb. give away.

verscher'zen, vb. throw away, lose frivolously.

verscheu'chen, vb. scare away.

verschic'ken, vb. send off.

verschie'ben*, vb. shift, displace; postpone.

Verschie'bung, -en, n.f. shift; postponement.

verschie'den, adj. different; distinct; various, assorted, separate.

verschie'denartig, adj. various; heterogeneous.

verschie'ßen*, vb. fire off; fade.

verschla'fen*, 1. vb. miss by sleeping too long; sleep off; (sich v.) oversleep. 2. adj. sleepy.

Verschlag', -̈e, n.m. partition, compartment.

verschla'gen*, 1. vb. drive away; (es verschlägt mir den Atem) it takes my breath away. 2. adj. sly.

verschlech'tern, vb. make worse, impair; (sich v.) become worse, deteriorate.

Verschlech'terung, -en, n.f. deterioration.

verschlei'ern, vb. veil.

verschlep'pen, vb. delay; abduct.

verschleu'dern, vb. squander.

verschlie'ßen*, vb. close, lock.

verschlim'mern, vb. make worse, aggravate; (sich v.) become worse, deteriorate.

verschlin'gen*, vb. devour.

verschlis'sen, adj. worn out, frayed.

verschlos'sen, adj. closed, locked; reserved, taciturn.

verschlu'cken, vb. swallow; (sich v.) swallow the wrong way, choke.

Verschluß', -̈sse, n.m. closure; lock, plug, stopper; fastening, fastener; (camera) shutter.

verschmach'ten, vb. languish.

verschmel'zen*, vb. fuse, merge.

Verschmel'zung, -en, n.f. fusion.

verschneit', adj. covered with snow.

Verschnitt', n.m. adulteration; watered spirits.

verschnupft', adj. having a cold.

verschol'len, adj. missing, never heard of again.

verscho'nen, vb. spare.

verschö'nern, vb. beautify.

verschrei'ben*, vb. prescribe.

verschüch'tern, vb. intimidate.

verschul'det, adj. indebted.

verschüt'ten, vb. spill.

verschwei'gen*, vb. keep quiet about.

verschwen'den, vb. squander, waste, dissipate.

Verschwen'der, -, n.m. spendthrift.

verschwen'derisch, adj. wasteful, extravagant, prodigal.

Verschwen'dung, -en, n.f. extravagance, wastefulness.

verschwie'gen, adj. silent, discreet, reticent.

verschwin'den*, vb. disappear.

Verschwin'den, n.nt. disappearance.

verschwom'men, adj. blurred.

verschwö'ren*, vb. renounce; (sich v.) conspire.

Verschwö'rer, -, n.m. conspirator.

Verschwö'rung, -en, n.f. conspiracy.

verse'hen*, vb. provide; perform; (sich v.) make a mistake.

Verse'hen, -, n.nt. oversight, error; (aus V.) by mistake.

versen'den*, vb. send off.

versen'gen, vb. singe, scorch.

versen'ken, vb. sink.

verset'zen, vb. move, transfer; (school) promote; pawn, hock; reply.

versi'chern, vb. insure, assure; affirm, assert.

Versi'cherung, -en, n.f. insurance, assurance.

versie'geln, vb. seal.

versie'gen, vb. dry up.

versin'ken*, vb. sink.

versinn'bildlichen, vb. symbolize.

Version', -en, n.f. version.

versöh'nen, vb. reconcile.

versöh'nend, adj. conciliation.

versöhn'lich, adj. conciliatory.

Versöh'nung, -en, n.f. reconciliation.

versor'gen, vb. provide, supply.

Versor'gung, n.f. supply, maintenance.

verspä'ten, vb. (sich v.) be late.

verspä'tet, adj. late.

Verspä'tung, -en, n.f. lateness.

versper'ren, vb. bar, obstruct.

verspie'len, vb. gamble away; (sich v.) misplay.

verspielt', adj. playful.

verspot'ten, vb. mock, deride.

verspre'chen*, vb. promise; (sich v.) make a slip of the tongue.

Verspre'chen, -, n.nt. promise.

verstaat'lichen, vb. nationalize.

Verstand', n.m. mind, intellect, brains.

verstän'dig, adj. sensible, intelligent.

verstän'digen, vb. inform; (sich v.) make oneself understood, make an agreement.

Verstän'digung, -en, n.f. agreement, understanding.

verständ'lich, adj. understandable.

Verständ'nis, n.nt. understanding.

verständ'nisvoll, adj. understanding.

verstär'ken, vb. strengthen, reinforce, intensify, amplify.

Verstär'ker, -, n.m. amplifier.

Verstär'kung, -en, n.f. reinforcement.

verstau'ben, vb. get covered with dust.

verstäu'ben, vb. atomize.

verstau'chen, vb. sprain.

Versteck', -e, n.nt. hiding place; ambush; (V. spielen) play hide-and-go-seek.

verste'cken, vb. hide.

versteckt', adj. hidden; veiled, oblique, ulterior.

verste'hen*, vb. understand.

Verstei'gerung, -en, n.f. auction.

verstell'bar, adj. adjustable.

verstel'len, vb. adjust; change, disguise.

Verstel'lung, -en, n.f. adjustment; disguise, sham, hypocrisy.

versteu'ern, vb. pay tax on.

verstim'men, vb. annoy, upset.

verstimmt', adj. annoyed, cross; (music) out of tune.

verstockt', adj. obdurate; impenitent.

verstoh'len, adj. stealthy, surreptitious.

verstop'fen, vb. stop up, clog.

Verstop'fung, -en, n.f. obstruction, jam; (med.) constipation.

verstor'ben, adj. deceased.

verstört', adj. distracted, bewildered.

Verstoß', ⸚e, n.m. violation, offence.

versto'ßen°, vb. expel, disown; (v. gegen) infringe on, offend.

verstrei'chen°, vb. elapse.

verstri'cken, vb. ensnare, enmesh.

verstüm'meln, vb. mutilate.

Verstüm'melung, -en, n.f. mutilation.

verstum'men, vb. become silent.

Versuch', -e, n.m. attempt; test, trial, experiment; effort.

versu'chen, vb. attempt, try, test; strive; entice, tempt.

versuchs'weise, adv. experimentally.

Versu'chung, -en, n.f. temptation.

versün'digen, vb. (sich v.) sin against.

versun'ken, adj. sunken; (v. sein°) be absorbed, be lost.

versü'ßen, vb. sweeten.

verta'gen, vb. adjourn.

Verta'gung, -en, n.f. adjournment.

vertau'schen, vb. exchange for; mistake for; substitute.

vertei'digen, vb. defend, advocate.

Vertei'diger, -, n.m. defender; (jur.) counsel for the defense.

Vertei'digung, -en, n.f. defense.

vertei'len, vb. distribute, disperse, divide.

Vertei'ler, -, n.m. distributor.

Vertei'lung, -en, n.f. distribution; dispersal, division.

vertie'fen, vb. deepen; (sich v.) deepen, become engrossed.

vertieft', adj. absorbed.

vertil'gen, vb. consume; exterminate.

Vertrag', ⸚e, n.m. contract, treaty, pact.

vertra'gen°, vb. endure, tolerate, stand; (sich v.) agree, get along.

vertrag'lich, adj. contractual.

verträg'lich, adj. compatible, good-natured.

vertrau'en, vb. trust; confide in; rely on.

Vertrau'en, n.f. trust, confidence, faith.

vertrau'ensvoll, adj. confident, reliant.

Vertrau'ensvotum, n.nt. vote of confidence.

vertrau'lich, adj. confidential.

Vertrau'lichkeit, -en, n.f. familiarity, intimacy; (in aller V.) in strict confidence.

vertraut', adj. acquainted, familiar; intimate.

Vertraut', -, n.m.&f. confidant(e).

Vertraut'heit, -en, n.f. familiarity; intimacy.

vertrei'ben°, vb. drive away, expel.

Vertrei'bung, -en, n.f. expulsion.

vertre'ten°, vb. represent; act as substitute; advocate.

Vertre'ter, -, n.m. representative, agent; deputy, substitute.

Vertre'tung, -en, n.f. representation, agency; substitution.

Vertrieb', -e, n.m. sale, market.

Vertrie'ben-, n.m.&f. expellee, refugee.

Vertriebs'stelle, -n, n.f. distributor.

vertu'schen, vb. hush up.

verü'beln, vb. take amiss.

verü'ben, vb. commit.

verun'glücken, vb. meet with an accident; fail.

verun'reinigen, vb. pollute.

verun'stalten, vb. disfigure.

verun'zieren, vb. mar.

verur'sachen, vb. cause, bring about; result in.

verur'teilen, vb. condemn; (jur.) sentence.

Verur'teilung, n.f. condemnation; (jur.) sentence.

verviel'fachen, vb. multiply.

verviel'fältigen, vb. multiply; mimeograph; (sich v.) multiply.

vervoll'kommnen, vb. perfect.

Vervoll'kommnung, n.f. perfection.

vervoll'ständigen, vb. complete.

verwach'sen°, vb. grow together; become deformed.

Verwach'sung, -en, n.f. deformity.

verwah'ren, vb. keep, hold in safe-keeping.

verwahr'losen, vb. neglect.

Verwah'rung, n.f. custody.

verwal'ten, vb. administer, manage.

Verwal'ter, -, n.m. administrator.

Verwal'tung, -en, n.f. administration, management.

verwan'deln, vb. change, transform.

Verwand'lung, -en, n.f. change, transformation; metamorphosis.

verwandt', adj. related.

Verwandt'-, n.m.&f. relation, relative.

Verwandt'schaft, -en, n.f. relationship, affinity.

verwech'seln, vb. mistake for, confuse.

Verwechs'lung, -en, n.f. mistake, mix-up.

verwe'gen, adj. daring, bold.

verweh'ren, vb. prevent from; refuse.

verwei'gern, vb. refuse.

Verwei'gerung, -en, n.f. refusal.

verwei'len, vb. linger.

Verweis', -e, n.m. reprimand; (einen V. erteilen) reprimand.

verwei'sen°, vb. banish; (v. auf) refer to.

verwend'bar, adj. usable, applicable.

Verwend'barkeit, n.f. usability, applicability.

verwen'den(°), vb. use, supply; expend.

Verwen'dung, -en, n.f. use, application.

verwer'fen°, vb. reject.

verwe'sen, vb. putrify, decay.

verwi'ckeln, vb. entangle, involve, implicate.

verwi'ckelt, adj. involved, intricate, complicated.

Verwick'lung, -en, n.f. entanglement, implication; complication.

verwin'den°, vb. get over, overcome.

verwir'ken, vb. forfeit.

verwirk'lichen, vb. realize, materialize.

Verwirk'lichung, -en, n.f. realization.

verwir'ren, vb. confuse, bewilder, confound, puzzle, mystify.

Verwir'rung, -en, n.f. confusion, bewilderment, perplexity.

verwi'schen, vb. wipe out; smudge.

verwit'wet, adj. widowed.

verwor'fen, adj. depraved.

verwor'ren, adj. confused.

verwun'den, vb. wound.

verwun'dern, vb. astonish.

Verwun'dung, -en, n.f. wound, injury.

verwun'schen, adj. enchanted.

verwün'schen, vb. curse; bewitch.

verwüs'ten, vb. devastate.

verza'gen, vb. despair.

verzagt', adj. despondent.

verzäh'len, vb. (sich v.) miscount.

verzär'teln, vb. pamper.

verzau'bern, vb. bewitch.

verzeh'ren, vb. consume.

verzeich'nen, vb. register, list.

Verzeich'nis, -se, n.nt. list, index.

verzei'hen°, vb. pardon, forgive.

Verzei'hung, -en, n.f. pardon, forgiveness; (ich bitte um V.) I beg your pardon.

verzer'ren, vb. distort.

Verzicht', -e, n.m. renunciation; (V. leisten) renounce.

verzich'ten, vb. renounce, forego, waive.

verzie'hen°, vb. pull out of shape; (child) spoil; (sich v.) withdraw; vanish, disperse; (wood) warp.

verzie'ren, vb. embellish.

Verzie'rung, -en, n.f. ornament, embellishment.

verzin'sen, vb. pay interest; (sich v.) bear interest.

Verzin'sung, -en, n.f. interest return; payment of interest; interest rate.

verzo'gen, adj. moved away; (child) spoiled.

verzö'gern, vb. delay.

Verzö'gerung, -en, n.f. delay.

verzol'len, vb. pay duty on.

verzückt, adj. enraptured.

Verzug', -e, n.m. delay; default.

verzwei'feln, vb. despair.

verzwei'felt, adj. desperate.

Verzweif'lung, -en, n.f. desperation.

verzwickt', adj. complicated.

Vesper, -n, n.f. vespers.

Veterinär', -e, n.m. veterinary.

Vetter, -n, n.m. cousin.

Viadukt', -e, n.m. viaduct.

Vibration', -en, n.f. vibration.

vibrie'ren, vb. vibrate.

Vieh, n.nt. cattle.

viehisch, adj. brutal.

Viehzucht, n.f. cattle breeding.

viel, adj. much; (pl.) many.

vielbedeutend, adj. significant.

vieldeutig, adj. ambiguous.

Vieleck, -e, n.nt. polygon.

vielerlei, adj. various, many.

vielfach, adj. manifold.

vielfältig, adj. multiple.

Vielfältigkeit, n.f. multiplicity.

vielfarbig, adj. multicolored.

Vielfraß, -e, n.m. glutton.

Vielheit, -en, n.f. multiplicity.

vielleicht', adv. perhaps.

vielmals, adv. many times.

vielmehr, adv. rather.

vielsagend, adj. significant, highly suggestive.

vielseitig, adj. many-sided; versatile.

vielverheißend, adj. very promising.

vielversprechend, adj. very promising.

vier, num. four.

Viereck, -e, n.nt. square.

viereckig, adj. square.

vierfach, adj. fourfold.

Vierfüßler, -, n.m. quadruped.

vierschrötig, adj. thick-set.

viert-, adj. fourth.

vierteilen, vb. quarter.

Viertel, -, n.nt. fourth part, quarter; (ein v.) one-fourth.

vierzehn, num. fourteen.

vierzig, num. forty.

vierzigst-, adj. fortieth.

Vierzigstel, -, n.nt. fortieth part; (ein v.) one-fortieth.

violett', adj. violet.

Violi'ne, -n, n.f. violin.

Violinist', -en, -en, n.m. violinist.

Virtuo'se, -n, -n, n.m. virtuoso.

Visier', -e, n.nt. visor; (gun) sight.

visuell', adj. visual.

Visum, -sa, n.nt. visa.

Vitalität', n.f. vitality.

Vogel, ², n.m. bird.

vogelartig, adj. birdlike.

Vogelbauer, -, n.nt. bird cage.

Vogelscheuche, -n, n.f. scarecrow.

Vogt, -e, n.m. overseer.

Vokal', -e, n.m. vowel.

Volant', -s, n.m. flounce.

Volk, ²er, n.nt. people, nation.

Völkerbund, n.m. League of Nations.

Völkerkunde, n.f. ethnology; (school) social studies.

Völkermord, n.m. genocide.

Völkerrecht, n.nt. international law,

Volksabstimmung, -en, n.f. plebiscite, referendum.

Volkscharakter, n.m. national character.

Volksentscheid, n.m. plebiscite, referendum.

Volksgenosse, -n, -n, n.m. fellow countryman.

Volkskunde, n.f. folklore.

Volkslied, -er, n.nt. folksong.

Volksmenge, n.f. crowd, mob.

Volksschule, -n, n.f. elementary school.

Volkstanz, ²e, n.m. folk-dance.

volkstümlich, adj. popular.

Volkszählung, -en, n.f. census.

voll, adj. full.

Vollblut, n.nt. thoroughbred.

vollblütig, adj. full-blooded.

vollbrin'gen°, vb. accomplish, fulfill.

vollen'den, vb. finish, complete.

vollen'det, adj. accomplished.

vollends, adv. completely.

Völlerei', n.f. gluttony.

vollfüh'ren, vb. accomplish.

Vollgas, n.nt. full throttle.

völlig, adj. complete, entire.

volljährig, adj. of age.

vollkom'men, adj. perfect.

Vollkom'menheit, n.f. perfection.

Vollmacht, -en, n.f. authority, warrant, proxy, power of attorney.

vollständig, adj. complete.

voll stopfen, vb. cram, stuff.

vollstre'cken, vb. execute, carry out.

Vollversammlung, n.f. (U.N.) General Assembly.

vollzählig, adj. complete.

vollzie'hen°, vb. execute, carry out; consummate; (sich v.) take place.

Volontär', -e, n.m. volunteer.

Volontär'arzt, ²e, n.m. intern.

Volt, -, n.nt. volt.

Volu'men, -, n.nt. volume.

von, prep. before; in front of; ago.

vor, prep. before; in front of; ago.

Vorabend, -e, n.m. eve.

Vorahnung, -en, n.f. premonition, foreboding.

voran', adv. in front of, ahead; onward.

voran'-gehen°, vb. precede.

voran'-kommen°, vb. get ahead.

Voranmeldung, -en, n.f. (telephone) (mit V.) person-to-person call.

Voranschlag, ²e, n.m. estimate.

Vorarbeit, -en, n.f. preparatory work.

Vorarbeiter, -, n.m. foreman.

vorauf', adv. before, ahead.

voraus', adv. in advance, ahead; (im v.) in advance.

voraus'-bedingen°, vb. precede.

voraus'-bestellen, vb. order ahead, make reservations.

voraus'-gehen°, vb. precede.

voraus'gesetzt, adv. (v. daß) provided that.

voraus'-nehmen°, vb. state now, anticipate.

Voraus'sage, -n, n.f. prediction, forecast.

voraus'-sagen, vb. predict, forecast.

voraus'-setzen, vb. presume, presuppose.

Voraus'setzung, -en, n.f. supposition, assumption; prerequisite.

Voraus'sicht, n.f. foresight.

voraus'sichtlich, 1. adj. probable, prospective. 2. adv. presumably.

voraus'-zahlen, vb. pay in advance, advance.

Vorbedacht, n.m. forethought.

Vorbedeutung, -en, n.f. omen.

Vorbedingung, -en, n.f. prerequisite.

Vorbehalt, n.m. reservation.

vor-behalten°, vb. reserve.

vorbei', adv. over, past.

vorbelastet, adj. having a questionable record; (jur.) having a criminal record.

vor-bereiten, vb. prepare.

vor-bestellen, vb. order in advance, make reservations.

vor-beugen, vb. prevent.

vorbeugend, adj. preventive.

Vorbild, -er, n.nt. model.

vorbildlich, adj. exemplary.

vor-bringen°, vb. state; propose.

vorder-, adj. front, anterior.

Vorderfront, -en, n.f. frontage; (fig.) forefront.

Vordergrund, n.m. foreground.

vorderhand, adv. for the time being; right now.

Vordermann, ²er, n.m. person ahead of one.

Vorderseite, -n, n.f. front.

Vorderteil, -e, n.nt. front part.

vor-drängen, vb. (sich v.) elbow one's way forward.

vor-dringen*, vb. press forward, advance.

Vordruck, -°e, n.m. form, blank.

voreilig, adj. rash, hasty.

voreingenommen, adj. prejudiced.

Voreingenommenheit, n.f. partiality.

vor-enthalten*, vb. withhold.

vorerst, adv. first of all.

Vorfahr, -en, -en, n.m. ancestor.

vor-fahren*, vb. drive up; (v. lassen*) let pass.

Vorfahrtsrecht, -e, n.nt. right of way.

Vorfall, -°e, n.m. incident.

vor-fallen*, vb. occur.

vor-finden*, vb. find.

vor-führen, vb. show, demonstrate, produce.

Vorführung, -en, n.f. demonstration, show, production.

Vorgang, -°e, n.m. occurrence, process, procedure.

Vorgänger, -, n.m. predecessor.

vor-geben*, vb. pretend, feign.

Vorgefühl, -e, n.nt. presentiment, hunch.

vor-gehen*, vb. advance; come first, precede.

Vorgehen, n.nt. procedure, policy.

Vorgericht, -e, n.nt. appetizer; first course.

Vorgeschichte, n.f. prehistory; history, background.

vorgeschrieben, adj. prescribed.

vorgesehen, adj. planned, scheduled.

Vorgesetzt-, n.m.&f. superior.

vorgestern, adv. the day before yesterday.

vorgetäuscht, adj. make-believe.

vor-greifen*, vb. anticipate.

vor-haben*, vb. plan, intention.

Vorhaben, n.nt. plan, intention.

Vorhalle, -n, n.f. lounge.

vor-halten*, vb. (fig.) reproach.

Vorhand, n.f. forehand.

vorhan'den, adj. existing, present, available.

Vorhang, -°e, n.m. curtain, drapery.

vorher, adv. before, beforehand, previously.

vorher'gehend, adj. previous.

vor-herrschen, vb. prevail.

Vorherrschaft, n.f. predominance.

vorherrschend, adj. prevalent, predominant.

Vorher'sage, -n, n.f. prediction.

vorher'sagen, vb. foretell.

vorher'sehen*, vb. foresee.

Vorhut, n.f. vanguard.

vorig, adj. previous, last.

Vorjahr, -e, n.nt. preceding year.

Vorkämpfer, -, n.m. pioneer, champion.

Vorkenntnis, -se, n.f. preliminary knowledge; rudiments.

Vorkommen, n.nt. occurrence.

vor-kommen*, vb. occur.

Vorkommnis, -se, n.nt. occurrence.

Vorkriegs-, cpds. prewar.

vor-laden*, vb. summon.

Vorladung, -en, n.f. summons.

vor-lassen*, vb. let pass; admit.

Vorlassung, -en, n.f. admittance.

vorläufig, 1. adj. preliminary, tentative; temporary. 2. adv. for the time being.

vorlaut, adj. flippant, fresh.

vor-legen, vb. show, submit, produce.

vor-lesen*, vb. read out loud.

Vorlesung, -en, n.f. reading; lecture.

Vorlesungsverzeichnis, -se, n.nt. university catalogue.

vorletzt, adj. last but one.

Vorliebe, n.f. preference, fondness.

vorlieb'nehmen*, vb. be satisfied with.

vor-liegen*, vb. exist.

vorliegend, adj. present, at hand, in question.

vor-machen, vb. show how to do; (einem etwas v.) deceive, fool.

Vormachtstellung, -en, n.f. predominance.

vormalig, adj. former.

vormals, adv. heretofore.

Vormann, -°er, n.m. foreman.

Vormarsch, -°e, n.m. advance.

vor-merken, vb. make a note of; reserve.

Vormittag, -e, n.m. forenoon.

Vormund, -e, n.m. guardian.

vorn, adv. in front.

Vorname(n), -, -n, n.m. first name.

vornehm, adj. noble, distinguished.

vor-nehmen*, vb. (sich v.) undertake, consider, take up, resolve.

vornehmlich, adv. chiefly.

Vorort, -e, n.m. suburb.

Vorortzug, -°e, n.m. local (train).

Vorplatz, -°e, n.m. hall; court.

Vorrang, n.m. priority, precedence.

Vorrat, -°e, n.m. supply, provision, stock, stockpile.

vorrätig, adj. in stock.

Vorratskammer, -n, n.f. storeroom; pantry.

Vorrecht, -e, n.nt. privilege, prerogative.

Vorrede, -n, n.f. preface.

Vorrichtung, -en, n.f. arrangement; contrivance, device, fixture.

vor-rücken, vb. move forward, advance.

Vorsatz, -°e, n.m. purpose, intention; (jur.) premeditation.

vorsätzlich, adj. willful, intentional; (jur.) premeditated.

Vorschein, n.m. (zum V. kommen*) appear.

Vorschlag, -°e, n.m. proposal, proposition, suggestion.

vor-schlagen*, vb. propose, suggest.

vorschnell, adj. rash.

vor-schreiben*, vb. prescribe.

Vorschrift, -en, n.f. regulation.

vorschriftsmäßig, adj. as prescribed, regulation.

Vorschub, n.m. assistance.

Vorschule, -n, n.f. elementary school.

Vorschuß, -°sse, n.m. advance payment.

vor-schützen, vb. pretend, plead.

vor-sehen*, vb. earmark, plan, schedule; (sich v.) be careful.

Vorsehung, n.f. providence.

Vorsicht, -en, n.f. caution.

vorsichtig, adj. careful, cautious.

vorsichtshalber, adv. as a precaution.

Vorsichtsmaßregel, -n, n.f. precaution.

Vorsilbe, -n, n.f. prefix.

Vorsitz, -e, n.m. chairmanship, presidency; (den V. führen) preside.

Vorsitzend-, n.m.&f. chairperson.

Vorsitzende(r), -n, n.m.&f. chairman; chairwoman.

Vorsorge, n.f. providence, foresight; (V. treffen*) take precautions.

vorsorglich, adv. as a precaution.

Vorspeise, -n, n.f. appetizer.

vor-spiegeln, vb. deceive, delude.

Vorspiel, -e, n.nt. prelude.

vor-springen*, vb. project.

Vorsprung, -°e, n.m. advantage; head start; (arch.) ledge.

Vorstadt, -°e, n.f. suburb, outskirts.

vorstellbar, adj. conceivable.

vor-stellen, vb. present, introduce; (clock) set ahead; (sich v.) imagine, picture.

Vorstellung, -en, n.f. presentation, introduction; imagination, idea, notion; (theater) performance, show.

Vorstoß, -°e, n.m. attack.

vor-stoßen*, vb. push forward.

vor-strecken, vb. stretch forward; (money) advance.

vor-täuschen, vb. make-believe, simulate.

Vorteil, -e, n.m. advantage.

vorteilhaft, adj. advantageous, profitable.

Vortrag, -°e, n.m. lecture, talk.

vor-tragen*, vb. lecture, recite, report.

Vortragend-, n.m.&f. lecturer.

vortrefflich, adj. excellent.

Vortritt, n.m. precedence.

vorü'ber, adv. past, gone.

vorü'ber-gehen*, vb. pass.

vorübergehend, *adj.* temporary.

Vorurteil, -e, *n.nt.* prejudice.

Vorväter, *n.pl.* forefathers.

Vorwahl, -en, *n.f.* primary election.

Vorwahlnummer, -n, *n.f.* area code (telephone).

Vorwand, ¨e, *n.m.* pretense, pretext.

Vorwarnung, -en, *n.f.* forewarning.

vorwärts, *adv.* forward.

vorwärts-kommen*, *vb.* get ahead, make headway.

vorweg-nehmen*, *vb.* anticipate; forestall.

vor-werfen*, *vb.* reproach.

Vorwort, -e, *n.nt.* preface.

Vorwurf, ¨e, *n.m.* reproach.

vor-zeigen, *vb.* show, produce.

vorzeitig, *adj.* premature.

vor-ziehen*, *vb.* prefer.

Vorzimmer, -, *n.nt.* antechamber, anteroom.

Vorzug, ¨e, *n.m.* preference; advantage.

vorzüg'lich, **1.** *adj.* excellent, exquisite. **2.** *adv.* especially.

Vorzüg'lichkeit, -en, *n.f.* excellence.

vorzugsweise, *adv.* preferably.

vulgär, *adj.* vulgar.

Vulkan', -e, *n.m.* volcano.

W

Waage, -n, *n.f.* scales.

waagerecht, *adj.* horizontal.

Waagschale, -n, *n.f.* scale.

Wabe, -n, *n.f.* honeycomb.

wach, *adj.* awake.

Wache, -n, *n.f.* watch, guard.

wachen, *vb.* be awake, stay awake; watch over.

wachhabend, *adj.* on duty.

Wachlokal, -e, *n.nt.* guardhouse, police station.

Wachposten, -, *n.m.* sentry.

Wachs, -e, *n.nt.* wax.

wachsam, *adj.* watchful, vigilant.

Wachsamkeit, *n.f.* vigilance.

wachsen*, *vb.* grow, increase.

wachsen, *vb.* wax.

Wachskerze, -n, *n.f.* candle.

Wachstum, *n.nt.* growth.

Wacht, *n.f.* guard, watch.

Wächter, -, *n.m.* watchman; keeper.

Wachtmeister, -, *n.m.* (police) sergeant.

wackelig, *adj.* shaky, wobbly.

wackeln, *vb.* shake, wobble.

wacker, *adj.* staunch, brave, stouthearted.

Wade, -n, *n.f.* calf (of the leg).

Waffe, -n, *n.f.* weapon, arm.

Waffel, -n, *n.f.* waffle.

Waffenfabrik, -en, *n.f.* arms factory.

Waffengattung, -en, *n.f.* arm; branch of the army.

waffenlos, *adj.* unarmed, defenseless.

Waffenstill'stand, ¨e, *n.m.* armistice, truce.

waffnen, *vb.* arm.

wagemutig, *adj.* venturesome.

wagen, *vb.* dare, risk, venture.

Wagen, -, *n.m.* carriage, coach, wagon, car.

wägen(*), *vb.* consider.

Wagenheber, -, *n.m.* auto jack.

Waggon', -s, *n.m.* railroad car.

Waggon'ladung, -en, *n.f.* carload.

waghalsig, *adj.* rash, risky.

Wagnis, -se, *n.nt.* venture.

Wahl, -en, *n.f.* choice, election, vote, ballot.

wählbar, *adj.* eligible; (**nicht w.**) ineligible.

wahlberechtigt, *adj.* eligible to vote.

Wahlbezirk, -e, *n.m.* constituency.

wählen, *vb.* choose; elect; vote; (telephone) dial.

Wähler, -, *n.m.* constituent, voter.

wählerisch, *adj.* choosy, fastidious.

Wählerschaft, *n.f.* electorate.

Wahlgang, ¨e, *n.m.* ballot.

Wahlkampf, ¨e, *n.m.* election campaign.

Wahlliste, -n, *n.f.* ticket, slate.

Wahlrecht, -e, *n.nt.* franchise, suffrage; (**W. erteilen***) enfranchise; (**W. entziehen***) disenfranchise.

Wählscheibe, -n, *n.f.* dial (on a telephone).

Wahlspruch, ¨e, *n.m.* slogan, motto.

Wahlstimme, -n, *n.f.* vote.

Wahn, *n.m.* delusion.

Wahnsinn, *n.m.* insanity.

wahnsinnig, *adj.* insane, delirious.

wahr, *adj.* true, truthful, real; (**nicht w.?**) isn't that so?

wahren, *vb.* keep, preserve.

während, *vb.* continue, last.

während, **1.** *prep.* during. **2.** *conj.* while.

wahrhaftig, *adj.* true, sincere.

Wahrheit, -en, *n.f.* truth.

wahrnehmbar, *adj.* perceptible.

wahr-nehmen*, *vb.* perceive.

Wahrnehmung, -en, *n.f.* perception.

wahr-sagen, *vb.* prophesy, tell fortunes.

Wahrsager, -, *n.m.* fortuneteller.

wahrschein'lich, *adj.* probable, likely.

Währung, -en, *n.f.* currency.

Wahrzeichen, -, *n.nt.* distinctive mark, landmark.

Waise, -n, *n.f.* orphan.

Waisenhaus, ¨er, *n.nt.* orphanage.

Wald, ¨er, *n.m.* wood, forest.

Walfisch, -e, *n.m.* whale.

Wall, ¨e, *n.m.* rampart.

wallen, *vb.* undulate; bubble.

Wallfahrer, -, *n.m.* pilgrim.

Wallfahrt, -en, *n.f.* pilgrimage.

Walnuß, -sse, *n.f.* walnut.

Walroß, -sse, *n.nt.* walrus.

walten, *vb.* rule.

Walze, -n, *n.f.* roll, roller.

walzen, *vb.* roll.

wälzen, *vb.* roll.

Walzer, -, *n.m.* waltz.

Wand, ¨e, *n.f.* wall.

Wandel, *n.m.* change.

wandelbar, *adj.* changeable.

Wandelhalle, -n, *n.f.* lobby.

wandeln, *vb.* change; go, wander.

wandern, *vb.* hike, wander, roam.

Wanderschaft, *n.f.* travels.

Wanderung, -en, *n.f.* hike, wandering; migration.

Wandgemälde, -, *n.nt.* mural.

Wandlung, -en, *n.f.* change, transformation.

Wandschrank, ¨e, *n.m.* (**eingebauter W.**) closet.

Wandtafel, -n, *n.f.* blackboard.

Wandteppich, -e, *n.m.* tapestry.

Wandverkleidung, -en, *n.f.* wallcovering.

Wange, -n, *n.f.* cheek.

wankelmütig, *adj.* fickle.

wanken, *vb.* stagger, sway.

wann, **1.** *conj.* when. **2.** *adv.* when.

Wanne, -n, *n.f.* tub.

Wanze, -n, *n.f.* bedbug.

Wappen, -, *n.nt.* coat of arms.

Ware, -n, *n.f.* article, commodity, merchandise, ware; (*pl.*) goods.

Warenhandel, *n.m.* trade, commerce.

Warenhaus, ¨er, *n.nt.* department store.

Warenrechnung, -en, *n.f.* invoice.

warm (¨), *adj.* warm.

Wärme, *n.f.* warmth, heat.

wärmen, *vb.* warm.

Wärmflasche, -n, *n.f.* hot water bottle.

warnen, *vb.* warn, caution.

Warnung, -en, *n.f.* warning.

Warte, -n, *n.f.* watch-tower, lookout.

warten, *vb.* wait.

Wärter, -, *n.m.* keeper, guard.

Warteraum, ¨e, *n.m.* waiting room.

Wartezeit, -en, *n.f.* wait.

Wartezimmer, -, *n.nt.* waiting room.

warum', *adv.&conj.* why.

Warze, -n, *n.f.* wart.

was, *pron.* what.

Waschanstalt, -en, *n.f.* laundry.

waschbar, *adj.* washable.

Waschbecken, -, *n.nt.* washbasin.

Wäsche, *n.f.* laundry, linen.

waschecht, *adj.* colorfast; (*fig.*) dyed in the wool.

waschen*, vb. wash, launder.

Wäscherei', -en, n.f. laundry.

Wäscheschrank, -̈e, n.m. linen closet.

Waschfrau, -en, n.f. laundress.

Waschlappen, -, n.m. face cloth.

Waschleder, n.nt. chamois.

Waschmaschine, -n, n.f. washing machine.

Waschpulver, n.nt. soap powder.

Waschraum, -̈e, n.m. washroom.

Waschseife, -n, n.f. laundry soap.

Waschtisch, -e, n.m. washstand, washbowl.

Waschzettel, -, n.m. laundry list; (book) blurb; memo.

Wasser, -, n.nt. water.

wasserdicht, adj. watertight, waterproof.

Wasserfall, -̈e, n.m. waterfall.

Wasserflugzeug, -e, n.nt. hydroplane.

Wasserhahn, -̈e, n.m. faucet.

wässerig, adj. watery, aqueous.

Wasserleitung, -en, n.f. water main; aqueduct.

wässern, vb. water.

Wasserrinne, -n, n.f. gully, gutter.

Wasserstoff, n.m. hydrogen.

Wasserstoffbombe, -n, n.f. hydrogen bomb.

Wasserstoffsu'peroxyd, n.nt. hydrogen peroxide.

Wassersucht, n.f. dropsy.

waten, vb. wade.

watscheln, vb. waddle.

weben(*), vb. weave.

Webeschiffchen, -, n.nt. shuttle.

Webstuhl, -̈e, n.m. loom.

Wechsel, -, n.m. change, shift, rotation; (comm.) draft.

Wechselgeld, n.nt. change.

Wechseljahre, n.pl. menopause.

Wechselkurs, -e, n.m. rate of exchange.

wechseln, vb. change, exchange.

wechselnd, adj. intermittent.

Wechselstrom, -̈e, n.m. alternating current.

wecken, vb. wake, awaken.

Wecker, -, n.m. alarm clock.

wedeln, vb. wag.

weder, adj. (w. . . . noch) neither . . . nor.

weg, adv. away; gone.

Weg, -e, n.m. way, path, route.

wegen, prep. because of.

weg·fahren*, vb. drive away, leave.

weg·fallen*, vb. be omitted; not take place.

weg·gehen*, vb. go away, leave.

weg·kommen*, vb. get away; get off.

weg·lassen*, vb. leave out.

weg·nehmen*, vb. take away.

weg·räumen, vb. remove.

weg·schicken, vb. send off.

weg·schnappen, vb. snatch.

Wegweiser, -, n.m. guidepost, signpost.

Wegzehrung, -en, n.f. provisions for a journey.

Weh, n.nt. woe, pain, ache.

weh, adj. sore; (w. tun*) hurt, be sore.

wehen, vb. (wind) blow; (flag) wave.

Wehen, n.pl. labor pains.

Wehklage, -n, n.f. lament, lamentation.

wehklagen, vb. wail, lament.

Wehmut, n.f. sadness.

wehmütig, adj. sad, melancholy.

Wehr, -e, n.nt. dam.

Wehr, -en, n.f. defense, resistance.

Wehrdienst, n.m. military service.

wehren, vb. (sich w.) defend oneself, fight.

wehrfähig, adj. fit to serve (in the army).

wehrlos, adj. defenseless.

Wehrmacht, n.f. armed forces; (specifically, German army to 1945).

Wehrpflicht, n.f. duty to serve in armed forces; (allgemeine W.) compulsory military service.

weh·tun*, vb. hurt, be sore.

Weib, -er, n.nt. woman.

Weibchen, -, n.nt. (zool.) female.

Weibersache, -n, n.f. women's affair.

weiblich, adj. female, feminine.

weich, adj. soft.

Weiche, -n, n.f. switch.

weichen*, vb. give way, yield.

weichen, vb. soften.

weichlich, adj. soft; effeminate.

Weide, -n, n.f. pasture; willow.

weiden, vb. graze; (sich w.) feast one's eyes, gloat.

weidlich, adv. thoroughly.

weigern, vb. (sich w.) refuse.

Weihe, -n, n.f. consecration.

weihen, vb. consecrate.

Weiher, -, n.m. pond.

weihevoll, adj. solemn.

Weihnachten, -, n.nt. Christmas.

Weihnachtslied, -er, n.nt. Christmas carol.

Weihnachtsmann, -̈er, n.m. Santa Claus.

Weihrauch, n.m. incense.

Weihung, -en, n.f. consecration.

weil, conj. because, since.

Weile, n.f. while.

weilen, vb. stay.

Weiler, -, n.m. hamlet.

Wein, -e, n.m. wine.

Weinbauer, -, n.m. wine grower.

Weinberg, -e, n.m. vineyard.

Weinbrand, -e, n.m. brandy.

weinen, vb. cry, weep.

Weingarten, -̈, n.m. vineyard.

Weinlese, n.f. vintage.

Weinrebe, -n, n.f. grapevine.

Weinstock, -̈e, n.m. grapevine.

Weinstube, -n, n.f. tap room.

Weintraube, -n, n.f. grape.

weise, adj. wise.

Weise, -n, n.f. manner, way, method.

weisen*, vb. show; (von sich w.) reject.

Weisheit, -en, n.f. wisdom.

weis·machen, vb. make someone believe, fool.

weiß, adj. white.

weissagen, vb. prophesy, tell fortunes.

Weissager, -, n.m. fortune teller.

Weißwaren, n.pl. linen goods.

Weisung, -en, n.f. order, direction.

weit, adj. far; wide, large.

weitab', adv. far away.

weitaus', adv. by far.

Weite, -n, n.f. width, largeness, expanse; size.

weiter, adv. farther, further; (und so w.) and so forth.

weiterhin, adv. furthermore.

weitgehend, adj. far-reaching.

weither', adv. from afar.

weitläufig, adj. lengthy, elaborate, complex.

weitreichend, adj. far-reaching.

weitsichtig, adj. far-sighted.

weittragend, adj. far-reaching.

weitverbreitet, adj. widespread.

weitverstreut, adj. far-flung.

Weizen, n.m. wheat.

welcher, -es, -e, pron.&adj. which, what.

welchergestalt, adv. in what manner.

welk, adj. wilted.

welken, vb. wilt.

Welle, -n, n.f. wave; (tech.) shaft.

wellen, vb. wave; (tech.) corrugate.

Wellenlänge, -n, n.f. wave length.

wellig, adj. wavy.

Welt, -en, n.f. world.

Weltall, n.nt. universe.

Weltanschauung, -en, n.f. philosophy of life.

Weltbürger, -, n.m. cosmopolite.

weltgeschichtlich, adj. historical.

weltgewandt, adj. sophisticated.

weltklug (-), adj. worldly-wise.

Weltkrieg, -e, n.m. world war.

Weltkugel, -n, n.f. globe.

weltlich, adj. worldly, secular.

Weltmeister, -, n.m. world's champion.

Weltmeisterschaft, -en, n.f. world's championship.

weltnah, adj. worldly, realistic.

Weltraum, n.m. outer space.

Weltreich, -e, n.nt. empire.

Weltschmerz, n.m. world-weariness.

Weltstadt, "e, n.f. metropolis.

weltweit, adj. world-wide.

Wende, -n, n.f. turn, bend.

Wendekreis, -e, n.m. tropic; (W. des Krebses) tropic of Cancer; (W. des Steinbocks) tropic of Capricorn.

wenden*, vb. turn; (sich w. an) appeal to.

wendig, adj. versatile, resourceful.

Wendung, -en, n.f. turn.

wenig, adj. few, little.

weniger, adj. fewer, less; minus.

Wenigkeit, -e, n.f. trifle; (meine W.) yours truly.

wenigstens, adv. at least.

wenn, conj. when, if.

wer, pron. who.

werben*, vb. recruit, enlist, advertise; woo.

Werbeplakat, -e, n.nt. poster.

Werber, -, n.m. suitor.

Werbung, -en, n.f. recruiting, advertising; courting.

Werdegang, "e, n.m. development; career.

werden*, vb. become, get, grow.

werfen*, vb. throw, cast; (über den Haufen w.) upset.

Werft, -en, n.f. dockyard, shipyard.

Werk, -e, n.nt. work, labor, deed; factory, plant.

werken, vb. work, operate.

Werkstatt, "en, n.f. plant, shop.

Werktag, -e, n.m. work day, weekday.

werktags, adv. weekdays.

Werkzeug, -e, n.nt. tool, instrument.

Wermut, n.m. vermouth.

Wert, -e, n.m. value, worth, merit.

wert, adj. worth, valued, esteemed.

Wertarbeit, -en, n.f. workmanship.

Wertbrief, -e, n.m. registered insured letter.

wertlos, adj. worthless, useless.

Wertlosigkeit, -en, n.f. worthlessness, uselessness.

Wertpapier, -e, n.nt. security, bond, stock.

Wertschätzung, -en, n.f. esteem, value.

Werturteil, -e, n.nt. value judgement.

Wertverminderung, -en, n.f. depreciation.

wertvoll, adj. valuable.

Wesen, -, n.nt. being, creature; nature, character; essence, substance.

Wesenheit, n.f. entity.

wesenlos, adj. unreal.

Wesenszug, "e, n.m. characteristic.

wesentlich, adj. essential, material; substantial, vital.

weshalb, 1. conj. for which reason. 2. adv. why.

Wespe, -n, n.f. wasp.

wessen, pron. whose.

West, Westen, n.m. west.

Weste, -n, n.f. vest, waistcoat.

westlich, adj. western; to the west.

westwärts, adv. westward.

Wettbewerb, -e, n.m. competition.

Wettbewerber, -, n.m. competitor, contestant.

Wette, -n, n.f. wager, bet.

wetteifern, vb. compete, rival.

wetten, vb. wager, bet.

Wetter, n.nt. weather.

Wetterfahne, -n, n.f. weather vane.

Wettermeldung, -en, n.f. weather report.

Wetterverhältnisse, n.pl. weather conditions.

Wettkampf, "e, n.m. match, contest; competition.

Wettlauf, "e, n.m. race (on foot).

Wettläufer, -, n.m. runner.

Wettrennen, -, n.nt. race.

Wettrüsten, n.nt. armament race.

Wettspiel, -e, n.nt. match, tournament.

Wettstreit, -e, n.m. contest, competition; match, race.

wetzen, vb. hone, sharpen.

Whisky, -s, n.m. whiskey.

wichsen, vb. shine; thrash.

Wicht, -e, n.m. little fellow.

wichtig, adj. important.

Wichtigkeit, n.f. importance.

Wichtigtuer, -, n.m. busybody, pompous fellow.

Wickel, -, n.m. wrapping, compress; curler.

wickeln, vb. wind, reel; wrap; curl.

wider, prep. against, contrary to.

widerfah'ren*, vb. happen to.

Widerhall, -e, n.m. reverberation.

wider-hallen, vb. resound, reverberate.

Widerhalt, n.m. support.

widerle'gen, vb. refute, disprove.

Widerle'gung, -en, n.f. refutation, disproof, rebuttal.

widerlich, adj. distasteful, repulsive.

widernatürlich, adj. perverse.

widerra'ten*, vb. dissuade.

widerrechtlich, adj. illegal.

Widerrede, -n, n.f. contradiction.

Widerruf, -e, n.m. revocation; cancellation.

widerru'fen*, vb. revoke, repeal; retract; cancel.

Widersacher, -, n.m. antagonist.

Widerschein, n.m. reflection.

widerset'zen, vb. (sich w.) oppose.

Widersinn, n.m. absurdity.

widersinnig, adj. absurd, preposterous.

widerspenstig, adj. recalcitrant, contrary.

wider-spiegeln, vb. reflect.

widerspre'chen*, vb. contradict.

widerspre'chend, adj. contradictory.

Widerspruch, "e, n.m. contradiction, disagreement.

Widerstand, "e, n.m. resistance.

widerstandsfähig, adj. resistant, tough.

Widerstandskraft, "e, n.f. power of resistance, resilience.

widerstandslos, adj. without resistance.

widerste'hen*, vb. resist, withstand.

widerstre'ben, vb. resist, be repugnant.

Widerstre'ben, n.nt. reluctance.

widerstre'bend, adj. reluctant.

Widerstreit, -e, n.m. antagonism, confict.

widerstrei'ten*, vb. resist, conflict with.

widerwärtig, adj. repugnant, repulsive.

Widerwille(n), n.m. distaste.

widerwillig, adj. unwilling, reluctant.

widmen, vb. dedicate, devote.

Widmung, -en, n.f. dedication.

widrig, adj. contrary.

widrigenfalls, adv. failing which, otherwise.

wie, 1. conj. how; as. 2. adv. how.

wieder, adv. again; back, in return.

Wiederauf'bau, n.m. reconstruction.

wieder auf-bereiten, vb. recycle.

Wiederauf'erstehung, n.f. resurrection.

Wiederauf'rüstung, -en, n.f. rearmament.

Wiederauf'wertung, -en, n.f. revaluation.

Wiederbelebung, -en, n.f. revival.

wiederein'setzen, vb. reinstate.

wiederein'stellen, vb. reinstate.

wiedererkennen*, vb. recognize.

Wiedererkennung, -en, n.f. recognition.

wiedererlangen, vb. retrieve.

wiedererstatten, vb. reimburse, refund.

wiederfinden*, vb. recover.

Wiedergabe, -n, *n.f.* return; rendition, reproduction.

wieder-geben*, *vb.* return, restore.

wiedergeboren, *adj.* born-again.

Wiedergeburt, *n.f.* rebirth.

wieder-gewinnen*, *vb.* recover, regain.

Wiedergewinnung, -en, *n.f.* recovery.

wiedergut-machen, *vb.* redress, make amends for.

Wiedergut-machung, -en, *n.f.* restitution, redress.

wiederher-stellen, *vb.* restore.

Wiederher-stellung, -en, *n.f.* restoration.

wiederho-len, *vb.* repeat.

Wiederho-lung, -en, *n.f.* repetition.

Wiederhören, *n.nt.* hearing again; (auf W.) good-bye (at the end of a telephone call).

Wiederinstand-setzung, -en, *n.f.* reconditioning.

Wiederkehr, *n.f.* return, recurrence.

wieder-kehren, *vb.* return.

Wiedersehen, *n.nt.* seeing again; (auf W.) good-bye.

Wiedervereinigung, -en, *n.f.* reunification.

wieder-verheiraten, *vb.* (sich w.) remarry.

wieder-versöhnen, *vb.* reconcile.

Wiederversöhnung, -en, *n.f.* reconciliation.

Wiege, -n, *n.f.* cradle.

wiegen, *vb.* rock.

wiegen*, *vb.* weigh.

Wiegenlied, -er, *n.nt.* lullaby.

wiehern, *vb.* neigh.

Wiese, -n, *n.f.* meadow.

wieso, *adv.* how so, why.

wild, *adj.* wild, ferocious, savage.

Wild, *n.nt.* game.

Wild-, *n.m.* savage.

Wildfang, -e, *n.m.* tomboy.

Wildheit, *n.f.* ferocity, fierceness.

Wildleder, -, *n.nt.* chamois, suede.

Wildnis, -se, *n.f.* wilderness.

Wille(n), *n.m.* will.

willenlos, *adj.* irresolute, passive, shifting.

Willenskraft, *n.f.* willpower.

willensstark (-̈), *adj.* strong-willed, resolute.

willfah'ren*, *vb.* comply with, gratify.

willfährig, *adj.* complaisant.

willig, *adj.* willing, ready.

Willkom'men, *n.nt.* welcome.

Willkür, *n.f.* arbitrariness, choice.

willkürlich, *adj.* arbitrary.

wimmeln, *vb.* swarm.

wimmern, *vb.* moan.

Wimper, -n, *n.f.* eyelash.

Wind, -e, *n.f.* wind.

Winde, -n, *n.f.* reel.

Windel, -n, *n.f.* diaper.

winden*, *vb.* wind, coil; (sich w.) squirm.

Windhund, -e, *n.m.* greyhound.

windig, *adj.* windy.

Windmühle, -n, *n.f.* windmill.

Windpocken, *n.pl.* chickenpox.

Windschutzscheibe, -n, *n.f.* windshield.

windstill, *adj.* calm.

Windstoß, -e, *n.m.* gust.

Windzug, *n.m.* draft.

Wink, -e, *n.m.* sign, wave; (fig.) hint, tip.

Winkel, -, *n.m.* angle, corner.

Winkelzug, -e, *n.m.* dodge, subterfuge.

winken, *vb.* wave, beckon.

winseln, *vb.* whimper, wail.

Winter, -, *n.m.* winter.

Winterfrische, -n, *n.f.* winter resort.

Wintergarten, -̈, *n.m.* conservatory.

winterlich, *adj.* wintry.

Winzer, -, *n.m.* wine-grower.

winzig, *adj.* tiny, minute.

Wippe, -n, *n.f.* seesaw.

wir, *pron.* we.

Wirbel, -, *n.m.* whirl, whirlpool; cowlick; vertebra.

wirbeln, *vb.* whirl.

Wirbelsäule, -n, *n.f.* vertebral column, spine.

Wirbelsturm, -e, *n.m.* cyclone.

Wirbeltier, -e, *n.nt.* vertebrate.

wirken, *vb.* work, effect; (w. auf) effect.

wirklich, *adj.* real, actual.

Wirklichkeit, *n.f.* reality.

Wirklichkeitsflucht, *n.f.* escapism.

wirklichkeitsnah, *adj.* realistic.

wirksam, *adj.* effective.

Wirksamkeit, *n.f.* effectiveness, validity; (in W. treten*), take effect.

Wirkung, -en, *n.f.* effect.

Wirkungskraft, *n.f.* effect, efficacy.

wirkungslos, *adj.* ineffectual.

wirkungsvoll, *adj.* effective.

wirr, *adj.* confused.

Wirrnis, -se, *n.f.* tangle, confusion.

Wirrwarr, *n.nt.* confusion, maze.

Wirt, -e, *n.m.* host; landlord; proprietor.

Wirtin, -nen, *n.f.* hostess; landlady.

Wirtschaft, -en, *n.f.* inn, tavern; household; economy.

wirtschaften, *vb.* manage; keep house.

Wirtschafterin, -nen, *n.f.* housekeeper.

wirtschaftlich, *adj.* economic(al).

Wirtschaftlichkeit, *n.f.* economy.

Wirtschaftsabkommen, -, *n.nt.* trade agreement.

Wirtschaftsprüfer, -, *n.m.* certified public accountant.

Wirtschaftswissenschaft, *n.f.* economics.

Wirtshaus, -er, *n.nt.* inn.

Wisch, -e, *n.m.* scrap.

wischen, *vb.* wipe.

Wischlappen, -, *n.m.* cleaning rag.

wispern, *vb.* whisper.

Wißbegier, *n.f.* desire for knowledge; curiosity.

wissen*, *vb.* know.

Wissen, *n.nt.* learning, knowledge.

Wissenschaft, -en, *n.f.* learning, knowledge, science, scholarship.

wissenschaftlich, *adj.* scientific, scholarly.

wissenswert, *adj.* worth knowing.

wissentlich, *adv.* knowingly.

wittern, *vb.* smell; suspect.

Witterung, *n.f.* weather.

Witterungsverhältnisse, *n.pl.* weather conditions.

Witwe, -n, *n.f.* widow.

Witwer, -, *n.m.* widower.

Witz, -e, *n.m.* joke, pun, gag.

Witzbold, -e, *n.m.* joker, wise guy.

witzeln, *vb.* quip.

witzig, *adj.* witty, humorous.

witzlos, *adj.* pointless, fatuous.

wo, *adv.* where, in what place.

woan'ders, *adv.* elsewhere.

wobei', *adv.* whereby.

Woche, -n, *n.f.* week.

Wochenblatt, -er, *n.nt.* weekly paper.

Wochenende, -n, *n.nt.* weekend.

Wochenschau, *n.f.* newsreel.

Wochentag, -e, *n.m.* weekday.

wöchentlich, *adj.* weekly.

wodurch', *adv.* through what; whereby.

wofern', *conj.* in so far as.

Woge, -n, *n.f.* wave, billow.

wogen, *vb.* wave, heave.

woher', *adv.* whence, from where.

wohin', *adv.* where.

wohl, *adv.* well; presumably, I suppose.

Wohl, *n.nt.* well-being, good health; (zum W.) here's to you.

wohlbedacht, *adj.* well-considered.

Wohlbehagen, *n.nt.* comfort.

Wohlergehen, *n.nt.* welfare.

wohlerzogen, *adj.* well brought up.

Wohlfahrt, *n.f.* welfare.

Wohlfahrtsstaat, -en, *n.m.* welfare state.

Wohlgefallen, *n.nt.* pleasure.

wohlgefällig, *adj.* pleasant, agreeable.

wohlgemerkt, *adv.* nota bene.

wohlgemut, *adj.* cheerful.

wohlgeneigt, *adj.* affectionate.

Wohlgeruch, -e, *n.m.* fragrance.

wohlhabend, *adj.* prosperous, well-to-do.
wohlig, *adj.* comfortable.
wohlklingend, *adj.* melodious.
wohlriechend, *adj.* fragrant.
wohlschmeckend, *adj.* tasty.
Wohlsein, *n.nt.* good health; (zum W.) your health.
Wohlstand, *n.m.* prosperity.
Wohltat, -en, *n.f.* benefit; pleasure.
Wohltäter, -, *n.m.* benefactor.
wohltätig, *adj.* charitable.
Wohltätigkeit, -en, *n.f.* charity.
wohltuend, *adj.* beneficial, pleasant, soothing.
wohlweislich, *adv.* wisely, prudently.
Wohlwollen, *n.nt.* benevolence, good will.
wohlwollend, *adj.* benevolent.
wohnen, *vb.* reside, live, dwell.
wohnhaft, *adj.* resident.
wohnlich, *adj.* comfortable, cozy.
Wohnort, -e, *n.m.* domicile, place of residence.
Wohnsitz, -e, *n.m.* residence.
Wohnung, -en, *n.f.* apartment, place of living.
Wohnwagen, -, *n.m.* trailer.
wölben, *vb.* (sich w.) arch over.
Wolf, -e, *n.m.* wolf.
Wolke, -n, *n.f.* cloud.
Wolkenbruch, -e, *n.m.* cloudburst.
wolkenlos, *adj.* cloudless.
Wolle, *n.f.* wool.
wollen, *adj.* woolen.
wollen*, *vb.* want, be willing, intend.
wollig, *adj.* fluffy, fleecy.
Wollust, *n.f.* voluptuousness, lust.
wollüstig, *adj.* lascivious.
womöglich, *adv.* if possible.
Wonne, -n, *n.f.* delight.
wonnig, *adj.* charming, delightful.
Wort, -e *or* -er, *n.nt.* word.
Wortart, -en, *n.f.* part of speech.
Wörterbuch, -er, *n.nt.* dictionary.
Wörterverzeichnis, -se, *n.nt.* vocabulary.
Wortführer, -, *n.m.* spokesman.
wortgetreu, *adj.* literal, verbatim.
wortkarg, *adj.* taciturn.
Wortlaut, -e, *n.m.* wording, text.
wörtlich, *adj.* literal.
wortlos, *adj.* speechless.
wortreich, *adj.* wordy, verbose.
Wortschatz, -e, *n.m.* vocabulary.
Wortspiel, -e, *n.nt.* pun.
Wortwechsel, -, *n.m.* altercation.
Wrack, -s, *n.nt.* wreck.
wringen*, *vb.* wring.
Wucher, *n.m.* usury.
wucherisch, *adj.* usurious.

Wuchs, *n.m.* growth, figure, height.
Wucht, *n.f.* weight; momentum.
wühlen, *vb.* burrow, rummage; (fig.) agitate.
wühlerisch, *adj.* inflammatory, subversive.
wulstig, *adj.* thick.
wund, *adj.* sore, wounded.
Wunde, -n, *n.f.* wound.
Wunder, -, *n.nt.* miracle, wonder.
wunderbar, *adj.* wonderful, miraculous.
Wunderdoktor, -en, *n.m.* quack.
Wunderkind, -er, *n.nt.* child prodigy.
wunderlich, *adj.* strange.
wundern, *vb.* surprise; (sich w.) be surprised.
wundersam, *adj.* wondrous.
wunderschön, *adj.* lovely, exquisite.
wundervoll, *adj.* wonderful.
Wundmal, -e, *n.nt.* scar; (pl.) stigmata.
Wunsch, -e, *n.m.* wish, desire.
wünschen, *vb.* wish, desire, want.
wünschenswert, *adj.* desirable.
Würde, *n.f.* dignity.
Würdenträger, -, *n.m.* dignitary.
würdig, *adj.* worthy, dignified.
würdigen, *vb.* honor, appreciate.
Wurf, -e, *n.m.* throw; litter, brood.
Würfel, -, *n.m.* cube; (pl.) dice.
Würfelzucker, *n.m.* lump sugar.
Wurfpfeil, -e, *n.m.* dart.
würgen, *vb.* choke; retch; strangle.
Wurm, -er, *n.m.* worm.
wurmen, *vb.* annoy, rankle.
wurmstichig, *adj.* wormy.
Wurst, -e, *n.f.* sausage.
Würstchen, -, *n.nt.* (heißes W.) frankfurter.
Würze, -n, *n.f.* seasoning, flavor.
Wurzel, -n, *n.f.* root.
würzen, *vb.* season, spice.
würzig, *adj.* aromatic, spicy.
wüst, *adj.* waste, desolate; unkempt; wild; vulgar.
Wüste, -n, *n.f.* desert.
Wut, *n.f.* rage, fury.
wüten, *vb.* rage.
wütend, *adj.* furious.

X

X-beinig, *adj.* knock-kneed.
x-beliebig, *adj.* any old, any . . . at all; (jeder x-beliebige) every Tom, Dick, and Harry.
X-Strahlen, *n.pl.* x-rays.
Xylophon', -e, *n.nt.* xylophone.

Y

Yacht, -en, *n.f.* yacht.

Z

Zacke, -n, *n.f.* jag; spike; (fork) prong; (dress) edging.
zacken, *vb.* indent, notch.
zackig, *adj.* jagged; notched; snappy.
zag, *adj.* faint-hearted.
zagen, *vb.* hesitate.
zaghaft, *adj.* timid.
zäh, *adj.* tough, tenacious.
zähflüssig, *adj.* viscous.
Zähigkeit, *n.f.* tenacity, perseverance.
Zahl, -en, *n.f.* number, figure.
zahlen, *vb.* pay; (Herr Ober, bitte z.) waiter, the check please.
zählen, *vb.* count.
Zahlenangaben, *n.pl.* figures.
zahlenmäßig, *adj.* numerical.
Zähler, -, *n.m.* meter.
Zahlkarte, -n, *n.f.* money order.
zahllos, *adj.* countless.
zahlreich, *adj.* numerous.
Zahltag, -e, *n.m.* payday.
Zahlung, -en, *n.f.* payment.
zahlungsfähig, *adj.* solvent.
Zahlungsmittel, -, *n.nt.* tender, currency.
zahlungsunfähig, *adj.* insolvent.
Zahlwort, -er, *n.nt.* numeral.
zahm, *adj.* tame.
zähmen, *vb.* tame, domesticate.
Zahn, -e, *n.m.* tooth; (tech.) cog.
Zahnarzt, -e, *n.m.* dentist.
Zahnbürste, -n, *n.f.* toothbrush.
zahnen, *vb.* teethe.
Zahnfleisch, *n.nt.* gum.
Zahnheilkunde, *n.f.* dentistry.
Zahnpaste, -n, *n.f.* toothpaste.
Zahnplombe, -n, *n.f.* filling.
Zahnputzmittel, -, *n.nt.* dentifrice.
Zahnradbahn, -en, *n.f.* cog railroad.
Zahnschmerzen, *n.pl.* toothache.
Zahnstein, *n.m.* tartar.
Zahnstocher, -, *n.m.* toothpick.
Zahnweh, *n.nt.* toothache.
Zange, -n, *n.f.* pliers; forceps.
Zank, *n.m.* quarrel.
zanken, *vb.* (sich z.) quarrel, bicker.
zapfen, *vb.* tap.
Zapfen, -, *n.m.* peg, plug.
Zapfenstreich, *n.m.* tattoo, retreat to quarters.
zappelig, *adj.* fidgety.
zappeln, *vb.* flounder, fidget.
Zar, -en, -en, *n.m.* czar.
zart, *adj.* tender, dainty.

Zartheit, -en, *n.f.* tenderness, daintiness.

zärtlich, *adj.* tender, affectionate.

Zauber, -, *n.m.* enchantment, spell, charm, fascination.

Zauberei', -, *n.f.* sorcery, magic.

Zauberer, -, *n.m.* magician, wizard.

zauberhaft, *adj.* enchanting.

Zauberkraft, ‑e, *n.f.* magic power.

Zauberkunst, ‑e, *n.f.* magic.

Zauberspruch, ‑e, *n.m.* incantation, charm.

zaudern, *vb.* hesitate.

Zaum, -e, *n.m.* bridle.

zäumen, *vb.* bridle.

Zaun, ‑e, *n.m.* fence.

zausen, *vb.* tousle.

Zebra, -s, *n.nt.* zebra.

Zeche, -n, *n.f.* bill for drinks; mine, colliery.

zechen, *vb.* drink, carouse.

Zeder, -n, *n.f.* cedar.

Zeh, -en, *n.m.* toe.

Zehe, -n, *n.f.* toe.

Zehenspitze, -n, *n.f.* tip of the toe; **(auf Z.n gehen)** tiptoe.

zehn, *num.* ten.

zehnt-, *adj.* tenth.

Zehntel, -, *n.nt.* tenth part; **(ein z.)** one-tenth.

zehren, *vb.* **(z. an)** wear out, consume; **(z. von)** live on.

Zeichen, -, *n.nt.* sign, mark, token.

Zeichenfilm, -e, *n.m.* animated cartoon.

zeichnen, *vb.* draw; initial; *(comm.)* subscribe.

Zeichner, -, *n.m.* draftsman.

Zeichnung, -en, *n.f.* drawing, *(comm.)* subscription.

Zeigefinger, -, *n.m.* forefinger.

zeigen, *vb.* show, indicate, point; demonstrate; exhibit.

Zeiger, -, *n.m.* (clock) hand.

Zeile, -n, *n.f.* line.

Zeit, -en, *n.f.* time.

Zeitalter, -, *n.nt.* age, era.

Zeitaufnahme, -n, *n.f.* time exposure.

Zeitdauer, *n.f.* period of time.

Zeitgeist, *n.m.* spirit of the times.

zeitgemäß, *adj.* timely.

Zeitgenosse, -n, -n, *n.m.* contemporary.

zeitgenössisch, *adj.* contemporary.

zeitig, *adj.* early.

zeitlich, *adj.* 1. *adj.* temporal. 2. *adv.* in time.

zeitlos, *adj.* timeless, ageless.

Zeitmangel, *n.m.* lack of time.

Zeitpunkt, -e, *n.m.* time, moment.

zeitraubend, *adj.* time-consuming.

Zeitraum, -e, *n.m.* period.

Zeitschrift, -en, *n.f.* magazine, journal, periodical.

Zeitspanne, -n, *n.f.* period of time.

Zeitung, -en, *n.f.* newspaper.

Zeitungsanzeige, -n, *n.f.* ad, announcement.

Zeitungsausschnitt, -e, *n.m.* newspaper clipping.

Zeitungshändler, -, *n.m.* newsdealer.

Zeitungsjunge, -n, -n, *n.m.* paper-boy.

Zeitungsnotiz, -en, *n.f.* press item.

Zeitvertreib, *n.m.* pastime.

zeitweilig, *adj.* temporary.

Zeitwort, ‑er, *n.nt.* verb.

Zelle, -n, *n.f.* cell.

zellig, *adj.* cellular.

Zellophan', *n.nt.* cellophane.

Zellstoff, -e, *n.m.* cellulose.

Zelluloid', *n.nt.* celluloid.

Zellulo'se, -n, *n.f.* cellulose.

Zelt, -e, *n.nt.* tent.

zelten, *vb.* live in a tent, camp.

Zelter, -, *n.m.* camper.

Zement', -e, *n.m.* cement, concrete.

zensie'ren, *vb.* censor; (school) grade, mark.

Zensor, -'oren, *n.m.* censor.

Zensur', -en, *n.f.* censorship; (school) grade, mark.

Zensus, *n.m.* census.

Zentime'ter, -, *n.nt.* centimeter.

Zentner, -, *n.m.* 100 German pounds.

zentral', *adj.* central.

Zentral'heizung, *n.f.* central heating.

zentralisie'ren, *vb.* centralize.

Zentrum, -tren, *n.nt.* center.

zerbre'chen*, *vb.* break to pieces, shatter.

zerbrech'lich, *adj.* fragile, frail.

zerbrö'ckeln, *vb.* crumble.

zerdrü'cken, *vb.* crush.

Zeremonie'-, -i'en, *n.f.* ceremony.

zeremoniell', *adj.* ceremonial.

zerfah'ren, *adj.* absent-minded, scatter-brained.

Zerfall', *n.m.* ruin, decay.

zerfal'len*, *vb.* fall into ruin, disintegrate; **(in Teile z.)** be divided.

zerfet'zen, *vb.* tear into shreds.

zerflei'schen, *vb.* mangle.

zerfres'sen*, *vb.* erode, corrode.

zerge'hen*, *vb.* dissolve, melt.

zerglie'dern, *vb.* dismember, dissect.

zerklei'nern, *vb.* reduce to small pieces; crush; (wood) chop.

zerknau'tschen, *vb.* crumple.

zerknirscht', *adj.* contrite.

zerknül'len, *vb.* crumple.

zerlas'sen*, *vb.* dissolve, melt.

zerle'gen, *vb.* separate, cut up, carve.

zerlumpt', *adj.* ragged.

zermal'men, *vb.* crunch.

zermar'tern, *vb.* torture; **(den Kopf z.)** rack one's brain.

zermür'ben, *vb.* wear down.

Zermür'bung, -en, *n.f.* attrition.

zerpflü'cken, *vb.* pick to pieces.

zerquet'schen, *vb.* squash.

Zerrbild, -er, *n.nt.* distorted picture, caricature.

zerrei'ßen*, *vb.* tear up, rend.

zerren, *vb.* tug, pull.

zerrin'nen*, *vb.* disappear, melt away.

zerrüt'ten, *vb.* ruin.

Zerrüt'tung, -en, *n.f.* ruin.

zerschla'gen*, *vb.* smash, shatter.

zerschmei'ßen*, *vb.* smash.

zerset'zen, *vb.* decompose.

zerset'zend, *adj.* subversive.

Zerset'zung, -en, *n.f.* decomposition; subversion.

zersprin'gen*, *vb.* burst.

zerstäu'ben, *vb.* pulverize; atomize; scatter.

zerstö'ren, *vb.* destroy, demolish.

zerstö'rend, *adj.* destructive.

Zerstö'rung, -en, *n.f.* destruction, demolition.

zerstreu'en, *vb.* scatter; divert, amuse.

zerstreut', *adj.* absent-minded.

Zerstreu'ung, -en, *n.f.* scattering; relaxation, amusement.

zertei'len, *vb.* cut up; separate, divide.

zertren'nen, *vb.* sever; (dress) cut up.

zertre'ten*, *vb.* trample.

zertrüm'mern, *vb.* wreck, demolish.

Zerwürf'nis, -se, *n.nt.* discord, quarrel.

zerzau'sen, *vb.* tousle, rumple.

Zettel, -, *n.m.* slip of paper, note, sticker, bill.

Zeug, -e, *n.nt.* stuff, material, cloth.

Zeuge, -n, -n, *n.m.* witness.

zeugen, *vb.* testify, give evidence; beget, create, produce.

Zeugenaussage, -n, *n.f.* testimony.

Zeugnis, -se, *n.nt.* testimony, evidence; reference (for a job); (school) report card.

Zicho'rie, -n, *n.f.* chickory.

Zickzack, -e, *n.m.* zigzag.

Ziege, -n, *n.f.* (she-)goat.

ziegel, -, *n.m.* brick.

Ziegelstein, -e, *n.m.* brick.

Ziegenbock, ‑e, *n.m.* billy-goat.

Ziegenpeter, *n.m.* mumps.

ziehen*, *vb. (intr.)* move, go, draw, be drafty; *(tr.)* pull, drag, draw, tug; cultivate.

Ziehharmonika, -s, *n.f.* accordion.

Ziehung, -en, *n.f.* drawing.

Ziel, -e, *n.nt.* goal, target, end, objective.

zielbewußt, *adj.* with a clear goal, resolute.

zielen, *vb.* aim.

ziellos, *adj.* aimless, erratic.

Zielscheibe, -n, *n.f.* target.

ziemen, *vb.* be fitting for; (sich z.) be proper.

ziemlich, 1. *adj.* suitable, fitting; pretty much of. 2. *adv.* pretty, rather, quite.

Zier, *n.f.* ornament(ation).

Zierat, -e, *n.m.*, or -en, *n.f.* ornament, decoration.

Zierde, -n, *n.f.* ornament; honor.

zieren, *vb.* adorn, ornament.

zierlich, *adj.* dainty.

Ziffer, -n, *n.f.* figure, numeral.

Zifferblatt, -er, *n.nt.* dial, face (of a clock).

Zigarette, -n, *n.f.* cigarette.

Zigarre, -n, *n.f.* cigar.

Zigeuner, -, *n.m.* gypsy.

Zimbel, -n, *n.f.* cymbal.

Zimmer, -, *n.nt.* room.

Zimmerdecke, -n, *n.f.* ceiling.

Zimmermädchen, -, *n.nt.* chambermaid.

Zimmermann, -leute, *n.m.* carpenter.

zimperlich, *adj.* finicky, prim.

Zimt, *n.m.* cinnamon.

Zinke, -n, *n.f.* prong.

Zinn, *n.nt.* tin, pewter.

Zins, -en, *n.m.* interest.

Zinseszins, -en, *n.m.* compound interest.

Zinssatz, -e, *n.m.* rate of interest.

Zipfel, -, *n.m.* tip.

Zirkel, -, *n.m.* compass (for making a circle).

zirkulieren, *vb.* circulate.

zirkulierend, *adj.* circulatory.

Zirkus, -se, *n.m.* circus.

zirpen, *vb.* chirp.

zischen, *vb.* hiss, sizzle; whiz.

ziselieren, *vb.* engrave, chase.

Zitadelle, -n, *n.f.* citadel.

Zitat, -e, *n.nt.* quotation.

zitieren, *vb.* quote, cite.

Zitrone, -n, *n.f.* lemon.

zittern, *vb.* quiver, shiver, tremble.

zivil, *adj.* civil; reasonable.

Zivil, *n.nt.* civilians; civilian clothes.

Zivilbevölkerung, -en, *n.f.* civilian population.

Zivilisation, -en, *n.f.* civilization.

zivilisieren, *vb.* civilize.

Zivilist, -en, -en, *n.m.* civilian.

Zobel, *n.m.* sable.

zögern, *vb.* hesitate.

Zögern, *n.nt.* hesitation.

zögernd, *adj.* hesitant.

Zölibat, *n.m.* or *nt.* celibacy.

Zoll, -, *n.m.* inch.

Zoll, -e, *n.m.* tariff, duty, toll.

Zollamt, -er, *n.nt.* custom house.

Zollbeamt-, *n.m.* customs officer.

zollfrei, *adj.* duty free.

Zöllner, -, *n.m.* customs collector; (Bible) publican.

zollpflichtig, *adj.* subject to duty.

Zolltarif, -e, *n.m.* tariff.

Zollverein, -e, *n.m.* customs union.

Zollverschluß, *n.m.* customs seal; (unter Z.) under bond.

Zone, -, *n.f.* zone.

Zoo, -s, *n.m.* zoo.

Zoologie, *n.f.* zoology.

zoologisch, *adj.* zoological.

Zorn, *n.m.* ire, wrath, anger.

zornig, *adj.* angry.

zottig, *adj.* shaggy.

zu, *adv.* too; closed.

zu, *prep.* to.

Zubehör, *n.nt.* accessories, appurtenances, trimmings.

zubereiten, *vb.* prepare.

Zubereitung, -en, *n.f.* preparation.

zubringen, *vb.* bring to; pass, spend.

Zucht, -en, *n.f.* breed(ing), rearing, education, training, decency.

züchten, *vb.* breed, raise.

Züchter, -, *n.m.* breeder.

Zuchthaus, -er, *n.nt.* penitentiary.

züchtig, *adj.* chaste, demure.

züchtigen, *vb.* chasten, chastise.

zucken, *vb.* twitch, jerk, flash.

Zucker, *n.m.* sugar.

Zuckerbäcker, -, *n.m.* confectioner.

Zuckerguß, -sse, *n.m.* icing.

Zuckerkrankheit, *n.f.* diabetes.

Zuckerwerk, *n.nt.* confectionery.

Zuckung, -en, *n.f.* twitch, convulsion.

zudecken, *vb.* cover up.

zudem, *adv.* in addition.

zudringlich, *adj.* intruding, obtrusive.

Zueignung, -en, *n.f.* dedication.

zueinander, *adv.* to one another.

zuerkennen, *vb.* award.

zuerst, *adv.* first, at first.

Zufall, -e, *n.m.* chance, coincidence.

zufällig, 1. *adj.* chance, fortuitous. 2. *adv.* by chance.

Zuflucht, *n.f.* refuge; recourse.

Zufluchtsort, -e, *n.m.* place of refuge.

Zufluß, -sse, *n.m.* flowing in, influx.

zufolge, *prep.* as a result of; according to.

zufrieden, *adj.* content, satisfied.

zufriedenstellen, *vb.* satisfy.

zufrieren, *vb.* freeze over, freeze up.

zufügen, *vb.* inflict.

Zufuhr, -en, *n.f.* bringing in, importation, supply.

zuführen, *vb.* bring to, import, supply.

Zug, -e, *n.m.* pull, drawing, draft; stroke; feature, trait;

move; train; procession; trend; flight; (mil.) squad.

Zugabe, -n, *n.f.* bonus, premium, encore.

Zugang, -e, *n.m.* access, approach.

zugänglich, *adj.* accessible, approachable.

zugeben, *vb.* give in addition; admit.

zugegebenermaßen, *adv.* admittedly.

zugegen, *adv.* present.

zugehörig, *adj.* belonging to, pertinent.

Zügel, -, *n.m.* rein; restraint.

zügellos, *adj.* unbridled, unrestrained.

zügeln, *vb.* bridle, curb, check.

zugestandenermaßen, *adv.* avowedly.

Zugeständnis, -se, *n.nt.* confession; concession.

zugestehen, *vb.* confess, concede.

zugetan, *adj.* devoted to, fond of.

zugig, *adj.* drafty.

Zugkraft, *n.f.* pull, thrust.

zugleich, *adv.* at the same time.

zugreifen, *vb.* lend a hand; help oneself.

zugrunde, *adv.* at the bottom, as a basis; (z. gehen*) go to ruin, perish; (z. richten) ruin, destroy.

zugunsten, *adv.&prep.* for the benefit of, in favor of.

zugute, *adv.* for the benefit of.

zuhaken, *vb.* hook.

zuhalten, *vb.* keep shut.

zuhanden, *adv.* at hand.

zuhören, *vb.* listen to.

Zuhörer, -, *n.m.* listener, auditor; (pl.) audience.

Zuhörerraum, -e, *n.m.* auditorium.

Zuhörerschaft, -en, *n.f.* audience.

zukleben, *vb.* paste together.

zuknallen, *vb.* slam.

zuknöpfen, *vb.* button up.

zuknüpfen, *vb.* tie, knot, fasten.

zukommen, *vb.* be one's due; be proper for.

Zukunft, *n.f.* future.

zukünftig, *adj.* future.

Zulage, -n, *n.f.* extra pay, pay raise.

zulangen, *vb.* help oneself.

zulänglich, *adj.* adequate.

zulassen, *vb.* leave closed; admit; permit.

zulässig, *adj.* permissible, admissible.

Zulauf, *n.m.* run; (Z. haben*) be popular.

zulaufen, *vb.* run up to.

zulegen, *vb.* add; (sich etwas z.) acquire.

zuleide, *adv.* (z. tun*) hurt, harm.

zu'leiten, vb. lead to, direct to.

zuletzt', adv. at last, finally.

zulie'be, adv. for the sake of.

zu'machen, vb. shut.

zumal', 1. adv. especially; together. 2. conj. especially; because.

zu'mauern, vb. wall up.

zumeist', adv. for the most part.

zu'messen*, vb. allot.

zumin'dest, adv. at least.

zumu'te, adv. (z. sein*) feel, be in a mood.

zu'muten, vb. expect, demand.

Zumutung, -en, n.f. imposition.

zunächst', adv. first of all.

Zunahme, -n, n.f. increase.

Zuname(n), -, n.m. surname, last name.

zünden, vb. ignite; (fig.) inflame.

zündend, adj. inflammatory.

Zünder, -, n.m. fuse.

Zündholz, ⸚er, n.nt. match.

Zündkerze, -n, n.f. spark plug.

Zündschlüssel, -, n.m. ignition key.

Zündstoff, -e, n.m. fuel.

Zündung, n.f. ignition; detonation.

zu'nehmen*, vb. grow, increase; (moon) wax; put on weight.

zu'neigen, vb. incline.

Zuneigung, -en, n.f. inclination; affection.

Zunft, ⸚e, n.f. guild.

Zunge, -n, n.f. tongue.

zungenfertig, adj. glib.

zunich'te, adv. to nothing, ruined; (z. machen) ruin, frustrate.

zunut'ze, adv. (z. machen) profit by, utilize.

zuo'berst, adv. at the top.

zu'packen, vb. (fig.) get to work.

zupfen, vb. pull, (wool) pick.

zu'raten*, vb. advise in favor of.

zurechnungsfähig, adj. accountable.

zurecht', adv. right, in good order.

zurecht'finden*, vb. (sich z.) find one's way.

zurecht'machen, vb. prepare.

zu'reden, vb. urge, encourage.

zureichend, adj. sufficient.

zu'richten, vb. prepare; (übel z.) maul.

zürnen, vb. be angry.

Zurschau'stellung, -en, n.f. display.

zurück', adv. back, behind.

zurück'behalten*, vb. keep back.

zurück'bleiben*, vb. lag behind.

zurück'bringen*, vb. return.

zurück'drängen, vb. drive back.

zurück'erstatten, vb. reimburse.

zurück'fahren*, vb. drive back; recoil.

zurück'fallen*, vb. fall back; relapse.

zurück'führen, vb. lead back; trace back, attribute.

zurück'geben*, vb. return.

zurück'geblieben, adj. backward.

Zurück'gebliebenheit, n.f. backwardness.

zurück'gehen*, vb. go back; decline.

zurück'gesetzt, adj. (prices) reduced.

zurück'gezogen, adj. secluded.

Zurück'gezogenheit, n.f. seclusion.

zurück'halten*, vb. retain; restrain; withhold.

zurück'haltend, adj. reticent.

Zurück'haltung, n.f. restraint.

zurück'kehren, vb. return, revert.

zurück'kommen*, vb. return.

zurück'lassen*, vb. leave behind.

zurück'legen, vb. lay aside; accomplish.

zurück'lehnen, vb. (sich z.) lean back, recline.

zurück'liegen*, vb. lie in the past.

zurück'nehmen*, vb. take back; retract.

zurück'prallen, vb. recoil, rebound.

zurück'rufen*, vb. recall.

zurück'schauen, vb. look back on; reflect.

zurück'schlagen*, vb. hit back, repulse.

zurück'schrecken, vb. be startled; shrink (from).

zurück'sehen*, vb. look back on; reflect.

zurück'sehnen, vb. (sich z.) long to return.

zurück'setzen, vb. put back; set aside; reduce.

zurück'stehen*, vb. stand back; (fig.) be inferior.

zurück'stellen*, vb. set back; set aside; (mil.) defer.

zurück'stoßen*, vb. repulse.

zurück'strahlen, vb. reflect.

zurück'treiben*, vb. repel.

zurück'treten*, vb. resign.

zurück'verfolgen, vb. trace.

zurück'versetzen, vb. put back; (sich z.) go back to a time.

zurück'weichen*, vb. retreat.

zurück'weisen*, vb. send back; reject.

Zurück'weisung, -en, n.f. rebuff.

zurück'zahlen, vb. refund, repay.

zurück'ziehen*, vb. pull back, withdraw; (sich z.) withdraw, back out.

Zuruf, -e, n.m. call, shout; acclamation.

Zusage, -n, n.f. acceptance.

zu'sagen, vb. accept; (es sagt mir zu) it pleases me, it agrees with me.

zusam'men, adv. together.

Zusam'menarbeit, n.f. cooperation, collaboration.

zusam'men-arbeiten, vb. cooperate, collaborate.

Zusam'menbau, n.m. assemblage.

zusam'men-brauen, vb. concoct.

zusam'men-brechen*, vb. collapse.

Zusam'menbruch, ⸚e, n.m. collapse.

zusam'men-drängen, vb. (sich z.) crowd together; huddle.

zusam'men-fahren*, vb. ride together; crash; be startled, wince.

zusam'men-fassen, vb. summarize, recapitulate.

zusam'menfassend, adj. comprehensive; summary.

Zusam'menfassung, -en, n.f. summary, condensation.

zusam'men-fügen, vb. join together.

zusam'men-gehören, vb. belong together.

zusam'men-geraten*, vb. collide.

zusam'mengesetzt, adj. composed; compound.

Zusam'menhang, ⸚e, n.m. connection, relation; context; association.

zusam'men-hängen*, vb. hang together, be connected, cohere.

zusam'menhängend, adj. coherent.

zusam'menhangslos, adj. disconnected, incoherent.

zusam'men-häufen, vb. pile up.

zusam'men-kauern, vb. huddle.

zusam'men-kommen*, vb. get together, convene.

Zusam'menkunft, ⸚e, n.f. meeting.

zusam'men-laufen*, vb. converge.

zusam'men-legen, vb. combine, pool, merge.

zusam'men-nehmen*, vb. (sich z.) pull oneself together.

zusam'men-passen, vb. go well together.

Zusam'menprall, -e, n.m. collision, impact.

zusam'men-pressen, vb. compress.

zusam'men-rechnen, vb. add up.

zusam'men-reißen*, vb. (sich z.) pull oneself together.

zusam'men-rotten, vb. (sich z.) band together.

zusam'men-rufen*, vb. summon, convene.

zusam'men-scharen, vb. scrape together; (sich z.) band together, cluster.

zusam'men-schließen*, vb. join together; (sich z.) close ranks.

Zusam'menschluß, -̈sse, n.m. federation, merger.

zusam'men-schrumpfen, vb. shrink, dwindle.

zusam'men-setzen, vb. combine, compound; (sich z.) consist, be composed.

Zusam'mensetzung, -en, n.f. combination, composition.

zusam'men-stehen*, vb. stand together, stick together.

zusam'men-stellen*, vb. make up, compile.

Zusam'menstellung, -en, n.f. composition, arrangement.

Zusam'menstoß, -̈e, n.m. collision, clash.

zusam'men-stoßen*, vb. get together; collide, clash, crash.

zusam'men-strömen, vb. flow together, flock together.

zusam'men-stürzen, vb. collapse.

zusam'men-tragen*, vb. compile.

zusam'men-treffen*, vb. meet, encounter; coincide.

Zusam'mentreffen, -, n.nt. encounter; coincide.

zusam'men-treten*, vb. convene.

zusam'men-tun*, vb. put together; (sich z.) unite.

zusam'men-wirken, vb. act to gether, collaborate.

zusam'men-zählen, vb. sum up.

zusam'men-ziehen*, vb. draw together; (sich z.) contract, constrict.

Zusam'menziehung, -en, n.f. contraction.

Zusatz, -̈e, n.m. addition.

zusätzlich, adj. additional, supplementary.

zuschan'den-machen, vb. ruin.

zu-schauen, vb. look on, watch.

Zuschauer, -, n.m. spectator.

zu-schicken, vb. send to, forward.

zu-schieben*, vb. shove towards; (die Schuld z.) put the blame on.

zu-schießen*, vb. contribute.

Zuschlag, -̈e, n.m. increase; additional charge.

zu-schlagen*, vb. strike; bang shut.

zu-schließen*, vb. lock.

zu-schneiden*, vb. cut out.

zu-schreiben*, vb. ascribe, attribute, impute.

Zuschrift, -en, n.f. communication.

Zuschuß, -̈sse, n.m. subsidy.

zu-sehen*, vb. look on, watch.

zusehends, adv. visibly.

zu-senden*, vb. send, forward.

zu-sichern, vb. assure, promise.

Zustand, -̈e, n.m. state, condition; situation.

zustan'de-bringen*, vb. bring about, achieve, accomplish.

zustan'de-kommen*, vb. come about, be accomplished.

zuständig, adj. competent, qualified.

Zuständigkeit, -en, n.f. competence; jurisdiction.

zustat'ten-kommen*, vb. be useful.

zu-stehen*, vb. be due to; become, suit; behoove.

zu-stellen, vb. deliver.

Zustellung, -en, n.f. delivery.

zu-stimmen, vb. agree, consent.

Zustimmung, -en, n.f. agreement, consent, approval.

zu-stopfen, vb. plug.

zu-stoßen*, vb. slam tight, meet with, befall.

Zustrom, n.m. influx.

Zutat, -en, n.f. ingredient.

zu-teilen, vb. allot, assign, allocate.

zu-trauen, vb. believe someone capable of doing.

Zutrauen, n.nt. confidence.

zu-treffen*, vb. prove right, apply.

zutreffend, adj. correct, applicable.

Zutritt, -e, n.m. admittance, admission.

Zutun, n.nt. assistance.

zuverlässig, adj. reliable, trustworthy.

Zuversicht, n.f. confidence, trust.

zuversichtlich, adj. confident, sure.

zuviel', adv. too much.

zuvor', adv. beforehand.

zuvor'derst, adv. up front.

zuvör'derst, adv. first of all.

zuvor'-kommen*, vb. anticipate, forestall.

zuvor'kommend, adj. obliging, polite.

Zuvor'kommenheit, n.f. civility.

Zuwachs, n.m. increase, rise, growth.

zu-wandern, vb. immigrate.

zuwe'ge-bringen*, vb. bring about, achieve.

zuwei'len, adv. at times.

zu-weisen*, vb. assign, apportion, allot.

Zuweisung, -en, n.f. assignment, allocation.

zu-wenden*, vb. turn towards; bestow upon.

Zuwendung, -en, n.f. donation.

zuwi'der, 1. adv. abhorrent, repugnant. 2. prep. contrary to.

zuwi'der-handeln, vb. act contrary to, disobey.

zu-zahlen, vb. pay extra.

zu-ziehen*, vb. pull closed; (sich etwas z.) contract, incur.

Zuzug, n.m. move, influx.

zuzüglich, adv. plus.

Zwang, n.m. compulsion, coercion, duress; constraint.

zwanglos, adj. unrestrained, informal, casual.

Zwangsarbeit, n.f. forced labor; hard labor.

zwangsläufig, adv. necessarily.

zwangsweise, adv. evict.

zwangsweise, adv. forcibly.

Zwangsverschleppt-, n.m.&f. displaced person.

Zwangswirtschaft, n.f. controlled economy.

zwanzig, num. twenty.

zwanzigst-, adj. twentieth.

Zwanzigstel, -, n.nt. twentieth part; (ein z.) one-twentieth.

zwar, adv. to be sure (means that a but is coming); (und z.) namely, to give further details.

Zweck, -e, n.m. purpose, end, aim.

zweckdienlich, adj. expedient.

Zwecke, -n, n.f. tack.

zweckmäßig, adj. expedient.

zwecks, prep. for the purpose of.

zwei, num. two.

zweideutig, adj. ambiguous.

Zweideutigkeit, -en, n.f. ambiguity.

zweierlei, adj. of two kinds.

zweifach, adj. twofold.

zweifältig, adj. twofold, double.

Zweifel, -, n.m. doubt.

zweifelhaft, adj. doubtful.

zweifellos, adj. doubtless.

zweifeln, vb. doubt.

Zweifler, -, n.m. doubter, sceptic.

Zweig, -e, n.m. branch, bough, twig.

Zweikampf, -̈e, n.m. duel.

zweimal, adv. twice.

zweimalig, adj. repeated, done twice.

zweimonatlich, adj. bimonthly.

Zweirad, -̈er, n.nt. bicycle.

zweiseitig, adj. two-sided, bilateral.

Zweisitzer, -, n.m. two-seater, roadster.

zweit-, adj. second.

zweitbest-, adj. second-best.

zweiteilig, adj. two-piece; bipartite.

zweitens, adv. in the second place, secondly.

zweitklassig, adj. second-class.

Zwerchfell, -e, n.nt. diaphragm.

Zwerg, -e, n.m. dwarf; midget.

zwergenhaft, adj. dwarfish, diminutive.

Zwetschge, -n, n.f. plum.

zwicken, vb. pinch.

Zwickmühle, -n, n.f. dilemma, jam.

Zwieback, -̈e or -e, n.m. zwieback, rusk.

Zwiebel, -n, n.f. onion.

zwiefach, adj. double.

Zwiegespräch, -e, n.nt. dialogue.

Zwielicht, n.nt. twilight.

zwielichtig, adj. shady.

Zwiespalt, -e, *n.m.* discrepancy; discord; schism.

zwiespältig, *adj.* discrepant, conflicting.

Zwilling, -e, *n.m.* twin.

zwingen*, *vb.* force, compel.

zwingend, *adj.* compelling.

Zwinger, -, *n.m.* cage; (dog) kennel.

zwinkern, *vb.* wink.

Zwirn, -e, *n.m.* thread; twine.

Zwirnfaden, ⸚, *n.m.* thread.

zwischen, *prep.* between, among.

Zwischenakt, -e, *n.m.* entr'acte; interval.

Zwischenbemerkung, -en, *n.f.* incidental remark, interruption.

Zwischendeck, -e, *n.nt.* steerage.

Zwischending, -e, *n.nt.* something halfway between, mixture, cross.

zwischendurch', *adv.* in between; now and then.

Zwischenfall, ⸚e, *n.m.* incident.

Zwischenhändler, -, *n.m.* jobber.

Zwischenlandung, -en, *n.f.* stopover.

Zwischenraum, ⸚e, *n.m.* space in between; interval.

Zwischenruf, -e, *n.m.* interjection, interruption.

Zwischenspiel, -e, *n.nt.* interlude, intermezzo.

Zwischenstock, ⸚e, *n.m.* mezzanine.

Zwischenzeit, *n.f.* interval, interim.

Zwist, -e, *n.m.* quarrel, discord.

zwitschern, *vb.* twitter, chirp.

Zwitter, -, *n.m.* hybrid.

zwo, *num.* two (used especially on the telephone to avoid having *zwei* misunderstood as *drei*).

zwölf, *num.* twelve.

Zwölffin'gerdarm, ⸚e, *n.m.* duodenum.

zwölft-, *adj.* twelfth.

Zwölftel, -, *n.nt.* twelfth part; (ein z.) one-twelfth.

zwot-, *adj.* second.

Zyklamat', -e, *n.nt.* cyclamate.

Zyklon', -e, *n.m.* cyclone.

Zyklotron, -e, *n.nt.* cyclotron.

Zyklus, -klen, *n.m.* cycle.

Zylin'der, -, *n.m.* cylinder; top hat.

Zyniker, -, *n.m.* cynic.

zynisch, *adj.* cynical.

Zypres'se, -n, *n.f.* cypress.

Zyste, -n, *n.f.* cyst.

English-German

A

a, *art.* ein, -, -e.
abandon, *vb.* verlas'sen*.
abandoned, *adj.* verlas'sen; (*depraved*) verwor'fen.
abandonment, *n.* Aufgeben *nt.*
abash, *vb.* beschä'men.
abate, *vb.* nach·las'sen*.
abatement, *n.* Vermin'derung, -en *f.*
abbess, *n.* Äbtis'sin, -nen *f.*
abbey, *n.* Abtei', -en *f.*, Kloster, - *nt.*
abbot, *n.* Abt, ⸗e *m.*
abbreviate, *vb.* ab·kürzen.
abbreviation, *n.* Abkürzung, -en *f.*
abdicate, *vb.* ab·danken.
abdication, *n.* Abdankung, -en *f.*
abdomen, *n.* Unterleib, -er *m.*
abdominal, *adj.* Leib- (*cpds.*).
abduct, *vb.* entfüh'ren.
abduction, *n.* Entfüh'rung, -en *f.*
abductor, *n.* Entfüh'rer, - *m.*
aberration, *n.* Abweichung, -en *f.*
abet, *vb.* an·treiben*, helfen*.
abetment, *n.* Beistand, -e *m.*
abettor, *n.* Helfershelfer, - *m.*
abeyance, *n.* Schwebezustand, ⸗e *m.*
abhor, *vb.* verab'scheuen.
abhorrence, *n.* Abscheu, -e *m.*
abhorrent, *adj.* zuwi'der.
abide, *vb.* (*dwell*) wohnen; (*remain*) bleiben*; (*tolerate*) leiden*.
abiding, *adj.* dauernd.
ability, *n.* Fähigkeit, -en *f.*
abject, *adj.* elend, iniedrig, unterwür'fig.
abjure, *vb.* ab·schwören*, entsa'gen.
ablative, *n.* Ablativ, -e *m.*
ablaze, *adj.* in Flammen.
able, *adj.* fähig, tüchtig; (to be a.) können*.
able-bodied, *adj.* kräftig.
ablution, *n.* Abwaschung, -en *f.*
ably, *adv.* fähig, tüchtig.
abnormal, *adj.* ungewöhnlich, abnorm'.
abnormality, *n.* Mißbildung, -en *f.*, Abnormität', -en *f.*
aboard, *adv.* an Bord.
abode, *n.* Wohnsitz, -e *m.*, Wohnung, -en *f.*
abolish, *vb.* ab·schaffen.
abolition, *n.* Aufhebung, -en *f.*
abominable, *adj.* abscheu'lich.
abominate, *vb.* verab'scheuen.
abomination, *n.* Abscheu, -e *m.*
aboriginal, *adj.* ursprüng'lich, Ur- (*cpds.*).
aborigine, *n.* Ureinwohner, - *m.*

abort, *vb.* fehl·gebären*, ab·treiben*.
abortion, *n.* Fehlgeburt, -en *f.*, Abtreibung, -en *f.*
abortive, *adj.* mißglückt'.
abound, *vb.* im Überfluß vorhanden sein.
about, 1. *adv.* (*approximately*) etwa, ungefähr; (*around*) herum', umher'; (be a. to) im Begriff sein*. 2. *prep.* (*around*) um; (*concerning*) über.
about-face, *n.* Kehrtwendung *f.*
above, 1. *adj.* obig. 2. *adv.* oben. 3. *prep.* über.
aboveboard, *adj.* offen, unverhoh'len.
abrasion, *n.* Abschaben *nt.*, Abschleifen *nt.*
abrasive, 1. *n.* Schleifmittel, -nt. 2. *adj.* abschaben, abschleifend.
abreast, *adv.* nebeneinan'der, Seite an Seite.
abridge, *vb.* ab·kürzen.
abridgment, *n.* Abkürzung, -en *f.*
abroad, *adv.* im Ausland.
abrupt, *adj.* schroff.
abruptness, *n.* Schroffheit, -en *f.*
abscess, *n.* Eitergeschwulst, -e *f.*
abscond, *vb.* durch·brennen*.
absence, *n.* Abwesenheit, -en *f.*
absent, *adj.* abwesend.
absentee, *n.* Abwesend- *m.*
absent-minded, *adj.* zerstreut'.
absinthe, *n.* Absinth', -e *m.*
absolute, *adj.* absolut', unbedingt'.
absoluteness, *n.* Unbedingt'heit, -en *f.*
absolution, *n.* Absolution', -en *f.*
absolve, *vb.* frei·sprechen*, entla'sten.
absorb, *vb.* auf·saugen, absorbie'ren.
absorbed, *adj.* (*fig.*) vertieft'.
absorbent, 1. *n.* Absorbie'rungsmittel, - *nt.* 2. *adj.* aufsaugend.
absorbing, *adj.* aufsaugend; (*interesting*) packend.
absorption, *n.* Absorption', -en *f.*
abstain, *vb.* sich enthal'ten*.
abstemious, *adj.* enthalt'sam.
abstinence, *n.* Enthalt'samkeit, -en *f.*
abstract, 1. *n.* (*book, article*) Auszug, ⸗e *m.* 2. *adj.* abstrakt'. 3. *vb.* abstrahie'ren.
abstraction, *n.* Abstraktion', -en *f.*
abstruse, *adj.* abstrus'.
absurd, *adj.* unsinnig.
absurdity, *n.* Unsinnigkeit, -en *f.*

abundance, *n.* Überfluß, ⸗sse *m.*
abundant, *adj.* überreich.
abuse, 1. *n.* mißbrau'chen; 2. *n.* Mißbrauch, ⸗e *m.*
abusive, *adj.* mißbräuchlich, beschimp'fend.
abut, *vb.* an·grenzen.
abutment, *n.* Angrenzung, -en *f.*
abyss, *n.* Abgrund, ⸗e *m.*
academic, *adj.* akade'misch.
academy, *n.* Akademie', -mi'en *f.*, Hochschule, -n *f.*
acanthus, *n.* Akan'thus, -se *m.*
accede, *vb.* ein·willigen.
accelerate, *vb.* beschleu'nigen.
acceleration, *n.* Beschleu'nigung, -en *f.*
accelerator, *n.* Gashebel, - *m.*
accent, 1. *n.* Akzent', -e *m.* 2. *vb.* beto'nen.
accept, *vb.* an·nehmen*.
acceptability, *n.* Annehmbar'keit, -en *f.*
acceptable, *adj.* annehmbar.
acceptance, *n.* Annahme, -n *f.*
access, *n.* Zugang, ⸗e *m.*
accessible, *adj.* zugänglich.
accessory, 1. *n.* (*person*) Mithelfer, - *m.*; (*thing*) Zubehör *nt.* 2. *adj.* zusätzlich.
accident, *n.* Unfall, ⸗e *m.*; (*chance*) Zufall, ⸗e *m.*
accidental, *adj.* zufällig.
acclaim, 1. *n.* Beifall, ⸗e *m.* 2. *vb.* Beifall rufen*.
acclamation, *n.* Zuruf, ⸗e *m.*, Beifall, ⸗e *m.*
acclimate, *vb.* akklamatisie'ren.
accommodate, *vb.* an·passen, (*lodge*) unter·bringen*.
accommodating, *adj.* entgegenkommend.
accommodation, *n.* Anpassung, -en *f.*, (*lodging*) Unterkunft, ⸗e *f.*
accompaniment, *n.* Beglei'tung, -en *f.*
accompanist, *n.* Beglei'ter, - *m.*
accompany, *vb.* beglei'ten.
accomplice, *n.* Mittäter, - *m.*
accomplish, *vb.* leisten.
accomplished, *adj.* vollen'det.
accomplishment, *n.* Leistung, -en *f.*
accord, *n.* Einvernehmen, - *nt.*
accordance, *n.* Überein'stimmung, -en *f.*
accordingly, *adv.* demgemäß.
according to, *prep.* laut, gemäß'.
accordion, *n.* Ziehharmonika, -s *f.*
accost, *vb.* an·sprechen*.
account, *n.* (*comm.*) Konto, -ten *nt.*, (*narrative*) Bericht', - e *m.*

accountable, *adj.* verant'wortlich.

accountant, *n.* Buchhalter, - *m.*

accounting, *n.* Buchführung, - en *f.*

accredit, *vb.* akkreditie'ren, beglau'bigen.

accrual, *n.* Zuwachs *m.*

accrue, *vb.* an·wachsen*.

accumulate, *vb.* (sich) an·häufen.

accumulation, *n.* Anhäufung, - en *f.*

accumulator, *n.* Ansammler, - *m.*, Akkumula'tor, -to'ren *m.*

accuracy, *n.* Genau'igkeit, -en *f.*

accurate, *adj.* genau'.

accursed, *adj.* verflucht'.

accusation, *n.* Anklage, -n *f.*

accusative, 1. *n.* Akkusativ, -e *m.* 2. *adj.* anklagend.

accuse, *vb.* an·klagen.

accused, *n.* Angeklagt- *m.&f.*

accuser, *n.* Ankläger, - *m.*

accustom, *vb.* gewöh'nen.

accustomed, *adj.* gewohnt', gewöhnt'; (**become a. to**) sich gewöh'nen an.

ace, *n.* As, -se *nt.*

acetate, *n.* Acetat', -e *nt.*

acetic, *adj.* ace'tisch.

acetylene, *n.* Acetylen' *nt.*

ache, 1. *n.* Schmerz, -en *m.* 2. *vb.* weh tun*, schmerzen.

achieve, *vb.* errei'chen.

achievement, *n.* Leistung, -en *f.*

acid, 1. *n.* Säure, -n *f.* 2. *adj.* sauer.

acidify, *vb.* in Säure verwandeln.

acidity, *n.* Säuerlichkeit, -en *f.*

acknowledge, *vb.* an·erkennen*, bestä'tigen.

acme, *n.* Höhepunkt, -e *m.*

acne, *n.* Akne, -n *f.*

acolyte, *n.* Altar'diener, - *m.*

acorn, *n.* Eichel, -n *f.*

acoustics, *n.* Aku'stik *f.*

acquaint, *vb.* bekannt'machen.

acquaintance, *n.* Bekannt'schaft, -en *f.*

acquainted, *adj.* bekannt', vertraut'.

acquiesce, *vb.* ein·willigen, ruhig hin·nehmen*.

acquiescence, *n.* Einwilligung, -en *f.*

acquire, *vb.* erwer'ben*.

acquisition, *n.* Erwer'bung, -en *f.*

acquisitive, *adj.* gewinn'süchtig.

acquit, *vb.* frei·sprechen*.

acquittal, *n.* Freispruch, ⁼e *m.*

acre, *n.* Morgen, - *m.*

acreage, *n.* Flächeninhalt nach Morgen.

acrimonious, *adj.* scharf, bitter.

acrimony, *n.* Bitterkeit, -en *f.*

acrobat, *n.* Akrobat', -en, -en *m.*

across, 1. *prep.* über. 2. *adv.* hinü'ber, herü'ber.

act, 1. *n.* (*deed*) Tat, -en *f.*; (*drama*) Akt, -e *m.*; (*law*) Gesetz', -e *nt.* 2. *vb.* handeln; (*stage*) spielen; (*behave*) sich beneh'men*.

acting, 1. *n.* (*stage*) Schauspielkunst, ⁼e *f.* 2. *adj.* stellvertretend.

action, *n.* Handlung, -en *f.*

activate, *vb.* aktivie'ren.

activation, *n.* Aktivie'rung, -en *f.*

active, *adj.* tätig, aktiv'.

activity, *n.* Tätigkeit, -en *f.*

actor, *n.* Schauspieler, - *m.*

actress, *n.* Schauspielerin, -nen *f.*

actual, *adj.* tatsächlich.

actuality, *n.* Wirklichkeit, -en *f.*

actually, *adv.* wirklich.

actuary, *n.* Gerichts'schreiber, - *m.*; Versi'cherungsmathema'tiker, - *m.*

acumen, *n.* Scharfsinn *m.*

acupuncture, *n.* Akupunktur', -en, *f.*

acute, *adj.* scharf, scharfsinnig, akut'; (*angle*) spitz.

acuteness, *n.* Schärfe, -n *f.*, Scharfsinnigkeit *f.*

adage, *n.* Sprichwort, ⁼er *nt.*

adamant, *adj.* hartnäckig.

adapt, *vb.* an·passen, bearbei'ten.

adaptability, *n.* Anpassungsfähigkeit, -en *f.*

adaptable, *adj.* anpassungsfähig.

adaptation, *n.* Anwendung, -en *f.*, Bear'beitung, -en *f.*

adapter, *n.* Bear'beiter, - *m.*

add, *vb.* hinzu'·fügen, addie'ren.

adder, *n.* Natter, -n *f.*

addict, *n.* (*drug a.*) Rauschgiftsüchtig- *m.&f.*; (*alcohol a.*) Alkoholsüchtig- *m.&f.*

addition, *n.* Zusatz, ⁼e *m.*

additional, *adj.* zusätzlich.

address, 1. *n.* (*on letters, etc.*) Adres'se, -n *f.*; (*speech*) Ansprache, -n *f.* 2. *vb.* (*a letter*) adressie'ren; (*a person*) an·sprechen*.

addressee, *n.* Empfäng'er, - *m.*

adenoid, *n.* Nasenwucherung *f.*; (*pl.*) Poly'pen *pl.*

adept, *adj.* erfah'ren, geschickt'.

adequacy, *n.* Angemessenheit, -en *f.*

adequate, *adj.* angemessen.

adhere, *vb.* haften, fest·halten*.

adherence, *n.* Festhalten *nt.*

adherent, *n.* Anhänger, - *m.*

adhesive, 1. *n.* Klebemittel, - *nt.* 2. *adj.* anhaftend; (a. tape) Leukoplast' *n.nt.*

adieu, *interj.* lebewohl'!, ade'! **adjacent**, *adj.* angrenzend.

adjective, *n.* Eigenschaftswort, ⁼er *nt.*, Adjektiv, -e *nt.*

adjoin, *vb.* an·grenzen.

adjourn, *vb.* verta'gen.

adjournment, *n.* Verta'gung, -en *f.*

adjunct, 1. *n.* Zusatz, ⁼e *m.* 2. *adj.* zusätzlich.

adjust, *vb.* passend machen, berich'tigen, aus·gleichen*.

adjuster, *n.* Ausgleicher, - *m.*

adjustment, *n.* Ausgleichung, -en *f.*

adjutant, *n.* Adjutant', -en, -en *m.*

administer, *vb.* verwal'ten; erteil'len.

administration, *n.* Verwal'tung, -en *f.*

administrative, *adj.* Verwal'tungs- (*cpds.*).

administrator, *n.* Verwal'ter, - *m.*

admirable, *adj.* bewun'dernswert.

admiral, *n.* Admiral', -e *m.*

admiralty, *n.* Admiralität', -en *f.*

admiration, *n.* Bewun'derung *f.*

admire, *vb.* bewun'dern.

admirer, *n.* Vereh'rer, - *m.*

admissible, *adj.* zulässig.

admission, *n.* (*entrance*) Eintritt, -e *m.*; (*confession*) Zugeständnis, -se *nt.*

admit, *vb.* (*permit*) zu·lassen*; (*concede*) zu·gestehen*.

admittance, *n.* Zutritt, -e *m.*

admittedly, *adv.* zugegebenerma'ßen.

admixture, *n.* Beimischung, - en *f.*

admonish, *vb.* ermah'nen.

admonition, *n.* Ermah'nung, - en *f.*

adolescence, *n.* das heran'wachsende Alter, Jugendzeit, -en *f.*

adolescent, 1. *n.* der heran'wachsende Junge, das heran'wachsende Mädchen. 2. *adj.* jugendlich.

adopt, *vb.* adoptie'ren, an·nehmen*.

adoption, *n.* Adoption', -en *f.*

adorable, *adj.* reizend, entzück'end.

adoration, *n.* Vereh'rung *f.*, Anbetung *f.*

adore, *vb.* vereh'ren, an·beten.

adorn, *vb.* schmücken, zieren.

adornment, *n.* Verzie'rung, -en *f.*

adrift, *adv.* treibend, Wind und Wellen preisgegeben.

adroit, *adj.* geschickt'.

adulation, *n.* Schmeichelei', -en *f.*

adult, 1. *n.* Erwach'sen- *m.&f.* 2. *adj.* erwach'sen.

adulterate, *vb.* verfäl'schen.

adultery, *n.* Ehebruch, ⁼e *m.*

advance, 1. *n.* Fortschritt, -e *m.*; (*mil.*) Vormarsch, ⁼e *m.*; (*pay*) Vorschuß, ⁼sse; (**in a.**)

im voraus'. **2.** *vb.* Fortschritte machen; *(mil.)* vor•rücken; *(pay)* voraus'zahlen; *(promote)* beför'dern.

advanced, *adj.* fortgeschritten, modern'.

advancement, *n.* Förderung, -en *f.*, Beför'derung, -en *f.*

advantage, *n.* Vorteil, -e *m.*

advantageous, *adj.* vorteilhaft.

advent, *n.* Ankunft, ⁼e *f.*; *(eccl.)* Advent' *m.*

adventure, *n.* Abenteuer, - nt.

adventurer, *n.* Abenteurer, - *m.*

adventurous, *adj.* abenteuerlich.

adverb, *n.* Adverb', -en *nt.*, Umstandswort, ⁼er *nt.*

adverbial, *adj.* adverbial'.

adversary, *n.* Gegner, - *m.*

adverse, *adj.* ungünstig, nachteilig.

adversity, *n.* Mißgeschick, -e *nt.*

advertise, *vb.* an•zeigen, annoncie'ren, Rekla'me machen.

advertisement, *n.* Annon'ce, -n *f.*, Inserat', -e *nt.*, Rekla'me, -n *f.*

advertiser, *n.* Inserent', -en, -en *m.*, Anzeiger, -*m.*

advertising, *n.* Rekla'me, -n *f.*

advice, *n.* Rat *m.*

advisability, *n.* Ratsamkeit *f.*

advisable, *adj.* ratsam.

advise, *vb.* raten*, bera'ten*.

advisedly, *adv.* absichtlich.

adviser, *n.* Bera'ter, - *m.*

advocacy, *n.* Befür'wortung *f.*

advocate, 1. *n.* Anwalt, ⁼e *m.* **2.** *vb.* vertei'digen, befür'worten.

aerate, *vb.* mit Luft vermen'gen.

aerial, 1. *n.* Anten'ne, -n *f.* **2.** *adj.* Luft- *(cpds.).*

aeronautics, *n.* Aeronau'tik *f.*

aesthetic, *adj.* ästhe'tisch.

aesthetics, *n.* Ästhe'tik *f.*

afar, *adv.* von ferne.

affability, *n.* Freundlichkeit *f.*

affable, *adj.* freundlich.

affair, *n.* Angelegenheit, -en *f.*; Affä're, -n *f.*

affect, 1. *n.* Affekt', -e *m.* **2.** *vb.* wirken auf.

affectation, *n.* Affektiert'heit, -en *f.*

affected, *adj.* betrof'fen; *(unnatural)* affektiert'.

affection, *n.* Zuneigung, -en *f.*, Liebe, -n *f.*

affectionately, *adv. (letter)* mit herzlichen Grüßen.

affidavit, *n.* eidesstattliche Erklä'rung, -en *f.*

affiliate, *vb.* an•gliedern.

affiliation, *n.* Angliederung, -en *f.*

affinity, *n.* Verwandt'schaft, -en *f.*

affirm, *vb. (declare)* erklä'ren;

(confirm) bestä'tigen; *(say yes to)* beja'hen.

affirmation, *n.* Bestä'tigung, -en *f.*; Beja'hung, -en *f.*

affirmative, *adj.* beja'hend.

affix, 1. *n. (gram.)* Affix, -e *nt.* **2.** *vb.* an•heften; *(add on)* bei•fügen.

afflict, *vb.* plagen.

affliction, *n.* Plage, -n *f.*, Leid *nt.*

affluence, *n.* Reichtum, ⁼er *m.*

affluent, *adj.* reich.

afford, *vb.* gewäh'ren; *(have the means to)* sich leisten.

affront, **1.** *n.* Belei'digung, -en *f.* **2.** *vb.* belei'digen.

afield, *adv.* **(far a.)** weit entfernt'.

afire, *adv.* in Flammen.

afraid, *adj.* bange; **(be a. of)** sich fürchten vor.

Africa, *n.* Afrika, *nt.*

African, 1. *n.* Afrika'ner, - *m.* **2.** *adj.* afrika'nisch.

aft, *adv.* achtern.

after, 1. *prep.* nach, hinter. **2.** *conj.* nachdem'.

aftermath, *n.* Nachernte, -n *f.*

afternoon, *n.* Nachmittage, -e *m.*

afterward(s), *adv.* hinterher', nachher.

again, *adv.* wieder, noch einmal.

against, *prep.* gegen.

age, 1. *n.* Alter, - *nt.*; *(era)* Zeitalter, - *nt.* **2.** *vb.* altern.

aged, *adj.* bejahrt'.

ageism, *n.* Vorurteil gegen, Benachteiligung von älteren Menschen.

ageless, *adj.* zeitlos.

agency, *n.* Vertre'tung, -en *f.*, Agentur', -en *f.*

agenda, *n.* Tagesordnung, -en *f.*

agent, *n.* Vertre'ter, -*m.*

aggrandizement, *n.* Machterweiterung, -en *f.*

aggravate, *vb.* verschlim'mern, erschwe'ren.

aggravation, *n.* Verschlim'merung, -en *f.*

aggregate, 1. *n.* Aggregat', -e *nt.* **2.** *adj.* Gesamt- *(cpds.).*

aggregation, *n.* Anhäufung, -en *f.*

aggression, *n.* Angriff, -e *m.*, Aggression', -en *f.*

aggressive, *adj.* aggresiv'.

aggressiveness, *n.* Angriffslust *f.*

aggressor, *n.* Angreifer, - *m.*

aghast, *adj.* entsetzt'.

agile, *adj.* flink, behen'd(e).

agility, *n.* Behen'digkeit *f.*

agitate, *vb.* bewe'gen, beun'ruhigen.

agitation, *n.* Bewe'gung, -en *f.*, Beun'ruhigung, -en *f.*

agitator, *n.* Hetzredner, -m.

agnostic, 1. *n.* Agno'stiker, - *m.* **2.** *adj.* agno'stisch.

ago, *adv.* vor.

agony, *n.* Qual, -en *f.*

agree, *vb.* überein'stimmen.

agreeable, *adj.* angenehm.

agreement, *n.* Überein'stimmung, -en *f.*

agricultural, *adj.* landwirtschaftlich.

agriculture, *n.* Landwirtschaft *f.*

ahead, *adv.* voraus'; **(straight a.)** gera'de aus.

aid, 1. *n.* Hilfe, -n *f.* **2.** *vb.* helfen*.

aide, *n.* Adjutant', -en, -en *m.*

ail, *vb.* kranken.

ailment, *n.* Krankheit, -en *f.*

aim, 1. *n. (goal)* Ziel, -e *nt.*; *(purpose)* Zweck, -e *m.* **2.** *vb.* zielen.

aimless, *adj.* ziellos.

air, 1. *n.* Luft, -e *f.* **2.** *vb.* lüften.

airbag, (automobile) Luftsack, ⁼e, *m.*

air base, *n.* Luftstützpunkt, -e *m.*

airborne, *adj.* in der Luft; **(a. troops)** Luftlandetruppen *pl.*

air-condition, *vb.* klimatisie'ren, mit Klima-Anlage verse'hen*.

air-conditioned, *adj.* klimatisiert', mit Klima-Anlage verse'hen.

air-conditioning, *n.* Klima-Anlage, -n *f.*

aircraft, *n.* Flugzeug, -e *nt.*

aircraft carrier, *n.* Flugzeugträger, -, *m.*, Flugzeugmut'terschiff, -e *nt.*

air line, *n.* Luftlinie, -n *f.*

air liner, *n.* Verkehrs'flugzeug, -e *nt.*

air mail, *n.* Luftpost *f.*

airplane, *n.* Flugzeug, -e *nt.*

air pollution, *n.* Luftverpestung, *f.*

airport, *n.* Flughafen, ⁼ *m.*

air pressure, *n.* Luftdruck, -e *m.*

air raid, *n.* Luftangriff, -e *m.*

airsick, *adj.* luftkrank (⁼).

airtight, *adj.* luftdicht.

airy, *adj.* luftig.

aisle, *n.* Gang, ⁼e *m.*; *(church)* Chorgang, ⁼e *m.*

ajar, *adj.* angelehnt, halb offen.

akin, *adj.* verwandt'.

alarm, 1. *n.* Alarm', -e *m.* **2.** *vb.* alarmie'ren, beun'ruhigen.

albino, *n.* Albi'no, -s *m.*

album, *n.* Album, -ben *nt.*

albumen, *n.* Eiweißstoff, -e *m.*, Albu'men *nt.*

alcohol, *n.* Alkohol, -e *m.*

alcoholic, 1. *n.* Alkoho'liker, - *m.* **2.** *adj.* alkoho'lisch.

alcove, *n.* Alko'ven, - *m.*

ale, *n.* englisches Bier, Ale *nt.*

alert, 1. *n.* Alarm', -e *m.*, Vorwarnung, -en *f.* **2.** *adj.* aufmerksam. **3.** *vb.* alarmie'ren.

alfalfa, *n.* Alfal'fa *m.*

algebra, *n.* Algebra *f.*

algebraic, *adj.* algebra'isch.

alias, *adv.* alias.

alibi, *n.* Alibi, -s *nt.*

alien, 1. *n.* Ausländer, - *m.* **2.** *adj.* fremd, ausländisch.

alienate, *vb.* entfrem'den.

alight, *vb.* sich nieder·lassen*; *(dismount)* ab·steigen*.

align, *vb.* aus·richten; *(ally)* zu·sam'men·tun*.

alike, *adj.* gleich.

alive, *adj.* leben'dig; **(be a.)** leben.

alkali, *n.* Alka'li *nt.*

alkaline, *adj.* alka'lisch.

all, *adj.* aller, -es, -e; **(above a.)** vor allem; **(a. at once)** auf einmal; **(a. the same)** gleich; **(a. of you)** Sie alle; **(not at a.)** gar nicht.

allay, *vb.* beru'higen, stillen.

allegation, *n.* Behaup'tung, -en *f.*

allege, *vb.* an·führen, behaup'ten.

allegiance, *n.* Treue *f.*, Gehor'sam *m.*

allegory, *n.* Allegorie', -i'en *f.*; Sinnbild, -er *nt.*

allergy, *n.* Allergie', -i'en *f.*

alleviate, *vb.* erleich'tern, lindern.

alley, *n.* Gasse, -n *f.*; Durchgang, ⸗e *m.*; **(blind a.)** Sackgasse, -n *f.*

alliance, *n.* Bündnis, -se *nt.*; Allianz', -en *f.*

allied, *adj.* verbün'det; *(related)* verwandt'.

alligator, *n.* Alliga'tor, -to'ren *m.*

allocate, *vb.* zu·teilen.

allot, *vb.* zu·weisen*; zu·teilen.

allotment, *n.* Zuweisung, -en *f.*

allow, *vb.* erlau'ben, gestat'ten.

allowance, *n.* *(money)* Taschengeld, -er *nt.*; *(permission)* Erlaub'nis, -se *f.*; **(make a.s for)** Rücksicht nehmenauf*.

alloy, 1. *n.* Legie'rung, -en *f.* **2.** *vb.* legie'ren.

all right, *interj.* gut, schön, in Ordnung.

allude, *vb.* hin·weisen*, an·spielen.

allure, 1. *n.* Charme *m.* **2.** *vb.* verlock'en.

allusion, *n.* Anspielung, -en *f.*

ally, 1. *n.* Verbün'det- *m.*, Alliiert'- *m.* **2.** *vb.* verbün'den.

almanac, *n.* Almanach, -e *m.*

almighty, *adj.* allmäch'tig.

almond, *n.* Mandel, -n *f.*

almost, *adv.* beinahe, fast.

alms, *n.* Almosen, - *nt.*

aloft, *adv.* hochoben; empor'.

alone, *adv.* allein'; **(leave a.)** in Ruhe lassen*.

along, 1. *adv.* entlang'; **(come a.)** mit·kommen*. **2.** *prep.* entlang, längs.

alongside, *prep.* neben.

aloof, 1. *adj.* gleichgültig. **2.** *adv.* abseits.

aloud, *adv.* laut.

alpaca, *n.* Alpa'ka, -s *nt.*

alphabet, *n.* Alphabet', -e *nt.*

alphabetical, *adj.* alphabe'tisch.

alphabetize, *vb.* alphabetisie'ren.

Alps, *n.pl.* Alpen *pl.*

already, *adv.* schon.

also, *adv.* auch.

altar, *n.* Altar', ⸗e *m.*

alter, *vb.* ändern.

alteration, *n.* Änderung, -en *f.*

alternate, 1. *n.* Stellvertreter, - *m.* **2.** *adj.* alternativ'. **3.** *vb.* ab·wechseln.

alternating current, *n.* Wechselstrom, ⸗e *m.*

alternative, 1. *n.* Alternati've, -n *f.* **2.** *adj.* alternativ'.

although, *conj.* obwohl', obgleich'.

altitude, *n.* Höhe, -n *f.*

alto, *n.* Altstimme, -n *f.*

altogether, *adv.* völlig, ganz und gar; alles in allem.

altruism, *n.* Altruis'mus *m.*

alum, *n.* Alaun', -e *f.*

aluminum, *n.* Alumi'nium *nt.*

always, *adv.* immer.

amalgamate, *vb.* amalgamie'ren.

amass, *vb.* an·sammeln.

amateur, *n.* Amateur', -e *m.*

amaze, *vb.* erstau'nen.

amazement, *n.* Erstau'nen *nt.*

amazing, *adj.* erstaun'lich.

ambassador, *n.* Botschafter, - *m.*, Gesandt' -*m.*

amber, *n.* Bernstein, -e *m.*

ambiguity, *n.* Zweideutigkeit, -en *f.*

ambiguous, *adj.* zweideutig.

ambition, *n.* Ehrgeiz *m.*, Ambition', -en *f.*

ambitious, *adj.* ehrgeizig.

ambulance, *n.* Krankenwagen, - *m.*, Krankenauto, -s *nt.*

ambush, 1. *n.* Hinterhalt *m.* **2.** *vb.* aus dem Hinterhalt überfallen*.

ameliorate, *vb.* verbes'sern.

amenable, *adj.* zugänglich.

amend, *vb.* verbes'sern, ergän'zen.

amendment, *n.* Gesetz'abänderung, -en *f.*, Verfas'sungszusatz, ⸗e *m.*

amenity, *n.* Annehmlichkeit, -en *f.*

America, *n.* Ame'rika *nt.*

American, 1. *n.* Amerika'ner, - *m.* **2.** *adj.* amerika'nisch.

amethyst, *n.* Amethyst', -e *m.*

amiable, *adj.* liebenswürdig.

amicable, *adj.* freundschaftlich.

amid, *prep.* inmit'ten.

amidships, *adv.* mittschiffs.

amiss, *adj.* los, schief; **(take a.)** übel·nehmen*.

amity, *n.* Freundschaft, -en *f.*

ammonia, *n.* Ammoniak *nt.*; **(household a.)** Salmiak'geist *m.*

ammunition, *n.* Munition', -en *f.*

amnesia, *n.* Amnesie' *f.*

amnesty, *n.* Amnestie', -i'en *f.*

amniocentesis, *n.* Amniokente'se *f.*

amoeba, *n.* Amö'be, -n *f.*

among, *prep.* unter, zwischen, bei.

amorous, *adj.* verliebt'.

amortize, *vb.* tilgen, amortisie'ren.

amount, 1. *n.* *(sum)* Betrag', ⸗e *m.*; **(large a.)** Menge, -n *f.* **2.** *vb.* **(a. to)** betra'gen*.

ampere, *n.* Ampere, - *(pron.* Ampär')* nt.*

amphibian, 1. *n.* Amphi'bie, -n *f.* **2.** *adj.* amphi'bisch.

amphibious, *adj.* amphi'bisch.

amphitheater, *n.* Amphi'theater, - *nt.*

ample, *adj.* reichlich.

amplify, *vb.* *(enlarge)* erweitern; *(make louder)* verstärken; *(state more fully)* ausführ'licher dar·stellen.

amputate, *vb.* amputie'ren.

amuse, *vb.* belus'tigen, amüsie'ren.

amusement, *n.* Unterhal'tung, -en *f.*; Belus'tigung, -en *f.*

an, *art.* ein, -, -e.

anachronism, *n.* Anachronis'mus, -men *m.*

analogical, *adj.* analo'gisch.

analogous, *adj.* analog'.

analogy, *n.* Analogie', -i'en *f.*

analysis, *n.* Analy'se, -n *f.*

analyst, *n.* Analy'tiker, - *m.*

analytic, *adj.* analy'tisch.

analyze, *vb.* analysie'ren.

anarchy, *n.* Anarchie', -i'en *f.*

anatomy, *n.* Anatomie', -i'en *f.*

ancestor, *n.* Vorfahr, -en, -en, *m.*

ancestral, *adj.* Stamm- *(cpds.)*.

ancestry, *n.* Abstammung, -en *f.*

anchor, 1. *n.* Anker, - *m.* **2.** *vb.* veran'kern.

anchovy, *n.* Sardel'le, -n *f.*

ancient, *adj.* alt, uralt.

and, *conj.* und.

anecdote, *n.* Anekdo'te, -n *f.*

anemia, *n.* Blutarmut *f.*

anemic, *adj.* blutarm.

anesthesia, *n.* Anästhesie' *f.*

anesthetic, 1. *n.* Narko'se, -n *f.*, Betäu'bungsmittel, - *nt.* **2.** *adj.* betäu'bend, narko'tisch.

anew, *adv.* aufs neue, von neuem.

angel, *n.* Engel, - *m.*

anger, *n.* Zorn *m.*, Ärger *m.*

angle, 1. *n.* *(geom.)* Winkel, - *m.*; *(point of view)* Gesichtspunkt, -e *m.* **2.** *vb.* *(fish)* angeln.

angry, *adj.* böse, ärgerlich; **(be a.)** sich ärgern.

anguish, *n.* Qual, -en *f.*

angular, *adj.* eckig.

animal, 1. *n.* Tier, -e *nt.* **2.** *adj.* tierisch.

animate, *vb.* bele'ben.

animated, *adj.* lebhaft.

animated cartoon, n. Trickfilm, -e m.

animation, n. Lebhaftigkeit, -en f.

animosity, n. Erbit'terung, -en f.

ankle, n. Fessel, -n f.; Fessel'gelenk, -e nt.

annals, n.pl. Anna'len pl.

annex, 1. n. Anhang, =e m.; (building) Nebengebäude, - nt. **2.** vb. annektie'ren.

annexation, n. Annektie'rung, -en f.

annihilate, vb. vernich'ten.

anniversary, n. Jahrestag, -e m.

annotate, vb. mit Anmerkungen verse'hen*, annotie'ren.

announce, vb. an•kündigen, bekannt'•geben*.

announcement, n. Bekannt'machung, -en f.

announcer, n. Ansager, - m.

annoy, vb. belās'tigen, ärgern.

annoyance, n. Ärger m.; Belā's'tigung, -en f.

annual, 1. n. Jahrbuch, ˝er nt. **2.** adj. jährlich.

annuity, n. jährliche Rente, -n f.

annul, vb. annullie'ren.

anoint, vb. salben.

anomaly, n. Anomalie', -i'en f.

anonymous, adj. anonym'.

another, adj. (different) ein ander-; (additional) noch ein; (one a.) sich, einan'der.

answer, 1. n. Antwort, -en f. **2.** vb. antworten, beant'worten.

answerable, adj. beant'wortbar; verant'wortlich.

ant, n. Ameise, -n f.

antagonism, n. Widerstreit, -e m.

antagonist, n. Widersacher, - m., Gegner, - m.

antagonistic, adj. widerstrei'tend.

antagonize, vb. vor den Kopf stoßen*.

antarctic, 1. n. Antark'tis, - f. **2.** adj. antark'tisch.

antecedent, 1. n. (gram.) Bezie'hungswort, ˝er nt. **2.** adj. vorher'gehend.

antelope, n. Antilo'pe, -n f.

antenna, n. (radio) Anten'ne, -n f.; (insect) Fühler, - m.

anterior, adj. vorder-.

anteroom, n. Vorzimmer, - nt.

anthem, Hymne, -n f.; (national a.) National'hymne, -n f.

anthology, n. Anthologie', -i'en f.

anthracite, n. Anthrazit' m.

anthropologist, n. Anthropolo'ge, -n, -n m.

anthropology, n. Anthropologie' -i'en f.

antiaircraft, adj. Flak (cpds.).

antibody, n. Antikörper, - m.

antic, n. Posse, -n f.; Mätzchen, - nt.

anticipate, vb. vorweg'•nehmen*; erwar'ten.

anticipation, n. Erwar'tung, -en f.

anticlimax, n. enttäu'schende Wendung, -en f.

antidote, n. Gegengift, -e nt.

antinuclear, adj. antinuklear'.

antiquated, adj. veral'tet.

antique, adj. antik'.

antiquity, n. Anti'ke f.; Altertum, ˝er nt.

antiseptic, 1. n. antisep'tisches Mittel nt. **2.** adj. antisep'tisch.

antisocial, adj. antisozial'.

antitoxin, n. Gegengift, -e nt.

antlers, n.pl. Geweih', -e nt.

anvil, n. Amboß, -sse m.

anxiety, n. Angst, =e f.; Sorg'nis, -se f.

anxious, adj. besorgt'; ängstlich.

any, adj. irgendein, -, -e; irgendwelcher, -es, -e; jeder, -es, -e; (not a.) kein, -, -e.

anybody, pron. jemand, irgendjemand; (not . . . a.) niemand.

anyhow, adv. sowieso'.

anyone, pron. jemand, irgendjemand; (not . . . a.) niemand.

anything, pron. etwas, irgendetwas; (not . . . a.) nichts.

anyway, adv. sowieso'.

anywhere, adv (location) irgendwo; (direction) irgendwohin.

apart, adv. abseits, beisei'te; (a. from) abgesehen von; (take a.) auseinan'der•nehmen*.

apartheid, n. Apart'heid f.

apartment, n. Mietswohnung, -en f.

ape, 1. n. Affe, -n, -n m. **2.** vb. nach•affen.

aperture, n. Öffnung, -en f.

apex, n. Gipfel, - m.

aphorism, n. Aphoris'mus, -men m.

apiece, adv. (ten dollars a.) je zehn Dollar.

apologetic, adj. entschul'digend.

apologize, vb. sich entschul'digen.

apology, n. Entschul'digung, -en f.

apoplexy, n. Schlaganfall, =e m.

apostle, n. Apos'tel, - m.

appall, vb. entset'zen.

apparatus, n. Apparat', -e m.; Ausrüstung, -en f.

apparel, n. Kleidung, -en f.

apparent, adj. (visible) sichtbar; (clear) klar; (obvious) offensichtlich; (probable) scheinbar.

apparition, n. Erschei'nung, -en f.; Gespenst', -er, nt.

appeal, 1. n. (request) Bitte, -n f.; (charm) Reiz, -e m.; (law) Beru'fung, -en f. **2.** vb. (law) Beru'fung ein•legen, ap-

pellie'ren; (a. to, turn to) sich wenden* an; (a. to, please) gefal'len*.

appear, vb. (seem) scheinen*; (come into view) erschei'nen*.

appearance, n. Erschei'nung, -en f., Anschein, -e m.

appease, vb. beschwich'tigen.

appeasement, n. Beschwich'tigung, -en f.

appendage, n. Anhang, ˝e m.

appendectomy, n. Blinddarmoperation -en f.

appendicitis, n. Blinddarmentzündung, -en f.

appendix, n. Anhang, ˝e m.; (med.) Blinddarm, ˝e m.

appetite, n. Appetit' m.

appetizer, n. Vorgericht, -e nt.

appetizing, adj. appetit'lich; lecker.

applaud, vb. applaudie'ren, Beifall klatschen.

applause, n. Beifall, =e m.

apple, n. Apfel, ˝ m.

applesauce, n. Apfelmus nt.

appliance, n. Gerät', -e nt.

applicable, adj. anwendbar.

applicant, n. Bewer'ber, - m.

application, n. (request) Bewer'bung, -en f.; (use) Anwendung, -en f.

appliqué, n. (a. work) Applikations'stickerei, -en f.

apply, vb. (make use of) an•wenden*; (request) sich bewer'ben*.

appoint, vb. ernen'nen*.

appointment, n. (to a position) Ernen'nung, -en f.; (doctor's) Anmeldung, -en f.; (date) Verab'redung, -en f.

apportion, vb. proportional'vertei'len; zu•teilen.

appraisal, n. Abschätzung, -en f.

appraise, vb. ab•schätzen.

appreciable, adj. beträcht'lich.

appreciate, vb. schätzen; an•er•kennen*.

appreciation, n. Anerkennung, -en f.

apprehend, vb. (grasp) erfas'sen; (arrest) verhaf'ten; (fear) befürch'ten.

apprehension, n. (worry) Besorg'nis, -se f.; (arrest) Verhaf'tung, -en f.

apprehensive, adj. besorgt'.

apprentice, n. Lehrling, -e m.

apprise, vb. benach'richtigen.

approach, 1. n. (nearing) Annäherung, -en f.; (access) Zugang, ˝e m. **2.** vb. (come nearer) sich nähern; (turn to) sich wenden* an.

approachable, adj. zugänglich.

approbation, n. Geneh'migung, -en f.

appropriate, 1. adj. angemessen, passend. **2.** vb. (seize) sich an•eignen; (vote funds) bewilligen.

appropriation, n. (seizure) Aneignung, -en f.; (approval) Bewilligung, -en f.

approval, n. Zustimmung, -en f., Einwilligung, -en f.

approve, vb. zu·stimmen, geneh'migen.

approximate, 1. vb. sich nähern. 2. adj. annähernd.

approximately, adv. ungefähr, etwa.

approximation, n. Annäherung, -en f.

apricot, n. Apriko'se, -n f.

April, n. April' m.

apron, n. Schürze, -n f.

apropos, 1. adj. treffend. 2. prep. hinsichtlich.

apt, adj. (fitting) passend; (likely) geneigt'; (able) fähig.

aptitude, n. Fähigkeit, -en f.

aquarium, n. Aqua'rium, -ien nt.

aquatic, adj. Wasser- (cpds.).

aqueduct, n. Wasserleitung, -en f.

Arab, 1. n. Araber, - m. 2. adj. ara'bisch.

Arabian, adj. ara'bisch.

Arabic, adj. ara'bisch.

arable, adj. bestell'bar.

arbiter, n. Schlichter, - m.

arbitrary, adj. willkürlich.

arbitrate, vb. schlichten.

arbitration, n. Schlichtung, -en f.

arbitrator, n. Schlichter, - m.

arbor, n. Laube, -n f.

arc, n. Bogen, ⁼ m.

arcade, n. Arka'de, -n f.

arch, n. Bogen, -(⁼) m.; (instep) Spann, -e m.

archaeology, n. Altertumskunde f., Archäologie' f.

archaic, adj. archa'isch, altertümlich.

archbishop, n. Erzbischof, ⁼e m.

archdiocese, n. Erzdiözese, -n f.

archduke, n. Erzherzog, ⁼e m.

archer, n. Bogenschütze, -n, -n m.

archery, n. Bogenschießen nt.

architect, n. Architekt', -en, -en m.

architectural, adj. architekto'nisch.

architecture, n. Architektur', -en f.

archives, n. Archiv', e nt.

archway, n. Torbogen, ⁼ m.

arctic, 1. n. Arktis f. 2. adj. arktisch.

ardent, adj. eifrig, inbrünstig.

ardor, n. Eifer m., Inbrunst f.

arduous, adj. mühsam.

area, n. Fläche, -n f., Gebiet', -e nt.

area code, n. (phone) Vorwahlnummer, -n f.

arena, n. Are'na, -nen f.

Argentina, n. Argenti'nien nt.

argue, vb. argumentie'ren; (quarrel) sich streiten*.

argument, n. Argument', -e nt.

argumentative, adj. streitsüchtig.

aria, n. Arie, -n f.

arid, adj. dürr, trocken.

arise, vb. auf·stehen*, sich erhe'ben*; (come into being) entste'hen*.

aristocracy, n. Aristokratie', -i'en f.

aristocrat, n. Aristokrat', -en, -en m.

aristocratic, adj. aristokra'tisch.

arithmetic, n. Rechnen nt., Arithmetik' f.

ark, n. Arche, -n f.; (Noah's a.) Arche Noah.

arm, 1. n. Arm, -e m.; (weapon) Waffe, -n f. 2. v. bewaff'nen, rüsten.

armament, n. Bewaff'nung, -en f.; (weapons) Waffen pl.

armchair, n. Lehnstuhl, ⁼e m.

armful, n. Menge, -n f.

armhole, n. Armloch, ⁼er nt.

armistice, n. Waffenstill'stand m.

armor, Rüstung, -en f., Panzer, - m.

armored, adj. gepan'zert; Panzer- (cpds.).

armory, n. Exerzier'halle, -n f.; Waffenfabrik, -en f.

armpit, n. Achselhöhle, -n f.

arms, n.pl. Waffen pl.

army, n. Heer, -e nt., Armee', -me'en f.

aroma, n. Aro'ma, -s nt.

aromatic, adj. würzig.

around, 1. adv. herum'; (approximately) etwa, ungefähr. 2. prep. um.

arouse, vb. (excite) erre'gen; (waken) wecken.

arraign, vb. richterlich vorführen.

arrange, vb. arrangie'ren, einrichten; (agree) verein'baren.

arrangement, n. Anordnung, -en f.

array, 1. n. Anordnung, -en f.; (fig.) Menge, -n f. 2. vb. ordnen.

arrears, n.pl. Schulden pl.; (in a.) in Rückstand.

arrest, 1. n. (law) Verhaf'tung, -en f. 2. vb. (law) verhaf'ten; (stop) an·halten*.

arrival, n. Ankunft, ⁼e f.

arrive, vb. an·kommen*.

arrogance, n. Anmaßung, -en f., Arroganz, -en f.

arrogant, adj. anmaßend, arrogant'.

arrow, n. Pfeil, -e m.

arsenal, n. Waffenlager, - nt.

arsenic, n. Arsen' nt.

arson, n. Brandstiftung, -en f.

art, n. Kunst, ⁼e f.

arterial, adj. Arte'rien- (cpds.); (a. highway) Hauptverkehrs'straße, -n f.

arteriosclerosis, n. Arte'rienverkalkung, -en f.

artful, adj. kunstvoll; (sly) schlau.

arthritis, n. Arthri'tis f.

artichoke, n. Artischock'e, -n f.

article, n. Arti'kel, - m.

articulate, 1. vb. (utter) artikulie'ren; (join) zusam'men·fügen. 2. adj. deutlich.

articulation, n. Artikulie'rung, -en f.

artifice, n. List, -en f.

artificial, adj. künstlich.

artificiality, n. Künstlichkeit, -en f.

artillery, n. Artillerie', -i'en f.

artisan, n. Handwerker, - m.

artist, n. Künstler, - m.

artistic, adj. künstlerisch.

artistry, n. Künstlertum nt.

artless, adj. kunstlos.

as, conj. & adv. (when) wie, als; (because) da; (a. if) als ob; (with X a. Hamlet) mit X als Hamlet; (a. big a.) so groß wie; (just a. big a.) ebenso groß wie; (he a. well a. I) er sowohl wie ich.

asbestos, n. Asbest', -e m.

ascend, vb. (intr.) steigen*; (tr.) bestei'gen*.

ascent, n. Aufstieg, -e m.

ascertain, vb. fest·stellen.

ascetic, 1. n. Asket', -en, -en m. 2. adj. aske'tisch.

ascribe, vb. zu·schreiben*.

ash, n. Asche, -n f.; (tree) Esche, -n f.

ashamed, adj. beschämt'; (be a.) sich schämen.

ashen, adj. aschgrau.

ashes, n.pl. Asche f.

ashore, adv. an Land.

ash tray, n. Aschenbecher, - m., Aschbecher, - m.

Asia, n. Asien nt.

Asian, 1. n. Asiat', -en, -en m. 2. adj. asia'tisch.

aside, adv. beisei'te; (a. from) außer.

ask, vb. (question) fragen; (request) bitten*; (demand) verlangen.

asleep, adj. schlafend; (be a.) schlafen*.

asparagus, n. Spargel, - m.

aspect, n. Anblick, -e m.; (fig.) Gesichts'punkt, -e m.

aspersion, n. Verleum'dung, -en f.

asphalt, n. Asphalt', -e m.

asphyxiate, vb. ersticken.

aspirant, n. Anwärter, - m.

aspirate, 1. n. Hauchlaut, -e m. 2. adj. aspiriert'. 3. vb. aspirie'ren.

aspiration, n. Aspiration', -en f., Bestre'bung, -en f.

aspire, vb. streben.

aspirin, n. Aspirin' nt.

ass, n. Esel, - m.

assail, vb. an·greifen*.

assailable, adj. angreifbar.

assailant, n. Angreifer, - m.

assassin, n. Attentä'ter, - m., Mörder, - m.

assassinate, vb. ermor'den.

assassination, n. Ermor'dung, -en f., Attentat, -e nt.

assault, 1. n. Angriff, -e m.; (law) tätliche Belei'digung, -en f. **2.** vb. an•greifen°.

assay, 1. n. Probe, -n f. **2.** vb. prüfen.

assemblage, n. Versamm'lung, -en f.

assemble, vb. versam'meln; (tech.) montie'ren.

assembly, n. Versamm'lung, -en f.; (tech.) Monta'ge, -n f.

assent, 1. n. Zustimmung, -en f. **2.** vb. zu•stimmen.

assert, vb. behaup'ten.

assertion, n. Behaup'tung, -en f.

assertive, adj. bestimmt'.

assess, vb. ein•schätzen.

assessor, n. Steuerabschätzer, - m.

asset, n. Vorzug, -̈e m.; (comm.) Guthaben, - nt.

asseverate, vb. beteu'ern.

assiduous, adj. emsig.

assign, vb. zu•teilen, zu•weisen°; (homework) auf•geben°.

assignable, adj. bestimm'bar.

assignation, n. Anweisung, -en f.; (tryst) Stelldichein, - nt.

assignment, n. Anweisung, -en f.; (homework) Aufgabe, -n f.

assimilate, vb. an•gleichen°, assimilie'ren.

assimilation, n. Angleichung, -en f., Assimilie'rung, -en f.

assimilative, adj. angleichend.

assist, vb. unterstüt'zen, helfen°.

assistance, n. Unterstüt'zung, -en f., Hilfe, -n f.

assistant, 1. n. Gehil'fe, -n -n m., Assistent', -en, -en m. **2.** adj. Hilfs- (cpds.) stellvertretend.

associate, 1. n. Partner, - m. **2.** vb. verkeh'ren, assoziie'ren.

association, n. Verbin'dung, -en f., Verei'nigung, -en f.

assonance, n. Assonanz', -en f.

assort, vb. sortie'ren.

assorted, adj. verschie'den.

assortment, n. Auswahl, -en f.

assuage, vb. beschwich'tigen.

assume, vb. an•nehmen°; (arrogate) sich an•maßen.

assuming, adj. anmaßend; (as that) angenommen, daß.

assumption, n. Annahme, -n f.; (eccles.) Himmelfahrt f.

assurance, n. Versi'cherung, -en f., Zusicherung, -en f.

assure, vb. versi'chern, zu•sichern.

assured, adj. sicher, zuversichtlich.

aster, n. Aster, -n f.

asterisk, n. Sternchen, - nt.

asthma, n. Asthma nt.

astigmatism, n. Astigmatis'mus, -men m.

astonish, vb. erstau'nen; (be astonished) staunen.

astonishment, n. Erstau'nen, - nt.

astound, vb. erstau'nen.

astray, adj. irre; (go a.) sich verir'ren, auf Abwege gera'ten°.

astringent, adj. gefäß'zusammennend, hautstraffend, adstringie'rend.

astrology, n. Astrologie', -i'en f.

astronaut, n. Astronaut', -en m.

astronomy, n. Astronomie', -i'en f.

astute, adj. scharf (-), schlau.

asylum, n. (refuge) Asyl', -e nt.; (institution) Anstalt, -en f.

at, prep. an; (at home) zu Hause.

atheist, n. Atheist', -en, -en m.

athlete, n. Athlet', -en, -en m., Sportler, - m.

athletic, adj. athle'tisch, sportlich.

athletics, n. Sport, -e m.

Atlantic, 1. n. Atlan'tik m. **2.** adj. atlan'tisch.

Atlantic Ocean, n. Atlan'tik m.

atlas, n. Atlas, -lan'ten m.

atmosphere, n. Atmosphä're, -n f.

atmospheric, adj. atmosphä'risch.

atoll, n. Atoll', -e nt.

atom, n. Atom', -e nt.

atomic, adj. atomar'; Atom'- (cpds.).

atomize, vb. atomisie'ren.

atone, vb. büßen, sühnen.

atonement, n. Buße, -n f., Sühne, -n f.

atrocious, adj. entsetz'lich, grausam.

atrocity, n. Grausamkeit, -en f.

atrophy, n. Atrophie', -i'en f.

attach, vb. an•heften, beifügen; (attribute) bei•messen°.

attaché, n. Attaché, -s m.

attachment, n. Beifügung, -en f.; (device) Vorrichtung, -en f., Zubehör nt.; (liking) Zuneigung, -en f.

attack, 1. n. Angriff, -e m. **2.** vb. an•greifen°.

attain, vb. errei'chen.

attainable, adj. erreich'bar.

attainment, n. Errun'genschaft, -en f.

attempt, 1. n. Versuch', -e m. **2.** vb. versu'chen.

attend, vb. (meeting) bei•wohnen; (lecture) besu'chen; (patient) behan'deln; (person) beglei'ten.

attendance, n. Anwesenheit, -en f., Besuch', -e m.

attendant, 1. n. Beglei'ter,

- m. **2.** adj. beglei'tend, anwesend.

attention, n. Aufmerksamkeit, -en f.; (a.!) Achtung!; (pay a.) auf•passen.

attentive, adj. aufmerksam.

attenuate, vb. verdün'nen, vermin'dern; (jur.) mildern.

attest, vb. bezeu'gen.

attic, n. Dachboden, -̈ m., Boden, -̈ m.

attire, 1. n. Kleidung, -en f. **2.** vb. kleiden.

attitude, n. n. Haltung, -en f.

attorney, n. Anwalt, -̈e m.

attract, vb. an•ziehen°.

attraction, n. Anziehungskraft, -̈e f.

attractive, adj. anziehend.

attribute, 1. n. Eigenschaft, -en f. **2.** vb. zu•schreiben°.

attribution, n. Beimessung, -en f.

auction, n. Verstei'gerung, -en f.

auctioneer, n. Verstei'gerer, - m., Auktiona'tor, -to'ren m.

audacious, adj. kühn.

audacity, n. Kühnheit, -en f.

audible, adj. hörbar.

audience, n. Zuhörerschaft, -en f., Publikum, -ka nt.; (of a king) Audienz', -en f.

audiovisual, adj. audiovisuell'.

audit, 1. n. Rechnungsprüfung, -en f. **2.** vb. prüfen.

audition, n. Vorführungsprobe, -n f.

auditor, n. Hörer, - m.; (comm.) Rechnungsprüfer, - m.

auditorium, n. Zuhörerraum, -̈ e m., Auditorium, -rien nt.

augment, vb. vermeh'ren.

augur, 1. n. Augur', -en, -en m. **2.** vb. weissagen.

August, n. August' m.

aunt, n. Tante, -n f.

auspices, n.pl. Auspi'zien.

auspicious, adj. günstig.

austere, adj. streng.

austerity, n. Enthalt'samkeit, -en f.

Austria, n. Österreich nt.

Austrian, 1. n. Österreicher, - m. **2.** adj. österreichisch.

authentic, adj. authen'tisch.

authenticate, vb. beglau'bigen.

authenticity, n. Echtheit, -en f.

author, n. Verfas'ser, - m.

authoritarian, adj. autoritär'.

authoritative, adj. maßgebend.

authority, n. Autorität', -en f.

authorization, n. Vollmacht, -̈e f.

authorize, vb. bevoll'mächtigen.

auto, n. Auto, -s nt.

autobiography, n. Selbstbiographie, -i'en f.

autocracy, n. Autokratie', i'en f.

autocrat, n. Autokrat', -en, -en m.

autograph, n. Autogramm', -e nt.

automatic, *adj.* automa'tisch.

automation, *n.* Automation' *f.*

automaton, *n.* Automat', -en, - en *m.*

automobile, *n.* Kraftwagen, - *m.*

automotive, *adj.* Auto *(cpds.).*

autonomous, *adj.* autonom'.

autonomy, *n.* Autonomie', -i'en *f.*

autopsy, *n.* Leichenöffnung, - en *f.*

autumn, *n.* Herbst, -e *m.*

auxiliary, *adj.* Hilfs- *(cpds.).*

avail, 1. *n.* Nutzen *m.* **2.** *vb.* nützen; **(a. oneself of)** benut'zen.

available, *adj.* vorhan'den.

avalanche, *n.* Lawi'ne, -n *f.*

avarice, *n.* Geiz, -e *m.*

avaricious, *adj.* geizig.

avenge, *vb.* rächen.

avenue, *n.* Allee', -e'en *f.*

average, 1. *n.* Durchschnitt, -e *m.* **2.** *adj.* durchschnittlich; Durchschnitts- *(cpds.).*

averse, *adj.* abgeneigt.

aversion, *n.* Abneigung, -en *f.*

aviation, *n.* Luftfahrt *f.*

aviator, *n.* Flieger, - *m.*

aviatrix, *n.* Fliegerin, -nen *f.*

avid, *adj.* begie'rig.

avocation, *n.* Nebenberuf, -e *m.*

avoid, *vb.* vermei'den*.

avoidable, *adj.* vermeid'lich.

avoidance, *n.* Vermei'dung, -en *f.*

avow, *vb.* geste'hen*.

avowal, *n.* Geständ'nis, -se *nt.*

await, *vb.* erwar'ten.

awake, *adj.* wach.

awaken, *vb. (tr.)* wecken, *(intr.)* erwach'en.

award, 1. *n.* Preis, -e *m.; (jur.)* Urteil, -e *nt.* **2.** *vb.* zu'erkennen*.

aware, *adj.* bewußt'.

away, *adv.* weg, fort.

awe, *n.* Ehrfurcht *f.*

awful, *adj.* schrecklich.

awhile, *adv.* eine Weile.

awkward, *adj. (clumsy)* ungeschickt; *(embarrassing)* peinlich.

awning, *n.* Marki'se, -n *f.*

awry, *adj.* schief.

axe, *n.* Axt, ⸗e *f.*

axiom, *n.* Axiom', -e *nt.*

axis, *n.* Achse, -n *f.*

axle, *n.* Achse, -n *f.*

ayatollah, *n.* Ajatol'lah, -s *m.*

azure, *adj.* azur'blau.

B

babble, 1. *n.* Geschwätz' *nt.* **2.** *vb.* schwatzen.

baboon, *n.* Pavian, -e *m.*

baby, *n.* Baby, -s *nt.,* Säugling, -e *m.*

bachelor, *n.* Junggeselle, -n, -n *m.*

back, 1. *n.* Rücken, - *m.,* Kreuz, -e *nt.; (chair)* Lehne, - n *f.* **2.** *vb.* rückwärts·fahren*; *(support)* unterstüt'zen. **3.** *adj.* hinter-. **4.** *adv.* zurück'.

backbone, *n.* Rückgrat, -e *nt.*

backfire, *n.* Fehlzündung, -en *f.*

background, *n.* Hintergrund, ⸗e *m.*

backing, *n.* Unterstüt'zung, -en *f.*

backlash, *n.* Rückprall *m;* Bewir'kung des Gegenteils *f.*

backpack, *vb.* mit Rucksack wandern.

backward, 1. *adj.* zurück'geblieben, rückständig. **2.** *adv.* rückwärts.

backwards, *adv.* rückwärts; *(wrongly)* verkehrt'.

bacon, *n.* Speck *m.*

bacterium, *n.* Bakte'rium, -rien *nt.*

bad, *adj. (not good)* schlecht; *(serious)* schlimm; **(too b.)** schade.

bag, *n.* Sack, ⸗e *m.; (paper)* Tüte, -n *f.; (luggage)* Koffer, - *m.; (woman's purse)* Tasche, -n *f.*

baggage, *n.* Gepäck' *nt.*

baggage cart, *n. (airport)* Kofferkuli, -s *m.*

baggy, *adj.* bauschig.

bail, *n.* Kaution', -en *f.,* Bürgschaft, -en *f.*

bail out, *vb (set free)* Kaution' stellen für; *(empty out water)* schöpfen, aus·schöpfen; *(make a parachute jump)* ab·springen*.

bake, *vb.* backen*.

baking, *n.* Backen *nt.*

baking soda, *n.* doppelkohlensaures Natron.

balance, 1. *n. (equilibrium)* Gleichgewicht *nt.; (remainder)* Rest, -e *m; (trade)* Bilanz', -en *f.* **2.** *vb.* balancie'ren; *(make come out equal)* aus·gleichen*.

balcony, *n.* Balkon', -s *or* -e *m.*

bald, *adj.* kahl; **(b. head)** Glatzkopf, ⸗e *m.;* **(b. spot)** Glatze, -n *f.*

balk, *vb. (hinder)* verhin'dern; **(b. at nothing)** vor nichts zurück'scheuen.

ball, *n. (for throwing, game, dance)* Ball, -e *m.; (spherical object, bullet)* Kugel, -n *f.*

ballerina, *n.* Balleri'na, -nen *f.*

ballot, *n. (paper)* Stimmzettel, - *m.; (voting)* Wahl, -en *f.*

ballroom, *n.* Tanzsaal, -säle *m.*

balm, *n.* Balsam, -e *m.*

balmy, *adj.* sanft.

balsam, *n.* Balsam, -e *m.*

Baltic Sea, *n.* Ostsee *f.*

bamboo, *n.* Bambus, -se *m.*

ban, 1. *n.* Bann, -e *m.* **2.** *vb.* bannen, verbie'ten*.

banal, *adj.* banal'.

banana, *n.* Bana'ne, -n *f.*

band, *n.* Band, ⸗er *nt.; (gang)* Bande, -n *f.; (music)* Musikkapelle, -n *f.*

bandage, 1. *n.* Verband', ⸗e *m.* **2.** *vb.* verbin'den*.

bandanna, *n.* Kopftuch, ⸗er *nt.,* Halstuch, ⸗er *nt.*

bandit, *n.* Bandit', -en, -en *m.*

baneful, *adj.* giftig, verderb'lich.

bang, 1. *n.* Knall, -e *m.* **2.** *vb.* knallen.

banish, *vb.* verban'nen.

banishment, *n.* Verban'nung, -en *f.*

banister, *n.* Treppengeländer, - *nt.*

bank, *n.* Bank, -en *f.; (river)* Ufer, - *nt.; (slope)* Böschung, -en *f.*

bankbook, *n.* Kontobuch, ⸗er *nt.*

banker, *n.* Bankier', -s *m.*

banking, *n.* Bankgeschäft, -e *nt.*

bank note, *n.* Banknote, -n, *f.*

bankrupt, *adj.* bankrott'.

bankruptcy, *n.* Konkurs', -e *m.*

banner, *n.* Banner, - *nt.*

banquet, *n.* Festessen, - *nt.*

banter, 1. *n.* Scherz, -e *m.* **2.** *vb.* scherzen.

baptism, *n.* Taufe, -n *f.*

baptismal, *adj.* Tauf- *(cpds.).*

Baptist, *n.* Baptist', -en, -en *m.*

baptistery, *n.* Taufkapelle, -n *f.,* Taufstein, -e *m.*

baptize, *vb.* taufen.

bar, 1. *n.* Stange, -n *f.; (for drinks)* Bar, -s *f.; (jur.)* Gericht', -e *nt.* **2.** *vb.* aus·schließen*.

barb, *n.* Widerhaken, - *m.*

barbarian, 1. *n.* Barbar', -en, -en *m.* **2.** *adj.* barba'risch.

barbarism, *n.* Barbarei', -en *f.*

barbarous, *adj.* barba'risch.

barber, *n.* Herrenfriseur, -e *m.*

barbiturate, *n.* Barbitur'säurepräparat, -e *nt.*

bare, 1. *adj.* bloß, nackt. **2.** *vb.* entblö'ßen.

barefoot, *adj.* barfuß.

barely, *adv.* kaum.

bargain, 1. *n.* Gele'genheitskauf, ⸗e *m.* **2.** *vb.* feilschen, handeln.

barge, 1. *n.* Schleppkahn, ⸗e *m.,* Leichter, - *m.* **2.** *vb.* stürmen.

baritone, *n.* Bariton, -e *m.*

barium, *n.* Barium *nt.*

bark, 1. *n. (tree)* Rinde, -n *f.; (boat)* Barke, -n *f.; (dog)* Bellen *nt.* **2.** *vb.* bellen.

barley, *n.* Gerste, -n *f.,* Graupen *pl.*

barn, *n. (hay, grain)* Scheune, - n *f.; (animals)* Stall, ⸗e *m.*

barnacle, *n.* Entenmuschel, -n *f.*

barnyard, *n.* Bauernhof, ⸗e *m.*

barometer, *n.* Barome'ter, - *nt.*

barometric, adj. barome'trisch.

baron, n. Baron', -e m.

baroness, n. Barones'se, -n f.

baroque, 1. n. Barock', nt. **2.** adj. barock'.

barracks, n. Kaser'ne, -n f.

barrage, n. Sperre, -n f.; (mil.) Sperrfeuer, - nt.

barrel, n. Faß, -sser nt.

barren, adj. unfruchtbar, dürr.

barricade, 1. n. Barrika'de, -n f. **2.** vb. verbarrikadie'ren.

barrier, n. Schranke, -n f.

barroom, n. Schankstube, -n f.

bartender, n. Barmixer, - m.

barter, 1. n. Tauschhandel m. **2.** vb. tauschen.

base, 1. n. der unterste Teil, -e m.; (geom.) Grundlinie, -n f.; (mil.) Stützpunkt, -e m. **2.** vb. basie'ren. **3.** adj. niederträchtig.

baseball, n. Baseball. -e m.

baseboard, n. Waschleiste, -n f.

basement, n. Keller, - m.

baseness, n. Niederträchtigkeit, -en f.

bashful, adj. schüchtern.

bashfulness, n. Schüchternheit, -en f.

basic, adj. grundlegend.

basin, n. Becken, - nt.

basis, n. Grundlage, -n f., Basis, -sen f.

basket, n. Korb, -e m.

bass, n. (singer) Baß, -sse m.; (fish) Barsch, -e m.

bassinet, n. Korbwiege, -n f.

bassoon, n. Fagott', -e nt.

bastard, n. uneheliches Kind nt., Bastard, -e m.

baste, vb. (thread) heften; (roast) begie'ßen*.

bat, n. Fledermaus, -e, f.; (sport) Schlagholz, -er nt.

batch, n. Schub, -e m.

bath, n. Bad, -er nt.

bathe, vb. baden.

bather, n. Badend- m.&f.

bathrobe, n. Bademantel, - m.

bathroom, n. Badezimmer, - nt.

bathtub, n. Bedewanne, -n f.

baton, n. Taktstock, -e m.

battalion, n. Bataillon', -e nt.

batter, 1. n. (one who bats) Schläger, - m.; (cooking) Teig, -e m. **2.** vb. schlagen*.

battery, n. Batterie', -i'en f.

battle, 1. n. Schlacht, -en f. **2.** vb. kämpfen.

battlefield, n. Schlachtfeld, -er nt.

battleship, n. Schlachtschiff, -e nt.

bawl, vb. brüllen.

bay, 1. n. (geography) Bucht, -en f.; (plant) Lorbeer, -en m.; (at b.) in Schach. **2.** adj. (color) rotbraun. **3.** vb. bellen.

bayonet, n. Bajonett', -e nt.

bazaar, n. Bazar', -e m.

be, vb. sein*.

beach, n. Strand, -e m.

beachhead, n. Landekopf, -e nt.

beacon, n. Leuchtfeuer, - nt.

bead, n. Perle, -n f.; (drop) Tropfen, - m.

beading, n. Perlstickerei, -en f.

beak, n. Schnabel, -- m.

beaker, n. Becher, - m.

beam, 1. n. (construction) Balken, - m.; (light) Strahl, -en m. **2.** vb. strahlen, glänzen.

beaming, adj. strahlend.

bean, n. Bohne, -n f.

bear, 1. n. (animal) Bär, -en, -en m. **2.** vb. (carry) tragen*; (endure) ertra'gen*; (give birth to) gebä'ren*.

bearable, adj. erträg'lich.

beard, n. Bart, -e m.

bearer, n. Überbrin'ger, - m.

bearing, n. (behavior) Haltung, -en f.; (affect) Bezug', -e m.; (machinery) Lager, - nt.

beast, n. Vieh nt., Tier, -e nt., Bestie, - f.

beat, 1. n. Schlag, -e m.; (music) Takt, -e m. **2.** vb. schlagen*.

beaten, adj. geschla'gen.

beatify, vb. selig-sprechen*.

beating, n. (punishment) Prügel pl., Schläge pl.; (defeat) Niederlage, -n f.

beatitudes, n.pl. (biblical) Seligpreisungen pl.

beau, n. Vereh'rer, - m.

beautiful, adj. schön.

beautify, vb. verschö'nern.

beauty, n. Schönheit, -en f.

beauty parlor, n. Schönheitssalon, -s m., Frisier'salon, -s m.

beaver, n. Biber, - m.

because, conj. weil; (b. of) wegen.

beckon, vb. winken.

become, vb. werden*.

becoming, adj. kleidsam.

bed, n. Bett, -en nt.; (garden) Beet, -e nt.

bedbug, n. Wanze, -n f.

bedding, n. Bettzeug nt.

bedroom, n. Schlafzimmer, - nt.

bedspread, n. Bettdecke, -n f.

bee, n. Biene, -n f.

beef, n. Rindfleisch nt.

beefsteak, n. Beefsteak, -s nt.

beehive, n. Bienenstock, -e m.

beer, n. Bier, -e nt.

beet, n. Bete, -n f., Runkelrübe, -n f., rote Rübe, -n f.

beetle, n. Käfer, - m.

befall, vb. zu-stoßen*.

befit, vb. gezie'men.

befitting, adj. schicklich; (be b.) sich schicken.

before, 1. adv. (time) vorher; (place) voran'. **2.** prep. vor. **3.** conj. ehe, bevor.

beforehand, adv. vorher.

befriend, vb. sich an-freunden mit.

befuddle, vb. verwir'ren.

beg, vb. betteln; (implore) bitten*.

beggar, n. Bettler, - m.

begin, vb. an-fangen*, begin'nen*.

beginner, n. Anfänger, - m.

beginning, n. Anfang, -e m.

begrudge, vb. mißgön'nen.

beguile, vb. bestrick'en.

behalf, n. (on b. of) zugun'sten von, im Namen von.

behave, vb. sich beneh'men*.

behavior, n. Beneh'men, nt.

behead, vb. enthaup'ten.

behind, 1. adv. hinten, zurück. **2.** prep. hinter.

behold, 1. vb. sehen*. **2.** interj. sieh(e) da.

beige, adj. beigefarben.

being, n. Sein nt., Wesen, - nt.

belated, adj. verspä'tet.

belch, vb. rülpsen.

belfry, n. Glockenturm, -e m.

Belgian, 1. n. Belgier, - m. **2.** adj. belgisch.

Belgium, n. Belgien nt.

belie, vb. Lügen strafen.

belief, n. Glaube(n), - m.

believable, adj. glaubhaft.

believe, vb. glauben.

believer, n. Gläubig- m.&f.

belittle, vb. bagatellisie'ren.

bell, n. (small) Klingel, -n f.; (large) Glocke, -n f.

bellboy, n. Hotel'boy, -s m.

belligerence, n. Kriegslust, -e f.; Kriegszustand, -e m.

belligerent, adj. kriegerisch, kriegsführend.

bellow, vb. brüllen.

bellows, n. Blasebalg, -e m.

belly, n. Bauch, -e m.

belong, vb. gehö'ren.

belongings, n.pl., Habseligkeiten pl.

beloved, adj. geliebt.

below, 1. adv. unten. **2.** prep. unter.

belt, n. Gürtel, - m.

bench, n. Bank, -e f.

bend, vb. biegen*.

beneath, 1. adv. unten. **2.** prep. unter.

benediction, n. Segen, - m.

benefactor, n. Wohltäter, - m.

benefactress, n. Wohltäterin, -nen f.

beneficent, adj. wohltätig.

beneficial, adj. wohltuend, nützlich.

beneficiary, n. Begün'stigt- m.&f.; Nutzniesser, - m.

benefit, 1. n. Wohltat, -en f.; (advantage) Nutzen, - m., Vorteil, -e m. **2.** vb. nützen; (b. from) Nutzen ziehen* aus.

benevolence, n. Wohlwollen nt.

benevolent, adj. wohlwollend.

benign, adj. gütig.

bent, adj. gebeugt; (out of shape) verbo'gen.

benzine, n. Benzin' nt.

bequeath, vb. verma'chen.

bequest, n. Vermächt'nis, -se nt. Legat', -e nt.

berate, vb. aus·schelten*.

bereave, vb. berau'ben.

bereavement, n. Verlust durch Tod.

berry, n. Beere, -n f.

berth, n. Bettplatz, -̈e m.

beseech, vb. an·flehen.

beset, vb. bedrän'gen.

beside, prep. neben; (b. oneself) außer sich.

besides, 1. adv. außerdem. 2. prep. außer.

besiege, vb. bela'gern.

best, 1. adj. best-. 2. vb. übertref'fen*.

bestial, adj. bestia'lisch, tierisch.

bestow, vb. verlei'hen*.

bestowal, n. Verlei'hung, -en f.

bet, 1. n. Wette, -n f. 2. vb. wetten.

betake oneself, vb. sich auf·machen.

betoken, vb. bezeich'nen.

betray, vb. verra'ten*.

betrayal, n. Verrat' m.

betroth, vb. verlo'ben; (be b.ed) sich verlo'ben.

betrothal, n. Verlo'bung, -en f.

better, 1. adj. besser. 2. vb. verbes'sern.

between, prep. zwischen.

bevel, n. schräger Anschnitt, -e m. 2. vb. schräg ab·schneiden*.

beverage, n. Getränk', -e nt.

bewail, vb. bekla'gen.

beware, vb. sich hüten.

bewilder, vb. verwir'ren.

bewilderment, n. Verwir'rung, -en f.

bewitch, vb. bezau'bern; verzau'bern.

beyond, 1. adv. jenseits. 2. prep. jenseits, über.

biannual, adj. halbjährlich.

bias, n. Vorurteil, -e nt.

bib, n. Lätzchen, - nt.

Bible, n. Bibel, -n f.

Biblical, adj. biblisch.

bibliography, n. Bibliographie', -i'en f.

bicarbonate, n. (of soda) doppelkohlensaures Natron nt.

biceps, n. Bizeps, -e m.

bicker, vb. sich zanken.

bicycle, n. Fahrrad, -̈er nt.

bicyclist, n. Radfahrer, - m.

bid, 1. n. Angebot, -e nt. 2. vb. bieten*.

bide, vb. ab·warten.

biennial, adj. zweijährlich.

bier, n. Bahre, -n f.

bifocal, adj. bifokal'.

big, adj. groß (größer, größt-).

bigamist, n. Bigamist', -en, -en m.

bigamous, adj. biga'misch.

bigamy, n. bigamie', -i'en f.

bigot, n. Frömmler, - m.

bigoted, adj. bigott'.

bigotry, n. Frömmelei', -en f.

bilateral, adj. zweiseitig.

bile, n. Galle, -n f.

bilingual, adj. zweisprachig.

bilious, adj. gallig.

bill, n. (bird) Schnabel, -̈ m.; (banknote) Geldschein, -e m.; (sum owed) Rechnung, -en f.; (legislative) Geset'zesvorlage, -n f.

billboard, n. Rekla'meschild, -er nt.

billet, 1. n. Quartier', -e nt. 2. vb. ein·quartieren.

billfold, n. Brieftasche, -n f.

billiards, n. Billard nt.

billion, n. Billion', -en f.

bill of fare, n. Speisekarte, -n f.

bill of health, n. Gesund'heitsattest, -e nt.

bill of lading, n. Frachtbrief, -e m.

bill of sale, n. Kaufkontrakt, -e m.

billow, 1. n. Woge, -n f. 2. vb. wogen.

bimonthly, adj. zweimo'natlich.

bin, n. Kasten, -̈ m.

bind, vb. binden*; verbin'den*.

bindery, n. Buchbinderei' f.

binding, 1. n. (book) Einband, -̈e m.; (ski) Bindung, -en f. 2. adj. bindend.

binocular, n. Fernglas, -̈er nt.

biochemistry, n. Biochemie' f.

biodegradable, adj. orga'nisch abbaubar.

biofeedback, n. Biosignalrückgabe, -n f.

biographer, n. Biograph' -en, -en m.

biographical, adj. biogra'phisch.

biography, n. Biographie', -i'en f.

biological, adj. biolo'gisch.

biology, n. Biologie', -i'en f.

bipartisan, adj. die Regierungs- und die Oppositionspartei vertretend.

bird, n. Vogel, -̈ m.

birth, n. Geburt', -en f.

birth control, n. Gebur'tenkontrolle f.

birthday, n. Geburts'tag, -e m.

birthmark, n. Muttermal, -e nt.

birthplace, n. Geburts'ort, -e m.

birth rate, n. Gebur'tenziffer, -n f.

birthright, n. Erstgeburtsrecht, -e nt.; angestammtes Recht nt.

biscuit, n. Biskuit', -e nt.; Keks, -e m.

bisect, vb. halbie'ren.

bishop, n. Bischof, -̈e m.

bismuth, n. Wismut nt.

bison, n. Bison, -s m.

bit, n. (piece) Bißchen, - nt.; (a b. of) ein bißchen; (harness)

Gebiß, -sse nt.; (computer) Bit, - nt.

bitch, n. Hündin, -nen f.

bite, 1. n. Bissen, - m. 2. vb. beißen*.

biting, adj. beißend.

bitter, adj. bitter.

bitterness, n. Bitterkeit, -en f.

biweekly, adj. zweiwöchentlich.

black, 1. adj. schwarz (-̈). 2. n. (person) Schwarz- m.&f.

blackberry, n. Brombeere, -n f.

blackbird, n. Amsel, -n f.

blackboard, n. Wandtafel, -n f.

blacken, vb. schwärzen.

blackmail, 1. n. Erpres'sung, -en f. 2. vb. erpres'sen.

black market, n. Schwarzmarkt, -̈e m.

blackout, n. Verdun'kelung, -en f.

blacksmith, n. Schmied, -e m.

bladder, n. Blase, -n f.

blade, n. (knife) Klinge, -n f.; (grass) Halm, -e m.

blame, 1. n. Schuld, -en f. 2. vb. beschul'digen.

blanch, vb. bleichen; bleich werden*.

bland, adj. mild.

blank, 1. n. (form) Formular', -e nt. 2. adj. unbeschrieben, leer.

blanket, n. Decke, -n f., Wolldecke, -n f.

blaspheme, vb. lästern.

blasphemer, n. Gotteslästerer, - m.

blasphemous, adj. gotteslästerlich.

blasphemy, n. Gotteslästerung, -en f., Blasphemie', -i'en f.

blast, 1. n. (of wind) Windstoß, -̈e m.; (explosion) Explosion', -en f. 2. vb. sprengen.

blatant, adj. laut, aufdring'lich.

blaze, 1. n. Flamme, -n f. 2. vb. lodern, leuchten.

bleach, vb. bleichen.

bleak, adj. öde.

bleed, vb. bluten.

blemish, n. Makel, - m.

blend, 1. n. Mischung, -en f. 2. vb. mischen.

bless, vb. segnen.

blessed, adj. gese'gnet, selig.

blessing, n. Segen, - m.

blight, 1. n. (bot.) Brand, -̈e m. 2. (fig.) verei'teln.

blind, 1. adj. blind. 2. vb. blenden.

blindfold, 1. n. Augenbinde -n f. 2. vb. die Augen verbin'den*.

blindness, n. Blindheit, -en f.

blink, vb. blinken, blinzeln.

blinker, n. Scheuklappe, -n f.; (signal) Blinklicht, -er nt.

bliss, n. Glückseligkeit, -en f.

blissful, adj. glückselig.

blister, n. Blase, -n f.

blithe, adj. fröhlich.

blizzard, n. Schneesturm, -̈e m.

bloat, vb. blähen.

bloc, n. Block, -e m.

block, 1. n. (wood) Holzblock, -e m.; (city) Häuserblock, -e m. 2. vb. sperren.

blockade, n. Blocka'de, -n f.

blond, adj. blond.

blood, n. Blut nt.

bloodhound, n. Bluthund, -e m.

blood plasma, n. Plasma, -men nt.

blood poisoning, n. Blutvergiftung, -en f.

blood pressure, n. Blutdruck, m.

bloodshed, n. Blutvergießen, nt.

bloodshot, adj. blutunterlaufen.

bloody, adj. blutig.

bloom, 1. n. Blüte, -n f. 2. vb. blühen.

blossom, n. Blüte, -n f.

blot, 1. n. Fleck, -e m. 2. vb. beflecken, (ink) löschen.

blotter, n. Löschpapier, -e nt.

blouse, n. Bluse, -n f.

blow, 1. n. Schlag, -¨e m, Stoß, -¨e, m. 2. vb. blasen*.

blowout, n. Reifenpanne, -n f.

blubber, 1. n. Walfischspeck m. 2. vb. flennen.

blue, adj. blau.

bluebird, n. Blaukehlchen, - nt.

blue jeans, n.pl. Jeans, Bluejeans.

blueprint, n. Blaudruck, -¨e m.; (fig.) Plan, -¨e m.

bluff, 1. n. (cliff) Klippe, -n f., schroffer Felsen, - m.; (cards) Bluff, -s m. 2. adj. schroff. 3. vb. bluffen.

bluffer, n. Bluffer, - m.

bluing, n. Waschblau nt.

blunder, 1. n. Fehler, - m. 2. vb. Fehler machen.

blunderer, n. Tölpel, - m.

blunt, adj. stumpf; (fig.) unverblümt.

blur, 1. n. Verschwom'menheit f. 2. vb. (intr.) verschwim'men*; (tr.) trüben.

blurred, adj. verschwommen.

blush, 1. n. Errö'ten f. 2. vb. errö'ten.

bluster, vb. toben; (swagger) prahlen.

boar, n. Eber, - m.

board, 1. n. (plank) Brett, -er nt., Bord, -e nt.; (food) Verpfle'gung, -en f.; (committee) Ausschuß, ¨sse m.; (council) Behör'de, -n f.; (ship) Bord, - e m. 2. vb. an Bord gehen*.

boarder, n. Kostgänger, - m.

boarding house, n. Pension', - en f.

boast, 1. n. Angeberei', -en f. 2. vb. prahlen, an·geben*.

boaster, n. Angeber, - m.

boastful, adj. angeberisch.

boastfulness, n. Angeberei', - en f.

boat, n. Boot, -e nt., Schiff, - e nt.

bob, 1. n. (hair) Bubikopf m. 2. vb. baumeln; (hair) kurz schneiden*.

bobby pin, n. Haarklammer, -n f.

bodice, n. Oberteil, -e nt.

bodily, adj. leiblich.

body, n. Körper, - m., Leib, -er m.

bodyguard, n. Leibwache, -n f.

bog, 1. n. Sumpf, -¨e m. 2. vb. (b. down) stecken bleiben*.

Bohemian, 1. n. Böhme, -n, -n m. 2. adj. böhmisch.

boil, 1. n. (med.) Furun'kel, -n f. 2. vb. kochen.

boiler, n. Kessel, - m.

boisterous, adj. ungestüm.

bold, adj. kühn.

boldface, n. Fettdruck, -e m.

boldness, n. Kühnheit, -en f.

Bolivian, 1. n. Bolivia'ner, - m. 2. adj. bolivia'nisch.

bolster, 1. n. Polster, - nt. 2. vb. (support) unterstüt'zen.

bolster up, vb. stärken.

bolt, 1. n. (lock) Riegel, - m.; (screw with nut) Schraube, -n f.; (lightning) Blitz, -e m. 2. vb. (lock) verrie'geln; (dash of persons) davon'·stürzen, (of horses) durch·gehen*.

bomb, 1. n. Bombe, -n f. 2. vb. bomben.

bombard, vb. bombardie'ren.

bombardier, n. Bombardier', - m.

bombardment, n. Beschie'ßung, -en f.

bomber, n. Bombenflugzeug, - e nt.

bombproof, adj. bombensicher.

bombshell, n. Bombe, -n f.

bombsight, n. Bombenziel'vorrichtung, -en f.

bonbon, n. Fondant', -s m.

bond, n. Band, -e n., Fessel, -n f.; (law) Bürgschaft, -en f.; (stock exchange) Obligation'- en f.

bondage, n. Knechtschaft, -en f.

bone, n. Knochen, - m.; (fish) Gräte, -n f.

bonfire, n. Freudenfeurer, - nt.

bonnet, n. Damenhut, -¨e m.

bonus, n. Extrazahlung, -en f.; Tantie'me, -n f.

bony, adj. knochig.

book, 1. n. Buch, -¨er nt. 2. vb. buchen.

bookcase, n. Bücherschrank, -¨e m.

bookkeeper, n. Buchhalter, - m.

bookkeeping, n. Buchführung, -en f.

booklet, n. Broschü're, -n f.

bookseller, n. Buchhändler, - m.

bookstore, n. Buchhandlung, - en f.

boom, 1. n. Baum, -¨e m.; (econ.) Hochkonjunktur,

-en f. 2. vb. brummen, dröhnen.

boon, n. Geschenk', -e nt.; (fig.) Segen, - m.

boor, n. Grobian, -e m.

boorish, adj. grob (-).

boost, 1. n. (increase) Aufschwung, -¨e m.; (push) Antrieb, -e m. 2. vb. (increase) steigern; (push) nachhelfen*.

boot, n. Stiefel, - m.

bootblack, n. Schuhputzer, - m.

booth, n. Bude, -n f.; (telephone) Fernsprechzelle, -n f.

border, 1. n. Grenze, -n f. 2. vb. grenzen an.

borderline, n. Grenze, -n f.

bore, 1. n. (hole) Bohrloch, -¨er nt.; (cylinder) Bohrung, -en f.; (person) langweiliger Mensch, -en, -en m. 2. vb. bohren; (annoy) langweilen.

boredom, n. Langeweile f.

boric, adj. Bor- (cpds.).

boring, adj. langweilig.

born, adj. gebo'ren.

born-again, adj. wiedergeboren.

borough, n. Stadtteil, -e m.

borrow, vb. borgen, leihen*.

bosom, n. Busen, - m.

boss, n. Chef, -s m.

bossy, adj. herrschsüchtig.

botanical, adj. bota'nisch.

botany, n. Bota'nik f.

both, adj.&pron. beide.

bother, 1. n. Verdruß' m. 2. vb. belās'tigen; (disturb) stören.

bothersome, adj. lästig.

bottle, n. Flasche, -n f.

bottom, n. Grund, -¨e m.

bottomless, adj. bodenlos.

boudoir, n. Boudoir', -s nt.

bough, n. Ast, -¨e m., Zweig, -e m.

bouillon, n. Kraftbrühe, -n f.

boulder, n. Felsblock, -¨e m.

boulevard, n. Boulevard', -s m.

bounce, vb. springen*.

bound, 1. n. (jump) Sprung, -¨e m.; (b.s.) Grenzen pl. 2. vb. (jump) springen*; (limit) begren'zen 3. adj. (tied) gebun'den; (duty b.) verpflich'tet; (b. for) unterwegs' nach.

boundary, n. Grenze, -n f.

bound for, adj. unterwegs' nach.

boundless, adj. grenzenlos.

bounty, n. Freigebigkeit, -en f.

bouquet, n. Blumenstrauß, -¨e m.

bourgeois, adj. bürgerlich.

bout, n. (boxing) Boxkampf, -¨e m.

bovine, adj. Rinder- (cpds.).

bow, 1. n. (for arrows, violin) Bogen, - m.; (greeting) Verbeu'gung, -en f.; (hair, dress) Schleife, -n f.; (of boats) Bug, -e m. 2. vb. sich verbeu'gen.

bowels, n.pl. Eingeweide pl.

bowl, 1. n. Schüssel -n f., Schale, -n f. 2. vb. kegeln.

bowlegged, adj. o-beinig.

bowler, n. Kegelspieler, - m.; (hat) Melo'ne, -n f.

bowling, n. Kegeln nt.

box, 1. n. (small) Schachtel, -n f.; (large) Kasten - m.; (theater) Loge, -n f.; (letter b.) Briefkasten, - m. 2. vb. (sport) boxen.

boxcar, n. Güterwagen, - m.

boxer, n. Boxer, - m.

boxing, n. Boxen nt.

box office, n. Thea'terkasse, - n, f.

boy, n. Junge, -n, -n m., Bube, -n, -n m.

Boycott, 1. n. boykott', -e m. 2. vb. boykottie'ren.

boyhood, n. Jugend, -en f.

boyish, adj. jungenhaft, jung.

brace, 1. n. Klammer, -n f., Stütze, -n f. 2. vb. absteifen.

bracelet, n. Armband, ⸚er nt.

bracket, n. Klammer, -n f.; (typography) Klammer, -n f.; (group) Gruppe, -n f.

brag, vb. prahlen, an'geben*.

braggart, n. Angeber, - m.

braid, 1. n. Flechte, -n f. 2. vb. flechten*.

brain, n. Gehirn', -e nt.

brake, 1. n. Bremse, -n f. 2. vb. bremsen.

bran, n. Kleie, -n f.

branch, n. Ast, ⸚e m., Zweig, -e m.

brand, 1. n. (sort) Sorte, -n f.; (mark) Marke, -n f. 2. vb. brandmarken.

brandish, vb. schwingen*.

brandy, n. Weinbrand, -e m., Kognak, -s m.

brash, adj. dreist.

brass, n. Messing nt.

brassiere, n. Büstenhalter, - m.

brat, n. Balg, ⸚e m.

bravado, n. Bravour' f., Schneid m.

brave, adj. tapfer.

bravery, n. Tapferkeit, -en f.

brawl, n. Rauferei', -en f.

brawn, n. Muskelkraft, ⸚e f.

bray, 1. n. Eselsgeschrei nt. 2. vb. schreien'.

brazen, adj. ehern; (insolent) unverschämt.

Brazil, n. Brasi'lien nt.

Brazilian, 1. n. Brasilia'ner, - m. 2. adj. brasilia'nisch.

breach, n. Bruch, ⸚e m.

bread, n. Brot, -e nt.

breadth, n. Breite, -n f.

break, 1. n. Bruch, ⸚e m.; Pause, -n f. 2. vb. brechen*.

breakable, adj. zerbrech'lich.

breakfast, n. Frühstück, -e nt.

breakneck, adj. halsbrecherisch.

breakwater, n. Mole, -n f.

breast, n. Brust, ⸚e f.

breath, n. Atem, - m.

breathe, vb. atmen.

breathing, n. Atmen nt.

breathless, adj. atemlos.

breeches, n. Kniehose -n f.

breed, 1. n. Zucht, -en f. 2. vb. (beget) erzeu'gen; (raise) züchten; (educate) erzie'hen*.

breeder, n. Züchter, - m.

breeding, n. Erzie'hung, -en f.

breeze, n. Brise, -n f.

breezy, adj. luftig.

brevity, n. Kürze, -n f.

brew, 1. n. Gebräu, -e nt. 2. vb. brauen.

brewer, n. Brauer, - m.

brewery, n. Brauerei', -en f.

briar, n. Dornbusch, ⸚e m.; Bruyèreholz m.

bribe, vb. beste'chen*.

briber, n. Beste'cher, - m.

bribery, n. Beste'chung, -en f.

brick, n. Backstein, -e m.; Ziegelstein, -e m.

bricklayer, n. Maurer, - m.

bridal, adj. Hochzeits- (cpds.).

bride, n. Braut, ⸚e f.

bridegroom, n. Bräutigam, -e m.

bridesmaid, n. Brautjungfer, -n f.

bridge, 1. n. Brücke, -n f.; (game) Bridge nt. 2. vb. überbrü'cken.

bridle, n. Zaum, ⸚e m.

brief, adj. kurz (⸚).

brief case, n. Aktenmappe, -n f.

bright, adj. hell; (smart) gescheit'.

brighten, vb. erhel'len.

brightness, n. Klarheit, -en f.

brilliance, n. Glanz, -e m.

brilliant, adj. glänzend; (smart) hochbegabt.

brim, n. (cup) Rand, ⸚er m.; (hat) Krempe, -n f.

brine, n. Salzwasser, - nt., Sole, -n f.

bring, vb. bringen*.

brink, n. Rand, ⸚er m.

briny, adj. salzig.

brisk, adj. lebhaft.

brisket, n. (meat) Bruststück, -e nt.

briskness, n. Lebhaftigkeit, -en f.

bristle, 1. n. Borste, -n f. 2. vb. sich sträuben.

Britain, n. Britan'nien nt.

British, adj. britisch.

Briton, n. Brite, -n, -n m.

brittle, adj. brüchig, spröde.

broad, adj. breit, weit.

broadcast, 1. n. Rundfunksendung, -en f., Übertra'gung, -en f. 2. vb. senden, im Radio übertra'gen*.

broadcaster, n. Rundfunksprecher, - m.

broadcloth, n. feiner Wäschestoff m.

broaden, vb. erwei'tern.

broadly, adv. allgemein'.

broadminded, adj. großzügig, tolerant'.

brocade, n. Brokat', -e m.

broil, vb. grillen.

broiler, n. Bratrost, -e m.

broke, adj. pleite.

broken, adj. gebro'chen; kaputt'.

broker, n. Makler, - m.

brokerage, n. (business) Maklergeschäft, -e nt.; (charge) Maklergebühr, -en f.

bronchial, adj. bronchial'.

bronchitis, n. Bronchi'tis f.

bronze, n. Bronze, -n f.

brooch, n. Brosche, -n f.

brood, 1. n. Brut, -en f. 2. vb. brüten.

brook, n. Bach, ⸚e m.

broom, n. Besen, - m.

broomstick, n. Besenstiel, -e m.

broth, n. Brühe, -n f.

brothel, n. Bordell', -e nt.

brother, n. Bruder, ⸚ m.

brotherhood, n. Brüderschaft, -en f.

brother-in-law, n. Schwager, ⸚ m.

brotherly, adj. brüderlich.

brow, n. Stirn, -en f.

brown, adj. braun.

browse, vb. schmökern.

bruise, 1. n. Quetschung, -en f.; 2 vb. quetschen, stoßen*.

brunette, n. Brünet'te, -n f.

brunt, n. (bear the b.) die Hauptlast tragen*.

brush, 1, n. Bürste, -n f.; (artist's) Pinsel, -n. 2. vb. bürsten.

brusque, adj. brüsk.

brutal, adj. brutal'.

brutality, n. Brutalität', -en f.

brutalize, vb. verro'hen.

brute, n. Unmensch, -en, -en m.

bubble, 1. n. Luftblase, -n f. 2. vb. sprudeln.

buck, 1. n. Bock, ⸚e m. 2. vb. bocken; (fig.) sich gegen etwas auf'bäumen.

bucket, n. Eimer, - m.

buckle, 1. n. Schnalle, - f. 2. vb. (fasten) schnallen; (bend) sich krümmen, sich biegen*.

buckwheat, n. Buchweizen m.

bud, 1. n. Knospe, -n f. 2. vb. knospen.

budge, vb. sich rühren.

budget, n. Etat', -s m.

buffalo, n. Büffel, - m.

buffer, n. Puffer, - m.; (b. state) Pufferstaat, -en m.

buffet, 1. n. Büfett' -e, Buffet', -s nt. 2. vb. schlagen*.

bug, n. Käfer, - m.

bugle, n. Signal'horn, ⸚er nt.

build, vb. bauen.

builder, n. Baumeister, - m.

building, n. Gebäu'de, - nt.

bulb, n. Knolle, -n f.; (electric) Glühbirne, -n f.

bulge, 1. n. Ausbuchtung, -en f. 2. vb. sich aus'buchten.

bulk, n. Umfang, ⸚e m., Hauptteil, -e m.

bulky, adj. umfangreich.

bull, n. Bulle, -n m.

bulldog, n. Bulldogge, -n f.

bullet, n. Kugel, -n f.

bulletin, n. Bericht', -e m.

bully, 1. n. Kraftmeier, - m. **2.** vb. kraftmeiern.

bulwark, n. Bollwerk, -e m.

bum, 1. n. (fam.) Lump, -en, - en m. **2.** vb. (fam.) pumpen.

bumblebee, n. Hummel, -n f.

bump, 1. n. Stoß, ⁼e m. **2.** vb. stoßen*.

bumper, n. Stoßstange, -n f.

bun, n. Brötchen, - nt.

bunch, n. Büschel, - nt.

bundle, n. Bündel, - nt.

bungle, vb. pfuschen.

bunion, n. Enzün'dung am großen Zeh.

bunny, n. Kanin'chen, - nt.

buoy, n. Boje, -n f.

buoyant, adj. schwimmend, tragfähig; (fig.) lebhaft.

burden, 1. n. Last, -en f. **2.** vb. belas'ten.

burdensome, adj. beschwer'lich.

bureau, n. Büro', -s nt.; (furniture) Kommo'de, -n f.

burglar, n. Einbrecher, - m.

burglary, n. Einbruch, ⁼e m.

burial, n. Begräb'nis, -se nt.

burlap, n. grobe Leinwand f.

burly, adj. stämmig.

burn, 1. n. Verbren'nung, -en f. **2.** vb. (intr.) brennen*, (tr.) verbren'nen*.

burner, n. Brenner, - m.

burrow, 1. n. (of an animal) Bau, -e m. **2.** vb. sich eingraben*.

burst, 1. n. Krach, -e m.; Explosion', -en f. **2.** vb. (intr.) platzen; (tr.) sprengen.

bury, vb. begra'ben*; eingraben*.

bus, n. Bus, -se m.

bush, n. Busch, ⁼e m.

bushel, n. Scheffel, - m.

bushy, adj. buschig.

business, n. Geschäft', -e nt.

businesslike, adj. geschäftsmäßig.

businessman, n. Geschäfts'mann, ⁼er or -leute m.

businesswoman, n. Geschäfts'frau, -en f.

bust, 1. n. Büste, -n f. **2.** vb. (fam.) kaputt' machen.

bustle, n. Geschäf'tigkeit, -en f.

busy, adj. beschäf'tigt; geschäf'tig.

but, 1. prep. außer. **2.** conj. aber.

butcher, n. Fleischer, - m.; Metzger, - m., Schlächter, - m., Schlachter, - m.

butler, n. Diener, - m.

butt, 1. n. (gun) Kolben, - m.; (aim) Ziel, -e nt. **2.** vb. mit dem Kopf stoßen*.

butter, n. Butter f.

butterfly, n. Schmetterling, - m.

buttermilk, n. Buttermilch f.

buttocks, n.pl. Gesäß', -e nt.

button, n. Knopf, ⁼e m.

buttonhole, n. Knopfloch, ⁼er nt.

buttress, 1. n. Stütze, -n f.; (arch.) Strebepfeiler, - m. **2.** vb. stützen.

buxom, adj. drall.

buy, vb. kaufen.

buyer, n. Käufer, - m.

buzz, vb. summen.

buzzard, n. Bussard, -e m.

buzzer, n. Klingel, -n f.

by, prep. von; (through) durch; (near) bei.

by-and-by, adv. später.

bygone, adj. vergan'gen.

by-pass, n. Umge'hungsstraße, -n f.

by-product, n. Nebenprodukt, -e nt.

bystander, n. Zuschauer, - m.

byte, n. Byte, -s nt.

byway, n. Nebenweg, -e m.

C

cab, n. (taxi) Taxe, -n f., Taxi, -s nt.; (locomotive) Führerstand, -e m.

cabaret, n. Kabarett' -e nt.

cabbage, n. Kohl m.

cabin, n. Kabi'ne, -n f.

cabinet, n. Kabinett', -e nt.

cabinetmaker, n. Kunsttischler, - m.

cable, 1. n. Kabel, - nt. **2.** vb. kabeln.

cablegram, n. Kabel, - nt.

cache, n. Versteck', -e nt.

cackle, vb. gackern.

cactus, n. Kaktus, -te'en m.

cad, n. Schuft, -e m.

cadaver, n. Leichnam, -e m.

cadet, n. Kadett', -en, -en m.

cadence, n. Tonfall, ⁼e m.; Kadenz', -en f.

cadmium, n. Kadmium nt.

café, n. Café, -s nt.; Konditorei', -en f.

caffeine, n. Koffein', -e nt.

cage, n. Käfig, -e m.

cajole, vb. beschwat'zen.

cake, n. Kuchen, - m.

calamity, n. Unglück, -e nt.

calcium, n. Kalzium nt.

calculable, adj. bere'chenbar.

calculate, vb. berech'nen.

calculating machine, n. Rechenmaschine, -n f.

calculation, n. Berech'nung, - en f.

calculus, n. Differential'rechnung, -en f.

caldron, n. Kessel, - m.

calendar, n. Kalen'der, - m.

calf, n. Kalb, ⁼er nt.

calfskin, n. Kalbleder, - nt.

caliber, n. Kali'ber, - nt.

calico, n. Kattun', -e m.

calipers, n.pl. Greifzirkel, - m.

callsthenics, n.pl. Leibesübungen pl.

call, 1. n. Ruf, -e m.; (telephone) Anruf, -e m. **2.** vb. rufen*.

calling card, n. Visi'tenkarte, - n f.

callous, adj. schwielig; (unfeeling) gefühl'los.

callus, n. Schwiele, -n f.

calm, 1. adj. ruhig. **2.** vb. beru'higen.

calmness, n. Ruhe f.

caloric, adj. kalo'risch.

calorie, n. Kalorie', -i'en f.

Calvary, n. Kalva'rienberg m.

calve, vb. kalben.

cambric, n. Batist', -e m.

camel, n. Kamel', -e nt.

cameo, n. Kame'e, -n f.

camera, n. Kamera, -s f.; Photoapparat, -e m.

camouflage, 1. n. Tarnung, -en f.; (natural c.) Mimikry f. Schutzfarbe, -n f. **2.** vb. tarnen.

camp, 1. n. Lager, - nt. **2.** vb. lagern.

campaign, 1. n. Feldzug, ⁼e m.; Kampag'ne, -n f. **2.** vb. (political) Wahlreden halten*.

camper, n. Zelter, - m.

camphor, n. Kampfer m.

camping, n. Zelten nt.

campus, n. Universitäts'gelände, - nt., College-Gelände, - nt.

can, 1. n. (tin) Büchse, -n f.; (large) Kanne, -n f. **2.** vb. (preserve) ein'machen; (be able) können*.

Canada, n. Kanada nt.

Canadian, 1. n. Kana'dier, - m. **2.** adj. kana'disch.

canal, n. Kanal', ⁼e m.

canapé, n. Cocktailgebäck nt.

canary, n. Kana'rienvogel, ⁼ m.

cancel, vb. entwer'ten, rückgängig machen, auf'heben*.

cancellation, n. Aufhebung, -en f., Entwer'tung, -en f.

cancer, n. Krebs, -e m.

candelabrum, n. Armleuchter, - m.

candid, adj. offen, ehrlich.

candidacy, n. Kandidatur', -en f.

candidate, n. Kandidat', -en, -en m.

candied, adj. kandiert'.

candle, n. Kerze, -n f.

candlestick, n. Leuchter, - m.

candor, n. Offenheit, -en f.

cane, n. Stock, ⁼e m; (sugar) Rohr, -e nt.

canine, adj. Hunde- (cpds.).

canister, n. Blechbüchse, -n f.

canker, n. Krebs, -e m.

canned, adj. eingemacht; Büchsen- (cpds.).

cannibal, n. Kanniba'le, -n, -n m.

canning, n. Einmachen nt.

cannon, n. Kano'ne, -n f.

cannot, vb. nicht können*.

canny, *adj.* schlau, umsichtig.

canoe, *n.* Kanu', -s *nt.*

canon, *n. (rule, song)* Kanon, -s *m.; (person)* Domherr, -n, -en *m.*

canonical, *adj.* kano'nisch.

canonize, *vb.* kanonisie'ren.

can opener, *n.* Büchsenöffner, - *m.*

canopy, *n.* Baldachin, -e *m.*

cant, *n.* Heuchelei', -en *f.*

cantaloupe, *n.* Melo'ne, -n *f.*

canteen, *n.* Kanti'ne, -n *f.*

canvas, *n. (material)* Segeltuch *nt.; (painter's)* Leinwand *f.*

canvass, **1.** *n.* Stimmenprüfung, -en *f.* **2.** *vb.* untersuchen, prüfen.

canyon, *n.* Schlucht, -en *f.*

cap, *n.* Mütze, -n *f.*

capability, *n.* Fähigkeit, -en *f.*

capable, *adj.* fähig.

capacious, *adj.* geräu'mig.

capacity, *n. (content)* Inhalt *m.; (ability)* Fähigkeit, -en *f.; (quality)* Eigenschaft, -en *f.*

cape, *n. (clothing)* Umhang, -e *m.; (geogr.)* Kap, -s *nt.*

caper, **1.** *n.* Luftsprung, -e *m.* **2.** *vb.* Luftsprünge machen.

capital, **1.** *n. (money)* Kapital', -ien *nt.; (city)* Hauptstadt, -e *f.* **2.** *adj.* kapital'.

capitalism, *n.* Kapitalis'mus *m.*

capitalist, *n.* Kapitalist', -en, -en *m.*

capitalistic, *adj.* kapitalistisch.

capitalization, *n.* Kapitalisie'rung, -en *f.*

capitalize, *vb.* kapitalisie'ren.

capitulate, *vb.* kapitulie'ren.

capon, *n.* Kapaun', -e *m.*

caprice, *n.* Laune, -n *f.*

capricious, *adj.* launenhaft.

capsize, *vb.* kentern.

capsule, *n.* Kapsel, -n *f.*

captain, *n.* Kapitän', -e *m.; (army)* Hauptmann, -leute *m.*

caption, *n.* Überschrift, -en *f.*

captious, *adj.* verfäng'lich.

captivate, *vb.* fesseln.

captive, **1.** *n.* Gefan'gen, - *m.&f.* **2.** *adj.* gefan'gen.

captivity, *n.* Gefan'genschaft, - en *f.*

captor, *n.* Fänger, - *m.*

capture, **1.** *n.* Gefan'gennahme, -n *f.* **2.** *vb. (person)* fangen*; *(city)* ero'bern.

car, *n.* Wagen, - *m.;* Auto, -s *nt.*

carafe, *n.* Karaf'fe, -n *f.*

caramel, *n.* Karamel' *nt.*

carat, *n.* Karat', - *m.*

caravan, *n.* Karawa'ne, -n *f.*

caraway, *n.* Kümmel *m.*

carbide, *n.* Karbid' *nt.*

carbine, *n.* Karabi'ner, - *m.*

carbohydrate, *n.* Kohlehydrat, -e *nt.*

carbon, *n.* Kohlenstoff, -e *m.*

carbon dioxide, *n.* Kohlendi-oxyd *nt.*

carbon monoxide, *n.* Kohle-oxyd' *nt.*

carbon paper, *n.* Kohlepapier, -e *nt.*

carbuncle, *n.* Karbun'kel, - *m.; (gem)* Karfun'kel, - *m.*

carburetor, *n.* Verga'ser, - *m.*

carcass, *n.* Kada'ver, - *m.*

carcinogenic, *adj.* krebserregend.

card, *n.* Karte, -n *f.*

cardboard, *n.* Pappe, -n *f.*

cardiac, *adj.* Herz- *(cpds.).*

cardinal, **1.** *n.* Kardinal', -e *m.* **2.** *adj.* hauptsächlich.

care, **1.** *n. (worry)* Sorge, -n *f.; (prudence)* Vorsicht *f.; (accuracy)* Sorgfalt *f.;* **(take c. of)** sorgen für. **2.** *vb. (attend)* sorgen für; **(c. for, like)** gern mögen*; **(c. about)** sich kümmern um.

careen, *vb.* wild fahren*.

career, *n.* Karrie're, -n *f.*

carefree, *adj.* sorglos.

careful, *adj. (prudent)* vorsichtig; *(accurate)* sorgfältig.

carefulness, *n. (prudence)* Vorsicht *f.; (accuracy)* Sorgfalt *f.*

careless, *adj. (imprudent)* unvorsichtig; *(inaccurate)* unsorgfältig, nachlässig.

carelessness, *n. (imprudence)* Unvorsichtigkeit, -en *f.; (inaccuracy)* Nachlässigkeit, -en *f.*

caress, **1.** *n.* Liebkosung, -en *f.* **2.** *vb.* liebkosen, streicheln.

caretaker, *n.* Verwal'ter, - *m.*

cargo, *n.* Ladung, -en *f.;* Fracht, -en *f.*

caricature, **1.** *n.* Karikatur', -en *f.* **2.** *vb.* karikie'ren.

caries, *n.* Karies *f.*

carload, *n.* Waggon'ladung, -en *f.*

carnal, *adj.* fleischlich.

carnation, *n.* Nelke, -n *f.*

carnival, *n.* Karneval, -s *m.*

carnivorous, *adj.* fleischfressend.

carol, **1.** *n.* Weihnachtslied, -er *nt.* **2.** *vb.* singen*.

carouse, *vb.* zechen.

carousel, *n.* Karussell', -s *nt.*

carpenter, *n. (construction)* Zimmermann, -leute *m; (finer work)* Tischler, - *m.*

carpet, *n.* Teppich, -e *m.*

car pool, *n.* Mitnehmen von anderen im Auto zwecks Benzin-und Zeitersparnis *nt.*

carriage, *n. (vehicle)* Wagen, - *m.; (posture)* Haltung, -en *f.*

carrier, *n.* Träger, - *m.*

carrot, *n.* Mohr'rübe, -n *f.*

carry, *vb.* tragen*; **(c. on, intr.)** fort'fahren*; **(c. on, tr.)** fort-setzen; **(c. out)** aus'führen; **(c. through)** durch-führen.

cart, *n.* Karren, - *m.*

cartage, *n.* Transport', -e *m.*

cartel, *n.* Kartell', -e *nt.*

cartilage, *n.* Knorpel, - *m.*

carton, *n.* Karton', -s *m.*

cartoon, *n.* Karikatur', -en *f.*

cartridge, *n.* Patro'en, -n *f.*

carve, *vb.* schneiden*; *(wood)* schnitzen; *(meat)* zerle'gen, tranchie'ren.

carving, *n.* Schnitzerk, -e *nt.*

case, *n.* Fall, -e *m.*

cash, **1.** *n.* Bargeld, -er *nt.* **2.** *vb.* ein-lösen. **3.** *adj.* bar.

cashier, *n.* Kassie'rer, - *m.*

cashmere, *n.* Kaschmir, -e *m.*

casing, *n.* Hülle, -n *f.*

casino, *n.* Kasi'no, -s *nt.*

cask, *n.* Tonne, -n *f.,* Faß, -sser *nt.*

casket, *n.* Sarg, -e *m.*

casserole, *n.* Schmorpfanne, -n *f.*

cassette, *n.* Kaset'te, -n *f.*

cast, **1.** *n. (theater)* Rollenverteilung, -en *f.* **2.** *vb. (throw)* werfen*; *(metal)* gießen*.

caste, *n.* Kaste, -n *f.*

castigate, *vb.* züchtigen.

castle, *n.* Schloß, -sser, *nt.*

castoff, *adj.* abgelegt.

castor oil, *n.* Rizinusöl, -e *nt.*

casual, *adj. (accidental)* zufällig; *(nonchalant)* zwanglos.

casualness, *n.* Zwanglosigkeit, -en *f.*

casualty, *n.* Opfer, - *nt.; (casualties)* Verlus'te *pl.*

cat, *n.* Katze, -n *f.; (tomcat)* Kater, - *m.*

cataclysm, *n.* Sündflut, -en *f.*

catacomb, *n.* Katakom'be, -n *f.*

catalogue, *n.* Katalog', -e *m.*

catapult, *n.* Katapult', -e *m.*

cataract, *n. (eye)* Katarakt', -e *m.,* grauer Star, -e *m.*

catarrh, *n.* Katarrh', -e *m.*

catastrophe, *n.* Katastro'phe, -n *f.*

catch, *vb.* fangen*; *(sickness, train)* bekom'men*.

catcher, *n.* Fänger, - *m.*

catechism, *n.* Katechis'mus, -men *m.*

categorical, *adj.* katego'risch.

category, *n.* Kategorie', -i'en *f.*

cater, *vb.* versor'gen.

caterpillar, *n.* Raupe, -n *f.*

cathartic, **1.** *n.* Abführmittel, - *nt.* **2.** *adj.* abführend.

cathedral, *n.* Kathedra'le, -n *f.;* Dom, -e *m.*

cathode, *n.* Katho'de, -n *f.*

Catholic, **1.** *n.* Katholik', -en, -en *m.* **2.** *adj.* katho'lisch.

Catholicism, *n.* Katholizis'mus, -men *m.*

catsup, *n.* Ketchup *nt.*

cattle, *n.* Vieh *nt.*

cauliflower, *n.* Blumenkohl, -e *m.*

cause, **1.** *n. (origin)* Ursache, -n *f.; (idea)* Sache, -n *f.* **2.** *vb.* verur'sachen.

caustic, *adj.* beißend.

cauterize, *vb.* aus'brennen*.

cautery, *n.* Ausbrennen *nt.*

caution, **1.** *n.* Vorsicht, -en *f.* **2.** *vb.* warnen.

cautious, adj. vorsichtig.

cavalcade, n. Kavalka'de, -n f.

cavalier, n. Kavalier', -e m.

cavalry, n. Kavallerie', -i'en f.

cave, n. Höhle, -n f.

cavern, n. Höhle, -n f.

caviar, n. Kaviar m.

cavity, n. Loch, -er nt., Höhle, -n f.

cease, vb. (intr.) auf•hören, (tr.) ein•stellen.

cedar, n. Zeder, -n f.

cede, vb. ab•treten*.

ceiling, n. Zimmerdecke, -n f.; (fig.) Höchstgrenze, -n f.

celebrate, vb. feiern.

celebrated, adj. berühmt'.

celebration, n. Feier, -n f.

celebrity, n. Berühmt'heit, -en f.

celery, n. Sellerie m.

celestial, adj. himmlisch.

celibacy, n. Zölibat', -n nt., Ehelosigkeit f.

celibate, adj. ehelos.

cell, n. Zelle, -n f.

cellar, n. Keller, - m.

cellist, n. Cellist', -en, -en m.

cello, n. Cello, -s nt.

cellophane, n. Zellophan' nt.

celluloid, n. Zelluloid' nt.

cellulose, n. Zellstoff, -e m.

Celtic, adj. keltisch.

cement, 1. n. Zement', -e m. 2. vb. zementie'ren.

cemetery, n. Friedhof, -e m.

censor, 1. n. Zensor, -o'ren m. 2. vb. zensie'ren.

censorship, n. Zensur', -en f.

censure, n. Tadel, - m., Verweis', -e m.

census, n. Volkszählung, -en f., Zensus, - m.

cent, n. Cent, -s m.

centenary, n. Hundertjahr'feier, -n f.

centennial, 1. n. Hundertjahr'feier, -n f. 2. adj. hundertjährig.

center, n. Mitte, -n f.; Mittelpunkt, -e m.; Zentrum, -tren nt.

centerfold, n. Mittelfaltblatt, -er nt.

centigrade, n. (c. thermometer) Celsiusthermometer, - nt.; (10 degrees c.) 10 Grad Celsius.

central, adj. zentral'.

centralize, vb. zentralisie'ren.

century, n. Jahrhun'dert, -e nt.

ceramic, adj. kera'misch.

ceramics, n. Kera'mik, -en f.

cereal, n. Getrei'de, - nt., Getrei'despeise, - n f.

cerebral, adj. Gehirn- (cpds.).

ceremonial, adj. zeremoniell'.

ceremonious, adj. feierlich.

ceremony, n. Zeremonie', -i'en f.; Feierlichkeit, -en f.

certain, adj. sicher.

certainty, n. Gewißheit, -en f.

certificate, n. Beschei'nigung, -en f.; Urkunde, -n f.

certification, n. Beschei'nigung, -en f.

certify, vb. beschei'nigen, beglau'bigen, beeiden.

cervix, n. Gebär'mutterhals m.

cessation, n. Aufhören nt.

cesspool, n. Senkgrube, -n f.

chafe, vb. reiben*.

chagrin, n. Kummer, - m.

chain, 1. n. Kette, -n f. 2. vb. an•ketten, fesseln.

chain reaction, n. Kettenreaktion, -en f.

chair, n. Stuhl, -e m.

chairman, n. Vorsitzend- m.

chairperson, n. Vorsitzend- m. & f.

chalice, n. Kelch, -e m.

chalk, n. Kreide, -n f.

chalky, adj. kreidig.

challenge, 1. n. Heraus'forderung, -en f. 2. vb. heraus'fordern, auf•fordern.

challenger, n. Heraus'forderer, - m.

chamber, n. Kammer, -n f.; (pol.) Haus, -er nt.

chambermaid, n. Zimmermädchen, - nt.

chamber music, n. Kammermusik f.

chamois, n. (animal) Gemse, -n f.; (leather) Wildleder nt.

champagne, n. Sekt, -e m., Champag'ner, - m.

champion, n. Kämpfer, - m.; (sport) Meister, - m.

championship, n. Meisterschaft, -en f.

chance, 1. n. Zufall, -e m.; (expectation) Aussicht, -en f.; (occasion) Gele'genheit, -en f. 2. vb. wagen. 3. adj. zufällig.

chancel, n. Altar'platz, -e m.

chancellery, n. Kanzlei', -en f.

chancellor, n. Kanzler, - m.

chandelier, n. Kronleuchter, - m.

change, 1. n. Verän'derung, -en f.; (alteration) Änderung, -en f.; (variety) Abwechslung, -en f.; (small coins) Kleingeld nt.; (money due) Rest m. 2. vb. verändern; (alter) ändern; (money) wechseln.

changeability, n. Unbeständigkeit, -en f.

changeable, adj. unbeständig.

channel, n. Fahrwasser nt., Kanal'; -e m.; (radio) Frequenz'band, Fer nt.

chant, 1. n. Gesang', -e m. 2. vb. singen*.

chaos, n. Chaos, nt.

chaotic, adj. chao'tisch.

chap, 1. n. Bursche, -n, -n m., Kerl, -e m. 2. vb. (become chapped) auf•springen*.

chapel, n. Kapel'le, -n f.

chaplain, n. Geistlich- m.; (mil.) Feldgeistlich-m.

chapter, n. Kapi'tel, - nt.

char, vb. verkoh'len.

character, n. Charak'ter, -te're m.

characteristic, adj. charakteri'stisch.

characterization, n. Charakterisie'rung, -en f.

characterize, vb. charakterisie'ren.

charcoal, n. Holzkohle, -n f.

charge, 1. n. (load) Ladung, -en f.; (attack) Angriff, -e m.; (price) Preis, -e m.; (custody) Obhut, -en f. 2. vb. (load) laden*; (set a price) berech'nen; (put on one's account) an•schreiben* lassen*.

chariot, n. Wagen, - m.

charisma, n. Charis'ma nt.

charitable, adj. wohltätig, nachsichtig.

charity, n. Wohltätigkeit, -en f., Nächstenliebe f.

charlatan, n. Scharlatan, -e m.

charm, 1. n. Charme m.; Liebreiz, -e m.; (magic saying) Zauberspruch, -e m. 2. vb. bezau'bern.

charming, adj. bezau'bernd, reizend.

chart, n. (map) Karte, -n f.; (graph) Tabel'le, -n f.

charter, n. Urkunde, -n f.

charter flight, n. Charterflug, -e m.

charwoman, n. Putzfrau, -en f.

chase, 1. n. Jagd, -en f. 2. vb. jagen.

chasm, n. Abgrund, -e m.

chassis, n. Fahrgestell, -e nt.

chaste, adj. züchtig, keusch.

chasten, vb. züchtigen.

chastise, vb. züchtigen.

chastity, n. Keuschheit f.

chat, 1. n. Plauderei', -en f. 2. vb. plaudern.

chateau, n. Chateau', -s nt.

chatter, 1. n. Geschwätz' nt. 2. vb. schwatzen; (teeth) klappern.

chauffeur, n. Fahrer, - m., Chauffeur', -e m.

cheap, adj. billig, (fig.) ordinär'.

cheapen, vb. im Wert herab'setzen.

cheapness, n. Billigkeit, -en f.

cheat, vb. betrü'gen*; (harmless) schummeln.

check, 1. n. (restraint) Hemmnis, -se ni.; (verification) Kontrol'le, -n f.; Überprü'fung, -en f.; (clothes, luggage) Kontroll'marke, -n f.; (bank) Scheck, -s m.; (bill) Rechnung, -en f. 2. vb. (verify) kontrollie'ren, überprü'fen; (luggage) auf•geben*, ab•geben*; (mark) ab•hacken.

checkerboard, n. Damebrett, -er nt.

checkers, n. Damespiel nt.

cheek, n. Backe, -n f., Wange, -n f.

cheer, 1. n. Beifallsruf, -e m. 2. vb. Beifall rufen*; (c. up) auf•muntern.

cheerful, adj. fröhlich.

cheerfulness, n. Fröhlichkeit f.

cheery, adj. heiter.

cheese, n. Käse m.

cheesecloth, n. grobe Gaze, -n f.

chef, n. Küchenchef, -s m.

chemical, 1. chemisches Präparat', -e nt.; **(c. s)** Chemikal'ien pl. **2.** adj. chemisch.

chemist, n. Chemiker, -m.

chemistry, n. Chemie' f.

chemotherapy, n. Chemotherapie' f.

chenille, n. Chenille', -n f.

cherish, vb. schätzen.

cherry, n. Kirsche, -n f.

cherub, n. Cherub, -s or -im or -i'nen m.

chess, n. Schach nt., Schachspiel nt.

chessboard, n. Schachbrett, -er nt.

chessman, n. Schachfigur, -en f.

chest, n. (box) Kiste, -n f.; Truhe, -n f.; (body) Brust f.

chestnut, n. Kasta'nie, -n f.

chevron, n. Dienstgradabzeichen, - nt.

chew, vb. kauen.

chic, adj. schick; elegant'.

chick, n. Küken, - nt.

chicken, n. Huhn, ⸚er nt.

chicken pox, n. Windpocken pl.

chicory, n. Zicho'rie, -n f.

chide, vb. schelten*.

chief, 1. n. Oberhaupt, ⸚er nt. **2.** adj. hauptsächlich; Haupt- (cpds.).

chieftain, n. Häuptling, -e m.

chiffon, n. Chiffon, -s m.

child, n. Kind, -er nt.

childbirth, n. Niederkunft f.

childhood, n. Kindheit, -en f.

childish, adj. kindisch.

childishness, n. Kindhaftigkeit, -en f.

childless, adj. kinderlos.

childlike, adj. kindlich.

chill, 1. n. Frost, ⸚e m.; (fever) Schauer, - m. **2.** vb. auf Eis stellen.

chilliness, n. Kühle f.

chilly, adj. kühl.

chime, 1. n. (chimes) Glockenspiel, -e nt. **2.** vb. läuten.

chimney, n. Schornstein, -e m.

chimpanzee, n. Schimpan'se, -n, -n m.

chin, n. Kinn, -e nt.

china, n. Porzellan', -e nt.

China, n. China nt.

chinchilla, n. Chinchil'la, -s m.

Chinese, 1. n. Chine'se, -n, -n m.; Chine'sin, -nen f. **2.** adj. chine'sisch.

chintz, n. Chintz, -e m.

chip, 1. n. Splitter, - m. **2.** vb. ab-brechen*; ab-splittern.

chiropodist, n. Fußpfleger, - m.

chiropractor, n. Chiroprak'tiker, - m.

chirp, 1. n. Gezirp' nt. **2.** vb. zirpen.

chisel, 1. n. (stone, metal) Meißel, - m.; (wood) Beitel, - m. **2.** vb. meißeln.

chivalrous, adj. ritterlich.

chivalry, n. Ritterlichkeit, -en f.

chive, n. Schnittlauch, m.

chloride, n. Chlorid', -e nt.

chlorine, n. Chlor, -s nt.

chloroform, n. Chloroform' nt.

chocolate, n. Schokola'de, -n f.

choice, n. Wahl, -en f.; (selection) Auswahl, -en f.

choir, n. Chor, ⸚e m.

choke, vb. erwür'gen, erstick'en.

choker, n. Halsband, ⸚er nt.

cholera, n. Cholera f.

choose, vb. wählen.

chop, 1. n. (meat) Kotelett', -s nt. **2.** vb. hacken.

choppy, adj. (sea) unruhig.

choral, adj. Chor- (cpds.).

chord, n. (string) Saite, -n f.; (harmony) Akkord', -e m.

chore, n. Alltagsarbeit, -en f.

choreographer, n. Choreograph', -en, -en m.

choreography, n. Choreographie', -i'en f.

chorus, n. Chor, ⸚e m.; Refrain', -s m.

Christ, n. Christus m.

christen, vb. taufen.

Christendom, n. Christenheit f.

christening, n. Taufe, -n f.

Christian, 1. n. Christ, -en, -en m. **2.** adj. christlich.

Christianity, n. Christentum nt.

Christmas, n. Weihnachten pl.

chrome, chromium, n. Chrom nt.

chronic, adj. chronisch.

chronicle, n. Chronik, -en f.

chronological, adj. chronolo'gisch.

chronology, n. Chronologie', -i'en f.

chrysanthemum, n. Chrysanthe'me, -n f.

chubby, adj. dicklich.

chuckle, vb. vergnügt'lachen.

chug, n. daher'keuchen.

chunk, n. Stück, -e nt.

church, n. Kirche, -n f.

churchyard, n. Kirchhof, ⸚e m.

churn, 1. n. Butterfaß, ⸚sser nt. **2.** vb. buttern; (fig.) auf-wühlen.

chute, n. (mail) Postschacht, ⸚e m.; (laundry) Wäscheschacht, ⸚e m.

cider, n. Apfelwein, -e m.

cigar, n. Zigar're, -n f.

cigarette, n. Zigaret'te, -n f.

cinch, n. Sattelgurt, -e m.; (fam.) Kleinigkeit, -en f.

cinder, n. Asche, -n f.

cinema, n. Kino, -s nt.

cinnamon, n. Zimt m.

cipher, n. (number) Ziffer, -n

f.; (zero) Null, -en f.; (code) Chiffre, -n f.

circle, n. Kreis, -en m.

circuit, n. (course) Umkreis, -e m.; (elec.) Stromkreis, -e m.; (short c.) Kurzschluß, ⸚sse m.

circuitous, adj. umwegig.

circular, 1. n. Rundschreiben, - nt. **2.** adj. kreisförmig.

circulate, vb. zirkulie'ren.

circulation, n. (blood) Kreislauf, ⸚e m.; (paper) Auflage, -n f.; (money) Umlauf, ⸚e m.

circulatory, adj. zirkulie'rend.

circumcise, vb. beschnei'den*.

circumcision, n. Beschnei'dung, -en f.

circumference, n. Umfang, ⸚e m.

circumlocution, n. Umschrei'bung, -en f.

circumscribe, vb. (geom.) umschrei'ben*; (delimit) begren'zen.

circumspect, adj. umsichtig.

circumstance, n. Umstand, ⸚e m.; (pl.) Verhält'nisse pl.

circumstantial, adj. eingehend; (c. evidence) Indi'zienbeweis, -e m.

circumvent, vb. umge'hen*.

circumvention, n. Umge'hung, -en f.

circus, n. Zirkus, -se m.

cirrhosis, n. Zirrho'se, -n f.

cistern, n. Zister'ne, -n f.

citadel, n. Zitadel'le, -n f.

citation, n. Auszeichnung, -en f.; (law) Vorladung, -en f.

cite, vb. an-führen, zitie'ren; (law) vor-laden*.

citizen, n. Bürger, - m.

citizenship, n. Staatsangehörigkeit, -en f.

city, n. Stadt, ⸚e f. (cpds.).

civic, adj. Bürger- (cpds.).

civil, adj. bürgerlich; (law) zivil'rechtlich; (polite) höflich.

civilian, 1. n. Zivilist', -en, -en m. **2.** adj. bürgerlich.

civility, n. Höflichkeit, -en f.

civilization, n. Zivilisation', -en f.

civilize, vb. zivilisie'ren.

civilized, adj. zivilisiert'.

clad, adj. geklei'det.

claim, 1 n. Anspruch, ⸚e m. **2.** vb. bean'spruchen, fordern.

claimant, n. Bean'spruchend- m.&f.

clairvoyance, n. Hellsehen nt.

clairvoyant, 1. n. Hellseher, - m. **2.** adj. hellseherisch.

clammy, adj. feuchtkalt.

clamor, 1. n. Geschrei' nt. **2.** vb. schreien*.

clamp, 1. n. Klammer, -n f. **2.** vb. fest-klammern.

clandestine, adj. heimlich.

clap, vb. klatschen.

claret, n. Rotwein, -e m.

clarification, n. Klarstellung, -en f.

clarify, vb. klar-stellen.

clarinet, n. Klarinet'te, -n f.

clarity, n. Klarheit, -en f.

clash, 1. n. Zusam'menstoß, ∺ m. **2.** vb. zusam'men-stoßen*; (fig.) sich nicht vertra'gen*.

clasp, 1. n. Schnalle, -n f.; (hands) Händedruck m. **2.** vb. fest-schnallen; (grasp) um-fas'sen; (embrace) umar'men.

class, n. Klasse, -n f.; (period of instruction) Stunde, -n f.

classic, classical, adj. klassisch.

classicism, n. Klassizis'mus, -men m.

classification, n. Klassifizie'rung, -en f.

classify, vb. klassifizie'ren.

classmate, n. Klassenkamerad, -en, -en m.

classroom, n. Klassenzimmer, - nt.

clatter, 1. n. Geklap'per nt. **2.** vb. klappern.

clause, n. Satzteil, -e m.; (main c.) Hauptsatz, ∺e m.; (subordinate c.) Nebensatz, ∺e m.; (law) Klausel, -n f.

claw, 1. n. Kralle, -n f., Klaue, -n f. **2.** vb. krallen.

clay, n. Ton, -e m., Lehm, -e m.

clean, 1. vb. sauber machen, reinigen. **2.** adj. sauber.

clean-cut, adj. sauber.

cleaner, n. (the c.s) Reinigung, -en f.

cleanliness, cleanness, n. Sauberkeit f.

cleanse, vb. reinigen.

clear, 1. vb. klären; (profit) rein verdie'nen; (weather) sich auf-klären. **2.** adj. klar.

clearance, n. (enough space) Raum m.; (sale) Räumung, -en f.; (approval) Gutheißung f.

clearing, n. Lichtung, -en f.

clearness, n. Klarheit, -en f.

cleat, n. (naut.) Klampe, -n f.; (on boots) Krampe, -n f.

cleavage, n. Spaltung, -en f.

cleave, vb. spalten*.

cleaver, n. Fleischerbeil, -e nt.

clef, n. Notenschlüssel, - m.

cleft, 1. n. Spalte, -n f. **2.** adj. gespal'ten.

clemency, n. Milde f.

clench, vb. zusam'men-pressen; (fist) ballen.

clergy, n. Geistlichkeit f.

clergyman, n. Geistlich, -en m.

clerical, adj. (eccles.) geistlich, klerikal'; (writing) Schreib- (cpds.).

clerk, n. Schreiber, - m.; (salesc.) Verkäu'fer, - m., Verkäu'ferin, -nen f.

clever, adj. klug (∺), geschickt', schlau.

cleverness, n. Klugheit, -en f., Geschick'lichkeit, -en f.

clew, n. (object) Knäuel, - nt.; (fact) Anhaltspunkt, -e m., Schlüssel, - m.

cliché, n. Klischee', -s nt.

click, 1. n. Klicken nt.; (lan-guage) Schnalzlaut, -e m. **2.** vb. klicken, knacken.

client, n. Kunde, -n, -n m., Klient', -en, -en m.

clientele, n. Kundschaft, -en f.

cliff, n. Klippe, -n f.

climate, n. Klima, -s or a'te nt.

climatic, adj. klima'tisch.

climax, n. Höhepunkt, -e m.

climb, vb. (intr.) steigen*, klettern; (tr.) erstei'gen*.

climber, n. Kletterer, - m.

clinch, vb. fest-machen; (fig.) den Ausschlag geben*.

cling, vb. sich an-klammern.

clinic, n. Klinik, -en f.

clinical, adj. klinisch.

clip, 1. n. Klammer, -n f.; (jewelry) Schmucknadel, -n f. **2.** vb. beschnei'den*.

clippers, n.pl. Schere, -n f.; (barber) Haarschneidemaschine, -n f.

clipping, n. (newspaper) Zeitungsausschnitt, -e m.

clique, n. Clique, -n f.

cloak, n. Mantel, ∺ m.

cloakroom, n. Gardero'be, -n f.

clock, n. Uhr, -en f.

clod, n. Klumpen, - m.

clog, 1. n. Holzschuh, -e m. **2.** vb. verstop'fen.

cloister, n. Kloster, ∺ nt.; (arch.) Kreuzgang, ∺e m.

clone, n. Klon, -s nt.

close, 1. adj. (narrow) eng. knapp; (near) nah (∺). **2.** vb. schließen*, zu-machen.

closeness, n. Enge, -n f., Nähe, -n f.

closet, n. Wandschrank, ∺e m.

clot, 1. n. Klumpen, - m. **2.** vb. gerin'nen*.

cloth, n. Tuch, ∺er nt., Stoff, -e m.

clothe, vb. kleiden.

clothes, n.pl. Kleider pl.

clothing, n. Kleidung, -en f.

cloud, n. Wolke, -n f.

cloudburst, n. Wolkenbruch, ∺e m.

cloudiness, n. Bewölkt'heit f.

cloudy, adj. bewölkt', trübe.

clove, n. Gewürz'nelke, -n f.

clover, n. Klee m.

clown, n. Clown, -s m.

cloy, vb. übersät'tigen.

club, n. (group) Klub, -s m.; (stick) Keule, -n f.

clubs, n. (cards) Treff nt.

clue, n. Anhaltspunkt, -e m., Schlüssel, - m.

clump, n. Klumpen, - m.

clumsiness, n. Ungeschicklichkeit, -en f.

clumsy, adj. ungeschickt.

cluster, 1. n. Büschel, - m. **2.** vb. sich zusam'men-scharen.

clutch, 1. n. (auto) Kuppelung, -en f. **2.** vb. packen.

clutter, vb. umher'-streuen.

coach, 1. n. Kutsche, -n f.; (train) Eisenbahnwagen, - m.; (sports) Trainer, - m.; (tutor) Privat'lehrer, - m. **2.** vb. (sports) trainie'ren; (tutor) Privat'stunden geben*.

coagulate, vb. gerin'nen*.

coagulation, n. Gerin'nen nt.

coal, n. Kohle, -n f.

coalesce, vb. verschmel'zen*.

coalition, n. Koalition', -en f.

coarse, adj. grob (∺).

coarsen, vb. vergrö'bern.

coarseness, n. Grobheit, -en f.

coast, n. Küste, -n f.

coastal, adj. Küsten- (cpds.).

coaster, n. Küstenfahrer, - m.

coat, n. (suit) Jacke, -n f.; (overcoat) Mantel, ∺ m.

coating, n. Überzug, ∺e m.

coat of arms, n. Wappen, - nt.

coax, vb. überre'den.

cobalt, n. Kobalt m.

cobblestone, n. Kopfstein, -e m.

cobweb, n. Spinngewebe, - nt.

cocaine, n. Kokain' nt.

cock, 1. n. Hahn, ∺e m. **2.** vb. (gun) spannen.

cockeyed, adj. schielend; (crazy) verrückt'.

cockpit, n. Führersitz, -e m.

cockroach, n. Küchenschabe, -n f.

cocktail, n. Cocktail, -s m.

cocky, adj. frech.

cocoa, n. Kaka'o, -s m.

coconut, n. Kokosnuß, ∺sse f.

cocoon, n. Kokon', -s m.

cod, n. Kabeljau, -e m.

C. O. D., adv. per Nachnahme.

coddle, vb. verpäp'peln.

code, n. (law) Kodex, -dizes m.; (secret) Kode, -s m.

codeine, n. Kodein' nt.

codfish, n. Kabeljau, -e m.

codify, vb. kodifizie'ren.

cod-liver oil, n. Lebertran m.

coeducation, n. Koedukation' f.

coerce, vb. zwingen*.

coercion, n. Zwang m.

coexist, vb. koexistie'ren.

coffee, n. Kaffee m.

coffin, n. Sarg, ∺e m.

cog, n. Zahn, ∺e m.; (c. railway) Zahnradbahn, -en f.

cogent, adj. zwingend.

cogitate, vb. nach-denken*.

cognizance, n. Kenntnis, -se f.

cognizant, adj. bewußt'.

cogwheel, n. Zahnrad, ∺er nt.

cohere, vb. zusam'men-hängen*.

coherent, adj. zusam'menhängend.

cohesion, n. Kohäsion' f.

cohesive, adj. kohärent'.

cohort, n. Kohor'te, -n f.

coiffure, n. Frisur', -en f.

coil, 1. n. Rolle, -n f.; (elec.) Spule, -n f. **2.** vb. auf-rollen; (rope) auf-schießen*.

coin, 1. n. Münze, -n f. **2.** vb. prägen.

coinage, *n.* Prägung, -en *f.*

coincide, *vb.* zusam·men·treffen*.

coincidence, *n.* Zufall, ⸗e *m.*

coincident, *adj.* gleichzeitig.

coincidental, *adj.* zufällig.

cold, 1. *n.* Kälte, -n *f.; (med.)* Erkäl·tung, -en *f.* **2.** *adj.* kalt (⸗).

cold-blooded, *adj.* kaltblütig.

collaborate, *vb.* zusam·men·arbeiten, mit·arbeiten.

collaboration, *n.* Mitarbeit *f.*

collaborator, *n.* Mitarbeiter, - *m.*

collapse, 1. *n.* Zusam·men·bruch ⸗e *m.* **2.** *vb.* zusam·men·brechen*.

collar, *n.* Krage, - *m.*

collarbone, *n.* Schlüsselbein, -e *nt.*

collate, *vb.* verglei·chen*.

collateral, 1. *n. (econ.)* Deckung *f.* **2.** *adj.* kollateral·.

colleague, *n.* Kolle·ge, -n, -n *m.*

collect, *vb.* sammeln; *(money)* ein·kassieren.

collection, *n.* Sammlung, -en *f.; (church)* Kollek·te, -n *f.*

collective, *adj.* kollektiv·.

collector, *n. (art.)* Sammler, - *m.; (tickets)* Schaffner, - *m.; (tax)* Steuereinnehmer, - *m.*

college, *n.* College, -s *nt.*

collegiate, *adj.* College- *(cpds.).*

collide, *vb.* zusam·men·stoßen*.

collision, *n.* Zusam·menstoß, ⸗e *m.*

colloquial, *adj.* umgangssprachlich.

colloquialism, *n.* umgangssprachlicher Ausdruck, ⸗e *m.*

collusion, *n.* Kollusion·, -en *f.*

Cologne, *n.* Köln *nt.*

colon, *n. (typogr.)* Doppelpunkt, -e *m., (med.)* Dickdarm, ⸗e *m.,* Kolon, -s or Kola *nt.*

colonel, *n.* Oberst, -en, -en *m.*

colonial, *adj.* kolonial·.

colonist, *n.* Siedler, - *m.,* Kolonist·, -en, -en *m.*

colonization, *n.* Kolonisation·, -en *f.*

colonize, *vb.* kolonisie·ren.

colony, *n.* Kolonie·, -i'en *f.*

color, 1. *n.* Farbe, -n *f.* **2.** *vb.* färben.

colored, *adj.* farbig.

colorful, *adj.* farbenreich.

coloring, *n.* Färbung, -en *f.*

colorless, *adj.* farblos.

colossal, *adj.* kolossal·.

colt, *n.* Fohlen, - *nt.*

column, *n. (arch.)* Säule, -n *f.; (typogr.)* Spalte, -n *f.; (mil.)* Kolon·ne, -n *f.*

columnist, *n.* Zeitungsartikelschreiber, - *m.*

coma, *n.* Koma *nt.*

comb, 1. *n.* Kamm, ⸗e *m.* **2.** *vb.* kämmen.

combat, 1. *n.* Kampf, ⸗e *m.* **2.** *vb.* bekäm·pfen.

combatant, *n.* Kämpfer, - *m.*

combination, *n.* Kombination·, -en *f.*

combine, *vb.* verbin·den*, verei·nigen, zusam·men·setzen, kombinie·ren.

combustible, *adj.* (ver)brenn·bar.

combustion, *n.* Verbren·nung *f.*

come, *vb.* kommen*.

comedian, *n.* Komiker, - *m.*

comedienne, *n.* Komikerin, -nen *f.*

comedy, *n.* Komö·die, -n *f.*

come in, *interj.* herein'!

comely, *adj.* hübsch.

comet, *n.* Komet·, -en, -en *m.*

comfort, 1. *n.* Behag·lichkeit, -en *f.,* Bequem·lichkeit, -en *f.* **2.** *vb.* trösten.

comfortable, *adj.* behag·lich, bequem·.

comforter, *n.* Steppdecke, -n *f.*

comic, comical, *adj.* komisch.

comma, *n.* Komma, -s or -ta *nt.*

command, 1. *n.* Befehl·, -e *m.* **2.** *vb.* befeh·len*.

commandeer, *vb.* requirie·ren.

commander, *n.* Befehls·haber, - *m.; (navy)* Fregat·tenkapitän, -e *m.*

commander in chief, *n.* Oberbefehlshaber, - *m.*

commandment, *n.* Gebot·, -e *nt.*

commemorate, *vb.* geden·ken*.

commemoration, *n.* Gedächt·nisfeier, -n *f.*

commemorative, *adj.* Gedächt·nis- *(cpds.).*

commence, *vb.* begin·nen*.

commencement, *n.* Anfang, ⸗e *m.; (college)* akade·mische Abschlußfeier, -n *f.*

commend, *vb. (praise)* loben; *(recommend)* empfeh·len*.

commendable, *adj.* lobenswert.

commendation, *n.* Lob *nt.,* Auszeichnung, -en *f.*

commensurate, *adj.* angemessen.

comment, 1. *n.* Bemerkung, -en *f.* **2.** *vb.* bemer·ken.

commentary, *n.* Kommentar·, - *e m.*

commentator, *n.* Kommenta·tor, -o'ren *m.*

commerce, *n.* Handel *m.*

commercial, *adj.* kommerziell·, kaufmännisch; *(cpds.)* Handels-.

commercialism, *n.* Handelsgeist *m.*

commercialize, *vb.* in den Handel bringen*.

commiserate, *vb.* bemit·leiden.

commissary, *n.* Kommissar·, -e *m.; (store)* Militärversor·gungsstelle, -n *f.*

commission, 1. *n. (committee)* Kommission·, -en *f.; (percentage)* Provision·, -en *f.; (assignment)* Auftrag, ⸗e *m.* **2.**

vb. beauf·tragen; *(mil.)* das Offiziers'patent verlei·hen*.

commissioner, *n.* Beauf·tragt· *m.*

commit, *vb. (give over)* an·vertrauen; *(crime)* bege·hen*; *(oneself)* sich verpflich·ten.

commitment, *n.* Verpflich·tung, -en *f.*

committee, *n.* Ausschuß, ⸗sse *m.*

commodity, *n.* Ware, -n *f.*

common, *adj.* allgemein·, gewöhn·lich; *(vulgar)* ordinär·.

Common Market, *n.* EG *f.;* Europä·ische Gemein·schaft *f.*

commonness, *n.* Häufigkeit *f.*

commonplace, 1. *n.* Gemein·platz, ⸗e *m.* **2.** *adj.* abgedroschen.

commonwealth, *n.* Commonwealth *nt.*

commotion, *n.* Aufruhr *m.*

communal, *adj.* Gemein·de- *(cpds.).*

commune, 1. *n.* Gemein·de, -n *f.* **2.** *vb.* Kommunizie·ren.

communicable, *adj.* mitteilbar; *(med.)* ansteckbar.

communicant, *n.* Kommunikant·, -en, -en *m.*

communicate, *vb.* mit·teilen.

communication, *n.* Mitteilung, -en *f.*

communicative, *adj.* mitteilsam.

communion, *n.* Gemein·schaft *f.; (eccl.)* Abendmahl *nt.; (Catholic)* Kommunion·, -en *f.*

communiqué, *n.* Kommuniqué· -s *nt.*

communism, *n.* Kommunismus *m.*

communist, 1. *n.* Kommunist·, -en, -en *m.* **2.** *adj.* kommunistisch.

communistic, *adj.* kommunistisch.

community, *n.* Gemein·de, -n *f.,* Gemein·schaft, -en *f.*

commutation, *n.* Austausch *m.; (law)* Milderung *f.*

commute, *vb.* täglich von der Vorstadt in die Stadt fahren und zurück; *(law)* herab·setzen.

commuter, *n.* Pendler *m.*

compact, 1. *n. (cosmetics)* Puderdose, -n *f.* **2.** *adj.* kompakt·.

compactness, *n.* Kompakt·heit *f.*

companion, *n.* Beglei·ter *m.*

companionable, *adj.* gesel·lig.

companionship, *n.* Kamerad·schaft, -en *f.*

company, *n.* Gesell·schaft, -en *f.,* Firma, -men *f.*

comparable, *adj.* vergleich·bar.

comparative, 1. *n. (gram.)* Komparativ·, -e *m.* **2.** *adj.* verhält·nismäßig.

compare, *vb.* verglei·chen*.

mparison, n. Vergleich', -e

mpartment, n. Abtei'lung, - n f., Fach, -er nt.; (train) Ab- zil, -e nt.

mpass, n. (naut.) Kompaß, -se m.; (geom.) Zirkel, - m.

mpassion, n. Mitleid nt., Er- ar'men nt.

mpassionate, adj. mitleidig.

mpatible, adj. verträg'lich.

mpatriot, n. Landsmann, ъcute m.

mpel, vb. zwingen*.

mpensate, vb. entschä'digen, ompensie'ren.

mpensation, n. Entschä'di- ung, -en f., Kompensation', en f.

mpete, vb. wetteifern, kon- urrie'ren.

mpetence, n. (ability) Fähig- eit, -en f.; (field of responsi- ility) Zuständigkeit, -en f.

mpetent, adj. (able) fähig; responsible) zuständig.

mpetition, n. Wettbewerb, -e n., Konkurrenz', -en f.

mpetitive, adj. auf Konkur- enz' eingestellt.

mpetitor, n. Mitbewerber, - n., Konkurrent', -en, -en m.

mpile, vb. zusam'men·tra- gen*.

mplacency, n. Selbstzufrie- denheit f.

mplacent, adj. selbstzufrie- den.

mplain, vb. sich bekla'gen, sich beschwe'ren.

mplaint, n. Klage, -n f., Be- schwer'de, -n f.

mplement, 1. n. Ergän'zung, -en f. 2. vb. ergän'zen.

mplete, 1. vb. vollen'den. 2. adj. vollständig, fertig.

mpletely, adv. völlig.

mpletion, n. Vollen'dung, -en f.

mplex, 1. n. Komplex', -e m. 2. adj. komplex', weitläufig.

mplexion, n. (type) Natur' f.; (skin) Teint, -s m.

mplexity, n. Weitläufigkeit, - en f.

mpliance, n. Bereit'willigkeit f., Einwilligen n.

mpliant, adj. bereit'willig, nachgiebig.

mplicate, vb. (make more complex) verwi'ckeln; (make harder) erschwe'ren.

mplicated, adj. kompliziert', verwi'ckelt.

mplication, n. Komplika- tion', -en f.

mpliment, 1. n. Kompli- ment', -e nt. 2. vb. beglück'- wünschen.

mplimentary, adj. schmei- chelhaft; (free) Frei- (cpds.).

mply, vb. ein·willigen, sich fügen.

mponent, n. Bestand'teil, -e m.

compose, vb. zusam'men· setzen; (music) komponie'- ren.

composer, n. Komponist', -en, -en m.

composite, adj. zusam'menge- setzt.

composition, n. Zusam'men- setzung, -en f.; (school) Auf- satz, -e m.; (mus.) Komposition', -en f.

composure, n. Fassung f.

compote, n. Kompott', -e nt.

compound, 1. n. Mischung, -en f.; (gram.) Kompo'situm, -ta nt.; (chem.) Verbin'dung, - en f.; (mil.) eingezäunte La- gerabteilung, -en f. 2. adj. zu- sam'mengesetzt; (c. interest) Zinseszins m. 3. vb. zusam'- men·setzen.

comprehend, vb. verste'hen*, begrei'fen*.

comprehensible, adj. ver- ständ'lich.

comprehension, n. Fassungs- vermögen, - nt.

comprehensive, adj. umfas'- send.

compress, 1. n. Kompres'se, -n f. 2 vb. zusam'men·pressen.

compressed, adj. Press- (cpds.).

compression, n. Kompression', -en f.

comprise, vb. umfas'sen, ent- hal'ten*.

compromise, 1. n. Kom- promiß', -sse m. 2. vb. einen Kompromiß schließen*; (em- barrass) kompromittie'ren.

compulsion, n. Zwang m.

compulsive, adj. Zwangs- (cpds.).

compulsory, adj. obligato'- risch.

compunction, n. Beden'ken, - nt.

computation, n. Berech'nung, -en f.

compute, vb. rechnen, berech'- nen.

computer, n. Komputer, - m.; Elektro'nenrechner, - m.

computerize, vb. auf Kompu- ter umstellen.

computer science, n. Kompu'- terwissenschaft f.

comrade, n. Kamerad', -en, -en m.

concave, adj. konkav'.

conceal, vb. verste'cken, ver- heim'lichen.

concealment, n. Versteck', -e nt., Verheim'lichung, -en f.

concede, vb. zu·gestehen*.

conceit, n. Einbildung, -en f.

conceited, adj. eingebildet.

conceivable, adj. vorstellbar.

conceivably, adv. unter Um- ständen.

conceive, vb. begrei'fen*, sich vor·stellen; (child) empfan'- gen*.

concentrate, vb. konzentrie'- ren.

concentration camp, n. Kon- zentrations'lager, - nt.

concept, n. Begriff', -e m.

concern, 1. n. (affair) Angele- genheit, -en f.; (interest) Inte- res'se, -n nt.; (firm) Konzern', -e m.; (worry) Sorge, -n f. 2. vb. an·gehen*.

concerning, prep. hinsichtlich.

concert, n. Konzert', -e nt.

concession, n. Konzession', - en f.

concierge, n. Portier', -s m.

conciliate, vb. versöh'nen, schlichten.

conciliation, n. Versöh'nung, -en f., Schlichtung, -en f.

conciliator, n. Schlichter, - m.

conciliatory, adj. versöh'nend.

concise, adj. knapp, gedrängt'.

conciseness, n. Gedrängt'heit f.

conclude, vb. schließen*.

conclusion, n. Abschluß, -sse m, Schluß, -sse m.

conclusive, adj. entschei'dend.

concoct, vb. zusam'men· brauen.

concoction, n. Gebräu, -e nt.

concomitant, adj. beglei'tend.

concord, n. Eintracht f.

concourse, n. Sammelplatz, -e m.

concrete, 1. n. Zement' m. 2. adj. konkret'.

concubine, n. Konkubi'ne, -n f.

concur, vb. überein'·stimmen.

concurrence, n. Zustimmung, - en f.

concurrent, adj. (simultaneous) gleichzeitig; (agreeing) über- ein'stimmend.

concussion, n. Erschüt'terung, -en f.; (brain) Gehirn'erschüt- terung, -en f.

condemn, vb. verur'teilen; (dis- approve) mißbil'ligen.

condemnable, adj. strafbar; nichtswürdig.

condemnation, n. Verur'teilung f.; Mißbilligung f.

condensation, n. Kondensa- tion', -en f.; (summary) Zu- sam'menfassung, -en f.

condense, vb. kondensie'ren; (summarize) zusam'men·fas- sen.

condenser, n. Kondensa'tor, -o'ren m.

condescend, vb. sich herab'· lassen*.

condescending, adj. herab'las- send.

condescension, n. Herab'las- sung, -en f.

condiment, n. Gewürz', -e nt.

condition, 1. n. (stipulation) Bedin'gung, -en f.; (state) Zu- stand, -e m. 2. vb. bedin'gen; (training) in Form bringen*.

conditional, adj. abhängig.

conditionally, *adv.* unter gewissen Bedingungen.

condolence, *n.* Beileid *nt.*

condominium, *n.* Eigentumswohnung, -en *f.*

condone, *vb.* entschul'digen.

conducive, *adj.* förderlich.

conduct, 1. *n.* Betra'gen *nt.* **2.** *vb.* leiten; *(behave)* sich betra'gen*; *(music)* dirigie'ren.

conductor, *n.* Leiter, - *m.;* *(train)* Schaffner, - *m.; (music)* Dirigent', -en, -en *m.*

conduit, *n.* Leitungsrohr, -e *nt.*

cone, *n.* Kegel, - *m.; (pine)* Tannenzapfen, - *m.*

confection, *n.* Konfekt', -e *nt.*

confectioner, *n.* Zuckerbäcker, - *m.*

confectionery, *n.* Zuckerwerk *nt.*

confederacy, *n.* Bündnis, -se *nt.; (conspiracy)* Verschwö'rung, -en *f.*

confederate, 1. *n.* Helfershelfer, - *m.* **2.** *adj.* verbün'det.

confederation, *n.* Staatenbund, ‑e *m.*

confer, *vb. (bestow)* verlei'hen*; *(counsel)* berat'schlagen.

conference, *n.* Bespre'chung, -en *f.,* Konferenz', -en *f.*

confess, *vb.* zu·geste'hen*; *(eccles.)* beichten.

confession, *n.* Geständ'nis, -se *nt.; (eccles.)* Beichte, -n *f.*

confessional, *n.* Beichtstuhl, ‑e *m.*

confessor, *n.* Beken'ner, - *m.; (father c.)* Beichtvater, ‑ *m.*

confidant, *n.* Vertraut'- *m.*

confidante, *n.* Vertraut'- *f.*

confide, *vb.* vertrau'en; sich an·vertrauen.

confidence, *n. (trust)* Vertrau'en *nt.; (assurance)* Zuversicht *f.*

confident, *adj.* zuversichtlich.

confidential, *adj.* vertrau'lich.

confidentially, *adv.* unter uns.

confine, *vb.* beschrän'ken; *(imprison)* ein·sperren.

confirm, *vb.* bestä'tigen; *(church)* konfirmie'ren.

confirmation, *n.* Bestä'tigung, -en *f.; (church)* Konfirmation', -en *f.*

confiscate, *vb.* beschlag'nahmen, konfiszie'ren.

confiscation, *n.* Beschlag'nahme, -n *f.*

conflagration, *n.* Brand, ‑e *m.,* Feuersbrunst *f.*

conflict, 1. *n.* Konflikt', -e *m.* **2.** *vb.* in Widerspruch stehen*, nicht überein'stimmen.

conform, *vb.* sich an·passen.

conformation, *n.* Anpassung, -en *f.; (shape)* Gestal'tung, -en *f.*

conformer, conformist, *n.* Mitmacher, - *m.*

conformity, *n.* Überein'stimmung, -en *f.*

confound, *vb. (make confused)* verwir'ren; **(c. A with B)** A mit B verwech'seln; **(c. it!)** zum Donnerwetter!

confront, *vb.* gegen'überstellen, konfrontie'ren.

confuse, *vb. (make confused)* verwir'ren; **(c. A with B)** A mit B verwech'seln.

confusion, *n.* Verwir'rung, -en *f.;* Durcheinan'der *nt.;* Verwechs'lung, -en *f.*

congeal, *vb.* erstar'ren.

congenial, *adj.* sympa'thisch.

congenital, *adj.* angeboren.

congestion, *n.* Stauung, -en *f.*

conglomerate, 1. *n.* Anhäufung, -en *f.* **2.** *vb.* zusam'men·ballen.

conglomeration, *n.* Anhäufung, -en *f.*

congratulate, *vb.* gratulie'ren, beglück'wünschen.

congratulation, *n.* Glückwunsch, ‑e *m.*

congratulatory, *adj.* Glückwunsch- *(cpds.).*

congregate, *vb.* sich versam'meln.

congregation, *n. (church)* Gemein'de, -n *f.*

congress, *n.* Kongreß', -sse *m.*

congressional, *adj.* Kon·greß'- *(cpds.).*

conjecture, 1. *n.* Mutmaßung, -en *f.* **2.** *vb.* mutmaßen.

conjugal, *adj.* ehelich.

conjugate, *vb.* konjugie'ren.

conjugation, *n.* Konjugation', -en *f.*

conjunction, *n.* Zusam'mentreffen, - *nt.; (gram.)* Bindewort, ‑er *nt.,* Konjunktion', -en *f.*

conjunctive, *adj.* verbin'dend.

conjunctivitis, *n.* Bindehautentzündung, -en *f.*

conjure, *vb.* zaubern.

connect, *vb.* verbin'den*.

connection, *n.* Verbin'dung, -en *f.*

connive, *vb.* in heimlichem Einverständnis stehen*.

connoisseur, *n.* Kenner, - *m.*

connotation, *n.* Nebenbedeutung, -en *f.,* Beiklang, ‑e *m.*

connote, *vb.* in sich schließen*.

conquer, *vb.* ero'bern.

conqueror, *n.* Ero'berer, - *m.*

conquest, *n.* Ero'berung, -en *f.*

conscience, *n.* Gewis'sen, - *nt.*

conscientious, *adj.* gewis'senhaft.

conscious, *adj.* bewußt', bei Bewußt'sein.

consciousness, *n.* Bewußt'sein *nt.*

conscript, *n.* Dienstpflichtige- *m.*

conscription, *n.* Militär'dienstpflicht *f.*

consecrate, *vb.* weihen.

consecration, *n.* Weihung, -en *f.*

consecutive, *adj.* aufeinan'derfolgend.

consensus, *n.* allgemeine Meinung, -en *f.*

consent, 1. *n.* Zustimmung, -en *f.* **2.** *vb.* zu·stimmen.

consequence, *n.* Folge, -n *f.*

consequent, *adj.* folgend.

consequential, *adj.* folgenreich.

consequently, *adv.* folglich.

conservation, *n.* Bewah'rung, -en *f.;* Konservie'rung, -en *f.*

conservatism, *n.* Konservatis'mus *m.*

conservative, *adj.* konservativ'.

conservatory, *n. (music)* Konservato'rium, -rien *nt.; (plants)* Treibhaus, ‑er *nt.*

conserve, *vb.* bewah'ren.

consider, *vb.* betrach'ten; *(take into account)* berück'sichtigen.

considerable, *adj.* beträcht'lich.

considerate, *adj.* rücksichtsvoll.

consideration, *n. (thought)* Erwä'gung, -en *f.; (kindness)* Rücksicht, -en *f.;* **(in c. of)** in Anbetracht.

consign, *vb.* übersen'den*.

consignment, *n.* Übersen'dung, -en *f.*

consist, *vb.* beste'hen*.

consistency, *n.* Folgerichtigkeit *f.; (substance)* Konsistenz' *f.*

consistent, *adj.* folgerichtig, konsequent'.

consolation, *n.* Trost *m.*

console, *vb.* trösten.

consolidate, *vb.* festigen, konsolidie'ren.

consommé, *n.* Bouillon', -s *f.*

consonant, *n.* Konsonant', -en, -en *m.*

consort, 1. *n.* Gemahl', -e *m.;* Gemah'lin, -nen *f.* **2.** *vb.* verkeh'ren.

conspicuous, *adj.* auffällig.

conspiracy, *n.* Verschwö'rung, -en *f.*

conspirator, *n.* Verschwö'rer, - *m.*

conspire, *vb.* sich verschwö'ren*.

constancy, *n.* Standhaftigkeit *f.*

constant, *adj.* bestän'dig, konstant'.

constantly, *adv.* dauernd.

constellation, *n.* Konstellation', -en *f.*

consternation, *n.* Bestür'zung, -en *f.*

constipated, *adj.* verstopft'.

constipation, *n.* Verstop'fung, -en *f.*

constituency, *n. (people)* Wählerschaft, -en *f.; (place)* Wahlbezirk, -e *m.*

constituent, *n.* Bestand'teil, -e *m.; (voter)* Wähler, - *m.*

constitute, vb. (make up) ausmachen; (found) gründen.

constitution, n. Konstitution', -en f.; (government) Verfas'sung, -en f.

constitutional, adj. konstitutionell'.

constrain, vb. zwingen*.

constrict, vb. zusam'menziehen*.

construct, vb. konstruie'ren.

construction, n. Konstruktion', -en f.

constructive, adj. positiv.

construe, vb. aus·legen.

consul, n. Konsul, -n, m.

consular, adj. konsula'risch.

consulate, n. Konsulat', -e nt.

consult, vb. zu Rate ziehen*; konsultie'ren.

consultant, n. Bera'ter, - m.

consultation, n. Konferenz', -en f.; (med.) Konsultation', -en f.

consume, vb. verzeh'ren, verbrau'chen.

consumer, n. Verbrau'cher, - m.

consummate, 1. vb. vollen'den. 2. adj. vollen'det.

consummation, n. Vollzie'hung, -en f.

consumption, n. Verbrauch' m.; (med.) Schwindsucht f.

consumptive, adj. schwindsüchtig.

contact, 1. n. Kontakt', -e m. 2. vb. sich in Verbin'dung setzen mit.

contagion, n. Ansteckung, -en f.

contagious, adj. ansteckend.

contain, vb. enthal'ten*.

container, n. Behäl'ter, - m.

contaminate, vb. verunrei'nigen.

contemplate, vb. betrach'ten.

contemplation, n. Betrach'tung, -en f.

contemplative, adj. nachdenklich.

contemporary, 1. n. Zeitgenosse, -n, -n, m. 2. adj. zeitgenössisch.

contempt, n. Verach'tung, -en f.

contemptible, adj. verach'tenswert.

contemptuous, adj. verächt'lich.

contend, vb. (assert) behaup'ten; (fight) streiten*.

contender, n. Streiter, - m.

content, 1. n. Inhalt m. 2. adj. zufrie'den.

contented, adj. zufrie'den.

contention, n. (assertion) Behaup'tung, -en f.; (fight) Streit, -e m.

contentment, n. Zufrie'denheit f.

contest, 1. n. Wettstreit, -e m.; (advertising) Preisausschreiben, - nt. 2. vb. bestrei'ten*.

contestant, n. Bewer'ber, - m.

context, n. Zusam'menhang, -̈e m.

continent, 1. n. Kontinent, -e m. 2. adj. enthalt'sam.

continental, adj. kontinental'.

contingency, n. Eventualität', -en f.

continual, adj. dauernd.

continuation, n. Fortsetzung, -en f.

continue, vb. (tr.) fort·setzen; (intr.) fort·fahren*.

continuity, n. Fortdauer f.

continuous, adj. fortdauernd.

contort, vb. verdre'hen.

contortion, n. Verdre'hung, -en f.

contour, n. Umriß, -sse m.

contraband, n. Schmuggelware, -n f.

contraception, n. Schwangerschaftsverhütung f.

contraceptive device, n. Verhütungsmittel, - nt.

contract, 1. n. Vertrag', -̈e m. 2. vb. vertrag'lich abschließen*; (disease) sich zuziehen*.

contraction, n. Zusam'menziehung, -en f.

contractor, n. Bauunternehmer, - m.

contradict, vb. widerspre'chen*.

contradiction, n. Widerspruch, -̈e m.

contradictory, adj. widerspre'chend.

contralto, n. Altstimme, -n f.

contraption, n. Vorrichtung, -en f.

contrary, 1. n. Gegenteil, -e nt. 2. adj. (opposite) entge'gengesetzt; (obstinate) widerspenstig.

contrast, 1. n. Gegensatz, -̈e m. 2. vb. entge'gen·setzen.

contribute, vb. bei·tragen*.

contribution, n. Beitrag, -̈e m.

contributor, n. Beiträger, - m.

contributory, adj. mitwirkend.

contrite, adj. zerknirscht'.

contrivance, n. Vorrichtung, -en f.

contrive, vb. fertig bringen*, erfin'den*.

control, 1. n. Kontrol'le, -n f. 2. vb. beherr'schen.

controllable, adj. kontrollier'bar.

controller, n. Überprü'fer, - m.

controversial, adj. strittig.

controversy, n. Streitfrage, -n f.

contusion, n. Quetschung, -en f.

convalesce, vb. gene'sen*.

convalescence, n. Konvaleszenz' f.

convalescent, adj. gene'send.

convene, vb. zusam'menkommen*.

convenience, n. Annehmlichkeit, -en f.

convenient, adj. bequem', geeig'net.

convent, n. Nonnenkloster, -̈ nt.

convention, n. Versamm'lung, -en f., Tagung, -en f.; (contract) Abkommen, - nt.; (tradition) Konvention', -en f.

conventional, adj. konventionell'.

converge, vb. zusam'menlaufen*.

convergence, n. Konvergenz', -en f.

convergent, adj. konvergie'rend.

conversant with, adj. bewan'dert in.

conversational, adj. Gesprächs'- (cpds.).

converse, 1. n. Kehrseite, -n f. 2. vb. sich unterhal'ten*. 3. adj. umgekehrt.

convert, 1. n. Konvertit', -en, -en m. 2. vb. (belief, goods, money) konvertie'ren; (missionary) bekeh'ren.

converter, n. Bekeh'rer, - m.; (elec.) Transforma'tor, -o'ren m.

convertible, 1. n. (auto) Kabriolett', -s nt. 2. adj. konvertier'bar.

convex, adj. konvex'.

convey, vb. beför'dern, übermit'teln.

conveyance, n. (vehicle) Beför'derungsmittel, - nt.; Übermitt'lung, -en f.

conveyor, n. Beför'derer, - m.

convict, 1. n. Sträfling, -e m. 2. vb. überfüh'ren.

conviction, n. Schuldigsprechung, -en f.; (belief) Überzeu'gung, -en f.

convince, vb. überzeu'gen.

convincing, adj. überzeu'gend.

convivial, adj. gesel'lig.

convocation, n. Versamm'lung, -en f.

convoy, 1. n. Geleit'zug, -̈e m. 2. vb. gelei'ten.

convulse, vb. in Zuckungen versetzen; (be c.d) sich krümmen.

convulsion, n. Krampf, -̈e m.

convulsive, adj. krampfhaft.

cook, 1. n. Koch, -̈e m.; Köchin, -nen f. 2. vb. kochen.

cookbook, n. Kochbuch, -̈er nt.

cookie, n. Keks, -e m.

cool, 1. adj. kühl. 2. vb. ab·kühlen.

coolness, n. Kühle, f.

coop, n. Hühnerkorb, -̈e m.

cooperate, vb. zusam'menarbeiten.

cooperation, n. Zusam'menarbeit, -en f.

cooperative, 1. *n.* Konsum've-rein, -e *m.* **2.** *adj.* hilfsbereit.

coordinate, 1. *adj.* beigeordnet, koordiniert'. **2.** *vb.* bei•orden, koordinie'ren.

coordination, *n.* Beiordnung, -en *f.;* Koordination', -en *f.*

coordinator, *n.* Organisations'-planer, - *m.*

cop, *n.* Schupo, -s *m.*

cope, *vb.* sich ab•mühen.

copier, *n.* Kopier'maschine, -n *f.*

copious, *adj.* reichlich.

copper, *n.* Kupfer *nt.*

copy, 1. *n.* Abschrift, -en *f.,* Kopie', -i'en *f.; (book)* Exem-plar', -e *nt.* **2.** *vb.* ab•schrei-ben*, kopie'ren.

copyright, *n.* Urheberrecht, -e *nt.*

coquette, 1. *n.* Koket'te, -n *f.* **2.** *adj.* kokett'.

coral, *n.* Koral'le, -n *f.*

cord, *n.* Schnur, -e *f.*

cordial, *adj.* herzlich.

cordiality, *n.* Herzlichkeit *f.*

cordovan, *n.* Korduanleder, - *nt.*

core, *n. (fruit)* Kernhaus, -er *nt.; (heart)* Kern, -e *m.*

cork, *n. (material)* Kork *m.; (stopper)* Korken, - *m.*

corkscrew, *n.* Korkenzieher, - *m.*

corn, *n. (grain)* Getrei'de *nt.; (maize)* Mais *m.; (foot)* Hüh-nerauge, -n *nt.*

cornea, *n.* Hornhaut, -e *f.*

corner, *n.* Ecke, -n *f.*

cornet, *n.* Kornett' *nt.*

cornice, *n.* Gesims', -e *nt.*

corn-plaster, *n.* Hühneraugen-pflaster, - *nt.*

cornstarch, *n.* Maize'na *nt.*

coronation, *n.* Krönung, -en *f.*

coronet, *n.* Adelskrone, -n *f.*

corporal, 1. *n. (mil.)* Gefreit-m *m.* **2.** *adj.* körperlich.

corporate, *adj.* körperschaft-lich.

corporation, *n.* Körperschaft, -en *f.; (comm.)* Aktiengesell-schaft, -en *f.*

corps, *n.* Korps, - *nt.*

corpse, *n.* Leichnam, -e *m.*

corpulent, *adj.* korpulent'.

corpuscle, *n.* Körperchen, - *nt.*

correct, 1. *adj.* richtig, kor-rekt'. **2.** *vb.* verbes'sern, be-rich'tigen, korrigie'ren.

correction, *n.* Verbes'serung, -en *f.,* Berich'tigung, -en *f.*

corrective, *adj.* korrektiv'.

correctness, *n.* Korrekt'heit, -en *f.*

correlate, *vb.* aufeinan'der be-zie'hen*.

correlation, *n.* Korrelation', -en *f.*

correspond, *vb.* entspre'chen*; *(agree)* überein'•stimmen; *(letters)* korrespondie'ren.

correspondence, *n.* Entspre'-chung, -en *f.; (agreement)* Überein'stimmung, -en *f.; (letters)* Korrespondenz, -en *f.*

correspondent, *n.* Korrespon-dent', -en, -en *m.*

corridor, *n.* Korridor, -e *m.*

corroborate, *vb.* bestä'tigen.

corroboration, *n.* Bestä'tigung, -en *f.*

corrode, *vb.* korrodie'ren.

corrosion, *n.* Korrosion', -en *f.*

corrugate, *vb.* wellen.

corrupt, 1. *vb.* korrumpie'ren. **2.** *adj.* korrupt'.

corrupter, *n.* Verführ'rer, *m.*

corruptible, *adj.* verführ'bar.

corruption, *n.* Korruption', -en *f.*

corsage, *n.* Blume or Blumen zum Anstecken.

corset, *n.* Korsett', -s *nt.*

cortège, *n.* Leichenzug, -e *m.*

cosmetic, 1. *n.* kosme'tisches Mittel, - *nt.* **2.** *adj.* kosme'-tisch.

cosmic, *adj.* kosmisch.

cosmopolitan, *adj.* kosmopoli'-tisch.

cosmos, *n.* Kosmos *m.*

cost, 1. *n.* Preis, -e *m.;* Kosten *pl.* **2.** *vb.* kosten.

costliness, *n.* Kostspieligkeit, -en *f.*

costly, *adj.* kostspielig.

costume, *n. (fancy)* Kostüm, -e *nt.; (native)* Tracht, -en *f.*

cot, *n.* Feldbett, -en *nt.*

cottage, *n.* Häuschen, - *nt.; Landhaus,* -er *nt.*

cotton, *n.* Baumwolle *f.*

couch, *n.* Couch, -es *f.*

cough, 1. *n.* Husten *m.* **2.** *vb.* husten.

could, *vb. (was able)* konnte: *(would be able)* könnte.

council, *n.* Rat, -e *m.*

counsel, 1. *n.* Rat, -e *m.; (law-yer)* Anwalt, -e *m.* **2.** *vb.* be-ra'ten*, raten*.

counselor, *n.* Bera'ter, - *m.*

count, 1. *n.* Gesamt'zahl, -en *f.; (noble)* Graf, -en, -en *m.* **2.** *vb.* zählen.

countenance, *n.* Gesicht, -er *nt.*

counter, 1. *n.* Zähler, - *m.; (store)* Ladentisch, -e *m.* **2.** *adv.* (c. to) entge'gen.

counteract, *vb.* entge'gen•ar-beiten.

counterattack, 1. *n.* Gegenan-griff, -e *m.* **2.** *vb.* einen Ge-genangriff machen.

counterbalance, 1. *n.* Gegenge-wicht, -e *nt.* **2.** *vb.* auf-wiegen*.

counterfeit, 1. *n.* Falschgeld, -er *nt.* **2.** *adj.* gefälscht'. **3.** *vb.* fälschen.

countermand, *vb.* widerru'fen*.

counteroffensive, *n.* Gegenof-fensive, -n *f.*

counterpart, *n.* Gegenstück, -e *nt.*

countess, *n.* Gräfin, -nen *f.*

countless, *adj.* zahllos.

country, *n.* Land, -er *nt.*

countryman, *n.* Landsmann, -leute *m.*

countryside, *n.* Landschaft, -en *f.*

county, *n.* Grafschaft, -en *f.*

coupé, *n.* geschlossenes Zwei-sitzer-Auto, -s *nt.*

couple, 1. *n.* Paar, -e *nt.* **2.** *vb.* koppeln.

coupon, *n.* Coupon', -s *m.*

courage, *n.* Mut *m.*

courageous, *adj.* mutig.

courier, *n.* Kurier', -e *m.*

course, *n.* Lauf, -e *m.; (race)* Rennbahn, -en *f.; (nautical)* Kurs, -e *m.; (school)* Kursus, Kurse *m.; (food)* Gang, -e *m.; (of c.)* natür'lich.

court, 1. *n.* Hof, -e *m.* **2.** *vb.* den Hof machen.

courteous, *adj.* höflich.

courtesan, *n.* Kurtisa'ne, -n *f.*

courtesy, *n.* Höflichkeit, -en *f.*

courthouse, *n.* Gerichts'ge-bäude, - *nt.*

courtier, *n.* Höfling, -e *m.*

courtly, *adj.* höfisch.

court-martial, *n.* Kriegsgericht, -e *nt.*

courtroom, *n.* Gerichts'saal, -säle *m.*

courtship, *n.* Freien *nt.*

courtyard, *n.* Hof, -e *m.*

cousin, *n.* Vetter, -n *m.;* Cou-si'ne, -n *f.*

covenant, *n.* Vertrag', -e *m.*

cover, 1. *n.* Deckel, - *m.* **2.** *vb.* bede'cken; (c. up) zu•decken.

covering, *n.* Bede'ckung, -en *f.*

covet, *vb.* begeh'ren.

covetous, *adj.* begie'rig.

cow, *n.* Kuh, -e *f.*

coward, *n.* Feigling, -e *m.*

cowardice, *n.* Feigheit, -en *f.*

cowardly, *adj.* feige.

cowboy, *n.* Cowboy, -s *m.*

cower, *vb.* kauern.

cowhide, *n.* Rindsleder, - *nt.*

coy, *adj.* spröde.

cozy, *adj.* behag'lich.

crab, *n.* Taschenkrebs, -e *m.*

crack, 1. *n.* Spalt, -e *m.,* Sprung, -e *m.,* Riß, -sse *m.* **2.** *vb.* brechen*, springen*.

cracker, *n.* Salzkeks, -e *m.*

cradle, *n.* Wiege, -n *f.*

craft, *n.* Kunstfertigkeit, -en *f.; (ship)* Schiff, -e *nt.*

craftsman, *n.* Handwerker, - *m.*

craftsmanship, *n.* Kunstfertig-keit, -en *f.*

crafty, *adj.* gewiegt.

cram, *vb.* voll•stopfen; *(exam)* pauken.

cramp, *n.* Krampf, -e *m.*

crane, *n.* Kran, -e *f.; (bird)* Kranich, -e *m.*

crank, 1. *n. (handle)* Kurbel, -n *f.; (crackpot)* Sonderling, -e *m.* **2.** *vb.* an•kurbeln.

cranky, *adj.* mißvergnügt.

cranny, n. Ritze, -n f.

crash, 1. n. Krach m.; (collision) Zusam'menstoß, -e m.; (plane) Absturz, -e m. 2. vb. krachen;   zusam'men-stoßen*; ab-stürzen.

crate, n. Kiste, -n f.

crater, n. Krater, - m.

crave, vb. verlan'gen nach.

craving, n. gieriges Verlan'-gen, - nt.

crawl, vb. kriechen*; (swimming) kraulen.

crayon, n. Buntstift, -e m.

crazed, adj. wahnsinnig.

crazy, adj. verrückt'.

creak, vb. knarren.

cream, n. Sahne f., Rahm m; (cosmetic) Creme, -s f., Krem, -s m.

creamery, n. Molkerei', -en f.

creamy, adj. sahnig.

crease, 1. n. Falte, -n f. 2. vb. falten.

create, vb. schaffen*, erschaf'fen*; erzeu'gen.

creation, n.   Erschaf'fung, -en f.; Schöpfung, -en f.

creative, adj. schöpferisch.

creator, n. Schöpfer, - m.

creature, n. Geschöpf', -e nt., Wesen, - nt.

credentials, n.pl. Beglau'bigungsschreiben, - nt.

credibility, n. Glaubwürdigkeit f.

credible, adj. glaubwürdig.

credit, 1. n. Verdienst', nt.; (comm.) Kredit', -e m. 2. vb. gut•schreiben*.

creditable, adj. anerkennenswert.

credit card, n. Kredit'karte, -n f.

creditor, n. Gläubig• - m.

credo, n.   Glaubensbekennt-nnis, -se nt.

credulity, n. Leichtgläubigkeit f.

credulous, adj. leichtgläubig.

creed, n. Glaubensbekenntnis, -se nt.

creek, n. Bach, -e m.

creep, vb. kriechen*.

cremate, vb. ein•äschern.

cremation, n. Einäscherung, -en f.

crematory, n. Kremato'rium, -rien nt.

crepe, n. Krepp m.

crescent, n. Mondsichel, -n f.

crest, n. Kamm, -e m.

crestfallen, adj. geknickt'.

cretonne, n. Kretonn'e, -s m.

crevasse, n. Gletscherspalte, -n f.

crevice, n. Riß, -sse m.

crew, n. Mannschaft, -en f.

crib, n. Krippe, -n f.; (bed) Kinderbett, -en nt.

cricket, n. Grille, -n f.

crime, n. Verbre'chen, - nt.

criminal, 1. n. Verbre'cher, - m. 2. adj. verbre'cherisch.

criminology, n. Kriminalis'tik f.

crimson, adj. karmin'rot.

cringe, vb. sich krümmen.

cripple, 1. n. Krüppel, - m. 2. vb. zum Krüppel machen; lähmen.

crippled, adj. verkrüp'pelt, gelähmt'.

crisis, n. Krise, -n f.

crisp, adj. (weather, vegetables) frisch; (bread, etc.) knusprig.

criterion, n.   Krite'rium, -rien nt.

critic, n. Kritiker, - m.

critical, adj. kritisch.

criticism, n. Kritik', -en f.

criticize, vb. kritisie'ren.

croak, vb. krächzen.

crochet, vb. häkeln.

crock, n. Steintopf, -e m.

crockery, n. Steingut nt.

crocodile, n. Korkodil', -e nt.

crook, n. (bend) Biegung, -en f.; (cheater) Schwindler, - m.

crooked, adj. (not straight) krumm, schief; (dishonest) unehrlich, betrü'gerisch.

croon, vb. summen; (jazz) Schlager singen*.

crop, n. Ernte, -n f.; (riding) Peitsche, -n f.

croquet, n. Kroket'spiel m.

croquette, n. Kroket'te, -n f.

cross, 1. n. Kreuz, -e nt.; (mixture) Kreuzung, -en f. 2. vb. kreuzen.

cross-eyed, adj. (be c.) schielen.

crossing, n. Kreuzung, -en f.

crossroads, n.pl. Scheideweg, - e m.; Kreuzung, -en f.

cross section, n. Querschnitt, -e m.

crossword puzzle, n. Kreuzworträtsel, - nt.

crotch, n. (trousers) Schritt, -e m.; (tree) Gabelung, -en f.

crouch, vb. kauern.

croup, n. Krupp m.

crouton, n. Crouton', -s m.

crow, 1. n. Krähe, -n f. 2. vb. krähen.

crowd, 1. n. Menge, -n f. 2. vb. drängeln.

crown, 1. n. Krone, -n f. 2. vb. krönen.

crucial, adj. entschei'dend.

crucible, n.   Schmelztiegel, - m.

crucifix, n. Kruzifix, -e nt.

crucifixion, n.   Kreuzigung, -en f.

crucify, vb. kreuzigen.

crude, adj. roh, grob (-).

crudeness, n. Grobheit, -en f., Unfeinheit, -en f.

crudity, n. Roheit, -en f., Unfeinheit, -en f.

cruel, adj. grausam.

cruelty, n. Grausamkeit, -en f.

cruise, 1. n. Seereise, -n f. 2. vb. kreuzen.

cruiser, n. Kreuzer, - m.

crumb, n. Krümel, - m.

crumble, vb. zerbrö'ckeln.

crumple, vb. zerknül'len.

crusade, n. Kreuzzug, -e m.

crusader, n.   Kreuzzügler, - m.

crush, 1. n. (crowd) Gedrän'ge nt. 2. vb. zerdrü'cken.

crust, n. Kruste, -n f.

crustacean, n.   Krustentier, -e nt.

crusty, adj. knusprig.

crutch, n. Krücke, -n f.

cry, 1. n. Schrei, -e m. 2. vb. schreien*; (weep) weinen.

crying, adj. (urgent) dringend.

cryosurgery, n. Kryochirurgie' f.

cryptic, adj. geheim'.

cryptography, n.   Geheim'-schrift, -en f.

crystal, 1. n. Kristall', -e nt. 2. adj. kristal'len.

crystalline, adj. kristal'len.

crystallize, vb. kristallisie'ren.

cub, n. Jung• - nt.

cube, n. Würfel, - m.

cubic, adj. würfelförmig, kubisch; Kubik'- (cpds.).

cubicle, n. kleiner Schlafraum, -e m.

cuckoo, n. Kuckuck, -e m.

cucumber, n. Gurke, -n f.

cud, n.   Widergekäut-   nt.; (chew the c.) wieder•käuen.

cuddle, vb. herzen.

cudgel, n. Keule, -n f.

cue, n. Stichwort, -er nt.

cuff, n. (sleeve) Manschet'te, -n f.; (trousers) Hosenaufschlag, -e m.

cuisine, n. Küche, -e f.

culinary, adj. kulina'risch.

cull, vb. pflücken.

culminate, vb. gipfeln.

culmination, n. Höhepunkt, -e m.

culpable, adj. schuldhaft.

culprit, n. Täter, - m.

cult, n. Kult, -e m.

cultivate, vb. kultivie'ren.

cultivated, adj. kultiviert'.

cultivation, n. Kultivie'rung f.

cultural, adj. kulturell'.

culture, n. Kultur', -ren f.

cultured, adj. kultiviert'.

cumbersome, adj. schwerfällig.

cumulative, adj. kumulativ'.

cunning, 1. n. List, -en f. 2. adj. listig; (sweet) goldig.

cup, n. Tasse, -n f.

cupboard, n. Schrank, -e m.

cupidity, n. Begier'de, -n f.

cupola, n. Kuppel, -n f.

curable, adj. heilbar.

curator, n. Kura'tor, -o'ren m.

curb, 1. n. (sidewalk) Bordstein, -e m., (harness) Zügel, - m.

curdle, vb. gerin'nen*.

cure, 1. n. Kur, -en f.; (medicine) Heilmittel, - nt. 2. vb. heilen.

curfew, n. Polizei'stunde, -n f.

curio, n. Kuriosität', -en f.

curiosity, n. Neugierde f.

curious, adj. neugierig.

curl, 1. n. Locke, -n f. **2.** vb. locken, kräuseln.

curly, adj. lockig, kraus.

currant, n. Johan'nisbeere, -n f.; (dried) Korin'the, -n f.

currency, n. Währung, -en f.

current, 1. n. Strom, ∺e m. **2.** adj. laufend.

currently, adv. zur Zeit.

curriculum, n. Lehrplan, ∺e m.

curry, n. Curry m.

curse, 1. n. Fluch, ∺e m. **2.** (intr.) fluchen, (tr.) verflu'chen.

cursed, adj. verflucht'.

curse-word, n. Schimpfwort, ∺er nt.

cursory, adj. flüchtig.

curt, adj. kurz angebunden.

curtail, vb. ein·schränken.

curtain, n. Gardi'ne, -n f.; (drapes) Vorhang, ∺e m.

curtsy, n. Knicks, -e m.

curvature, n. Krümmung, -en f.

curve, n. Kurve, -n f.

cushion, n. Kissen, - nt.

custard, n. Eierpudding, -s m.

custodian, n. Hausmeister, - m.

custody, n. Verwah'rung f.

custom, n. Sitte, -n f., Brauch, ∺e m.; (habit) Gewohn'heit, -en f.

customary, adj. gebräuch'lich.

customer, n. Kunde, -n, -n m.

custom house, n. Zollamt, ∺er nt.

customs, n. Zoll, ∺e m.

customs officer, n. Zollbeamt- m.

cut, 1. n. Schnitt, -e m.; (wound) Schnittwunde, -n f.; (salary) Kürzung, -en f.; (taxes) Senkung, -en f. **2.** vb. schneiden*; kürzen; senken; (class) schwänzen.

cute, adj. niedlich, süß, goldig.

cut glass, n. geschlif'fenes Glas nt.

cuticle, n. Nagelhaut, ∺e f.

cutlery, n. Stahlwaren pl.

cutlet, n. Kotelett', -s nt.

cutter, n. Zuschneider, - m.; (boat) Kutter, - m.

cyclamate, n. Zyklamat', -e nt.

cycle, 1. n. Kreislauf, ∺e m.; Zyklus, -klen m. **2.** vb. radeln.

cyclist, n. Radfahrer, - m.

cyclone, n. Wirbelsturm, ∺e m.

cyclotron, n. Zyklotron, -e nt.

cylinder, n. Zylin'der, - m.

cylindrical, adj. zylin'drisch.

cymbal, n. Zimbel, -n f.

cynic, n. Zyniker, - m.

cynical, adj. zynisch.

cynicism, n. Zynis'mus, -men m.

cypress, n. Zypres'se, -n f.

cyst, n. Zyste, -n f.

D

dab, vb. tupfen.

dabble, vb. sich dilettan'tenhaft mit einer Sache ab·geben*.

daffodil, n. Narzis'se, -n f.

dagger, n. Dolch, -e m.

dahlia, n. Dahlie, -n f.

daily, 1. n. (newspaper) Tageszeitung, -en f. **2.** adj. täglich.

daintiness, n. Zartheit, -en f.

dainty, adj. zart, delikat', zierlich.

dairy, n. Milchwirtschaft, -en f., Molkerei' -en f.

dairyman, n. Milchhändler, - m.

dais, n. Podium, -ien nt.

daisy, n. Margeri'te, -n f.

dale, n. Tal, ∺er nt.

dally, vb. tändeln; (dawdle) trödeln.

dam, 1. n. Damm, ∺e m. **2.** vb. ein·dämmen.

damage, 1. n. Schaden, ∺ m.; (damages, law) Schadenersatz m. **2.** vb. schädigen; beschädigen.

damask, n. Damast, -e m.

damn, vb. verdam'men; (curse) verflu'chen.

damnation, n. Verdam'mung, -en f.

damp, adj. feucht.

dampen, vb. (moisten) einfeuchten; (quiet) dämpfen; (fig.) nieder·schlagen*.

dampness, n. Feuchtigkeit, -en f.

dance, 1. n. Tanz, ∺e m. **2.** vb. tanzen.

dancer, n. Tänzer, - m.

dancing, n. Tanzen nt.

dandelion, n. Löwenzahn m.

dandruff, n. Kopfschuppen pl.

dandy, 1. n. Geck, -en, -en m. **2.** adj. prima.

Dane, n. Däne, -n, -n m.

danger, n. Gefahr', -en f.

dangerous, adj. gefähr'lich.

dangle, vb. baumeln; baumeln lassen*.

Danish, adj. dänisch.

dapper, adj. klein und elegant'.

dare, vb. wagen.

daredevil, n. Draufgänger, - m.

daring, adj. gewagt'.

dark, 1. n. Dunkel nt.; Dunkelheit, -en f. **2.** adj. dunkel.

darken, vb. verdun'keln.

darkness, n. Dunkel nt.; Dunkelheit, -en f.

darling, 1. n. Liebling, -e m. **2.** adj. goldig.

darn, vb. (socks) stopfen.

dart, 1. n. Wurfpfeil, -e m. **2.** vb. fliezen*.

dash, 1. n. (pen) Strich, -e m; (sport) Lauf, ∺e m. **2.** vb. (intr.) sich stürzen; (tr.) stoßen*, schleudern.

dashboard, n. Armatu'renbrett, -er nt.

dashing, adj. schneidig.

data, n.pl. Angaben pl.

data processing, n. Datenverarbeitung, -en f.

date, 1. n. Datum, -ten nt.; (appointment) Verab'redung, -en f.; (fruit) Dattel, -n f. **2.** vb. datie'ren; aus·gehen* mit.

daub, vb. schmieren.

daughter, n. Tochter, ∺ f.

daughter-in-law, n. Schwiegertochter, ∺ f.

daunt, vb. entmu'tigen.

dauntless, adj. kühn.

dawdle, vb. trödeln.

dawn, 1. n. Morgendämmerung, -en f. **2.** vb. dämmern.

day, n. Tag, -e m.

daybreak, n. Tagesanbruch m.

daydream, 1. n. Träumerei', -en f. **2.** vb. vor sich hin träumen; sinnie'ren.

daylight, n. Tageslicht nt.

daze, 1. n. Benom'menheit f. **2.** vb. betäu'ben.

dazzle, vb. blenden.

deacon, n. Diakon', -e m.

dead, adj. tot.

deaden, vb. dämpfen.

dead end, n. Sackgasse, -n f.

deadline, n. Termin', -e m.

deadlock, n. Stockung, -en f.

deadly, adj. tödlich.

deaf, adj. taub.

deafen, vb. betäu'ben.

deafness, n. Taubheit f.

deal, 1. n. Anzahl f.; (business) Geschäft', -e nt. **2.** vb. (cards) geben*; (d. with) behan'deln; (d. in) handeln mit.

dealer, n. Händler, - m.; (cards) Geber, - m.

dean, n. Dekan', -e m.

dear, adj. lieb, teuer.

dearly, adv. sehr.

dearth, n. Mangel, ∺ m.

death, n. Tod m.; Todesfall, -e m.

deathless, adj. unsterblich.

debase, vb. ernie'drigen.

debatable, adj. bestreit'bar.

debate, 1. n. Debat'te, -n f. **2.** vb. debattie'ren.

debauch, 1. n. Orgie, -n f. **2.** vb. verfüh'ren.

debenture, n. Obligation', -en f.

debilitate, vb. entkräf'ten.

debit, n. Debet, -s nt.

debonair, adj. zuvor'kommend; heiter und sorglos.

debris, n. Trümmer pl.

debt, n. Schuld, -en f.

debtor, n. Schuldner, - m.

debunk, vb. mit etwas auf·räumen, den Nimbus rauben.

debut, n. Debüt', -s nt.

debutante, n. Debütan'tin, -nen f.

decade, n. Jahrzehnt', -e nt.

decadence, n. Dekadenz' f.

decadent, adj. dekadent'.

decaffeinated, adj. koffein'frei.

decanter, n. Karaf'fe, -n f.

decapitate, vb. enthaup'ten.

decay, 1. n. Verfall' m.; Ver'we'sung, -en f. 2. vb. verfal'len*; verwe'sen.

deceased, adj. verstor'ben.

deceit, n. Täuschung, -en f.; Betrug', -̈e m.

deceitful, adj. falsch; betrü'gerisch.

deceive, vb. täuschen; betrü'gen*.

December, n. Dezem'ber m.

decency, n. Anständigkeit, -en f.

decent, adj. anständig.

decentralization, n. Dezentrali-sation', -en f.

decentralize, vb. dezentralisie'ren.

deception, n. Täuschung, -en f.

deceptive, adj. irreführend, täuschend.

decibel, n. Dezi'bel, -n f.

decide, vb. entschei'den*; sich entschlie'Ben*.

decimal, 1. n. Dezimal'bruch, -̈e m. 2. adj. Dezimal'- (cpds.)

decimate, vb. dezimie'ren.

decipher, vb. entzif'fern.

decision, n. Entschei'dung, -en f.; Beschluß', -̈sse m.

decisive, adj. entschei'dend.

deck, n. (ship) Deck, -s nt.; (cards) Spiel, -e nt.

declaration, n. Erklä'rung, -en f.

declarative, adj. erklä'rend; (d. sentence) Aussagesatz, -̈e m.

declare, vb. erklä'ren, behaup'ten; (customs) deklarie'ren.

declension, n. Deklination', -en f.

decline, 1. n. Niedergang m. 2. vb. neigen; (refuse) ab'lehnen; (gram.) deklinie'ren.

décolleté, n. Dekolleté', -s nt.

decompose, vb. (tr.) zerset'zen; (intr.) verwe'sen.

decomposition, n. Zerset'zung, -en f.; Verwe'sung, -en f.

decongestant, n. schleimlösendes Mittel nt.

décor, n. Ausstattung, -en f.

decorate, vb. schmücken, dekorie'ren.

decoration, n. Dekoration', -en f.

decorative, adj. dekorativ'.

decorator, n. Dekorateur', -e m.; (interior d.) Innenarchi-tekt, -en, -en m.

decorous, adj. schicklich.

decorum, n. Schicklichkeit f.

decoy, 1. n. Lockvogel, -̈ m. 2. vb. locken.

decrease, 1. n. Abnahme, -n f. 2. vb. (tr.) verrin'gern; (intr.) ab'nehmen*.

decree, 1. n. Erlaß', -̈sse m. 2. vb. verord'nen.

decrepit, adj. gebrech'lich, klapprig.

decry, vb. mißbil'ligen, tadeln.

dedicate, vb. widmen.

dedication, n. Widmung, -en f.

deduce, vb. folgern.

deduct, vb. ab'ziehen*.

deduction, n. Abzug, -̈e m.; (logic) Folgerung, -en f.

deductive, adj. deduktiv'.

deed, n. Tat, -en f.; (document) Urkunde, -n f.

deem, vb. denken*; halten*.

deep, adj. tief.

deepen, vb. vertie'fen.

deep freeze, n. Tiefkühltruhe, -n f.

deer, n. Reh, -e nt.; Hirsch, -e m.

deerskin, n. Rehleder, - nt.; Hirschleder, - nt.

deface, vb. entstel'len.

defamation, n. Verleum'dung, -en f.

defame, vb. in schlechten Ruf bringen*.

default, 1. n. Versäum'nis, -se nt.; Unterlas'sung, -en f. 2. vb. im Verzug' sein*.

defeat, 1. n. Niederlage, -n f. 2. vb. besie'gen.

defect, 1. n. Fehler, - m., Defekt', -e m. 2. vb. über'lau-fen*.

defection, n. Versa'gen nt.; Treubruch, -̈e m.

defective, adj. fehlerhaft.

defend, vb. vertei'digen.

defendant, n. Angeklagt- m.&f.

defender, n. Vertei'diger, - m., Beschüt'zer, - m.

defense, n. Vertei'digung, -en f.

defenseless, adj. wehrlos.

defensible, adj. verfecht'bar, zu vertei'digen.

defensive, 1. n. Defensi've, -n f. 2. adj. defensiv'.

defer, vb. (put off) auf'schie-ben*; (yield) nach'geben*.

deference, n. Achtung f.

deferential, adj. ehrerbietig.

defiance, n. Heraus'forderung, -en f.; Trotz m.

defiant, adj. trotzig, heraus'-fordernd.

deficiency, n. Mangel, -̈ m.

deficient, adj. unzureichend.

deficit, n. Defizit, -e nt.

defile, 1. n. Engpaß, -̈sse m. 2. vb. (march) defilie'ren; (soil) besu'deln.

definite, adj. bestimmt'.

definition, n. Definition', -en f.

definitive, adj. definitiv'.

deflate, vb. die Luft heraus'lassen*.

deflation, n. Deflation', -en f.

deflect, vb. ab'wenden*.

deform, vb. entstel'len.

deformity, n. Verwachs'ung, -en f.

defraud, vb. betrü'gen*.

defray, vb. bestrei'ten*.

defrost, vb. entfros'ten.

deft, adj. geschickt'.

defy, vb. trotzen.

degenerate, 1. adj. degene-riert'. 2. vb. entar'ten.

degeneration, n. Degeneration' f.

degradation, n. Ernie'drigung, -en f.

degrade, vb. ernie'drigen.

degree, n. Grad, -e m.

deify, vb. vergött'lichen.

deign, vb. geru'hen.

deity, n. Gottheit, -en f.

dejected, adj. niedergeschla-gen.

dejection, n. Trübsinn m.

delay, 1. n. Verzö'gerung, -en f. 2. vb. auf'schieben*, verzö'gern.

delectable, adj. ergötz'lich.

delegate, 1. n. Delegiert'-m.&f. 2. vb. delegie'ren.

delegation, n. Abordnung, -en f., Delegation', -en f.

delete, vb. aus'streichen*.

deliberate, 1. vb. erwä'gen*. 2. adj. bedäch'tig; (on purpose) absichtlich.

deliberation, n. Überle'gung, -en f., Erwä'gung, -en f.

delicacy, n. (food) Delikates'se, -n f.; (fig.) Feinheit, -en f.

delicate, adj. delikat'.

delicious, adj. köstlich.

delight, 1. n. Entzü'cken, - nt. 2. vb. entzü'cken.

delightful, adj. entzü'ckend.

delineate, vb. dar'stellen.

delinquency, n. Verge'hen, - nt.; Unterlas'sung, -en f.

delinquent, 1. n. Kriminell'-m.&f.; (juvenile d.) Jugend-verbrecher, - m. 2. adj. ver-bre'cherisch, kriminell'; (in default) säumig.

delirious, adj. im Fieberwahn-sinn; wahnsinnig.

delirium, n. Deli'rium, -rien nt.

deliver, vb. (set free) erlö'sen; (hand over) überge'ben*, ab'liefern.

deliverance, n. Erlö'sung, -en f., Befrei'ung, -en f.

delivery, n. Lieferung, -en f.; (childbirth) Entbin'dung, -en f.

delude, vb. täuschen, verlei'ten.

deluge, 1. n. Überschwem'mung, -en f.; (Bible) Sintflut f. 2. vb. überflu'ten.

delusion, n. Täuschung, -en f., Wahn m.

de luxe, adj. Luxus- (cpds.)

delve, vb. graben*; (fig.) sich vertie'fen.

demand, 1. n. Forderung, -en f.; (claim) Anspruch, -̈e m.; (econ.) Nachfrage f. 2. vb. fordern, verlan'gen; fragen.

demean (oneself), vb. sich ent-wür'digen.

demeanor, n. Betra'gen nt.

demerit, n. (school) Tadel, - m.

demilitarize, vb. entmilitarisie'ren.

demobilization, n. Demobilisie'rung, -en f.

demobilize, vb. demobilisie'ren.

democracy, n. Demokratie', -n f.

democrat, n. Demokrat', -en, -en m.

democratic, adj. demokra'tisch.

demolish, vb. ab·reißen*, zerstö'ren.

demolition, n. Zerstö'rung, -en f.

demon, n. Dämon, -o'nen m.

demonstrable, adj. nachweisbar.

demonstrate, vb. zeigen, vorführen, demonstrie'ren.

demonstration, n. Beweis' -e m., Darlegung, -en f.; Kundgebung, -en f.

demonstrative, adj. demonstrativ'.

demonstrator, n. Demonstrie'rend- m.&f.

demoralize, vb. demoralisie'ren.

demote, vb. degradie'ren.

demur, vb. Einwendungen machen.

demure, adj. züchtig.

den, n. Höhle, -n f.

denaturalize, vb. denaturalisie'ren.

denial, n. Vernei'nung, -en f.

denim, n. Jeansstoff, -e m.

Denmark, n. Dänemark nt.

denomination, n. (money) Nennwert, -e m.; (church) Sekte, -n f.

denominator, n. Nenner, - m.

denote, vb. kennzeichnen.

dense, adj. dicht.

density, n. Dichte f.

dent, n. Einbuchtung, -en f.

dental, adj. Zahn- (cpds.).

dentifrice, n. Zahnputzmittel, - nt.

dentist, n. Zahnarzt, -e m.

dentistry, n. Zahnheilkunde f.

denture, n. künstliches Gebiß', -sse nt.

denunciation, n. Denunzie'rung, -en f.

deny, vb. leugnen, vernei'nen.

deodorant, n. Desodorisie'rungsmittel, - nt.

depart, vb. ab·fahren*; (deviate) ab·weichen*.

department, n. Abtei'lung, -en f.; (government) Ministe'rium, -rien nt.

departmental, adj. Abtei'lungs- (cpds.).

departure, n. Abfahrt, -en f.; (deviation) Abweichung, -en f.

depend, vb. ab·hängen*; (rely) sich verlas'sen*.

dependability, n. Verläß'lichkeit f.

dependable, adj. zuverlässig.

dependence, n. Abhängigkeit f.

dependent, 1. n. Angehörig- m.&f. **2.** adj. abhängig.

depict, vb. dar·stellen.

depiction, n. Darstellung, -en f.

deplete, vb. erschöp'fen.

deplorable, adj. bekla'genswert.

deplore, vb. bekla'gen.

deport, vb. deportie'ren.

deportation, n. Deportation', - en f.

deportment, n. Betra'gen nt.

depose, vb. ab·setzen.

deposit, 1. n. Anzahlung, -en f.; (bank) Einzahlung, -en f.; (ore, etc.) Lager, - nt. **2.** vb. ein·zahlen; hinterle'gen.

deposition, n. (eidesstattliche) schriftliche Aussage, -n f.

depositor, n. Einzahler, - m., Bankkunde, -n, -n m.

depot, n. Lager, - nt.; Depot', - s nt.; (railroad) Kleinbahnhof, -e m.

depravity, n. Verwor'fenheit f.

deprecate, vb. mißbilligen.

depreciate, vb. (tr.) entwer'ten, den Wert mindern; (intr.) im Wert sinken*.

depreciation, n. Wertminderung f.

depress, vb. deprimie'ren.

depression, n. Depression', -en f.

deprivation, n. Berau'bung, -en f.

deprive, vb. berau'ben.

depth, n. Tiefe, -n f.

deputy, n. (substitute) Stellvertreter, - m.; (parliament) Abgeordnet- m.&f.

derail, vb. entglei'sen lassen*; (be d.ed) entglei'sen.

deranged, adj. geistesgestört.

derelict, 1. n. Wrack, -s or -e nt. **2.** adj. nachlässig.

dereliction, n. Vernach'lässigung, -en f.

deride, vb. verspot'ten.

derision, n. Hohn m.

derisive, adj. spöttisch.

derivation, n. Ableitung, -en f.

derivative, adj. abgeleitet.

derive, vb. ab·leiten.

derogatory, adj. abfällig.

derrick, n. Ladebaum, -e m.; (oil) Bohrturm, -e m.

descend, vb. herab'steigen*; (ancestry) ab·stammen.

descendant, n. Nachkomme, - n, -n m.

descent, n. Abstieg, -e m.

describe, vb. beschrei'ben*.

description, n. Beschrei'bung, -en f.

descriptive, adj. beschrei'bend.

desecrate, vb. entwei'hen.

desert, 1. n. Wüste, -n f.; (merit) Verdienst, -e nt. **2.** vb. verlas'sen*.

deserter, n. Fahnenflüchtigm.&f., Deserteur', -e m.

desertion, n. (law) böswilliges Verlas'sen nt.; (army) Desertion', -en f., Fahnenflucht f.

deserve, vb. verdie'nen.

deserving, adj. verdienst'voll.

design, 1. n. Entwurf', -e m., Muster, - nt.; (aim) Absicht, -en f. **2.** vb. entwer'fen*; beab'sichtigen.

designate, vb. bezeich'nen, bestim'men.

designation, n. Bezeich'nung, -en f., Bestim'mung, -en f.

designer, n. Konstrukteur', -e m.; (fashion) Modeschöpfer, - m.

desirability, n. Erwünscht'heit, -en f.

desirable, adj. wünschenswert.

desire, 1. n. Verlan'gen, - nt., Wunsch, -e m. **2.** vb. verlan'gen, wünschen.

desirous, adj. begie'rig.

desist, vb. ab·lassen*.

desk, n. Schreibtisch, -e m.

desolate, 1. adj. trostlos. **2.** vb. verhee'ren.

desolation, n. Verwüs'tung, -en f.; Trostlosigkeit f.

despair, 1. n. Verzweif'lung, -en f. **2.** vb. verzwei'feln.

despatch, 1. n. Absendung, -en f. **2.** vb. ab·senden*, eilig weg·schicken.

desperado, n. Bandit', -en, -en m., Despera'do, -s m.

desperate, adj. verzwei'felt.

desperation, n. Verzweif'lung, -en f.

despicable, adj. verach'tenswert, gemein'.

despise, vb. verach'ten.

despite, prep. trotz.

despondent, adj. verzagt'.

despot, n. Despot', -en, -en m.

despotic, adj. despo'tisch.

despotism, n. Gewalt'herrschaft f.

dessert, n. Nachtisch, -e m.

destination, n. Bestim'mung f.; Bestim'mungsort, -e m.

destine, vb. bestim'men.

destiny, n. Schicksal, -e nt.

destitute, adj. mittellos.

destitution, n. Armut f., Not, - e f.

destroy, vb. zerstö'ren.

destroyer, n. Zerstö'rer, - m.

destruction, n. Zerstö'rung, -en f.

destructive, adj. zerstö'rend.

desultory, adj. flüchtig.

detach, vb. ab·trennen; (mil.) ab·kommandieren.

detachment, n. (mil.) Abtei'lung, -en f.; Objektivität' f.

detail, n. Einzelheit, -en f.

detain, vb. ab·halten*; fest·halten*; auf·halten*.

detect, vb. entde'cken, ermit'teln.

detection, n. Entde'cken nt.; Ermitt'lung, -en f.

detective, n. Detektiv'- -e m.

détente, n. Entspan'nung f.

detention, n. Haft f.

deter, v. ab•halten*, hindern.

detergent, n. chemisches Seifenmittel, -nt.

deteriorate, vb. sich verschlech'tern.

deterioration, n. Verschlech'terung, -en f.

determination, n. Bestim'mung, -en f.; (resolve) Entschlos'senheit f.

determine, vb. bestim'men.

determined, adj. entschlos'sen.

deterrence, n. Abschreckung f.

detest, vb. verab'scheuen.

detonate, vb. explodie'ren.

detonation, n. Explosion', -en f.

detour, n. Umweg, -e m.; (traffic) Umleitung, -en f.

detract, vb. ab•ziehen*; (d. from) schmälern.

detriment, n. Nachteil, -e m., Schaden, - m.

detrimental, adj. nachteilig.

devaluate, vb. ab•werten.

devastate, vb. verwüs'ten.

devastation, n. Verwüs'tung, -en f.

develop, vb. entwi'ckeln.

developer, n. Entwick'ler, - m.

developing nation, n. Entwicklungsland, -er nt.

development, n. Entwick'lung, -en f.

deviate, vb. ab•weichen*.

deviation, n. Abweichung, -en f.

device, n. Vorrichtung, -en f.

devil, n. Teufel, - m.

devilish, adj. teuflisch.

devious, adj. abweichend.

devise, vb. ersin'nen*.

devoid, adj. (d. of) leer an, ohne.

devote, vb. widmen.

devoted, adj. erge'ben.

devotee, n. Verfech'ter, - m.

devotion, n. Hingebung f.; (religious) Andacht, -en f.

devour, vb. verschlin'gen*.

devout, adj. andächtig, fromm.

dew, n. Tau m.

dewy, adj. betaut'.

dexterity, n. Gewandt'heit, -en f.

dexterous, adj. gewandt'.

diabetes, n. Zuckerkrankheit f.

diabolic, adj. teuflisch.

diadem, n. Diadem', -e nt.

diagnose, vb. diagnostizie'ren.

diagnosis, n. Diagno'se, -n f.

diagnostic, adj. diagnos'tisch.

diagonal, 1. n. Diagona'le, -n f. 2. adj. diagonal', schräg.

diagram, n. graphische Darstellung, -en f.

dial, 1. n. Zifferblatt, -er nt.; (telephone) Wählscheibe, -n f. 2. vb. (telephone) wählen.

dialect, n. Dialekt', -e m., Mundart, -en f.

dialogue, n. Dialog', -e m.

diameter, n. Durchmesser, -m.

diametrical, adj. diametral'.

diamond, n. Diamant', -en, -en m.; (cards) Karo nt.

diaper, n. Windel, -n f.

diaphragm, n. Zwerchfell, -e nt.

diarrhea, n. Durchfall m.

diary, n. Tagebuch, -er nt.

diathermy, n. Diathermie' f.

diatribe, n. Schmähschrift, -en f.

dice, n.pl. Würfel, - m.

dicker, vb. feilschen.

dictate, vb. diktie'ren.

dictation, n. Diktat', -e nt.

dictator, n. Dikta'tor, -o'ren m.

dictatorial, adj. diktato'risch.

dictatorship, n. Diktatur', -en f.

diction, n. Aussprache, -n f.

dictionary, n. Wörterbuch, -er nt., Lexikon, -ka nt.

didactic, adj. didak'tisch.

die, 1. n. (gaming cube) Würfel, - m.; (stamper) Prägestempel, - m. 2. vb. sterben*.

diet, n. Diät' -en f.; (government) Parlament', -e nt.

dietary, adj. diät'gemäß.

dietetic, adj. diäte'tisch.

dietitian, n. Diät'planer, - m.

differ, vb. sich unterschei'den*, ab•weichen*, verschiedener Meinung sein*.

difference, n. Unterschied, -e m.

different, adj. verschie'den, ander-.

differential, 1. n. Unterschied, - m.; (d. gear) Differential', -e nt., Ausgleichsgetriebe, - nt. 2. adj. differential'.

differentiate, vb. unterschei'den*.

difficult, adj. schwer, mühsam, schwierig.

difficulty, n. Schwierigkeit, -en f.

diffident, adj. zurück'haltend, schüchtern.

diffuse, 1. adj. weitverbreitet, diffus'. 2. vb. verbrei'ten.

diffusion, n. Diffusion', -en f.

dig, vb. graben*.

digest, vb. verdau'en.

digestible, adj. verdau'lich.

digestion, n. Verdau'ung f.

digestive, adj. Verdau'ungs- (cpds.).

digital, adj. digital'.

digitalis, n. Digita'lis nt.

dignified, adj. würdig.

dignify, vb. ehren, aus•zeichnen.

dignitary, n. Würdenträger, -m.

dignity, n. Würde f.

digress, vb. ab•schweifen.

digression, n. Abschweifung, -en f.

dike, n. Deich, -e m.

dilapidated, adj. baufällig.

dilate, vb. aus•dehnen.

dilemma, n. Dilem'ma, -s nt.

dilettante, n. Dilettant', -en, -en m.

diligence, n. Fleiß m.

diligent, adj. fleißig.

dill, n. Dill m.

dilute, vb. verdün'nen.

dilution, n. Verdün'nung, -en f.

dim, 1. adj. trübe, dunkel. 2, vb. trüben; (auto lights) ab•blenden.

dimension, n. Ausmaß, -e nt., Dimension', -en f.

diminish, vb. vermin'dern.

diminution, n. Vermin'derung, -en f.

diminutive, 1. n. Diminutiv', -e nt. 2. adj. winzig.

dimness, n. Dunkelheit f.

dimple, n. Grübchen, - nt.

din, n. Lärm m.

dine, vb. speisen.

diner, n. (noon) Mittagessen, -nt.; (evening) Abendessen, -nt.

diner, dining-car, n. Speisewagen, - m.

dingy, adj. schäbig.

dinner, n. (noon) Mittagessen, -nt.; (evening) Abendessen, -nt.

dinosaur, n. Dinosau'rier, - m.

diocese, n. Diöze'se, -n f.

dip, vb. tauchen, ein•tauchen; sich senken.

diphtheria, n. Diphtherie' f.

diploma, n. Diplom', -e nt.

diplomacy, n. Diplomatie', -en f.

diplomat, n. Diplomat', -en, -en m.

diplomatic, adj. diploma'tisch.

dipper, n. Schöpflöffel, - m., Schöpfkelle, -n f.; (Big D.) Großer Bär m.; (Little D.) Kleiner Bär m.

dire, adj. gräßlich.

direct, 1. adj. direkt'. 2. vb. führen; an•weisen*; leiten.

direct current, n. Gleichstrom, -e m.

direction, n. (leadership) Leitung, -en f., Führung, -en f.; (instruction) Anweisung, -en f.; (course) Richtung, -en f.

directional, adj. Leitungs-, Richtungs- (cpds.).

directive, 1. adj. leitend; Richtung gebend. 2. n. Direkti've, -n f.

directness, n. Gerad'heit f., Offenheit f.

director, n. Leiter, - m., Direk'tor, -o'ren m.

directory, n. (addresses) Adreß'buch, -er nt.; (telephone d.) Telephon'buch, -er nt.

dirigible, n. Luftschiff, -e nt.

dirt, n. Schmutz m.

dirty, adj. schmutzig.

disability, n. Unfähigkeit f.; Körperbehinderung, -en f.

disable, vb. untauglich machen.

disabled, *adj.* untauglich; kriegsversehrt.

disadvantage, *n.* Nachteil, -e *m.*

disagree, *n.* anderer Meinung sein*; *(food)* nicht bekom'men*.

disagreeable, *adj.* unangenehm.

disagreement, *n.* Uneinigkeit, -en *f.*, Widerspruch, -̈e *m.*

disappear, *vb.* verschwin'den*.

disappearance, *n.* Verschwin'den *nt.*

disappoint, *vb.* enttäu'schen.

disappointment, *n.* Enttäu'schung, -en *f.*

disapproval, *n.* Mißbilligung, -en *f.*

disapprove, *vb.* mißbilligen.

disarm, *vb.* entwaff'nen, ab·rü'sten.

disarmament, *n.* Abrüstung, -en *f.*

disarray, *n.* Unordnung *f.*

disaster, *n.* Unglück, -e *nt.*, Katastro'phe, -n *f.*

disastrous, *adj.* verhee'rend.

disavow, *vb.* ab·leugnen.

disband, *vb.* auf·lösen.

disburse, *vb.* aus·zahlen.

discard, *vb.* ab·legen.

discern, *vb.* unterschei'den*.

discerning, *adj.* scharfsinnig.

discernment, *n.* Scharfsinn *m.*, Einsicht *f.*

discharge, 1. *n.* Entlas'sung, -en *f.*; *(medicine)* Ausschei'dung, -en *f.* 2. *vb.* entlas'sen*, aus·scheiden*; *(gun)* ab·feuern.

disciple, *n.* Jünger, - *m.*

disciplinary, *adj.* maßregelnd.

discipline, 1. *n.* Disziplin' *f.* 2. *vb.* schulen, disziplinie'ren.

disclaim, *vb.* ab·leugnen; ver·zich'ten.

disclose, *vb.* enthül'len.

disclosure, *n.* Enthül'lung, -en *f.*

discomfort, *n.* Unbehagen *nt.*

disconcert, *vb.* in Verwir'rung bringen*.

disconnect, *vb.* los·lösen; *(elec.)* aus·schalten.

discontent, 1. *n.* Unzufriedenheit *f.* 2. *adj.* unzufrieden.

discontinue, *vb.* ein·stellen.

discord, *n.* Mißklang, -̈e *m.*; *(fig.)* Uneinigkeit, -en *f.*

discotheque, *n.* Diskothek', -en *f.*

discount, 1. *n.* Rabatt' *m.* 2. *vb.* ab·ziehen*.

discourage, *vb.* entmu'tigen.

discouragement, *n.* Entmu'tigung, -en *f.*

discourse, 1. *n.* Gespräch', -e *nt.*; Abhandlung, -en *f.* 2. *vb.* sprechen*.

discourteous, *adj.* unhöflich.

discourtesy, *n.* Unhöflichkeit, -en *f.*

discover, *vb.* entde'cken.

discovery, *n.* Entde'ckung, -en *f.*

discredit, 1. *n.* Nichtachtung *f.* 2. *vb.* nicht glauben; in schlechten Ruf bringen*.

discreet, *adj.* diskret'.

discrepancy, *n.* Zwiespalt, -e *m.*

discretion, *n.* Diskretion' *f.*; Beson'nenheit *f.*

discriminate, *vb.* unterschei'den*; diskriminie'ren.

discrimination, *n.* Diskriminie'rung, -en *f.*

discuss, *vb.* diskutie'ren.

discussion, *n.* Diskussion', -en *f.*

disdain, *vb.* verach'ten.

disdainful, *adj.* verächt'lich.

disease, *n.* Krankheit, -en *f.*

disembark, *vb.* landen.

disembarkation, *n.* Landung, -en *f.*

disenchantment, *n.* Enttäu'schung, -en *f.*, Ernüch'terung *f.*

disengage, *vb.* los·lösen.

disentangle, *vb.* entwir'ren.

disfavor, *n.* Mißfallen *nt.*; Ungnade *f.*

disfigure, *vb.* entstel'len.

disgrace, 1. *n.* Schande, -n *f.*, Unehre *f.* 2. *vb.* schänden, blamie'ren.

disgraceful, *adj.* schändlich.

disgruntled, *adj.* mürrisch.

disguise, 1. *n.* Verklei'dung, -en *f.* 2. *vb.* verklei'den.

disgust, 1. *n.* Ekel *m.* 2. *vb.* an·ekeln.

disgusting, *adj.* ekelhaft, widerlich.

dish, *n.* Schüssel, -n *f.*; *(food)* Gericht', -e *nt.*

dishcloth, *n.* Abwaschtuch, -̈er *nt.*

dishearten, *vb.* entmu'tigen.

dishonest, *adj.* unehrlich.

dishonesty, *n.* Unehrlichkeit, -en *f.*

dishonor, 1. *n.* Schande, -n *f.* 2. *vb.* enteh'ren.

dishonorable, *adj.* unehrenhaft.

dishtowel, *n.* Geschirr'handtuch, -̈er *nt.*

disillusion, 1. *n.* Enttäu'schung, -en *f.* 2. *vb.* enttäu'schen.

disinfect, *vb.* desinfizie'ren.

disinfectant, *n.* Desinfizie'rungsmittel, - *nt.*

disinherit *vb.* enter'ben.

disintegrate, *vb.* zerfal'len*.

disinterested, *adj.* gleichgültig.

disjointed, *adj.* unzusammenhängend.

disk, *n.* Scheibe, -n *f.*

dislike, 1. *n.* Abneigung, -en *f.* 2. *vb.* nicht mögen*.

dislocate, *vb.* aus·renken.

dislodge, *vb.* los·reißen*, vertrei'ben*.

disloyal, *adj.* treulos.

disloyalty, *n.* Untreue, -n *f.*

dismal, *adj.* jämmerlich.

dismantle, *vb.* demontie'ren.

dismay, 1. *n.* Bestür'zung, -en *f.* 2. *vb.* erschre'cken.

dismember, *vb.* zerstü'ckeln.

dismiss, *vb.* entlas'sen*; fallen lassen*.

dismissal, *n.* Entlas'sung, -en *f.*

dismount, *vb.* ab·steigen*.

disobedience, *n.* Ungehorsam *m.*

disobedient, *adj.* ungehorsam.

disobey, *vb.* nicht gehor'chen.

disorder, *n.* Unordnung *f.*

disorderly, *adj.* unordentlich, liederlich.

disorganize, *vb.* in Unordnung bringen*.

disown, *vb.* verleug'nen.

disparage, *vb.* herab'·setzen.

disparity, *n.* Ungleichheit, -en *f.*

dispassionate, *adj.* leidenschaftslos.

dispatch, 1. *n.* Absendung, -en *f.* 2. *vb.* ab·senden*, eilig weg·schicken.

dispatcher, *n.* Absender, - *m.*

dispel, *vb.* vertrei'ben*.

dispensable, *adj.* entbehr'lich.

dispensary, *n.* Arznei'ausgabestelle, -n *f.*

dispensation, *n.* Befrei'ung, -en *f.*

dispense, *vb.* aus·geben*; *(d. with)* verzich'ten auf.

dispersal, *n.* Vertei'lung, -en *f.*

disperse, *vb.* vertei'len.

displace, *vb.* verdrän'gen.

displaced person, *n.* Zwangsverschleppt- *m.&f.*

display, 1. *n.* Aufwand *m.*; *(window)* Schaufensterauslage, -n *f.* 2. *vb.* entfal'ten, zeigen.

displease, *vb.* mißfal'len*.

displeasure, *n.* Mißfallen *nt.*

disposable, *adj.* verfüg'bar.

disposal, *n.* Verfü'gung, -en *f.*

dispose, *vb.* bestim'men.

disposition, *n.* Verfü'gung, -en *f.*; *(character)* Anlage *f.*

dispossess, *vb.* enteig'nen.

disproof, *n.* Widerle'gung, -en *f.*

disproportion, *n.* Mißverhältnis, -se *nt.*

disproportionate, *adj.* unverhältnismäßig.

disprove, *vb.* widerle'gen.

disputable, *adj.* bestreit'bar.

dispute, 1. *n.* Streit, -e *m.* 2. *vb.* bestrei'ten*.

disqualification, *n.* Disqualifizie'rung, -en *f.*

disqualify, *vb.* disqualifizie'ren.

disregard, 1. *n.* Nichtbeachtung *f.* 2. *vb.* nicht beach'ten.

disrepair, *n.* Verfall' *m.*

disreputable, *adj.* verru'fen.

disrespect, *n.* Nichtachtung *f.*, Mißachtung *f.*

disrespectful, adj. unehrerbietig, unhöflich.

disrobe, vb. entklei'den.

disrupt, vb. auseinan'derreißen*.

dissatisfaction, n. Unzufriedenheit, -en f.

dissatisfy, vb. nicht befrie'digen.

dissect, vb. zerglie'dern; (med.) sezie'ren.

disseminate, vb. verbrei'ten.

dissension, n. Uneinigkeit, -en f.

dissent, 1. n. Meinungsverschiedenheit, -en f. 2. vb. anderer Meinung sein*.

dissertation, n. Dissertation', -en f.

dissimilar, adj. unähnlich.

dissipated, adj. ausschweifend, verlebt'.

dissipation, n. Ausschweifung, -en f.

dissociate, vb. trennen.

dissolute, adj. verkom'men.

dissolution, n. Auflösung, -en f.

dissolve, vb. auf·lösen.

dissonance, n. Dissonanz', -en f.

dissonant, adj. dissonant'.

dissuade, vb. ab·raten*.

distance, n. Entfer'nung, -en f.; Abstand, -̈e m.

distant, adj. entfernt'; (fig.) zurück'haltend.

distaste, n. Widerwille(n), - m., Abneigung, -en f.

distasteful, adj. widerwärtig, widerlich.

distemper, n. (dog) Staupe f.

distend, vb. aus·dehnen.

distill, vb. destillie'ren.

distillation, n. Destillation', -en f.

distiller, n. Destillateur', -e m.

distillery, n. Branntweinbrennerei, -en f.

distinct, adj. deutlich; (different) verschie'den.

distinction, n. (difference) Unterschied, -e m.; (elegance) Vornehmheit f.; (honor) Auszeichnung, -en f.

distinctive, adj. kennzeichnend.

distinctness, n. Deutlichkeit f.

distinguish, vb. (differentiate) unterschei'den*; (honor) aus·zeichnen.

distinguished, adj. (famous) berühmt'; (elegant) vornehm.

distort, vb. verzer'ren.

distract, vb. ab·lenken.

distraction, n. Ablenkung, -en f.

distress, 1. n. Not, -̈e f. 2. vb. betrü'ben.

distribute, vb. vertei'len.

distribution, n. Vertei'lung, -en f.

distributor, n. Vertei'ler, - m.; (agent) Vertriebs'stelle, -n f.

district, n. Bezirk', -e m.

distrust, 1. n. Mißtrauen nt. 2. vb. mißtrau'en.

distrustful, adj. mißtrauisch.

disturb, vb. stören, beun'ruhigen.

disturbance, n. Störung, -en f., Unruhe, -n f.

ditch, n. Graben, -̈ m.

diva, n. Diva, -s f.

divan, n. Diwan, -e m.

dive, 1. n. Kopfsprung, -̈e m. 2. vb. tauchen.

diver, n. Taucher, - m.

diverge, vb. auseinan'dergehen*.

divergence, n. Divergenz', -en f.

divergent, adj. divergie'rend.

diverse, adj. verschie'den.

diversion, n. Ablenkung, -en f.; (pastime) Zeitvertreib, -e m.

diversity, n. Mannigfaltigkeit, -en f.

divert, vb. ab·lenken, um·leiten.

divest, vb. entklei'den.

divide, vb. teilen.

dividend, n. Dividen'de, -n f.

divine, adj. göttlich.

divinity, n. Gottheit, -en f.; (study) Theologie', -i'en f.

divisible, adj. teilbar.

division, n. Teilung, -en f.; (mil.) Division', -en f.

divorce, 1. n. Scheidung, -en f. 2. vb. (get d.d) sich scheiden lassen*; (d. a person) sich von einem Menschen scheiden lassen*.

divorcée, n. geschie'dene Frau, -en f.

divulge, vb. enthül'len.

dizziness, n. Schwindel m.

dizzy, adj. schwindlig.

do, vb. tun*, machen.

docile, adj. fügsam.

dock, n. Dock, -s nt.

docket, n. Gerichts'kalender, - m.; Geschäfts'ordnung, -en f.

doctor, n. Doktor, -o'ren m.; (physician) Arzt, -̈e m.

doctorate, n. Doktorat', -e nt.

doctrine, n. Lehre, -n f.; Grundsatz, -̈e m.

document, n. Urkunde, -n f.; Dokument', -e nt.

documentary, adj. urkundlich, dokumenta'risch.

documentation, n. Dokumentation', -en f.

dodge, vb. aus·weichen*.

doe, n. Reh, -e nt.

doeskin, n. Rehleder nt.

dog, n. Hund, -e m.

dogma, n. Dogma, -men nt.

dogmatic, adj. dogma'tisch.

dogmatism, n. Dogma'tik f.

dole, 1. n. Arbeitslosenunterstützung, -en f.; (be on the d.) stempeln gehen*. 2. vb. (d. out) vertei'len.

doleful, adj. kummervoll.

doll, n. Puppe, -n f.

dollar, n. Dollar, -s m.

domain, n. Bereich', -e m.

dome, n. Dom, -e m., Kuppel, -n f.

domestic, adj. häuslich; (d. policy) Innenpolitik f.

domesticate, vb. zähmen.

domicile, n. Wohnort, -e m.

dominance, n. Herrschaft, -en f.

dominant, adj. vorherrschend.

dominate, vb. beherr'schen.

domination, n. Herrschaft, -en f.

domineer, vb. tyrannisie'ren.

dominion, n. Domi'nion, -s nt.

domino, n. Domino, -s m.

don, vb. an·ziehen*; (hat) auf·setzen.

donate, vb. stiften.

donation, n. Gabe, -n f., Schenkung, -en f.

done, adj. (food) gar.

donkey, n. Esel, - m.

doom, n. Verder'ben nt.

door, n. Tür, -en f.

doorman, n. Portier', -s m.

doorway, n. Türeingang, -̈e m.

dope, n. (drug) Rauschgift, -e nt.; (fool) Trottel, - m.

dormant, adj. ruhend, latent'.

dormitory, n. (room) Schlafsaal, -säle m.; (building) Studentenheim, -e nt.

dosage, n. Dosie'rung, -en f.

dose, n. Dosis, -sen f.

dossier, n. Akte, -n f.

dot, n. Punkt, -e m.

double, 1. n. Doppelgänger, - m. 2. adj. doppelt.

double-breasted, adj. zweireihig.

double-cross, vb. hintergeh'en*.

doubt, 1. n. Zweifel, - m. 2. vb. zweifeln, bezwei'feln.

doubtful, adj. zweifelhaft.

doubtless, adj. zweifellos.

dough, n. Teig, -e m.

douse, vb. begie'ßen; (fire) löschen.

dove, n. Taube, -n f.

dowdy, adj. schlampig.

down, 1. n. Flaum m.; (material) Daune, -n f. 2. vb. niederwerfen*, (fig.) besie'gen. 3. adv. unten, nieder, ab; hin-, herun'ter; hin-, herab'

downcast, adj. niedergeschlagen.

downfall, n. Untergang, -̈e m.

downhearted, adj. betrübt'.

downhill, adv. bergab'.

down payment, n. Anzahlung, -en f.

downpour, n. Regenguß, -̈sse m.

downstairs, adv. unten.

downtown, 1. n. Geschäfts'viertel, - nt. 2. adv. (direction) in die Stadt; (location) in der Stadt.

downward, adv. nach unten.

dowry, n. Mitgift, -en f.

doze, vb. dösen.

dozen, n. Dutzend, -e nt.

drab, *adj.* *(color)* bräunlich gelb; *(dull)* farblos.

draft, 1. *n.* *(plan)* Entwurf´, -e *m.;* *(money)* Wechsel, - *m.;* *(air)* Zug, ⁼e *m.;* *(military service)* militä´rische Dienstpflicht *f.* 2. *vb.* ent-wer´fen*; *(mil.)* ein·ziehen*.

draftee, *n.* Rekrut´, -en, -en *m.*

draftsman, *n.* Zeichner, - *m.*

drafty, *adj.* zugig.

drag, *vb.* schleppen, schleifen.

dragon, *n.* Drache, -n, -n *m.*

drain, 1. *n.* Abfluß, ⁼sse *m.* 2. *vb.* ab·laufen lassen*; ent-wäs´sern.

drainage, *n.* Abfluß, ⁼sse *m.;* Entwäs´serung, -en *f.*

dram, *n.* Drachme, -n *f.*

drama, *n.* Drama, -men *nt.;* Schauspiel, -e *nt.*

dramatic, *adj.* drama´tisch.

dramatics, *n.* Thea´terwissenschaft, -en *f.*

dramatist, *n.* Drama´tiker, - *m.*

dramatize, *vb.* dramatisie´-ren.

drape, 1. *n.* Vorhang, ⁼e *m.* 2. *vb.* drapie´ren.

drapery, *n.* Vorhang, ⁼e *m.;* Be-hang´, ⁼e *m.*

drastic, *adj.* drastisch.

draught, see draft.

draw, *vb.* *(pull)* ziehen*; *(picture)* zeichnen; **(d. up)** ab·fassen.

drawback, *n.* Nachteil, -e *m.;* Schattenseite, -n *f.*

drawbridge, *n.* Zugbrücke, -n *f.*

drawer, *n.* Schublade, -n *f.*

drawing, *n.* *(picture)* Zeichnung, -en *f.;* *(lottery)* Ziehung, -en *f.*

drawl, *vb.* langsam und ausgedehnt sprechen*.

dread, 1. *n.* Furcht *f.,* Angst, ⁼e *f.* 2. *vb.* fürchten.

dreadful, *adj.* furchtbar.

dream, 1. *n.* Traum, ⁼e *m.* 2. *vb.* träumen.

dreamy, *adj.* träumerisch, ver-träumt´.

dreary, *adj.* trostlos.

dredge, 1. *n.* Bagger, - *m.* 2. *vb.* baggern.

dregs, *n.pl.* Bodensatz, ⁼e *m.;* *(fig.)* Abschaum, ⁼e *m.*

drench, *vb.* durchnäs´sen.

dress, 1. *n.* Kleid, -er *nt.* 2. *vb.* an·ziehen*, kleiden.

dresser, *n.* Kommo´de, -n *f.*

dressing, *n.* *(food)* Soße, -n *f.;* *(med.)* Verband´, ⁼e *m.*

dressing gown, *n.* Schlafrock, ⁼e *m.,* Morgenrock, ⁼e *m.*

dressmaker, *n.* Schneiderin, -nen *f.*

drier, *n.* *(hair)* Trockenhaube, -n *f.;* *(clothes)* Trockenautomat, -en, -en *m.*

drift, 1. *n.* *(snow)* Schneewehe, -n *f.;* *(tendency)* Richtung, -en *f.;* Strömung, -en *f.* 2. *vb.* treiben*.

drill, 1. *n.* *(tool)* Drillbohrer, - *m.;* *(practice)* Schulung, -en *f.;* *(mil.)* Exerzie´ren *nt.* 2. *vb.* bohren; schulen; exerzie´-ren.

drink, 1. *n.* Getränk´, -e *nt.* 2. *vb.* trinken*.

drinkable, *adj.* trinkbar.

drip, *vb.* tropfen.

drive, 1. *n.* *(ride)* Spazier´fahrt, -en *f.;* *(energy)* Schwungkraft *f.* 2. *vb.* treiben*; *(auto)* fah-ren*.

driver, *n.* Fahrer, - *m.*

driveway, *n.* Auffahrt, -en *f.*

drizzle, 1. *n.* Sprühregen, - *m.* 2. *vb.* nieseln.

drone, 1. *n.* *(bee)* Drohne, -n *f.;* *(hum)* Gesum´me *nt.* 2. *vb.* summen.

droop, *vb.* herab´·hängen*.

drop, 1. *n.* Tropfen, - *m.* 2. *vb.* *(fall)* fallen*; *(let fall)* fallen* lassen*.

dropout, *n.* jemand, der absichtlich seine ordnungsgemäße Tätigkeit, Ausbildung, Lebensart, aufgibt.

dropper, *n.* Tropfer, - *m.*

dropsy, *n.* Wassersucht *f.*

drought, *n.* Dürre, -n *f.,* Trockenheit, -en *f.*

drown, *vb.* *(intr.)* ertrin´ken*; *(tr.)* erträn´ken*.

drowsiness, *n.* Schläfrigkeit *f.*

drowsy, *adj.* schläfrig.

drudgery, *n.* Plackerei´, -en *f.*

drug, *n.* Droge, -n *f.,* Medika-ment´, -e *nt.*

druggist, *n.* Drogist´, -en, -en *m.,* Apothe´ker, - *m.*

drug store, *n.* Drogerie´, -i´en *f.,* Apothe´ke, -n *f.*

drum, *n.* Trommel, -n *f.*

drummer, *n.* Trommler, - *m.*

drumstick, *n.* Trommelschlegel, - *m.;* *(fowl)* Geflü´gel-schlegel, - *m.*

drunk, *adj.* betrun´ken; **(get d.)** sich betrin´ken*.

drunkard, *n.* Trinker, - *m.;* Trunkenbold, -e *m.*

drunken, *adj.* betrun´ken.

drunkenness, *n.* Trunkenheit *f.*

dry, 1. *adj.* trocken. 2. *vb.* trocknen.

dry cell, *n.* Trockenelement, -e *nt.*

dry-cleaner, *n.* Reinigung, -en *f.*

dry-cleaning, *n.* chemische Reinigung, -en *f.*

dry goods, *n.pl.* Texti´lien *pl.*

dryness, *n.* Trockenheit, -en *f.*

dual, *adj.* Doppel- *(cpds.).*

dubious, *adj.* zweifelhaft.

duchess, *n.* Herzogin, -nen *f.*

duchy, *n.* Herzogtum, ⁼er *nt.*

duck, 1. *n.* Ente, -n *f.* 2. *vb.* sich ducken.

duct, *n.* Rohr, -e *nt.;* Kanal´, ⁼e *m.*

due, *adj.* schuldig; fällig.

duel, *n.* Duell´, -e *nt.*

dues, *n.pl.* Gebüh´ren *pl.,* Bei-trag, ⁼e *m.*

duet, *n.* Duett´, -e *nt.*

duffle bag, *n.* Seesack, ⁼e *m.*

duke, *n.* Herzog, ⁼e *m.*

dull, *adj.* *(not sharp)* stumpf; *(boring)* langweilig.

dullness, *n.* Stumpfheit *f.;* Langweiligkeit *f.*

duly, *adv.* gebüh´rend.

dumb, *adj.* stumm; *(stupid)* dumm (⁼), blöde.

dumbwaiter, *n.* Drehaufzug, ⁼e *m.*

dumfound, *vb.* verblüf´fen.

dummy, *n.* *(posing as someone)* Strohmann, ⁼er *m.;* *(window-display)* Schaufensterpuppe, -n *f.;* *(bridge)* Tisch *m.;* *(theater)* Statist´, -en, -en *m.*

dump, 1. *n.* Abladeplatz, ⁼e *m.;* *(refuse)* Schuttablade, -n *f.* 2. *vb.* ab·laden*.

dumpling, *n.* Kloß, ⁼e *m.*

dun, 1. *adj.* graubraun. 2. *vb.* zur Zahlung mahnen.

dunce, *n.* Schafskopf, ⁼e *m.,* Dummkopf, ⁼e *m.*

dune, *n.* Düne, -n *f.*

dung, *n.* Dung *m.*

dungarees, *n.pl.* Arbeitshose, -n *f.*

dungeon, *n.* Kerker, - *m.*

dunk, *vb.* tunken.

dupe, 1. *n.* düpie´ren. 2. *n.* Düpiert´- *m.&f.*

duplex, *adj.* Doppelt- *(cpds.).*

duplicate, *vb.* verdop´peln, kopie´ren.

duplication, *n.* Verdop´pelung, -en *f.*

duplicity, *n.* Dupliziät´, -en *f.*

durability, *n.* Dauerhaftigkeit *f.*

durable, *adj.* dauerhaft.

duration, *n.* Dauer *f.*

duress, *n.* Zwang *m.*

during, *prep.* während.

dusk, *n.* Abenddämmerung, -en *f.*

dust, 1. *n.* Staub *m.* 2. *vb.* ab·stauben.

dusty, *adj.* staubig.

Dutch, *adj.* holländisch.

Dutchman, *n.* Holländer, - *m.*

dutiful, *adj.* pflichtgetreu.

duty, *n.* Pflicht, -en *f.;* *(tax)* Zoll, ⁼e *m.*

duty-free, *adj.* zollfrei.

dwarf, *n.* Zwerg, -e *m.*

dwell, *vb.* wohnen.

dweller, *n.* Bewoh´ner, - *m.*

dwelling, *n.* Wohnung, -en *f.;* Wohnsitz, -e *m.*

dwindle, *vb.* schrumpfen.

dye, 1. *n.* Farbe, -n *f.;* Farbstoff, -e *m.* 2. *vb.* färben.

dyer, *n.* Färber, - *m.*

dyestuff, *n.* Farbstoff, -e *m.*

dynamic, *adj.* dyna´misch.

dynamite, *n.* Dynamit´ *nt.*

dynamo, *n.* Dyna´mo, -s *m.*

dynasty, *n.* Dynastie´, -i´en *f.*

dysentery, *n.* Ruhr *f.*

E

dyslexia, n. Dysle'xia f.

dyspepsia, n. Dyspepsie' f.

each, adj. jeder, -es, -e.

each other, pron. einan'der.

eager, adj. eifrig.

eagerness, n. Eifer m.

eagle, n. Adler, - m.

ear, n. Ohr, -en nt.

earache, n. Ohrenschmerzen pl.

eardrum, n. Trommelfell, -e nt.

earl, n. Graf, -en, -en m.

early, adj. früh.

earmark, 1. n. Anzeichen, - nt. **2.** vb. bestim'men; (be e.ed) vorgesehen sein*.

earn, vb. verdie'nen.

earnest, adj. ernst.

earnestness, n. Ernst m.

earnings, n.pl. Einnahmen pl.

earring, n. Ohrring, -e m.

earth, n. Erde, -n f.

earthenware, n. Steingut nt.

earthly, adj. irdisch.

earthquake, n. Erdbeben, - nt.

earthy, adj. erdig; (fig.) derb.

ease, n. Leichtigkeit, -en f.; (comfort) Behag'lichkeit, -en f. **2.** vb. erleich'tern, lindern.

easel, n. Staffelei', -en f.

easiness, n. Leichtigkeit, -en f.

east, 1. n. Osten m., Orient m. **2.** adj. östlich; Ost (cpds.).

Easter, n. Ostern nt.

easterly, adj. östlich.

eastern, adj. östlich.

eastward, adv. ostwärts.

easy, adj. leicht.

easygoing, adj. gutmütig, ungezwungen.

eat, vb. essen*.

eatable, adj. eßbar.

eaves, n.pl. Dachrinne, -n f.

ebb, 1. n. Ebbe, -n f. **2.** vb. abneh'men*.

ebony, n. Ebenholz, ⁻er nt.

eccentric, adj. exzen'trisch.

eccentricity, n. Exzentrizität', -en f.

ecclesiastic, adj. kirchlich, geistlich.

ecclesiastical, adj. kirchlich, geistlich.

echelon, n. Staffel, -n f.

echo, 1. n. Echo, -s nt. **2.** vb. wider'hallen.

eclipse, n. Finsternis, -se f.

ecological, adj. ökolo'gisch.

ecology, n. Ökologie' f.

economic, adj. wirtschaftlich.

economical, adj. sparsam.

economics, n. Volkswirtschaft f., National'ökonomie f.

economist, n. Volkswirtschaftler, - m.

economize, vb. haus·halten*.

economy, n. Wirtschaft f.; Sparsamkeit f.

ecstasy, n. Verzü'ckung, -en f.

ecumenical, adj. ökume'nisch.

eczema, n. Ekzem', -e nt.

eddy, n. Strudel, - m.

edge, n. Rand, ⁻er m.; (knife, etc.) Schneide, -n f.

edible, adj. eßbar.

edict, n. Verord'nung, -en f., Edikt', -e nt.

edifice, n. Gebäu'de, - nt.

edify, vb. erbau'en.

edit, vb. heraus'·geben*.

edition, n. Ausgabe, -n f., Auflage, -n f.

editor, n. Heraus'geber, - m.

editorial, 1. n. Leitartikel, - m. **2.** adj. Redaktions'- (cpds.).

educate, vb. (bring up) erzie'hen*; (train) aus·bilden.

education, n. (upbringing) Erzie'hung f.; (training) Ausbildung f.; (culture) Bildung f.

educational, adj. erzie'herisch.

educator, n. Erzie'her, - m.; Pädago'ge, -n, -n m.

eel, n. Aal, -e m.

effect, n. Wirkung, -en f.

effective, adj. wirkungsvoll.

effectiveness, n. Wirksamkeit f.

effectual, adj. wirksam.

effeminate, adj. verweich'licht.

effervescence, n. Sprudeln nt.

effete, adj. entkräf'tet.

efficiency, n. Leistungsfähigkeit f., Tüchtigkeit f., Wirksamkeit f.

efficient, adj. leistungsfähig, tüchtig, wirksam.

effigy, n. Abbild, -er nt.

effort, n. Mühe, -n f.; (exertion) Anstrengung, -en f.; (attempt) Versuch, -e m.

effrontery, n. Frechheit, -en f.

effusive, adj. überschwenglich.

egg, n. Ei, -er nt.

eggplant, n. Aubergi'ne, -n f.

ego, n. Ich nt.

egoism, n. Egois'mus m.

egotism, n. Egotis'mus m.

egotist, n. Egoist', -en, -en m.

Egypt, n. Ägyp'ten nt.

Egyptian, 1. n. Ägyp'ter, - m. **2.** adj. ägyp'tisch.

eight, num. acht.

eighteen, num. achtzehn.

eighteenth, 1. adj. achtzehnt-. **2.** n. Achtzehntel, - nt.

eighth, 1. adj. acht-. **2.** n. Achtel, - nt.

eightieth, 1. adj. achtzigst-. **2.** n. Achtzigstel, - nt.

eighty, num. achtzig.

either, 1. pron.&adj. jeder, -es, -e; beides, pl. beide. **2.** conj. (e. . . . or) entweder . . . oder. **3.** adv. (not . . . e.) auch nicht, auch kein, -, -e.

ejaculation, n. Ausruf, -e m.

eject, vb. hinaus'·werfen*; vertrei'ben*.

ejection, n. Hinaus'werfen nt.

eke out, vb. sich durch·helfen*.

elaborate, 1. adj. weitläufig;

kunstvoll. 2. vb. ins einzelne gehen*.

elapse, vb. verge'hen*.

elastic, 1. n. Gummiband, ⁻er nt. **2.** adj. elas'tisch.

elasticity, n. Elastizität' f.

elate, vb. erfreu'en.

elated, adj. hocherfreut.

elation, n. Freude, -n f.

elbow, n. Ellbogen, - m.

elder, 1. n. (tree) Holun'der, - m.; (church) Ältest- m. **2.** adj. älter.

elderly, adj. ältlich.

eldest, adj. ältest-.

elect, vb. wählen.

election, n. Wahl, -en f.

elective, adj. Wahl- (cpds.).

electorate, n. Wählerschaft, -en f.

electric, electrical, adj. elek'trisch.

electrician, n. Elek'triker, - m.

electricity, n. Elektrizität' f.

electrocardiogram, n. EKG, -s nt.; Elektrokardiogramm', -e nt.

electrocution, n. Tötung durch elektrischen Strom; Hinrichtung auf dem elektrischen Stuhl.

electrode, n. Elektro'de, -n f.

electrolysis, n. Elektroly'se f.

electron, n. Elektron, -o'nen nt.

electronic, adj. Elektro'nen- (cpds.).

electronics, n. Elektro'nenwissenschaft f.

elegance, n. Eleganz' f.

elegant, adj. elegant'.

elegy, n. Elegie', -i'en f.

element, n. Element', -e nt.

elemental, elementary, adj. elementar'.

elephant, n. Elefant', -en, -en m.

elephantine, adj. elefan'tenartig.

elevate, vb. erhö'hen.

elevation, n. Erhö'hung, -en f.; Höhe, -n f.

elevator, n. Fahrstuhl, ⁻e m.

eleven, num. elf.

eleventh, 1. adj. elft-. **2.** n. Elftel, - nt.

elf, n. Kobold, -e m.

elfin, adj. koboldartig.

elicit, vb. heraus'·holen, erwir'ken.

eligibility, n. Qualifiziert'heit f.

eligible, adj. qualifiziert'.

eliminate, vb. besei'tigen, aus·scheiden*.

elimination, n. Besei'tigung, -en f.; Ausscheidung, -en f.

elixir, n. Elixier', -e nt.

elk, n. Elch, -e m.

elm, n. Ulme, -n f.

elocution, n. Redekunst, ⁻e f.

elongate, vb. verlän'gern.

elope, vb. mit einem Mädchen oder einem Jungen durchbrennen*.

eloquence, n. Bered'samkeit f.

eloquent, adj. redegewandt.

else, adv. anders, sonst.

elsewhere, adv. anderswo.

elucidate, vb. erläu'tern.

elude, vb. entge'hen*.

elusive, adj. nicht greifbar; aalglatt.

emaciated, adj. abgezehrt.

emanate, vb. aus-strömen.

emancipate, vb. emanzipie'ren.

emancipation, n. Emanzipa'tion', -en f.

emancipator, n. Befrei'er, - m.

emasculate, vb. entman'nen.

embalm, vb. ein-balsamieren.

embankment, n. Uferanlage, -n f.

embargo, n. Embar'go, -s nt.

embark, vb. ein-schiffen.

embarrass, vb. in Verle'genheit bringen*.

embarrassed, adj. verle'gen.

embarrassment, n. Verle'genheit, -en f.

embassy, n. Botschaft, -en f.

embellish, vb. aus-schmücken.

embellishment, n. Ausschmückung, -en f.

embezzle, vb. unterschla'gen*.

embitter, vb. verbit'tern.

emblem, n. Wahrzeichen, - nt. , Emblem', -e nt.

embody, vb. verkör'pern.

embrace, vb. umar'men.

embroider, vb. sticken.

embroidery, n. Stickerei', -en f.

embroil, vb. verwi'ckeln.

embryo, n. Embryo, -s m.

emerald, n. Smaragd', -e m.

emerge, vb. hervor'treten*, auf-tauchen.

emery, n. Schmirgel m.

emetic, n. Brechmittel, - nt.

emigrant, n. Auswanderer, - m.

emigrate, vb. aus-wandern.

emigration, n. Auswanderung, -en f.

eminence, n. (hill) Anhöhe, -n f.; (distinction) Auszeichnung, -en f.; (title) Eminenz', -en f.

eminent, adj. erha'ben.

emissary, n. Gesandt'- m.&f.

emission controls, n.pl. Abgasbestimmungen f.pl.

emit, vb. von sich geben*.

emotion, n. Gefühl', -e nt.; Erre'gung, -en f.

emotional, adj. gefühls'mäßig; erreg'bar.

emperor, n. Kaiser, - m.

emphasis, n. Nachdruck m.

emphasize, vb. beto'nen, hervor'heben*.

emphatic, adj. nachdrücklich.

empire, n. Kaiserreich, -e nt.

empirical, adj. empi'risch.

employ, vb. an-stellen, beschäf'tigen.

employee, n. Arbeitnehmer, - m., Angestellt- m.&f.

employer, n. Arbeitgeber, - m.

employment, n. Anstellung, -en f.; Beschäf'tigung, -en f.

empower, vb. ermäch'tigen.

empress, n. Kaiserin, -nen f.

emptiness, n. leere f.

empty, 1. vb. leeren. 2. adj. leer.

emulate, vb. nach-eifern.

emulsion, n. Emulsion', -en f.

enable, vb. ermög'lichen; (enabling act) Ermäch'tigungsgesetz, -e nt.

enact, vb. (law) erlas'sen; (role) spielen.

enactment, n. Verord'nung, -en f.

enamel, n. Emai'lle f.

enamor, vb. (be e.ed of) in jemand verliebt' sein*; (become e.ed of) sich in jemand verlie'ben.

encamp, vb. sich lagern.

encampment, n. Lager, - nt.

encephalitis, n. Gehirn'entzündung, -en f.

enchant, vb. entzü'cken; bezau'bern.

enchantment, n. Bezau'berung f.; Zauber m.

encircle, vb. umrin'gen.

enclose, vb. ein-schließen*; (letter) bei-fügen.

enclosure, n. Einzäunung, -en f.; (letter) Beilage, -n f.

encompass, vb. umschlie'ßen*, ein-schließen*.

encounter, n. treffen*, begeg'nen.

encourage, vb. ermu'tigen.

encouragement, n. Ermu'tigung, -en f.

encroach upon, vb. sich ein-drängen.

encyclical, n. Enzy'klika, -ken f.

encyclopedia, n. Konversations'lexikon, -ka nt.; Enzyklopädie', -i'en f.

end, 1. n. Ende, -n nt.; (purpose) Zweck, -e m.; (goal) Ziel, -e nt. 2. vb. been'den, vollen'den, been'digen.

endanger, vb. gefähr'den.

endear, vb. lieb, teuer, wert machen.

endearment, n. Zärtlichkeit, -en f.

endeavor, vb. sich bemü'hen, streben.

ending, n. Ende, -n nt., Schluß, -sse m.

endless, adj. endlos.

endocrine, adj. endokrin'.

endorse, vb. gut-heißen*; (check) girie'ren.

endorsement, n. Billigung, -en f.; (check) Giro nt.

endow, vb. aus-statten; stiften.

endowment, n. Ausstattung, -en f.; Stiftung, -en f.

endurance, n. Ausdauer f.

endure, vb. (last) dauern; (bear) ertra'gen*.

enema, n. Klistier', -e nt.

enemy, n. Feind, -e m.

energetic, adj. tatkräftig.

energy, n. Tatdrft, -e f., Energie', -n f.

enfold, vb. ein-hüllen.

enforce, vb. durch-setzen; auf-swingen*.

enforcement, n. Durchführung -en f., Durchsetzung, -en f.

engage, vb. (hire) an-stellen; (affiance) verlo'ben; (rent) mieten.

engaged, adj. (busy) beschäf'tigt; (affianced) verlobt'.

engagement, n. (date) Verab'redung, -en f.; (betrothal) Verlo'bung, -en f.

engaging, adj. anziehend.

engender, vb. hervor'bringen*.

engine, n. Maschi'ne, - f.; Motor, -o'ren, m.; Lokomoti've, -n f.

engineer, n. Ingenieur', -e m; (locomotive) Lokomotiv'führer, - m.; (mil.) Pionier, -e m.

engineering, n. Ingenieur'wesen nt.

England, n. England nt.

English, adj. englisch.

Englishman, n. Engländer, - m.

Englishwoman, n. Engländerin, -en f.

engrave, vb. gravie'ren.

engraver, n. Graveur', -e m.

engraving, n. Kupferstich, -e m.

engross, vb. in Anspruch nehmen*.

enhance, vb. erhö'hen.

enigma, n. Rätsel, - nt.

enigmatic, adj. rätselhaft, dunkel.

enjoin, vb. (command) befeh'len*; (forbid) verbie'ten*.

enjoy, vb. genie'ßen*, sich erfreu'en.

enjoyable, adj. erfreu'lich, angenehm, nett.

enjoyment, n. Freude, -n f., Genuß', -sse m.

enlarge, vb. vergrö'ßern.

enlargement, n. Vergrö'ßerung, -en f.

enlarger, n. Vergrö'ßerungsapparat, -e m.

enlighten, vb. auf-klären.

enlightenment, n. Aufklärung f.

enlist, vb. ein-spannen; (mil.) sich freiwillig melden.

enlisted man, n. Soldat', -en, - en m.

enlistment, n. freiwillige Meldung zum Militärdienst.

enliven, vb. bele'ben.

enmity, n. Feindschaft, -en f.

ennui, n. Langeweile f.

enormity, n. Ungeheuerlichkeit, -en f.

normous, adj. ungeheuer, enorm'.

nough, adv. genug', genü'gend.

nrage, vb. rasend machen.

nrapture, vb. entzü'cken.

nrich, vb. berei'chern.

nroll, vb. als Mitglied ein·tragen*.

nrollment, n. Eintragung (f.) als Mitglied; Mitgliederzahl,-en f.

nsemble, n. Ensem'ble, -s nt.

nshrine, vb. als Heiligtum verwah'ren.

nsign, n. (rank) Fähnrich, -e m.; (flag) Fahne, -n f.

nslave, vb. verskla'ven, knechten.

nsnare, vb. verstri'cken.

nsue, vb. folgen.

ntail, vb. ein·schließen*.

ntangle, vb. verwi'ckeln.

nter, vb. ein·treten*, ein·dringen*.

nterprise, n. Unterneh'men, - nt.

nterprising, adj. unternehmend.

ntertain, vb. unterhal'ten*.

ntertainment, n. Unterhal'tung, -en f.

nthrall, vb. bezau'bern.

nthusiasm, n. Begeis'terung, f.

nthusiastic, adj. begeis'tert.

ntice, vb. verlo'cken.

ntire, adj. ganz, gesamt'.

ntirety, n. Ganz- nt., Ganzheit f., Gesamt'heit f.

ntitle, vb. berech'tigen; (name) beti'teln.

ntity, n. Wesenheit f.

ntrails, n.pl. Eingeweide pl.

ntrain, vb. den Zug bestei'gen*.

ntrance, n. Eingang, -e m.

ntrant, n. Teilnehmer, - m.

ntrap, vb. in einer Falle fangen*; verstri'cken.

ntreat, vb. an·flehen.

ntreaty, n. Gesuch', -e nt.

ntrench, vb. verschan'zen.

ntrepreneur, n. Unterneh'mer, - m.

ntrust, vb. an·vertrauen.

ntry, n. Eintritt, -e m.; (writing) Eintragung, -en f.

numerate, vb. auf·zählen.

numeration, n. Aufzählung, -en f.

nunciate, vb. aus·sprechen*.

nunciation, n. Aussprache, -n f.

nvelop, vb. ein·hüllen.

nvelope, n. Umschlag, -e m., Kuvert', -s nt.

nviable, adj. benei'denswert.

nvious, adj. neidisch.

nvironment, n. Umge'bung, -en f., Umwelt f.

nvironmentalist, n. Umweltschützer, - m.

nvironmental protection, n. Umweltschutz m.

nvirons, n. Umge'bung, -en f.

---

envisage, vb. vergegenwär'tigen.

envoy, n. Gesandt'- m.

envy, n. Neid m.

eon, n. Äon', -en m.

ephemeral, adj. vergäng'lich.

epic, 1. n. Epos, -pen nt. 2. adj. episch.

epicure, n. Feinschmecker, - m.

epidemic, 1. n. Epidemie', i'en f. 2. adj. epide'misch.

epidermis, n. Epider'mis f.

epigram, n. Epigramm', -e nt.

epilepsy, n. Epilepsie' f.

episode, n. Episo'de, -n f.

epistle, n. Schreiben, - nt.

epitaph, n. Epitaph', -e nt.

epithet, n. Beiwort, -er nt.

epitome, n. Kurzfassung, -en f.; (fig.) Verkör'perung, -en f.

epitomize, vb. zusam'men·fassen; bezeich'nend sein* für.

epoch, n. Epo'che, -n f.

equal, 1. adj. gleich. 2. vb. gleichen*.

equality, n. Gleichheit f.

equalize, vb. gleich·machen; aus·gleichen*.

equanimity, n. Gleichmut m.

equate, vb. gleich·setzen.

equation, n. Gleichung, -en f.

equator, n. Äqua'tor m.

equatorial, adj. äquatorial'.

equestrian, n. Reiter, - m.

equilateral, adj. gleichseitig.

equilibrium, n. Gleichgewicht nt.

equinox, n. Tag- und Nachtgleiche, -n f.

equip, vb. aus·rüsten.

equipment, n. Ausrüstung, -en f.

equitable, adj. gerecht', billig.

equity, n. Billigkeit f.; Billigkeitsrecht nt.; (mortgage, etc.) Rückkaufswert, -e m.

equivalent, adj. gleichwertig.

equivocal, adj. zweideutig.

equivocate, vb. zweideutig sein*.

era, n. Zeitalter, - nt.

eradicate, vb. aus·rotten.

erase, vb. aus·radieren.

erasure, n. Ausradierung, -en f.

erect, 1. adj. gera'de. 2. vb. er·rich'ten.

erection, n. Errich'tung, -en f.

erectness, n. Gerad'heit f.

ermine, n. Hermelin' m.

erode, vb. erodie'ren, zerfres'sen*.

erosion, n. Erosion', -en f.

erotic, adj. ero'tisch.

err, vb. irren.

errand, n. Besor'gung, -en f.

errant, adj. wandernd; abwegig.

erratic, adj. verirrt'; ziellos.

erroneous, adj. irrtümlich.

error, n. Fehler, - m.; Irrtum, -er m.

---

erudite, adj. gelehrt'.

erudition, n. Gelehr'samkeit f.

erupt, vb. hervor'·brechen*, aus·brechen*.

eruption, n. Ausbruch, -e m.

escalate, vb. steigern.

escalator, n. Rolltreppe, -n f.

escapade, n. Streich, -e m.

escape, 1. n. Flucht f. 2. vb. entkom'men*, entge'hen*.

escapism, n. Wirklichkeitsflucht f.

escort, 1. n. Beglei'ter, - m. 2. vb. beglei'ten.

escutcheon, n. Wappenschild, -er nt.

esophagus, n. Speiseröhre, -n f.

esoteric, adj. esote'risch.

especial, adj. beson'der-.

especially, adv. beson'ders.

espionage, n. Spiona'ge f.

espousal, n. Vermäh'lung, -en f.; (e. of) Eintreten für nt.

espouse, vb. vermäh'len; (e. a cause) ein·treten* für.

essay, 1. n. Essay, -s m. 2. vb. versu'chen.

essence, nt. Wesen nt., Wesentlich- nt.

essential, adj. wesentlich.

establish, vb. fest·setzen; er·rich'ten; ein·richten.

establishment, n. Einrichtung, -en f.; Betrieb', -e m.

estate, n. (inheritance) Nachlaß, -sse m.; (possessions) Vermö'gen nt.; (condition) Zustand, -e m., Stand, -e m.

esteem, 1. n. Achtung f. 2. vb. achten, schätzen.

estimable, adj. schätzenswert.

estimate, 1. n. Kostenanschlag, -e m. 2. vb. schätzen.

estimation, n. Achtung f.; (view) Ansicht, -en f.

estrange, vb. entfrem'den.

etch, vb. ätzen.

etching, n. Radie'rung, -en f.

eternal, adj. ewig.

eternity, n. Ewigkeit, -en f.

ether, n. Äther m.

ethereal, adj. äthe'risch.

ethical, adj. ethisch, sittlich, mora'lisch.

ethics, n. Ethik f.

ethnic, adj. ethnisch.

etiquette, n. Etikett'e f.

etymology, n. Etymologie', -i'en f.

eucalyptus, n. Eukalyp'tus, -ten m.

eugenic, adj. euge'nisch.

eugenics, n. Eugene'tik f.

eulogize, vb. lobpreisen*.

eulogy, n. Lobrede, -n f.

eunuch, n. Eunuch', -en, -en m.

euphonious, adj. wohlklingend.

Europe, n. Euro'pa nt.

European, 1. n. Europä'er, - m. 2. adj. europä'isch.

euthanasia, n. Gnadentod m., Euthanasie' f.

evacuate, vb. evakuie'ren.

evade, vb. aus'weichen*, vermei'den*.

evaluate, vb. ab'schätzen, den Wert berech'nen.

evaluation, n. Abschätzung, -en f., Wertbestimmung, -en f.

evangelist, n. Evangelist', -en, -en m.

evaporate, vb. verdam'pfen.

evaporation, n. Verdam'pfung f.

evasion, n. Umge'hen, - nt.

evasive, adj. ausweichend.

eve, n. Vorabend, -e m.

even, 1. adj. gleich, gera'de, eben. 2. adv. eben, sogar', selbst.

evening, n. Abend, -e m.

evenness, n. Ebenheit, -en f.; Gleichheit, -en f.; Gleichmut m.

event, n. Ereig'nis, -se nt.

eventful, adj. ereig'nisreich.

eventual, adj. (approximate) etwaig; (final) schließlich.

ever, adv. je, jemals.

evergreen, adj. immergrün.

everlasting, adj. ewig.

every, adj. jeder, -es, -e.

everybody, pron. jeder m.; alle pl.

everyday, adj. Alltags (cpds.).

everyone, pron. jeder m.; alle pl.

everything, pron. alles.

everywhere, adv. überall'.

evict, vb. aus'weisen*; zwangsräumen.

eviction, n. Ausweisung, -en f.; Zwangsräumung, -en f.

evidence, n. Beweis', -e m.; Augenschein, m.; (law) Beweis'material, -ien nt.; (give e.) aus'sagen.

evident, adj. klar, deutlich.

evidently, adv. offenbar.

evil, 1. n. Bös- nt. 2. adj. böse, übel.

evince, vb. offenba'ren.

evoke, vb. hervor'rufen*.

evolution, n. Evolution', -en f.

evolve, vb. entwi'ckeln.

ewe, n. Mutterschaf, -e nt.

exact, 1. adj. genau'. 2. vb. erzwin'gen*.

exaggerate, vb. übertrei'ben*.

exaggeration, n. Übertrei'bung, -en f.

exalt, vb. erhö'hen, verherr'lichen.

exaltation, n. Erhö'hung f.; Erre'gung, -en f.

examination, n. Prüfung, -en f., Exa'men, - nt.; Unter-su'chung, -en f.

examine, vb. prüfen; untersu'chen.

example, n. Beispiel, -e nt.

exasperate, vb. reizen, verär'gern.

exasperation, n. Gereizt'heit f.

excavate, vb. aus'graben*.

excavation, n. Ausgrabung, -en f.; Aushöhlung, -en f.

exceed, vb. übertref'fen*.

exceedingly, adv. außerordent-lich.

excel, vb. sich aus'zeichnen.

excellence, n. Vorzüg'lichkeit, -en f.

Excellency, n. Excellenz', -en f.

excellent, adj. ausgezeich'net.

except, 1. vb. aus'schließen*. 2. prep. außer, ausgenom-men; (e. for) außer.

exception, n. Ausnahme, -n f.

exceptional, adj. außerge-wöhnlich.

excerpt, n. Auszug, -̈e m.

excess, n. Übermaß nt.

excessive, adj. übermäßig.

exchange, 1. n. Tausch m.; (rate of e.) Wechselkurs m.; (foreign e.) Valu'ta f.; (student) Austausch m.; (stock e.) Börse, -n f. 2. vb. tauschen; wechseln; aus'tauschen; (goods) um'tauschen.

exchangeable, adj. austausch-bar; umtauschbar.

excise, 1. n. Verbrauchs'-steuer, -n f. 2. vb. heraus'-schneiden*.

excite, vb. auf'regen, erre'gen (get e.d) sich auf'regen.

excitement, n. Erre'gung, -en f.; Aufregung, -en f.

exclaim, vb. aus'rufen*.

exclamation, n. Ausruf, -e m.

exclamation point or mark, n. Ausrufungszeichen, - nt.

exclude, vb. aus'schließen*.

exclusion, n. Ausschluß, -sse m.

exclusive, adj. ausschließlich; (e. of) abgesehen von; (select) exklusiv'.

excommunicate, vb. exkommuni-zie'ren.

excommunication, n. Exkom-munikation', -en f.

excrement, n. Exkrement', -e nt.

excruciating, adj. qualvoll.

excursion, n. Ausflug, -̈e m.

excusable, adj. entschuld'bar.

excuse, vb. entschul'digen, ver-zei'hen*.

execute, vb. aus'führen; (legal killing) hin'richten.

execution, n. Ausführung, -en f.; (legal killing) Hinrich-tung, -en f.

executioner, n. Scharfrichter, - m.

executive, 1. n. Mann in lei-tender Stellung; (gov't.) Exe-kuti've f. 2. adj. vollzie'hend, ausübend.

executor, n. Testaments'voll-strecker, - m.

exemplary, adj. musterhaft.

exemplify, vb. als Beispiel die-nen.

exempt, 1. adj. befreit'. 2. vb. befrei'en.

exercise, 1. n. Übung, -en f.; (carrying out) Ausübung, -en f.; (physical) Bewe'gung, -en f. 2. vb. üben; aus'üben; bewe'gen.

exert, vb. aus'üben; (e. oneself) sich an'strengen.

exertion, n. Anstrengung, -en f.

exhale, vb. aus'atmen.

exhaust, 1. n. (auto.) Auspuff, -e m. 2. vb. erschöp'fen.

exhaustion, n. Erschöp'fung, -en f.

exhaustive, adj. erschöp'fend.

exhibit, 1. n. Ausstellung, -en f. 2. vb. aus'stellen; zei'gen.

exhibition, n. Ausstellung, -en f.

exhibitionism, n. Exhibitionis-mus m.

exhilarate, vb. auf'heitern.

exhort, vb. ermah'nen.

exhortation, n. Ermah'nung, -en f.

exhume, vb. aus'graben*.

exigency, n. Dringlichkeit, -en f.

exile, n. Verban'nung, -en f. 2. vb. verban'nen.

exist, vb. beste'hen*, existie'ren.

exodus, n. Auszug, -̈e m.; Auswanderung, -en f.

exonerate, vb. entlas'ten.

exorbitant, adj. übermäßig.

exotic, adj. exo'tisch.

expand, vb. aus'dehnen, aus'-breiten, erwei'tern.

expanse, n. Ausdehnung, -en f., Weite, -n f.

expansion, n. Ausdehnung, -en f., Ausbreitung, -en f.; Expansion' f.

expansive, adj. umfas'send.

expatriate, n. Emigrant', -en, -en m.

expect, vb. erwar'ten.

expectancy, n. Erwar'tung, -en f.

expectation, n. Erwar'tung, -en f.

expectorate, vb. (aus')spuken.

expediency, n. Zweckmäßig-keit, -en f.

expedient, adj. zweckmäßig.

expedite, vb. beschleu'nigen.

expedition, n. Expedition', -en f.

expel, vb. vertrei'ben*.

expend, vb. (money) aus'ge-ben*; (energy) auf'wenden*.

expenditure, n. Ausgabe, -n f.; Aufwand m.

expense, n. Ausgabe, -n f., Kosten pl., Unkosten pl.; (on an e. account) auf Spesen.

expensive, adj. teuer, kostspie-lig.

experience, 1. n. Erfah'rung, -en f. 2. vb. erfah'ren*.

experienced, adj. erfah'ren.

experiment, n. Versuch', -e

n., Experiment', -e nt. 2. vb.
xperimentie'ren.
perimental, adj. Versuchs'-
cpds.).
perimentally, adv. versuchs'-
veise.
pert, 1. n. Sachverständig-
n., Exper'te, -n, -n m. 2. adj.
rfah'ren.
piate, vb. büßen.
piration, n. (breath) Ausat-
nung, -en f.; (end) Ablauf m.
pire, vb. (breathe out) aus·at-
nen; (die) verschei'den; (end)
b·laufen*.
plain, vb. erklä'ren.
planation, n. Erklä'rung,
en f.
planatory, adj. erklä'rend.
pletive, 1. n. Füllwort, -er
nt.; Ausruf, -e m. 2. adj. aus-
üllend.
plicit, adj. ausdrücklich.
plode, vb. explodie'ren.
ploit, vb. aus·beuten, aus·
utzen.
ploitation, n. Ausbeutung, -
n f., Ausnutzung, -en f.
ploration, n. Erfor'schung,
n f.
ploratory, adj. untersu'-
hend, erkun'dend.
plore, vb. erfor'schen, unter·
u'chen.
plorer, n. Forscher, - m.,
orschungsreisend- m.
plosion, n. Explosion', -en f.
plosive, 1. n. Sprengstoff, -e
n. 2. adj. explosiv'.
ponent, n. Exponent', -en, -
n m.
port, 1. n. Export', -e m.,
usfuhr f. 2. vb. exportie'
en, aus·führen.
portation, n. Ausfuhr f.
pose, vb. aus·setzen; (photo)
elich'ten; (disclose) enthül'-
en.
posé, n. Darlegung, -en f.;
disclosure)   Enthül'lung,
en f.
position,   n.   Darlegung,
en f.; (exhibit) Ausstellung, -
n f.
pository, adj. erklä'rend.
posure, n. Aussetzung, -en
f.; (photo) Belich'tung, -en f.;
isloßtellung, -en f.
pound, vb. aus·legen, erklä'-
en.
press, 1. n. (train) Schnell-
ug, -e m. 2. vb. aus·drücken.
, adj. ausdrücklich.
pression, n. Ausdruck, -e m.
pressive, adj. ausdrucksvoll.
propriate, vb. enteig'nen.
pulsion,   n.   Vertrei'bung,
en f., Entlas'sung, -en f.
purgate, vb. reinigen.
quisite, adj. vorzüg'lich.
tant, adj. vorhan'den.
temporaneous, adj. aus dem
tegreif.
tend, vb. (intr.) sich er-

stre'cken, reichen; (tr.) aus·
dehnen.
extension, n. Ausdehnung,
-en f.; Verlän'gerung, -en f.
extensive, adj. umfangreich.
extent, n. Umfang, -e m.
exterior, adj. äußer-, äußerlich.
exterminate, vb. aus·rotten,
vernich'ten.
extermination, n. Ausrottung,
-en   f.,   Vernich'tung,
-en f.
external, adj. äußer-; auswärtig.
extinct, adj. ausgestorben.
extinction, n. Aussterben nt.
extinguish, vb. aus·löschen.
extol, vb. loben, preisen*.
extort, vb. ab·zwingen*.
extortion, n.   Erpres'sung,
-en f.
extra, adj. extra, beson'der-.
extra-, (cpds.) außer-.
extract, 1. n. Auszug, -e m.,
Extrakt', -e m. 2. vb. heraus·
ziehen*, heraus'·holen.
extraction, n. Ausziehen nt.;
(ethnic) Herkunft, -e f., Abstammung, -en f.
extradite, vb. aus·liefern.
extradition, n. Auslieferung, -
en f.
extraneous, adj. fremd.
extraordinary, adj. außerge-
wöhnlich.
extravagance, n. Verschwen-
dung, -en f., Extravaganz', -
en f.
extravagant, adj. verschwen-
derisch; übertrie'ben.
extravaganza, n.   phanta-
s'tische, überspann'te Komposition', -en f.
extreme, adj. äußerst-.
extremely,   adv.   äußerst,
höchst.
extremity, n. Äußerst- nt.;
(limbs) Gliedmaßen pl.
extricate, vb. heraus·winden*.
exuberant, adj. überschwenglich.
exult, vb. frohlo'cken.
exultant, adj. frohlo'ckend.
eye, n. Auge, -n nt.
eyeball, n. Augapfel, -̈ m.
eyebrow, n. Augenbraue, -n f.
eyeglasses, n.pl. Brille, -n f.
eyelash, n. Augenwimper, -n f.
eyelet, n. Öse, -n f.
eyelid, n. Augenlid -er nt.
eyesight, n. Augensicht f.; Augen pl.

F

fable, n. Fabel, -n f.
fabric, n. Stoff, -e m.
fabricate, vb. her·stellen; (lie)
erdich'ten.
fabrication,   n.   Herstellung,
-en f.; (lie) Erdich'tung, -en f.
fabulous, adj. sagenhaft.

façade, n. Fassa'de, -n f.
face, 1. n. Gesicht', -er nt.;
(surface) Oberfläche, -n f. 2.
vb. ins Gesicht' sehen*; (be
opposite) gegenü'ber·liegen*.
facet, n. Facet'te, -n f.
facetious, adj. scherzhaft.
face value, n. Nennwert, -e m.
facial, 1. n. Gesichts'massage, -
n f. 2. adj. Gesichts'- (cpds.).
facile, adj. gewandt'.
facilitate, vb. erleich'tern.
facility, n. (ease) Leichtigkeit
f.; (skill) Geschick'lichkeit f.;
(possibility) Möglichkeit, -en
f.
facing, n. (clothing) Besatz' m.
facsimile, n. Faksi'mile, -s nt.
fact, n. Tatsache, -n f.
faction, n. Gruppe, -n f.
factor, n. Faktor, -o'ren m.
factory, n. Fabrik', -en f.
factual, adj. auf Tatsachen beschränkt'; Tatsachen- (cpds.).
faculty, n. Fähigkeit, -en f.,
Gabe, -n f.; (college) Fakultät', -en f.
fad, n. Mode, -n f.
fade, vb. verblas'sen.
fail, vb. versa'gen; (school)
durch·fallen*; (f. to do) nicht
tun*.
failure,   n.   Versa'gen nt.,
Mißerfolg, -e m.; (bank-
ruptcy) Bankrott', -e m.
faint, 1. adj. schwach. 2. vb. in
Ohnmacht fallen*.
fair, 1. n. Messe, -n f., Jahrmarkt, -e m. 2. adj. (weather)
heiter; (blond) blond; (just)
gerecht'.
fairness,   n.   Gerech'tigkeit,
-en f.
fairy, n. Fee, Fe'en f.
fairy tale, n. Märchen, - nt.
faith, n. (trust) Vertrau'en nt.;
(belief) Glaube(n), - m.
faithful, adj. treu.
faithfulness, n. Treue f.
faithless, adj. treulos.
fake, 1. adj. falsch. 2. vb. vor·
täuschen.
faker, n. Schwindler, - m.
falcon, n. Falke, -n, -n m.
fall, 1. n. Fall, -e m., Sturz -e
m.; (autumn) Herbst, -e m. 2.
vb. fallen*.
fallacious, adj. trügerisch.
fallacy, n. Trugschluß, -sse m.
fallible, adj. fehlbar.
fallout, n. (radioaktiver) Niederschlag, -e m.
fallow, adj. brach.
false, adj. falsch.
falsehood, n. Lüge, -n f.
falseness, n. Falschheit, -en f.
falsetto, n. Falsett', -e nt.
falsification, n. Verfäl'schung,
-en f.
falsify, vb. verfäl'schen.
falter, vb. straucheln, stocken.
fame, n. Ruhm m.
famed, adj. berühmt'.
familiar, adj. vertraut'.
familiarity, n. Vertraut'heit, -

en f.; Vertrau'lichkeit, -en f.
familiarize, vb. vertraut'machen.
family, n. Fami'lie, -n f.
famine, n. Hungersnot, -e f.
famished, adj. ausgehungert.
famous, adj. berühmt'.
fan, 1. n. Fächer, - m.; Ventila'tor, -o'ren m.; (enthusiast) Vereh'rer, - m., Anhänger, - m. **2.** vb. fächern.
fanatic, 1. n. Fana'tiker, - m. **2.** adj. fana'tisch.
fanatical, adj. fana'tisch.
fanaticism, n. Fanatis'mus m.
fanciful, adj. phantas'tisch.
fancy, 1. n. (imagination) Einbildung, -en f.; (mood) Laune, -n f.; (liking) Vorliebe f. **2.** adj. apart', ausgefallen; Luxus- (cpds.). **3.** vb. sich ein·bilden.
fanfare, n. Fanfa're, -n f.; (fig.) Getu'e nt.
fang, n. Fang, ‿e, m.
fantastic, adj. phantas'tisch.
fantasy, n. Phantasie', -i'en f.
far, adj. weit, fern.
faraway, adj. entfernt'; (fig.) träumerisch.
farce, n. Farce, -n f.
fare, 1. n. (passenger) Fahrgeld, -er nt.; (price) Fahrpreis, -e m.; (food) Kost f. **2.** vb. gehen*.
farewell, 1. n. Abschied, -e m.; Abschieds- (cpds.). **2.** interj. lebe wohl! leben Sie wohl!
far-fetched, adj. gesucht'.
farina, n. Griessmehl nt.
farm, 1. n. landwirtschaftlicher Betrieb', -e m., Farm, -en f. **2.** vb. Landwirtschaft betrei'ben*, Landwirt sein*.
farmer, n. Landwirt, -e m., Farmer, - m., Bauer, (-n), -n m.
farmhouse, n. Farmhaus, ‿er nt.; Bauernhaus, ‿er nt.
farming, n. Landwirtschaft f.; Ackerbau m.
farmyard, n. Bauernhof, ‿e m.
far-sighted, adj. weitsichtig.
farther, adj. weiter.
farthest, adj. weitest-.
fascinate, vb. faszinie'ren, bezau'bern.
fascination, n. Faszination f., Zauber m.
fascism, n. Faschis'mus m.
fascist, 1. n. Faschist', -en, -en m. **2.** adj. faschis'tisch.
fashion, n. Mode, -n f.; (manner) Art, -en f.
fashionable, adj. modern', schick.
fast, 1. n. Fasten nt. **2.** adj. (speedy) schnell; (be f., of a clock) vor·gehen*; (firm) fest. **3.** vb. fasten.
fasten, vb. fest·machen.
fastener, fastening, n. Verschluß', ‿sse m.
fastidious, adj. wählerisch; eigen.

fat, 1. n. Fett, -e nt. **2.** adj. fett, dick.
fatal, adj. tötlich; verhäng'nisvoll.
fatality, n. Verhäng'nis, -se nt.; Todesfall, ‿e m.
fate, n. Schicksal, -e nt.
fateful, adj. schicksalsschwer; verhäng'nisvoll.
father, n. Vater, ‿ m.
fatherhood, n. Vaterschaft, -en f.
father-in-law, n. Schwiegervater, ‿ m.
fatherland, n. Vaterland nt.
fatherless, adj. vaterlos.
fatherly, adj. väterlich.
fathom, 1. n. Klafter, -n f. **2.** vb. loten; (fig.) ergrün'den.
fatigue, 1. n. Ermü'dung f. **2.** vb. ermü'den.
fatten, vb. mästen.
fatty, adj. fettig.
faucet, n. Wasserhahn, ‿e m.
fault, n. Fehler, - m.; (it's my f.) es ist meine Schuld.
faultless, adj. fehlerlos, makellos.
faulty, adj. fehlerhaft.
favor, 1. n. Gunst, -en f.; (do a f.) einen Gefallen tun*. **2.** vb. begün'stigen, bevor'zugen; (a sore limb) schonen.
favorable, adj. günstig.
favorite, 1. n. Liebling, -e m.; (sport) Favorit', -en, -en m. **2.** adj. Lieblings- (cpds.).
favoritism, n. Begün'stigung f.
fawn, n. Rehkalb, -er nt.
faze, vb. in Verle'genheit bringen*.
fear, 1. n. Furcht f., Angst, ‿e f. **2.** vb. fürchten.
fearful, adj. (afraid) furchtsam; (terrible) furchtbar.
fearless, adj. furchtlos.
fearlessness, n. Furchtlosigkeit f.
feasible, adj. durchführbar.
feast, n. Fest, -e nt., Festmahl, -e nt.
feat, n. Tat, -en f.; Kunststück, -e nt.
feather, n. Feder, -n f.
feature, n. (quality) Eigenschaft, -en f.; (face) Gesichtszug, ‿e m.; (distinguishing mark) Kennzeichen, - nt.
February, n. Februar m.
feces, n.pl. Exkremen'te pl.
federal, adj. bundesstaatlich; Bundes- (cpds.).
federation, n. Staatenbund, -e m., Föderation', -en f.; Bundesstaat, -en m.
fee, n. Gebühr', -en f.
feeble, adj. schwach (‿).
feeble-minded, adj. schwachsinnig.
feebleness, n. Schwäche, -n f.
feed, 1. n. Futter, - nt. **2.** vb. füttern.

feedback, n. Feedback m., Rückkopplung f.
feel, vb. fühlen.
feeling, n. Gefühl', -e nt.
feign, vb. Vor·geben*, heucheln.
felicitate, vb. beglück'wünschen.
felicity, n. Glück nt.
fell, vb. fällen.
fellow, n. Kerl, -e m., Bursche, -n, -n m.; (member) Mitglied, -er nt.
fellowship, n. Gemein'schaft, -en f.
felony, n. Gewalt'verbrechen, - nt.
felt, n. Filz, -e m.
female, 1. n. (human) Frau, -en f.; (animal) Weibchen, - nt. **2.** adj. weiblich.
feminine, adj. weiblich, feminin'.
femininity, n. Weiblichkeit f.
fence, 1. n. Zaun, ‿e m. **2.** vb. ein·zäunen; (sport) fechten*.
fencing, n. Fechten nt.
fender, n. (auto) Kotflügel, - m.
ferment, vb. gären*.
fermentation, n. Gärung, -en f.
fern, n. Farnkraut, ‿er nt.
ferocious, adj. wild.
ferocity, n. Wildheit f.
ferry, n. Fähre, -n f.
fertile, adj. fruchtbar.
fertility, n. Fruchtbarkeit f.
fertilization, n. Befruch'tung, -en f.
fertilize, vb. befruch'ten; düngen.
fertilizer, n. Dünger m., Kunstdünger m.
fervent, adj. inbrünstig.
fervid, adj. brennend.
fervor, n. Inbrunst f., Eifer m.
fester, vb. eitern.
festival, n. Fest, -e nt.
festive, adj. festlich.
festivity, n. Festlichkeit, -en f.
festoon, n. Girlan'de, -n f.
fetch, vb. holen.
fetching, adj. reizend.
fête, n. Fest, -e nt.
fetid, adj. stinkend.
fetish, n. Fetisch, -e m.
fetters, n.pl. Fesseln pl.
fetus, n. Foetus, -se m.
feud, n. Feindschaft, -en f.; (historical) Fehde, -n f.
feudal, adj. feudal'.
feudalism, n. Feudalis'mus m.
fever, n. Fieber, - nt.
feverish, adj. fieberhaft.
few, adj. wenig; (a f.) ein paar
fiancé, n. Verlobt'- m.
fiancée, n. Verlobt'- f.
fiasco, n. Fias'ko, -s nt.
fib, n. Lüge, -n f.
fiber, n. Faser, -n f.
fickle, adj. wankelmütig.
fickleness, n. Wankelmütigkeit f.
fiction, n. Erdich'tung, f.

(novel writing) Prosadichtung, -en *f.*

fictional, *adj.* erdich'tet.

fictitious, *adj.* fingiert'.

fiddle, 1. *n.* Geige, -n *f.* 2. *vb.* geigen.

fidelity, *n.* Treue *f.*

fidget, *vb.* zappeln.

field, *n.* Feld, -er *nt.*

fiend, *n.* Teufel, - *m.*

fiendish, *adj.* teuflisch.

fierce, *adj.* wild.

fiery, *adj.* feurig.

fife, *n.* Querpfeife, -n *f.*

fifteen, *num.* fünfzehn.

fifteenth, 1. *adj.* fünfzehnt-. 2. *n.* Fünfzehntel, - *nt.*

fifth, 1. *adj.* fünft-. 2. *n.* Fünftel, - *nt.*

fiftieth, 1. *adj.* fünfzigst-. 2. *n.* Fünfzigstel, - *nt.*

fifty, *num.* fünfzig.

fig, *n.* Feige, -n *f.*

fight, 1. *n.* Kampf, ⸗e *m.; (brawl)* Schlägerei', -en *f.; (quarrel)* Streit, -e *m.* 2. *vb.* kämpfen; bekämp'fen.

fighter, *n.* Kämpfer, - *m.*

figment, *n.* Fiktion', -en *f.*

figurative, *adj.* bildlich; *(f. meaning)* übertra'gene Bedeu'tung, -en *f.*

figure, 1. *n.* Figur', -en *f.*, Gestalt', -en *f.; (number)* Zahl, -en *f.* 2. *vb.* rechnen; berech'nen.

figurehead, *n.* Galionsfigur, -en *f.; (fig.)* Repräsentations'figur, -en *f.*

figure of speech, *n.* Redewendung, -en *f.*

figurine, *n.* Porzellan'figur, -en *f.*

filament, *n.* Faser, -n *f.*, Faden, ⸗ *m.*

file, 1. *n. (tool)* Feile, -n *f.; (row)* Reihe, -n *f.; (papers, etc.)* Akte, -n *f.; (cards)* Kartothek', -en *f.* 2. *vb. (tool)* feilen; *(papers)* ein'ordnen.

filigree, *n.* Filigran', -e *nt.*

fillet, *n.* Filet', -s *nt.*

fill, *vb.* füllen.

filling, *n. (tooth)* Plombe, -n *f.*

filling station, *n.* Tankstelle, -n *f.*

film, 1. *n.* Film, -e *m.* 2. *vb.* filmen.

filmy, *adj.* mit einem Häutchen bedeckt; duftig.

filter, 1. *n.* Filter, - *m.* 2. *vb.* filtrie'ren.

filth, *n.* Dreck *m.*

filthy, *adj.* dreckig; *(fig.)* unanständig.

fin, *n.* Flosse, -n *f.*

final, *adj.* endgültig.

finale, *n.* Fina'le, -s *nt.*

finalist, *n.* Teilnehmer (-, *m.)* in der Schlußrunde.

finality, *n.* Endgültigkeit *f.*

finance, 1. *n.* Finanz', -en *f.; (study)* Finanz'wesen *nt.; (f.s.)* Finan'zen *pl.* 2. *vb.* finanzie'ren.

financial, *adj.* finanziell'.

financier, *n.* Finanz'mann, ⸗er *m.*

find, *vb.* finden*.

findings, *n.pl.* Tatbestand, ⸗e *m.*

fine, 1. *n.* Geldstrafe, -n *f.* 2. *adj.* fein. 3. *vb.* zu einer Geldstrafe verur'teilen.

fine arts, *n.* Kunstwissenschaft *f.*

finery, *n.* Putz *m.*

finesse, *n.* Fines'se, -n *f.*

finger, *n.* Finger, - *m.*

fingernail, *n.* Fingernagel, *m.*

fingerprint, *n.* Fingerabdruck, ⸗e *m.*

finicky, *adj.* zimperlich.

finish, 1. *n.* Ende, -n *nt.;* Abschluß', ⸗sse *m.* 2. *vb.* beenden; vollen'den.

finite, *adj.* endlich.

fir, *n.* Fichte, -n *f.*

fire, 1. *n.* Feuer, - *nt.* 2. *vb. (shoot)* feuern; *(dismiss)* entlas'sen*.

fire alarm, *n.* Feueralarm *m.*

fire-alarm box, *n.* Feuermelder, - *m.*

firearm, *n.* Feuerwaffe, -n *f.*

fire engine, *n.* Feuerspritze, -n *f.*

fire escape, *n.* Feuerleiter, -n *f.*

fire extinguisher, *n.* Feuerlöscher, - *m.*

fireman, *n.* Feuerwehrmann, ⸗er *m.*

fireplace, *n.* Kamin, -e *m.*

fireproof, *adj.* feuerfest.

fireworks, *n.* Feuerwerk, -e *nt.*

firm, 1. *n.* Firma, -men *f.* 2. *adj.* fest.

firmness, *n.* Festigkeit *f.*

first, 1. *adj.* erst. 2. *adv.* zuerst'.

first aid, *n.* erste Hilfe *f.*

first-class, *adj.* erstklassig, erster Klasse.

fiscal, *adj.* fiska'lisch.

fish, 1. *n.* Fisch, -e *m.* 2. *vb.* fischen, angeln.

fisherman, *n.* Fischer, - *m.*, Angler, - *m.*

fishing, *n.* Angeln *nt.*

fission, *n.* Spaltung, -en *f.; (nuclear f.)* Kernspaltung *f.*

fissure, *n.* Spalt, -e *m.*

fist, *n.* Faust, ⸗e *f.*

fit, 1. *n. (attack)* Anfall, ⸗e *m.* 2. *adj.* in Form. 3. *vb.* passen; *(adapt)* an'passen.

fitful, *adj.* unregelmäßig.

fitness, *n.* Tauglichkeit *f.;* Gesund'heit *f.*

fitting, 1. *n.* Anprobe, -n *f.* 2. *adj.* passend.

five, *num.* fünf.

fix, 1. *n. (predicament)* Verle'genheit, -en *f.* 2. *vb.* festsetzen; *(prepare)* zubereiten; *(repair)* reparie'ren.

fixation, *n.* Fixie'rung, -en *f.*

fixed, *adj. (repaired)* heil; *(set)* fest.

fixture, *n.* Vorrichtung, -en *f.;* Zubehör *nt.*

flabby, *adj.* schlaff.

flag, *n.* Fahne, -n *f.*, Flagge, -n *f.*

flagpole, *n.* Fahnenstange, -n *f.*

flagrant, *adj.* schreiend.

flagship, *n.* Flaggschiff, -e *nt.*

flair, *n.* Flair *nt.*

flake, *n.* Flocke, -n *f.*

flamboyant, *adj.* flammend; *(fig.)* überla'den.

flame, 1. *n.* Flamme, -n *f.* 2. *vb.* flammen.

flank, 1. *n.* Flanke, -n *f.* 2. *vb.* flankie'ren.

flannel, *n.* Flanell', -e *m.*

flap, 1. *n.* Klappe, -n *f.; (wings)* Flügelschlag, ⸗e *m.* 2. *vb.* flattern.

flare, 1. *n.* Leuchtsignal, -e *nt.* 2. *vb.* flackern.

flash, 1. *n.* Lichtstrahl, -en *m.* 2. *vb.* auf'flammen.

flashcube, *n.* Blitzwürfel, - *m.*

flashlight, *n.* Taschenlampe, -n *f.*

flashy, *adj.* auffällig; *(clothes, etc.)* laut.

flask, *n.* Flasche, -n *f.*

flat, 1. *n.* Mietswohnung, -en *f.* 2. *adj.* flach, platt.

flatcar, *n.* offener Güterwagen, - *m.*

flatness, *n.* Flachheit, -en *f.*

flatten, *vb.* flach machen.

flatter, *vb.* schmeicheln.

flattering, *adj.* schmeichelhaft.

flattery, *n.* Schmeichelei', -en *f.*

flaunt, *vb.* zur Schau stellen.

flavor, *n. (taste)* Geschmack', ⸗e *m.; (odor)* Geruch', ⸗e *m.* 2. *vb.* würzen.

flavoring, *n.* Geschmack', ⸗e *m.;* Essenz', -en *f.*

flavorless, *adj.* fade.

flaw, *n.* Fehler, - *m.*, Makel, - *m.*

flawless, *adj.* fehlerfrei, makellos.

flax, *n.* Flachs *m.*

flay, *vb.* schinden*.

flea, *n.* Floh, ⸗e *m.*

fleck, *n.* Fleck, -e *m.*

flee, *vb.* fliehen*, flüchten.

fleece, *n.* Vlies, -e *nt.*

fleecy, *adj.* wollig.

fleet, *n.* Flotte, -n *f.*

fleeting, *adj.* flüchtig.

Fleming, *n.* Flame, -n, -n *m.*

Flemish, *adj.* flämisch.

flesh, *n.* Fleisch *nt.*

fleshy, *adj.* fleischig.

flex, *vb.* biegen*; beugen.

flexibility, *n.* Biegsamkeit *f.*

flexible, *adj.* biegsam, flexi'bel.

flicker, *vb.* flackern.

flier, *n.* Flieger, - *m.*

flight, *n.* Flug, ⸗e *m.; (escape)* Flucht, -en *f.*

flight attendants, *n.pl.* Flugpersonal *m.*

flimsy, *adj.* dünn; lose.

flinch, *vb.* zurück'zucken.

fling, vb. schleudern.

flint, n. Feuerstein, -e m.

flip, vb. schnellen.

flippant, adj. vorlaut.

flirt, 1. n. Flirt, -s m. 2. vb. flirten, kokettie'ren.

flirtation, n. Flirt, -s m.

float, 1. n. Floß, ⸗e nt. 2. vb. treiben*, schwimmen*.

flock, n. Herde - f., Schar, -en f.

flog, vb. peitschen.

flood, 1. n. Flut, -en f.; Überschwem'mung, -en f. 2. vb. überschwem'men.

floodlight, n. Scheinwerfer, - m.

floor, n. Fußboden, ⸗ m.; (story) Stockwerk, -e nt.

floorwalker, n. Abteilungsaufseher (, - m.) in einem Warenhaus.

flop, 1. n. (thud) Plumps m.; (failure) Reinfall, ⸗e m. 2. vb. plumpsen: rein·gallen*.

floral, adj. Blumen- (cpds.).

florid, adj. gerö'tet.

florist, n. Blumenhändler, - m.

flounce, 1. n. Volant', -s m. 2. vb. tänzeln.

flounder, 1. n. Flunder, -n f. 2. vb. taumeln.

flour, n. Mehl nt.

flourish, vb. (grow) gedei'hen*, blühen; (shake) schwenken.

flow, vb. fließen*.

flower, 1. n. Blume, -n f. 2. vb. blühen.

flowerpot, n. Blumentopf, ⸗e m.

flowery, adj. blumig.

fluctuate, vb. schwanken.

fluctuation, n. Schwankung, -en f.

flue, n. Rauchfang, ⸗e m.

fluency, n. Geläu'figkeit f.

fluent, adj. fließend.

fluffy, adj. flaumig, wollig.

fluid, 1. n. Flüssigkeit, -en f. 2. adj. flüssig.

fluidity, n. flüssiger Aggregat'zustand m.; Flüssigsein nt.

fluorescent, adj. fluoreszie'rend.

fluoroscope, n. Leuchtschirm, - e m.; Fluroskop', -e nt.

flurry, n. Wirbel, - m.

flush, 1. n. Röte f.; (fig.) Flut f. 2. vb. errö'ten; (wash out) aus·spülen; (toilet) aufzie'hen*.

flute, n. Flöte, -n f.

flutter, vb. flattern.

flux, n. Fluss m.; Strömen nt.

fly, 1. n. Fliege, -n f. 2. vb. fliegen*.

foam, 1. n. Schaum, ⸗e m. 2. vb. schäumen.

focal, adj. fokal'.

focus, 1. n. Brennpunkt, -e m. 2. vb. (scharf, richtig) ein·stellen.

fodder, n. Futter nt.

foe, n. Feind, -e m.

fog, n. Nebel m.

foggy, adj. neblig.

foil, 1. n. Rapier', -e nt. 2. vb. verei'teln.

foist, vb. unterschie'ben*.

fold, 1. n. Falte, -n f. 2. vb. falten.

folder, n. (for papers) Mappe, - n f.; Hefter, - m.; (brochure) Broschü're, -n f.; Prospekt', - e m.

foliage, n. Laub nt.

folio, n. Folio, -lien nt.

folk, n. Volk, ⸗er nt.

folklore, n. Volkskunde f.

folks, n.pl. Leute pl.

follow, vb. folgen.

follower, n. Anhänger, - m.

folly, n. Torheit, -en f.

foment, vb. schüren.

fond, adj. (be f. of) gern haben*.

fondle, vb. liebkosen.

fondness, n. Vorliebe f.

food, n. Nahrung, f., Essen nt.

foodstuffs, n. Nahrungsmittel pl.

fool, 1. n. Narr, -en, -en m. 2. vb. täuschen, zum Narren halten*.

foolhardiness, n. Tollkühnheit, -en f.

foolhardy, adj. tollkühn.

foolish, adj. dumm, närrisch.

foolproof, adj. narrensicher.

foot, n. Fuss, ⸗e m.

footage, n. Länge in Fuß gemessen.

football, n. Fußball, ⸗e m.

foothills, n.pl. Vorgebirge nt.

foothold, n. Halt m.

footing, n. Stand m.; Boden m.

footlights, n.pl. Rampenlicht, - er nt.

footnote, n. Fußnote, -n f.

footprint, n. Fußstapfe, -n f.

footstep, n. Fußstapfe, -n f.

for, 1. prep. für. 2. conj. denn.

forage, 1. n. Futter nt. 2. vb. furagie'ren.

foray, n. Überfall, ⸗e m.

forbearance, n. Enthal'tung f.; Nachsicht f.

forbid, vb. verbie'ten*.

forbidding, adj. abschreckend.

force, 1. n. Kraft, ⸗e f., Gewalt', -en f. 2. vb. zwingen*.

forceful, adj. kräftig, wirkungsvoll.

forcefulness, n. Überzeu'gungskraft f.

forceps, n. Zange, -n f.

forcible, adj. kräftig, heftig, mit Gewalt'.

ford, n. Furt, -en f.

fore, adv. vorn.

forearm, n. Unterarm, -e m.

forebears, n.pl. Vorfahren pl.

foreboding, n. Vorahnung, -en f.

forecast, 1. n. Voraus'sage, -n f. 2. vb. voraus'sagen.

forecaster, n. Wetterprophet, en, -en m.

foreclosure, n. Zwangsvollstreckung, -en f.

forefather, n. Vorfahr, -en, -en m.

forefinger, n. Zeigefinger, - m.

forefront, n. Vordergrund m.

foreground, n. Vordergrund m.

forehead, n. Stirn, -en f.

foreign, adj. fremd, ausländisch.

foreign aid, n. Entwick'lungshilfe f.

foreigner, n. Ausländer, - m.

foreman, n. Vorarbeiter, - m.

foremost, adj. vorderst-.

forenoon, n. Vormittag, -e m.

forerunner, n. Vorläufer, - m.

foresee, vb. vorher'·sehen*.

foreshadow, vb. ahnen lassen*.

foresight, n. Voraus'sicht f.

forest, n. Wald, ⸗er m.

forestall, vb. verhin'dern, vorweg'·nehmen*.

forester, n. Förster, - m.

forestry, n. Forstwirtschaft f.

foretaste, n. Vorgeschmack, ⸗e m.

foretell, vb. vorher'·sagen, prophezei'en.

forever, adv. ewig.

forevermore, adv. für, auf immer und ewig.

forewarn, vb. vorher warnen.

foreword, n. Vorwort, -e nt.

forfeit, vb. verwir'ken, ein·büßen.

forfeiture, n. Verwir'kung f., Einbuße f.

forgather, vb. sich versam'meln.

forge, 1. n. Schmiede, -n f. 2. vb. schmieden; (falsify) fälschen.

forger, n. Fälscher, - m.

forgery, n. Fälschung, -en f.

forget, vb. verges'sen*.

forgetful, adj. vergeß'lich.

forgive, vb. verge'ben*, verzei'hen*.

forgiveness, n. Verge'bung f.

forgo, vb. verzich'ten auf.

fork, n. Gabel, -n f.

forlorn, adj. verlas'sen.

form, 1. n. Form, -en f.; (blank) Formular', -e nt. 2. vb. bilden, formen.

formal, adj. formell'; offiziell'.

formaldehyde, n. Formaldehyd', -e nt.

formality, n. Formalität', -en f.; Förmlichkeit, -en f.

format, n. Format', -e nt.

formation, n. Gestal'tung, -en f.; (mil.) Formation', -en f.

former, adj. ehemalig, früher; (the f.) jener, -es, -e.

formerly, adv. früher.

formidable, adj. beacht'lich.

formless, adj. formlos.

formula, n. Formel, -n f.

formulate, vb. formulie'ren.

formulation, n. Formulie'rung, -en f.

forsake, vb. verlas'sen*.

fort, n. Feste, -n f.

forte, n. Stärke, -n f.

forth, adv. fort; (and so f.) und so weiter.

forthcoming, adj. angekündigt.

forthright, adj. offen, ehrlich.

fortieth, 1. adj. vierzigst-. 2. n. Vierzigstel, - nt.

fortification, n. Befes'tigungswerk, -e nt.

fortify, vb. stärken, befes'tigen.

fortissimo, adj. fortis'simo.

fortitude, n. seelische Stärke f., Mut m.

fortnight, n. vierzehn Tage pl.

fortress, n. Festung, -en f.

fortuitous, adj. zufällig.

fortunate, adj. glücklich.

fortune, n. Glück nt.; (money) Vermö'gen, - nt.

fortune-teller, n. Wahrsager, - m.

forty, adj. vierzig.

forum, n. Forum, -ra nt.

forward, adv. vorwärts.

forwardness, n. Dreistigkeit f.

fossil, n. Fossil', -ien nt.

foster, vb. (nourish) nähren; (raise) auf'ziehen*; Pflege- (cpds.).

foul, adj. schmutzig.

found, vb. gründen.

foundation, n. (building) Fundament', -e nt.; (fund) Stiftung, -en f.

founder, n. Gründer, - m.

foundling, n. Findling, -e m.

foundry, n. Gießerei', -en f.

fountain, n. Springbrunnen, - m.

fountainhead, n. Urquell, -e m.

fountain pen, n. Füllfederhalter, - m.

four, num. vier.

fourteen, num. vierzehn.

fourteenth, 1. adj. vierzehnt- 2. n. Vierzehntel, - nt.

fourth, 1. adj. viert-. 2. n. Viertel, - nt.

fowl, n. Geflü'gel nt.; Huhn, ⁼er nt.

fox, n. Fuchs, ⁼e m.

foxglove, n. Fingerhut, ⁼e m.

foxhole, n. Schüt'zenloch, ⁼er nt.

foxy, adj. schlau.

foyer, n. Foyer', -s nt.

fracas, n. Keilerei', -en f.

fraction, n. (number) Bruchstück, -e nt.; (part) Bruchteil, -e m.; (f.s.) Bruchrechnung f.

fracture, 1. n. Bruch, ⁼e m. 2. vb. brechen*.

fragile, adj. zerbrech'lich.

fragment, n. Bruchstück, -e nt.

fragmentary, adj. fragmenta'risch.

fragrance, n. Duft, ⁼e m.

fragrant, adj. wohlriechend.

frail, adj. zerbrech'lich, schwach (⁼).

frailty, n. Schwachheit, -en f.

frame, 1. n. Rahmen, - m. 2. vb. (shape) formen; (enclose) ein·rahmen.

framework, n. Rahmen, - m.

France, n. Frankreich nt.

franchise, n. Wahlrecht, -e nt.

frank, adj. frei, offen.

frankfurter, n. Frankfurter Würstchen, - nt.

frankly, adv. ehrlich gesagt'.

frankness, n. Offenheit f.

frantic, adj. wahnsinnig.

fraternal, adj. brüderlich.

fraternity, n. Brüderlichkeit f.; (students) Studen'tenverbindung, -en f.

fraternize, vb. fraternisie'ren.

fraud, n. Betrug' m.

fraudulent, adj. betrügerisch.

fraught, adj. voll.

fray, n. Tumult', -e m.; Schlägerei', -en f.

freak, 1. n. Mißgebert, -en f.; Kurio'sum, -sa nt. 2. adj. monströs', bizarr'.

freckle, n. Sommersprosse, -n f.

freckled, adj. sommersprossig.

free, 1. adj. frei; kostenlos. 2. vb. befrei'en; frei·lassen*.

freedom, n. Freiheit, -en f.

freeze, vb. (be cold) frieren*; (turn to ice) (intr.) gefrie'ren*; (tr.) gefrie'ren lassen*; (food) tief kühlen; (wages) stoppen (Löhne).

freezer, n. Tiefkühler, - m.; (in refrigerator) Gefrier'fach, ⁼er nt.

freezing, adj. eisig.

freight, n. Fracht, -en f.; Frachtgut nt.

freightage, n. Frachtspesen pl.

freighter, n. Frachter, - m.

French, adj. franzö'sisch.

Frenchman, n. Franzo'se, -n, - n m.

Frenchwoman, n. Franzö'sin, -nen f.

frenzied, adj. rasend.

frenzy, n. Raserie', -en f.

frequency, n. Häufigkeit, -en f.; (physics) Frequenz', -en f.

frequent, adj. häufig.

fresh, adj. frisch; (impudent) frech.

freshen, vb. erfri'schen.

freshman, n. Student' im ersten College-Jahr.

freshness, n. Frische f.

fresh water, n. Süßwasser nt.

fret, vb. nervös' sein*; nervös' werden*.

fretful, adj. nervös', unruhig.

fretfulness, n. Reizbarkeit f.

friar, n. Bettelmönch, -e m.

fricassee, n. Frikassee', -s nt.

friction, n. Reibung, -en f.

Friday, n. Freitag, -e m.

friend, n. Freund, -e m.; Freundin, -nen f.

friendless, adj. freundlos.

friendliness, n. Freundlichkeit, -en f.

friendly, adj. freundlich.

friendship, n. Freundschaft, -en f.

frigate, n. Fregat'te, -n f.

fright, n. Angst, ⁼e f., Schreck m.

frighten, vb. ängstigen, erschre'cken; (be f.ed) erschre'cken*.

frightful, adj. schrecklich.

frigid, adj. kalt (⁼); (sexual) frigid'.

frill, n. Krause, -n f.

fringe, n. Franse, -n f.; Rand, ⁼er m.

frisky, adj. lebhaft.

fritter, n. eine Art Pfannkuchen.

frivolity, n. Frivolität', -en f.

frivolous, adj. leichtsinnig, frivol'.

frivolousness, n. Leichtsinnigkeit, -en f.

frock, n. Kleid, -er nt.; (monk) Kutte, -n f.

frog, n. Frosch, ⁼e m.

frolic, vb. ausgelassen sein*.

from, prep. von, aus.

front, n. Vorderseite, -n f.; (mil.) Front, -en f.; (in f.) vorn; (in f. of) vor.

frontage, n. Vorderfront, -en f.

frontal, adj. frontal'.

frontier, n. Grenze, -n f.

frost, n. Frost, ⁼e m.

frostbite, n. Frostbeule, -n f.

frosting, n. Kuchenglasur, -en f.

frosty, adj. frostig.

froth, n. Schaum, ⁼e m.

frown, vb. die Stirn runzeln.

frugal, adj. sparsam, frugal'.

frugality, n. Sparsamkeit f.

fruit, n. Frucht, ⁼e f., Obst nt.

fruitful, adj. fruchtbar.

fruition, n. Reife f.

fruitless, adj. unfruchtbar; (fig.) vergeblich.

frustrate, vb. verdrän'gen; (nullify) verei'teln.

frustration, n. Verdrän'gung, -en f.; Verei'telung, -en f.

fry, vb. braten*.

fryer, n. junges Brathuhn, ⁼er nt.

frying pan, n. Bratpfanne, -n f.

fuchsia, n. Fuchsie, -n f.

fuel, n. Brennstoff, -e m.

fugitive, n. Flüchtling, -e m.

fugue, n. Fuge, -n f.

fulcrum, n. Drehpunkt, -e m.

fulfill, vb. erfül'len.

fulfillment, n. Erfül'lung, -en f.

full, adj. voll.

full dress, n. Frack, ⁼e m.; Gala-Uniform, -en f.

fullness, n. Fülle f.

fully, adv. völlig.

fumble, vb. umher·tappen.

fume, 1. n. Dampf, ⁼e m., Dunst, ⁼e m. 2. vb. dampfen, dunsten; (fig.) wüten.

fumigate, vb. aus·räuchern.

fumigator, n. Räucherapparat, -e m.

fun, n. Vergnügen nt., Spaß m., Jux m.

function, 1. n. Funktion', -en f. **2.** vb. funktionie'ren.

functional, adj. sachlich.

fund, n. Fond, -s m.

fundamental, adj. grundlegend.

funeral, n. Begräb'nis, -se nt., Beer'digung, -en f.

funereal, adj. düster.

fungicide, n. Pilzvernichtungsmittel, - nt.

fungus, n. Fungus, - m.

funnel, n. Trichter, - m.; (smoke-stack) Schornstein, -e m.

funny, adj. komisch, drollig.

fur, n. Pelz, -e m.

furious, adj. wütend.

furlough, n. Urlaub, -e m.

furnace, n. Ofen, - m.

furnish, vb. möblie'ren.

furnishings, n.pl. Ausstattung, -en f.

furniture, n. Möbel pl.

furor, n. Aufsehen nt.

furrier, n. Pelzhändler, - m.

furrow, n. Furche, -n f.

furry, adj. pelzartig.

further, 1. vb. fördern. **2.** adj. weiter, ferner.

furtherance, n. Förderung, -en f.

furthermore, adv. ausserdem, überdies'.

fury, n. Wut f.; Zorn m.; (mythology) Furie, -n f.

fuse, 1. n. (elec.) Sicherung, -en f.; (explosives) Zünder, - m. **2.** vb. verschmel'zen*.

fuselage, n. Rumpf, -e m.

fusillade, n. Gewehr'feuerer nt.

fusion, n. Verschmel'zung, -en f.; Fusion', -en f.

fuss, n. Aufheben nt, Umstand, -e m.

fussy, adj. umständlich, genau', betu'lich.

futile, adj. vergeb'lich, nutzlos.

futility, n. Nutzlosigkeit f.

future, 1. n. Zukunft f. **2.** adj. zukünftig.

futurity, n. Zukunft f.

futurology, n. Futurologie' f.

fuzz, n. Flaum m.

fuzzy, adj. flaumig.

G

gab, vb. schwatzen.

gabardine, n. Gabardine m.

gable, n. Giebel, -m.

gadget, n. Vorrichtung, -en f.

gag, 1. n. Knebel, - m.; (joke) Witz, -e m. **2.** vb. knebeln.

galety, n. Ausgelassenheit f.

gain, 1. n. Gewinn', -e m. **2.** vb. gewin'nen*.

gainful, adj. einträglich.

gait, n. Gang, -e m.

gala, adj. festlich.

galaxy, n. Milchstrasse, -n f.

gale, n. Sturm, -e m.

gall, 1. n. (bile) Galle, -n f.; (insolence) Unverschämtheit, -en f. **2.** vb. ärgern.

gallant, adj. aufmerksam, galant'.

gallantry, n. Höflichkeit, -en f., Galante'rie, -i'en f.

gall bladder, n. Gallenblase, -n f.

gallery, n. Galerie', -i'en f.

galley, n. (ship) Galee're, -n f.; (kitchen) Kombü'se, -n f.; (typogr.) Setzschiff, -e nt.

Gallic, adj. gallisch.

gallivant, vb. bummeln.

gallon, n. Gallo'ne, -n f.

gallop, 1. n. Galopp', -s m. **2.** vb. galoppie'ren.

gallows, n.pl. Galgen, - m.

gallstone, n. Gallenstein, -e m.

galore, adv. in Hülle und Fülle.

galosh, n. Überschuh, -e m.

gamble, 1. n. (game) Glücksspiel, -e nt.; (risk) Risiko, -s nt. **2.** vb. um Geld spielen; riskie'ren.

gambler, n. Glücksspieler,- m.

gambling, n. Glücksspiel, -e nt.

game, 1. n. Spiel, -e nt.; (hunting) Wild nt., Wildbret nt. **2.** adj. beherzt'; (lame) lahm.

gander, n. Gänserich, -e m.

gang, n. Bande, -n f.

gangplank, n. Laufplanke, -n f.

gangrene, n. Gangrän', -e nt.

gangrenous, adj. gangränös', brandig.

gangster, n. Gangster, - m.

gangway, n. Laufplanke, -n f.

gap, n. Lücke, -n f.; Spalte, -n f.

gape, vb. gaffen.

garage, n. Gara'ge, -n f.

garb, n. Gewand', -er nt.

garbage, n. Abfall, -e m., Müll m.

garble, vb. entstel'len, verzer'ren.

garden, n. Garten, - m.

gardener, n. Gärtner, - m.

gardenia, n. Garde'nia, -ien f.

gargle, vb. gurgeln.

gargoyle, n. Wasserspeier, - m.

garish, adj. grell.

garland, n. Girlan'de, -n f.

garlic, n. Knoblauch m.

garment, n. Kleidungsstück, -e nt.

garner, vb. auf-speichern.

garnet, n. Granat', -e m.

garnish, vb. garnie'ren.

garret, n. Dachstube, -n f.

garrison, n. Garnison', -en f.

garrulous, adj. schwatzhaft.

garter, n. Strumpfband, -er nt.; Hosenband, -er nt.; Sockenhalter, - m.

gas, n. Gas, -e nt.; (gasoline) Benzin' nt.

gaseous, adj. gasförmig.

gash, 1. n. klaffende Wunde, -n f. **2.** vb. eine tiefe Wunde schlagen*.

gasket, n. Dichtung f.

gas mask, n. Gasmaske, -n f.

gasohol, n. Benzin-Alkohol-Gemisch' nt.

gasoline, n. Benzin' nt.

gasp, vb. keuchen; nach Luft schnappen.

gastric, adj. gastrisch.

gastritis, n. Magenschleimhautentzündung, -en f.

gastronomical, adj. gastrono'misch.

gate, n. Tor, -e nt., Pforte, -n f.

gateway, n. Einfahrt, -en f., Tor, -e nt.

gather, vb. sammeln, pflücken; (infer) schließen*.

gathering, n. Versamm'lung, -en f.

gaudiness, n. auffälliger Protz m.

gaudy, adj. protzig.

gauge, 1. n. (measurement) Maß, -e nt.; (instrument) Messer, - m., Zeiger, - m.; (railway) Spurweite, -n f. **2.** vb. ab·messen*.

gaunt, adj. hager.

gauntlet, n. Handschuh, -e m.

gauze, n. Gaze, -n f.

gavel, n. Hammer, - m.

gawky, adj. linkisch.

gay, adj. fröhlich, heiter; (homosexual) homosexuell, schwul.

gaze, vb. starren.

gazelle, n. Gazel'le, -n f.

gazette, n. Zeitung, -en f.

gazetteer, n. geogra'phisches Namensverzeichnis, -se nt.

gear, n. Zahnrad, -er nt.; (auto) Gang, -e m.; (equipment) Zeug nt.

gearing, n. Getrie'be, - nt.

gearshift, n. Schalthebel, - m.

gelatin, n. Gelati'ne, -n f.

gelatinous, adj. gallertartig.

geld, vb. kastrie'ren.

gelding, n. Wallach, -e m.

gem, n. Edelstein, -e m.

gender, n. Geschlecht', -er nt., Genus, -nera nt.

gene, n. Gen, -e nt.

genealogical, adj. genealo'gisch.

genealogy, n. Genealogie', -i'en f.

general, 1. n. General', -e m. **2.** adj. allgemein.

generality, n. Allgemein'heit, -en f.

generalization, n. Verallgemei'nerung, -en f.

generalize, vb. verallgemei'nern.

generally, adv. (in general) im allgemei'nen; (usually) gewöhn'lich, meistens.

generate, vb. erzeu'gen.

generation, n. Generation', -en f.

generator, n. Genera'tor, -o'ren m.

generic, adj. Gattungs- (cpds.).

generosity, n. Großzügigkeit f.

generous, adj. großzügig, freigebig.

genetic, adj. gene'tisch.

genetics, n. Verer'bungslehre f.

Geneva, n. Genf nt.

genial, adj. freundlich, froh.

geniality, n. Freundlichkeit f.

genital, adj. genital'.

genitals, n. Geschlechts'organe pl.

genitive, n. Genitiv, -e m.

genius, n. Genie', -s nt.

genocide, n. Völkermord m.

genre, n. Genre, -s nt.

genteel, adj. vornehm.

gentile, 1. n. Nichtjude, -n -n m. 2. adj. nichtjüdisch.

gentility, n. Vornehmheit f.

gentle, adj. sanft, mild.

gentleman, n. Gentleman, -men m.

gentleness, n. Sanftheit f.

gentry, n. niederer Adel m.

genuflect, vb. das Knie beugen.

genuine, adj. echt.

genuineness, n. Echtheit f.

genus, n. Geschlecht', -er nt., Gattung, -en f.

geographer, n. Geograph', -en, -en m.

geographical, adj. geographisch.

geography, n. Geographie' f., Erdkunde f.

geometric, adj. geome'trisch.

geometry, n. Geometrie' f.

geopolitics, n. Geopolitik' f.

geranium, n. Gera'nie, -n f.

germ, n. Keim, -e m.; Bakte'rie, -n f.

German, 1. n. Deutsch- m.&f. 2. adj. deutsch.

germane, adj. zur Sache gehö'rig.

Germanic, adj. germa'nisch.

German measles, n. Röteln pl.

Germany, n. Deutschland nt.; (West G.) Bundesrepublik' f. Westdeutschland nt.; (East G.) Deutsche Demokratische Republik f.; Ostdeutschland nt.

germicide, n. keimtötendes Mittel, - nt.

germinal, adj. Keim- (cpds.).

germinate, vb. keimen.

gestate, vb. aus'tragen*.

gestation, n. Gestation', -en f.

gesticulate, vb. gestikulie'ren.

gesticulation, n. Gebär'de, -n f.

gesture, n. Gebär'de, -n f., Geste, -n f.

get, vb. (receive) bekom'men*, kriegen; (fetch) holen; (become) werden*; (arrive) an'kommen*; (g. to) hin'kommen*; (g. up) auf'stehen*; (g. in) ein'steigen*; (g. out) aus'steigen*.

geyser, n. Geiser, - m.

ghastly, adj. grauenhaft.

ghost, n. Geist, -er m., Gespenst', -er nt.

giant, 1. n. Riese, -n, -n m. 2. adj. riesenhaft.

gibberish, n. Kauderwelsch nt.

gibbon, n. Gibbon, -s m.

giblets, n. Geflü'gelklein nt.

giddy, adj. schwindlig.

gift, n. Gabe, -n f., Geschenk', -e nt.

gifted, adj. begabt'.

gigantic, adj. riesenhaft.

giggle, vb. kichern.

gigolo, n. Eintänzer, - m.

gild, vb. vergol'den.

gill, n. Kieme, -n f.

gilt, n. Vergol'dung, -en f.

gimlet, n. Handbohrer, - m.

gin, n. Gin, -s m.; (cotton) Entker'nungsmaschine, -n f.

ginger, n. Ingwer m.

gingerly, adv. sachte.

gingham, n. Kattun', -e m.

giraffe, n. Giraf'fe, -n f.

gird, vb. gürten.

girder, n. Träger, - m.

girdle, n. Gürtel, - m.; Strumpfbandgürtel, - m.

girl, n. Mädchen, - nt.

girlish, adj. mädchenhaft.

girth, n. Umfang, =e m.

gist, n. Kern, -e m.

give, vb. geben*.

given name, n. Vorname(n), - m.

gizzard, n. Geflü'gelmagen, = m.

glacé, adj. glaciert'.

glacial, adj. Eis- (cpds.).

glad, adj. froh.

gladden, vb. erfreu'en.

gladiolus, n. Schwertlilie, -n f.

gladly, adv. gern.

gladness, n. Freude, -n f.

glamor, n. äußerer Glanz m.; beste'chende Schönheit f.

glamorous, adj. äußerlich beste'chend, blendend.

glance, 1. n. Blick, -e m. 2. vb. blicken.

gland, n. Drüse, -n f.

glandular, adj. Drüsen- (cpds.).

glare, 1. n. blendendes Licht nt. 2. vb. blenden; (look) starren; (g. at) an'starren.

glaring, adj. grell.

glass, n. Glas, =er nt.

glasses, n. pl. Brille, -n f.

glassware, n. Glasware, -n f.

glassy, adj. glasig.

glaucoma, n. Glaukom', -e nt.

glaze, 1. n. Glasur', -en f. 2. vb. glasie'ren.

glazier, n. Glaser, - m.

gleam, 1. n. Lichtstrahl, -en m. 2. vb. strahlen, glänzen.

glee, n. Freude, -n f.

gleeful, adj. fröhlich.

glen, n. enges Tal, =er nt.

glib, adj. zungenfertig.

glide, 1. n. Gleitflug, =e m. 2. vb. gleiten*.

glider, n. Segelflugzeug, -e nt.

glimmer, 1. n. Schimmer, - m. 2. vb. schimmern.

glimpse, n. flüchtiger Blick, -e m.

glint, n. Lichtschimmer, - m.

glisten, vb. glänzen.

glitter, 1. n. Glanz m. 2. vb. glitzern.

gloat, vb. sich weiden; schadenfroh sein*.

global, adj. global.

globe, n. Erdkugel, -n f.; Globus, -se m.

globular, adj. kugelförmig.

globule, n. Kügelchen, - nt.

gloom, n. Düsternis f.; (fig.) Trübsinn m.

gloomy, adj. düster; trübsinnig.

glorification, n. Verherr'lichung f.

glorify, vb. verherr'lichen.

glorious, adj. ruhmvoll, glorreich.

glory, n. Ruhm m.; Herrlichkeit f.

gloss, n. Glanz m.

glossary, n. Glossar', -e nt.

glossy, adj. glänzend.

glove, n. Handschuh, -e m.

glow, 1. n. Glühen nt. 2. vb. glühen.

glucose, n. Traubenzucker m.

glue, 1. n. Leim m. 2. vb. leimen.

glum, adj. mürrisch.

glumness, n. Mürrischkeit f.

glut, 1. n. Überfluß m. 2. vb. übersät'tigen.

glutinous, adj. leimig.

glutton, n. Vielfraß, -e m.

gluttonous, adj. gefrä'ßig.

glycerine, n. Glyzerin' nt.

gnarled, adj. knorrig.

gnash, vb. knirschen.

gnat, n. Schnake, -n f.

gnaw, vb. knabbern.

go, vb. gehen*; (become) werden*; (g. without) entbeh'ren.

goad, 1. n. Treibstock, =e m. 2. vb. an'stacheln.

goal, n. Ziel, -e nt.; (soccer) Tor, -e nt.

goal-keeper, n. Torwart, =er m.

goat, n. Ziege, -n f.; Geiß, -en f.; (billy g.) Ziegenbock, =e m.

goatee, n. Spitzbart, =e m.

goatskin, n. Ziegenleder nt.

gobble, vb. verschlin'gen*.

go-between, n. Vermitt'ler, - m.

goblet, n. Kelchglas, =er nt.

goblin, n. Kobold, -e m.

god, n. Gott, =er m.

godchild, n. Patenkind, -er nt.

goddess, n. Göttin, -nen f.

godfather, n. Patenonkel, - m.

godless, adj. gottlos.

godlike, adj. gottähnlich.

godly, adj. göttlich.

godmother, n. Patentante, -n f.

godsend, n. Gottesgabe, -n f.

Godspeed, n. Lebewohl' nt.

go-getter, n. Draufgänger, - m.

goiter, n. Kropf, =e m.

gold, n. Gold nt.

golden, adj. golden.

goldfinch, n. Stieglitz, -e m.

goldfish, n. Goldfisch, -e m.

goldsmith, n. Goldschmied, -e m.

golf, n. Golf nt.

gondola, n. Gondel, -n f.

gondolier, n. Gondelführer, - m.

gone, adv. weg.

gong, n. Gong, -s m.

gonorrhea, n. Tripper m.

good, adj. gut (besser, best-).

good-by, interj. auf Wiedersehen.

Good Friday, n. Karfrei'tag m.

good-hearted, adj. gutherzig.

good-humored, adj. gutmütig.

good-looking, adj. gutaussehend.

good-natured, adj. gutmütig.

goodness, n. Güte f.

goods, n.pl. Waren pl.

good will, n. Wohlwollen n.

goose, n. Gans, ẅe f.

gooseberry, n. Stachelbeere, -n f.

gooseneck, n. Gänsehals, ẅe m.

goose step, n. Stechschritt m.

gore, 1. n. Blut nt. **2.** vb. aufspießen.

gorge, n. (anatomical) Gurgel, -n f.; (ravine) Schlucht, -en f.

gorgeous, adj. prachtvoll.

gorilla, n. Goril'la, -s m.

gory, adj. blutig.

gospel, n. Evange'lium, -ien nt.

gossamer, 1. n. hauchdünner Stoff m. **2.** adj. hauchdünn.

gossip, 1. n. Klatsch m. **2.** vb. klatschen.

Gothic, 1. n. Gotik f. **2.** adj. gotisch.

gouge, 1. n. Hohleisen, - nt. **2.** vb. aus·höhlen.

gourd, n. Kürbis, -se m.

gourmand, n. Vielfraß, ẅe m.

gourmet, n. Feinschmecker, - m.

govern, vb. regie'ren.

governess, n. Erzie'herin, -nen f.

government, n. Regie'rung, -en f.

governmental, adj. Regie'rungs- (cpds.).

governor, n. Gouverneur', -e m.

governorship, n. Gouverneurs'amt, ẅer nt.

gown, n. Kleid, -er nt.

grab, vb. greifen*.

grace, n. Anmut f.; (mercy) Gnade f.

graceful, adj. anmutig.

graceless, adj. unbeholfen.

gracious, adj. gnädig, gütig.

grade, 1. n. Grad, -e m., Rang, ẅe m.; (mark) Zensur', -en f.; (class) Klasse, -n f.; (rise) Steigung, -en f. **2.** vb. bewer'ten; (smooth) ebnen.

grade crossing, n. Bahnübergang, ẅe m.

gradual, adj. allmäh'lich.

graduate, vb. graduie'ren.

graft, 1. n. Beste'chung, -en f., Korruption' f. **2.** vb. (bot.) propfen.

grail, n. Gral m.

grain, n. Körnchen, - nt; (wheat, etc.) Getrei'de n.; (wood) Maserung, -en f.

gram, n. Gramm, - nt.

grammar, n. Gramma'tik, -en f.

grammar school, n. Grundschule, -n f.

grammatical, adj. gramma'tisch.

gramophone, n. Grammophon', -e nt.

granary, n. Kornspeicher, - m.

grand, adj. großartig.

grandchild, n. Enkelkind, -er nt.

granddaughter, n. Enkelin, -nen f.

grandeur, n. Erha'benheit f.

grandfather, n. Großvater, ẅ m.

grandiloquent, adj. schwülstig.

grandiose, adj. grandios'.

grandmother, n. Großmutter, ẅ f.

grandparents, n.pl. Großeltern pl.

grandson, n. Enkel, - m.

grandstand, n. Tribü'ne, -n f.

granite, n. Granit' m.

grant, 1. n. finanziel'le Beihilfe, -n f.; Stipen'dium, -en nt. **2.** vb. gewäh'ren.

granular, adj. körnig.

granulated sugar, n. Streuzucker m.

granulation, n. Körnung f.

granule, n. Körnchen, - nt.

grape, n. Weintraube, -n f.

grapefruit, n. Pampelmu'se, - f.

grapevine, n. Weinstock, ẅe m.; (rumor) Amtstratsch m.

graph, n. graphische Darstellung, -en f., Diagramm', -e nt.

graphic, adj. graphisch.

graphite, n. Graphit' m.

graphology, n. Graphologie' f.

grapple, 1. n. Enterhaken, - m. **2.** vb. packen; ringen*.

grasp, 1. n. Griff, -e m.; (mental) Fassungsvermögen nt. **2.** vb. ergrei'fen*.

grasping, adj. habgierig.

grass, n. Gras, ẅer nt.; (lawn) Rasen, - m; (marijuana) Hasch m.

grasshopper, n. Heuschrecke, -n f.

grassy, adj. grasartig.

grate, 1. n. Rost m. **2.** vb. (cheese, etc.) reiben*, (irritate) irritie'ren.

grateful, adj. dankbar.

grater, n. Reibe, -n f.

gratify, vb. befrie'digen.

grating, n. Gitter, - nt.

gratis, adj. gratis.

gratitude, n. Dankbarkeit, -en f.

gratuitous, adj. unentgeltlich.

gratuity, n. Geschenk', -e nt.; (tip) Trinkgeld, -er nt.

grave, 1. n. Grab, ẅer nt. **2.** adj. schwerwiegend.

gravel, n. Kies m.

graveyard, n. Friedhof, ẅe m.

gravitate, vb. angezogen werden*; gravitie'ren.

gravity, n. Schwerkraft f.; Ernst m.

gravure, n. Gravü're, -n f.

gravy, n. Soße, -n f.

gray, adj. grau.

graze, vb. grasen, weiden.

grease, 1. n. Fett, -e nt. **2.** vb. fetten; schmieren.

greasy, adj. fettig, schmierig.

great, adj. groß (größer, größt-).

greatness, n. Größe, -n f.

Greece, n. Griechenland f.

greed, n. Gier f., Habsucht f.

greediness, n. Gier f., Habsucht f.

greedy, adj. gierig, habsüchtig.

Greek, 1. n. Grieche, -n, -n m. **2.** adj. griechisch.

green, adj. grün.

greenery, n. Grün nt.

greenhouse, n. Gewächs'haus, ẅer nt., Treibhaus, ẅer nt.

greet, vb. begrü'ßen.

greeting, n. Gruß, ẅe m.

gregarious, adj. gesel'lig.

grenade, n. Grana'te, -n f.

grenadine, n. Granat'apfellikör m.

greyhound, n. Windhund, -e m.

grid, n. Gitter, - nt.; (elec.) Stromnetz, -e nt.

griddle, n. Bratpfanne, -n f.

grief, n. Kummer m.

grievance, n. Beschwer'de, -n f.

grieve, vb. (intr.) trauern; (tr.) betrü'ben.

grievous, adj. schmerzlich; (serious) schwerwiegend.

grill, n. Grill, -s m.

grim, adj. grimmig.

grimace, n. Grimas'se, -n f., Fratze, -n f.

grime, n. Ruß m.

grimy, adj. schmutzig.

grin, 1. n. Grinsen nt. **2.** vb. grinsen.

grind, vb. mahlen*.

grindstone, n. Schleifstein, -e m.

grip, 1. n. Griff, -e m.; (suitcase) Koffer, - m. **2.** vb. fassen.

gripe, 1. n. (complaint) Ärgernis, -se nt. **2.** vb. (complain) nörgeln.

grippe, n. Grippe, -n f.

gristle, n. Knorpel, - m.

grit, 1. n. Kies m.; (courage) Mut m. **2.** vb. (g. one's teeth) die Zähne zusam'men-beis-sen*.

grizzled, adj. grau.

groan, 1. n. Stöhnen nt. 2. vb. stöhnen.

grocer, n. Kolonial'waren-händler, - m.

groceries, n.pl. Kolonial'waren pl.

grocery store, n. Kolonial'wa-rengeschäft, -e nt., Lebens-mittelgeschäft, -e nt.

grog, n. Grog, -s m.

groggy, adj. benom'men; (be g.) taumeln.

groin, n. Leistengegend f.

groom, n. Reitknecht, - e m.; (footman) Diener, - m.; (bridegroom) Bräutigam -e m.

groove, n. Rinne, -n f.

grope, vb. tappen.

gross, 1. n. Gros, -se nt. 2. adj. grob (-); (weight) brutto.

grossness, n. Kraßheit, -en f.

grotesque, adj. grotesk'.

grotto, n. Grotte, -n f.

grouch, n. Griesgram, -e m. 2. vb. verdrieß'lich sein*.

ground, 1. n. Grund, -e m., Bo-den m.; Gebiet', -e nt. 2. vb. (elec.) erden.

groundless, adj. grundlos.

groundwork, n. Grundlage, -n f.

group, 1. n. Gruppe, -n f. 2. vb. gruppie'ren.

groupie, n. Mitläufer im Ge-folge Prominenter, besonders Rockmusikstars.

grouse, n. schottisches Schnee-huhn, -er nt.

grove, Hain, -e m.

grovel, vb. kriechen*, speichel-leckerisch sein*.

grow, vb. wachsen*.

growl, vb. knurren.

grown, adj. erwach'sen.

grown-up, 1. n. Erwach'sen-m.&f. 2. adj. erwach'sen.

growth, n. Wachstum nt.; (med.) Gewächs', -e nt.

grub, 1. n. Larve, -n f.; (food) Fressa'lien pl. 2. vb. wühlen.

grudge, n. Groll m.

gruel, n. dünne Hafergrütze f.

gruesome, adj. schauerlich.

gruff, adj. bärbeißig.

grumble, vb. murren.

grumpy, adj. mürrisch.

grunt, 1. n. Grunzen, - nt. 2. vb. grunzen.

guarantee, 1. n. Garantie', -i'en f. 2. vb. garantie'ren.

guarantor, n. Bürge, -n, -n m.

guaranty, n. Sicherheit, -en f.; Bürgschaft, -en f.

guard, 1. n. Wache, -n f.; 2. vb. bewa'chen.

guarded, adj. vorsichtig.

guardian, n. Vormund, -e m.

guerrilla, n. Partisan' (-en,) -en m.

guess, vb. raten*.

guesswork, n. Raterei' f.

guest, n. Gast, -e m.

guidance, n. Leitung f., Füh-rung f.

guide, 1. n. Führer, - m. 2. vb. führen, leiten.

guidebook, n. Reiseführer, - m.

guidepost, n. Wegweiser, - m.

guild, n. Gilde, -n f.

guile, n. Arglist f.

guillotine, n. Guilloti'ne, -n f.

guilt, n. Schuld f.

guiltless, adj. schuldlos.

guilty, adj. schuldig.

guinea fowl, n. Perlhuhn, -er nt.

guinea pig, n. Meerschwein-chen, - nt.

guise, n. Art, -en f.; (clothes) Aussehen nt.

guitar, n. Gitar're, -n f.

gulf, n. Golf, -e m.

gull, n. Möwe, -n f.

gullet, n. Kehle, -n f.

gullible, adj. leichtgläubig.

gully, n. Wasserrinne, -n f.

gulp, vb. schlucken.

gum, n. Gummi, -s nt.; (teeth) Zahnfleisch nt.; (chewing g.) Kaugummi, -s nt.

gummy, adj. gummiartig, kleb-rig.

gun, n. (small) Gewehr', -e nt.; (large) Geschütz', -e nt.

gunboat, n. Kano'nenboot, -e nt.

gunner, n. Kanonier', -e m.

gunpowder, n. Schießpulver nt.

gunshot, n. Schuß, -sse m.

gurgle, vb. gluckern.

guru, n. Guru, -s m.

gush, vb. hervor'-quellen*.

gusher, n. sprudelnde Petrole-umquelle, -n f.

gusset, n. Zwickel, - m.

gust, n. Windstoß, -e m.

gustatory, adj. Geschmacks'- (cpds.).

gusto, n. Schwung m.

gusty, adj. windig.

guts, n. Eingeweide pl.; (cour-age) Mumm m.

gutter, n. (street) Rinnstein, -e m., Gosse, -n f.; (house) Dachtraufe, -n f.

guttural, adj. guttural'.

guy, n. Kerl, -e m.

guzzle, vb. saufen*.

gymnasium, n. Turnhalle, -n f.

gymnast, n. Turner, - m.

gymnastic, adj. gymnas'tisch.

gymnastics, n. Gymnas'tik f.

gynecologist, n. Frauenarzt, -e m., Gynäkolo'ge, -n, -n m.

gynecology, n. Gynäkologie' f.

gypsum, n. Gips m.

gypsy, n. Zigeu'ner, - m.

gyrate, vb. kreiseln.

gyroscope, n. Kreiselkompaß, -sse m.

H

haberdashery, n. Geschäft' für Herrenartikel.

habit, n. Gewohn'heit, -en f.; Kleidung, -en f.

habitable, adj. bewohn'bar.

habitat, n. Wohnbereich, -e m.

habitual, adj. gewöhn'lich; Ge-wohn'heits- (cpds.).

habitué, n. Stammgast, -e m.

hack, 1. n. Droschke, -n f.; (horse) Klepper, - m. 2. vb. hacken.

hacksaw, n. Metall'säge, -n f.

hag, n. Vettel, -n f.

haggard, adj. abgehärmt.

haggle, vb. feilschen.

Hague, n. Den Haag m.

hail, 1. n. Hagel m. 2. vb. ha-geln; (greet) begrü'ßen. 3. interj. heil!

hailstone, n. Hagelkorn, -er nt.

hailstorm, n. Hagelwetter, - nt.

hair, n. Haar, -e nt.

haircut, n. Haarschnitt, -e m.; (get a h.) sich die Haare schneiden lassen*.

hairdo, n. Frisur', -en f.

hairdresser, n. Friseur', - m., Friseu'se, -n f.

hairline, n. Haaransatz, -e m.; Haarstrich, -e m.

hairpin, n. Haarnadel, -n f.

hair-raising, adj. haarsträu-bend.

hairspray, n. Haarspray m.

hairy, adj. haarig.

hale, adj. kräftig.

half, 1. n. Hälfte, -n f. 2. adj. halb.

half-breed, n. Mischling, -e m.

half-brother, n. Stiefbruder, - m.

half-hearted, adj. lauwarm.

half-mast, n. Halbmast m.

halfway, adv. halbwegs.

half-wit, n. Narr, -en, -en m.

halibut, n. Heilbutt, -e m.

hall, n. (auditorium) Halle, -n f.; (large room) Saal, Säle m.; (corridor) Gang, -e m., Korridor, -e m.; (front h.) Diele, -n f.

hallmark, n. Stempel der Echt-heit m.

hallow, vb. heiligen.

Halloween, n. Abend (m.) vor Allerhei'ligen.

hallucination, n. Wahnvorstel-lung, -en f., Halluzination', -en f.

hallway, n. Gang, -e m., Korri-dor, -e m.

halo, n. Heiligenschein, -e m.

halt, 1. n. Halt, -e m.; (fig.) Stillstand m. 2. vb. an-hal-ten*. 3. interj. halt!

halter, n. (horse) Halfter, - nt.; (female clothing) Ober-teil eines Bade- oder Luftan-zuges.

halve, vb. halbie'ren.

ham, n. Schinken, - m.

Hamburg, n. Hamburg nt.

hamlet, n. Flecken, - m.

hammer, 1. n. Hammer, ≈ m. 2. vb. hämmern.

hammock, n. Hängematte, -n f.

hamper, 1. n. Korb, ≈e m. 2. vb. hemmen.

hamstring, vb. lähmen.

hand, 1. n. Hand, ≈e f. 2. vb. reichen.

handbag, n. Handtasche, -n f.

handbook, n. Handbuch, ≈er nt.

handcuffs, n.pl. Handschellen pl.

handful, n. Handvoll f.

handicap 1. n. Handikap, -s nt.; Hindernis, -se nt. 2. vb. hemmen.

handicraft, n. Handwerk nt.

handiwork, n. Handarbeit, -en f., Handwerk nt.

handkerchief, n. Taschentuch, ≈er nt.

handle, 1. n. Henkel, - m., Griff, -e m. 2. vb. handhaben.

hand-made, adj. handgearbeitet.

handout, n. Almosen, - nt.

hand-rail, n. Gelän'der, - nt.

handsome, adj. gutaussehend; ansehnlich.

handwriting, n. Handschritt, -en f.

handy, adj. handlich; (skilled) geschickt'.

handy man, n. Fakto'tum, -s nt.

hangar, n. Schuppen, - m.

hanger, n. Aufhänger, - m.; (clothes) Kleiderbügel, - m.

hanger-on, n. Schmarot'zer, - m.

hang glider, n. Drachenflieger, - m.

hanging, n. Hinrichtung (-en f.) durch Hängen.

hangman, n. Henker, - m.

hangnail, n. Niednagel, ≈ m.

hangout, n. Stammlokal, -e nt.

hang-over, n. Kater, - m., Katzenjammer m.

hangup, n. (to have a h.) mit etwas nicht fertig werden, einen Komplex haben, verklemmt sein.

haphazardly, adv. aufs Geratewohl'.

happen, vb. sich ereig'nen, geschehen*, passie'ren.

happening, n. Ereig'nis, -se nt.

happiness, n. Glück nt.

happy, adj. glücklich.

happy-go-lucky, adj. sorglos.

harangue, 1. n. marktschreierische Ansprache, -n f. 2. vb. eine marktschreierische Ansprache halten*.

harass, vb. plagen.

harbinger, n. Vorbote, -n, -n m.

harbor, n. Hafen, ≈ m.

hard, adj. (not soft) hart (≈); (not easy) schwer, schwierig.

hard-boiled, adj. hartgekocht; (fig.) abgebrüht.

hard coal, n. Anthrazit', -e m.

harden, vb. (intr.) hart werden*; (tr.) ab'härten.

hard-headed, adj. praktisch, realis'tisch.

hard-hearted, adj. hartherzig.

hardiness, n. Rüstigkeit f.

hardly, adv. kaum.

hardness, n. Härte, -n f.

hardship, n. Not, ≈e f.; (exertion) Anstrengung, -en f.

hardware, n. Eisenwaren pl.

hardwood, n. Hartholz nt.

hardy, adj. rüstig.

hare, n. Hase, -n, -n m.

harem, n. Harem, -s m.

hark, vb. horchen.

Harlequin, n. Harlekin, -e m.

harm, 1. n. Schaden, ≈ m.; Unrecht, -e nt. 2. vb. schaden; Unrecht zu-fügen.

harmful, adj. schädlich.

harmless, adj. harmlos.

harmonic, adj. harmo'nisch.

harmonica, n. Harmo'nika, -s f.

harmonious, adj. harmo'nisch.

harmonize, vb. harmonisie'ren.

harmony, n. Harmonie', -i'en f.; (fig.) Eintracht f.

harness, 1. n. Geschirr', -e nt. 2. vb. ein-spannen.

harp, n. Harfe, -n f.

harpoon, 1. n. Harpu'ne, -n f. 2. vb. harpunie'ren.

harpsichord, n. Spinett', -e nt.

harrow, 1. n. Egge, -n f. 2. vb. eggen.

harry, vb. plündern; plagen.

harsh, adj. rauh; streng.

harshness, n. Rauheit f.; Strenge f.

harvest, 1. n. Ernte, -n f. 2. vb. ernten.

hassle, n. Hetze f.

hassock, n. gepolsterter Hocker, - m.

haste, n. Eile f.

hasten, vb. eilen; sich beei'len.

hat, n. Hut, ≈e m.

hatch, 1. n. Luke, -n f. 2. vb. aus-brüten.

hatchet, n. Beil, -e nt.

hate, 1. n. Haß m. 2. vb. hassen.

hateful, adj. verhaßt'; widerlich.

hatred, n. Haß m.

haughtiness, n. Hochmut m.

haughty, adj. hochmütig.

haul, vb. schleppen.

haunch, n. Keule, -n f.

haunt, vb. verfol'gen.

have, vb. haben*; (I h. it made) ich lasse* es machen; (I h. him make it) ich lasse* ihn es machen.

haven, n. Hafen, ≈ m.; Zufluchtsort, -e m.

havoc, n. Verwüs'tung, -en f.

hawk, n. Habicht, -e m.

hawser, n. Trosse, -n f.

hay, n. Heu nt.

hay fever, n. Heuschnupfen, - m.

hayloft, n. Heuboden, ≈ m.

haystack, n. Heuhaufen, - m.

hazard, 1. n. Risiko, -s nt. 2. vb. riskie'ren.

hazardous, adj. gewagt'.

haze, n. Dunst, ≈e m.

hazel, adj. haselnußbraun.

hazelnut, n. Haselnuß, ≈sse f.

hazy, adj. dunstig, unklar.

he, pron. er.

head, n. Kopf, ≈e m., Haupt, ≈er nt.

headache, n. Kopfschmerzen pl.

headfirst, adv. Hals über Kopf.

headgear, n. Kopfbedeckung, -en f.

heading, n. Überschrift, -en f., Rubrik', -en f.

headlight, n. Scheinwerfer, - m.

headline, n. Überschrift, -en f.; (newspaper) Schlagzeile, -n f.

headlong, adj. überstürzt'.

headmaster, n. Schuldirektor, -en m.

head-on, adv. direkt von vorn.

headquarters, n.pl. Hauptquartier, -e nt.

headstone, n. (grave) Grabstein, -e m.; (arch.) Eckstein, -e m.

headstrong, adj. dickköpfig.

headwaters, n.pl. Quelle, -n f.

headway, n. (make h.) vorwärts kommen*.

heal, vb. heilen.

health, n. Gesund'heit, -en f.

healthful, adj. gesund' (≈).

healthy, adj. gesund'(≈).

heap, 1. n. Haufen, - m. 2. vb. häufen.

hear, vb. hören.

hearing, n. Gehör' nt.; (jur.) Verhör', -e nt.

hearsay, n. Hörensagen nt.

hearse, n. Leichenwagen, - m.

heart, n. Herz(en), - nt.

heartache, n. Herzenskummer m.

heart-breaking, adj. herzzerbrechend.

heartbroken, adv. tieftraurig.

heartburn, n. Sodbrennen, - nt.

heartfelt, adj. aufrichtig.

hearth, n. Kamin', -e m.

heartless, adj. herzlos.

heart-rending, adj. herzzerreißend.

heart-sick, adj. niedergeschlagen.

heart-to-heart, adj. freimütig.

hearty, adj. herzhaft.

heat, 1. n. Hitze f., Wärme f.; (house) Heizung f. 2. vb. heiß machen, erhit'zen; (house) heizen.

heated, adj. geheizt'; (fig.) hitzig.

heater, *n.* Heizvorrichtung, -en *f.*

heathen, 1. *n.* Heide, -n, -n *m.* 2. *adj.* heidnisch.

heather, *n.* Heidekraut *nt.*

heat-stroke, *n.* Hitzschlag, ⁼e *m.*

heat wave, *n.* Hitzewelle, -n *f.*

heave, *vb.* heben*; wogen; (*utter*) aus⸱stoßen*.

heaven, *n.* Himmel, - *m.*

heavenly, *adj.* himmlisch.

heavy, *adj.* schwer; *(fig.)* heftig.

heavyweight, *n.* Schwergewicht *nt.*

Hebrew, 1. *n.* Hebrä'er, - *m.* 2. *adj.* hebrä'isch.

heckle, *vb.* hecheln.

hectic, *adj.* hektisch.

hedge, *n.* Hecke, -n *f.*

hedgehog, *n.* Igel, - *m.*

hedge-hop, *vb. (mil.)* im Tiefflug an⸱fliegen*.

hedgerow, *n.* Baumhecke, -n *f.*

hedonism, *n.* Hedonis'mus *m.*

heed, *vb.* beach'ten.

heedless, *adj.* achtlos.

heel, *n. (shoes)* Absatz, ⁼e *m.; (foot)* Ferse, -n *f.; (scoundrel)* Schuft, -e *m.*

heifer, *n.* junge Kuh, ⁼e *f.*

height, *n.* Höhe, -n *f.; (person)* Größe -n *f.*

heighten, *vb.* erhö'hen.

heinous, *adj.* abscheu'lich, verrucht'.

heir, *n.* Erbe, -n, -n *m.*

heirloom, *n.* Erbstück, -e *nt.*

helicopter, *n.* Hubschrauber, - *m.*

heliotrope, *n.* Heliotrop', -e *nt.*

helium, *n.* Helium *nt.*

hell, *n.* Hölle, -n *f.*

Hellenic, *adj.* helle'nisch.

Hellenism, *n.* Hellenis'mus *m.*

hello, *interj.* guten Tag (Morgen, Abend); *(call for attention)* hallo.

helm, *n.* Steuerruder, - *nt.*

helmet, *n.* Helm, -e *m.*

helmsman, *n.* Steuermann, ⁼er *m.*

help, 1. *n.* Hilfe *f.* 2. *vb.* helfen*.

helper, *n.* Helfer, - *m.*

helpful, *adj.* hilfreich, hilfsbereit.

helpfulness, *n.* Hilfsbereitschaft *f.*

helping, *n.* Portion', -en *f.*

helpless, *adj.* hilflos.

helter-skelter, *adv.* hol'terdiepol'ter.

hem, 1. *n.* Saum, ⁼e *m.* 2. *vb.* säumen.

hematite, *n.* Hematit', -e *m.*

hemisphere, *n.* Halbkugel, -n *f.*

hemlock, *n.* Schierling *m.*

hemoglobin, *n.* Hämoglobin' *nt.*

hemophilia, *n.* Bluterkrankheit *f.*

hemorrhage, *n.* Bluterguß, ⁼sse *m.*

hemorrhoid, *n.* Hämorrhoi'de, -n *f.*

hemp, *n.* Hanf *m.*

hemstitch, *n.* Hohlsaum, ⁼e *m.*

hen, *n.* Henne, -n *f.*

hence, *adv. (time)* von nun an; *(place)* von hier aus; *(therefore)* daher, deshalb, deswegen, also.

henceforth, *adv.* von nun an.

henchman, *n.* Trabant', -en, -en *m.*

henna, *n.* Henna *f.*

henpecked, *adj.* unter dem Pantof'fel stehend.

hepatic, *adj.* Leber- *(cpds.)*

hepatica, *n.* Hepa'tika, -ken *f.*

her, 1. *pron.* sie, ihr. 2. *adj.* ihr, -, -e.

heraldic, *adj.* heral'disch.

heraldry, *n.* Wappenkunde *f.*

herb, *n.* Kraut, ⁼er *nt.*, Gewürz'kraut, ⁼er *nt.*

herculean, *adj.* herku'lisch.

herd, *n.* Herde, -n *f.*

here, *adv. (in this place)* hier; *(to this place)* hierher'; *(from h.)* hierhin'.

hereabout, *adv.* hier.

hereafter, 1. *n.* Leben *(nt.)* nach dem Tode. 2. *adv.* in Zukunft.

hereby, *adv.* hiermit.

hereditary, *adj.* erblich.

heredity, *n.* Erblichkeit *f.;* Verer'bung, -en *f.*

herein, *adv.* hierbei, hiermit.

heresy, *n.* Ketzerei', -en *f.*

heretic, 1. *n.* Ketzer, - *m.* 2. *adj.* ketzerisch.

heritage, *n.* Erbe *nt.*

hermetic, *adj.* herme'tisch.

hermit, *n.* Einsiedler, - *m.*

hernia, *n.* Bruch, ⁼e *m.*

hero, *n.* Held, -en, -en *m.*

heroic, *adj.* heldenhaft.

heroin, *n.* Heroin' *nt.*

heroine, *n.* Heldin, -nen *f.*

heroism, *n.* Heldenmut *m.*

heron, *n.* Reiher, - *m.*

herring, *n.* Hering, -e *m.*

herringbone, *n.* Heringsgräte, - *n f.*

hers, *pron.* ihrer, -es, -e.

hertz, *n.* Hertz *nt.*

hesitancy, *n.* Zögern *nt.*

hesitant, *adj.* zögernd.

hesitate, *vb.* zögern.

hesitation, *n.* Zögern *nt.*

heterodox, *adj.* heterodox'.

heterogeneous, *adj.* heterogen'.

heterosexual, *adj.* heterosexuell'.

hew, *vb.* hauen*.

hexagon, *n.* Sechseck, -e *nt.*

heyday, *n.* Blütezeit, -en *f.*

hi, *interj.* hallo.

hibernate, *vb.* überwin'tern.

hibernation, *n.* Überwin'terung, -en *f.*

hibiscus, *n.* Hibis'kus, -ken *m.*

hiccup, *n.* Schluckauf *m.*

hickory, *n.* Hickoryholz, ⁼er *nt.*

hide, 1. *n.* Haut, ⁼e *f.;* Fell, -e *nt.* 2. *vb.* verber'gen*, verste'cken; verheim'lichen.

hideous, *adj.* gräßlich.

hide-out, *n.* Schlupfwinkel, - *m.*

hierarchy, *n.* Rangordnung, -en *f.*, Hierarchie', -i'en *f.*

hieroglyphic, *adj.* hierogly'phisch.

high, *adj.* hoch, hoh- (höher, höchst); *(tipsy)* beschwipst'.

high fidelity, *n.* Hifi *nt.*

high-handed, *adj.* anmaßend.

highland, *n.* Hochland, ⁼er *nt.*

highlight, *n.* Höhepunkt, -e *m.*

highly, *adv.* höchst.

high-minded, *adj.* edelmütig.

Highness, *n.* Hoheit, -en *f.*

high school, *n.* höhere Schule, - *n f.*

high seas, *n.* hohe See *f.*

high-strung, *adj.* nervös, kribbelig.

high tide, *n.* Flut, -en *f.*

highway, *n.* Landstraße, -n *f.*, Chaussee', -n *f.*

hijacker, *n.* Flugzeugentführer, - *m.;* Luftpirat, -en, -en *m.*

hike, 1. *n.* Wanderung, -en *f.* 2. *vb.* wandern.

hilarious, *adj.* ausgelassen.

hilarity, *n.* Ausgelassenheit *f.*

hill, *n.* Hügel, - *m.*

hilt, *n.* Heft, -e *nt.*

him, *pron.* ihn; ihm.

hind, *adj.* hinter-.

hinder, *vb.* hindern; verhin'dern.

hindmost, *adj.* letzt-, hinterst-.

hindrance, *n.* Hindernis, -se *nt.; (disadvantage)* Nachteil, - *e m.*

hinge, *n.* Scharnier, -e *nt.*

hint, 1. *n.* Wink, -e *m.* 2. *vb.* an⸱deuten.

hinterland, *n.* Hinterland *nt.*

hip, *n.* Hüfte, -n *f.*

hippopotamus, *n.* Nilpferd, -e *nt.*

hire, *vb.* mieten; *(persons)* an⸱stellen.

his, 1. *adj.* sein, -, -e. 2. *pron.* seiner, -es, -e.

Hispanic, *n.* erste oder zweite Generation Amerikaner spanisch sprechender Herkunft.

hiss, *vb.* zischen.

historian, *n.* Histo'riker, - *m.*

historic, historical, *adj.* histo'risch.

history, *n.* Geschich'te, -en *f.*

hit, 1. *n.* Stoß, ⁼e *m.*, Schlag, ⁼e *m.; (success)* Treffer, - *m.* 2. *vb.* stoßen*, schlagen*, treffen*.

hitch, 1. *n. (knot)* Knoten, - *m.; (obstacle)* Hindernis, -se *nt.* 2. *vb.* fest⸱machen.

hitchhike, *vb.* per Anhalter fahren*.

hive, *n.* Bienenstock, ⁼e *m.*

hives, *n.* Nesselsucht *f.*

hoard, 1. n. Vorrat, ⁼e m. **2.** vb. hamstern.

hoarse, adj. heiser.

hoax, n. Schabernack, -e m.

hobble, vb. humpeln.

hobby, n. Liebhaberei', -en f.

hobgoblin, n. Kobold, -e m.

hobnob with, vb. mit jemand auf vertrau'tem Füße stehen*.

bobo, n. Landstreicher, - m.

hockey, n. Hockey nt.

hocus-pocus, n. Ho'kuspo'kus m.

hod, n. Traggestell, -e nt.

hodgepodge, n. Mischmasch, -e m.

hoe, 1. n. Hacke, -n f. **2.** vb. hacken.

hog, n. Schwein, -e nt.

hogshead, n. Oxhoft, -e nt.

hoist, vb. hoch·ziehen*, hissen.

hold, 1. n. Halt m.; (ship) Laderaum, ⁼e m. **2.** vb. halten*; (contain) enthal'ten*; (h. up) auf·halten*.

holder, n. Halter, - m.

holdup, n. Überfall, ⁼e m.

hole, n. Loch, ⁼er nt.

holiday, n. Feiertag, -e m., Festtag, -e m.

holiness, n. Heiligkeit f.

Holland, n. Holland nt.

hollow, adj. hohl.

holly, n. Stechpalme, -n f.

hollyhock, n. Malve, -n f.

holocaust, n. Brandopfer, - nt., Großfeuer, - nt.

hologram, n. Hologramm', -e nt.

holography, n. Holografie' f.

holster, n. Pisto'lenhalter, - m.

holy, adj. heilig.

holy day, n. Kirchenfeiertag, -e m.

Holy See, n. der Heilige Stuhl m.

Holy Spirit, n. der Heilige Geist m.

Holy Week, n. Karwoche f.

homage, n. Huldigung, -en f.

home, 1. n. Heim, -e nt.; (h. town) Heimat, -en f.; (place of residence) Wohnort, -e m.; (house) Haus, ⁼er nt.; (institution) Heim, -e nt. **2.** adv. (location) zu Hause, daheim'; (direction) nach Hause, heim.

homeland, n. Heimatland, ⁼er nt.

homeless, adj. heimatlos; obdachlos.

homelike, adj. behag'lich.

homely, adj. häßlich.

home-made, adj. selbstgefertigt.

home rule, n. Selbstverwaltung f.

homesick, be, vb. Heimweh haben*.

homesickness, n. Heimweh nt.

homestead, n. Fami'liensitz, -e m.

homeward, adv. heimwärts.

homework, n. Hausaufgabe, -n f., Schularbeiten pl.

homicide, n. Mord, -e m.

homogeneous, adj. homogen'.

homogenize, vb. homogenisie'ren.

homonym, n. Homonym', -e nt.

homosexual, adj. homosexuell'.

hone, n. Wetzstein, -e m.

honest, adj. ehrlich, aufrichtig.

honesty, n. Ehrlichkeit, -en f.

honey, n. Honig m.

honey-bee, n. Honigbiene, -n f.

honeycomb, n. Honigwabe, -n f.

honeymoon, n. Hochzeitsreise, -n f., Flitterwochen pl.

honeysuckle, n. Geißblatt nt.

honor, 1. n. Ehre, -n f. **2.** vb. ehren; honorie'ren.

honorable, adj. ehrbar, ehrenvoll.

honorary, adj. Ehren- (cpds.).

hood, n. Haube, -n f., (monk) Kapu'ze, -n f.

hoodlum, n. Rowdy, -s m.

hoodwink, vb. übertöl'peln.

hoof, n. Huf, -e nt.

hook, 1. n. Haken, - m. **2.** vb. zu·haken; (catch) fangen*.

hoop, n. Reifen, - m.

hoot, vb. schreien*.

hop, 1. n. (plant) Hopfen m.; (jump) Sprung, ⁼e m. **2.** vb. hüpfen, springen*.

hope, 1. n. Hoffnung, -en f. **2.** vb. hoffen.

hopeful, adj. hoffnungsvoll.

hopeless, adj. hoffnungslos.

hopelessness, n. Hoffnungslosigkeit f.

horde, n. Horde, -n f.

horizon, n. Horizont', -e m.

horizontal, adj. waagerecht, horizontal'.

hormone, n. Hormon', -e nt.

horn, n. Horn, ⁼er nt.

horny, adj. hornig, hörnern.

horoscope, n. Horoskop', -e nt.

horrible, adj. grauenhaft.

horrid, adj. gräßlich.

horrify, vb. entset'zen.

horror, n. Grauen nt.

horse, n. Pferd, -e nt.

horseback, on, adv. zu Pferde.

horsehair, n. Roßhaar, -e nt.

horseman, n. Reiter, - m.

horsemanship, n. Reitkunst f.

horse-power, n. Pferdestärke, -n f.

horseradish, n. Meerrettich, -e m.

horseshoe, n. Hufeisen, - nt.

horticulture, n. Gartenbau m.

hose, n. (tube) Schlauch, ⁼e m.; (stocking) Strumpf, ⁼e m.

hosiery, n. Strumpfwaren pl.

hospitable, adj. gastfreundlich, gastfrei.

hospital, n. Krankenhaus, ⁼er nt.

hospitality, n. Gastfreundschaft, Gastfreiheit f.

hospitalization, n. Krankenhausaufenthalt m.

hospitalize, vb. ins Krankenhaus stecken; (be h.d) im Krankenhaus liegen müssen*.

host, n. Gastgeber, - m.; (innkeeper) Wirt, -e m.; (crowd) Menge, -n f.; (Eucharist) Hostie f.

hostage, n. Geisel, -n m.

hostel, n. Herberge, -n f.; (youth h.) Jugendherberge, -n f.

hostess, n. Gastgeberin, -nen f.

hostile, adj. feindlich.

hostility, n. Feindseligkeit, -en f., Krieg, -e m.

hot, adj. heiß.

hotbed, n. Mistbeet, -e nt.; (fig.) Brutstätte, -n f.

hot dog, n. Bockwurst, ⁼e f.

hotel, n. Hotel', -s nt.

hothouse, n. Treibhaus, ⁼er nt.

hound, n. Hund, -e m.

hour, n. Stunde, -n f.

hourglass, n. Stundenglas, ⁼er nt.

hourly, adj. stündlich.

house, n. Haus, ⁼er nt.

housefly, n. Stubenfliege, -n f.

household, n. Haushalt, -e m.

housekeeper, n. Haushälterin, -nen f.

housekeeping, n. Haushaltung f.

housemaid, n. Hausmädchen, - nt.

housewife, n. Hausfrau, -en f.

housework, n. Hausarbeit, -en f.

hovel, n. Hütte, -n f.

hover, vb. schweben.

hovercraft, n. Hovercraft m. & nt.; Luftkissenboot, -e nt.

how, adv. wie.

however, 1. conj. aber, doch, jedoch'. **2.** adv. wie . . . auch.

howitzer, n. Haubit'ze, -n f.

howl, 1. n. Gebrüll' nt. **2.** vb. brüllen.

hub, n. Nabe, -n f.; (fig.) Mittelpunkt, -e m.

hubbub, n. Tumult, -e m.

huckleberry, n. Heidelbeere, -n f.

huddle, vb. zusam'men·kauern, sich zusam'men·drängen.

hue, n. Färbung, -en f.

hug, 1. n. Umar'mung, -en f. **2.** vb. umar'men.

huge, adj. sehr groß, ungeheuer.

hull, n. Hülse, -n f.; (fruit) Schale, -n f.; (ship) Rumpf, ⁼e m.

hum, 1. n. (people) Gemur'mel nt.; (insects) Summen nt. **2.** vb. murmeln; summen.

human, adj. menschlich.

humane, adj. human', menschlich.

humanism, n. Humanis'mus m.

humanitarian, adj. menschenfreundlich.

humanity, n. (mankind) Menschheit f.; (humaneness) Menschlichkeit f.

humble, adj. demütig, bescheiden.

humbug, n. Schwindel m., Quatsch m.

humdrum, adj. langweilig, eintönig.

humid, adj. feucht.

humidity, n. Feuchtigkeit f.

humidor, n. Tabakstopf, -e m

humiliate, vb. demütigen.

humiliation, n. Demütigung, -en f.

humility, n. Demut f.

humor, n. Humor' m.; (mood) Laune, -n f.

humorist, n. Humorist', -en, -en m

humorous, adj. humor'voll, witzig.

hump, n. Buckel,- m., Höcker, - m.

hunch, 1. n. Höcker, - m., Buckel, - m.; (suspicion) Ahnung, -en f., Riecher, - m. **2.** vb. krümmen.

hunchback, 1. n. Buckel, - m.; (person) Bucklig- m.&f. **2.** adj. bucklig.

hundred, num. hundert.

hundredth, 1. adj. hundertst-. **2.** n. Hundertstel, - nt.

Hungarian, 1. n. Ungar, -n, -n m. **2.** adj. ungarisch.

Hungary, n. Ungarn nt.

hunger, n. Hunger m.

hungry, adj. hungrig.

hunt, 1. n. Jagd, -en f. **2.** vb. jagen.

hunter, n. Jäger, - m.

hunting, n. Jagd, -en f.

hurdle, 1. n. Hürde, -n f. **2.** vb. hinü'berspringen*.

hurl, vb. schleudern.

hurrah, interj. (h. for him) er lebe hoch!

hurricane, n. Orkan', -e m.

hurry, vb. eilen, sich beei'len.

hurt, vb. weh tun*, verlet'zen.

hurtful, adj. schädlich.

husband, n. Mann, =er m., Gatte, -n, -n m.

husbandry, n. Landwirtschaft f.; (management) Wirtschaften nt

hush, 1. n. Stille f. **2.** vb. zum Schweigen bringen*. **3.** interj. still!

husk, 1. n. Hülse, -n f. **2.** vb. enthül'sen.

husky, adj. (hoarse) rauh; (strong) stark (-).

hustle, vb. rührig sein*.

hut, n. Hütte, -n f.

hyacinth, n. Hyazin'the, -n f.

hybrid, adj. hybrid'.

hydrangea, n. Horten'sie, -n f.

hydrant, n. Hydrant', -en, -en m.

hydraulic, adj. hydrau'lisch.

hydrochloric acid, n. Salzsäure f.

hydroelectric, adj. hydroelek'trisch.

hydrogen, n. Wasserstoff m.

hydrogen bomb, n. Wasserstoffbombe, -n f.

hydrophobia, n. krankhafte Wasserscheu f.

hydroplane, n. Wasserflugzeug, -e nt.

hydrotherapy, n. Hydrotherapie' f.

hyena, n. Hyä'ne, -n f.

hygiene, n. Hygie'ne f.

hygienic, adj. hygie'nisch.

hymn, n. Hymne, -n f., Choral', =e m., Kirchenlied, -er nt.

hymnal, n. Gesang'buch, =er nt.

hyperacidity, n. Hyperacidität', f.

hyperbole, n. Hyper'bel, -n f.

hypercritical, adj. überkritisch.

hypersensitive, adj. überempfindlich.

hypertension, n. übernormaler Blutdruck m.

hyphen, n. Bindestrich, -e m.

hyphenate, vb. trennen.

hypnosis, n. Hypno'se, -n f.

hypnotic, adj. hypno'tisch.

hypnotism, n. Hypnotis'mus m.

hypnotize, vb. hypnotisie'ren.

hypochondria, n. Schwermut f.

hypochondriac, 1. n. Hypochon'der, - m. **2.** adj. schwermütig.

hypocrisy, n. Heuchelei', -en f.

hypocrite, n. Heuchler, - m.

hypocritical, adj. heuchlerisch.

hypodermic, n. Spritze, -n f.

hypothesis, n. Hypothe'se, -n f.

hypothetical, adj. hypothe'tisch.

hysterectomy, n. Hysterek'tomie f.

hysteria, hysterics, n. Hysterie' f.

hysterical, adj. hyste'risch.

I

I, pron. ich.

ice, n. Eis nt.

iceberg, n. Eisberg, -e m.

ice-box, n. Eisschrank, =e m.

ice cream, n. Eis nt., Sahneneis nt.

ice skate, 1, n. Schlittschuh, -e m. **2.** vb. Schlittschuh laufen*.

icing, n. Zuckerguß, =sse m.

icon, n. Iko'ne, -n f.

icy, adj. eisig.

idea, n. Idee', -de'en f., Gedan'ke(n), - m.

ideal, 1. n. Ideal', -e nt. **2.** adj. ideal'.

idealism, n. Idealis'mus m.

idealist, n. Idealist', -en, -en m.

idealistic, adj. idealis'tisch.

idealize, vb. idealisie'ren.

identical, adj. iden'tisch.

identifiable, adj. identifizier'bar.

identification, n. Identifizie'rung, -en f.; (card) Ausweis, -e m

identify, vb. identifizie'ren.

identity, n. Identität', -en f.

ideology, n. Ideologie', -i'en f.

idiocy, n. Blödsinn m.

idiom, n. Idiom', -e nt.

idiot, n. Idiot', -en, -en m.

idiotic, adj. idio'tisch, blödsinnig.

idle, adj. müßig; arbeitslos.

idleness, n. Müßigkeit f.

idol, n. Götzenbild, -er nt.

idolatry, n. Abgötterei', -en f.

idolize, vb. vergöt'tern.

if, conj. wenn; (as if) als ob.

ignite, vb. an·zünden.

ignition, n. Zündung f.

ignition key, n. Zündschlüssel, - m.

ignominious, adj. schmachvoll.

ignoramus, n. Nichtswisser, - m.

ignorance, n. Unwissenheit f.

ignorant, adj. unwissend.

ignore, vb. überse'hen*, unbeachtet lassen*.

ill, adj. krank (-).

illegal, adj. illegal, ungesetzlich.

illegible, adj. unleserlich.

illegitimate, adj. ungesetzlich; (unmarried) unehelich.

illicit, adj. unerlaubt.

illiteracy, n. Analphabe'tentum, nt.

illiterate, 1. n. Analphabet', -en, -en m. **2.** adj. des Lesens und Schreibens unkundig.

illness, n. Krankheit, -en f.

illogical, adj. unlogisch.

illuminate, vb. beleuch'ten, erleuch'ten.

illumination, n. Beleuch'tung, -en f

illusion, n. Illusion', -en f.

illusive, illusory, adj. trügerisch, illuso'risch.

illustrate, vb. erläu'tern; (with pictures) illustrie'ren.

illustration, n. Erläu'terung, -en f.; (picture) Illustration', -en f

illustrative, adj. erläu'ternd.

illustrious, adj. berühmt'.

image, n. Abbild, -er nt.

imaginable, adj. denkbar.

imaginary, adj. scheinbar, imaginär'.

imagination, n. Einbildung, -en f., Vorstellung, -en f.

imaginative, adj. phantasievoll.

imagine, vb. sich ein·bilden, sich vorstellen.

imam, n. Imam, -e m.

imbecile, adj. schwachsinnig.

imitate, vb. nach·ahmen, imitie'ren.

imititation, n. Nachahmung, -en f., Imitation', -en f.

immaculate, adj. unbefleckt, makellos, blitzsauber; **(i. conception)** unbefleckte Empfäng'nis f.

immaterial, adj. unwesentlich.

immature, adj. unreif.

immediate, adj. ummittelbar.

immediately, adv. sofort'.

immense, adj. unermeßlich.

immerse, vb. unter·tauchen, versen'ken.

immigrant, n. Einwanderer, - m.

immigrate, vb. ein·wandern.

imminent, adj. bevor'stehend.

immobile, adj. unbeweglich.

immobilize, vb. unbeweglich machen.

immoderate, adj. unbescheiden.

immodest, adj. unbescheiden, anstößig.

immoral, adj. unsittlich, unmoralisch.

immorality, n. Unsittlichkeit, -en f.

immortal, adj. unsterblich.

immortality, n. Unsterblichkeit f.

immortalize, vb. unsterblich machen.

immune, adj. immun'.

immunity, n. Immunität', -en f.

immunize, vb. immunisie'ren.

impact, n. Zusam'menprall m.; (fig.) Auswirkung, -en f.

impair, vb. verrin'gern, verschlechtern.

impart, vb. zu·kommen lassen*.

impartial, adj. umparteiisch.

impatience, n. Ungeduld f.

impatient, adj. ungeduldig.

impeach, vb. an·klagen, beschul'digen.

impeachment, n. Anklage, -n f.; Beschul'digung, -en f.; (U.S.) Verhandlung gegen einen Beamten vor dem Kongress.

impede, vb. behin'dern.

impediment, n. Behin'derung, -en f. (speech i.) Sprachfehler, - m.

impel, vb. an·treiben*, zwingen*.

impenetrable, adj. undurchdringlich.

imperative, 1. n. Imperativ, -e m. **2.** adj. zwingend.

imperceptible, adj. unmerklich, unwahrnehmbar.

imperfect, 1. n. Imperfekt, -e nt. **2.** adj. unvollkommen, fehlerhaft.

imperfection, n. Unvollkommenheit, -en f., Fehler, - m.

imperial, adj. kaiserlich.

imperialism, n. Imperialis'mus m.

impersonal, adj. unpersönlich.

impersonate, vb. verkör'pern; (theater) dar·stellen.

impersonation, n. Verkör'perung, -en f.; (theater) Darstellung, -en f.

impersonator, n. Imita'tor, -o'ren m.; (swindler) Hochstapler, - m.

impertinence, n. Frechheit, -en f., Unverschämtheit, -en f.

impertinent, adj. frech, unverschämt.

impervious, adj. unzugänglich; (fig.) gefühl'los.

impetuous, adj. ungestüm.

impetus, n. Anstoß m., Antrieb m.

implement, 1. n. Werkzeug, -e nt. **2.** vb. durch·führen.

implicate, vb. verwi'ckeln.

implication, n. implizier'ter Gedan'ke(n), - m.; Verwick'lung, -en f.; (by i.) impli'cite.

implicit, adj. inbegriffen, stillschweigend.

implied, adj. miteinbegriffen.

implore, vb. an·flehen.

imply, vb. in sich schliessen*, impli'cite sagen, an·deuten.

impolite, adj. unhöflich.

import, 1. n. Einfuhr f., Import', -e m.; (meaning) Bedeu'tung, -en f. **2.** vb. ein·führen, importie'ren.

importance, n. Wichtigkeit f.

important, adj. wichtig, bedeu'tend.

importation, n. Einfuhr f.

impose, vb. auf·erlegen.

imposition, n. Belas'tung, -en f.

impossibility, n. Unmöglichkeit, -en f.

impossible, adj. unmöglich.

impotence, n. Unfähigkeit, -en f.; (med.) Impotenz, -en f.

impotent, adj. unfähig; (med.) impotent.

impoverish, vb. arm machen; (fig.) aus·saugen.

impregnable, adj. uneinnehmbar.

impregnate, vb. durchdrin'gen*; (make pregnant) schwängern.

impresario, n. Impresa'rio, -s m.

impress, vb. (imprint) prägen, ein·prägen; (affect) beein'drucken.

impression, n. Druck, -e m.; (copy) Abdruck, -e m.; (fig.) Eindruck, -e m.

impressive, adj. eindrucksvoll.

imprison, vb. ein·sperren.

imprisonment, n. Haft f.

improbable, adj. unwahrscheinlich.

impromptu, adv. aus dem Stegreif.

improper, adj. unrichtig; unschicklich.

improve, vb. verbes'sern.

improvement, n. Verbes'serung, -en f.; Besserung f.

improvise, vb. improvisie'ren.

impudent, adj. frech.

impulse, n. Impuls', -e m.

impulsive, adj. impulsiv'.

impunity, n. (with i.) ungestraft.

impure, adj. unrein.

impurity, n. Unreinheit, -en f.

in, prep. in.

inadvertent, adj. achtlos, unaufmerksam.

inalienable, adj. unveräußerlich.

inane, adj. leer, geistlos.

inaugural, adj. Antritts- (cpds.).

inaugurate, vb. ins Amt einführen.

inauguration, n. Einweihung, -en f.; Amtseinführung, -en f.

incandescence, n. Glühen nt.

incandescent, adj. glühend; Glüh- (cpds.).

incantation, n. Beschwö'rung f., Zauberspruch, -e m.

incapacitate, vb. unfähig machen.

incapacity, n. Unfähigkeit, -en f.

incarcerate, vb. ein·kerkern.

incarnate, adj. verkör'pert, fleischgeworden.

incarnation, n. Verkör'perung, -en f., Fleischwerdung f.

incendiary, adj. Brand- (cpds.); aufwieglerisch.

incense, n. Weihrauch m.

incentive, n. Anreiz, -e m., Antrieb, -e m.

inception, n. Begin'nen nt.

incessant, adj. unaufhörlich.

incest, n. Blutschande f.

inch, n. Zoll, - m.

incidence, n. Vorkommen nt.

incident, n. Vorfall, -e m.

incidental, adj. zufällig.

incidentally, adv. übrigens.

incision, n. Einschnitt, -e m.

incisor, n. Schneidezahn, -e m.

incite, vb. an·regen, an·stacheln.

inclination, n. Neigung, -en f.

incline, vb. neigen; (be i.d) geneigt sein*.

inclose, vb. ein·schließen*.

include, vb. ein·schließen*.

including, prep. einschließlich.

inclusive, adj. einschließlich.

incognito, adv. inkog'nito.

income, n. Einkommen, - nt.

incomparable, adj. unvergleichlich.

inconsiderate, adj. unüberlegt, rücksichtslos.

inconvenience, n. Mühe, -n f., Belas'tung, -en f.

inconvenient, adj. mühsam, ungelegen.

incorporate, vb. verei'nigen; auf·nehmen*.

incorrigible, adj. unverbesserlich.

increase, 1. n. Zunahme, -n f.

2. *vb.* zu·nehmen*, wachsen*.

incredible, *adj.* unglaublich.

incredulity, *n.* Zweifel, - *m.*

incredulous, *adj.* zweifelnd.

increment, *n.* Zunahme, -n *f.*

incriminate, *vb.* belas'ten, beschul'digen.

incrimination, *n.* Beschul'digung, -en *f.*, Belas'tung, -en *f.*

incrust, *vb.* überkrus'ten.

incubator, *n.* Brutapparat, -e *m.*

incumbent, **1.** *n.* Amtsinhaber, - *m.* **2.** *adj.* verpflich'tend.

incur, *vb.* auf sich laden*.

incurable, *adj.* unheilbar.

indebted, *adj.* verschul'det.

indeed, *adv.* in der Tat.

indefatigable, *adj.* unermüdlich.

indefinite, *adj.* unbestimmt.

indefinitely, *adv.* endlos.

indelible, *adj.* unauslöschlich.

indemnify, *vb.* sicher·stellen; entschä'digen.

indemnity, *n.* Sicherstellung, -en *f.*; Entschä'digung, -en *f.*

indent, *vb.* zacken; *(paragraph)* ein·rücken; *(damage)* verbeu'len.

indentation, *n.* Einkerbung, -en *f.*; *(paragraph)* Einrückung, -en *f.*; *(damage)* Verbeu'lung, -en *f.*

independence, *n.* Unabhängigkeit *f.*

independent, *adj.* unabhängig.

in-depth, *adj.* gründlich, Tiefen- *(cpds.).*

index, *n.* Verzeich'nis, -se *nt.*, Regis'ter, - *nt.*; **(i. finger)** Zeigefinger, - *m.*

India, *n.* Indien *nt.*

Indian, **1.** *n.* Inder, - *m.*; **(American I.)** India'ner, - *m.* **2.** *adj.* indisch; india'nisch.

indicate, *vb.* zeigen, an·deuten.

indication, *n.* Hinweis, -e *m.*, Anzeichen, - *nt.*

indicative, **1.** *n.* Indikativ, -e *m.* **2.** *adj.* bezeich'nend.

indicator, *n.* Zeiger, - *m.*, Indika'tor, -o'ren *m.*; *(sign)* Zeichen, - *nt.*

indict, *vb.* an·klagen.

indictment, *n.* Anklage, -n *f.*

indifference, *n.* Gleichgültigkeit.

indifferent, *adj.* gleichgültig.

indigestion, *n.* Verdau'ungsstörung, -en *f.*

indignant, *adj.* entrüs'tet.

indignation, *n.* Entrüs'tung, -en *f.*

indignity, *n.* Unwürdigkeit, -en *f.*; *(insult)* Belei'digung, -en *f.*

indirect, *adj.* indirekt.

indiscreet, *adj.* indiskret.

indiscretion, *n.* Indiskretion', -en *f.*

indispensable, *adj.* unabkömmlich.

indisposed, *adj.* unpäßlich; *(disinclined)* abgeneigt.

indisposition, *n.* Unpäßlichkeit, -en *f.*; Abneigung, -en *f.*

individual, **1.** *n.* Einzeln- *m.*, Indivi'duum, -duen *nt.* **2.** *adj.* einzeln, individuell'.

individually, *n.* Individualität', -en *f.*

indivisible, *adj.* unteilbar.

indoctrinate, *vb.* schulen.

indolent, *adj.* träge.

Indonesia, *n.* Indone'sien *nt.*

indoor, *adj.* Haus-, Zimmer- *(cpds.).*

indoors, *adv.* zu Hause, drinnen.

indorse, *vb.* gut·heißen*; *(check)* girie'ren.

induce, *vb.* veran'lassen; *(elec.)* induzie'ren.

induct, *vb.* ein·führen; *(physics)* induzie'ren; *(mil.)* verei'digen.

induction, *n.* Einführung, -en *f.*; *(physics)* Induktion', -en *f.*; *(mil.)* Verei'digung, -en *f.*

inductive, *adj.* induktiv'.

indulge, *vb.* nach·sehen*; frönen.

indulgence, *n.* Nachsicht, *f.*, Langmut *m.*, Frönen *nt.*; *(eccles.)* Ablaß, ¨sse *m.*

indulgent, *adj.* nachsichtig, langmütig, kommend.

industrial, *adj.* industriell', Industrie'- *(cpds.).*

industrialist, *n.* Industriell'- *m.*

industrious, *adj.* fleißig.

industry, *n.* Industrie', -i'en *f.*; *(hard work)* Fleiß *m.*

ineligible, *adj.* nicht wählbar; nicht in Frage kommend.

inept, *adj.* ungeschickt, unfähig.

inert, *adj.* träge.

inertia, *n.* Trägheit, -en *f.*

inevitable, *adj.* unvermeidlich.

infallible, *adj.* unfehlbar.

infamous, *adj.* berüch'tigt.

infamy, *n.* Niedertracht, -en *f.*, Schande, -n *f.*

infancy, *n.* Kindheit, -en *f.*; *(fig.)* Anfang, ¨e *m.*

infant, *n.* Säugling, -e *m.*

infantile, *adj.* kindlich, kindisch.

infantry, *n.* Infanterie', -i'en *f.*

infantryman, *n.* Infantorist', -en, -en *m.*

infatuate, *vb.* betö'ren, hin·reißen*.

infect, *vb.* an·stecken.

infected, *adj.* entzün'det.

infection, *n.* Entzün'dung, -en *f.*

infectious, *adj.* ansteckend.

infer, *vb.* folgern, an·nehmen*.

inference, *n.* Folgerung, -en *f.*, Annahme, -n *f.*

inferior, *adj.* minderwertig, unterle'gen.

inferiority, *n.* Minderwertig-

keit, -en *f.*, Unterle'genheit *f.*

infernal, *adj.* höllisch.

inferno, *n.* Hölle *f.*; Fegefeuer *nt.*

infest, *vb.* heim·suchen.

infidel, *n.* Ungläubig- *m.&f.*

infidelity, *n.* Untreue *f.*

infiltrate, *vb.* ein·dringen*, infiltrie'ren.

infinite, *adj.* unendlich.

infinitesimal, *adj.* unendlich klein; winzig.

infinitive, *n.* Infinitiv, -e *m.*

infinity, *n.* Unendlichkeit, -en *f.*

infirm, *adj.* schwach (¨).

infirmary, *n.* Schul- oder Studen'tenkrankenhaus, ¨er *nt.*

infirmity, *n.* Schwachheit, -en *f.*

inflame, *vb.* entzün'den.

inflammable, *adj.* entzünd'bar, feuergefährlich.

inflammation, *n.* Entzün'dung, -en *f.*

inflate, *vb.* auf·blasen*; *(tires)* auf·pumpen.

inflation, *n.* Inflation', -en *f.*

inflection, *n.* Biegung, -en *f.*; *(voice)* Tonfall, ¨e *m.*; *(gram.)* Beugung, -en *f.*

inflict, *vb.* zu·fügen.

infliction, *n.* Last, -en *f.*

influence, **1.** *n.* Einfluß, ¨sse *m.* **2.** *vb.* beein'flussen.

influential, *adj.* einflußreich.

influenza, *n.* Grippe, -n *f.*

inform, *vb.* benach'richtigen, mit·teilen; **(i. on)** denunzie'ren.

informal, *adj.* zwanglos, nicht formell'.

information, *n.* Auskunft, ¨e *f.*

infringe, *vb.* übertre'ten*; *(jur.)* verlet'zen.

infuriate, *vb.* wütend machen, rasend machen, erbo'sen.

ingenious, *adj.* erfin'derisch, genial'.

ingenuity, *n.* Findigkeit *f.*, Genialität' *f.*

ingredient, *n.* Bestand'teil, -e *m.*; *(cooking)* Zutat, -en *f.*

inhabit, *vb.* bewoh'nen.

inhabitant, *n.* Bewoh'ner, - *m.*, Einwohner, - *m.*

inhale, *vb.* ein·atmen.

inherent, *adj.* angeboren, eigen.

inherit, *vb.* erben.

inheritance, *n.* Erbe *nt.*; Erbschaft, -en *f.*

inhibit, *vb.* hindern, ab·halten*.

inhibition, *n.* Hemmung, -en *f.*

inhuman, *adj.* unmenschlich.

inimitable, *adj.* unnachahmlich.

iniquity, *n.* Ungerechtigkeit, - *f.*; Schändlichkeit, -en *f.*

initial, **1.** *n.* Anfangsbuchstabe, -n, -n *m.* **2.** *adj.* anfänglich; Anfangs- *(cpds.).*

initiate, vb. ein·führen, ein·weihen.
initiation, n. Einführung, -en f., Einweihung, -en f.
initiative, n. Initiati've, -n f.
inject, vb. ein·spritzen.
injection, n. Einspritzung, -en f.
injunction, n. gerichtlicher Unterlas'sungsbefehl, -e m.
injure, vb. verlet'zen.
injurious, adj. schädlich; (fig.) nachteilig.
injury, n. Verlet'zung, -en f.; Schaden, = m.
injustice, n. Ungerechtigkeit, -en f.
ink, n. Tinte, -n f.
inland, 1. n. Binnenland, =er nt. 2. adj. inländisch.
inlet, n. kleine Bucht, -en f.
inmate, n. Insasse, -n, -n m.
inn, n. Gasthaus, =er nt., Wirtshaus, =er nt.
inner, adj. inner-.
innermost, adj. innerst-.
innocence, n. Unschuld f.
innocent, adj. unschuldig.
innovation, n. Neuerung, -en f.
innuendo, n. Unterstel'lung, -en f.
innumerable, adj. zahllos.
inoculate, vb. ein·impfen.
inoculation, n. Einimpfung, -en f.
input, n. Input, -s m.; Eingabe, -n f.
inquest, n. gerichtliche Untersuchung, -en f.
inquire, vb. fragen, sich erkun·digen.
inquiry, n. Nachfrage, -n f., Erkun'digung, -en f.
inquisition, n. Untersu'chung, -en f.; (eccles.) Inquisition', -en f.
inquisitive, adj. neugierig.
insane, adj. wahnsinnig.
insanity, n. Wahnsinn m.
inscribe, vb. ein·zeichnen, ein·schreiben*.
inscription, n. Inschrift, -en f.
insect, n. Insekt', -en nt.
insecticide, n. Insek'tenpulver, - nt.
insensible, adj. gefühl'los.
insensitive, adj. unempfindlich.
inseparable, adj. unzertrennlich.
insert, 1. n. Beilage, -n f. 2. vb. ein·fügen, ein·setzen.
insertion, n. Einsatz, =e m.
inside, 1. n. Innenseite, -n f., Inner- nt. 2. adj. inner-. 3. adv. innen, drinnen.
insidious, adj. hinterlistig.
insight, n. Einsicht, -en f.
insignia, n.pl. Abzeichen, - nt.; Insig'nien pl.
insignificance, n. Bedeu'tungslosigkeit f.
insignificant, adj. bedeu'tungslos.
insinuate, vb. an·spielen auf;

(i. oneself) sich ein·schmeicheln.
insinuation, n. Anspielung, -en f.
insipid, adj. fade.
insist, vb. beste'hen*, behar'ren.
insistence, n. Beste'hen nt., Behar'ren nt.
insistent, adj. beharr'lich, hartnäckig.
insolence, n. Unverschämtheit, -en f.
insolent, adj. unverschämt.
insomnia, n. Schlaflosigkeit f.
inspect, vb. besich'tigen.
inspection, n. Besich'tigung, -en f.
inspector, n. Inspek'tor, -o'ren m.
inspiration, n. Eingebung, -en f., Inspiration', -en f.
inspire, vb. an·feuern, begeis'tern.
install, vb. ein·bauen; (fig.) ein·führen.
installation, n. Installation', -en f.
installment, n. Rate, -n f.; (i. plan) Ratenzahlung, -en f.
instance, n. (case) Fall, =e m.; (example) Beispeil, -e nt.; (law) Instanz', -en f.; (for i.) zum Beispiel.
instant, 1. n. Augenblick, -e nt. 2. adj. augenblicklich.
instantaneous, adj. sofor'tig.
instantly, adv. sofort', auf der Stelle.
instead, adv. statt dessen, dafür; (i. of) statt, anstatt'.
instigate, vb. veran'lassen, an·stacheln.
instill, vb. ein·flößen.
instinct, n. Instinkt', -e m.
instinctive, adj. unwillkürlich, instinktiv'.
institute, 1. n. Institut', -e nt. 2. vb. ein·leiten, an·ordnen.
institution, n. Einrichtung, -en f.; Institut', -e nt., Anstalt, -en f.
instruct, vb. unterrich'ten, an·weisen*.
instruction, n. Anweisung, -en f.; (school) Unterricht m.
instructive, adj. lehrreich.
instructor, n. Lehrer, - m.
instructress, n. Lehrerin, -nen f.
instrument, n. Werkzeug, -e nt., Instrument', -e nt.
instrumental, adj. behilf'lich; (music) Instrumental'- (cpds.).
insufferable, adj. unerträglich.
insufficient, adj. ungenügend.
insulate, vb. insolie'ren.
insulation, n. Isolie'rung, -en f.
insulator, n. Isola'tor, -o'ren m.
insulin, n. Insulin' nt.
insult, 1. n. Belei'digung, -en f. 2. vb. belei'digen.
insurance, n. Versi'cherung, -en f.
insure, vb. versi'chern.

insurgent, 1. n. Aufständisch - m. 2. adj. aufständisch.
insurrection, n. Aufstand, =e m.
intact, adj. intakt'.
intangible, adj. nicht greifbar.
integral, 1. n. (math.) Integral', -e nt. 2. adj. unerläßlich.
integrate, vb. integrie'ren.
integrity, n. Unbescholtenheit f.
intellect, n. Verstand' m., Intellekt' m.
intellectual, 1. n. Intellektuell- m.&f. 2. adj. intellektuell'.
intelligence, n. Intelligenz' f.
intelligent, adj. intelligent'.
intelligentsia, n. geistige Oberschicht f.
intelligible, adj. verständ'lich.
intend, vb. beab'sichtigen.
intense, adj. angespannt, intensiv'.
intensify, vb. verstär'ken.
intensive, adj. intensiv'.
intent, 1. n. Absicht, -en f. 2. adj. erpicht'.
intention, n. Absicht, -en f.
intentional, adj. absichtlich.
inter, vb. beer'digen.
intercede, vb. dazwi'schentreten*.
intercept, vb. ab·fangen*.
intercourse, n. Verkehr' m., Umgang m.
interest, 1. n. Interes'se, -n nt.; (comm.) Zins, -en m. 2. vb. interessie'ren.
interesting, adj. interessant'.
interface, n. Schnittstelle, -n f.
interfere, vb. sich ein·mischen; ein·greifen*.
interference, n. Einmischung, -en f.; (radio) Störung, -en f.
interim, 1. n. Zwischenzeit, -en f. 2. adj. Interims- (cpds.).
interior, 1. n. Inner- nt. 2. adj. inner-; Innen- (cpds.).
interject, vb. dazwi'schenwer'fen*.
interjection, n. Ausruf, -e m.; (gram.) Interjektion', -en f.
interlude, n. Zwischenspiel, -e nt.
intermarry, vb. untereinander heiraten.
intermediary, 1. n. Vermitt'ler, - m. 2. adj. Zwischen- (cpds.).
intermediate, adj. Zwischen- (cpds.).
interment, n. Begräb'nis, -se nt.
intermission, n. Unterbre'chung, -en f.; (theater) Pause, -n f.
intermittent, adj. wechselnd, perio'disch.
intern, vb. internie'ren.
internal, adj. inner-, innerlich.
international, adj. international'.
internationalism, n. Internationalis'mus m.

interne, n. Volontär'arzt, ⁼e m.

interpose, vb. ein·fügen.

interpret, vb. interpretie'ren; *(language)* dolmetschen.

interpretation, n. Interpretation', -en f., Auslegung, -en f.

interpreter, n. Dolmetscher, - m.

interrogate, vb. aus·fragen; *(law)* verneh'men*, verhö'ren.

interrogation, n. Verhör', -e nt.

interrogative, 1. n. Fragewort, ⁼er nt. **2.** adj. fragend, Frage- *(cpds.).*

interrupt, vb. unterbre'chen*.

interruption, n. Unterbre'chung, -en f.

intersect, vb. *(intr.)* sich schneiden; sich kreuzen; *(tr.)* durchschnei'den, durchkreu'zen.

intersection, n. Kreuzung, -en f.

intersperse, vb. durchset'zen.

interval, n. Abstand, ⁼e m.

intervene, vb. dazwi'schen·kommen*, sich ein·mischen.

intervention, n. Dazwi'schentreten nt., Einmischung, -en f.

interview, 1. n. Interview' -s nt. **2.** vb. interview'en.

intestine, n. Darm, ⁼e m.

intimacy, n. Vertrau'lichkeit, -en f.

intimate, adj. vertraut', innig.

intimidate, vb. ein·schüchtern.

intimidation, n. Einschüchterung, -en f.

into, prep. in.

intolerant, adj. intolerant.

intonation, n. Tonfall, ⁼e m.

intoxicate, vb. berau'schen.

intoxication, n. Rausch, ⁼e m.

intravenous, adj. intravenös'.

intrepid, adj. furchtlos.

intricacy, n. Kompliziert'heit, -en f.

intricate, adj. verwi'ckelt; kompliziert'.

intrigue, 1. n. Intri'ge, -n f. **2.** vb. intrigie'ren.

intrinsic, adj. innerlich; wahr.

introduce, vb. ein·führen, ein·leiten; *(persons)* vor·stellen.

introduction, n. Einführung, -en f., Einleitung, -en f.; Vorstellung, -en f.

introductory, adj. einleitend.

introvert, n. nach innen gekehr'ter Mensch, -en, -en m.

intrude, vb. ein·dringen*.

intruder, n. Eindringling, -e m.

intuition, n. Intuition', -en f.

inundate, vb. überschwem'men.

invade, vb. ein·dringen*, ein·fallen*.

invader, n. Angreifer, - m.

invalid, 1. n. Invali'de, -n, -n m. **2.** adj. ungültig.

invariable, adj. unveränderlich.

invasion, n. Invasion', -en f.

inveigle, vb. verlei'ten.

invent, vb. erfin'den*.

invention, n. Erfin'dung, -en f.

inventive, adj. erfin'derisch.

inventor, n. Erfin'der, - m.

inventory, n. Inventar', -e nt.; Inventur', -en f.

inverse, adj. umgekehrt.

invertebrate, adj. ohne Wirbelsäule.

invest, vb. investie'ren, an·legen.

investigate, vb. untersu'chen.

investigation, n. Untersu'chung, -en f.

investment, n. Kapitals'anlage, -n f.

inveterate, adj. eingefleischt.

invigorate, vb. bele'ben, erfri'schen.

invincible, adj. unbesiegbar.

invisible, adj. unsichtbar.

invitation, n. Einladung, -en f., Aufforderung, -en f.

invite, vb. ein·laden*, auf·fordern.

invocation, n. Anrufung, -en f.; *(eccles.)* Bittgebet, -e nt.

invoice, n. Warenrechnung, -en f.

invoke, vb. an·rufen*; erbit'ten.

involuntary, adj. unfreiwillig.

involve, vb. ein·schließen*; verwi'ckeln.

involved, adj. verwi'ckelt.

invulnerable, adj. unverletz'lich; uneinnehmbar.

inward, adj. inner-, innerlich.

inwardly, adv. innerlich.

iodine, n. Jod nt.

Iran, n. Iran' nt.

Iraq, n. Irak' m.

irate, adj. zornig.

Ireland, n. Irland nt.

iridium, n. Iri'dium nt.

iris, n. Iris f.; *(flower)* Schwertlilie, -n f.

Irish, adj. irisch.

Irishman, n. Irländer,- m., Ire, -n, -n m.

Irishwoman, n. Irländerin, -nen f.

irk, vb. ärgern.

iron, 1. n. Eisen nt.; *(flati.)* Bügeleisen, - nt. **2.** adj. eisern. **3.** vb. bügeln.

ironical, adj. spöttisch, iro'nisch.

irony, n. Spott m., Ironie' f.

irrational, adj. irrational'.

irrefutable, adj. unwiderlegbar.

irregular, adj. unregelmäßig.

irregularity, n. Unregelmäßigkeit, -en f.

irrelevant, adj. belang'los; unanwendbar.

irresistible, adj. unwiderstehlich.

irresponsible, adj. unverantwortlich.

irreverent, adj. unehrerbietig.

irrevocable, adj. unwiderruflich.

irrigate, vb. bewäs'sern.

irrigation, n. Bewäs'serung, -en f.

irritability, n. Reizbarkeit f.

irritable, adj. reizbar.

irritant, n. Reizfaktor, -en m.

irritate, vb. reizen, irritie'ren.

irritation, n. Reizung, -en f.; Ärger m.

island, n. Insel, -n f.

isolate, vb. isolie'ren.

isolation, n. Isolie'rung, -en f.

isolationist, n. Isolationist', -en, -en m.

Israel, n. Israel nt.

Israeli, 1. n. Israe'li, -s m. **2.** adj. israe'lisch.

Israelite, 1. n. Israelit', -en, -en m. **2.** adj. israeli'tisch.

issuance, n. Ausgabe, -n f.

issue, 1. n. Ausgabe, -n f.; Problem', -e nt.; *(result)* Erbeg'nis, -se nt. **2.** vb. aus·geben*, aus·stellen.

isthmus, n. Isthmus, -men m.

it, pron. es.

Italian, 1. n. Italie'ner, - m. **2.** adj. italie'nisch.

italic, adj. ita'lisch.

italics, n. Kursiv'schrift f.

Italy, n. Ita'lien nt.

itch, 1. n. Jucken nt. **2.** vb. jucken.

item, n. Arti'kel, - m., Posten, - m.

itemize, vb. auf·zählen.

itinerary, n. Reiseroute, -n f.

ivory, n. Elfenbein nt.

ivy, n. Efeu m.

J

jab, 1. n. Stoß, ⁼e m., Stich, -e m. **2.** vb. stoßen*, stechen*.

jack, n. *(auto)* Wagenheber, - m.; *(card)* Bube, -n, -n m.

jackal, n. Schakal', -e m.

jackass, n. Esel, - m.

jacket, n. Jacke, -n f.

jack-knife, n. Klappmesser, - nt.

jack-of-all-trades, n. Hans Dampf in allen Gassen m.

jade, n. Jade m.

jaded, adj. ermat'tet.

jagged, adj. zackig.

jail, n. Gefäng'nis, -se nt.

jailer, n. Gefäng'niswärter, - m.

jam, 1. n. Marmela'de, -n f., Konfitüre, -n f.; *(trouble)* Klemme, -n f. **2.** vb. klemmen.

jangle, vb. rasseln.

janitor, n. Pförtner, - m., Hausmeister, - m.

January, n. Januar m.

Japan, n. Japan nt.

Japanese, 1. n. Japa'ner, - m. **2.** adj. japa'nisch.

jar, 1. n. Krug, ⁼e m., Glas, ⁼er nt. **2.** vb. rütteln.

jargon, n. Jargon', -s m.

jasmine, n. Jasmin', -e m.

jaundice, n. Gelbsucht f.

jaunt, n. kurze Reise, -n f.

javelin, n. Speer, -e m.

jaw, n. Kiefer, - m.

jay, n. Eichelhäher, - m.

jaywalk, vb. quer über eine Straßenkreuzung gehen*.

jazz, n. Jazz m.

jealous, adj. eifersüchtig.

jealousy, n. Eifersucht f.

jeans, n. Jeans pl.

jeer, vb. spotten.

jelly, n. Gelee', -s nt.

jeopardize, vb. gefähr'den.

jeopardy, n. Gefahr', -en f.

jerk, 1. n. Ruck, -e m. **2.** vb. ruckartig bewe'gen.

jerky, adj. ruckartig.

jersey, n. Jersey, -s nt.

Jerusalem, n. Jeru'salem nt.

jest, 1. n. Scherz, -e m. **2.** vb. scherzen.

jester, n. Spaßmacher, - m.; (court j.) Hofnarr, -en, -en m.

Jesuit, 1. n. Jesuit', -en, -en m. **2.** adj. jesui'tisch; Jesui'ten-(cpds.).

Jesus Christ, n. Jesus Christus m.

jet, n. Strahl, -en m.; (tech.) Düse, -n f.; (plane) Düsenflugzeug, -e nt.; (mineral) Pechkohle, -n f.

jet lag, n. Jet-lag m.; körperliches Unbehagen durch Zeitverschiebung.

jetsam, n. Strandgut nt.; über Bord geworf'enes Gut nt.

jetty, n. Mole, -n f.

Jew, n. Jude, -n, -n m.

jewel, n. Juwel', -en nt., Edelstein, -e m.

jeweler, n. Juwelier', -e m.

jewelry, n. Schmucksachen pl., Schmuck m.

Jewish, adj. jüdisch.

jib, n. Klüver, - m.

jibe, vb. (sailing) halsen; (agree) sich decken.

jiffy, n. Nu m.

jig, n. Gigue f.

jilt, vb. sitzen lassen*.

jingle, vb. klingeln.

job, n. Stellung, -en f.; Aufgabe, -n f.

jobber, n. Zwischenhändler, - m.

jockey, n. Jockey, -s m.

jocular, adj. scherzhaft.

jog, vb. schubsen.

joggle, vb. (tr.) stubsen; (intr.) wackeln.

join, vb. verbin'den*; (club, etc.) bei'treten*.

joint, 1. n. Gelenk', -e nt. **2.** adj. gemein'sam.

joist, n. Querbalken, - m.

joke, 1. n. Witz, -e m., Scherz, -e m., Spaß, =e m. **2.** vb. einen Witz machen, scherzen.

joker, n. Witzbold, -e m.; (cards) Joker, - m.

jolly, adj. heiter.

jolt, 1. n. Stoß, =e m. **2.** vb. rütteln.

jonquil, n. gelbe Narzis'se, -n f.

jostle, vb. stoßen*.

journal, n. Journal', -e nt.; (diary) Tagebuch, =er m.; (newspaper) Zeitung, -en f.; (periodical) Zeitschrift, -en f.

journalism, n. Zeitungswesen nt.

journalist, n. Journalist', -en, -en m.

journey, n. Reise, -n f.

journeyman, n. Gesel'le, -n, -n m.

jovial, adj. jovial'.

jowl, n. Backe, -n f.

joy, n. Freude, -n f.

joyful, adj. freudig.

joyous, adj. freudig.

jubilant, adj. frohlockend.

jubilee, n. Jubilä'um, -ä'en nt.

Judaism, n. Judentum nt.

judge, 1. n. Kenner, - m.; (law) Richter, - m. **2.** vb. beur'teilen; (law) richten, Recht sprechen*.

judgment, n. Urteil, -e nt.; (law also:) Rechtsspruch, =e m.

judicial, adj. richterlich; Gerichts'-(cpds.).

judiciary, 1. n. Justiz'gewalt f.; Richterstand m. **2.** adj. richterlich.

judicious, adj. weise, klug.

jug, n. Krug, =e m.

juggle, vb. jonglie'ren.

juggler, n. Jongleur', -e m.

juice, n. Saft, =e m.

juicy, adj. saftig.

July, n. Juli m.

jumble, n. Durcheinan'der nt.

jump, 1. n. Sprung, =e m. **2.** vb. springen*.

junction, n. Verbin'dung, -en f.; (railroad) Knotenpunkt, -e m.

juncture, n. Zusam'mentreffen, - nt.

June, n. Juni m.

jungle, n. Dschungel, - m. or nt. (or -n f.).

junior, adj. jünger.

juniper, n. Wachol'der, - m.

junk, n. Altwaren pl.; (fig.) Kram m.

junket, n. (food) Milchpudding m.; (trip) Reise, -n f.

jurisdiction, n. Rechtsprechung, -en f.; Gerichts'barkeit f.; Zuständigkeit f.

jurisprudence, n. Rechtswissenschaft f.

jurist, n. Rechtsgelehrt- m.

juror, n. Geschwo'ren- m.&f.

jury, n. Geschwo'ren- pl.

just, 1. adj. gerecht'. **2.** adv. gera'de, eben.

justice, n. Gerech'tigkeit f.

justifiable, adj. berech'tigt.

justification, n. Rechtfertigung, -en f., Berech'tigung, -en f.

justify, vb. rechtfertigen.

jut, vb. hervor'stehen*.

jute, n. Jute f.

juvenile, adj. jugendlich.

K

kale, n. Grünkohl m.

kaleidoscope, n. Kaleidoskop', -e nt.

kangaroo, n. Känguruh', -s nt.

karat, n. Karat', -e nt.

karate, n. Kara'te nt.

keel, n. Kiel, -e m.

keen, adj. scharf; (fig.) eifrig.

keep, 1. n. (lodging) Unterhalt m. **2.** vb. behal'ten*, bewah'ren; (animals, etc.) halten*; (k. doing something) etwas immer wieder tun*; (k. on doing something) etwas weiter tun*.

keeper, n. Wärter, - m., Wächter, - m.

keepsake, n. Andenken, - nt.

keg, n. Faß, =sser nt.

kennel, n. Hundezwinger, - m.

kerchief, n. Halstuch, =er nt.; Kopftuch, =er nt.

kernel, n. Kern, -e m.; (grain) Korn, =er nt.

kerosene, n. Kerosin' nt.

ketchup, n. Ketchup m.

kettle, n. Kessel, - m.

kettledrum, n. Kesselpauke, -n f.

key, n. Schlüssel, - m.; (piano) Taste, -n f.; (musical structure) Tonart, -en f.

keyhole, n. Schlüsselloch, =er nt.

khaki, n. Khaki nt.

kick, 1. n. Stoß, =e m., Tritt, -e m. **2.** vb. stoßen*, treten*.

kid, 1. n. (goat) Zicklein, - nt.; (child) Kind, -er nt. **2.** vb. necken, rein·legen.

kidnap, vb. gewalt'sam entführen.

kidnaper, n. Kinderräuber, - m.

kidnaping, n. Kinderraub m.

kidney, n. Niere, -n f.

kidney bean, n. Schminkbohne, -n f.

kill, vb. töten, um·bringen*.

killer, n. Mörder, - m.

kiln, n. Brennofen, - m.

kilocycle, n. Kilohertz, - nt.

kilogram, n. Kilo, - nt.

kilohertz, n. Kilohertz nt.

kilometer, n. Kilome'ter, - nt.

kilowatt, n. Kilowatt, - nt.

kilt, n. Kilt, -s m.

kimono, n. Kimo'no, -s m.

kin, n. Verwandt'schaft, -en f.

kind, 1. n. Art, -en f., Sorte, -n f. **2.** adj. gütig, freundlich.

kindergarten, n. Kindergarten, - m.

kindle, vb. an·zünden, entzünden.

kindly, adj. freundlich.

kindness, n. Güte f., Freundlichkeit f.

kindred, adj. verwandt'.

king, n. König, -e m.

kingdom, n. Königreich, -e nt.

kink, n. Knoten, - m.

kiosk, n. Kiosk, -e m.

kiss, 1. n. Kuß, ⸗sse m. **2.** vb. küssen.

kitchen, n. Küche, -n f.

kite, n. Drachen, - m.; *(bird)* Milan, -e m.

kitten, n. Kätzchen, - nt.

kleptomaniac, n. Kleptoma'ne, -n, -n m.

knack, n. Talent', -e nt.

knapsack, n. Rucksack, ⸗e m.

knead, vb. kneten.

knee, n. Knie, Knie nt.

kneel, vb. knien.

knickers, n.pl. Kniehose, -n f.

knife, n. Messer, - m.

knight, nn. Ritter, - m.; *(chess)* Springer, - m.

knit, vb. stricken; *(fig.)* verknüp'fen.

knock, 1. n. Klopfen nt. **2.** vb. klopfen.

knot, 1. n. Knoten, - m.; *(wood)* Knorren, - m. **2.** vb. knoten.

knotty, adj. knotig; *(wood)* knorrig; *(fig.)* schwierig.

know, vb. *(facts)* wissen°; *(people, places, things)* kennen°.

knowledge, n. Kenntnis, -se f.; Wissen nt.

knuckle, n. Knöchel, - m.

Korea, n. Kore'a nt.

L

label, n. Etiket'te, -n f.

labor, 1. n. Arbeit, -en f.; *(workers)* Arbeiterschaft f.; *(birth)* Wehen pl. **2.** vb. arbeiten.

laboratory, n. Laborato'rium, -rien nt.

laborer, n. Arbeiter, - m.

laborious, adj. arbeitsam, mühselig.

labor union, n. Gewerk'schaft, -en f.

labyrinth, n. Labyrinth', -e nt.

lace, n. Spitze, -n f.

lacerate, vb. auf⸗reißen°.

laceration, n. Riß, -sse m.

lack, 1. n. Mangel, = m. (i. Mangel leiden° an; (i I. something) es fehlt, mangelt mir an etwas.

lackadaisical, adj. schwunglos, unlustig.

laconic, adj. lako'nisch.

lacquer, 1. n. Lack, -e m. **2.** vb. lackie'ren.

lacy, adj. spitzenartig; Spitzen-*(cpds.).*

lad, n. Knabe, -n, -n m.

ladder, n. Leiter, -n f.

ladle, n. Schöpflöffel, - m.

lady, n. Dame, -n f.

ladybug, n. Mari'enkäfer, - m.

lag, n. Verzö'gerung, -en f.

lag behind, vb. zurück'-bleiben°.

lagoon, n. Lagu'ne, -n f.

laid-back, adj. entspannt, unverkrampft, die Dinge auf sich zukommen lassend.

lair, n. Lagerstatt, ⸗e f.; Höhle, -n f.

laity, n. Laienstand m., Laien pl.

lake, n. See, Se'en m.

lamb, n. Lamm, ⸗er nt.

lame, adj. lahm.

lament, 1. n. Wehklage, -n f. **2.** vb. bekla'gen.

lamentable, adj. bekla'genswert.

lamentation, n. Wehklage, -n f.

laminate, vb. *(metal)* auswalzen, plattie'ren; **(l.d wood)** Furnier'holz nt.

lamp, n. Lampe, -n f.

lance, 1. n. Lanze, -n f. **2.** vb. durchsto'ßen°; *(med.)* mit der Lanzet'te öffnen.

land, 1. n. *(country)* Land, ⸗er nt.; *(ground)* Grund und Boden m. **2.** vb. landen.

landing, n. Landung, -en f.; *(stairs)* Treppenabsatz, ⸗e m.

landlady, n. Wirtin, -nen f.; Hausbesitzerin, -nen f.

landlord, n. Wirt, -e m.; Hausbesitzer, - m.

landmark, n. Markstein, -e m.

landscape, n. Landschaft, -en f.

landslide, n. Erdrutsch, -e m.; *(election)* überwäl'tigender Wahlsieg, -e m.

lane, n. Pfad, -e m.; *(boat)* Fahrrinne, -n f.; *(auto)* Fahrbahn, -en f.

language, n. Sprache, -n f.

languid, adj. energie'los, schlaff.

languish, vb. schmachten.

lanky, adj. baumlang.

lanolin, n. Lanolin' nt.

lantern, n. Later'ne, -n f.

lap, 1. n. Schoß, ⸗e m.; *(sport)* Runde, -n f. **2.** vb. übereinan'der⸗legen.

lapel, n. Revers', - m.

lapin, n. Kanin'chenpelz m.

lapse, 1. n. *(error)* Lapsus, - m., Verse'hen, - nt.; *(time)* Zwischenzeit, -en f. **2.** vb. verstrei'chen°.

larceny, n. Diebstahl, ⸗e m.

lard, n. Schweinefett nt.

large, adj. groß (größer, größt-); weit; umfangreich.

largely, adv. größtenteils.

largo, n. Largo, -s nt.

lariat, n. Lasso, -s nt.

lark, n. Lerche, -n f.; *(fun)* Vergnü'gen nt.

larkspur, n. Rittersporn m.

larva, n. Larve, -n f.

laryngitis, n. Kehlkopfentzündung, -en f.

larynx, n. Kehlkopf, ⸗e m.

lascivious, adj. wöllüstig.

laser, n. Laser m.

lash, 1. n. Peitsche, -n f.; Peitschenhieb, -e m.; *(eye)* Wimper, -n f. **2.** vb. peitschen.

lass, n. Mädchen, - nt.

lasso, n. Lasso, -s nt.

last, 1. n. Leisten, - m. **2.** adj. letzt-. **3.** vb. dauern.

lasting, adj. dauernd, anhaltend, bestän'dig.

latch, 1. n. Klinke, -n f. **2.** vb. ein⸗klinken.

late, adj. spät, verspä'tet; *(dead)* verstor'ben.

lately, adv. in letzter Zeit.

latent, adj. latent.

lateral, adj. seitlich.

lath, n. Latte, -n f.

lathe, n. Drehbank, ⸗e f.

lather, n. Schaum m.

Latin, 1. n. *(language)* Latein' nt.; *(person)* Roma'ne, -n, -n m. **2.** adj. latei'nisch; roma'nisch.

latitude, n. Breite, -n f.

latrine, n. Latri'ne, -n f.

latter, 1. adj. letzter-. **2.** pron. (the l.) dieser, -es, -e.

lattice, n. Gitterwerk nt.

laud, vb. loben, preisen°.

laudable, adj. lobenswert.

laudanum, n. Laudanum nt.

laudatory, adj. Lob- *(cpds.).*

laugh, 1. n. Lachen nt. **2.** vb. lachen.

laughable, adj. lächerlich.

laughter, n. Geläch'ter nt.

launch, 1. n. Barkas'se, -n f. **2.** vb. *(throw)* schleudern; *(boat)* vom Stapel lassen°.

launching, n. Stapellauf, ⸗e m.

launder, vb. waschen°.

laundress, n. Waschfrau, -en f.

laundry, n. *(clothes)* Wäsche f.; *(establishment)* Wäscherei', -en f.

laundryman, n. Wäscherei'angestellt- m.

laurel, n. Lorbeer, -en m.

lava, n. Lava f.

lavatory, n. Waschraum, ⸗e m.

lavender, n. Laven'del m.

lavish, adj. üppig.

law, n. *(individual)* Gesetz' -e nt.; *(system)* Recht nt.

lawful, adj. gesetz'lich, rechtmäßig.

lawless, adj. gesetz'los; *(fig.)* zügellos.

lawn, n. Rasen m.

lawsuit, n. Prozeß', -sse m.

lawyer, n. Rechtsanwalt, ⸗e m.; Jurist', -en, -en m.

lax, adj. lax.

laxative, n. Abführmittel, - nt.

laxity, n. Laxheit f.

lay, 1. adj. Laien- *(cpds.).* **2.** vb. legen.

layer, n. Schicht, -en f.

layman, n. Laie, -n, -n m.

lazy, adj. faul.

lead, 1. n. Führung f., Leitung f.; *(metal)* Blei nt. **2.** vb. führen, leiten.

leaden, *adj.* bleiern.

leader, *n.* Führer, - *m.,* Leiter, - *m.*

leadership, *n.* Führung *f.*

lead pencil, *n.* Bleistift, - e *m.*

leaf, *n.* Blatt, ⁻er *nt.*

leaflet, *n.* Broschü're, -n *f.,* Flugblatt, ⁻er *nt.*

league, *n.* Bund, ⁻e *m.,* Bündnis, -se *nt.*

League of Nations, *n.* Völkerbund *m.*

leak, 1. *n.* Leck, -e *nt.* **2.** *vb.* lecken.

leakage, *n.* Durchsickern *nt.*

leaky, *adj.* leck, undicht.

lean, 1. *adj.* mager. **2.** *vb.* lehnen.

leap, 1. *n.* Sprung, ⁻e *m.* **2.** *vb.* springen*.

leap year, *n.* Schaltjahr, -e *nt.*

learn, *vb.* lernen; erfah'ren*.

learned, *adj.* gelehrt'.

learning, *n.* Wissen *nt.,* Bildung *f.*

lease, 1. *n.* Mietvertrag, ⁻e *m.,* Pacht, -en *f.* **2.** *vb.* mieten, pachten.

leash, *n.* Leine, -n *f.*

least, *adj. (slightest)* geringst'-; *(smallest)* kleinst-; **(at l.,** *in any case)* wenigstens; **(at l.,** *surely this much)* mindestens, zum mindesten.

leather, 1. *n.* Leder, - *nt.* **2.** *adj.* ledern.

leathery, *adj.* ledern.

leave, 1. *n. (farewell)* Abschied, -e *m.; (permission)* Erlaub'nis, -e *f.; (furlough)* Urlaub, - e *m.* **2.** *vb. (depart)* ab'fahren*; *(go away)* fort'gehen*; *(abandon)* verlas'sen*; *(let)* lassen*.

leaven, *n.* Sauerteig, -e *m.*

lecherous, *adj.* lüstern.

lecture, 1. *n.* Vortrag, ⁻e *m.; (academic)* Vorlesung, -en *f.* **2.** *vb.* einen Vortrag halten*; eine Vorlesung halten*.

lecturer, *n.* Vortragend-e.

ledge, *n.* Felsvorsprung, ⁻e *m.,* Sims, -e *m.*

ledger, *n.* Hauptbuch, ⁻er *nt.*

lee, *n.* Lee *f.*

leech, *n.* Blutegel, - *m.*

leek, *n.* Lauch, -e *m.*

leer, *vb.* begehr'lich schielen.

leeward, *adv.* leewärts.

left, 1. *n. (pol.)* Link- *f.* **2.** *adj.* link-; **(l. over)** übriggeblieben. **3.** *adv.* links.

leftist, *adj.* links orientiert'.

left-over, *n.* Überbleibsel, - *nt.,* Rest, -e *m.*

leg, *n.* Bein, -e *nt.*

legacy, *n.* Vermächt'nis, -se *nt.,* Erbschaft, -en *f.*

legal, *adj.* gesetz'lich, gesetz'mäßig.

legalize, *vb.* legalisie'ren.

legation, *n.* Gesandt'schaft, - en *f.*

legend, *n.* Legen'de, -n *f.*

legendary, *adj.* legendär'.

legible, *adj.* leserlich.

legion, *n.* Legion', -e *f.*

legislate, *vb.* Gesetze geben*.

legislation, *n.* Gesetz'gebung *f.*

legislator, *n.* Gesetz'geber, - *m.*

legislature, *n.* gesetz'gebende Gewalt' *f.;* gesetz'gebende Versamm'lung, -en *f.*

legitimate, *adj.* legitim'.

leisure, *n.* Muße *f.*

leisurely, *adj.* gemäch'lich.

lemon, *n.* Zitro'ne, -n *f.*

lemonade, *n.* Limona'de, -n *f.*

lend, *vb.* leihen*.

length, *n.* Länge, -n *f.; (time)* Dauer *f.*

lengthen, *vb.* verlän'gern.

lengthwise, *adv.* der Länge nach.

lengthy, *adj.* langwierig.

lenient, *adj.* mild, nachsichtig.

lens, *n.* Linse, -n *f.; (photo)* Objectiv', -e *nt.*

Lent, *n.* Fastenzeit *f.*

Lenten, *adj.* Fasten- *(cpds.).*

lentil, *n.* Linse, -n *f.*

leopard, *n.* Leopard', -en, -en *m.*

leper, *n.* Aussätzig- *m.&f.*

leprosy, *n.* Aussatz *m.*

lesbian, *adj.* lesbisch.

lesion, *n.* Verlet'zung, -en *f.*

less, *adj.* weniger.

lesser, *adj. (size)* kleiner; *(degree)* gerin'ger.

lesson, *n.* Lehre, -n *f.; (school)* Lehrstunde, -n *f.; (assignment)* Aufgabe, -n *f.*

lest, *conj.* damit' . . . nicht.

let, *vb. (allow)* lassen*; *(lease)* vermie'ten.

letdown, *n.* Enttäu'schung, -en *f.*

lethal, *adj.* tödlich.

lethargic, *adj.* teilnahmslos, lethar'gisch.

lethargy, *n.* Teilnahmslosigkeit *f.,* Lethargie' *f.*

letter, *n. (alphabet)* Buchstabe(n), - *(or* -n, -n) *m.; (communication)* Brief, -e *m.*

letterhead, *n.* Briefkopf, ⁻e *m.*

lettuce, *n.* Kopfsalat, -e *m.*

leukemia, *n.* Leukämie' *f.*

levee, *n.* Damm, ⁻e *m.*

level, 1. *n.* Stand, ⁻e *m.,* Niveau', -s *nt.* **2.** *adj.* eben, gera'de; flach. **3.** *vb.* ebnen; gleich'machen.

lever, *n.* Hebel, - *m.*

levity, *n.* Leichtsinn *m.*

levy, 1. *n.* Abgabe, -n *f.,* Steuer, -n *f.*

lewd, *adj.* unzüchtig.

lexicon, *n.* Lexikon, -ka *nt.*

liability, *n.* Verant'wortlichkeit, -en *f.;* Verpflich'tung, - en *f.*

liable, *adj.* verant'wortlich; *(law)* haftbar.

liaison, *n.* Verbin'dung, -en *f.;* Liaison', -s *f.*

liar, *n.* Lügner, - *m.*

libel, *n.* Verleum'dung, -en *f.*

libelous, *adj.* verleum'derisch.

liberal, 1. *n.* Liberal'- *m.* **2.** *adj.* liberal'.

liberalism, *n.* Liberalis'mus *m.*

liberality, *n.* Freigebigkeit *f.;* Freisinnigkeit *f.*

liberate, *vb.* befrei'en.

liberation, *n.* Befrei'ung, -en *f.*

libertine, *n.* Lüstling, -e *m.*

liberty, *n.* Freiheit, -en *f.*

libido, *n.* Libido *f.*

librarian, *n.* Bibliothekar', -e *m.;* Bibliotheka'rin, -nen *f.*

library, *n.* Bibliothek', -en *f.,* Bücherei', -en *f.*

libretto, *n.* Libret'to, -s *nt.*

license, *n.* Erlaub'nis, -se *f.;* Geneh'migung, -en *f.* **(driver's l.)** Führerschein, -e *m.*

lick, *n.* lecken.

licorice, *n.* Lakrit'ze, -n *f.*

lid, *n.* Deckel, - *m.; (eye)* Lid, - er *nt.*

lie, 1. *n.* Lüge, -n *f.* **2.** *vb. (tell untruths)* lügen*; *(recline)* liegen*; **(l. down)** sich *(hin-)*legen.

lien, *n.* dinglich gesi'chertes Anrecht *nt.*

lieutenant, *n.* Leutnant, -s *m.*

life, *n.* Leben, - *nt.*

lifeboat, *n.* Rettungsboot, -e *nt.*

lifeguard, *n.* Bademeister, - *m.*

life insurance, *n.* Lebensversicherung, -en *f.*

lifeless, *adj.* leblos.

life preserver, *n.* Rettungsring, -e *m.; (vest)* Schwimmweste, - n *f.*

life style, *n.* Lebensstil *m.*

lifetime, *n.* Lebenszeit, -en *f.*

lift, 1. *n.* Fahrstuhl, ⁻e *m.* **2.** *vb.* heben*.

ligament, *n.* Sehne, -n *f.*

ligature, *n.* Ligatur', -en *f.*

light, 1. *n.* Licht, -er *nt.* **2.** *adj. (color)* hell; *(weight)* leicht. **3.** *vb. (fire)* an'zünden; *(illuminate)* beleuch'ten.

lighten, *vb.* leichter machen; *(fig.)* erleich'tern; *(lightning)* blitzen.

lighter, *n. (cigar, cigarette)* Feuerzeug, -e *nt.*

lighthouse, *n.* Leuchtturm, ⁻e *m.*

lightness, *n. (color)* Helligkeit *f.; (ease)* Leichtfertigkeit *f.*

lightning, *n.* Blitz, -e *m.*

like, 1. *adj.* gleich. **2.** *vb.* gern haben*, *(gern)* mögen*; **(I l. it)** es gefällt* mir; **(I l. to do it)** ich tue(*) es gern. **3.** *prep.* wie; **(l. this, l. that)** so.

likeable, *adj.* angenehm, liebenswert.

likelihood, *n.* Wahrschein'lichkeit, -en *f.*

likely, *adj.* wahrschein'lich.

liken, vb. verglei'chen*.

likeness, n. Ähnlichkeit, -en f.

likewise, adv. ebenso.

lilac, n. Flieder m.

lilt, n. wiegender Rhythmus m.

lily, n. Lilie, -n f.

lily of the valley, n. Maiglöckchen, - nt.

limb, n. Glied, -er nt.

limber, adj. biegsam.

limbo, n. Vorhölle f.

lime, n. Kalk m.; (fruit) Limo'ne, -n f.

limelight, n. Rampenlicht, -er nt.

limestone, n. Kalkstein m.

limit, 1. n. Grenze, -n f.; Höchstgrenze, -n f. 2. vb. begren'zen, beschrän'ken.

limitation, n. Begren'zung, -en f., Beschrän'kung, -en f.

limited, adj. begrenzt', beschränkt'.

limitless, adj. unbegrenzt.

limousine, n. Limousi'ne -n f.

limp, 1. adj. schlaff. 2. vb. hinken.

linden, n. Linde, -n f.

line, n. Linie, -n f.; (mark) Strich, -e m. (row) Reihe, -n f.; (writing) Zeile, -n f.; (rope) Leine, -n f.

lineage, n. Geschlecht', -er nt.

lineal, adj. in gerader Linie.

linear, adj. linear'.

linen, 1. n. Leinen, - nt.; (household) Wäsche f. 2. adj. leinen.

liner, n. (boat) Ozeandampfer, - m.

linger, vb. verwei'len.

lingerie, n. Damenunterwäsche f.

linguist, n. Sprachwissenschaftler, - m., Linguist', -en, -en m.

linguistic, adj. sprachlich; sprachwissenschaftlich, linguis'tisch.

linguistics, n. Sprachwissenschaft, -en f., Linguis'tik f.

liniment, n. Einreibemittel, - nt.

lining, n. Futter, - nt.

link, 1. n. (bond) Band, -e nt.; (chain) Glied, -er nt. 2. vb. verbin'den*; verket'ten.

linoleum, n. Lino'leum nt.

linseed oil, n. Leinöl nt.

lint, n. Fussel, -n f.

lion, n. Löwe, -n, -n m.

lip, n. Lippe, -n f.

lip-stick, n. Lippenstift, -e m.

liquefy, vb. flüssig machen.

liqueur, n. Likör', -e m.

liquid, 1. n. Flüssigkeit, -en f. 2. adj. flüssig.

liquidate, vb. liquidie'ren.

liquidation, n. Liquidation', -en f.

liquor, n. Alkohol m., Spirituo'sen pl.

lira, n. Lira, -re f.

lisp, vb. lispeln.

---

lisle, n. Baumwollfaden m.

list, 1. n. Liste, -n f., Verzeich'nis, -se nt.; (ship) Schlagseite f. 2. vb. verzeich'nen.

listen, vb. zu·hören, horchen.

listless, adj. lustlos.

litany, n. Litanei' f.

liter, n. Liter, - m.

literacy, n. Lesen und Schreiben Können nt.

literal, adj. buchstäblich, wörtlich.

literary, adj. litera'risch.

literate, adj. des Lesens und Schreibens kundig.

literature, n. Literatur', -en f.

lithe, adj. geschmei'dig.

lithograph, 1. n. Lithographie', -i'en f. 2. vb. lit'hgraphie'ren.

litigant, n. Rechtsstreitführer, - m.

litigation, n. Rechtsstreit, -e m.

litter, 1. n. (rubbish) Abfall, ⸚e m.; (stretcher) Tragbahre, -n f.; (puppies, kittens, etc.) Wurf, -e m. 2. vb. Sachen herum'liegen lassen*.

little, adj. (size) klein; (amount) wenig; (a.) ein bißchen, ein wenig.

liturgical, adj. litur'gisch.

liturgy, n. Liturgie', -i'en f.

live, 1. adj. leben'dig. 2. vb. (be alive) leben; (dwell) wohnen.

livelihood, n. Lebensunterhalt m.

lively, adj. lebhaft.

liver, n. Leber, -n f.

livery, n. Livree', -s f.

livestock, n. Viehbestand m.

livid, adj. aschfahl.

living, 1. n. Lebensweise f. 2. adj. lebend.

lizard, n. Eidechse, -n f.

lo, interj. siehe!

load, 1. n. Ladung, -en f., (burden) Last, -en f. 2. vb. laden*.

loaf, 1. n. Laib, -e m. 2. vb. faulenzen.

loafer, n. Faulenzer, - m.

loam, n. Lehm m.

loan, 1. n. Anleihe, -n f. 2. vb. leihen*.

loath, adj. abgeneigt.

loathe, vb. verab'scheuen.

loathing, n. Abscheu f.

loathsome, adj. widerlich, ekelhaft.

lobby, n. Wandelhalle, -n f.; (political) Interes'sengruppe, -n f.

lobe, n. Lappen, - m.

lobster, n. Hummer, - m.

local, 1. n. (train) Vorortzug, ⸚e m. 2. adj. of lich, lokal'.

locale, n. Schaup.. - ⸚e m.

locality, n. Ort, -e m.

localize, vb. lokalisie'ren.

locate, vb. finden*; (be l.d) liegen*.

location, n. Lage, -n f.

lock, 1. n. Schloß, ⸚sser nt.; (canal) Schleuse, -n f.; (hair) Locke, -n f. 2. vb. abschließen*.

---

locker, n. Schrank, ⸚e m.; (baggage) Schließfach, ⸚er nt.

locket, n. Medaillon', -s nt.

lockjaw, n. Kieferkrampf.

locksmith, n. Schlosser, - m.

locomotion, n. Fortbewegung, -en f.

locomotive, n. Lokomoti've, -n f.

locust, n. Heuschrecke, -n f.

lode, n. Erzader, -n f.

lodge, 1. n. Häuschen, - nt.; (fraternal) Loge, -n f. 2. vb. (intr.) logie'ren; (tr.) beherbergen.

lodger, n. Untermieter, - m.

lodging, n. Unterkunft, ⸚e f.

loft, n. Boden, ⸚ m.; (warehouse) Speicher, - m.

lofty, adj. erha'ben.

log, n. Holzklotz, ⸚e m.; (tree trunk) Baumstamm, ⸚e m.; (ship's l.) Logbuch, ⸚er nt.

loge, n. Loge, -n f.

logic, n. Logik f.

logical, adj. logisch.

loin, n. Lende, -n f.

loiter, vb. herum'stehen*.

London, n. London nt.

lone, lonely, lonesome, adj. einsam.

loneliness, n. Einsamkeit f.

long, 1. adj. lang (⸚). 2. vb. sich sehnen.

longevity, n. Langlebigkeit f.

longing, 1. n. Sehnsucht f. 2. adj. sehnsüchtig.

longitude, n. Länge f.

longitudinal, adj. Längen- (cpds.)

long-lived, adj. langlebig.

long playing record, n. Langspielplatte, -n f.

look, 1. n. Blick, -e m.; (appearance, l.s) Aussehen nt. 2. vb. sehen*, schauen, blicken, gucken; (l. at) an·sehen*, ·schauen ·blicken, ·gucken; (l. good, etc.) gut (etc.) aus·sehen*; (l. out, be careful) auf·passen.

looking glass, n. Spiegel, - m.

loom, n. Webstuhl, ⸚e m.

loop, n. Schlaufe, -n f.

loophole, n. Schlupfloch, ⸚er nt.

loose, adj. lose, locker.

loosen, vb. lockern.

loot, 1. n. Beute f. 2. vb. plündern.

lop off, vb. ab·schlagen*.

lopsided, adj. schief.

loquacious, adj. schwatzhaft.

lord, n. Herr, -n, -en m.; (title) Lord, -s m.

lordship, n. Herrschaft, -en f.

lose, vb. verlie'ren*.

loss, n. Verlust', -e m.

lot, n. Los, -e nt.; (quantity) Menge, -n f.; (ground) Grundstück, -e nt.

lotion, n. Lotion', -en f.

lottery, n. Lotterie', -i'en f.

lotus, n. Lotosblume, -n f.

loud, *adj.* laut; *(color)* grell.
loud-speaker, *n.* Lautsprecher, - *m.*
lounge, 1. *n.* Vorhalle, -n *f.* **2.** *vb.* herum'=lungern.
louse, *n.* Laus, =e *f.*
lout, *n.* Lümmel, - *m.*
louver, *n.* Lattenfenster, - *nt.*
lovable, *adj.* liebenswert.
love, 1. *n.* Liebe, -n *f.* **2.** *vb.* lie'ben; **(fall in l.)** sich verlie'ben.
lovely, *adj.* lieblich, reizend.
lover, *n.* Liebhaber, - *m.*
low, *adj.* niedrig, tief; *(nasty)* gemein'.
lowbrow, *adj.* unintellektuell, ungeistig.
lower, 1. *adj.* tiefer, niedriger; gemei'ner. **2.** *vb.* herun'ter=lassen*; herab'=setzen, senken.
lowly, *adj.* beschei'den.
loyal, *adj.* treu.
loyalist, *n.* Regie'rungstreu, - *m.*
loyalty, *n.* Treue *f.*, Loyalität' *f.*
lozenge, *n.* Pastil'le, -n *f.*
lubricant, *n.* Schmiermittel, - *nt.*
lubricate, *vb.* schmieren.
lucid, *adj.* klar.
luck, *n.* Glück *nt.*, Zufall, =e *m.*
lucky, *adj.* glücklich; **(be l.)** Glück haben*.
lucrative, *adj.* gewinn'bringend.
ludicrous, *adj.* lächerlich.
lug, *vb.* schleppen.
luggage, *n.* Gepäck' *nt.*
lukewarm, *adj.* lauwarm.
lull, 1. *n.* Pause, -n *f.* **2.** *vb.* beru'higen; **(l. to sleep)** ein'schläfern.
lullaby, *n.* Wigenlied, -er *nt.*
lumbago, *n.* Hexenschuß *m.*
lumber, *n.* Holz. *nt.*
luminous, *adj.* leuchtend.
lump, *n.* Klumpen, - *m.*, *(skin)* Beule, -n *f.*
lumpy, *adj.* klumpig.
lunacy, *n.* Irrsinn *m.*
lunar, *adj.* Mond- *(cpds.)*.
lunatic, 1. *n.* Irrsinnig- *m.* **2.** *adj.* irrsinnig.
lunch, *n.* leichtes Mittagessen, - *nt.* **2.** *vb.* zu Mittag essen*.
luncheon, *n.* leichtes Mittagessen, - *nt.*
lung, *n.* Lunge, -n *f.*
lunge, *vb.* vor=stoßen*.
lurch, *vb.* torkeln; **(leave in the l.)** sitzen lassen*.
lure, *vb.* locken.
lurid, *adj.* grell; *(fig.)* grausig.
lurk, *vb.* lauren.
luscious, *adj.* saftig, lecker.
lush, *adj.* saftig, üppig.
lust, 1. *n.* Wollust *f.* **2.** *vb.* gelü's'ten.
luster, *n.* Glanz *m.*
lustful, *adj.* lüstern.
lustrous, *adj.* glänzend.
lusty, *adj.* munter; kräftig.
lute, *n.* Laute, -n *f.*

Lutheran, 1. *n.* Luthera'ner, - *m.* **2.** *adj.* luthe'risch.
luxuriant, *adj.* üppig.
luxurious, *adj.* verschwen'derisch.
luxury, *n.* Luxus *m.*
lying, *adn.* lügnerisch.
lymph, *n.* Lymphe, -n *f.*
lynch, *vb.* lynchen.
lyre, *n.* Leier, -n *f.*
lyric, *adj.* lyrisch.
lyricism, *n.* Lyrik *f.*

M

macabre, *adj.* maka'ber.
macaroni, *n.* Makkaro'ni *pl.*
machine, *n.* Maschi'ne, -n *f.*
machine gun, *n.* Maschi'nengewehr, -e *nt.*
machinery, *n.* Mechanis'mus *m.;* Maschi'nen *pl.*
machinist, *n.* Maschinist', -en, -en *m.*
machismo, *n.* Männlichkeit, Virilität' *f.*
macho, *adj.* protzig männlich.
mackerel, *n.* Makre'le, -n *f.*
mackinaw, *n.* kurzer wollener Mantel, = *m.*
mad, *adj.* verrückt'; *(angry)* böse.
madam, *n.* gnädige Frau *f.*
madden, *vb.* verrückt' machen.
mafia, *n.* Mafia *f.*
magazine, *n.* Magazin', -e *nt.*, Zeitschrift, -en *f.*
magic, 1. *n.* Zauberkunst, =e *f.* **2.** *adj.* magisch.
magician, *n.* Zauberer, - *m.*
magistrate, *n.* Polizei'richter, - *m.*
magnanimous, *adj.* großzügig.
magnate, *n.* Magnat', -en, -en *m.*
magnesium, *n.* Magne'sium *nt.*
magnet, *n.* Magnet', (-en,) -en *m.*
magnetic, *adj.* magne'tisch.
magnificence, *n.* Herrlichkeit *f.*, Pracht *f.*
magnificent, *adj.* großartig, prächtig.
magnify, *vb.* vergrö'ßern.
magnitude, *n.* Größe, -n *f.*
mahogany, *n.* Mahago'ni *nt.*
maid, *n.* Dienstmädchen, - *nt.;* **(old m.)** alte Jungfer, -n *f.*
maiden, *adj.* Jungfern- *(cpds.)*; **(m. name)** Mädchenname(n), - *m.*
mail, 1. *n.* Post *f.* **2.** *vb.* mit der Post schicken; zur Post bringen*.
mail-box, *n.* Briefkasten, = *m.*
mailman, *n.* Postbote, -n, -n *m.*, Briefträger, - *m.*
maim, *vb.* verstüm'meln.
main, *adj.* hauptsächlich.
mainland, *n.* Festland *nt.*
mainspring, *n.* Triebfeder, -n *f.*

maintain, *vb.* aufrecht=erhalten*; *(assert)* behaup'ten.
maintenance, *n.* Aufrechterhaltung *f.*, Instand'haltung *f.*
mainframe, *n.* Großrechenanlage, -n *f.*
maize, *n.* Mais *m.*
majestic, *adj.* majestä'tisch.
majesty, *n.* Majestät', -en *f.*
major, 1. *n.* Major', -e *m.* **2.** *adj.* größer; Haupt- *(cpds.)*; *(music)* Dur *nt.*, **(A-major)** A-dur.
majority, *n.* Mehrzahl, -en *f.*, Mehrheit, -en *f.*, Majorität', -en *f.*
make, *vb.* machen; *(manufacture)* her=stellen; *(compel)* zwingen*.
make-believe, 1. *n.* Vorspiegelung, -en *f.* **2.** *adj.* vorgetäuscht. **3.** *vb.* vor'täuschen.
maker, *n.* Hersteller, - *m.*
makeshift, *n.* Notbehelf *m.*
make-up, *n.* Struktur', -en *f.;* Aufmachung, -en *f.; (face)* Schminke *f.*, Make-up *nt.*
malady, *n.* Krankheit, -en *f.*
malaria, *n.* Mala'ria *f.*
male, 1. *n.* *(human)* Mann, =er *m.; (animal)* Männchen, - *nt.* **2.** *adj.* männlich.
malevolent, *adj.* böswillig.
malice, *n.* Bosheit, -en *f.*
malicious, *adj.* boshaft.
malignant, *adj.* bösartig.
malnutrition, *n.* Unterernährung *f.*
malt, *n.* Malz *nt.*
maltreat, *vb.* mißhan'deln.
mammal, *n.* Säugetier, -e *nt.*
man, *n.* Mann, =er *m.; (human being)* Mensch, -en, -en *m.*
manage, *n.* handhaben; *(administer)* verwal'ten; *(direct)* leiten.
management, *n.* Verwal'tung, -en *f.;* Leitung, -en *f.*
manager, *n.* Leiter, - *m.;* Unterneh'mer, - *m.*
mandate, *n.* Mandat', -e *nt.*
mandatory, *adj.* unerläßlich.
mandolin, *n.* Mandoli'ne, -n *f.*
mane, *n.* Mähne, -n *f.*
maneuver, 1. *n.* Manö'ver, - *nt.* **2.** *vb.* manövrie'ren.
manganese, *n.* Mangan' *nt.*
manger, *n.* Krippe, -n *f.*
mangle, *vb.* zerflei'schen; *(laundry)* mangeln.
manhood, *n.* Mannesalter *nt.;* Mannhaftigkeit *f.*
mania, *n.* Manie', -i'en *f.*
maniac, *n.* Wahnsinnig- *m.*
manicure, 1. *n.* Maniкü're, -n *f.* **2.** *vb.* manikü'ren.
manifest, 1. *adj.* offenkundig. **2.** *vb.* bekun'den.
manifesto, *n.* Manifest', -e *nt.*
manifold, *adj.* mannigfaltig.
manipulate, *vb.* manipulie'ren.
mankind, *n.* Menschheit *f.*
manly, *adj.* mannhaft.

manner, n. Art, -en f., Weise, -n f.; Manier', -en f.

mannerism, n. Manieris'mus m.

mansion, n. Haus, ⁼er nt.

manslaughter, n. Totschlag, ⁼e m.

mantelpiece, n. Kamin'sims, -e m.

mantle, n. Mantel, ⁼ m.

manual, 1. n. Handbuch, ⁼er nt. 2. adj. Hand- (cpds.).

manufacture, 1. n. Herstellung, -en f. 2. vb. her·stellen.

manufacturer, n. Fabrikant', -en, -en m.

manure, n. Mist m.

manuscript, n. Handschrift, -en f., Manuskript', -e nt.

many, adj. pl. viele.

map, n. Landkarte, -n f.; (of a small area) Plan, ⁼e m.

maple, n. Ahorn, -e m.

mar, vb. verun'zieren.

marble, n. Marmor, -e m.

march, 1. n. Marsch, ⁼e m. 2. vb. marschie'ren.

March, n. März m.

mare, n. Stute, -n f.

margarine, n. Margari'ne f.

margin, n. (edge) Rand, ⁼er m.; (latitude) Spielraum, ⁼e m.

marginal, adj. Rand- (cpds.).

marijuana, n. Marihua'na nt.

marinate, vb. marinie'ren.

marine, adj. Meeres-, See- (cpds.).

mariner, n. Seemann, -leute m.

marionette, n. Marionet'te, -n f.

marital, adj. ehelich.

maritime, adj. Schiffahrts-, Seemanns- (cpds.).

mark, 1. n. Zeichen, - nt.; (school) Zensur', -en f., Note, -n f. 2. vb. kennzeichnen.

market, n. Markt, ⁼e m.

market place, Marktplatz, ⁼e m.

marmalade, n. Oran'genmarmelade, -n f.

maroon, 1. adj. rotbraun. 2. vb. aus·setzen.

marquee, n. Überda'chung, -en f.

marquis, n. Marquis', - m.

marriage, n. Heirat, -en f.; (ceremony) Trauung, -en f.; (institution) Ehe, -n f., (matrimony) Ehestand f.

marrow, n. Mark nt.

marry, vb. heiraten; (join in marriage) trauen; (get married) heiraten, sich verheira'ten; (m. off) verhei'raten.

marsh, n. Marsch, -en f.

marshal, n. Marschall, ⁼e m.

martial, adj. kriegerisch; Kriegs- (cpds.).

martyr, n. Märtyrer, - m.

martyrdom, n. Märtyrertum m.

marvel, 1. n. Wunder, - nt. 2. vb. (m. at) bewun'dern.

marvelous, adj. wunderbar.

mascara, n. Augenwimperntusche f.

mascot, n. Maskot'te, -n f.

masculine, adj. männlich, maskulin.

mash, 1. n. Brei, -e m. 2. vb. zerstoßen*.

mask, 1. n. Maske, -n f. 2. vb. maskie'ren.

mason, n. Maurer, - m.

masquerade, n. Maskera'de, -n f.

mass, n. Masse, -n f., (church) Messe, -n f.

massacre, 1. n. Gemet'zel, - nt. 2. vb. nieder·metzeln.

massage, 1. n. Massa'ge, -n f. 2. vb. massie'ren.

masseur, n. Masseur', -e m.

massive, adj. massiv'.

mass meeting, n. Massenversammlung, -en f.

mast, n. Mast, -en m.

master, 1. n. Meister, - m.; Herr, -n, -en m. 2. vb. beherr'schen.

masterpiece, n. Meisterstück, -e nt.

mastery, n. Beherr'schung f.; Herrschaft f.

mat, n. Matte, -n f.

match, 1. n. (light) Streichholz, ⁼er nt.; (contest) Wettkampf, ⁼e m.; (marriage) Heirat, -en f., Partie', -i'en f. 2. vb. passen zu; sich messen* mit.

mate, 1. n. (spouse) Ehemann, ⁼er m.; Ehefrau, -en f.; (naut.) Maat, -e m. 2. vb. sich paaren.

material, 1. n. Material', -ien nt.; (cloth) Stoff, -e m. 2. adj. materiell'; wesentlich.

materialism, n. Materialis'mus m.

materialize, vb. sich verwirk'lichen.

maternal, adj. mütterlich.

maternity, n. Mutterschaft f.

mathematical, adj. mathema'tisch.

mathematics, n. Mathematik' f.

matinée, n. Nachmittagsvorstellung, -en f.

matrimony, n. Ehestand m.

matron, n. Matro'ne, -n f.

matter, 1. n. Stoff, -e m., Mate'rie, -n f.; (fig.) Sache, -n f., Angelegenheit, -en f. 2. vb. von Bedeu'tung sein*; aus·machen; (it doesn't m.) es macht nichts.

mattress, n. Matrat'ze, -n f.

mature, 1. adj. reif. 2. vb. reifen; (fall due) fällig werden*.

maturity, n. Reife f.; Fälligkeit f.

maul, vb. übel zu·richten.

mausoleum, n. Mausole'um, -le'en nt.

maxim, n. Grundsatz, ⁼e m.

maximum, 1. n. Maximum, -ma nt. 2. adj. höchst- (cpds.).

may, vb. (be permitted) dürfen*; (he m. come) er wird vielleicht kommen*; (that m. be) das kann o mag sein*.

May, n. Mai m.

maybe, adv. vielleicht'.

mayhem, n. Mord und Totschlag m.

mayonnaise, n. Mayonnai'se, -n f.

mayor, n. Bürgermeister, - m.

maze, n. Wirrwarr nt.

me, pron. mir; mich.

meadow, n. Wiese, -n f.

meager, adj. dürftig.

meal, n. Mahlzeit, -en f.; (flour) Mehl nt.

mean, 1. n. (average) Durchschnitt, -e m. 2. adj. mittler-, durchschnittlich; Mittel-, Durchschnitts- (cpds.); (nasty) gemein'. 3. vb. (signify) bedeu'ten; (intend to say) meinen.

meaning, n. Bedeu'tung, -en f., (sense) Sinn, -e m.

means, n. Mittel pl.

meantime, meanwhile, n. Zwischenzeit f.; (in the m.) inzwi'schen, unterdes'sen.

measles, n. Masern pl.

measure, 1. n. Maß -e nt.; (fig.) Maßnahme, -n f. 2. vb. messen*.

measurement, n. Maß, -e nt.

measuring, n. Messen nt.

meat, n. Fleisch nt.

mechanic, n. Mecha'niker, - m.

mechanical, adj. mecha'nisch.

mechanism, n. Mechanis'mus, -men m.

mechanize, vb. mechanisie'ren.

medal, n. Orden, - m.

meddle, vb. sich ein·mischen.

mediaeval, adj. mittelalterlich.

median, n. Mittelwert, -e m.

mediate, vb. vermit'teln.

mediator, n. Vermitt'ler, - m.

medical, adj. ärztlich, medizi'nisch.

medicate, vb. medizi'nisch behan'deln.

medicine, n. Medizin', -en f.

mediocre, adj. mittelmäßig.

mediocrity, n. Mittelmäßigkeit f.

meditate, vb. nach·denken*.

meditation, n. Nachdenken nt.

Mediterranean, adj. Mittelmeer- (cpds.).

Mediterranean Sea, n. Mittelmeer nt.

medium, 1. n. Mittel, - nt.; Medium, -ien nt. 2. adj. mittler-.

medley, n. (music) Potpourri, -s nt.

meek, adj. sanft.

meekness, n. Sanftmut f.

meet, vb. treffen*; sich treffen*; begeg'nen.

meeting, n. Versamm'lung, -en f., Zusam'menkunft, ⁼e f., Tagung, -en f.; (encounter) Begeg'nung, -en f.

melancholy, 1. *n.* Schwermut *f.,* Melancholie' *f.* **2.** *adj.* schwermütig, melancho'lisch.

megahertz, *n.* Megahertz *nt.*

mellow, *adj.* gereift'.

melodious, *adj.* wohlklingend, melo'disch.

melodrama, *n.* Melodrama, -men *nt.*

melody, *n.* Melodie', -i'en *f.*

melon, *n.* Melo'ne, -n *f.*

melt, *vb.* schmelzen*.

meltdown, *n. (Atomkraftwerk)* Zerschmel'zen *nt.*

member, *n.* Mitglied, -er *nt.*

membership, *n.* Mitgliedschaft *f.*

membrane, *n.* Membra'ne, -n *f.*

memento, *n.* Andenken, - *nt.*

memoirs, *n.pl.* Memoi'ren *pl.*

memorable, *adj.* denkwürdig.

memorandum, *n.* Memoran'dum, -den *nt.*

memorial, 1. *n.* Denkmal, -:er *nt.;* Andenken, - *nt.* **2.** *adj.* Gedenk- *(cpds.).*

memorize, *vb.* auswendig lernen.

memory, *n. (retentiveness)* Gedächt'nis, -se *nt.; (remembrance)* Erin'nerung, -en *f.*

menace, 1. *n.* drohende Gefahr', -en *f.* **2.** *vb.* drohen, bedro'hen.

menagerie, *n.* Menagerie', -i'en *f.*

mend, *vb.* aus'bessern.

menial, *adj.* niedrig.

menopause, *n.* Wechseljahre *pl.*

menstruation, *n.* Regel *f.,* Menstruation' *f.*

menswear, *n.* Herrenkleidung *f.*

mental, *adj.* geistig.

mentality, *n.* Mentalität', -en *f.*

menthol, *n.* Menthol' *nt.*

mention, 1. *n.* Erwäh'nung, -en *f.* **2.** *vb.* erwäh'nen.

menu, *n.* Menü', -s *nt.;* Speisekarte, -n *f.*

mercantile, *adj.* kaufmännisch.

mercenary, *adj.* gewinnsüchtig.

merchandise, *n.* Ware, -n *f.*

merchant, *n.* Kaufmann, -leute *m.;* Geschäfts'mann, -leute *m.*

merchant marine, *n.* Handelsmarine, -n *f.*

merciful, *adj.* barmher'zig, gütig, gnädig.

merciless, *adj.* unbarmherzig, schonungslos.

mercury, *n.* Quecksilber *nt.*

mercy, *n.* Gnade *f.,* Mitleid *nt.* Erbar'men *nt.*

mere, *adj.* bloß, nichts als.

merely, *adv.* nur, bloß.

merge, *vb.* verschmel'zen*.

merger, *n.* Zusam'menschluß, -:sse *m.;* Fusion', -en *f.*

meringue, *n.* Baiser', -s *nt.*

merit, 1. *n.* Verdienst', -e *nt.;* Wert, -e *m.;* Vorzug, -:e *m.* **2.** *vb.* verdie'nen.

meritorious, *adj.* verdienst'lich.

mermaid, *n.* Nixe, -n *f.*

merriment, *n.* Fröhlichkeit, -en *f.*

merry, *adj.* fröhlich, lustig.

merry-go-round, *n.* Karussell', -s *nt.*

mesh, *n.* Netz, -e *nt.*

mess, *n.* Durcheinan'der *nt.;* Unordnung *f.;* Schlamas'sel *nt.; (mil.)* Eßsaal, -säle *m.*

message, *n.* Botschaft, -en *f.,* Nachricht, -en *f.*

messenger, *n.* Bote, -n, -n *m.*

messy, *adj.* unordentlich, schlampig.

metabolism, *n.* Stoffwechsel *m.*

metal, *n.* Metall', -e *nt.*

metallic, *adj.* metal'len.

metamorphosis, *n.* Metamor'pho'se, -n *f.*

metaphysics, *n.* Metaphysik' *f.*

meteor, *n.* Meteor', -e *m.*

meteorite, *n.* Meteorit', -e *m.*

meteorology, *n.* Meteorologie' *f.*

meter, *n. (unit of measure)* Meter, -r. -r or -r *m.; (recording device)* Zähler, - *m.*

method, *n.* Metho'de, -n *f.*

meticulous, *adj.* sorgfältig.

metric, *adj.* metrisch.

metropolis, *n.* Großstadt, -:e *f.*

metropolitan, *adj.* zur Großstadt gehö'rend.

mettle, *n.* Mut *m.*

Mexican, 1. *n.* Mexika'ner, - *m.* **2.** *adj.* mexika'nisch.

Mexico, *n.* Mexiko *nt.*

mezzanine, *n.* Zwischenstock *m.*

microbe, *n.* Mikro'be, -n *f.*

microfiche, *n.* Mikrofiche *f.*

microfilm, *n.* Mikrofilm, -e *m.*

microform, *n.* Mikroform *f.*

microphone, *n.* Mikrophon', -e *nt.*

microscope, *n.* Mikroskop', -e *nt.*

mild, *adj.* Mittel- *(cpds.); (in m. air)* mitten in der Luft.

middle, *n.* Mitte, -n *f.* **2.** *adj.* mittler-.

middle-aged, *adj.* in mittlerem Alter.

Middle Ages, *n.* Mittelalter *nt.*

middle class, *n.* Mittelstand, -:e *m.*

Middle East, *n.* Mittler-Osten *m.;* Nahost- *(cpds.)*

midget, *n.* Lilliputa'ner, - *m.*

midnight, *n.* Mitternacht *f.*

midwife, *n.* Hebamme, -n *f.*

mien, *n.* Miene, -n *f.*

might, *n.* Macht, -:e *f.*

mighty, *adj.* mächtig.

migraine, *n.* Migrä'ne *f.*

migrate, *vb.* wandern.

migration, *n.* Wanderung *f.*

migratory, *adj.* wandernd, Zug- *(cpds.).*

mildew, *n.* Schimmel *m.*

mildness, *n.* Milde *f.*

mile, *n.* Meile, -n *f.*

mileage, *n.* Meilenzahl *f.*

militant, *adj.* kriegerisch.

militarism, *n.* Militaris'mus *m.*

military, 1. *n.* Militär', -s *nt.* **2.** *adj.* militä'risch.

militia, *n.* Miliz', -en *f.*

milk, 1. *n.* Milch *f.* **2.** *vb.* melken*.

milkman, *n.* Milchmann, -:er *m.*

milky, *adj.* milchig.

mill, 1. *n.* Mühle, -n *f.; (factory)* Fabrik', -en *f.* **2.** *vb.* mahlen*.

miller, *n.* Müller, - *m.*

millimeter, *n.* Millime'ter, - *nt.*

millinery, *n.* Putzwaren *pl.*

million, *n.* Million', -en *f.*

millionaire, *n.* Millionär', -e *m.*

mimic, *n.* Schauspieler, - *m.* **2.** *vb.* nach'ahmen.

mince, *vb.* klein schneiden*; (he doesn't m. his words)* er nimmt kein Blatt vor den Mund.

mind, 1. *n.* Geist *m.,* Verstand' *m.,* Sinn *m.* **2.** *vb. (obey)* gehor'chen; *(watch over)* aufpassen auf; *(never m.)* das macht nichts.

mindful, *adj.* eingedenk.

mine, 1. *n.* Bergwerk, -e *nt.; (mil.)* Mine, -n *f.* **2.** *pron.* meiner, -es, -e. **3.** *vb.* ab'bauen; *(mil.)* Minen legen.

miner, *n.* Bergarbeiter, - *m.*

mineral, 1. *n.* Mineral', -e *nt.* **2.** *adj.* minera'lisch.

mingle, *vb.* mischen.

miniature, *n.* Miniatur', -en *f.*

miniaturize, *vb.* miniaturisie'ren.

minimal, *adj.* minimal'; Mindest-, Minimal'- *(cpds.).*

minimize, *vb.* herab'setzen.

minimum, *n.* Minimum, -ma *nt. & f.* **2.** *adj.* Mindest-, Minimal'- *(cpds.).*

mining, *n.* Bergbau *m.*

minister, *n. (government)* Mini'ster, - *m.; (church)* Pfarrer, - *m.,* Pastor, -o'ren *m.,* Geistlich- *m.*

ministry, *n. (government)* Mini'ste'rium, -rien *nt.; (church)* Geistlicher Stand *m.*

mink, *n.* Nerz, -e *m.*

minnow, *n.* Elritze, -n *f.*

minor, 1. *n.* Minderjährig *m.& f.* **2.** *adj.* gering'; minderjährig; *(music)* Moll *nt.,* (A-minor) a-Moll.

minority, *n.* Minderzahl, -en *f.,* Minderheit, -en *f.,* Minorität', -en *f.*

minstrel, *n.* Spielmann, -leute *m.*

mint, 1. *n. (plant)* Minze, -n *f.; (coin factory)* Münze, -n *f.* **2.** *vb.* münzen.

minus, *prep.* minus, weniger.

minute, 1. *n.* Minu'te, -n *f.* **2.** *adj.* winzig.

miracle, *n.* Wunder, - *nt.*

miraculous, *adj.* wie ein Wunder.

mirage, *n.* Luftspiegelung, -en *f.*

mire, *n.* Sumpf, ⸗e *m.;* Schlamm *m.*

mirror, *n.* Spiegel, - *m.*

mirth, *n.* Fröhlichkeit *f.*

misappropriate, *vb.* verun'treuen.

misbehave, *vb.* sich schlecht beneh'men*.

miscellaneous, *adj.* divers'.

mischief, *n.* Unfug *m.*

mischievous, *adj.* schelmisch.

misconstrue, *vb.* mißdeu'ten.

misdemeanor, *n.* Verge'hen, - *nt.*

miser, *n.* Geizhals, ⸗e *m.*

miserable, *adj.* jämmerlich, kläglich.

miserly, *adj.* geizig.

misery, *n.* Elend *nt.,* Jammer *m.*

misfit, *n.* Blindgänger, - *m.*

misfortune, *n.* Unglück, -e *nt.,* Pech *nt.*

misgiving, *n.* Beden'ken, - *nt.*

mishap, *n.* Unglück, -e *nt.*

mislay, *vb.* verle'gen.

mislead, *vb.* irre'führen.

misplace, *vb.* verle'gen.

mispronounce, *vb.* falsch aus-sprechen*.

miss, 1. *n.* Fehlschlag, ⸗e *m.* 2. *vb.* verfeh'len; *(feel the lack of)* vermis'sen; *(fail to obtain)* verpas'sen.

Miss, *n.* Fräulein, - *nt.*

missile, *n.* Wurfgeschoß, ⸗sse *nt.;* **(guided m.)** ferngesteuertes Rake'tengeschoß, -sse *nt.*

mission, *n.* Mission', -en *f.*

missionary, 1. *n.* Missionar', -e *m.* 2. *adj.* Missionars'-*(cpds.)*

misspell, *vb.* falsch buchstabie'ren.

mist, *n.* *(fog)* Nebel, - *m.;* *(haze)* Dunst, ⸗e *m.*

mistake, 1. *n.* Fehler, - *m.,* Irrtum, ⸗er *m.* 2. *vb.* verken'nen*.

mistaken, *adj.* falsch; irrig; **(be m.)** sich irren.

mister, *n.* Herr, -n, -en *m.*

mistletoe, *n.* Mistel, -n *f.*

mistreat, *vb.* mißhan'deln.

mistress, *n.* Herrin, -nen *f.; (of the house)* Hausfrau, -en *f.; (of a pet)* Frauchen, - *nt.; (lover)* Geliebt'-*f.*

mistrust, 1. *n.* Mißtrauen *nt.* 2. *vb.* mißtrau'en.

misty, *adj.* neblig; dunstig.

misunderstand, *vb.* mißverstehen*.

misuse, 1. *n.* Mißbrauch, ⸗e *m.* 2. *vb.* mißbrau'chen.

mite, *n.* Bißchen *nt.; (bug)* Milbe, -n *f.*

mitigate, *vb.* mildern.

mitten, *n.* Fausthandschuh, -e *m.*

---

mix, *vb.* mischen.

mixture, *n.* Mischung, -en *f.*

mix-up, *n.* Verwir'rung, -en *f.;* Verwechs'lung, -en *f.*

moan, *n.* stöhnen.

mob, *n.* Menschenmenge, -n *f.;* Pöbel *m.*

mobile, *adj.* beweg'lich; mobilisiert'.

mobilization, *n.* Mobil'machung, -en *f.*

mobilize, *vb.* mobilisie'ren.

mock, *vb.* *(tr.)* verspot'ten; *(intr.)* spotten.

mockery, *n.* Spott *m.,* Hohn *m.*

mod, *adj.* auffällig modern in Kleidung, Benehmen.

mode, *n.* *(way)* Art und Weise *f.; (fashion)* Mode, -n *f.*

model, 1. *n.* Vorbild, -er *nt.,* Muster, - *nt.;* Modell', -e *nt.* 2. *vb.* modellie'ren.

moderate, 1. *adj.* mäßig, gemä'ßigt. 2. *vb.* mäßigen; vermit'teln.

moderation, *n.* Mäßigung *f.*

modern, *adj.* modern'.

modernize, *vb.* modernisie'ren.

modest, *adj.* beschei'den.

modesty, *n.* Beschei'denheit *f.*

modify, *vb.* modifizie'ren.

modish, *adj.* modisch.

modulate, *vb.* modulie'ren.

moist, *adj.* feucht.

moisten, *vb.* befeuch'ten.

moisture, *n.* Feuchtigkeit *f.*

molar, *n.* Backenzahn ⸗e *m.*

molasses, *n.* Melas'se *f.;* Sirup *m.*

mold, 1. *n.* Form, -en *f.; (mildew)* Schimmel *m.* 2. *vb.* formen; schimmelig werden*.

moldy, *adj.* schimmelig.

mole, *n.* *(animal)* Maulwurf, ⸗e *m.; (mark)* Muttermal, -e *nt.*

molecule, *n.* Molekül', -e *nt.*

molest, *vb.* beläs'tigen.

molten, *adj.* flüssig.

moment, *n.* Augenblick, -e *m.,* Moment', -e *nt.; (factor)* Moment', -e *nt.*

momentary, *adj.* augenblick'lich, momentan'.

momentous, *adj.* folgenschwer.

monarch, *n.* Monarch', -en, -en *m.*

monarchy, *n.* Monarchie', -i'en *f.*

monastery, *n.* Kloster, ⸗ *nt.*

Monday, *n.* Montag, -e *m.*

monetary, *adj.* Geld'-*(cpds.)*

money, *n.* Geld, -er *nt.*

money changer, *n.* Geldwechsler, - *m.*

money order, *n.* Postanweisung, -en *f.*

mongrel, *n.* Bastard, -e *m.*

monitor, *n.* *(man)* Abhörer, - *m.; (apparatus)* Kontroll'gerät, -e *nt.*

monk, *n.* Mönch, -e *m.*

monkey, *n.* Affe, -n, -n *m.*

monocle, *n.* Mono'kel, - *nt.*

---

monologue, *n.* Monolog', -e *m.*

monopolize, *vb.* monopolisie'ren.

monopoly, *n.* Monopol', -e *nt.*

monotone, *n.* einförmiger Ton, ⸗e *m.*

monotonous, *adj.* eintönig, monoton'.

monotony, *n.* Eintönigkeit *f.,* Monotonie' *f.*

monster, *n.* Ungeheuer, - *nt.*

monstrosity, *n.* Ungeheuerlichkeit, -en *f.*

monstrous, *adj.* ungeheuerlich, haarsträubend.

month, *n.* Monat, -e *m.*

monthly, 1. *n.* Monatschrift, -en *f.* 2. *adj.* monatlich.

monument, *n.* Denkmal, ⸗er *nt.*

monumental, *adj.* monumental'.

mood, *n.* Stimmung, -en *f.;* Laune, -n *f.*

moody, *adj.* launisch; schwermütig.

moon, *n.* Mond, -e *m.*

moonlight, *n.* Mondschein *m.*

moor, 1. *n.* Moor, -e *nt.* 2. *vb.* veran'kern.

mooring, *n.* Ankerplatz, ⸗e *m.*

moot, *adj.* strittig.

mop, *n.* Mop, -s *m.*

moped, *n.* Mofa, -s *nt.*

moral, 1. *n.* Moral, -en *f.* 2. *adj.* sittlich, mora'lisch.

morale, *n.* Stimmung, -en *f.,* Moral' *f.*

moralist, *n.* Moralist', -en, -en *m.*

morality, *n.* Sittlichkeit *f.,* Moral' *f.;* Sittenlehre *f.*

morbid, *adj.* morbid'.

more, *adv.* mehr.

moreover, *adv.* außerdem.

morgue, *n.* Leichenhaus, ⸗er *nt.*

morning, *n.* Morgen, - *m.,* Vormittag, -e *m.*

moron, *n.* Schwachsinnige *m.&f.*

morose, *adj.* verdrieß'lich.

morphine, *n.* Morphium *nt.*

morsel, *n.* Bissen, - *m.*

mortal, *adj.* sterblich; tödlich.

mortality, *n.* Sterblichkeit *f.*

mortar, *n.* *(vessel)* Mörser, - *m.; (building material)* Mörtel *m.*

mortgage, *n.* Hypothek', -en *f.*

mortician, *n.* Leichenbestatter, - *m.*

mortify, *vb.* kastei'en; demütigen.

mortuary, *n.* Leichenhalle, -n *f.*

mosaic, *n.* Mosaik', -e *nt.*

mosquito, *n.* Mücke, -n *f.*

moss, *n.* Moos, -e *nt.*

mossy, *adj.* meist-.

mostly, *adv.* meistens, hauptsächlich.

moth, *n.* Motte, -n *f.*

mother, *n.* Mutter, ⸗ *f.*

mother-in-law, *n.* Schwiegermutter, ⸗ *f.*

motif, *n.* Motiv', -e *nt.*

motion, n. Bewe'gung, -en f.; (parliament) Antrag, -e m.

motionless, adj. bewe'gungslos.

motion picture, n. Film, -e m.

motivate, vb. veran'lassen, motivie'ren.

motivation, n. Motivie'rung, -en f.

motive, n. Beweg'grund, -e m.

motor, n. Motor, -o'ren m.

motorboat, n. Motorboot, -e nt.

motorcycle, n. Motorrad, -er nt.

motorist, n. Kraftfahrer, - m.

motto, n. Motto, -s nt.

mound, n. Erdhügel, - m.

mount, vb. (get on) bestei'gen*; (put on) montie'ren.

mountain, n. Berg, -e m.

mountaineer, n. Bergbewohner, - m.; Bergsteiger, - m.

mountainous, adj. bergig, gebir'gig.

mourn, vb. (intr.) trauern; (tr.) betrau'ern.

mournful, adj. trauervoll.

mourning, n. Trauer f.

mouse, n. Maus, -e f.

mouth, n. Mund, -er m.; (river) Mündung, -en f.

mouthpiece, n. (instrument) Mundstück, -e nt.; (spokesman) Wortführer, - m.

movable, adj. beweg'lich.

move, 1. n. (household goods) Umzug, -e m.; (motion) Bewe'gung, -en f.; (games) Zug, -e m. 2. vb. um-ziehen*; bewe'gen, sich bewe'gen; ziehen*; (parliamentary) bean'tragen.

movement, n. Bewe'gung, -en f.; (music) Satz, -e m.

movie, n. Kino, -s nt; Film, -e m.

moving, 1. n. Umzug, -e m. 2. adj. ergrei'fend.

mow, vb. mähen.

Mr., n. Herr m.

Mrs., n. Frau f.

much, adj. viel.

mucilage, n. Klebstoff, -e m.

muck, n. Schlamm m.

mucous, adj. schleimig.

mucus, n. Nasenschleim m.

mud, n. Schlamm m., Dreck m.

muddy, adj. schlammig, trübe.

muff, 1. n. Muff, -e m. 2. vb. vermas'seln.

muffle, vb. (wrap up) ein-hüllen; (silence) dämpfen.

muffler, n. (scarf) Schal, -s m.; (auto) Auspufftopf, -e m.

mug, n. Krug, -e m.

mulatto, n. Mulat'te, -n, -n m.

mule, n. Esel, - m.

mullah, n. Mullah, -s m.

multinational, adj. multinational'.

multiple, adj. vielfältig.

multiplication, n. Multiplikation', -en f.

multiply, vb. (math.) multiplizie'ren; (increase) verviel'fältigen.

multitude, n. Menge, -n f.

mummy, n. Mumie, -n f.

mumps, n. Ziegenpeter m.

Munich, n. München nt.

municipal, adj. städtisch.

munificent, adj. freigebig.

munition, n. Munition', -en f.

mural, n. Wandgemälde, - nt.

murder, 1. n. Mord, -e m. 2. vb. morden, ermor'den.

murderer, n. Mörder, - m.

murmur, 1. n. Gemur'mel, - nt. 2. vb. murmeln.

muscle, n. Muskel, -n m.

muscular, adj. muskulös; Muskel- (cpds.).

muse, 1. n. Muse, -n f. 2. vb. nach-denken*.

museum, n. Muse'um, -se'en nt.

mushroom, n. Pilz, -e m.

music, n. Musik' f.

musical, adj. musika'lisch.

musical comedy, n. Operet'te, -n f.

musician, n. Musiker, - m.

muslin, n. Musselin', -e m.

must, n. müssen*.

mustache, n. Schnurrbart, -e m.

mustard, n. Senf m., Mostrich m.

muster, 1. n. Musterung, -en f. 2. vb. mustern.

musty, adj. muffig.

mutation, n. Mutation', -en f.

mute, adj. stumm.

mutilate, vb. verstüm'meln.

mutiny, 1. n. Meuterei', -en f. 2. vb. meutern.

mutter, vb. murmeln.

mutton, n. Hammelfleisch nt.

mutual, adj. gegenseitig, gemein'sam.

muzzle, n. (gun) Mündung, -en f.; (animal's mouth) Maul, -er nt.; (mouth covering) Maulkorb, -e m.

my, adj. mein, -, -e.

myopia, n. Kurzsichtigkeit f.

myriad, 1. n. Myria'de, -n f.; (fig.) Unzahl, -en f. 2. adj. unzählig.

myrtle, n. Myrte, -n f.

mysterious, adj. geheim'nisvoll.

mystery, n. Geheim'nis, -se nt.; Rätsel, - nt.

mystic, 1. n. Mystiker, - m. 2. adj. mystisch; Geheim'- (cpds.).

mystify, vb. verwir'ren; verdun'keln.

myth, n. Sage, -n f.; Mythus, -then m.

mythical, adj. sagenhaft, mythisch.

mythology, n. Mythologie', -i'en f.

N

nag, 1. n. Gaul, -e m. 2. vb. herum'-nörgeln; keifen.

nail, 1. n. Nagel, - m. 2. vb. nageln.

naïve, adj. naiv', unbefangen.

naked, adj. nackt.

name, 1. n. Name(n), - m. 2. vb. nennen*.

namely, adv. nämlich.

namesake, n. Namensvetter, - m.

nap, 1. n. (sleep) Nickerchen, - nt., Nachmittagsschläfchen, - nt.; (cloth) Noppe, -n f. 2. vb. ein-nicken.

naphtha, n. Naphtha nt.

napkin, n. Serviet'te, -n f.; (sanitary n.) Binde, -n f.

narcissus, n. Narzis'se, -n f.

narcotic, 1. n. Rauschgift, -e nt. 2. adj. narko'tisch.

narrate, vb. erzäh'len.

narration, n. Erzäh'lung, -en f.

narrative, 1. n. Erzäh'lung, -en f. 2. adj. erzäh'lend.

narrow, adj. (tight, confined) eng; (not broad) schmal (-, -).

nasal, adj. nasal'.

nasty, adj. häßlich.

natal, adj. Geburts'- (cpds.).

nation, n. Nation', -en f., Volk -er nt.

national, 1. n. Staatsangehörig-m.&f. 2. adj. national'.

nationalism, n. Nationalis'mus m.

nationality, n. Staatsangehörigkeit, -en f., Nationalität', -en f.

nationalization, n. Verstaat'lichung, -en f.

nationalize, vb. verstaat'lichen.

native, 1. n. Eingeborenem.&f., Einheimisch- m.&f. 2. adj. gebür'tig, einheimisch.

nativity, n. Geburt', -en f.

natural, adj. natür'lich.

naturalist, n. Natur'forscher, - m., Naturalist', -en, -en m.

naturalize, vb. naturalisie'ren.

naturalness, n. Natür'lichkeit f.

nature, n. Natur', -en f.; (essence) Wesen nt.

naughty, adj. unartig.

nausea, n. Übelkeit f.

nauseating, adj. ekelerregend.

nautical, adj. nautisch.

naval, adj. See-, Schiffs-, Marı'ne- (cpds.).

nave, n. Kirchenschiff, -e nt.

navel, n. Nabel, - m.

navigable, adj. schiffbar.

navigate, vb. schiffen, steuern.

navigation, n. Schiffahrt f., Navigation' f.

navigator, n. Seefahrer, - m.; (airplane) Orter, - m.

navy, n. Mari'ne f.; Flotte, -n f.

navy yard, n. Mari'newerft, -en f.

near, 1. prep. in der Nähe von. 2. adj. nahe (näher, nächst-).

nearby, 1. adj. naheliegend, nahe gele'gen. 2. adv. in der Nähe.

nearly, adv. beinahe, fast.

near-sighted, adj. kurzsichtig.

neat, adj. sauber.

neatness, n. Sauberkeit f.

nebula, n. Nebelfleck, -e m.

nebulous, adj. nebelhaft.

necessary, adj. nötig, notwendig.

necessity, n. Notwendigkeit, -en f.

neck, n. Hals, ∸e m.

necklace, n. Halskette, -n f.

necktie, n. Schlips, -e m., Krawat'te, -n f.

nectar, n. Nektar m.

need, 1. n. Not, ∸e f.; Bedürf'nis, -se nt. 2. vb. benö'tigen, brauchen.

needful, adj. notwendig.

needle, n. Nadel, -n f.

needless, adj. unnötig.

needy, adj. notleidend.

negative, 1. n. (photo) Negativ, -e nt. 2. adj. vernei'nend, negativ.

neglect, 1. n. Vernach'lässigung, -en f. 2. vb. vernach'lässigen.

negligee, n. Negligé', -s nt.

negligent, adj. nachlässig, fahrlässig.

negligible, adj. gering'fügig.

negotiate, vb. verhan'deln.

negotiation, n. Verhand'lung, -en f.

Negro, n. Neger, - m.

neighbor, n. Nachbar, (-n), -n m.

neighborhood, n. Nachbarschaft, -en f.

neither, 1. pron. keiner, -es, -e (von beiden). 2. conj. (n. . . nor) weder . . . noch.

neon, n. Neon nt.

nephew, n. Neffe, -n, -n m.

nepotism, n. Nepotis'mus m.

nerve, n. Nerv, -en m.; (effrontery) Dreistigkeit f.

nervous, adj. nervös'.

nest, n. Nest, -er m.

nestle, vb. nisten; (fig.) sich an'schmiegen.

net, 1. n. Netz, -e nt. 2. adj. netto.

network, n. Netz, -e nt.

neuralgia, n. Neuralgie' f.

neurology, n. Neurologie' f.

neurotic, adj. neuro'tisch.

neutral, adj. neutral', unparteiisch.

neutrality, n. Neutralität' f.

neutron, n. Neutron, -o'nen nt.

neutron bomb, n. Neutro'nenbombe, -n f.

never, adv. nie, niemals.

nevertheless, adv. dennoch, trotzdem.

new, adj. neu.

news, n. Nachrichten pl.; (item of n.) Nachricht, -en f.

newsboy, n. Zeitungsjunge, -n, -n m.

newscast, n. Nachrichtensendung, -en f.

newspaper, n. Zeitung, -en f.

newsreel, n. Wochenschau f.

next, adj. nächst-.

nibble, vb. knabbern.

nice, adj. nett, hübsch.

nick, n. Kerbe, -n f.

nickel, n. Nickel nt.

nickname, n. Spitzname(n), - m.

nicotine, n. Nikotin' nt.

niece, n. Nichte, -n f.

niggardly, adj. knauserig.

night, n. Nacht, ∸e f.

night club, n. Nachtlokal, -e nt.

nightgown, n. Nachthemd, -en nt.

nightingale, n. Nachtigall, -en f.

nightly, adj. nächtlich, jede Nacht.

nightmare, n. böser Traum, ∸e m., Alpdruck m.

nimble, adj. flink.

nine, num. neun.

nineteen, num. neunzehn.

nineteenth, 1. adj. neunzehnt-. 2. n. Neunzehntel, - nt.

ninetieth, 1. adj. neunzigst-. 2. n. Neunzigstel, - nt.

ninety, num. neunzig.

ninth, 2. adj. neunt-. 2. n. Neuntel, - nt.

nip, 1. n. Zwick, -e m.; (drink) Schlückchen, - nt. 2. vb. zwicken.

nipple, n. Brustwarze, -n f.; (baby's bottle) Sauger, - m.

nitrate, n. Nitrat', -e nt.

nitrogen, n. Stickstoff m.

no, 1. adj. kein, -e, -e. 2. interj. nein.

nobility, n. Adel m.

noble, adj. (rank) adlig; (character) edel.

nobleman, n. Adlig- m.

nobody, pron. niemand, keiner.

nocturnal, adj. nächtlich.

nocturne, n. Noktur'ne, -n f.

nod, vb. nicken.

no-frills, adj. einfach, ohne Verschönerung.

noise, n. Geräusch', -e nt.; Lärm m.

noiseless, adj. geräusch'los.

noisy, adj. laut.

nomad, n. Noma'de, -n, -n m.

nominal, adj. nominal'.

nominate, vb. ernen'nen*; (candidate) auf'stellen.

nomination, n. Ernen'nung, -en f.; Kandidatur', -en f.

nominee, n. Kandidat', -en, -en m.

non-aligned, adj. blockfrei.

nonchalant, adj. zwanglos, nonchalant.

noncombatant, n. Nichtkämpfer, - m.

non-commissioned officer, n. Unteroffizier, -e m.

noncommittal, adj. nichtverpflich'tend.

nondescript, adj. unbestimmbar.

none, pron. keiner, -es, -e.

nonpartisan, adj. unparteiisch.

nonsense, n. Unsinn m.

nonstop, adj. durchgehend.

noodle, n. Nudel, -n f.

nook, n. Ecke, -n f., Winkel, - m.

noon, n. Mittag m.

noose, n. Schlinge, -n f.

nor, conj. noch.

normal, adj. normal', gewöhn'lich.

north, 1. n. Norden m. 2. adj. nördlich; Nord- (cpds.).

northeast, 1. n. Nordos'ten m. 2. adj. nordöst'lich; Nordost-(cpds.).

northeastern, adj. nordöst'lich.

northern, adj. nördlich.

North Pole, n. Nordpol m.

northwest, 1. n. Nordwes'ten m. 2. adj. nordwest'lich; Nordwest- (cpds.).

Norway, n. Norwegen nt.

Norwegian, 1. n. Norweger, - m. 2. adj. norwegisch.

nose, n. Nase, -n f.

nosebleed, n. Nasenbluten nt.

nose dive, n. Sturz, ∸e m.; (airplane) Sturzflug m.

nostalgia, n. Heimweh nt.; Sehnsucht f.

nostril, n. Nasenloch, ∸er nt., Nüster, -n f.

not, adv. nicht; (n. a, n. any) kein, -, -e.

notable, adj. bemer'kenswert.

notary, n. Notar', -e m.

notation, n. Aufzeichnung, -en f.

notch, 1. n. Kerbe, -n f. 2. vb. ein-kerben.

note, 1. n. Notiz', -en f.; (comment) Anmerkung, -en f.; (music) Note, -n f.; (letter) kurzer Brief, -e m. 2. vb. bemer'ken.

note-book, n. Notiz'buch, ∸er nt., Heft, -e nt.

noted, adj. bekannt'.

notepaper, n. Notiz'block, ∸e m.; Schreibblock, ∸e m.

noteworthy, adj. beach'tenswert.

nothing, pron. nichts.

notice, 1. n. (attention) Beach'tung, -en f.; (poster) Bekannt'machung, -en f.; (announcement) Anzeige, -n f.; (give n.) kündigen. 2. vb. beach'ten; bemer'ken.

noticeable, adj. bemer'kenswert; (conspicuous) auffällig.

notification, n. Benach'richtigung, -en f.

notify, vb. benach'richtigen.

notion, n. Vorstellung, -en f., Idee', -de'en f.; (n.s, articles) Kurzwaren pl.

notoriety, n. Verruf' m., Verru'fenheit f.

notorious, adj. berüch'tigt.

notwithstanding, 1. prep. ungeachtet, trotz. **2.** adv. nichtsdestoweniger.

noun, n. Hauptwort, ⸗er nt., Substantiv, -e nt.

nourish, vb. nähren; ernäh'ren.

nourishment, n. Nahrung, -en f.

novel, 1. n. Roman', -e m. **2.** adj. neu.

novelist, n. Roman'schriftsteller, - m.

novelty, n. Neuheit, -en f.

November, n. Novem'ber m.

novena, n. Nove'ne, -n f.

novice, n. Neuling, -e m.

novocaine, n. Novocain' nt.

now, adv. jetzt, nun.

nowhere, adv. nirgends.

nozzle, n. Düse, -n f.; (gun) Mündung, -en f.

nuance, n. Nuan'ce, -n f.

nuclear, adj. Kern- (cpds.); nukleaf.

nuclear warhead, n. nuklea'rer Sprengkopf m.

nuclear waste, n. Atom'müll m.

nucleus, n. Kern, -e m.

nude, adj. nackt.

nugget, n. Klumpen, - m.

nuisance, n. Ärgernis, -se nt.; (be a n.) ärgerlich, lästig sein°.

nuke, n. Rakete mit nuklearem Sprengkopf.

nullify, vb. annullie'ren, aufheben°.

number, 1. n. Zahl, -en f.; (figure) Ziffer, -n f.; (magazine, telephone, house) Nummer, -n f.; (amount) Anzahl, -en f. **2.** vb. numerie'ren; (amount to) sich belau'fen auf.

numerical, adj. zahlenmäßig.

numerous, adj. zahlreich.

nun, n. Nonne, -n f.

nuptial, adj. Hochzeits-, Ehe- (cpds.).

nurse, 1. n. Krankenschwester, -n f. **2.** vb. pflegen; (suckle) stillen.

nursery, n. Kinderzimmer, - nt.; (plants) Pflanzschule, -n f.

nurture, vb. ernäh'ren, nähren; (fig.) hegen.

nut, n. Nuß, ⸗sse f.

nutcracker, n. Nußknacker, - m.

nutrition, n. Ernäh'rung f.

nutritious, adj. nahrhaft.

nylon, n. Nylon nt.

nymph, n. Nymphe, -n f.

O

oak, n. Eiche, -n f.

oar, n. Ruder, - nt.

oasis, n. Oa'se, -n f.

oath, n. (pledge) Eid, -e m., Schwur, ⸗e m.; (curse) Fluch, ⸗e m.

oatmeal, n. Hafergrütze f.

oats, n. Hafer m.; Haferflocken pl.

obedience, n. Gehor'sam m.

obedient, adj. gehor'sam.

obeisance, n. Ehrerbietung, -en f.

obese, adj. fettleibig.

obey, vb. gehor'chen, befol'gen.

obituary, n. Nachruf, -e m.

object, 1. n. Gegenstand, ⸗e m.; (aim) Ziel, -e nt.; (purpose) Zweck, -e m.; (gram.) Objekt', -e nt. **2.** vb. einwenden°, Einspruch erhe'ben°.

objection, n. Einwand, ⸗e m., Einspruch, ⸗e m.

objectionable, adj. widerwärtig.

objective, 1. n. Ziel, -e nt.; (photo) Objektiv', -e nt. **2.** adj. sachlich, objektiv'.

obligation, n. Verpflich'tung, -en f.

obligatory, adj. obligato'risch.

oblige, vb. verpflich'ten; jemandem gefäl'lig sein°.

obliging, adj. gefäl'lig.

oblique, adj. schief, schräg.

obliterate, vb. aus·radieren, vernich'ten.

oblivion, n. Verges'senheit f.

oblong, adj. länglich; rechteckig.

obnoxious, adj. widerlich.

obscene, adj. unanständig, obszön'.

obscure, adj. dunkel.

obsequious, adj. unterwür'tig.

observance, n. Beach'tung, -en f.; (celebration) Feier f.

observation, n. Beob'achtung, -en f.

observatory, n. Sternwarte, -n f.

observe, vb. beob'achten; befol'gen.

observer, n. Beob'achter, - m.

obsession, n. fixe Idee', -de'en f.

obsolete, adj. veral'tet, überholt'.

obstacle, n. Hindernis, -se nt.

obstetrical, adj. geburts'hilflich.

obstetrician, n. Geburts'helfer, - m.

obstinate, adj. hartnäckig.

obstreperous, adj. lautmäulig.

obstruct, vb. versper'ren, hindern.

obstruction, n. Hindernis, -se nt.

obtain, vb. erhal'ten°, bekom'men°.

obviate, vb. besei'tigen.

obvious, adj. selbstverständlich, offensichtlich.

occasion, n. Gele'genheit, -en f.

occasional, adj. gele'gentlich.

Occident, n. Abendland nt.

occidental, adj. abendländisch.

occult, adj. verbor'gen, okkult'.

occupant, n. Inhaber, - m., Insasse, -n, -n m., Bewoh'ner, - m.

occupation, n. (profession) Beruf', -e m.; (mil.) Beset'zung, -en f.; (o. forces) Besat'zung, -en f.

occupy, vb. (take up) einnehmen°; (keep busy) beschäf'tigen; (mil.) beset'zen.

occur, vb. vor'kommen°, gesche'hen°, passie'ren.

occurrence, n. Ereig'nis, -se nt.

ocean, n. Ozean, -e m.

o'clock, n. Uhr f.

octagon, n. Achteck, -e nt.

octave, n. Okta've, -n f.

October, n. Okto'ber m.

octopus, n. Tintenfisch, -e m.

ocular, adj. Augen- (cpds.).

oculist, n. Augenarzt, ⸗e m.

odd, adj. (numbers) ungerade; (queer) merkwürdig.

oddity, n. Merkwürdigkeit, -en f.

odds, n.pl. Chance, -n f.; (probability) Wahrschein'lichkeit, -en f.; (advantage) Vorteil, -e m.

odious, adj. verhaßt'.

odor, n. Geruch', ⸗e m.

of, prep. von.

off, adv. ab.

offend, vb. verlet'zen, belei'digen.

offender, n. Missetäter, - m.

offense, n. (crime) Verge'hen, - nt.; (offensive) Offensi've, -n f.; (insult) Kränkung, -en f.

offensive, 1. n. Offensi've, -n f. **2.** adj. anstößig.

offer, 1. n. Angebot, -e nt. **2.** vb. an·bieten°.

offering, n. Opfer, - nt., Spende, -n f.

offhand, adj. beiläufig.

office, n. Amt, ⸗er nt.; (room) Büro, -s nt.; (doctor's, dentist's o.) Praxis f.

officer, n. Offizier', -e m.; (police) Polizist', -en, -en m.

official, 1. n. Beamt'- me 2. adj. amtlich, offiziell'.

officiate, vb. amtie'ren.

offspring, n. Abkömmling, -e m.

often, adv. oft, häufig.

oil, n. Öl, -e nt.; Petro'leum nt. **2.** vb. ölen.

oily, adj. ölig, fettig.

ointment, n. Salbe, -n f.

okay, adj. okay.

old, adj. alt (⸗).

old-fashioned, adj. altmodisch.

olive, n. Oli've, -n f.

ombudsman, n. Ombudsmann, ⸗er m.

omelet, n. Omelett', -e nt.

omen, n. Omen nt.

ominous, adj. unheilvoll.

omission, n. Versäum'nis, -se nt., Überse'hen, - nt.

omit, vb. aus·lassen*, unter·las'sen*.

omnibus, n. Omnibus, -se m.

omnipotent, adj. allmäch'tig.

on, prep. auf, an.

once, adv. einmal.

one, 1. pron. man; einer, -es, -e. 2. adj. ein, -, -e. 3. num. eins.

one-sided, adj. einseitig.

one-way, adj. Einbahn- (cpds.).

onion, n. Zwiebel, -n f.

only, 1. adj. einzig. 2. adv. nur.

onslaught, n. Angriff, -e m.

onward, adv. vorwärts.

ooze, vb. hervor'·quellen*.

opacity, n. Undurchsichtigkeit f.

opal, n. Opal', -e m.

opaque, adj. undurchsichtig.

open, 1. adj. offen. 2. adv. offen, auf. 3. vb. öffnen, auf·machen; (inaugurate) eröff'nen.

opening, 1. n. (hole) Öffnung, -en f.; (inauguration) Eröff'nung, -en f. 2. adj. eröff'nend.

opera, n. Oper, -n f.

opera-glasses, n.-pl. Opernglas, -er nt.

operate, vb. operie'ren.

operatic, adj. Opern- (cpds.).

operation, n. Verfah'ren, - nt.; Unterneh'men, - nt.; (med.) Operation', -en f.

operator, n.(of a machine) Bedie'ner, - m.; (telephone) Telefon'fräulein, - nt., Vermitt'lung f.; (manager) Manager, - m.

operetta, n. Operet'te, -n f.

ophthalmic, adj. Augen- (cpds.).

opinion, n. Meinung, -en f., Ansicht, -en f.

opponent, n. Gegner, - m.

opportunism, n. Opportunis'mus m.

opportunity, n. günstige Gele'genheit, -en f., Chance, -n f.

oppose, vb. sich widerset'zen.

opposite, 1. n. Gegenteil, -e nt.; (contrast) Gegensatz, -e m. 2. adj. entge'gengesetzt. 3. adv. gegenü'ber.

opposition, n. Opposition', -en f.

oppress, vb. unterdrü'cken.

oppression, n. Unterdrü'ckung, -en f.

oppressive, adj. tyran'nisch; bedrü'ckend, drü'ckend.

oppressor, n. Unterdrü'cker, - m.

optic, adj. optisch.

optician, n. Optiker, - m.

optics, n. Optik f.

optimism, n. Optimis'mus m.

optimistic, adj. optimis'tisch.

option, n. Wahl, -en f.; (privi-

lege of buying) Vorkaufsrecht, -e nt.

optional, adj. freigestellt, fakultativ'.

optometry, n. praktische Augenheilkunde f.

opulence, n. Üppigkeit f.

opulent, adj. üppig.

or, conj. oder.

oracle, n. Ora'kel, - nt.

oral, adj. mündlich.

orange, 1. n. Apfelsi'ne, -n f., Oran'ge, -n f. 2. adj. orange'farbig; (pred. adj. only) orange'.

oration, n. Rede, -n f.

orator, n. Redner, - m.

oratory, n. Redekunst f.

orbit, n. Bahn, -en f.; Gestirns'-, Plane'tenbahn, -en f.

orchard, n. Obstgarten, -e m.

orchestra, n. (large) Orches'ter, - nt.; (small) Kapel'le, -n f.

orchid, n. Orchide'e, -n f.

ordain, vb. in den geistlichen Stand auf·nehmen*.

ordeal, n. Qual, -en f.

order, 1. n. (command) Befehl', -e m.; (neatness) Ordnung f.; (decree) Erlaß, -sse m., Verord'nung, -en f.; (fraternity, medal) Orden, - m. 2. vb. (command) befehl'len*; (put in o.) ordnen; (decree) verord'nen.

orderly, adj. ordentlich; geord'net.

ordinance, n. Verord'nung, -en f.

ordinary, adj. gewöhn'lich.

ore, n. Erz, -e nt.

organ, n. Organ', -e nt.; (music) Orgel, -n f.

organic, adj. orga'nisch.

organism, n. Organis'mus, -men m.

organist, n. Organist', -en, -en m.

organization, n. Organisation', -en f.

organize, vb. organisie'ren.

organdy, n. Organ'dy m.

orgy, n. Orgie, -n f.

orient, vb. orientie'ren.

Orient, n. Orient m.

Oriental, adj. orienta'lisch.

orientation, n. Orientie'rung, -en f.

origin, n. Ursprung, -e m.

original, adj. ursprünglich; (novel) originell'.

originality, n. Originalität' -en f.

ornament, 1. n. Verzie'rung, -en f., Schmuck m. 2. vb. verzie'ren, schmücken.

ornamental, adj. dekorativ'.

ornate, adj. überla'den.

ornithology, n. Vogelkunde f.

orphan, n. Waise, -n f.

orphanage, n. Waisenhaus, -er nt.

orthodox, adj. orthodox'.

orthography, n. Rechtschrei-

bung, -en f., Orthographie', -i'en f.

orthopedic, adj. orthopä'disch.

oscillate, vb. schwingen*.

osmosis, n. Osmo'se f.

ostensible, adj. augenscheinlich.

ostentation, n. Schaustellung f.

ostentatious, adj. ostentativ'.

ostracize, vb. ächten.

ostrich, n. Strauß, -e m.

other, adj. ander-.

otherwise, adv. sonst.

ouch, interj. au!

ought, vb. sollte; (o. to have) hätte . . . sollen.

ounce, n. Unze, -n f.

our, adj. unser, -, -e.

ours, pron. unserer, -es, -e.

oust, vb. enthe'ben* (eines Amtes).

out, adv. aus, hin-, heraus'.

outbreak, n. Ausbruch, -e m.

outburst, n. Ausbruck, -e m.

outcast, n. Ausgestoßen- m.&f.

outcome, n. Ergeb'nis, -se nt.

outdoors, adv. draußen, im Freien.

outer, adj. äußer-.

outfit, 1. n. Ausrüstung, -en f.; (mil.) Einheit, -en f. 2. vb. aus·rüsten.

outgrowth, n. Folge, -n f.

outing, n. Ausflug, -e m.

outlandish, adj. bizarr'.

outlaw, 1. n. Gesetz'los- m. 2. vb. verbie'ten*.

outlet, n. Abfluß, -sse m.; (fig.) Ventil', -e nt.; (elec.) Steckdose, -n f.

outline, 1. n. Umriß, -sse m., Kontur', -en f.; (summary) Übersicht, -en f. 2. vb. um·rei'ßen*.

outlive, vb. überle'ben, überdau'ern.

out of, prep. aus.

out-of-date, adj. veral'tet, überholt'.

outpost, n. Vorposten, - m.

output, n. Leistung, -en f., Produktion', -en f.; (computer) Output, -s m., Ausgabe, -n f.

outrage, n. Frevel, - m.

outrageous, adj. unerhört.

outrank, vb. einen höheren Rang bekleiden.

outright, adj. uneingeschränkt.

outrun, vb. hinter sich lassen*.

outside, 1. n. Außenseite, -n f.; 2. adj. äußer-. 3. adv. draußen. 4. prep. außer, außerhalb.

outskirts, n. Außenbezirke pl.

outward, adj. äußerlich.

oval, adj. oval'.

ovary, n. Eierstock, -e m.

ovation, n. Huldigung, -en f.

oven, n. Ofen, -e m.

over, 1. prep. über. 2. adv. über; hin-, herü'ber; (past) vorbei'.

overbearing, adj. anmaßend.

overcoat, n. Mantel, -e m., Überzieher, - m.

overcome, vb. überwin'den*.
overdue, adj. überfällig.
overflow, 1. n. Überfluß, -sse m. 2. vb. über-fließen*.
overhaul, vb. überho'len.
overhead, 1. n. laufende Unkosten pl. 2. adv. oben.
overkill, n. Overkill nt.; übertriebenes Vernichtungsvermögen nt.
overlook, vb. überse'hen*.
overnight, adv. über Nacht.
overpass, n. Unterführ'rung, -en f.
overpower, vb. überwäl'tigen.
overrule, vb. überstim'men.
overrun, vb. überlau'fen*, (flood) überflu'ten.
oversee, vb. beauf'sichtigen.
oversight, n. Überse'hen, - nt.
overt, adj. offen.
overtake, vb. ein·holen.
overthrow, 1. n. Sturz m. 2. vb. stürzen; um·werfen*.
overtime, n. Überstunden pl.
overture, n. (music) Ouvertü're, -n f.; Annäherung, -en f.
overturn, vb. um·stürzen.
overview, n. Übersicht f.
overweight, n. Übergewicht nt.
overwhelm, vb. überwäl'tigen.
overwork, vb. überar'beiten.
owe, vb. schulden.
owing, adj. schuldig; (o. to) dank.
owl, n. Eule, -n f.
own, 1. adj. eigen. 2. vb. besit'zen*.
owner, n. Besitz'er,- m., Eigentümer, - m., Inhaber, - m.
ox, n. Ochse, -n m.
oxygen, n. Sauerstoff m.
oyster, n. Auster, -n f.

P

pace, n. Schritt, -e m.; (fig.) Tempo, -pi nt.
pacific, adj. friedlich.
Pacific Ocean, n. Stiller Ozean m.
pacifier, n. (baby's) Schnuller, - m.
pacifism, n. Pazifis'mus m.
pacifist, n. Pazifist', -en, -en m.
pacify, vb. beschwich'tigen.
pack, 1. n. Bündel, - nt.; (gang) Bande, -n f.; (cards) Kartenspiel, -e nt.; (animals) Rudel, - nt. 2. vb. packen.
package, n. Paket', -e nt.
packing, n. Dichtung, -en f.
pact, n. Pakt, -e m.
pad, 1. n. Polster, - nt.; (paper) Block, -s m. 2. vb. polstern.
padding, n. Polsterung, -en f.
paddle, 1. n. Paddel, - nt. 2. vb. paddeln.
padlock, n. Vorlegeschloß, -sser nt.
pagan, adj. heidnisch.

page, 1. n. (book) Seite, -n f.; (servant) Page, -n, -n m. 2. vb. suchen lassen.
pageant, n. prunkvoller Aufzug, -e m.
pail, n. Eimer, - m.
pain, 1. n. Schmerz, -en m. 2. vb. schmerzen.
painful, adj. schmerzlich, schmerzhaft.
painstaking, adj. sorgfältig.
paint, 1. n. Farbe, -n f. 2. vb. malen.
painter, n. Maler, - m.
painting, n. Bild, -er nt., Malerei', -en f.
pair, n. Paar, -e nt.
palace, n. Schloß, -sser nt., Palast', -e m.
palatable, adj. schmackhaft.
palate, n. Gaumen, - m.
palatial, adj. palast'artig.
pale, adj. blaß (-, -).
paleness, n. Blässe f.
palette, n. Palet'te, -n f.
pall, vb. schal werden*.
pallbearer, n. Sargträger, - m.
palm, n. (tree) Palme, -n f.; (hand) Handfläche, -n f.
palpitate, vb. klopfen.
paltry, adj. armselig.
pamper, vb. verzär'teln.
pamphlet, n. Broschü're, -n f.
pan, 1. n. Pfanne, -n f. 2. vb. herun'ter·machen.
panacea, n. Universal'mittel, - nt.
pancake, n. Pfannkuchen, - m.
pane, n. Glasscheibe, -n f.
panel, n. (wood) Einsatzstück, -e nt., Täfelung f.; (group of men) Diskussionsgruppe, -n f.; (dashboard) Armatu'renbrett, -er nt.
pang, n. plötzlicher Schmerz, -en m.
panic, n. Panik f.
panorama, n. Panora'ma, -men nt.
pant, vb. keuchen, schnaufen.
panther, n. Panther, - m.
pantomime, n. Pantomi'me, -n f.
pantry, n. Speisekammer, -n f.
pants, n. Hose, -n f.
pantyhose, n. Strumpfhose, -n f.
papal, adj. päpstlich.
paper, 1. n. Papier', -e nt.; (news) Zeitung, -en f. 2. adj. papieren; Papier'- (cpds.).
paperback, n. Taschenausgabe, -n f.
paper-hanger, n. Tapezie'rer, - m.
par, n. Pari nt.
parachute, n. Fallschrim, -e m.
parade, n. Para'de, -n f.
paradise, n. Paradies' nt.
paradox, n. Paradox', -e m.
paraffin, n. Paraffin', -e nt.
paragraph, n. Paragraph', -en, -en m.; (typing) Absatz, -e m.

parallel, 1. n. Paralle'le, -n f. 2. adj. parallel'.
paralysis, n. Lähmung, -en f.
paralyze, vb. lähmen.
paramedic, n. jemand, der Erste Hilfe bei Unglücksfällen leistet.
parameter, n. Para'meter, - m.
paramount, adj. oberst-.
paraphrase, vb. umschrei'ben*.
parasite, n. Schmarot'zer, - m.
parcel, n. Päckchen, - nt.; Paket', -e nt.
parch, vb. dörren.
parchment, n. Pergament', -e nt.
pardon, 1. n. Verzei'hung, -en f.; (legal) Begna'digung, -en f. 2. vb. verzei'hen*; begna'digen.
pare, vb. schälen.
parentage, n. Herkunft. -e f.
parenthesis, n. Klammer, -n f.
parents, n. pl. Eltern pl.
Paris, n. Paris' nt.
parish, n. Kirchspiel, -e nt., Gemein'de, -n f.
Parisian, 1. n. Pari'ser, - m. 2. adj. pari'sisch.
park, 1. n. Park, -s m. 2. vb. parken.
parking meter, n. Parkuhr, -en f.
parkway, n. Ausfallstrasse, -n f.
parliament, n. Parlament', -e nt.
parliamentary, adj. parlamenta'risch.
parlor, n. gute Stube, -n f., Salon', -s m.
parochial, adj. Pfarr-, Gemein'de- (cpds.); (fig.) beschränkt'.
parody, n. Parodie', -i'en f.
parrot, n. Papagei', -en m.
parsimony, n. Geiz m.
parsley, n. Petersi'lie f.
parson, n. Geistlich-m.
part, 1. n. Teil, -e m.; (hair) Scheitel, - m.; (theater) Rolle -n f. 2. vb. trennen.
partake, vb. teil·nehmen*.
partial, adj. Teil- (cpds.); partei'isch.
partiality, n. Voreingenommenheit f.
participant, n. Teilnehmer, - m.
participate, vb. teil·nehmen*.
participation, n. Teilnahme f.
participle, n. Partizip', -ien nt.
particle, n. Teilchen, - nt.
particular, adj. beson'der-.
parting, n. Abschied, -e m.
partisan, 1. n. Anhänger, - m., Partisan', (-en,) -en m. 2. adj. partei'isch.
partition, n. Teilung, -en f.; (wall) Scheidewand, -e f.
partly, adv. teilweise, teils.
partner, n. Teilhaber, - m.; (games) Partner, - m.

part of speech, *n.* Redeteil, -e *m.*, Wortart, -en *f.*

party, *n. (pol.)* Partei', -en *f.; (social)* Gesell'schaft, -en *f.*

pass, 1. *n. (mountain)* Paß, ֿsse *m; (identification)* Ausweis, -e *m.* **2.** *vb.* vorü'ber·gehen*; *(car)* überho'len; *(exam)* beste'hen*; *(to hand)* reichen.

passable, *adj. (roads)* befahr'bar; *(fig.)* erträg'lich, passa'bel.

passage, *n.* Durchgang, ֿe *m.*, Durchfahrt, -en *f.; (steamer)* Überfahrt, -en *f.; (law)* Annahme, -n *f.*

passenger, *n.* Passagier', -e *m.*

passer-by, *n.* Passant', -en, -en *m.*

passion, *n.* Leidenschaft, -en *f.; (Christ)* Passion' *f.*

passionate, *adj.* leidenschaftlich.

passive, 1. *n.* Passiv *nt.* **2.** *adj.* passiv.

passport, *n.* Paß, ֿsse *m.*

past, 1. *n.* Vergan'genheit *f.* **2.** *adj.* vergan'gen, früher. **3.** *adv.* vorbei', vorü'ber.

paste, 1. *n.* Paste, -n *f.; (mucilage)* Klebstoff, -e *m.* **2.** *vb.* kleben.

pasteurize, *vb.* pasteurisie'ren.

pastime, *n.* Zeitvertreib *m.*

pastor, *n.* Pfarrer, - *m.*

pastry, *n.* Gebäck' *nt.*

pastry shop, *n.* Bäckerei', -en *f.*

pasture, *n.* Weide, -n *f.*

pat, 1. *n.* Klaps, -e *m.* **2.** *vb.* einen leichten Schlag geben*.

patch, 1. *n.* Flicken, - *m.* **2.** *vb.* flicken.

patchwork, *n.* Flickwerk *nt.*

patent, *n.* Patent', -e *nt.*

patent leather, *n.* Lackleder *nt.*

paternal, *adj.* väterlich.

path, *n.* Weg, -e *m.*, Pfad, -e *m.*

pathetic, *adj.* rührend, armselig.

pathology, *n.* Pathologie' *f.*

patience, *n.* Geduld' *f.*

patient, 1. *n.* Patient', -en, -en *m.* **2.** *adj.* geduld'dig.

patio, *n.* Patio, -s *m.*

patriarch, *n.* Patriarch', -en, -en *m.*

patriot, *n.* Patriot', -en, -en *m.*

patriotic, *adj.* patrio'tisch.

patriotism, *n.* Patriotis'mus *m.*

patrol, 1. *n.* Streife, -n *f.* **2.** *vb.* patrouillie'ren.

patrolman, *n.* Polizist', -en, -en *m.*

patron, *n.* Schutzherr, -n, -en *m.; (client)* Kunde, -n, -n *m.*

patronage, *n.* Schirmherrschaft *f.*

patronize, *vb.* begün'stigen.

pattern, *n.* Muster, - *m.; (sewing)* Schnittmuster, - *nt.*

pauper, *n.* Arm- *m.&f.*

pause, *n.* Pause, -n *f.*

pave, *vb.* pflastern.

pavement, *n.* Pflaster, - *nt.*

pavillion, *n.* Pavillon, -s *m.*

paw, *n.* Pfote, -n *f.*

pawn, 1. *n.* Pfand, ֿer *m.; (chess)* Bauer, (-n,) -n *m.* **2.** *vb.* pfänden.

pay, 1. *n.* Bezah'lung *f.*, Gehalt', ֿer *nt.* **2.** *vb.* bezah'len.

payment, *n.* Bezah'lung *f.; (installment)* Rate, -n *f.*

pea, *n.* Erbse, -n *f.*

peace, *n.* Friede(n), - *m.*

peaceful, *adj.* friedlich.

peach, *n.* Pfirsich, -e *m.*

peacock, *n.* Pfau, -e *m.*

peak, *n.* Gipfel, - *m.*

peal, *vb.* läuten, dröhnen.

peanut, *n.* Erdnuß, ֿsse *f.*

pear, *n.* Birne, -n *f.*

pearl, *n.* Perle, -n *f.*

peasant, *n.* Bauer, (-n,) -n *m.*

pebble, *n.* Kieselstein, -e *m.*

peck, *vb.* picken.

peculiar, *adj.* merkwürdig, beson'der-.

peculiarity, *n.* Beson'derheit, -en *f.*

pedal, *n.* Pedal', -e *nt.*

pedant, *n.* Pedant', -en, -en *m.*

peddler, *n.* Hausie'rer, - *m.*

pedestal, *n.* Sockel, - *m.*

pedestrian, *n.* Fußgänger, - *m.*

pediatrician, *n.* Kinderarzt, ֿe *m.*

pedigree, *n.* Stammbaum, ֿe *m.*

peek, *vb.* gucken.

peel, 1. *n.* Schale, -n *f.* **2.** *vb.* schälen.

peep, *vb. (look)* lugen; *(chirp)* piepsen.

peer, *n.* Ebenbürtig- *m.*

peg, *n.* Pflock, ֿe *m.; Stift, -e *m.*

pelt, 1. *n.* Fell, -e *nt.* **2.** *vb.* bewer'fen*; nieder·prasseln.

pelvis, *n.* Becken, - *nt.*

pen, *n.* Feder, -n *f.; (sty)* Stall, ֿe *m.* **2.** *vb.* schreiben*.

penalty, *n.* Strafe, -n *f.*

penchant, *n.* Hang *m.*

pencil, *n.* Bleistift, -e *m.*

pendant, *n.* Anhänger, - *m.*

penetrate, *vb. (tr.)* durchdrin'gen*; *(intr.)* ein·dringen*.

penetration, *n.* Eindringen *nt.*, Durchdrin'gung *f.*

penicillin, *n.* Penicillin' *nt.*

peninsula, *n.* Halbinsel, -n *f.*

penitent, *adj.* reuig.

penitentiary, *n.* Zuchthaus, ֿer *nt.*

pen-knife, *n.* Federmesser, - *nt.*

penniless, *adj.* mittellos.

penny, *n.* Pfennig, -e *m.*

pension, *n.* Pension', -en *f.*

pensive, *adj.* nachdenklich.

people, *n.* Leute *pl.*, Menschen *pl.; (nation)* Volk, ֿer *nt.*

pepper, *n.* Pfeffer *m.*

per, *prep.* pro.

perambulator, *n.* Kinderwagen, - *m.*

perceive, *vb.* wahr·nehmen*.

percent, *n.* Prozent', -e *nt.*

percentage, *n.* Prozent'satz, ֿe *m.;* Provision', -en *f.*

perceptible, *adj.* wahrnehmbar.

perception, *n.* Wahrnehmung, -en *f.*

perch, 1. *n. (fish)* Barsch, -e *m.; (pole)* Stange, -n *f.* **2.** *vb.* sich nieder·setzen.

peremptory, *adj.* endgültig, diktato'risch.

perennial, 1. *n. (plant)* Staude, -n *f.* **2.** *adj.* alljähr'lich.

perfect, 1. *n. (gram.)* Perfekt, -e *nt.* **2.** *adj.* vollkom'men, perfekt'. **3.** *vb.* vervoll'kommnen.

perfection, *n.* Vollkom'menheit *f.*

perforate, *vb.* durchlö'chern.

perforation, *n.* Durchlö'cherung, -en *f.*

perform, *vb.* aus·führen; *(drama)* auf·führen.

performance, *n.* Ausführung, -en *f.; (accomplishment)* Leistung, -en *f.; (drama)* Aufführung, -en *f.*, Vorstellung, -en *f.*

perfume, *n.* Parfüm', -s *nt.*

perfunctory, *adj.* oberflächlich, mecha'nisch.

perhaps, *adv.* vielleicht'.

peril, *n.* Gefahr', -en *f.*

perimeter, *n.* Umfang, ֿe *m.*

period, *n.* Zeitraum, ֿe *m.*, Perio'de, -n *f.; (punctuation)* Punkt, -e *m.*

periodic, *adj.* perio'disch.

periphery, *n.* Umkreis, -e *m.*, Peripherie', -i'en *f.*

perish, *vb.* unter·gehen*; verder'ben*.

perishable, *adj.* verderb'lich.

perjure oneself, *vb.* Meineid bege'hen*.

perjury, *n.* Meineid, -e *m.*

permanent, 1. *n. (hair)* Dauerwelle, -n *f.* **2.** *adj.* bestän'dig.

permissible, *adj.* zulässig.

permission, *n.* Erlaub'nis, -se *f.*

permit, 1. *n.* Erlaub'nisschein, -e *m.* **2.** *vb.* erlau'ben, zu·lassen*.

perpendicular, *adj.* senkrecht.

perpetrate, *vb.* bege'hen*.

perpetual, *adj.* ewig.

perplex, *vb.* verwir'ren.

perplexity, *n.* Verwir'rung, -en *f.*

persecute, *vb.* verfol'gen.

persecution, *n.* Verfol'gung, -en *f.*

perseverance, *n.* Beharr'lichkeit *f.*

persevere, *vb.* behar'ren.

persist, *vb.* behar'ren, beste'hen*.

persistent, *adj.* beharr'lich.

person, *n.* Mensch, -en, -en *m.*, Person', -en *f.*

personal, *adj.* persön'lich.

personality, n. Persön'lichkeit, -en f.

personnel, n. Personal' nt.

perspective, n. Perspekti've, -n f.

perspiration, n. Schweiß m.

perspire, vb. schwitzen.

persuade, vb. überre'den.

persuasive, adj. überzeu'gend.

pertain, vb. betref'fen*.

pertinent, adj. zugehörig.

perturb, vb. beun'ruhigen.

perverse, adj. verkehrt; widernatürlich; pervers'.

perversion, n. Verdre'hung, -en f.

pervert, 1. n. perver'ser Mensch, -en, -en m. 2. vb. verdre'hen; verfüh'ren

pessimism, n. Pessimis'mus m.

pestilence, n. Pest f.

pet, 1. n. Liebling, -e m.; (animal) Haustier, -e nt. 2. vb. streicheln.

petal, n. Blütenblatt, ̈er nt.

petition, n. Eingabe, -n f., Antrag, ̈e m.

petrify, vb. verstei'nern; (be petrified) wie gelähmt' sein*.

petrol, n. Benzin' nt.

petroleum, n. Petro'leum nt.

petticoat, n. steifer Unterrock, -e m.

petty, adj. gering'fügig; kleinlich.

petulant, adj. mürrisch.

pew, n. Kirchenstuhl, ̈e m.

phantom, n. Phantom', -e nt.

pharmacist, n. Apothe'ker, - m.

pharmacy, n. Apothe'ke, -n f.

phase, n. Phase, -n f.

pheasant, n. Fasan', -e(n) m.

phenomenal, adj. erstaun'lich.

phenomenon, n. Erschei'nung, -en f.; Phänomen', -e nt.

philanthropy, n. Menschenliebe f., Wohltätigkeit, -en f.

philately, n. Briefmarkenkunde f.

philosopher, n. Philosoph', -en, -en m.

philosophical, adj. philoso'phisch.

philosophy, n. Philosophie', -i'en f.

phlegm, n. Phlegma nt.; (med.) Schleim m.

phlegmatic, adj. phlegma'tisch.

phobia, n. krankhafte Angst f., Phobie, -i'en f.

phonetic, adj. phone'tisch.

phonetics, n. Phone'tik f.

phonograph, n. Grammophon', -e nt.

phosphorus, n. Phosphor m.

photocopier, n. Photokopier'-maschine, -n f.

photocopy, n. Photokopie', -en f.; Ablichtung, -en f.

photocopy, vb. photokopie'ren.

photogenic, adj. photogen'.

photograph, n. Photographie', -i'en f., Lichtbild, -er nt.

photographer, n. Photograph', -en, -en m.

photography, n. Photographie' f.

photostat, 1. n. Photokopie', -i'en f. 2. vb. photokopie'ren.

phrase, 1. n. Satz, ̈e m.; Redewendung, -en f. 2. vb. ausdrücken.

physical, adj. körperlich, physisch.

physician, n. Arzt, ̈e m.

physicist, n. Physiker, - m.

physics, n. Physik' f.

physiology, n. Physiologie' f.

physiotherapy, n. Physiothera-pie' f.

physique, n. Körperbau m.

pianist, n. Klavier'spieler, - m., Pianist', -en, -en m.

piano, n. Klavier', -e nt.

piccolo, n. Piccoloflöte, -n f.

pick, 1. n. Spitzhacke, -n f. 2. vb. (gather) pflücken; (select) auswählen.

picket, 1. n. Holzpfahl, ̈e m.; (striker) Streikposten, - m. 2. vb. Streikposten stehen*.

pickle, n. saure Gurke f.

pickpocket, n. Taschendieb, -e m.

picnic, n. Picknick, -s nt.

picture, 1. n. Bild, -er nt.; (fig.) Vorstellung, -en f. 2. vb. darstellen; sich vorstellen.

picturesque, adj. malerisch.

pie, n. eine Art Backwerk.

piece, n. Stück, -e nt.

pier, n. Pier, -s m.

pierce, vb. durchboh'ren.

piety, n. Frömmigkeit f.

pig, n. Schwein, -e nt.; (young) Ferkel, -e nt.

pigeon, n. Taube, -n f.

pigment, n. Pigment', -e nt.

pile, 1. n. (heap) Haufen, m.; (post) Pfahl, ̈e m. 2. vb. aufhäufen.

pilfer, vb. stehlen*.

pilgrim, n. Pilger, - m.

pilgrimage, n. Wallfahrt, -en f.

pill, n. Pille, -n f.

pillage, 1. n. Plünderung, -en f. 2. vb. plündern.

pillar, n. Säule, -n f.

pillow, n. Kissen, - nt.

pillowcase, n. Kissenbezug, ̈e m.

pilot, n. Pilot', -en, -en m.; (ship) Lotse, -n, -n m.

pimple, n. Pickel, - m.

pin, 1. n. Stecknadel, -n f. 2. vb. stecken.

pinch, 1. n. (of salt, etc.) Prise, -n f. 2. vb. kneifen*, zwicken.

pine, n. Fichte, -n f.; Kiefer, -n f. 2. vb. sich sehnen.

pineapple, n. Ananas, -se f.

ping-pong, n. Tischtennis nt.

pink, adj. rosa.

pinnacle, n. Gipfel, - m.

pint, n. etwa ein halber Liter.

pioneer, n. Pionier', -e m.

pious, adj. fromm(̈, -).

pipe, n. Rohr, -e nt.; Röhre, -n f.; (smoking) Pfeife, -n f.

piquant, adj. pikant'.

pirate, n. Seeräuber, - m.

pistol, n. Pisto'le, -n f.

piston, n. Kolben, - m.

pit, n. (stone) Kern, -e m; (hole) Grube, -n f.

pitch, 1. n. (tar) Pech nt.; (resin) Harz, -e nt.; (throw) Wurf, ̈e m.; (music) Tonhöhe, -n f. 2. vb. (throw) werfen*; (a tent) auf'schlagen*.

pitcher, n. (jug) Krug, ̈e m.; (thrower) Ballwerfer beim Baseball m.

pitchfork, n. Heugabel, -n f.; Mistgabel, -n f.; (music) Stimmgabel, -n f.

pitfall, n. Falle, -n f.

pitiful, adj. erbärm'lich.

pitiless, adj. erbar'mungslos.

pity, n. Mitleid nt., Erbar'men nt.

pivot, n. Drehpunkt, -e m.

pizza, n. Pizza, -s f.

placard, n. Plakat', -e nt.

placate, vb. beschwich'tigen.

place, 1. n. Platz, ̈e m., Ort, -e m. 2. vb. setzen, stellen, legen; unter'bringen*.

placid, adj. gelas'sen.

plagiarism, n. Plagiat' nt.

plague, 1. n. Seuche, -n f. 2. vb. plagen.

plain, 1. n. Ebene, -n f. 2. adj. eben; (fig.) einfach, schlicht.

plaintiff, n. Kläger, - m.

plan, 1. n. Plan, ̈e m. 2. vb. planen.

plane, 1. n. (geom.) Fläche, -n f.; (tool) Hobel, - m.; (airplane) Flugzeug, -e nt. 2. vb. hobeln.

planet, n. Planet', -en, -en m.

planetarium, n. Planeta'rium, -ien nt.

plank, n. Brett, -er nt., Planke, -n f.

plant, 1. n. Pflanze, -n f.; (factory) Fabrik', -en f.; (installation) Werk, -e nt. 2. vb. pflanzen.

planter, n. Pflanzer, - m.

plasma, n. Plasma, -men nt.

plaster, n. Gips m.; (med.) Pflaster, - nt.; (walls) Verputz' m.

plastic, 1. n. Kunststoff, -e m. 2. adj. plastisch.

plate, n. Platte, -n f.; (dish) Teller, - m.

plateau, n. Hochebene, -n f., Plateau', -s nt.

platform, n. Plattform, -en f.; (train) Bahnsteig, -e m.

platinum, n. Platin nt.

platitude, n. Plattheit, -en f.

platoon, n. Zug, ̈e m.

platter, n. Servier'platte, -n f.

plausible, adj. einleuchtend.

play, 1. n. Spiel, -e nt.; (theater) Thea'terstück, -e nt. 2. vb. spielen.

player, n. (game) Mitspieler, -

m.; *(theater)* Schauspieler, -m.; *(music)* Spieler, - m.
playful, adj. spielerisch.
playground, n. Spielplatz, ⸗e m.
playmate, n. Spielgefährte, -n, -n m.
playwright, n. Drama'tiker, - m.
plea, n. Bitte, -n f.; *(excuse)* Vorwand, ⸗e m.; *(jur.)* Plädoyer', -s nt.
plead, vb. bitten*, plädie'ren.
pleasant, adj. angenehm.
please, 1. vb. gefal'len*. 2. interj. bitte.
pleasing, adj. angenehm.
pleasure, n. Vergnü'gen nt., Freude, -n f.
pleat, n. Falte, -n f.
plebiscite, n. Volksabstimmung, -en f.
pledge, 1. n. Gelüb'de, - nt. 2. vb. gelo'ben.
plentiful, adj. reichlich.
plenty, n. Fülle f.; *(p. of)* reichlich, genug'.
pleurisy, n. Rippenfellentzündung, -en f.
pliable, pliant, adj. biegsam.
pliers, n. Zange, -n f., Kneifzange, -n f.
plight, n. schwierige Lage, -n f.
plot, 1. n. Stück Erde nt.; *(story)* Handlung, -en f.; *(intrigue)* Komplott', -e nt.; intrigie'ren; *(plan)* entwer'fen*.
plow, 1. n. Pflug, ⸗e m. 2. vb. pflügen.
pluck, 1. n. Mut m. 2. vb. rupfen.
plug, 1. n. Stöpsel, - m., Pfropfen, - m.; *(spark p.)* Zündkerze, -n f.; *(fire p.)* Feuerhydrant, -en, -en m. 2. vb. zu·stopfen.
plum, n. Pflaume, -n f.
plumage, n. Gefie'der nt.
plumber, n. Klempner, - m.
plume, n. Feder, -n f.
plump, adj. dicklich.
plunder, 1. n. Beute f., Raub m. 2. vb. plündern.
plunge, vb. rauchen, stürzen.
plural, n. Mehrzahl, -en f., Plural, -e m.
plus, prep. plus.
plutocrat, n. Plutokrat', -en, -en m.
pneumatic, adj. pneuma'tisch.
pneumonia, n. Lungenentzündung, -en f.
poach, vb. *(hunt illegally)* wildern; *(eggs)* pochie'ren.
pocket, n. Tasche, -n f.
pocketbook, n. Handtasche, -n f.
pod, n. Schote, -n f.
podiatry, n. Fußheilkunde f.
poem, n. Gedicht', -e nt.
poet, n. Dichter, - m.
poetic, adj. dichterisch, poe'tisch.
poetry, n. Dichtung, -en f., Poesie' f.

poignant, adj. treffend.
point, 1. n. Punkt, -e m. 2. vb. zeigen, hin·weisen*.
pointed, adj. spitz.
pointless, adj. sinnlos, witzlos.
poise, n. Schwebe f.; *(assuredness)* sicheres Auftreten nt.
poison, 1. n. Gift, -e nt. 2. vb. vergif'ten.
poisonous, adj. giftig.
poke, vb. stoßen*.
Poland, n. Polen nt.
polar, adj. polar'.
pole, n. *(post)* Pfahl, ⸗e m.; *(rod)* Stange, -n f.; *(electrical, geographic)* Pol, -e m.
Pole, n. Pole, -n, -n m.
police, n. Polizei' f.
policeman, n. Polizist', -en, -en m.
policy, n. Politik' f.; *(insurance)* Poli'ce, -n f.
polish, 1. n. Politur', -en f.; *(shoe p.)* Schuhkrem, -s f. 2. vb. polie'ren, putzen.
Polish, adj. polnisch.
polite, adj. höflich.
politeness, n. Höflichkeit, -en f.
politic, political, adj. poli'tisch.
politician, n. Poli'tiker, - m.
politics, n. Politik' f.
poll, 1. n. Wahl, -en f., Abstimmung, -en f.; Meinungsumfrage, -n f. 2. vb. befra'gen.
pollen, n. Blütenstaub m.
pollute, vb. verun·reinigen.
polonaise, n. Poloña'se, -n f.
polygamy, n. Polygamie' f.
pomp, n. Pomp m.
pompous, adj. prunkvoll; *(fig.)* hochtrabend.
poncho, n. Poncho, -s m.
pond, n. Teich, -e m.
ponder, vb. *(tr.)* erwä'gen; *(intr.)* nach·denken*.
ponderous, adj. schwerfällig.
pontiff, n. Papst, ⸗e m.
pontoon, n. Schwimmer, - m.
pony, n. Pony, -s nt.
pool, 1. n. *(pond)* Tümpel, - m.; *(swimming p.)* Schwimmbad, ⸗er, nt.; *(group)* Interes'sengemeinschaft, -en f. 2. vb. zusam'men·legen.
poor, adj. arm (⸗).
pop, 1. n. Knall, -e m.; *(father)* Papi, -s m. 2. vb. knallen.
pope, n. Pabst, ⸗e m.
popular, adj. volkstümlich; beliebt'.
popularity, n. Beliebt'heit f.
population, n. Bevöl'kerung, -en f.
porcelain, n. Porzellan', -e nt.
porch, n. Veran'da, -den f.
pore, n. Pore, -n f.
pork, n. Schweinefleisch nt.
pornography, n. Pornographie' f.
porous, adj. porös'.
port, n. Hafen, ⸗ m.; *(wine)* Port m.

portable, adj. tragbar.
portal, n. Portal', -e nt.
portend, vb. Unheil verkün'den.
porter, n. Gepäck'träger, -m.
portfolio, n. Mappe, -n f.; Portefeuille' nt.
porthole, n. Luke, -n f.
portion, n. Teil, -e m.; *(serving)* Portion', -en f.
portrait, n. Porträt', -s nt.
portray, vb. schildern.
Portugal, n. Portugal nt.
Portuguese, 1. n. Portugie'se, - n, -n m. 2. adj. portugie'sisch.
pose, 1. n. Haltung, -en f., Pose, -n f. 2. vb. stellen; (p. as) sich aus·geben* für.
position, n. Stellung, -en f.
positive, adj. positiv.
possess, vb. besit'zen*.
possession, n. Besitz, -e m., Eigentum, ⸗er nt.
possessive, adj. besitz'gierig.
possessor, n. Besit'zer, - m., Eigentümer, - m.
possibility, n. Möglichkeit, -en f.
possible, adj. möglich.
possibly, adv. möglicherweise.
post, 1. n. *(pole)* Pfahl, ⸗e m.; *(place)* Posten, - m.; *(mail)* Post f. 2. vb. auf·stellen; zur Post geben*.
postage, n. Porto nt.
postal, adj. Post- (cpds.).
postcard, n. Postkarte, -n f.
poster, n. Plakat', -e nt.
posterior, adj. hinter-; Hinter-(cpds.).
posterity, n. Nachwelt f.
postmark, n. Postempel, - m.
postman, n. Postbote, -n, -n m., Briefträger, - m.
post office, n. Post f., Postamt, ⸗er nt.
postpone, vb. auf·schieben*, verschie'ben*.
postscript, n. Nachschrift, -en f.
posture, n. Haltung, -en f.
pot, n. Topf, ⸗e m.; *(marijuana)* Hasch m.
potassium, n. Kalium nt.
potato, n. Kartof'fel, -n f.
potent, adj. stark (⸗).
potential, 1. n. Möglichkeit, -en f. 2. adj. möglich.
potion, n. Trank, ⸗e m.
pottery, n. Töpferware, -n f.
pouch, n. Tasche, -n f., Beutel, - m.
poultry, n. Geflü'gel nt.
pound, 1. n. Pfund, -e nt. 2. vb. hämmern, schlagen*.
pour, vb. gießen*.
poverty, n. Armut f.
powder, 1. n. Pulver, -n f.; *(cosmetic)* Puder, - m. 2. vb. pudern.
power, n. Macht, ⸗e f.
powerful, adj. mächtig.
powerless, adj. machtlos.

practicable, *adj.* durchführbar.

practical, *adj.* praktisch.

practice, 1. *n.* Übung, -en *f.;* *(carrying out)* Ausübung *f.;* *(custom)* Gewohn'heit, -en *f.;* *(doctor)* Praxis, -xen *f.* **2.** *vb.* üben; *(carry out)* aus'üben.

practitioner, *n.* Vertre'ter, - *m.;* *(med.)* praktischer Arzt, -̈e *m.*

prairie, *n.* Prairie', -i'en *f.*

praise, 1. *n.* Lob, -e *nt.* **2.** *vb.* loben.

prank, *n.* Streich, -e *m.*

pray, *vb.* beten.

prayer, *n.* Gebet', -e *nt.*

preach, *n.* predigen.

preacher, *n.* Prediger, - *m.*

precarious, *adj.* heikel.

precaution, *n.* Vorsichtsmaßregel, -n *f.*

precede, *vb.* voran'gehen*.

precedence, *n.* Vorrang *m.*

precedent, *n.* Präzedenz'fall, -̈e *m.*

precept, *n.* Vorschrift, -en *f.*

precinct, *n.* Bezirk', -e *m.*

precious, *adj.* kostbar.

precipice, *n.* Abgrund, -̈e *m.*

precipitate, 1. *adj.* überstürzt'. **2.** *vb.* überstür'zen.

precise, *adj.* genau.

precision, *n.* Genau'igkeit *f.,* Präzision' *f.*

preclude, *vb.* aus'schließen*.

precocious, *adj.* frühreif, altklug (-).

predecessor, *n.* Vorgänger, - *m.*

predestination, *n.* Prädestination' *f.*

predicament, *n.* Dilem'ma, -s *nt.*

predicate, 1. *n.* Prädikat', -e *nt.* **2.** *vb.* begrün'den.

predict, *vb.* voraus'sagen.

predisposed, *adj.* geneigt'; *(med.)* anfällig.

predominant, *adj.* vorherrschend.

prefabricated, *adj.* Fertig- *(cpds.).*

preface, *n.* Vorwort, -e *nt.*

prefer, *vb.* vor'ziehen*.

preferable, *adj.* vorzuziehend (is p.) ist vorzuziehen.

preferably, *adv.* vorzugsweise.

preference, *n.* Vorzug *m.,* Vorliebe *f.*

prefix, *n.* Vorsilbe, -n *f.,* Präfix, -e *nt.*

pregnancy, *n.* Schwangerschaft, -en *f.*

pregnant, *adj.* schwanger.

prehistoric, *adj.* vorgeschichtlich, prähisto'risch.

prejudice, *n.* Vorurteil, -e *nt.*

prejudiced, *adj.* voreingenommen.

preliminary, *adj.* einleitend.

prelude, *n.* Einleitung, -en *f.,* Vorspiel, -e *nt.*

premature, *adj.* vorzeitig.

premeditate, *vb.* vorher überle'gen.

premeditated, *adj.* vorbedacht; mit Vorbedacht.

premier, *n.* Minis'terpräsident, -en, -en *m.*

première, *n.* Urauffführung, -en *f.*

premise, *n.* Prämis'se, -n *f.*

premium, *n.* Prämie, -n *f.*

premonition, *n.* Vorahnung, -en *f.*

prenatal, *adj.* vorgeburtlich.

preparation, *n.* Vorbereitung, -en *f.;* *(of food)* Zubereitung *f.*

preparatory, *adj.* vorbereitend; Vorbereitungs- *(cpds.).*

prepare, *vb.* vor'bereiten; *(food)* zu'bereiten.

preponderant, *adj.* überwiegend.

preposition, *n.* Präposition', -en *f.*

preposterous, *adj.* widersinnig.

prerequisite, *n.* Vorbedingung, -en *f.*

prerogative, *n.* Vorrecht, -e *nt.*

prescribe, *vb.* vor'schreiben*; *(med.)* verschrei'ben*.

prescription, *n.* Rezept', -e *nt.*

presence, *n.* Anwesenheit *f.,* Gegenwart *f.*

present, 1. *n.* *(time)* Gegenwart *f.;* *(gram.)* Präsens *nt.;* *(gift)* Geschenk', -e *nt.* **2.** *adj.* anwesend, gegenwärtig. **3.** *vb.* dar'bieten*; *(introduce)* vor'stellen; *(arms)* präsentie'ren.

presentable, *adj.* präsenta'bel.

presentation, *n.* Darstellung, -en *f.;* Vorstellung, -en *f.*

presently, *adv.* gleich.

preservation, *n.* Erhal'tung *f.*

preservative, *n.* Konservie'rungsmittel, - *nt.*

preserve, *vb.* bewah'ren, erhal'ten*; *(food)* konservie'ren, ein'machen.

preside, *vb.* den Vorsitz führen.

presidency, *n.* Vorsitz, -e *m.;* Präsident'schaft *f.*

president, *n.* Präsident', -en, -en *m.*

press, 1. *n.* Presse *f.* **2.** *vb.* pressen, drücken; *(iron)* bügeln.

pressing, *adj.* dringend.

pressure, *n.* Druck *m.*

pressure cooker, *n.* Dampfkochtopf, -̈e *m.*

prestige, *n.* Prestige' *nt.*

presume, *vb.* an'nehmen*; voraus'setzen.

presumptuous, *adj.* anmaßend.

presuppose, *vb.* voraus'setzen.

pretend, *vb.* vor'geben*.

pretense, *n.* Vorwand, -̈e *m.*

pretentious, *adj.* prätentiös'.

pretext, *n.* Vorwand, -̈e *m.*

pretty, 1. *adj.* hübsch, niedlich. **2.** *adv.* ziemlich.

prevail, *vb.* vor'herrschen; *(win)* siegen; **(p. upon)** überre'den.

prevalent, *adj.* vorherrschend.

prevent, *vb.* verhin'dern, verhü'ten.

prevention, *n.* Verhin'derung *f.,* Verhü'tung, -en *f.*

preventive, *adj.* Verhü'tungs-, Präventiv'- *(cpds.).*

preview, *n.* Vorschau *f.,* Voranzeige, -n *f.*

previous, *adj.* vorher'gehend.

prey, *n.* Raub *m.,* Beute *f.*

price, *n.* Preis, -e *m.*

priceless, *adj.* unbezahl'bar.

prick, *vb.* stechen*.

pride, *n.* Stolz *m.,* Hochmut *m.*

priest, *n.* Priester, - *m.,* Pfarrer, - *m.*

prim, *adj.* spröde, prüde.

primary, *adj.* primär'.

prime, 1. *n.* Blüte *f.* **2.** *adj.* Haupt- *(cpds.);* erstklassig; **(p. number)** Primzahl, -en *f.*

prime minister, *n.* Premier'minister, - *m.*

primitive, *adj.* primitiv'.

prince, *n.* *(king's son)* Prinz, -en, -en *m.; (other ruler)* Fürst, -en, -en *m.*

princess, *n.* Prinzes'sin, -nen *f.*

principal, 1. *n.* *(school)* Schuldirektor, -o'ren *m.* **2.** *adj.* hauptsächlich, Haupt- *(cpds.).*

principle, *n.* Prinzip', -ien *nt.,* Grundsatz, -̈e *m.*

print, 1. *n.* Druck, -e *m.* **2.** *vb.* drucken.

printing, *n.* Buchdruck *m.*

printing-press, *n.* Druckerpresse, -n *f.*

printout, *n.* Printout, -s *m.*

priority, *n.* Vorrang *m.,* Priorität', -en *f.*

prism, *n.* Prisma, -men *nt.*

prison, *n.* Gefäng'nis, -se *nt.*

prisoner, *n.* Gefan'gen- *m.&f.*

privacy, *n.* ungestörtes Allein'sein *nt.*

private, 1. *n.* *(mil.)* Soldat', -en, -en *m.* **2.** *adj.* privat'.

privation, *n.* Berau'bung, -en *f.;* Not, -̈e *f.*

privilege, *n.* Vorrecht, -e *nt.,* Privileg', -ien *nt.*

privy, 1. *n.* Abort, -e *m.* **2.** *adj.* geheim'.

prize, 1. *n.* Preis, -e *m.* **2.** *vb.* schätzen.

probability, *n.* Wahrschein'lichkeit, -en *f.*

probable, *adj.* wahrschein'lich.

probation, *n.* Probezeit, -en *f.;* *(jur.)* Bewäh'rungsfrist *f.*

probe, *vb.* sondie'ren.

problem, *n.* Problem', -e *nt.*

procedure, *n.* Verfah'ren *nt.*

proceed, *vb.* *(go on)* fort'fahren*; *(act)* verfah'ren*.

process, *n.* Verfah'ren, - *nt.*

procession, *n.* Prozession', -en *f.*

proclaim, *vb.* aus'rufen*, verkün'den.

proclamation, *n.* Bekannt'machung, -en *f.,* Proklamation', -en *f.*

procrastinate, *vb.* zögern.

procure, vb. besor'gen, verschaf'fen

prodigy, n. Wunder, - nt.; (infant p.) Wunderkind, -er nt.

produce, vb. (show) vor'legen, vorführen; (create) erzeu'gen, her'stellen, produzie'ren.

product, n. Erzeug'nis, -se nt., Produkt', -e nt.

production, n. Herstellung, -en f., Produktion', -en f.

productive, adj. produktiv'.

profane, adj. profan'.

profanity, n. Fluchen nt.

profess, vb. beken'nen*; (pretend) vor'geben*.

profession, n. Bekennt'nis, -se nt.; (calling) Beruf', -e m.

professional, adj. berufs'-mäßig

professor, n. Profes'sor, -o'ren m.

proficient, adj. erfah'ren, beschla'gen.

profile, n. Profil', -e nt.

profit, 1. n. Gewinn' m. 2. vb. profitie'ren.

profitable, adj. einträglich; (fig.) vorteilhaft.

profiteer, n. Schieber, - m.

profound, adj. tief, tiefsinnig.

profundity, n. Tiefe f.; Tiefgründigkeit f.

profuse, adj. überreich.

program, n. Programm', -e nt.

progress, 1. n. Fortschritt, -e m. 2. vb. fort'schreiten*.

progressive, adj. fortschrittlich.

prohibit, vb. verbie'ten*; verhin'dern.

prohibition, n. Verbot', -e nt.

prohibitive, adj. verbie'terisch.

project, 1. n. Projekt', -e nt. 2. vb.(plan) projizie'ren; (stick out) vor'springen*.

projectile, n. Geschoß', -sse nt.

projection, n. Projektion', -en f.

projector, n. Projek'tor, -o'ren m.

proliferation, n. Verbreitung f.

prolific, adj. fruchtbar.

prologue, n. Prolog', -e m.

prolong, vb. verlän'gern, aus'dehnen.

prominent, adj. prominent'.

promiscuous, adj. unterschiedslos; sexuell' zügellos.

promise, 1. n. Verspre'chen, -nt. 2. vb. verspre'chen*.

promote, vb. fördern; (in rank) beför'dern.

promotion, n. Förderung f.; Beför'derung, -en f.

prompt, adj. prompt.

promulgate, vb. verkün'den.

pronoun, n. Fürwort, -er nt., Pro'no'men, -mina nt.

pronounce, vb. aus'sprechen*.

pronunciation, n. Aussprache, -n f.

proof, n. Beweis, -e m.; (printing) Korrektur'bogen, - m.; (photo) Abzug, -e m.

prop, 1. n. Stütze, -n f. 2. vb. stützen.

propaganda, n. Propagan'da f.

propagate, vb. fort'pflanzen; verbrei'ten.

propel, vb. an'treiben*.

propeller, n. Propel'ler, - m.

proper, adj. passend, angebracht.

property, n. Besitz' m., Eigentum nt.

prophecy, n. Prophezei'ung, -en f.

prophesy, vb. prophezei'en.

prophet, n. Prophet', -en, -en m.

prophetic, adj. prophe'tisch.

propitious, adj. günstig.

proponent, n. Verfech'ter, - m.

proportion, n. Verhält'nis, -se nt., Proportion', -en f., Ausmaß, -e nt.

proportionate, adj. angemessen.

proposal, n. Vorschlag, -e m.; (marriage) Heiratsantrag, -e m.

propose, vb. vor'schlagen*; (intend) beab'sichtigen; einen Heiratsantrag machen.

proposition, n. Vorschlag, -e m.; (logic) Lehrsatz, -e m.

proprietor, n. Inhaber, - m., Eigentümer, - m.

propriety, n. Anstand m.

prosaic, adj. prosa'isch.

prose, n. Prosa f.

prosecute, vb. verfol'gen; (jur.) an'klagen.

prospect, n. Aussicht, -en f.

prospective, adj. voraus'sichtlich.

prosper, vb. gedei'hen*.

prosperity, n. Wohlstand m.

prosperous, adj. blühend, wohlhabend.

prostitute, n. Prostituiert'- f.

prostrate, 1. adj. hingestreckt. 2. vb. zu Boden werfen*.

protect, vb. schützen, beschützen.

protection, n. Schutz m.

protective, adj. Schutz- (cpds.).

protector, n. Beschüt'zer, - m.

protégé, n. Protegé', -s m.

protein, n. Protein' nt.

protest, 1. n. Einspruch, -e m., Protest', -e m. 2. vb. Einspruch erhe'ben*, protestie'ren.

Protestant, 1. n. Protestant', -en, -en m. 2. adj. protestan'tisch.

Protestantism, n. Protestantis'mus m.

protocol, n. Protokoll', -e nt.

proton, n. Proton, -o'nen nt.

protrude, vb. hervor'stehen*.

protuberance, n. Auswuchs, -e m., Buckel, - m.

proud, adj. stolz.

prove, vb. bewei'sen*.

proverb, n. Sprichwort, -er nt.

proverbial, adj. sprichwörtlich.

provide, vb. (p. for) sorgen für; (p. with) versor'gen mit, verse'hen-* mit.

provided, adv. voraus'gesetzt daß.

providence, n. Vorsehung f.; Vorsorge f.

province, n. Provinz', -en f.

provincial, adj. provinziell'.

provision, n. (stipulation) Bestim'mung, -en f.; (food) Proviant' m.; (stock) Vorrat, -e m.

provocation, n. Provokation', -en f.

provoke, vb. provozie'ren; (call forth) hervor'rufen*.

prowess, n. Tüchtigkeit f.

prowl, vb. umher'schleichen*.

proximity, n. Nähe f.

proxy, n. (thing) Vollmacht, -en f.; (person) Stellvertreter, - m.

prudence, n. Vorsicht f.; Klugheit f.

prudent, adj. klug (-); umsichtig.

prune, n. Backpflaume, -n f.

pry, vb. (break open) auf'brechen*; (peer about) herum'-schnüffeln.

psalm, n. Psalm, -en m.

pseudonym, n. Pseudonym', -e nt.

psychedelic, adj. psychede'lisch, halluzinie'rend

psychiatrist, n. Psychia'ter, - m.

psychiatry, n. Psychiatrie' f.

psychoanalysis, n. Psychoanaly'se, -n f.

psychological, adj. psycholo'gisch.

psychology, n. Psychologie' f.

psychosis, n. Psycho'se, -n f.

ptomaine, n. Ptomain', -e nt.

public, 1. n. Öffentlichkeit f. 2. adj. öffentlich

publication, n. Veröf'fentlichung, -en f., Publikation', -en f.

publicity, n. Rekla'me f., Propagan'da f.

publish, vb. veröf'fentlichen, publizie'ren; (make known) bekannt'machen.

publisher, n. Heraus'geber, - m., Verle'ger, - m.

pudding, n. Pudding, -s m.

puddle, n. Pfütze, -n f.

puff, 1. n. (wind) Windstoß, -e m.; (smoke) Rauchwolke, -n f.; (powder) Puderquaste, -n f. 2. vb. blasen*; paffen.

pull, 1. n. Zugkraft f., Anziehungskraft f.; (influence) Bezie'hung, -en f. 2. vb. ziehen*.

pulley, n. Flaschenzug, -e m.

pulmonary, adj. Lungen- (cpds.).

pulp, n. Brei m.; (fruit) Fruchtfleisch nt.

pulpit, n. Kanzel, -n f.

pulsar, n. Pulsar m.

pulsate, vb. pulsie'ren.

pulse, n. Puls, -e m.

pump, 1. n. Pumpe, -n f.; (shoe) Pump -s m. **2.** vb. pumpen.

pumpkin, n. Kürbis, -se m.

pun, n. Wortspiel, -e nt.

punch, 1. n. Schlag, ¨e m., Stoß, ¨e m.; (drink) Punsch m. **2.** vb. schlagen*, stossen*; (make holes) lochen.

punctual, adj. pünktlich.

punctuate, vb. interpunktie'ren.

punctuation, n. Interpunktion' f.

puncture, 1. n. Loch, ¨er nt.; (tire) Reifenpanne, -n f.; (med.) Punktion', -en f. **2.** vb. durchste'chen*.

pungent, adj. stechend, beißend.

punish, vb. strafen, bestra'fen.

punishment, n. Strafe, -n f.

puny, adj. mickrig.

pupil, n. Schüler, - m.; Schülerin, -nen f.

puppet, n. Marionet'te, -n f.

puppy, n. junger Hund, -e m.

purchase, 1. n. Kauf, ¨e m., Einkauf, ¨e m. **2.** vb. kaufen, erwer'ben*.

pure, adj. rein.

purée, n. Püree', -s nt.

purgative, n. Abführmittel, - nt.

purge, 1. n. Säuberungsaktion, -en f. **2.** vb. säubern.

purify, vb. reinigen, läutern.

puritanical, adj. purita'nisch.

purity, n. Reinheit f., Echtheit f.

purple, adj. purpurn; lila.

purport, 1. n. Sinn m. **2.** vb. den Anschein erwecken als ob.

purpose, n. Zweck, -e m.; Absicht, -en f.

purposely, adv. absichtlich.

purse, n. (handbag) Handtasche, -n f.; Geldbeutel, - m.

pursue, vb. verfol'gen.

pursuit, n. Verfol'gung, -en f.

push, 1. n. Stoß, ¨e m.; (fig.) Energie, -i'en f. **2.** vb. stossen*, schieben*.

put, vb. setzen; stellen; legen.

putrid, adj. faul, verfault'.

puzzle, 1. n. Rätsel, - nt.; (game) Puzzle, -s nt. **2.** vb. verwir'ren, zu denken geben*.

pyjamas, n.pl. Pyja'ma, -s m.

pyramid, n. Pyrami'de, -n f.

Q

quadrangle, n. Viereck, -e nt.

quadraphonic, adj. quadra'phon'.

quadruped, n. Vierfüßler, - m.

quail, n. Wachtel, -n f.

quaint, adj. seltsam; altmodisch.

quake, 1. n. Beben nt. **2.** vb. beben, zittern.

qualification, n. Befä'higung, -en f., Qualifikation', -en f.; (reservation) Einschränkung, -en f.

qualified, adj. geeig'net; (limited) eingeschränkt.

qualify, vb. qualifizie'ren; (limit) ein·schränken.

quality, n. (characteristic) Eigenschaft, -en f.; (grade) Qualität, -en f.

qualm, n. Beden'ken nt.

quandary, n. Dilem'ma nt.

quantity, n. Menge, -n f., Quantität', -en f.

quarantine, n. Quaranta'ne f.

quarrel, 1. n. Streit m., Zank m. **2.** vb. streiten*, sich streiten*, sich zanken.

quarry, n. Steinbruch, ¨e m.

quarter, 1. n. Viertel, - nt. **2.** vb. ein·quartieren.

quarterly, 1. n. Vierteljah'resschrift, -en f. **2.** adj. vierteljäh'rlich.

quartet, n. Quartett', -e nt.

quasar, n. Quasar m.

queen, n. Königin, -nen f.

queer, adj. merkwürdig, sonderbar.

quell, vb. unterdrü'cken.

quench, vb. löschen, stillen.

query, 1. n. Frage, -n f. **2.** vb. fragen.

quest, n. Suche, -n f.

question, 1. n. Frage, -n f. **2.** vb. fragen, befra'gen; anzweifeln.

questionable, adj. fraglich, fragwürdig.

question mark, n. Fragezeichen, - nt.

questionnaire, n. Fragebogen, ¨ m.

quick, adj. schnell, rasch.

quiet, 1. adj. leise, ruhig, still. **2.** vb. beru'higen.

quilt, n. Steppdecke, -n f.

quinine, n. Chinin' nt.

quintet, n. Quintett', -e nt.

quip, 1. n. witziger Seitenhieb, -e m., spitze Bemer'kung, -en f. **2.** vb. witzeln.

quit, vb. (leave) verlas'sen*; (stop) auf·hören; (resign) kündigen.

quite, adj. ziemlich; (completely) ganz, völlig.

quiver, 1. n. Köcher, - m. **2.** vb. beben, zittern.

quiz, 1. n. Quiz m.; (school) Klassenarbeit, -en f. **2.** vb. aus·fragen.

quorum, n. beschluß'fähige Versamm'lung f.

quota, n. Quote, -n f.

quotation, n. Zitat', -e nt.; (price) Notie'rung, -en f.

quotation mark, n. Anfüh-

rungsstrich, -e m., Anführungszeichen, - nt.

quote, vb. an·führen, zitie'ren.

R

rabbi, n. Rabbi'ner, - m.

rabbit, n. Kanin'chen, - nt.

rabble, n. Volksmenge f., Pöbel m.

rabid, adj. fana'tisch.

rabies, n. Tollwut f.

race, 1. n. (contest) Rennen, - nt., Wettrennen, - nt.; (breed) Rasse, -n f. **2.** vb. rennen*, um die Wette rennen*.

race-track, n. Rennbahn, -en f.

rack, 1. n. (torture) Folterbank, ¨e f.; (feed) Futtergestell, -e nt.; (luggage) Ständer, - m.; (train) Gepäcknetz, -e nt. **2.** vb. foltern.

racket, n. (tennis) Schläger, -m.; (uproar) Krach m.; (crime) Schiebung, -en f.

radar, n. Radar nt.

radiance, n. Glanz m., Strahlen nt.

radiant, adj. strahlend.

radiate, vb. aus·strahlen.

radiation, n. Ausstrahlung, -en f.

radiator, n. Heizkörper, - m.; (auto) Kühler, - m.

radical, adj. radikal'.

radio, n. Rundfunk m.; Rundfunkgerät, -e nt.; Radio, -s nt.

radioactive, adj. radioaktiv'; (r. fall-out) radioakti'ver Niederschlag, ¨e m.

radish, n. Radies'chen, - nt.; (white) Rettich, -e m.; (horser.) Meerrettich, -e m.

radium, n. Radium nt.

radius, n. Radius, -ien m.

raffle, 1. n. Lotterie', -i'en f. **2.** vb. (r. off) aus·losen.

raft, n. Floß, ¨e nt.

rag, n. Lumpen, - m., Lappen, - m.

rage, 1. n. Wut f.; (fashion) Schrei m. **2.** vb. wüten, rasen.

ragged, adj. zerlumpt'; (jagged) zackig.

raid, 1. n. Überfall, ¨e m., Razzia, -ien f. **2.** vb. überfal'len*, plündern.

rail, n. Schiene, -n f.

railing, n. Gelän'der, - nt.

railroad, n. Eisenbahn, -en f.

rain, 1. n. Regen m. **2.** vb. regnen.

rainbow, n. Regenbogen, ¨ m.

raincoat, n. Regenmantel, ¨ m.

rainy, adj. regnerisch.

raise, 1. n. (pay) Gehalts'erhöhung, -en f. **2.** vb. (increase) erhö'hen; (lift) heben*; (erect) auf·stellen; (collect) auf·treiben*; (bring up) groß·ziehen*.

raisin, n. Rosi'ne, -n f.

rake, 1. n. (tool) Harke, -n f., Rechen, - m.; (person) Roué', -s m. 2. vb. harken.

rally, 1. n. (recovery) Erho'lung, -en f.; (meeting) Kundgebung, -en f., Massenversammlung, -en f. 2. vb. sich erho'len; sich sammeln.

ram, 1. n. Widder, - m. 2. vb. rammen.

ramble, vb. umher·schweifen.

ramp, n. Rampe, -n f.

rampart, n. Burgwall, ¨-e m.

ranch, n. Ranch, -es f.

rancid, adj. ranzig.

rancor, n. Groll m.

random, n. (at r.) aufs Geratewohl'.

range, 1. n. (distance) Entfer'nung, -en f.; (scope) Spielraum, ¨-e m.; (mountains) Bergkette, -n f.; (stove) Herd, -e m. 2. vb. (extend) sich erstre'cken.

rank, 1. n. Rang, ¨-e m. 2. vb. ein·reihen.

ransack, vb. durchwüh'len.

ransom, n. Lösegeld, -er nt.

rap, vb. schlagen*, klopfen.

rape, 1. n. Vergewal'tigung, -en f. 2. vb. vergewal'tigen.

rapid, adj. schnell.

rare, adj. selten.

rascal, n. Schlingel, - m.

rash, adj. übereilt', waghalsig.

raspberry, n. Himbeere, -n f.

rat, n. Ratte, -n f.

rate, 1. n. (proportion) Maßstab, ¨-e m.; (price) Preis, -e m.; (exchange r.) Kurs, -e m.; (speed) Geschwin'digkeit, -en f. 2. vb. ein·schätzen.

rather, adv. (preferably) lieber; (on the other hand) vielmehr.

ratify, vb. ratifizie'ren.

ratio, n. Verhält'nis, -se nt.

ration, n. Ration', -en f. 2. vb. rationie'ren.

rational, adj. vernunft'gemäß.

rattle, vb. klappern.

ravage, 1. n. Verwüs'tung, -en f. 2. vb. verwüs'ten.

rave, vb. (fury) toben; (enthusiasm) schwärmen.

raven, 1. n. Rabe, -n, -n m. 2. adj. rabenschwarz.

raw, adj. rauh; (uncooked) roh.

ray, n. Strahl, -en m.

rayon, n. Kunstseide, -n f.

razor, n. (straight) Rasier'messer, - nt.; (safety) Rasier'apparat, -e m.

reach, 1. n. Reichweite f. 2. vb. (tr.) errei'chen; (intr.) reichen.

react, vb. reagie'ren.

reaction, n. Wirkung, -en f., Reaktion', -en f.

reactionary, 1. n. Reaktionär', -e m. 2. adj. reaktionär'.

reactor, n. Reak'tor, -o'ren m.

read, vb. lesen*.

reader, n. (person) Leser, - m.; (book) Lesebuch, ¨-er nt.

readily, adv. gern; (easily) leicht.

reading, n. Lesen nt.

ready, adj. (prepared) bereit'; (finished) fertig.

real, adj. wirklich, tatsächlich; (genuine) echt.

realist, n. Realist', -en m.

reality, n. Wirklichkeit f.

realization, n. (understanding) Erkennt'nis, -se f.; (making real) Verwirk'lichung, -en f., Realisie'rung, -en f.

realize, vb. (understand) erken'nen, begrei'fen, (I r. it) ich bin mir darüber im klaren; (make real, attain) verwirk'lichen, realisie'ren.

realm, n. Reich, -e nt.; (fig.) Bereich', -e m.

reap, vb. ernten.

rear, 1. n. (back) Rückseite, -n f.; (r.-guard) Nachhut, -en f. 2. vb. (bring up) erzie'hen*; (erect) errich'ten; (of horses) sich bäumen.

rear-view mirror, n. Rückspiegel, - m.

reason, 1. n. Vernunft' f.; (cause) Grund, ¨-e m. 2. vb. überle'gen, denken*; (r. with) vernünf'tig reden mit.

reasonable, adj. vernünf'tig.

reassure, vb. versi'chern; beru'higen.

rebate, n. Rabatt', -e m.

rebel, 1. n. Rebell', -en, -en m. 2. vb. rebellie'ren.

rebellion, n. Aufstand, ¨-e m., Rebellion', -en f.

rebellious, adj. rebel'lisch.

rebound, vb. zurück'prallen.

rebuild, vb. wider auf·bauen.

rebuke, 1. n. Tadel, - m. 2. vb. tadeln.

rebuttal, n. Widerle'gung, -en f.

recalcitrant, adj. starrköpfig.

recall, vb. zurück'rufen*; (remember) sich erin'nern an, (revoke) widerru'fen*.

recapitulate, vb. zusam'menfassen.

recede, vb. zurück'weichen*.

receipt, n. Quittung, -en f.; (recipe) Rezept', -e nt.

receiver, n. Empfän'ger, - m.; (telephone) Hörer, - m.

recent, adj. neu.

recently, adv. neulich, kürzlich.

receptacle, n. Behäl'ter, - m.

reception, n. Aufnahme, -n f.; (ceremony) Empfang', ¨-e m.

receptive, adj. empfäng'lich.

recess, n. (in wall) Nische, -n f.; (intermission) Pause, -n f.

recipe, n. Rezept', -e nt.

recipient, n. Empfän'ger m.

reciprocate, vb. aus·tauschen; erwi'dern.

recitation, n. Rezitation', -en f.

recite, vb. auf·sagen, vor·tragen*.

reckless, adj. rücksichtslos; leichtsinnig.

reclaim, vb. ein·fordern; (land) urbar machen; (waste product) aus·werten.

reclamation, n. (land) Urbarmachung f.

recline, vb. sich zurück'lehnen.

recognition, n. (acknowledgment) Anerkennung, -en f.; (know again) Wiedererkennen, -en f.

recognize, vb. (acknowledge) an·erkennen*; (know again) wieder·erkennen*.

recoil, vb. zurück'prallen.

recollect, vb. sich erin'nern an.

recommend, vb. empfeh'len*.

recommendation, n. Empfeh'lung, -en f.

recompense, 1. n. Erstat'tung, -en f. 2. vb. wieder·erstatten.

reconcile, vb. versöh'nen.

reconsider, vb. wieder erwägen.

reconstruct, vb. rekonstruie'ren.

record, 1. n. (document) Urkunde, -n f.; (top achievement) Rekord', -e m.; (phonograph) Schallplatte, -n f.; (r. player) Plattenspieler, - m. 2. vb. ein·tragen*; auf·zeichnen; (phonograph, tape) auf·nehmen*.

recording, n. (phonograph, tape) Aufnahme, -n f.

recourse, n. Zuflucht f.

recover, vb. wieder·gewinnen*; (health) sich erho'len, gene'sen.

recovery, n. Wiedergewinnung, -en f.; (health) Erho'lung, -en f., Gene'sung, -en f.

recruit, 1. n. Rekrut', -en, -en m. 2. vb. an·werben*.

rectangle, n. Rechteck, -e nt.

rectifier, n. Gleichrichter, - m.

rectify, vb. berich'tigen.

recuperate, vb. sich erho'len.

recur, vb. wieder·kommen*, zurück'kommen*.

recycle, vb. wieder auf·bereiten.

red, adj. rot (¨-).

Red Cross, n. Rotes Kreuz nt.

redeem, vb. ein·lösen; (eccles.) erlö'sen.

redeemer, n. (eccles.) Erlö'ser m., Heiland m.

redemption, n. Einlösung, -en f.; (eccles.) Erlö'sung f.

reduce, vb. verrin'gern, mindern, reduzie'ren; (prices) herab'setzen; (weight) ab·nehmen*.

reduction, n. Vermin'derung, -en f.; Herab·setzung, -en f.;

Ermäßigung, -en f.; Reduktion', -en f.

reed, n. Schilf nt.; *(music)* Rohrflöte, -n f.

reef, 1. n. Riff, -e nt.; *(sail)* Reff, -e nt. 2. vb. reffen.

reel, 1. n. Winde, -n f., Spule, -n f., Rolle, -n f. 2. vb. wickeln, spulen, drehen.

refer, vb. (r. to) sich bezie'hen* auf; sich beru'fen* auf; ver-wei'sen* auf.

referee, n. Schiedsrichter, - m.

reference, n. Bezug'nahme, -n f., Hinweis, -e m.; *(recommendation)* Zeugnis, -se nt.; **(cross-r.)** Querverweis, -e m.; **(r. library)** Handbibliothek, -en f.

refill, vb. wiederfüllen, nach-füllen.

refine, vb. verfei'nern; *(tech.)* raffinie'ren.

refinement, n. Verfei'nerung, -en f.; *(culture)* Bildung f.

reflect, vb. zurück'strahlen; wi-der-spiegeln; *(think)* nach-denken*.

reflection, n. Widerspiegelung, -en f., Reflexion', -en f.

reflex, n. Reflex', -e m.

reform, 1. n. Reform', -en f. 2. vb. verbes'sern, reformie'ren.

reformation, n. Reformation' f.

refrain, 1. n. Refrain', -s m. 2. vb. sich enthal'ten*.

refresh, vb. auf-frischen; erfri'-schen.

refreshment, n. Erfri'schung, -en f.

refrigerator, n. Kühlschrank, -e m.

refuge, n. Zuflucht f.

refugee, n. Flüchtling, -e m.

refund, 1. n. Rückzahlung, -en f. 2. vb. zurück'-zahlen.

refusal, n. Verwei'gerung, -en f.

refuse, 1. n. *(waste matter)* Ab-fall, -e m. 2. vb. verwei'gern; ab-schlagen*.

refute, vb. widerle'gen.

regain, vb. wieder-gewinnen*.

regal, adj. königlich.

regard, 1. n. Achtung, f.; *(greetings)* Grüße pl.; **(in r. to)** hinsichtlich. 2. vb. be-trach'ten.

regarding, prep. hinsichtlich.

regardless, adv. (r. of) ohne Rücksicht auf.

regime, n. Regi'me, -s nt.

regiment, n. Regiment', -er nt.

region, n. Gebiet', -e nt., Ge-gend, -en f.

register, 1. n. Verzeich'nis, -se nt.; *(music)* Regis'ter, - nt. 2. vb. verzeich'nen; ein-tragen*; *(letter)* ein-schrei-ben*.

registration, n. Registrie'rung, -en f.

regret, 1. n. Bedau'ern nt. 2. vb. bedau'ern, bereu'en.

regular, adj. regelmäßig; or-dentlich; gewöhn'lich.

regularity, n. Regelmäßigkeit f.

regulate, vb. regeln, ordnen, regulie'ren.

regulation, n. Regelung, -en f., Vorschrift, -en f.

rehabilitate, vb. rehabilitie'ren.

rehearsal, n. Probe, -n f.

rehearse, vb. proben.

reign, 1. n. Herrschaft f. 2. vb. herrschen.

reimburse, vb. zurück'-erstat-ten.

rein, n. Zügel, - m.

reindeer, n. Renntier, -e nt.

reinforce, vb. verstär'ken.

reinforcement, n. Verstär'k-ung, -en f.

reinstate, vb. wiederein'-setzen.

reiterate, vb. wiederho'len.

reject, vb. ab-lehnen, verwer'-fen*.

rejoice, vb. frohlo'cken.

rejuvenate, vb. verjün'gen.

relapse, 1. n. Rückfall, -e m. 2. vb. zurück'-fallen*.

relate, vb. *(tell)* berich'ten er-zäh'len; *(connect)* verknüp'-fen; *(be connected with)* sich bezie'hen*.

related, adj. verwandt'.

relate (to), vb. gemein haben (mit), zurechtkommen* (mit).

relation, n. *(story)* Erzäh'lung, -en f.; *(connection)* Bezie'-hung, -en f.; *(person)* Ver-wandt' m.&f.

relationship, n. Bezie'hung, -en f.; *(kinship)* Verwandt'-schaft, -en f.

relative, 1. n. Verwandt'- m.&f. 2. adj. relativ'.

relativity, n. Relativität' f.

relax, vb. sich entspan'nen; lockern.

relay, 1. n. Relais', - nt. 2. vb. übermit'teln.

release, 1. n. Entlas'sung, -en f., Befrei'ung, -en f. 1. vb. entlas'sen*; frei'lassen*.

relent, vb. sich erwei'chen las-sen*.

relevant, adj. einschlägig.

reliable, adj. zuverlässig.

relic, n. Reli'quie, -n f.; Uber-rest, -e m.

relief, n. Erleich'terung, -en f.; *(social work)* Unterstüt'zung, -en f.; *(replacement)* Ablö-sung, -en f.; *(art)* Relief', -s nt.

relieve, vb. erleich'tern; ab-lösen.

religion, n. Religion', -en f.

religious, adj. religiös', fromm.

relinquish, vb. auf-geben*.

relish, 1. n. Genuß', -sse m. 2. vb. genie'ßen*.

reluctance, n. Widerstre'ben nt.

reluctant, adj. widerstre'bend.

rely, vb. (r. on) sich verlas'sen* auf.

remain, vb. bleiben*; übrig bleiben*.

remainder, n. Rest, -e m.

remark, 1. n. Bemer'kung, -en f. 2. vb. bemer'ken.

remarkable, adj. bemer'kens-wert, beacht'lich.

remedy, 1. n. Heilmittel, - nt. 2. vb. heilen; ab-helfen*.

remember, vb. sich erin'nern an.

remind, vb. erin'nern; ermah'-nen.

reminiscence, n. Erin'nerung, -en f.

remiss, adj. nachlässig.

remit, vb. *(send)* übersen'den*; *(send money)* überwei'sen*; *(forgive)* verzei'hen*.

remittance, n. Überwei'sung, -en f.

remnant, n. Rest, -e m.

remorse, n. Gewis'senbiß, -sse m.

remote, adj. entle'gen.

removable, adj. abnehmbar, entfern'bar.

removal, n. Entfer'nung f., Be-sei'tigung f.

remove, vb. entfer'nen, weg-räumen, besei'tigen.

renaissance, n. Renaissance' f.

rend, vb. zerrei'ßen*.

render, vb. geben*; erwei'sen*.

rendezvous, n. Stelldichein, - nt., Rendezvous', - nt.

rendition, n. Wiedergabe, -n f.

renew, vb. erneu'ern; *(subscrip-tion)* verlän'gern.

renewal, n. Erneu'erung, -en f.; *(subscription)* Verlän'gerung, -en f.

renounce, vb. entsa'gen, ver-zich'ten auf.

renovate, vb. renovie'ren.

renowned, adj. berühmt', nam-haft.

rent, 1. n. Miete, -n f. 2. vb. *(from someone)* mieten; *(to someone)* vermie'ten.

rental, n. Miete, -n f.

repair, 1. n. Ausbesserung, -en f., Reparatur', -en f. 2. vb. aus-bessern, reparie'ren.

reparation, n. Reparation', -en f.

repatriate, 1. n. Repatriiert'- m.&f. 2. vb. repatriie'ren.

repay, vb. zurück'-zahlen.

repeat, vb. wiederho'len.

repel, vb. zurück'-treiben*; ab-schlagen*.

repent, vb. bereu'en.

repentance, n. Reue f.

repercussion, n. Auswirkung, -en f.

repertoire, n. Repertoire', -s nt.

repetition, n. Wiederho'lung, -en f.

replace, vb. erset'zen.

replenish, vb. wieder auf-fül-len.

reply, 1. *n.* Antwort, -en *f.* 2. *vb.* antworten, erwi'dern.

report, 1. *n.* Bericht', -e *m.;* *(bang)* Knall, -e *m.; (rumor)* Gerücht', -e *nt.* 2. *vb.* berich'ten; *(complain of)* an·zeigen.

reporter, *n.* Bericht'erstatter, - *m.,* Repor'ter, - *m.*

repose, 1. *n.* Ruhe *f.* 2. *vb.* ruhen.

represent, *vb.* dar·stellen; vertre'ten°.

representation, *n.* Darstellung, -en *f.;* Vertre'tung, -en *f.*

representative, 1. *n.* Vertre'ter, - *m.; (pol.)* Abgeordnet- *m.&f.* 2. *adj.* bezeich'nend, typisch.

repress, *vb.* unterdrü'cken.

repression, *n.* Unterdrü'ckung, -en *f.,* Repression', -en *f.*

reprimand, 1. *n.* Tadel, - *m.,* Verweis', -e *m.* 2. *vb.* einen Verweis' ertei'len.

reprisal, *n.* Vergel'tungsmaßnahme, -n *f.*

reproach, 1. *n.* Vorwurf, ·e *m.* 2. *vb.* vor·werfen°.

reproduce, *vb.* reproduzie'ren.

reproduction, *n.* Wiedergabe, - n *f.,* Reproduktion', -en *f.*

reptile, *n.* Reptil', -e *nt.*

republic, *n.* Republik', -en *f.*

republican, 1. *n.* Republika'ner, - *m.* 2. *adj.* republika'nisch.

repudiate, *vb.* ab·leugnen.

repudiation, *n.* Zurück'weisung, -en *f.,* Nichtanerkennung, -en *f.*

repulse, *vb.* zurück'schlagen°.

repulsive, *adj.* widerwärtig.

reputation, *n.* Ruf *m.,* Ansehen *nt.*

repute, *n.* Ansehen *nt.*

request, 1. *n.* Bitte, -n *f.,* Gesuch', -e *nt.* 2. *vb.* bitten°, ersu'chen.

require, *vb.* verlan'gen, erfor'dern.

requirement, *n.* Erfor'dernis, -se *nt.;* Bedin'gung, -en *f.*

requisite, 1. *n.* Erfor'dernis, -se *nt.* 2. *adj.* erfor'derlich.

requisition, 1. *n.* Forderung, - en *f.,* Requisition', -en *f.* 2. *vb.* an·fordern; beschlag'nahmen.

rescind, *vb.* rückgängig machen, auf·heben°.

rescue, 1. *n.* Rettung, -en *f.* 2. *vb.* retten.

research, *n.* Forschung, -en *f.*

resemble, *vb.* gleichen°, ähneln.

resent, *vb.* übel·nehmen°.

reservation, *n.* vorbehalt *m.; (tickets)* Vorbestellung, -en *f.;* **(Indian r.)** Reservation', -en *f.*

reserve, 1. *n.* Reser've, -n *f.* 2. *vb.* vor·behalten°; *(seats)* reservie'ren.

reservoir, *n.* Reservoir', -s *nt.*

reside, *vb.* wohnen.

residence, *n.* Wohnsitz, -e *m.*

---

resident, 1. *n.* Einwohner, - *m.* 2. *adj.* wohnhaft.

residue, *n.* Rest, -e *m.,* Restbestand, ·e *m.*

resign, *vb.* zurück'treten°; (r. oneself) sich ab·finden° mit, resignie'ren.

resignation, *n.* Rücktritt, -e *m.;* Resignation', -en *f.*

resist, *vb.* widerste'hen°.

resistance, *n.* Widerstand, ·e *m.*

resolute, *adj.* entschlos'sen.

resolution, *n.* Beschluß', ·sse *m.;* Entschlos'senheit *f.*

resolve, *vb.* entschei'den°; beschlie'ßen°.

resonance, *n.* Resonanz', -en *f.*

resonant, *adj.* resonant'.

resort, *n.* Ferienort, -e *m.;* Kurort, -e *m.*

resound, *vb.* wider·hallen.

resources, *n.pl.* Hilfsquellen *pl.;* (natural r.) Bodenschätze *pl.*

respect, 1. *n. (esteem)* Achtung *f.; (reference)* Hinsicht, -en *f.* 2. *vb.* achten.

respectable, *adj.* angesehen, ansehnlich.

respectful, *adj.* ehrerbietig, höflich.

respective, *adj.* entspre'chend.

respiration, *n.* Atmung *f.*

respite, *n.* Frist, -en *f.;* Atempause, -n *f.*

respond, *vb. (answer)* antworten; *(react)* reagie'ren.

response, *n.* Antwort, -en *f.;* Reaktion', -en *f.*

responsibility, *n.* Verant'wortung, -en *f.*

responsible, *adj.* verant'wortlich.

responsive, *adj.* zugänglich.

rest, 1. *n. (remainder)* Rest, -e *m.; (repose)* Ruhe *f.* 2. *vb.* ruhen; *(be based on)* beru'hen auf.

restaurant, *n.* Restaurant', -s *nt.*

restful, *adj.* ausruhsam.

restitution, *n.* Wiedergutmachung, -en *f.*

restless, *adj.* unruhig.

restoration, *n.* Wiederherstellung, -en *f.*

restore, *vb.* wiederher'stellen.

restrain, *vb.* zurück'halten°.

restraint, *n.* Zurück'haltung *f.*

restrict, *vb.* beschrän'ken, ein·schränken.

restriction, *n.* Einschränkung, -en *f.,* Beschrän'kung, -en *f.*

result, 1. *n.* Ergeb'nis, -se *nt.,* Resultat', -e *nt.* 2. *vb.* erge'ben°; zur Folge haben°.

resume, *vb.* wieder auf·nehmen°.

résumé, *n.* Resümee', -s *nt.*

resurrect, *vb.* wiedererwecken; wieder hervor·holen.

resurrection, *n. (eccles.)* Auferstehung *f.*

---

retail, 1. *n.* Einzelhandel *m.* 2. *vb.* im Einzelhandel vertrei'ben°.

retain, *vb.* bei·behalten°; zurück'halten°; auf·halten°.

retaliate, *vb.* vergel'ten°.

retaliation, *n.* Vergel'tung, -en *f.*

retard, *vb.* verzö'gern, zurück'halten°.

retention, *n.* Beibehaltung, -en *f.*

reticence, *n.* Zurück'haltung *f.;* Verschwie'genheit *f.*

reticent, *adj.* zurück'haltend, schweigsam.

retina, *n.* Netzhaut, ·e *f.*

retinue, *n.* Gefol'ge *nt.*

retire, *vb.* sich zurück'ziehen°; *(from office)* sich pensionie'ren lassen°, in den Ruhestand treten°.

retort, 1. *n.* Retor'te, -n *f.; (answer)* Erwi'derung, -en *f.* 2. *vb.* erwi'dern.

retract, *vb. (pull back)* zurück'ziehen°, *(recant)* widerru'fen°.

retreat, 1. *n. (withdrawal)* Rückzug, ·e *m.; (refuge)* Zuflucht *f.; (privacy)* Zurück'gezogenheit *f.* 2. *vb.* zurück'weichen°.

retribution, *n.* Strafe, -n *f.,* Vergel'tung *f.*

retrieve, *vb.* wieder·erlangen.

retroactive, *adj.* rückwirkend.

retrospect, *n.* Rückblick *m.*

return, 1. *n.* Rückkehr *f.,* Heimkehr *f.;* Rückgabe *f.* 2. *vb.* zurück'kehren, zurück'kommen°; zurück'geben°.

reunion, *n.* Wiederzusam'menkommen *nt.*

reunite, *vb.* wieder verei'nigen.

reveal, *vb.* offenba'ren; zeigen.

revel, *vb.* schwelgen.

revelation, *n.* Offenba'rung, -en *f.*

revelry, *n.* Schwiegerei, -en *f.*

revenge, 1. *n.* Rache *f.* 2. *vb.* rächen.

revenue, *n.* Einkommen, - *nt.*

reverberate, *vb.* wider·hallen.

revere, *vb.* vereh'ren.

reverence, *n.* Vereh'rung, -en *f.;* Ehrfurcht *f.*

reverend, *adj.* ehrwürdig.

reverent, *adj.* ehrerbietig.

reverie, *n.* Träumerei', -en *f.*

reverse, 1. *n. (opposite)* Gegenteil *nt.; (back)* Rückseite, -n *f.; (misfortune)* Rückschlag, ·e *m.; (auto)* Rückwärtsgang, ·e *m.* 2. *vb.* um·drehen; *(auto)* rückwärts·fahren°; *(tech.)* um·steuern.

revert, *vb.* zurück'kehren.

review, 1. *n.* nochmalige Durchsicht, -en *f.,* Überblick, -e *m.; (book r.)* Kritik', -en *f.,* Bespre'chung, -en *f.* 2. *vb.* überbli'cken, revidie'ren; bespre'chen°.

revise, vb. ab·ändern, revidie'ren.

revision, n. Revision', -en f.

revival, n. Wiederbelebung, -en f., Neubelebung, -en f.

revive, vb. (person) wieder zu Bewußt'sein bringen*; (fashion) wieder auf·leben lassen*.

revocation, n. Aufhebung, -en f.

revoke, vb. widerru'fen*, auf·heben*.

revolt, 1. n. Aufstand, =e m. **2.** vb. revolte'ren.

revolution, n. Revolution', -en f.; (turn) Umdre'hung, -en f.

revolutionary, adj. revolutio-när'.

revolve, vb. sich drehen.

revolver, n. Revol'ver, - m.

reward, 1. n. Beloh'nung, -en f. **2.** vb. beloh'nen.

rhetorical, adj. rheto'risch.

rheumatic, adj. rheuma'tisch.

rheumatism, n. Rheumatis'mus m.

rhinoceros, n. Nashorn, =er nt.

rhubarb, n. Rhabar'ber m.

rhyme, n. Reim, -e m.

rhythm, n. Rhythmus, -men m.

rhythmical, adj. rhythmisch.

rib, n. Rippe, -n f.

ribbon, n. Band, =er nt.

rice, n. Reis m.

rich, adj. reich.

rid, vb. los·werden*; sich los·machen.

riddle, n. Rätsel, - m.

ride, 1. n. (horse) Ritt, -e m.; (vehicles) Fahrt, -en f. **1.** vb. reiten*; fahren*.

rider, n. Reiter, - m.

ridge, n. (mountain) Grat, -e m.; (mountain range) Bergrücken, - m.

ridicule, 1. n. Spott m. **2.** vb. lächerlich machen, bespöt'teln.

ridiculous, adj. lächerlich.

rifle, n. Gewehr', -e nt.

rig, 1. n. (gear) Ausrüstung, -en f.; (ship) Takela'ge, -n f.; (oil) Ölbohrer, - m. **2.** vb. auf·takeln.

right, 1. n. Recht, -e nt. **2.** adj. (side) recht-; (just) gerecht'; (be r.) recht haben*. **3.** adv. rechts. **4.** vb. (set upright) auf·richten; (correct) wiedergut'·machen.

righteous, adj. rechtschaffen; (smug) selbstgerecht.

righteousness, n. Rechtschaffenheit f.; Selbstgerechtheit f.

right of way, n. Vorfahrtsrecht, -e nt.

rigid, adj. steif; starr.

rigidity, n. Starrheit f.

rigor, n. Härte, -n f.

rigorous, adj. hart (-), streng.

rim, n. Rand, =er m.

ring, 1. n. Ring, -e m.; (circle) Kreis, -e m.; (of bell) Klingeln nt. **2.** vb. klingeln.

rinse, vb. spülen.

riot, 1. n. Aufruhr, -e m. **2.** vb. in Aufruhr gera'ten*.

rip, vb. reißen*; auf·trennen.

ripe, adj. reif.

ripen, n., vb. reifen.

ripoff, n. Übervor'teilung f.

rip off, vb. jemand reinlegen.

ripple, 1. n. leichte Welle, -n f. **2.** vb. leichte Wellen schlagen*.

rise, 1. n. (increase) Zuwachs m.; (emergence) Aufgang, =e m.; (advance) Aufstieg, -e m. **2.** vb. an·steigen*; auf·gehen*; (get up) auf·stehen*.

risk, 1. n. Risiko, -s nt. **2.** vb. wagen.

rite, n. Ritus, -ten m.

ritual, 1. n. Rituell', -e nt. **2.** adj. rituell'.

rival, 1. n. Riva'le, -n, -n m., Konkurrenz', -en f. **2.** n. Konkurrenz- (cpds.). **3.** vb. wetteifern, rivalisie'ren.

rivalry, n. Konkurrenz', -en f., Wettstreit m.

river, n. Fluß, =sse m.

rivet, n. Niete, -n f. **2.** vb. nieten.

road, n. Straße, -n f., Landstraße, -n f.

roam, vb. umher·schweifen.

roar, 1. n. Gebrüll' nt. **2.** vb. brüllen; brausen.

roast, 1. n. Braten, - m. **2.** vb. braten*; rösten.

rob, vb. rauben; berau'ben.

robber, n. Räuber, - m.; Dieb, -e m.

robbery, n. Raub m.

robe, n. Gewand', =er nt.

robin, n. Rotkehlchen, - nt.

robot, n. Roboter, - m.

robust, adj. robust'.

rock, 1. n. Stein, m.; Felsen, - m.; (music) Rock m., Rockmusik f. **2.** vb. schaukeln.

rocker, n. Schaukelstuhl, =e m.

rocket, n. Rake'te, -n f.

rocky, adj. felsig; (shaky) wackelig.

rod, n. Stab, =e m., Stange, -n f.

rodent, n. Nagetier, -e nt.

roe, n. Rogen, - m.; (deer) Reh, -e nt.

role, n. Rolle, -n f.

roll, 1. n. Rolle, -n f.; Walze, -n f.; (bread) Brötchen, - nt. **2.** vb. rollen; (ship) schlingern.

roller, n. Rolle, -n f.; Walze, -n f.

Roman, 1. n. Römer, - m. **2.** adj. römisch.

romance, n. Roman'ze, -n f.; Liebesaffä're, -n f.

Romance, adj. roma'nisch.

romantic, adj. roman'tisch.

romanticism, n. Roman'tik f.

Rome, n. Rom nt.

roof, n. Dach, =er nt.

room, n. Zimmer, - nt., Raum, =e m.; (space) Raum m.

roommate, n. Zimmergenosse, -n, -n m.

rooster, n. Hahn, =e m.

root, 1. n. Wurzel, -n f. **2.** vb. (be rooted) wurzeln.

rope, n. Tau, -e m., Seil, -e nt., Strick, -e m.

rosary, n. Rosenkranz, =e m.

rose, n. Rose, -n f.

rosy, adj. rosig.

rot, vb. verfau'len, verwe·sen.

rotate, vb. rotie'ren; sich ab·wechseln.

rotation, n. Umdre'hung, -en f., Rotation', -en f.; Wechsel, - m.

rotten, adj. faul; (base) niederträchtig.

rouge, n. Rouge nt.

rough, adj. rauh; (coarse) grob (-); (sea) stürmisch.

round, 1. n. Runde, -n f. **2.** adj. rund. **3.** prep. um, um . . . herum'.

rout, 1. n. wilde Flucht f. **2.** vb. in die Flucht schlagen*.

route, n. Weg, -e m. Route, -n f.

routine, 1. n. Routi'ne, -n f. **2.** adj. alltäg'lich.

rove, vb. umher·streifen.

row, 1. n. (line, series) Reihe, -n f.; (fight) Krach m. **2.** vb. rudern.

rowboat, n. Ruderboot, -e nt.

royal, adj. königlich.

royalty, n. Königstum nt.; Mitglied eines Königshauses; (share of profit) Gewinn'anteil, -e m.

rub, vb. reiben*.

rubber, n. Gummi nt.

rubbish, n. Abfall, =e m.; (nonsense) Quatsch m.

ruby, n. Rubin', -e m.

rudder, n. Steuerruder, - nt.

rude, adj. rauh, unhöflich.

rudiment, n. erster Anfang, =e m.; Anfangsgrund, =e m.

ruffle, 1. n. Rüsche, -n f. **2.** vb. kräuseln.

rug, n. Teppich, -e m.

rugged, adj. rauh, hart (-).

ruin, 1. n. Untergang m.; Rui'ne, -n f.; (r.s) Trümmer pl. **2.** vb. ruinie'ren.

ruinous, adj. verderb'lich, katastrophal'.

rule, 1. n. (reign) Herrschaft f.; (regulation) Regel, -n f. **2.** vb. herrschen; entschei'den*.

ruler, n. Herrscher, - m.; (measuring stick) Lineal', -e nt.

rum, n. Rum m.

rumor, 1. n. Gerücht', -e nt. **2.** vb. munkeln.

run, 1. n. Lauf m.; (stocking) Laufmasche, -n f. **2.** vb. laufen*; (flow) fließen*.

rung, n. Sprosse, -n f.

runner, n. Läufer, - m.

runway, n. Startbahn, -en f.

rupture, 1. n. Bruch, =e m. **2.** vb. brechen*; reißen*.

rural, adj. ländlich.

rush, 1. n. Andrange m.; (hurry) Eile f. **2.** vb. drängen; eilen, sich stürzen.

Russia, n. Rußland nt.

Russian, 1. n. Russe, -n, -n m. **2.** adj. russisch.

rust, 1. n. Rost m. **2.** vb. rosten.

rustic, adj. bäurisch.

rustle, vb. rascheln.

rusty, adj. rostig.

rut, n. Rinne, -n f.; Radspur, -en f.

ruthless, adj. erbar'mungslos, rücksichtslos.

rye, n. Roggen m.

S

Sabbath, n. Sabbat, -e m.

saber, n. Säbel, - m.

sable, n. Zobel m.

sabotage, 1. n. Sabota'ge f. **2.** vb. sabotie'ren.

saboteur, n. Saboteur', -e m.

saccharine, n. Sacharin' nt.

sack, 1. n. Sack, ⸗e m. **2.** vb. (plunder) plündern; (discharge) auf der Stelle entlas'sen*.

sacrament, n. Sakrament', -e nt.

sacred, adj. heilig.

sacrifice, 1. n. Opfer, - nt. **2.** vb. opfern.

sacrilege, n. Sakrileg', -e nt.

sacrilegious, adj. gottesläster-lich.

sad, adj. traurig.

sadden, vb. betrü'ben.

saddle, 1. n. Sattel, - m. **2.** vb. satteln.

sadism, n. Sadis'mus m.

safe, 1. n. Geldschrank, ⸗e m. **2.** adj. sicher.

safeguard, 1. n. Schutz m. **2.** vb. schützen; sichern.

safety, n. Sicherheit f.

safety-pin, n. Sicherheitsnadel, -n f.

sage, adj. weise.

sail, 1. n. Segel, - nt. **2.** vb. se-geln.

sailboat, n. Segelboot, -e nt.

sailor, n. Matro'se, -n, -n m.

saint, 1. n. Heilig- m.&f. **2.** adj. heilig.

sake, n. (for the s. of) um . . . willen.

salad, n. Salat', -e m.

salary, n. Gehalt', ⸗er nt.

sale, n. Verkauf' m.; (bargain s.) Ausverkauf m.

salesman, n. Verkäufer, - m.; (traveling s.) Handelsreisend-m.

sales tax, n. Umsatzsteuer, -n f.

saliva, n. Speichel m.

salmon, n. Lachs m.

salon, n. Salon', -s m.

salt, 1. n. Salz, -e nt. **2.** vb. sal-zen.

salty, adj. salzig.

salutation, n. Gruß, ⸗e m.; Be-grü'ßung, -en f.

salute, 1. n. Gruß, ⸗e m. **2.** vb. salutie'ren.

salvage, 1. n. (act) Bergung f.; (material) Bergegut nt. **2.** vb. bergen*, retten.

salvation, n. Rettung f., Heil nt.

salve, n. Salbe, -n f.

same, adj. selb-; (the s.) der-selbe, dasselbe, dieselbe.

sample, 1. n. Probe, -n f., Mus-ter, - nt. **2.** vb. probie'ren.

sanatorium, n. Sanato'rium, -rien nt.

sanctify, vb. heiligen.

sanction, 1. n. Sanktion', -en f. **2.** vb. sanktionie'ren.

sanctity, n. Heiligkeit f.

sanctuary, n. Heiligtum, ⸗er nt.; (refuge) Zufluchtsort, -e m.

sand, n. Sand, -e m.

sandal, n. Sanda'le, -n f.

sandwich, n. belegtes Brot, -e nt.

sandy, adj. sandig.

sane, adj. vernünf'tig; geistig gesund'.

sanitary, adj. Gesund'heits-(cpds.).; hygie'nisch.

sanitation, n. Gesund'heitswe-sen nt.

sanity, n. geistige Gesund'heit f.

Santa Claus, n. Weihnachts-mann, ⸗er m.

sap, 1. n. Saft, ⸗e m. **2.** vb. schwächen.

sapphire, n. Saphir', -e m.

sarcasm, n. Sarkas'mus m.

sarcastic, adj. sarkas'tisch.

sardine, n. Sardi'ne, -n f.

sash, n. Schärpe, -n f.; (window) Fensterrahmen, - m.

satellite, n. Satellit', -en, -en m.

satin, n. Satin', -s m.

satire, n. Sati're, -n f.

satirize, vb. verspot'ten.

satisfaction, n. Genug'tuung, -en f.; Befrie'digung, -en f.

satisfactory, adj. befrie'digend, genü'gend.

satisfy, vb. befrie'digen, genü-gen.

saturate, vb. sättigen.

saturation, n. Sättigung f.

Saturday, n. Sonnabend, -e m., Samstag, -e m.

sauce, n. Soße, -n f.

saucer, n. Untertasse, -n f.

sausage, n. Wurst, ⸗e f.

savage, 1. n. Wild- m.&f. **2.** adj. wild.

save, 1. vb. (preserve) bewah'ren; (rescue) retten; (economize) sparen. **2.** prep. außer.

savings, n.pl. Erspar'nisse pl.

savior, n. Retter, - m.; (eccles.) Heiland m.

savor, 1. n. Geschmack', ⸗e m. **2.** vb. aus-kosten.

saw, 1. n. Säge, -n f.; (proverb)

Sprichwort, ⸗er nt. **2.** vb. sä-gen.

say, vb. sagen.

saying, n. Redensart, -en f.

scab, n. Schorf m.; (strike breaker) Streikbrecher, - m.

scaffold, n. Gerüst', -e nt.; (exe-cution) Schafott', -e nt.

scald, n. brühen; verbrü'hen.

scale, 1. n. Maßstab, ⸗e m., Skala, -len f.; (music) Tonlei-ter, -n f.; (weight measuring) Waage, -n f.; (fish) Schuppe, -n f. **2.** vb. (climb) erklet'tern.

scalp, n. Kopfhaut, ⸗e f.; (In-dian) Skalp, -e m.

scan, vb. überflie'gen*; (verse) skandie'ren.

scandal, n. Skandal', -e m.

scandalous, adj. schimpflich, unerhört'.

scant, adj. knapp.

scar, n. Narbe, -n f.

scarce, adj. selten; knapp.

scarcely, adv. kaum.

scarcity, n. Knappheit f., Man-gel m.

scare, 1. n. Schreck m. **2.** vb. erschre'cken; (be s.d) er-schre'cken*.

scarf, n. Schal, -s m., Halstuch, ⸗er nt.

scarlet, adj. scharlachrot.

scarlet fever, n. Scharlach m.

scatter, vb. zerstreu'en.

scenario, n. Inszenie'rung, -en f.; (film) Drehbuch, ⸗er nt.

scene, n. Szene, -n f.

scenery, n. Landschaft, -en f.; (stage) Bühnenausstattung, -en f.

scent, n. Geruch', ⸗e m.; (track) Spur, -en f.

schedule, 1. n. Liste, -n f.; Pro-gramm', -e nt.; (timetable) Fahrplan, ⸗e m.; (school) Stundenplan, ⸗e m. **2.** vb. an-setzen.

scheme, 1. n. Plan, ⸗e m.; Schema, -s nt. **2.** vb. intrigie'-ren.

scholar, n. Gelehrt'- m.&f.

scholarship, n. (knowledge) Ge-lehr'samkeit f.; (stipend) Sti-pen'dium, -dien nt.

school, n. Schule, -n f.

science, n. Wissenschaft, -en f.

science fiction, n. Science fic-tion f.

scientific, adj. wissenschaft-lich.

scientist, n. Natur'wissen-schaftler, - m.

scissors, n.pl. Schere, -n f.

scold, vb. schelten*.

scolding, n. Schelte f.

scoop, n. (ladle) Schöpfkelle, -n f.; (newspaper) Erstmel-dung, -en f.

scope, n. Reichweite f., Be-reich', -e m.

scorch, vb. sengen, brennen*.

score, 1. n. (points) Punktzahl, -en f.; (what's the s.?) wie steht das Spiel?; *(music)* Partitur', -en *f.* 2. *vb.* an·schrei-ben*; *(mark)* markie'ren.

scorn, 1. *n.* Verach'tung *f.* 2. *vb.* verach'ten.

scornful, *adj.* verächt'lich.

Scotland, *n.* Schottland *nt.*

Scotsman, *n.* Schotte, -n, -n *m.*

Scottish, *adj.* schottisch.

scour, *vb.* scheuern.

scout, 1. *n.* Kundschafter - *m.; (boy s.)* Pfadfinder, - *m.* 2. *vb.* erkun'den.

scowl, *vb.* finster blicken.

scramble, *vb. (tr.)* durcheinan-der·werfen*; *(intr.)* klettern; *(s. for)* sich reißen*um.

scrambled eggs, *n.* Rührei, -er *nt.*

scrap, 1. *n.* Fetzen, - *m.; (fight)* Streit *m.* 2. *vb.* aus·rangieren; *(fight)* streiten*.

scrape, *vb.* kratzen.

scratch, 1. *n.* Schramme, -n *f.* 2. *vb.* kratzen; streichen*; *(start from s.)* von Anfang an begin'nen*.

scream, 1. *n.* Schrei, -e *m.* 2. *vb.* schreien*, brüllen.

screen, 1. *n. (furniture)* Wand-schirm, -e *m.; (window)* Flie-gengitter, - *nt.; (movie)* Leinwand, -e *f.; (TV, radar)* Schirm, -e *m.f.* 2. *vb. (sift)* sieben; *(hide)* tarnen.

screw, 1. *n.* Schraube, -n *f.* 2. *vb.* schrauben.

scribble, *vb.* kritzeln, schmie-ren.

scripture, *n. (eccles.)* Heilige Schrift, -en *f.*

scroll, *n.* Schriftrolle, -n *f.*

scrub, *vb.* schrubben.

scruple, *n.* Skrupel, - *m.*, Be-den'ken, - *nt.*

scrupulous, *adj.* gewis'senhaft.

scrutinize, *vb.* genau' betrach'-ten.

sculptor, *n.* Bildhauer, - *m.*

sculpture, 1. *n.* Skulptur', -en *f.* 2. *vb.* bildhauern.

scythe, *n.* Sense, -n *f.*

sea, *n.* See, Se'en *f.*, Meer, -e *nt.; (waves)* Seegang *m.*

seabed, *n.* Meeresboden *m.*

seal, 1. *n.* Siegel, - *nt.; (animal)* Seehund, -e *m.*, Robbe, -n *f.* 2. *vb.* siegeln, versie'geln.

seam, 1. *n.* Saum, -e *m.* 2. *vb.* säumen.

seaport, *n.* Hafen, - *m.*

search, 1. *n.* Suche *f.; (Durch-su'chung, -en *f.* 2. *vb.* suchen; durch·su'chen.

seasick, *adj.* seekrank (-).

seasickness, *n.* Seekrankheit *f.*

season, 1. *n.* Jahreszeit, -en *f.; (Saison', -s *f.* 2. *vb.* würzen.

seasoning, *n.* Gewürz', -e *nt.*

seat, 1. *n.* Platz, -e *m.*, Sitz-platz, -e *m.; (headquarters)* Sitz, -e *m.* 2. *vb.* Sitzplätze haben* für.

second, 1. *n.* Sekun'de, -n *f.* 2.

adj. zweit-. 3. *vb.* **(s. a motion)** einen Antrag unterstüt'zen.

secondary, *adj.* sekundär'.

secret, 1. *n.* Geheim'nis, -se *nt.* 2. *adj.* geheim', heimlich.

secretary, *n.* Sekretär'-e *m.;* Sekretä'rin, -nen *f.; (organization)* Schriftführer, - *m.*

sect, *n.* Sekte, -n *f.*

section, *n.* Schnitt, -e *m.;* Teil, -e *m.;* Abschnitt, -e *m.;* Ab-tei'lung, -en *f.*

secular, *adj.* weltlich.

secure, 1. *adj.* sicher. 2. *vb.* si-chern.

security, *n.* Sicherheit, -en *f.*

sedative, *n.* Beru'higungsmit-tel, - *nt.*

seduce, *vb.* verfüh'ren.

seductive, *adj.* verfüh'rerisch.

see, *vb.* sehen*, schauen.

seed, *n. (individual)* Samen, - *m.; (collective & fig.)* Saat, -en *f.*

seek, *vb.* suchen.

seem, *vb.* scheinen*.

seep, *vb.* sickern.

seesaw, 1. *n.* Wippe, -n *f.* 2. *vb.* schaukeln.

segment, *n.* Segment', -e *nt.*

segregate, *vb.* ab·sondern.

seize, *vb.* fassen, ergrei'fen*; *(confiscate)* beschlag'nahmen.

seldom, *adv.* selten.

select, 1. *adj.* ausgesucht. 2. *vb.* aus·wählen, aus·suchen.

selection, *n.* Auswahl, -en *f.*

selective, *adj.* auswählend.

self, *adv.* selbst, selber.

selfish, *adj.* selbstsüchtig.

selfishness, *n.* Selbstsucht *f.*

sell, *vb.* verkau'fen.

semantic, *adj.* seman'tisch.

semantics, *n.* Seman'tik *f.*

semester, *n.* Semes'ter, - *nt.*

semicircle, *n.* Halbkreis, -e *m.*

semicolon, *n.* Strichpunkt, -e *m.*, Semiko'lon *nt.*

seminary, *n.* Seminar', -e *nt.*

senate, *n.* Senat', -e *m.*

senator, *n.* Sena'tor, -o'ren *m.*

send, *vb.* senden*, schicken.

senile, *adj.* senil'.

senior, *adj.* älter-.

senior citizen, *n.* Senior, -o'ren *m.;* Senio'rin, -nen *f.*

sensation, *n.* Sensation', -en *f.; (feeling)* Gefühl', -e *nt.*

sensational, *adj.* sensationell'.

sense, 1. *n.* Sinn, -e *m.; (feel-ing)* Gefühl', -e *nt.; (meaning)* Bedeu'tung, -en *f.* 2. *vb.* füh-len, empfin'den*.

sensible, *adj.* vernünf'tig.

sensitive, *adj.* empfind'lich; sensitiv'.

sensual, *adj.* sinnlich.

sentence, 1. *n.* Satz, -e *m.; (judgment)* Urteil, -e *nt.* 2. *vb.* verur'teilen.

sentiment, *n.* Gefühl', -e *nt.*, Empfin'dung, -en *f.*

sentimental, *adj.* gefühl'voll, sentimen'tal'.

separate, 1. *adj.* getrennt'. 2. *vb.* trennen.

separation, *n.* Trennung, -en *f.*

September, *n.* Septem'ber, - *m.*

sequence, *n.* Reihenfolge, -n *f.*

serenade, *n.* Ständchen, - *nt.*

serene, *adj.* klar, ruhig.

sergeant, *n.* Unteroffizier, -e *m.; (police)* Wachtmeister, - *m.*

serial, 1. *n.* fortlaufende Er-zäh'lung, -en *f.* 2. *adj.* Reihen- *(cpds.)*

series, *n.* Reihe, -n *f.*

serious, *adj.* ernst.

seriousness, *n.* Ernst *m.*

sermon, *n.* Predigt, -en *f.*

serpent, *n.* Schlange, -n *f.*

serum, *n.* Serum, -ra *nt.*

servant, *n.* Diener, - *m.; (do-mestic)* Hausangestell-t- *m.&f.*

serve, *vb.* dienen; *(offer food)* servie'ren.

service, *n.* Dienst, -e *m.; (hotel, etc.)* Bedie'nung *f.; (china, etc.)* Servi'ce *nt.; (church)* Gottesdienst, -e *m.*

session, *n.* Sitzung, -en *f.*

set, 1. *n. (dishes, tennis)* Satz, -e *m.; (articles belonging to-gether)* Garnitur', -en *f.* 2. *adj.* bestimmt'. 3. *vb.* setzen; stellen; legen; *(sun)* unter·ge-hen*.

settle, *vb. (dwell)* sich nieder-lassen*; *(conclude)* erle'digen; *(decide)* entschei'den*.

settlement, *n.* Niederlassung, -en *f.;* Siedlung, -en *f.; (deci-sion)* Überein'kommen, - *nt.*

settler, *n.* Siedler, - *m.*

seven, *num.* sieben.

seventeen, *num.* siebzehn.

seventeenth, 1. *adj.* siebzehnt-. 2. *n.* Siebzehntel, - *nt.*

seventh, 1. *adj.* sieb(en)t-. 2. *n.* Sieb(en)tel, - *nt.*

seventieth, 1. *adj.* siebzigst-. 2. *n.* Siebzigstel, - *nt.*

seventy, *num.* siebzig.

sever, *vb.* ab·trennen, ab·brechen*.

several, *adj.* mehrer-.

severe, *adj.* streng; hart (-); ernst.

severity, *n.* Strenge *f.;* Härte *f.;* Ernst *m.*

sew, *vb.* nähen.

sewer, *n.* Kanalisation' *f.*

sex, *n.* Geschlecht', -er *nt.;* Sexus *m.*

sexism, *n.* Vorurteil gegen das andere Geschlecht *nt.*

sexist, *n.* jemand, der ein Vor-urteil gegen das andere Ge-schlecht hat.

sexual, *adj.* geschlecht'lich, se-xuell'.

shabby, *adj.* schäbig.

shack, *n.* Bretterbude, -n *f.*

shade, 1. *n.* Schatten, - *m.;*

(color) Farbton, -e *m*. 2. *vb*. beschat'ten; schattie'ren.

shadow, *n*. Schatten, - *m*.

shady, *adj*. schattig; *(dubious)* zwielechtig.

shaft, *n*. Schaft, -̈e *m*.; *(mine)* Schacht, -̈e *m*.; *(transmission)* Welle, -n *f*.; *(wagon)* Deichsel, -n *f*.

shaggy, *adj*. zottig.

shake, *vb*. schütteln.

shall, *vb*. (we s. do it) wir werden* es tun; (what s. we do?) was sollen* wir tun?

shallow, *adj*. flach.

shame, 1. *n*. Schande *f*.; (what a s.) wie schade. 2. *vb*. beschä'men.

shameful, *adj*. schandbar.

shameless, *adj*. schamlos.

shampoo, 1. *n*. Schampun', -s *f*. 2. *vb*. die Haare waschen*.

shape, 1. *n*. Form, -en *f*., Gestalt', -en *f*. 2. *vb*. formen, gestal'ten.

share, 1. *n*. Anteil, -e *m*.; *(stock)* Aktie, -n *f*. 2. *vb*. teilen; teil-haben*.

shark, *n*. Haifisch, -e *m*.

sharp, 1. *n*. *(music)* Kreuz, -e *nt*. 2. *adj*. scharf (-); *(clever)* schlau.

sharpen, *vb*. schärfen.

sharpness, *n*. Schärfe *f*.

shatter, *vb*. zerbre'chen*.

shave, 1. *vb*. rasie'ren. 2. *n*. Rasie'ren *nt*.; (get a s.) sich rasie'ren lassen.

shawl, *n*. Schal, -s *m*.

she, *pron*. sie.

shear, *vb*. scheren*.

shears, *n.pl*. Schere, -n *f*.

sheath, *n*. Scheide, -n *f*.; *(dress)* körperenges Kleid, -er *nt*.

shed, 1. *n*. Schuppen, - *m*. 2. *vb*. ab-werfen*; *(tears, blood)* vergie'ßen*.

sheep, *n*. Schaf, -e *nt*.

sheet, *n*. *(bed)* Laken, - *nt*.; *(paper)* Bogen, -̈ *m*.; *(metal)* Platte, -n *f*.

shelf, *n*. Bord, -e *nt*.

shell, 1. *n*. Schale, -n *f*.; *(conch)* Muschel, -n *f*.; *(explosive)* Grana'te, -n *f*. 2. *vb*. beschie'ßen*.

shellac, *n*. Schellack, -e *m*.

shelter, 1. *n*. Schutz *m*., Obdach *nt*. 2. *vb*. beschir'men; beher'bergen.

shepherd, *n*. Schäfer, - *m*., Hirt, -en, -en *m*.

sherbet, *n*. Sorbett, -e *nt*.

sherry, *n*. Sherry, -s *m*.

shield, 1. *n*. Schild, -e *m*. 2. *vb*. schützen.

shift, 1. *n*. Wechsel, - *m*.; *(workers)* Schicht, -en *f*.; *(auto)* Schalthebel, - *m*. 2. *vb*. wechseln; schalten; verschie'ben*.

shin, *n*. Schienbein, -e *nt*.

shine, *vb*. scheinen*, glänzen; *(shoes)* putzen.

shingle, *n*. Schindel, -n *f*., Dachschindel, -n *f*.

shiny, *adj*. glänzend.

ship, 1. *n*. Schiff, -e *nt*. 2. *vb*. senden*.

shipment, *n*. Ladung, -en *f*., Sendung, -en *f*.

shipper, *n*. Verfrach'ter, - *m*., Verla'der, - *m*.

shipping agent, *n*. Spediteur', -e *m*.

shipwreck, *n*. Schiffbruch, -̈e *m*.

shirk, *vb*. sich drücken vor.

shirt, *n*. Hemd, -en *nt*.

shiver, *vb*. zittern.

shock, 1. *n*. Schock, -s *m*. 2. *vb*. schockie'ren.

shoe, *n*. Schuh, -e *m*.

shoelace, *n*. Schnürsenkel, - *m*.

shoemaker, *n*. Schuhmacher, - *m*., Schuster, -m.

shoot, 1. *n*. *(sprout)* Schößling, -e *m*. 2. *vb*. *(gun)* schießen*; *(person)* erschie'ßen*.

shop, 1. *n*. Laden, -̈ *m*., Geschäft', -e *nt*.; *(factory)* Werkstatt, -̈e *f*. 2. *vb*. Einkäufe machen.

shopping, *n*. Einkaufen *nt*.

shore, *n*. Küste, -n *f*.; *(beach)* Strand, -e *m*.

short, *adj*. kurz (-); *(scarce)* knapp.

shortage, *n*. Knappheit, -en *f*.

shorten, *vb*. kürzen.

shorthand, *n*. Stenographie' *f*.

shortly, *adv*. bald (-).

shorts, *n.pl*. Shorts, *pl*.

shot, *n*. Schuß, -̈sse *m*.; *(photo)* Aufnahme, -n *f*.

should, *vb*. sollte; (s. have) hätte . . . sollen.

shoulder, 1. *n*. Schulter, -n *f*. 2. *vb*. schultern.

shout, *vb*. schreien*.

shovel, *n*. Schaufel, -n *f*.

show, 1. *n*. *(theater, film)* Vorstellung, -en *f*.; *(spectacle)* Thea'ter, - *nt*.; *(exhibit)* Ausstellung, -en *f*. 2. *vb*. zeigen; vor-führen; aus-stellen.

shower, *n*. *(rain)* Schauer, - *m*.; *(bath)* Dusche, -n *f*.

shrapnel, *n*. Schrapnell', -s *nt*.

shrewd, *adj*. scharfsinnig; *(derogatory)* geris'sen.

shriek, *vb*. kreischen.

shrill, *adj*. schrill, gellend.

shrimp, *n*. Garne'le, -n *f*., Krabbe, -n *f*.; *(small person)* Dreikä'sehoch, -s *m*.

shrine, *n*. Schrein, -e *m*.

shrink, *vb*. schrumpfen; *(cloth)* ein-laufen*.

shroud, *n*. Leichentuch, -̈er *nt*.

shrub, *n*. Strauch, -̈er *m*., Busch, -̈e *m*.

shudder, *vb*. schaudern.

shun, *vb*. vermei'den*.

shut, 1. *vb*. schließen*, zu-machen. 2. *adj*. geschlos'sen. 3. *adv*. zu.

shutter, *n*. Fensterladen, -̈ *m*.; *(camera)* Verschluß', -̈sse *m*.

shy, 1. *adj*. scheu, schüchtern. 2. *vb*. scheuen.

Sicily, *n*. Sizi'lien *nt*.

sick, *adj*. krank (-); (be s. of) satt-haben*.

sickness, *n*. Krankheit, -en *f*.

side, *n*. Seite, -n *f*.; *(edge)* Rand, -̈er *m*.

sidewalk, *n*. Bürgersteig, -e *m*.

siege, *n*. Bela'gerung, -en *f*.

sieve, *n*. Sieb, -e *nt*.

sift, *vb*. sieben; sichten.

sigh, 1. *n*. Seufzer, - *m*. 2. *vb*. seufzen.

sight, 1. *n*. Sicht *f*.; *(vision)* Sehkraft *f*.; *(view)* Anblick, -e *m*.; *(sights)* Sehenswürdigkeit, -en *f*. 2. *vb*. sichten.

sightseeing, *n*. Besich'tigung *(f.)* von Sehenswürdigkeiten.

sign, 1. *n*. Zeichen, -*nt*.; Schild, -er *nt*. 2. *vb*. unterzeich'nen, unterschrei'ben*.

signal, 1. *n*. Signal', -e *nt*. 2. *vb*. signalisie'ren.

signature, *n*. Unterschrift, -en *f*.

significance, *n*. Bedeu'tung, -en *f*., Wichtigkeit *f*.

significant, *adj*. bezeich'nend, bedeu'tend.

signify, *vb*. bezeich'nen, bedeu'ten.

silence, 1. *n*. Schweigen *nt*., Ruhe *f*. 2. *vb*. zum Schweigen bringen*.

silent, *adj*. still, schweigsam.

silk, 1. *n*. Seide *f*. 2. *adj*. seiden.

silken, silky, *adj*. seidig.

sill, *n*. *(door)* Schwelle, -n *f*.; *(window)* Fensterbrett, -er *nt*.

silly, *adj*. albern.

silo, *n*. Silo, -s *m*.

silver, 1. *n*. Silber *nt*. 2. *adj*. silbern.

silverware, *n*. (silbernes) Besteck', -e *nt*.

similar, *adj*. ähnlich.

similarity, *n*. Ähnlichkeit, -en *f*.

simple, *adj*. einfach, schlicht; *(ignorant)* einfältig.

simplicity, *n*. Einfachheit *f*., Schlichtheit *f*.

simplify, *vb*. verein'fachen.

simulate, *vb*. vor-geben*; nach-ahmen.

simultaneous, *adj*. gleichzeitig.

sin, 1. *n*. Sünde, -n *f*. 2. *vb*. sündigen.

since, 1. *prep*. seit. 2. *conj*. seit, seitdem'; *(because)* da. 3. *adv*. seitdem'.

sincere, *adj*. aufrichtig, ehrlich.

sincerely, *adv*. (s. yours) Ihr erge'bener, Ihre erge'bene.

sincerity, *n*. Aufrichtigkeit *f*.

sinful, *adj*. sündhaft.

sing, *vb*. singen*.

singe, vb. sengen.

singer, n. Sänger, - m.

single, adj. einzeln; (unmarried) ledig.

singular, 1. n. (gram.) Einzahl f., Singular m. **2.** adj. einzig; (unusual) eigentümlich.

sinister, adj. düster, unheimlich.

sink, 1. n. Ausguß, ⁼sse m., Spülstein, -e m. **2.** vb. (tr.) versen'ken; (intr.) sinken*.

sinner, n. Sünder, - m.

sinus, n. Stirnhöhle, -n f.

sinusitis, n. Stirnhöhlenentzündung, -en f.

sip, 1. n. Schluck, -e m. **2.** vb. schlürfen.

siphon, n. Siphon, -s m.

sir, n. (yes, s.) jawohl'.

siren, n. Sire'ne, -n f.

sirloin, n. Lendenstück, -e nt.

sister, n. Schwester, -n f.

sister-in-law, n. Schwägerin, -nen f.

sit, vb. sitzen*; (s. down) sich (hin-)setzen.

site, n. Lage, -n f.

sitting, n. Sitzung, -en f.

situated, adj. gele'gen.

situation, n. Lage, -n f., Situation', -en f.

six, num. sechs.

sixteen, num. sechzehn.

sixteenth, 1. adj. sechzehnt-. **2.** n. Sechzehntel, - f.

sixth, 1. adj. sechst-. **2.** n. Sechstel, - f.

sixtieth, 1. adj. sechzigst-. **2.** n. Sechzigstel, - nt.

sixty, num. sechzig.

size, n. Größe, -n f., Ausmaß, -e nt.

skate, 1. n. Schlittschuh, -e m. **2.** vb. Schlittschuh laufen*.

skateboard, n. Skatebord nt.; Rollbrett nt.

skeleton, n. Skelett', -e nt.

skeptic, n. Skeptiker, - m.

skeptical, adj. skeptisch.

sketch, 1. n. Skizze, -n f.; Sketch, -e m. **2.** vb. skizzie'ren.

ski, 1. n. Ski, -er m. **2.** vb. Ski'laufen*.

skid, 1. n. Hemmschuh, -e m. **2.** vb. rutschen.

skill, n. Geschick', nt., Fertigkeit, -en f.

skillful, adj. geschickt'.

skim, vb. (remove cream) entrah'men; (go over lightly) flüchtig lesen*.

skim milk, n. Magermilch f.

skin, 1. n. Haut, ⁼e f.; (fur) Fell, -e nt.; (of fruit) Schale, -n f. **2.** vb. häuten.

skip, vb. springen*; (omit) überschla'gen*.

skirt, 1. n. Rock, ⁼e m. **2.** vb. umge'hen*.

skull, n. Schädel, - m.

skunk, n. Stinktier, -e nt.; (person) Schuft, -e m.

sky, n. Himmel, - m.

skyscraper, n. Wolkenkratzer, - m.

slab, n. Platte, -n f.

slack, adj. schlaff, flau.

slacken, vb. nach-lassen*.

slacks, n.pl. Slacks pl.

slam, vb. knallen, zu-knallen.

slander, 1. n. Verleum'dung, -en f. **2.** vb. verleum'den.

slang, n. Slang m., Jargon', -s m.

slant, 1. n. Neigung, -en f.; schiefe Ebene, -n f.; Aspekt', -e m. **2.** vb. neigen.

slap, 1. n. Klaps, -e m. **2.** vb. schlagen*.

slash, 1. n. Schlitz, -e m.; Schnittwunde, -n f. **2.** vb. schlitzen.

slat, n. Latte, -n f.

slate, n. Schiefer m.; (list) Liste, -n f.

slaughter, 1. n. Schlachten nt.; Gemet'zel, - nt. **2.** vb. schlachten; nieder-metzeln.

Slav, n. Slawe, -n, -n m.

slave, n. Sklave, -n, -n m.

slavery, n. Sklaverei' f.

Slavic, adj. slawisch.

slay, vb. erschla'gen*.

sled, n. Schlitten, - m.; (go sledding) Schlitten fahren*, rodeln.

sleek, adj. glatt (⁼-, -); geschniegelt.

sleep, 1. n. Schlaf m. **2.** vb. schlafen*. (go to s.) ein-schlafen*.

sleeper, sleeping car, n. Schlafwagen, - m.

sleepy, adj. schläfrig, müde.

sleet, n. Eisregen m.

sleeve, n. Ärmel, - m.

sleigh, n. Schlitten, - m.

slender, adj. schlank; (slight) schwach (⁼-).

slice, 1. n. Scheibe, -n f. **2.** vb. in Scheiben schneiden*.

slide, vb. gleiten*, rutschen.

slight, adj. leicht, gering'; (thin) schmächtig.

slim, adj. schlank; gering'.

slime, n. Schlamm m.; Schleim m.

slip, 1. n. (plant) Steckling, -e m.; (error) Verse'hen, - nt.; (underwear) Unterrock, ⁼e m.; (paper) Zettel, - m.; (bedding) Bezug', ⁼e m. **2.** vb. gleiten*, aus-leiten*.

slipper, n. Hausschuh, -e m., Pantof'fel, -n m.

slippery, adj. glatt (⁼-, -), schlüpfrig.

slit, 1. n. Schlitz, -e m. **2.** vb. schlitzen.

slogan, n. Schlagwort, -e or ⁼er nt.; (election s.) Wahlspruch, ⁼e m.

slope, n. Abhang, ⁼e m.; Neigung, -en f.

sloppy, adj. schlampig.

slot, n. Schlitz, -e m.

slovenly, adj. liederlich.

slow, adj. langsam; (be s., of a clock) nach-gehen*.

slowness, n. Langsamkeit f.

sluggish, adj. träge.

slum, n. Elendsviertel, - nt.

slur, 1. n. Anwurf, ⁼e m. **2.** vb. nuscheln.

slush, n. Matsch m.

sly, adj. schlau, verschla'gen.

small, adj. klein.

smallpox, n. Blattern, pl.

smart, adj. intelligent'; elegant'.

smash, vb. zerschla'gen*, zerschmei'ßen*.

smear, vb. schmieren, beschmie'ren.

smell, 1. n. Geruch', ⁼e m. **2.** vb. riechen*.

smelt, 1. n. Stint, -e m. **2.** vb. schmelzen, ein-schmelzen.

smile, 1. n. Lächeln m. **2.** vb. lächeln.

smock, n. Kittel, - m.

smoke, 1. n. Rauch f. **2.** vb. rauchen; (meat, fish) räuchern.

smooth, 1. adj. glatt (⁼-, -). **2.** vb. glätten.

smother, vb. ersti'cken.

smug, adj. selbstgefällig; blasiert'.

smuggle, vb. schmuggeln.

snack, n. Imbiß, -sse m.

snag, n. (stocking) Zugmasche, -n f.; (obstacle) Hindernis, -se nt.

snail, n. Schnecke, -n f.

snake, n. Schlange, -n f.

snap, 1. n. Druckknopf, ⁼e m. **2.** vb. schnappen; (break) zerrei'ßen*.

snapshot, n. Schnappschuß, ⁼sse m.

snare, n. Falle, -n f.

snarl, 1. n. Verhed'derung, -en f. **2.** vb. verhed'dern; (growl) drohend knurren.

snatch, vb. erha'schen, weg-schnappen.

sneak, vb. schleichen*.

sneer, vb. höhnisch grinsen.

sneeze, vb. niesen.

snob, n. Snob, -s m.

snore, vb. schnarchen.

snow, 1. n. Schnee m. **2.** vb. schneien.

snub, 1. n. Affront', -s m. **2.** vb. schneiden*.

snug, adj. eng; (fig.) mollig.

so, adv. so.

soak, vb. durchnäs'sen; ein-weichen.

soap, n. Seife, -n f.

soar, vb. sich empor'-schwingen*.

sob, vb. schluchzen.

sober, adj. nüchtern.

sociable, adj. gesel'lig.

social, adj. gesell'schaftlich, sozial'.

socialism, n. Sozialis'mus m.

socialist, n. Sozialist', -en, -en m.

society, n. Gesell'schaft, -en f.

sociology, n. Soziologie' f.

sock, 1. n. Socke, -n f. 2. vb. schlagen*.

socket, n. (eye) Augenhöhle, -n f.; (elec.) Steckdose, -n f.

sod, n. Sode, -n f.

soda, n. Soda nt.

sofa, n. Sofa, -s nt.

soft, adj. (not hard) weich; (not loud) leise; (not rough) sanft, sacht.

soft drink, n. alkoholfreies Getränk', -e nt.

soften, vb. weich machen*; (fig.) mildern.

soil, 1. n. Boden, - m. 2. vb. beschmut'zen.

soiled, adj. schmutzig.

sojourn, 1. n. Aufenthalt, -e m. 2. vb. sich auf-halten*.

solace, n. Trost m.

solar, adj. Sonnen- (cpds.).

soldier, n. Soldat', -en, -en m.

sole, 1. n. Sohle, -n f.; (fish) Seezunge, -n f. 2. adj. allei'nig, einzig.

solemn, adj. feierlich.

solicit, vb. an-halten* um.

solicitous, adj. besorgt'; eifrig.

solid, adj. fest; solid', kompakt'.

solidify, vb. festigen; verdich'ten.

solitary, adj. einzeln.

solitude, n. Einsamkeit, -en f.

solo, n. Solo, -s nt.

soloist, n. Solist', -en, -en m.

so long, interj. Wiedersehen.

solution, n. Lösung, -en f.

solve, vb. lösen.

solvent, 1. n. Lösungsmittel, - nt. 2. adj. (financially capable) zahlungsfähig.

somber, adj. düster.

some, pron.&adj. (with singulars) etwas; (with plurals) einig-, ein paar.

somebody, pron. jemand.

somehow, adv. irgendwie.

someone, pron. jemand.

somersault, n. Purzelbaum, ¨-e m.

something, pron. etwas.

sometime, adv. irgendwann.

sometimes, adv. manchmal.

somewhat, adv. etwas.

somewhere, adv. irgendwo.

son, n. Sohn, ¨-e m.

song, n. Lied, -er nt.

son-in-law, n. Schwiegersohn, ¨-e m.

soon, adv. bald.

soot, n. Ruß m.

soothe, vb. beschwich'tigen.

soothing, adj. wohltuend.

sophisticated, adj. anspruchsvoll verfei'nert, lebenserfahren, weltgewandt.

soprano, n. Sopran', -e m.

sorcery, n. Zauberei' f.

sordid, adj. dreckig; gemein'.

sore, 1. n. wunde Stelle, -n f., offene Wunde, -n f. 2. adj. wund; schmerzhaft; (angry)

eingeschnappt; (be s.) weh'-tun*.

sorrow, n. Kummer, - m.

sorrowful, adj. kummervoll.

sorry, adj. traurig, betrübt'; (I am s.) es tut* mir leid.

sort, 1. n. Sorte, -n f., Art, -en f. 2. vb. sortie'ren.

soul, n. Seele, -n f.

sound, 1. n. Ton, ¨-e m., Laut, -e m., Klang, ¨-e m. 2. adj. gesund (¨-, -); (valid) einwandfrei. 3. vb. Klingen*; (take soundings) loten.

soup, n. Suppe, -n f.

sour, adj. sauer.

source, n. Quelle, -n f.

south, 1. n. Süden m. 2. adj. südlich; Süd- (cpds.).

southeast, 1. n. Südos'ten m. 2. adj. südöst'lich; Südost'- (cpds.).

southeastern, adj. südlich.

southern, adj. südlich.

South Pole, n. Südpol m.

southwest, 1. n. Südwes'ten m. 2. adj. südwest'lich; Südwest'- (cpds.).

southwestern, adj. südwest'lich.

souvenir, n. Andenken, - nt.; Reiseandenken, - nt.

Soviet, 1. n. Sowjet, -s m. 2. adj. sowje'tisch.

sow, 1. n. Sau, ¨-e f. 2. vb. säen.

space, n. Raum, ¨-e m.

space shuttle, n. Raumtransporter, -.

spacious, adj. geräu'mig.

spade, n. Spaten, - m.; (cards) Pik nt.

spaghetti, n. Spaghet'ti pl.

Spain, n. Spanien nt.

span, 1. n. Spanne, -n f. 2. vb. überspan'nen.

Spaniard, n. Spanier, - m.

Spanish, adj. spanisch.

spank, vb. hauen*.

spanking, n. Haue f.

spar, 1. n. Sparren, - m. 2. vb. boxen.

spare, 1. adj. Ersatz'-, Reser've- (cpds.). 2. vb. sparen, scheuen.

spark, n. Funke(n), - m.

sparkle, vb. funkeln.

spark-plug, n. Zündkerze, -n f.

sparrow, n. Sperling, -e m.

sparse, adj. spärlich.

spasm, n. Krampf, ¨-e m.

spasmodic, adj. krampfhaft; sprunghaft.

spatter, vb. spritzen, bespritzen.

speak, vb. sprechen*, reden.

speaker, n. Redner, - m.; (presiding officer) Präsident', -en, -en m.

spear, 1. n. Speer, -e m.; Spieß, -e m. 2. vb. auf-spießen.

special, adj. beson'der-.

specialist, n. Spezialist', -en, - en m.

specially, adv. beson'ders.

specialty, n. Spezialität', -en f.

species, n. Art, -en f.; Gattung, -en f.

specific, adj. spezi'fisch.

specify, vb. spezifizie'ren; (stipulate) bestim'men.

specimen, n. Muster, - nt., Exemplar', -e nt., Probe, -n f.

spectacle, n. Schauspiel, -e nt.; Anblick, -e m.; (s.s) Brille, -n f.

spectacular, adj. aufsehenerregend.

spectator, n. Zuschauer, - m.

spectrum, n. Spektrum, -tren nt.

speculate, vb. spekulie'ren.

speculation, n. Spekulation', -en f.

speech, n. Sprache, -n f.; (address) Rede, -n.

speechless, adj. sprachlos.

speed, 1. n. Geschwin'digkeit, -en f., Tempo nt. 2. vb. hasten; (s. up) beschleu'nigt er-le'digen; (auto) die Geschwin'digkeitsgrenze überschrei'ten*.

speedometer, n. Geschwin'digkeitsmesser, - m.

speedy, adj. schnell; unverzüglich.

spell, 1. n. Zauber, - m. 2. vb. buchstabie'ren.

spelling, n. Rechtschreibung f.

spend, vb. (money) aus-geben*; (time) verwen'den*, verbrin'gen*.

sphere, n. Kugel, -n f., Sphäre, -n f.

spice, n. Gewürz', -e nt.

spider, n. Spinne, -n f.

spike, n. langer Nagel, ¨- m.; (thorn) Dorn, -en m., Stachel, -n m.

spill, vb. verschüt'ten; (make a spot) kleckern.

spin, vb. spinnen*.

spinach, n. Spinat' m.

spine, n. Rückgrat, -e nt.

spiral, 1. n. Spira'le, -n f. 2. adj. spiral'förmig.

spire, n. spitzer Turm, ¨-e m.

spirit, n. Geist, m.; (ghost) Gespenst', -er nt.; (vivacity) Schwung m.; (s.s) Spirituo'sen pl.

spiritual, 1. n. geistliches Negerlied, -er nt. 2. adj. geistig, seelisch.

spiritualism, n. Spiritualis'mus m.; Spiritis'mus m.

spit, 1. n. (saliva) Speichel m.; (roasting) Spieß, -e m. 2. vb. spucken.

spite, 1. n. Trotz m.; (in s. of) trotz. 2. vb. ärgern.

splash, vb. spritzen; planschen.

splendid, adj. prächtig.

splendor, n. Pracht f.

splice, vb. spleißen.

splint, n. Schiene, -n f.

splinter, n. Splitter, - m.

split, 1. n. Spalt, -e m. 2. vb. spalten.

spoil, vb. verder'ben*; schlecht

werden*; *(child)* verwöh'nen, verzie'hen*.

spoke, *n.* Speiche, -n *f.*

spokesman, *n.* Sprecher, - *m.*

sponge, 1. *n.* Schwamm, ⸗e *m.* **2.** *vb. (live off)* nassauern.

sponsor, 1. *n.* Bürge, -n, -n *m.;* Förderer, - *m.; (radio, TV, etc.)* Rekla'meauftraggeber, - *m.* **2.** *vb.* fördern; *(advertising)* in Auftrag geben*.

spontaneity, *n.* Impulsivität' *f.*

spontaneous, *adj.* spontan'.

spool, *n.* Spule, -n *f.*

spoon, *n.* Löffel, - *m.*

sport, *n.* Sport *m.;* Vergnü'gen, - *nt.*

spot, *n. (place)* Stelle, -n *f.; (blot)* Fleck, -en *m.*

spouse, *n.* Gatte, -n, -n *m.;* Gattin, -nen *f.*

spout, 1. *n.* Tülle, -n *f.; (water)* Strahl, -en *m.* **2.** *vb.* hervor'- sprudeln; speien*.

sprain, 1. *n.* Verren'kung, -en *f.,* Verstau'chung, -en *f.* **2.** *vb.* verren'ken, verstau'chen.

sprawl, *vb.* sich aus'breiten; alle Viere aus'strecken.

spray, *vb.* spritzen; zerstäu'- ben.

spread, 1. *n.* Spanne, -n *f.;* Umfang, ⸗e *m.* **2.** *vb.* aus'- breiten.

spree, *n.* Bummel, - *m.* Aus- flug, ⸗e *m.*

sprightly, *adj.* munter.

spring, 1. *n. (season)* Frühling, -e *m.,* Frühjahr, -e *nt.; (source)* Quelle, -n *f.; (leap)* Sprung, ⸗e *m.; (metal)* Feder, -n *f.* **2.** *vb.* springen*.

sprinkle, *vb.* sprengen; streuen.

sprint, 1. *n.* Kurzstreckenlauf, ⸗e *m.* **2.** *vb.* sprinten.

sprout, 1. *n.* Sproß, sse *m.* **2.** *vb.* sprießen*.

spry, *adj.* flink.

spur, 1. *n.* Sporn, Sporen *m.* **2.** *vb.* an'spornen.

spurn, *vb.* verschmä'hen.

spurt, *vb.* hervor'schießen*.

spy, 1. *n.* Spion', -e *m.* **2.** *vb.* spionie'ren.

squabble, 1. *n.* Zank *m.* **2.** *vb.* zanken.

squad, *n.* Trupp, -s *m.; (sport)* Mannschaft, -en *f.*

squadron, *n. (air)* Staffel, -n *f.; (navy)* Geschwa'der, - *nt.*

squall, *n.* Bö, -en *f.*

squalor, *n.* Schmutz *m.*

squander, *vb.* vergeu'den.

square, 1. *n.* Viereck, -e *nt.,* Quadrat', -e *nt.; (open place)* Platz, ⸗e *m.* **2.** *adj.* viereckig, quadra'tisch. **3.** *vb.* quadrie'- ren.

squash, 1. *n.* Kürbis, -se *m.* **2.** *vb.* quetschen, zerquet'schen.

squat, 1. *adj.* kurz und dick. **2.** *vb.* hocken, kauern.

squeak, *vb.* quietschen.

squeamish, *adj.* zimperlich.

squeeze, *vb.* drücken; *(juice)* aus'pressen.

squirrel, *n.* Eichhörnchen, - *nt.*

squirt, *vb.* spritzen.

stab, 1. *n.* Stich, -e *m.* **2.** *vb.* stechen*; erste'chen*.

stability, *n.* Bestän'digkeit *f.,* Stabilität' *f.*

stabilize, *vb.* stabilisie'ren.

stable, 1. *n.* Stall, ⸗e *m.* **2.** *adj.* bestän'dig; stabil'.

stack, 1. *n.* Haufen, - *m.* **2.** *vb.* auf'stapeln.

stadium, *n.* Stadion, -dien *nt.*

staff, *n.* Stab, ⸗e *m.; (personnel)* Personal' *nt.; (music)* Noten- linien *pl.*

stag, *n.* Hirsch, -e *m.*

stage, 1. *n. (theater)* Bühne, -n *f.; (phase)* Stadium, -dien *nt.* **2.** *vb.* insze'nieren.

stagflation, *n.* Stagflation' *f.*

stagger, *vb.* taumeln; *(amaze)* verblüf'fen; *(alternate)* staf- feln.

stagnant, *adj.* stagnie'rend.

stagnate, *vb.* stagnie'ren.

stain, 1. *n.* Fleck, -e *m.; (color)* Färbstoff, -e *m.; (paint)* Beize *f.* **2.** *vb.* befle'cken, färben; beizen.

staircase, stairs, *n.* Treppe, -n *f.*

stake, 1. *n. (post)* Pfahl, ⸗e *m.; (sum, bet)* Einsatz, ⸗e *m.* **2.** *vb.* aufs Spiel setzen.

stale, *adj.* alt (⸗), schal.

stalk, *n.* Stiel, -e *m.,* Halm, -e *m.*

stall, 1. *n.* Stall, ⸗e *m.; (vendor's)* Bude, -n *f.* **2.** *vb. (hesitate)* Zeit schinden*; *(engine)* ab'würgen.

stamina, *n.* Energie' *f.,* Ausdauer *f.*

stammer, *vb.* stammeln.

stamp, 1. *n.* Stempel, - *m.; (mark)* Geprä'ge *nt.; (postal)* Freimarke, -n *f.,* Briefmarke, -n *f.* **2.** *vb.* stempeln; prägen.

stand, 1. *n.* Stellung, -en *f.; (vendor's)* Bude, -n *f.; (grandstand)* Tribü'ne, -n *f.* **2.** *vb.* stehen*; *(endure)* ertra'gen*.

standard, 1. *n.* Norm, -en *f.,* Standard, -s *m.* **2.** *adj.* Standard- *(cpds.).*

standardize, *vb.* standardisie'- ren.

standing, *n.* Bestand' *m.; (reputation)* Ruf *m.*

standpoint, *n.* Standpunkt, -e *m.*

star, *n.* Stern, -e *m.; (movie)* Star, -s *m.*

starch, 1. *n.* Stärke *f.* **2.** *vb.* stärken.

stare, *vb.* starren, glotzen.

stark, *adj.* kraß; *(bare)* kahl.

start, 1. *n.* Anfang, ⸗e *m.,* Start, -s *m.* **2.** *vb.* an'fangen*, star- ten.

startle, *vb.* erschre'cken, auf'- schrecken.

starvation, *n.* Verhun'gern *nt.;* Hungertod *m.*

starve, *vb.* hungern; **(s. to death)** verhun'gern.

state, 1. *n.* Staat, -en *m.; (condition)* Zustand, ⸗e *m.* **2.** *vb.* dar'legen, erklä'ren.

statement, *n.* Erklä'rung, -en *f.;* Behaup'tung, -en *f.*

stateroom, *n.* Kabi'ne, -n *f.*

statesman, *n.* Staatsmann, ⸗er *m.*

static, 1. *n.* atmosphä'rische Störung, -en *f.* **2.** *adj.* statisch.

station, *n.* Station', -en *f.; (position)* Stellung, -en *f.; (R.R.)* Bahnhof, ⸗e *m.*

stationary, *adj.* feststehend, stationär'.

stationer, *n.* Schreibwaren- händler, - *m.*

stationery, *n.* Schreibwaren *pl.;* Briefpapier *nt.*

station wagon, *n.* Kombiwa- gen, - *m.*

statistics, *n.pl.* Statis'tik *f.*

statue, *n.* Statue, -n *f.*

stature, *n.* Wuchs *m.,* Statur' *f.; (fig.)* Format', -e *nt.*

status, *n.* Stand, ⸗e *m.*

statute, *n.* Statut', -e *nt.,* Satzung, -en *f.*

staunch, *adj.* treu, wacker.

stay, 1. *n. (sojourn)* Aufenthalt *m.; (delay)* Einstellung, -en *f.* **2.** *vb.* bleiben*; *(hold back)* zurück'halten*.

steady, *adj.* fest; sicher; bestän'dig.

steak, *n.* Beefsteak, -s *nt.*

steal, *vb.* stehlen*.

stealth, *n.* Verstoh'lenheit *f.*

stealthy, *adj.* verstoh'len.

steam, 1. *n.* Dampf, ⸗e *m.* **2.** *vb.* dampfen.

steamboat, *n.* Dampfboot, -e *nt.*

steamship, *n.* Dampfer, - *m.*

steel, 1. *n.* Stahl, -e en *m.* stählern; Stahl- *(cpds.).*

steep, *adj.* steil; *(price)* hoch (hoh-, höher, höchst-).

steeple, *n.* Kirchturm, ⸗e *m.*

steer, 1. *n.* Stier, -e *m.* **2.** *vb.* steuern.

stellar, *adj.* Sternen- *(cpds.).*

stem, 1. *n.* Stiel, -e *m.* **2.** *vb.* stammen.

stenographer, *n.* Stenotypi'- stin, -nen *f.*

stenography, *n.* Kurzschrift, -en *f.;* Stenographie', -i'en *f.*

step, 1. *n.* Schritt, -e *m.; (stair)* Stufe, -n *f.* **2.** *vb.* treten*.

stepfather, *n.* Stiefvater, ⸗ *m.*

stepladder, *n.* Trittleiter, -n *f.*

stepmother, *n.* Stiefmutter, ⸗ *f.*

stereophonic, *adj.* stereophon'.

sterile, *adj.* unfruchtbar; steril'.

sterility, *n.* Sterilität' *f.*

sterilize, *vb.* sterilisie'ren.

sterling, *adj.* münzecht; *(silver)*

echt; (pound s.) Pfund Sterling nt.

stern, adj. streng.

stethoscope, n. Stethoskop', -e nt.

stew, 1. n. Stew, -s nt. 2. vb. dämpfen.

steward, n. Steward, -s m.

stewardess, n. Stewardess', -en f.

stick, 1. n. Stock, -̈e m. 2. vb. (adhere) kleben; (pin) stecken.

sticker, n. Etiket'te, -n f.

sticky, adj. klebrig.

stiff, adj. steif.

stiffen, vb. steif werden*; (fig.) verhär'ten.

stiffness, r. Steifheit, -en f.

stifle, vb. ersti'cken.

stigma, n. Stigma, -men nt., Schandfleck, -e m.

still, 1. n. Destillier'apparat, -e m. 2. adj. still, 3. vb. stillen. 4. adv. noch; doch; dennoch.

stillness, n. Stille f.

stimulant, n. Reizmittel, - nt.

stimulate, vb. an·regen.

stimulus, n. Anreiz, -e m.

sting, 1. n. Stache, - m.; (bite) Stich, -e m. 2. vb. stechen*; (burn) brennen.

stingy, adj. geizig.

stink, vb. stinken*.

stipulate, vb. bestim'men.

stir, 1. n. Aufregung, -en f. 2. vb. rühren; erre'gen.

stitch, 1. n. Stich, -e m.; (knitting) Masche, -n f. 2. vb. steppen.

stock, 1. n. (supply) Vorrat, -̈e m., Lager, - nt.; (lineage) Fami'lie, -n f.; (livestock) Viehbestand, -̈e m.; (gun) Schaft, -̈e m. 2. vb. versorgen; auf Lager haben*.

stockbroker, n. Börsenmakler, - m.

stock exchange, n. Börse, -n f.

stocking, n. Strumpf, -̈e m.

stodgy, adj. schwerfällig; untersetzt'.

stole, n. Stola, -len f.

stomach, 1. n. Magen, -̈ m. 2. vb. (fig.) schlucken.

stone, 1. n. Stein, -e m.; (fruit) Kern, -e m. 2. vb. steinigen.

stool, n. Schemel, - m.

stoop, vb. sich bücken; (demean oneself) sich ernied'rigen.

stop, 1. n. Haltestelle, -n f. 2. vb. halten*; stoppen; (cease) auf·hören.

stop-over, n. Fahrtunterbrechung, -en f.

storage, n. Lagern nt.; Lagerhaus, -̈er nt.

store, 1. n. Laden, -̈ m., Geschäft', -e nt.; (supplies) Vorräte pl. 2. vb. lagern.

storehouse, n. Lagerhaus, -̈er nt.

storm, 1. n. Sturm, -̈e m. 2. vb. stürmen.

stormy, adj. stürmisch.

story, n. Erzäh'lung, -en f., Geschich'te, -n f.

stout, adj. dick; (strong) wacker.

stove, n. (cooking) Herd, -e m.; (heating) Ofen, -̈ m.

straight, adj. gera'de; (honest) ehrlich.

straighten, vb. gera'de machen; in Ordnung bringen*.

straightforward, adj. offen.

strain, 1. n. Anstrengung, -en f.; Belas'tung, -en f. 2. vb. an·strengen; belas'ten; (filter) seihen.

strait, n. Meeresenge, -n f.

strand, 1. n. Strähne, -n f. 2. vb. stranden.

strange, adj. merkwürdig; (foreign) fremd.

stranger, n. Fremd- m.&f.

strangle, vb. erwür'gen.

strap, n. Riemen, - m.

stratagem, n. Kriegslist, -en f.

strategic, adj. strate'gisch.

strategy, n. Strategie' f.

stratosphere, n. Stratosphä're f.

stratum, n. Schicht, -en f.

straw, n. Stroh, nt.; (for drinking) Strohalm, -e m.

strawberry, n. Erdbeere, -n f.

stray, 1. adj. verein'zelt. 2. vb. ab·weichen, ab·schweifen.

streak, n. Strähne, -n f.

stream, n. Strom, -̈e m.; (small) Bach, -̈e m.

streamlined, adj. stromlinienförmig.

street, n. Straße, -n f.

streetcar, n. Straßenbahn, -en f.

strength, n. Kraft, -̈e f., Stärke, -n f.

strengthen, vb. stärken.

strenuous, adj. anstrengend.

stress, 1. n. Belas'tung, -en f.; (accent) Beto'nung, -en f. 2. vb. belas'ten; beto'nen.

stretch, 1. n. Strecke, -n f.; Spanne, -n f. 2. vb. strecken; spannen.

stretcher, n. Tragbahre, -n f.

strew, vb. streuen.

stricken, adj. getrof'fen.

strict, adj. streng.

stride, 1. n. Schritt, -e m. 2. vb. schreiten*.

strife, n. Streit m.

strike, 1. n. (workers') Streik, -s m. 2. vb. streiken; (hit) schlagen*.

string, 1. n. Bindfaden, -̈ m., Schnur, -̈e f.; (music) Saite, -n f. 2. vb. auf·reihen.

string bean, n. grüne Bohne, -n f.

strip, 1. n. Streifen, - m. 2. vb. ab·streifen; entklei'den.

stripe, n. Streifen, - m.

strive, vb. streben.

stroke, 1. n. Schlag, -̈e m.; (pen, brush, etc.) Strich, -e m.;

(med.) Schlaganfall, -̈e m. 2. vb. streicheln.

stroll, 1. n. kleiner Spazier'gang, -̈e m. 2. vb. spazie'rengehen*.

stroller, n. Spazier'gänger, m.; (baby-carriage) Kindersportwagen, - m.

strong, adj. stark (-̈), kräftig.

stronghold, n. Feste, -n f.

structure, n. Struktur', -en f.

struggle, 1. n. Ringen nt. 2. vb. ringen*.

strut, vb. stolzie'ren.

stub, 1. n. Kontroll'abschnitt, -e m. 2. vb. an·stoßen*.

stubborn, adj. hartnäckig; (person) dickköpfig.

student, n. Student', -en, -en m.

studio, n. Atelier', -s nt.

studious, adj. eifrig.

study, 1. n. Studium, -dien nt.; (room) Arbeitszimmer, - nt. 2. vb. studie'ren; (do homework) arbeiten.

stuff, 1. n. Zeug nt. 2. vb. stopfen.

stuffing, n. Füllung, -en f.

stumble, vb. stolpern.

stump, n. Stumpf, -̈e m.

stun, vb. betäu'ben; verblüffen.

stunt, n. Kunststück, -e nt.

stupid, adj. dumm (-̈), blöde.

stupidity, n. Dummheit, -en f.

stupor, n. Betäu'bungszustand m.

sturdy, adj. stark (-̈), stämmig.

stutter, vb. stottern.

sty, n. Schweinestall, -̈e m.; (eye) Gerstenkorn, -̈er nt.

style, n. Stil, -e m.

stylish, adj. elegant'.

suave, adj. verbind'lich.

subconscious, adj. unterbewußt.

subdue, vb. unterdrü'cken.

subject, 1. n. (gram.) Subjekt, -e nt.; (topic) Thema, -men nt.; (of king) Untertan, -en, -en m. 2. adj. unterwor'fen. 3. vb. unterwer'fen*; aus·setzen.

subjugate, vb. unterjo'chen.

subjunctive, n. Konjunktiv, -e m.

sublime, adj. erha'ben.

submarine, n. Unterseeboot, -e nt., U-Boot, -e nt.

submerge, vb. unter·tauchen.

submission, n. Unterwer'fung, -en f.

submit, vb. (lay before) unterbrei'ten; (offer opinion) anheim'·stellen; (yield) sich fügen; (surrender) sich unterwer'fen*.

subnormal, adj. unternormal.

subordinate, 1. n. Unterge'ben- m. 2. adj. untergeordnet; (s. clause) Nebensatz, -̈e m.

subscribe, vb. (underwrite) zeichnen; (take regularly)

abonnie'ren; *(approve)* billigen.

subscription, *n.* Abonnement', -s *nt.*; Zeichnung, -en *f.*

subsequent, *adj.* folgend.

subside, *vb.* nach-lassen*.

subsidy, *n.* Zuschuß, ¨sse *m.*

substance, *n.* Substanz', -en *f.*

substantial, *adj.* wesentlich; beträcht'lich.

substitute, 1. *n.* Ersatz' *m.*; Vertre'tung, -en *f.* 2. *vb.* erset'zen; als Ersatz' geben*; die Vertre'tung überneh'men*.

substitution, *n.* Ersat'zung, -en *f.*

subtle, *adj.* subtil', fein.

subtract, *vb.* ab-ziehen*.

suburb, *n.* Vorort, -e *m.*

subversive, *adj.* zerset'zend, statsfeindlich.

subway, *n.* Untergrundbahn, -en *f.*, U-Bahn, -en *f.*

succeed, *vb.* erfolg'reich sein*; *(come after)* folgen.

success, *n.* Erfolg', -e *m.*

successful, *adj.* erfolg'reich.

succession, *n.* *(to throne)* Erbfolge, -n *f.*; *(sequence)* Reihenfolge, -n *f.*

successive, *adj.* aufeinan'derfolgend.

successor, *n.* Nachfolger, - *m.*

succumb, *vb.* erlie'gen*.

such, *adj.* solch.

suck, *vb.* saugen, lutschen.

suction, *n.* Saugen *nt.*; Saug- *(cpds.).*

sudden, *adj.* plötzlich, jäh.

sue, *vb.* verkla'gen, gericht'lich belan'gen.

suffer, *vb.* leiden*.

suffice, *vb.* genü'gen, aus'reichen.

sufficient, *adj.* genü'gend.

suffocate, *vb.* ersti'cken.

sugar, *n.* Zucker *m.*

suggest, *vb.* vor-schlagen*.

suggestion, *n.* Vorschlag, ¨e *m.*

suicide, *n.* Selbstmord, -e *m.*

suit, 1. *n.* *(man's clothing)* Anzug, ¨e *m.*; *(woman's clothing)* Kostüm', -e *nt.*; *(cards)* Farbe, -n *f.*; *(law)* Prozeß', -sse *m.* 2. *vb.* passen; *(be becoming)* stehen*.

suitable, *adj.* passend; angemessen.

suitcase, *n.* Koffer, - *m.*

suitor, *n.* Freier, - *m.*

sullen, *adj.* griesgrämig.

sum, *n.* Summe, -n *f.*

summarize, *vb.* zusam'men-fassen.

summary, 1. *n.* Übersicht, -en *f.* 2. *adj.* summa'risch.

summer, *n.* Sommer, - *m.*

summit, *n.* Gipfel, - *m.*

summon, *vb.* zusam'men-rufen*, ein-berufen*; *(law)* vor-laden*.

sun, *n.* Sonne, -n *f.*

sunburn, *n.* Sonnenbrand, ¨e *m.*

sunburned, *adj.* sonnenverbrannt.

Sunday, *n.* Sonntag, -e *m.*

sunken, *adj.* versun'ken.

sunny, *adj.* sonnig.

sunshine, *n.* Sonnenschein *m.*

superb, *adj.* hervor'ragend.

superficial, *adj.* oberflächlich.

superfluous, *adj.* überflüssig.

super-highway, *n.* Autobahn -en *f.*

superior, 1. *n.* Vorgesetzt-*m.&f.* 2. *adj.* höher; überle'gen.

superiority, *n.* Überle'genheit *f.*

superlative, 1. *n.* Superlativ, -e *m.* 2. *adj.* überra'gend.

supernatural, *adj.* übernatür-lich.

supersede, *vb.* verdrän'gen; erset'zen.

supersonic, *adj.* Überschall-*(cpds.).*

superstar, *n.* Superstar, -s *m.*

superstition, *n.* Aberglaube (n), - *m.*

superstitious, *adj.* abergläubisch.

supervise, *vb.* beauf'sichtigen.

supper, *n.* Abendbrot, -e *nt.*, Abendessen, - *nt.*; *(Lord's S.)* Abendmahl, -e *nt.*

supplement, *n.* Ergän'zung, -en *f.*, Nachtrag, ¨e *m.*

supply, 1. *n.* Versor'gung *f.*; Vorrat, ¨e *m.*; (s. and demand) Angebot *(nt.)* und Nachfrage *(f.).* 2. *vb.* versor'gen, liefern.

support, 1. *n.* Stütze, -n *f.*; Unterstüt'zung, -en *f.* 2. *vb.* stützen; unterstüt'zen.

suppose, *vb.* an-nehmen*, vermu'ten.

suppress, *vb.* unterdrü'cken.

suppression, *n.* Unterdrü'ckung, -en *f.*

supreme, *adj.* oberst-, höchst-; Ober- *(cpds.).*

sure, *adj.* sicher.

surely, *adv.* sicherlich, gewiß'.

surf, *n.* Brandung, -en *f.*

surface, *n.* Oberfläche, -n *f.*

surge, *vb.* wogen, branden.

surgeon, *n.* Chirurg', -en, -en *m.*

surgery, *n.* Chirurgie' *f.*; Operation', -en *f.*

surmise, 1. *n.* Vermu'tung, -en *f.* 2. *vb.* vermu'ten.

surmount, *vb.* überwin'den*.

surname, *n.* Zuname(n), - *m.*, Fami'liennname(n), - *m.*

surpass, *vb.* überstei'gen*, übertref'fen*.

surplus, 1. *n.* Überschuß, ¨sse *m.* 2. *adj.* überschüssig; Über- *(cpds.).*

surprise, 1. *n.* Überra'schung, -en *f.* 2. *vb.* überra'schen.

surrender, 1. *n.* Übergabe *f.*, Erge'bung, -en *f.*

surround, *vb.* umge'ben*; umzin'geln.

surroundings, *n.pl.* Umge'bung, -en *f.*

survey, 1. *n.* Überblick, -e *m.*; *(measuring)* Vermes'sung, -en *f.* 2. *vb.* überbli'cken; vermes'sen*.

survival, *n.* Überle'ben *nt.*

survive, *vb.* überle'ben.

susceptible, *adj.* empfäng'lich, zugänglich.

suspend, *vb.* *(debar)* suspendie'ren; *(stop temporarily)* zeitweilig auf-heben*; *(payment)* ein-stellen; *(sentence)* aus-setzen; *(hang)* auf-hängen.

suspense, *n.* Schwebe *f.*; Spannung, -en *f.*

suspension, *n.* Schwebe *f.*; Suspension', -en *f.*

suspicion, *n.* Verdacht' *m.*, Argwohn *m.*

suspicious, *adj.* *(doubting)* misstrauisch; *(doubtful looking)* verdäch'tig.

sustain, *vb.* aufrecht-erhalten*; *(suffer)* erlei'den*.

swallow, 1. *n.* *(bird)* Schwalbe, -n *f.*; *(gulp)* Schluck, -e *m.* 2. *vb.* schlucken.

swamp, 1. *n.* Sumpf, ¨e *m.* 2. *vb.* überschwem'men.

swan, *n.* Schwan, ¨e *m.*

swarm, 1. *n.* Schwarm, ¨e *m.* 2. *vb.* schwärmen; *(fig.)* wimmeln.

sway, *vb.* schwingen*; schwanken.

swear, *vb.* schwören*; *(curse)* fluchen.

sweat, 1. *n.* Schweiß *m.* 2. *vb.* schwitzen.

sweater, *n.* Pullo'ver, - *m.*, Strickjacke, -n *f.*

Swede, *n.* Schwede, -n, -n *m.*

Sweden, *n.* Schweden *nt.*

Swedish, *adj.* schwedisch.

sweet, *adj.* süß.

sweetheart, *n.* Liebst- *m.&f.*

sweetness, *n.* Süße *f.*; *(fig.)* Anmut *f.*

swell, 1. *adj.* prima. 2. *vb.* schwellen*.

swift, *adj.* rasch, geschwind'.

swim, *vb.* schwimmen*.

swindle, *vb.* schwindeln.

swindler, *n.* Schwindler, - *m.*

swine, *n.* Schwein, -e *nt.*

swing, 1. *n.* Schaukel, -n *f.* 2. *vb.* schwingen*, schaukeln.

Swiss, 1. *n.* Schweizer, - *m.* 2. *adj.* schweizerisch; Schweizer- *(cpds.).*

switch, 1. *n.* *(whip)* Gerte, -n *f.*; *(railway)* Weiche, -n *f.*; *(elec.)* Schalter, - *m.* 2. *vb.* *(railway)* rangie'ren; um-schalten; *(exchange)* vertau'schen.

Switzerland, *n.* die Schweiz *f.*

sword, *n.* Schwert, -er *nt.*

syllabic, *adj.* silbisch.

syllable, *n.* Silbe, -n *f.*

symbol, *n.* Symbol', -e *nt.*

symbolic, *adj.* symbo'lisch.
sympathetic, *adj.* mitfühlend; *(med.)* sympa'thisch.
sympathize, *vb.* mit·fühlen.
sympathy, *n.* Sympathie', -i'en *f.*
symphonic, *adj.* sympho'nisch.
symphony, *n.* Symphonie', -i'en *f.*
symptom, *n.* Anzeichen, - *nt.,* Symptom', -e *nt.*
symptomatic, *adj.* symptoma'tisch; charakteris'tisch.
syndicate, *n.* Syndikat', -e *nt.*
syndrome, *n.* Syndrom', -e *nt.*
synonym, *n.* Synonym', -e *nt.*
synonymous, *adj.* sinnverwandt, synonym'.
synthetic, *adj.* synthe'tisch, künstlich; Kunst- *(cpds.).*
syphilis, *n.* Syphilis *f.*
syringe, *n.* Spritze, -n *f.*
syrup, *n.* Sirup *m.*
system, *n.* System', -e *nt.*
systematic, *adj.* systema'tisch.

T

table, *n.* Tisch, -e *m.; (list)* Verzeich'nis, -se *nt.*
tablecloth, *n.* Tischdecke, -n *f.,* Tischtuch, ⸗er *nt.*
tablespoon, *n.* Eßlöffel, - *m.*
tablet, *n.* Tafel, -n *f.; (pill)* Tablet'te, -n *f.*
tack, 1. *n.* Stift, -e *m.; (thumb t.)* Heftzwecke, -n *f.* 2. *vb. (sew)* heften; *(sail)* kreuzen.
tact, *n.* Takt *m.*
tag, *n.* Etikett, -e *nt.; (play t.)* Fangen spielen.
tail, *n.* Schwanz, ⸗e *m.*
tailor, *n.* Schneider, - *m.*
take, *vb.* nehmen*; *(carry)* bringen*; *(need)* erfor'dern.
tale, *n.* Geschich'te, -n *f.,* Erzäh'lung, -en *f.*
talent, *n.* Bega'bung, -en *f.,* Talent', -e *nt.*
talk, 1. *n.* Gespräch', -e *nt.; (lecture)* Vortrag, ⸗e *m.* 2. *vb.* reden, sprechen*.
talkative, *adj.* gesprä'chig.
tall, *adj.* groß (⸗); hoch (hoh-, höher, höchst-); lang (⸗).
tame, 1. *adj.* zahm. 2. *vb.* zähmen.
tamper, *vb.* herum'·pfuschen.
tan, 1. *n. (sun)* Sonnenbräune *f.* 2. *adj.* gelbbraun. 3. *vb.* bräunen; *(leather)* gerben.
tangle, 1. *n.* Gewirr' *nt.* 2. *vb.* sich zu schaffen machen mit.
tank, *n.* Tank, -s *m.; (mil.)* Panzer, - *m.*
tap, 1. *n. (blow)* Taps, -e *m.; (faucet)* Hahn, ⸗e *m.* 2. *vb.* leicht schlagen*; an·zapfen.
tape, *n.* Band, ⸗er *nt.*
tape recorder, *n.* Tonbandgerät, -e *nt.,* Magnetophon', -e *nt.*

tapestry, *n.* Wandteppich, -e *m.;* Tapisserie', -i'en *f.*
tar, 1. *n.* Teer *m.* 2. *vb.* teeren.
target, *n.* Ziel, -e *nt.;* Zielscheibe, -n *f.*
tariff, *n.* Zolltarif, -e *m.*
tarnish, *vb. (fig.)* befle'cken; *(silver)* sich beschla'gen*.
tart, 1. *n.* Törtchen, - *nt.* 2. *adj.* sauer, herb.
task, *n.* Aufgabe, -n *f.*
taste, 1. *n.* Geschmack', ⸗e *m.* 2. *vb.* schmecken, kosten.
tasty, *adj.* schmackhaft.
taut, *adj.* straff.
tavern, *n.* Bierlokal, -e *nt.*
tax, 1. *n.* Steuer, -n *f.* 2. *vb.* besteu'ern, belas'ten.
taxi, *n.* Taxe, -n *f.,* Taxi, -s *nt.*
taxpayer, *n.* Steuerzahler, - *m.*
tea, *n.* Tee, -s *m.*
teach, *vb.* lehren, unterrich'ten.
teacher, *n.* Lehrer, - *m.*
tea-pot, *n.* Teekanne, -n *f.*
tear, 1. *n.* Träne, -n *f.; (rip)* Riß, -sse *m.* 2. *vb.* reißen*.
tease, *vb.* necken.
teaspoon, *n.* Teelöffel, - *m.*
technical, *adj.* technisch.
technique, *n.* Technik, -en *f.,* Kunstfertigkeit *f.*
tedious, *adj.* langweilig, mühsam.
telegram, *n.* Telegramm', -e *nt.*
telegraph, 1. *n.* Telegraph', -en, -en *m.* 2. *vb.* telegraphie'ren.
telephone, 1. *n.* Telephon', -e *nt.,* Fernsprecher, - *m.* 2. *vb.* telephonie'ren.
telescope, *n.* Fernrohr, -e *nt.*
televise, *vb.* im Fernsehen übertra'gen*.
television, *n.* Fernsehen *nt.*
television set, *n.* Fernsehapparat, -e *m.*
tell, *vb.* erzäh'len, berich'ten, sagen.
teller, *n.* Kassie'rer, - *m.*
temper, 1. *n.* Laune, -n *f.;* Temperament' *nt.; (anger)* Zorn *m.* 2. *vb.* mäßigen; *(steel)* härten.
temperament, *n.* Gemüts'art, -en *f.*
temperamental, *adj.* Gemüts- *(cpds.);* temperament'voll.
temperate, *adj.* mäßig.
temperature, *n.* Temperatur', -en *f.*
tempest, *n.* Sturm, ⸗e *m.*
temple, *n.* Tempel, - *m.*
temporary, *adj.* zeitweilig, vorü'bergehend, proviso'risch.
tempt, *vb.* versu'chen; reizen.
temptation, *n.* Versu'chung, - *f.*
ten, *num.* zehn.
tenant, *n.* Mieter, - *m.,* Pächter, - *m.*
tend, *vb.* pflegen, hüten; *(incline)* neigen zu.
tendency, *n.* Neigung, -en *f.,* Tendenz', -en *f.*

tender, 1. *n. (money)* Zahlungsmittel, - *nt.; (train, boat)* Tender, - *m.* 2. *adj.* zart; zärtlich. 3. *vb.* an·bieten*.
tenderness, *n.* Zartheit, -en *f.,* Zärtlichkeit, -en *f.*
tendon, *n.* Sehne, -n *f.*
tennis, *n.* Tennis *nt.*
tenor, *n.* Tenor', -e *m.*
tense, *adj.* gespannt'; kribbelig.
tension, *n.* Spannung, -en *f.*
tent, *n.* Zelt, -e *nt.*
tentative, *adj.* probeweise.
tenth, 1. *adj.* zehnt-. 2. *n.* Zehntel, - *nt.*
term, *n.* Perio'de, -n *f.; (of office)* Amtszeit, -en *f.; (college)* Semes'ter, - *nt.; (expression)* Ausdruck, ⸗e *m.; (condition)* Bedin'gung, -en *f.*
terminate, *vb.* been'den; begren'zen.
terrace, *n.* Terras'se, -n *f.*
terrible, *adj.* schrecklich, furchtbar.
terrify, *vb.* erschre'cken.
territory, *n.* Gebiet', -e *nt.*
terror, *n.* Schrecken, - *m.*
test, 1. *n.* Prüfung, -en *f.;* Probe, -n *f.;* Test, -s *m.;* Versuch', -e *m.* 2. *vb.* prüfen.
testify, *vb.* bezeu'gen; *(court)* aus·sagen.
testimony, *n.* Zeugnis, -se *nt.;* Zeugenaussage, -n *f.*
textile, 1. *n.* Textil'ware, -n *f.* 2. *adj.* Textil'- *(cpds.).*
texture, *n.* Gewe'be, - *nt.;* Aufbau *m.;* Beschaf'fenheit, -en *f.*
than, *conj.* als.
thank, *vb.* danken.
thankful, *adj.* dankbar.
that, 1. *pron.&adj.* der, das, die; jener, -es, -e. 2. *conj.* daß.
the, *art.* der, das, die.
theater, *n.* Thea'ter, - *nt.; (fig.)* Schauplatz, ⸗e *m.*
thee, *pron.* dich; dir.
theft, *n.* Diebstahl, ⸗e *m.*
their, *adj.* ihr, -, -e.
theirs, *pron.* ihrer, -es, -e.
them, *pron.* sie; ihnen.
theme, *n.* Thema, -men *nt.*
then, *adv. (after that)* dann; *(at that time)* damals; *(therefore)* dann, also.
thence, *adv.* von da, von dort.
theology, *n.* Theologie' *f.*
theoretical, *adj.* theore'tisch.
theory, *n.* Theorie', -i'en *f.*
therapy, *n.* Therapie' *f.*
there, *adv. (in that place)* da, dort; *(to that place)* dahin', dorthin'; *(from t.)* daher', dorther'.
therefore, *adv.* daher, darum, deshalb, deswegen, also.
thermometer, *n.* Thermome'ter, - *nt.*
thermonuclear, *adj.* kernphysikalisch.
these, *adj.* diese.

they, *pron.* sie.

thick, *adj.* dick; *(dense)* dicht.

thicken, *vb.* dicken, verdi'cken; verdich'ten.

thickness, *n.* Dicke *f.;* Dichtheit *f.; (layer)* Schicht, -en *f.*

thief, *n.* Dieb, -e *m.*

thigh, *n.* Schenkel, - *m.*

thimble, *n.* Fingerhut, ‒e *m.*

thin, *adj.* dünn; mager.

thing, *n.* Ding, -e *nt.;* Sache, -n *f.*

think, *vb.* meinen, glauben; denken*, nach•denken*.

thinker, *n.* Denker, - *m.*

third, 1. *adj.* dritt-. 2. *n.* Drittel, - *nt.*

Third World, *n.* Dritte Welt *f.*

thirst, 1. *n.* Durst *m.* 2. *vb.* dürsten.

thirsty, *adj.* durstig.

thirteen, *num.* dreizehn.

thirteenth, 1. *adj.* dreizehnt-. 2. *n.* Dreizehntel, - *nt.*

thirtieth, 1. *adj.* dreißigst-. 2. *n.* Dreißigstel, - *nt.*

thirty, *num.* dreißig.

this, *pron.&adj.* dieser, -es, -e.

thorough, *adj.* gründlich.

thou, *pron.* du.

though, 1. *adv.* doch. 2. *conj.* obwohl', obgleich'.

thought, *n.* Gedan'ke(n), - *m.*

thoughtful, *adj.* gedan'kenvoll; *(considerate)* rücksichtsvoll.

thousand, *num.* tausend.

thousandth, 1. *adj.* tausendst-. 2. *n.* Tausendstel, - *nt.*

thread, *n.* Faden, ‒ *m.;* Garn, -e *nt.*

threat, *n.* Drohung, -en *f.*

threaten, *vb.* drohen.

three, *num.* drei.

thrift, *n.* Sparsamkeit *f.*

thrill, 1. *n.* Aufregung, -en *f.;* Sensation', -en *f.;* Nervenkitzel, - *m.* 2. *vb.* erre'gen, packen.

throat, *n.* Hals, ‒e *m.,* Kehle, -n *f.*

throb, *vb.* pochen, pulsie'ren.

throne, *n.* Thron, -e *m.*

through, 1. *prep.* durch. 2. *adj.* fertig.

throughout, 1. *adv.* überall; völlig. 2. *prep.* durch.

throw, 1. *n.* Wurf, ‒e *m.* 2. *vb.* werfen*, schleudern.

thrust, 1. *n.* Stoß, ‒e *m.; (tech.)* Schub *m.* 2. *vb.* stoßen*.

thumb, *n.* Daumen, - *m.*

thunder, 1. *n.* Donner, - *m.* 2. *vb.* donnern.

thunderstorm, *n.* Gewit'ter, - *nt.*

Thursday, *n.* Donnerstag, -e *m.*

thus, *adv.* so.

ticket, *n.* Karte, -n *f.,* Billett', -s or -e *nt.; (admission)* Eintrittskarte, -n *f.; (travel)* Fahrkarte, -n *f.,* Fahrschein, -

thick, *e m.; (traffic)* Strafmandat, -e *nt.*

tickle, *vb.* kitzeln.

ticklish, *adj.* kitzlig; *(delicate, risky)* heikel.

tide, *n.* Gezei'ten *pl.; (low t.)* Ebbe *f.; (high t.)* Flut *f.*

tidy, *adj.* sauber, ordentlich.

tie, 1. *n. (bond)* Band, -e *nt.; (necktie)* Krawat'te, -n *f.,* Schlips, -e *m.; (equal score)* Punktgleichheit *f.,* Stimmengleichheit *f.* 2. *vb.* binden*, knüpfen.

tiger, *n.* Tiger, - *m.*

tight, *adj.* eng; *(taut)* straff; *(firm)* fest; *(drunk)* beschwipst'.

tighten, *vb.* straffen, enger machen.

tile, *n. (wall, stove)* Kachel, - *f.; (floor)* Fliese, -n *f.; (roof)* Ziegel, -n *m.*

till, 1. *n.* Ladenkasse, -n *f.* 2. *vb.* bebau'en, bestel'len. 3. *adv., conj.* bis.

tilt, 1. *n.* Neigung, -en *f.* 2. *vb.* neigen, kippen.

timber, *n.* Holz *nt.*

time, 1. *n.* Zeit, -en *f.; (o'clock)* Uhr *f.* 2. *vb.* die Zeit nehmen*.

timetable, *n.* Fahrplan, ‒e *m.,* Kursbuch, ‒er *nt.*

timid, *adj.* ängstlich, schüchtern.

timidity, *n.* Ängstlichkeit *f.,* Schüchternheit *f.*

tin, *n. (metal)* Zinn *nt.; (t. plate)* Blech *nt.; (t. can)* Konser'vendose, -n *f.*

tint, *n.* Farbtönung, -en *f.*

tiny, *adj.* winzig.

tip, 1. *n. (end)* Spitze, -n *f.; (gratuity)* Trinkgeld, -er *nt.* 2. *vb. (tilt)* kippen; *(give gratuity)* ein Trinkgeld geben*.

tire, *n.* Reifen, - *m.* 2. *vb.* ermü'den.

tired, *adj.* müde.

tissue, *n.* Gewe'be, - *nt.; (facial t.)* Papier'taschentuch, ‒er *nt.*

title, *n.* Titel, - *m.; (heading)* Überschrift, -en *f.*

to, *prep.* zu.

toast, 1. *n.* Toast *m.; (drink to health)* Trinkspruch, ‒e *m.* 2. *vb.* rösten; auf jemandes Wohl trinken*.

tobacco, *n.* Tabak *m.*

today, *adv.* heute.

toe, *n.* Zehe, -n *f.*

together, *adv.* zusam'men.

toil, 1. *n.* Arbeit, -en *f.,* Mühe, -n *f.* 2. *vb.* arbeiten, sich ab•mühen.

toilet, *n.* Toilet'te, -n *f.*

token, *n.* Zeichen, - *nt.;* Symbol', -e *nt.*

tolerance, *n.* Duldsamkeit *f.,* Toleranz' *f.*

tolerant, *adj.* duldsam, tolerant'.

tolerate, *vb.* dulden.

toll, 1. *n.* Zoll *m.; (highway)*

Wegegeld, -er *nt.; (bridge)* Brückengeld, -er *nt.* 2. *vb.* läuten.

tomato, *n.* Toma'te, -n *f.*

tomb, *n.* Grab, ‒er *nt.,* Grabmal, ‒er *nt.*

tomorrow, *adv.* morgen.

ton, *n.* Tonne, -n *f.*

tone, *n.* Ton, ‒e *m.*

tongue, *n.* Zunge, -n *f.*

tonic, 1. *n.* Stärkungsmittel *nt.* 2. *adj.* tonisch.

tonight, *adv.* heute abend.

tonsil, *n.* Mandel, -n *f.*

too, *adv.* zu; *(also)* auch.

tool, *n.* Werkzeug, -e *nt.*

tooth, *n.* Zahn, ‒e *m.*

toothache, *n.* Zahnschmerzen *pl.*

toothbrush, *n.* Zahnbürste, -n *f.*

toothpaste, *n.* Zahnpaste, -n *f.*

top, 1. *n.* Spitze, -n *f.,* oberstes Ende, -n *nt.; (surface)* Oberfläche, -n *f.; (on t. of all)* auf. 2. *vb. (fig.)* krönen.

topcoat, *n.* Mantel, ‒ *m.*

topic, *n.* Thema, -men *nt.*

torch, *n.* Fackel, -n *f.*

torment, 1. *n.* Qual, -en *f.* 2. *vb.* quälen.

torrent, *n.* reißender Strom, ‒e *m.*

torture, 1. *n.* Folter, -n *f.,* Qual, -en *f.* 2. *vb.* foltern, quälen.

toss, *vb.* werfen*, schleudern.

total, 1. *n.* Summe, -n *f.* 2. *adj.* gesamt'; total'.

totalitarian, *adj.* totalitär'.

touch, 1. *n.* Berüh'rung, -en *f.; (sense of t.)* Tastsinn *m.; (final t.)* letzter Schliff, -e *f.; (t. of fever, etc.)* Anflug *m.* 2. *vb.* berüh'ren.

touching, *adj.* rührend.

tough, 1. *n.* Rabau'ke, -n, -n *m.* 2. *adj.* zäh; *(hard)* hart (‒).

tour, 1. *n.* Reise, -n *f.,* Tour, -en *f.* 2. *vb.* berei'sen.

tourist, *n.* Tourist', -en, -en *m.*

tow, *vb.* schleppen.

toward, *prep.* nach; gegen; zu.

towel, *n.* Handtuch, ‒er *nt.*

tower, *n.* Turm, ‒e *m.*

town, *n.* Stadt, ‒e *f.,* Ort, -e *m.*

toy, 1. *n.* Spielzeug, -e *nt.* 2. *vb.* spielen.

trace, 1. *n.* Spur, -en *f.* 2. *vb. (delineate)* nach•zeichnen; *(track)* zurück'•verfolgen.

track, 1. *n.* Spur, -en *f.,* Fährte, -n *f.; (sports)* Leichtathletik *f.; (R.R.)* Gelei'se, ‒ *nt.,* Gleis, -e *nt.* 2. *vb. (t. down)* nachspüren.

tract, *n. (land)* Gebiet, -e *nt.; (pamphlet)* Traktat', -e *nt.*

tractor, *n.* Trecker, - *m.*

trade, 1. *n.* Handel *m.; (exchange)* Tausch *m.* 2. *vb.* Handel treiben*; aus•tauschen.

trader, *n.* Händler, - *m.*

tradition, n. Tradition', -en f.

traditional, adj. traditionell'.

traffic, n. Verkehr' m.; (trade) Handel m.

traffic light, n. Verkehrs'licht, -er nt., Verkehrs'ampel, -n f.

tragedy, n. Tragö'die, -n f.

tragic, adj. tragisch.

trail, n. Fährte, -n f.

trailer, n. Anhänger, - m.; (for living) Wohnwagen, - m.

train, 1. n. Zug, ⸚e m.; (of dress) Schleppe, -n f. 2. vb. aus·bilden.

traitor, n. Verrä'ter, - m.

tramp, n. Landstreicher, - m.

tranquil, adj. ruhig.

tranquillity, n. Ruhe f.

transaction, n. Transaktion', -en f.

transfer, 1. n. (ticket) Umsteigefahrschein, -e m. 2. vb. (change cars) um·steigen*; (money) überwei'sen*; (ownership) übertra'gen*; (move to new location) verset'zen.

transfix, vb. durchboh'ren.

transform, vb. um·wandeln, um·formen.

transfusion, n. Transfusion', -en f.

transition, n. Übergang, ⸚e m.

translate, vb. überset'zen.

translation, n. Überset'zung, -en f.

transmit, vb. übertra'gen*; übersen'den.

transparent, adj. durchsichtig.

transport, 1. n. Beför'derung, -en f., Transport', -e m. 2. vb. beför'dern, transportie'ren.

transportation, n. Beför'derung, -en f.

transsexual, adj. transsexual'.

transvestite, n. Transvestit', -en, -en m.

trap, n. Falle, -n f.

trash, n. Abfall, ⸚e m.; (fig.) Kitsch m.

travel, 1. n. Reise, -n f. 2. vb. reisen.

travel agency, n. Reisebüro, -s nt.

traveler, n. Reisend - m.&f.

traveler's check, n. Travelerscheck, -s m.; Reisescheck, -s m.

tray, n. Tablett', -e nt.

treacherous, adj. verrä'terisch; tückisch.

tread, 1. n. Schritt, -e m. 2. vb. treten*.

treason, n. Verrat' m.

treasure, 1. n. Schatz, ⸚e m. 2. vb. hoch·schätzen.

treasurer, n. Schatzmeister, - m.

treasury, n. Finanz'ministerium, -rien nt.

treat, 1. n. Extragenuß, ⸚sse m. 2. vb. gehandeln; (pay for) frei·halten*.

treatment, n. Behand'lung, -en f.

treaty, n. Vertrag', ⸚e m.

tree, n. Baum, ⸚e m.

tremble, vb. zittern.

tremendous, adj. ungeheuer.

trench, n. Graben, ⸚ m.

trend, n. Trend, -s m.

trespass, vb. widerrechtlich betre'ten*; übertre'ten*.

triage, n. Einteilung je nach Priorität f.

trial, n. Versuch', -e m.; (law) Prozeß', -sse m.

triangle, n. Dreieck, -e nt.

tribute, n. Tribut', -e m.; (fig.) Ehrung, -en f.

trick, 1. n. Kniff, -e m., Trick, -s m. 2. vb. rein·legen.

tricky, adj. knifflig; heikel.

trifle, n. Kleinigkeit, -en f., Lappa'lie, -n f.

trigger, n. (gun) Abzug, ⸚e m.

trim, 1. adj. adrett'. 2. vb. (clip) stutzen; (adorn) beset'zen.

trip, 1. n. Reise, -n f. 2. vb. stolpern; (tr.) einem ein Bein stellen.

triple, 1. adj. dreifach. 2. vb. verdrei'fachen.

trite, adj. abgedroschen.

triumph, 1. n. Triumph', -e m. 2. vb. triumphie'ren.

triumphant, adj. triumphie'rend.

trivial, adj. trivial'.

trolley-bus, n. Obus, -se m.

trolley-car, n. Strassenbahn, -en f.

troop, n. Trupp, -s m.

troops, n.pl. Truppen pl.

trophy, n. Trophä'e, -n f.

tropic, n. Wendekreis, -e m.

tropical, adj. tropisch.

tropics, n.pl. Tropen pl.

trot, 1. n. Trab m. 2. vb. traben.

trouble, 1. n. Mühe, -n f.; (difficulty) Schwierigkeit, -en f.; (unpleasantness) Unannehmlichkeit, -en f.; (jam) Klemme, -n f. 2. vb. bemü'hen; beun'ruhigen.

troublesome, adj. lästig.

trough, n. Trog, ⸚e m.

trousers, n.pl. Hose, -n f.

trousseau, n. Aussteuer, -n f.

trout, n. Forel'le, -n f.

truce, n. Waffenstillstand, ⸚e m.

truck, n. Lastauto, -s nt., Lastwagen, - m., Lastkraftwagen, - m.

true, adj. wahr; wahrhaf'tig; (faithful) treu.

truly, adv. wahrhaf'tig; (yours t.) Ihr erge'bener, Ihre erge'bene.

trumpet, n. Trompe'te, -n f.

trunk, n. (tree) Stamm, ⸚e m.; (luggage) Koffer, - m.

trust, 1. n. Zuversicht f., Vertrau'en f.; (comm.) Trust, -s m.; (in t.) zu treuen Händen. 2. vb. vertrau'en.

trustworthy, adj. zuverlässig.

truth, n. Wahrheit, -en f.

truthful, adj. wahr; ehrlich.

try, 1. n. Versuch', -e m. 2. vb. versu'chen, probie'ren.

T-shirt, n. T-Shirt nt.

tub, n. Wanne, -n f.

tube, n. Röhre, -n f.; (container) Tube, -n f.

tuberculosis, n. Tuberkulo'se f.

tuck, 1. n. Falte, -n f. 2. vb. falten.

Tuesday, n. Dienstag, -e m.

tuft, n. Büschel, - nt., Quaste, -n f.

tug, vb. ziehen*.

tuition, n. Schulgeld, -er nt.; (university) Studiengeld, -er nt.

tulip, n. Tulpe, -n f.

tumor, n. Tumor, -o'ren m.

tumult, n. Tumult', -e m.

tuna, n. Thunfisch, -e m.

tune, 1. n. Melodie', -i'en f. 2. vb. stimmen.

tuneful, adj. melo'disch.

tunnel, n. Tunnel, - m.

turbine, n. Turbi'ne, -n f.

turbo-jet, n. (plane) Turbi'nenjäger, - m.

turbo-prop, n. Turbi'nenpropellertriebwerk, -e nt.

Turk, n. Türke, -n, -n m.

turkey, n. Truthahn, ⸚e m., Puter, - m.

Turkey, n. die Türkei' f.

Turkish, adj. türkisch.

turmoil, n. Durcheinan'der nt.

turn, 1. n. Umdre'hung, -en f.; Wendung, -en f., Kurve, -n f.; (to take t.s) sich ab·wechseln; (it's my t.) ich bin dran. 2. vb. drehen, wenden*; (t. around) um·drehen.

turnip, n. Steckrübe, -n f.

turret, n. Turm, ⸚e m.

turtle, n. Schildkröte, -n f.

tutor, 1. n. Lehrer, - m.; Nachhilfelehrer, - m. 2. vb. Nachhilfeunterricht geben*.

twelfth, 1. adj. zwölft-. 2. n. Zwölftel, - nt.

twelve, num. zwölf.

twentieth, 1. adj. zwanzigst-. 2. n. Zwanzigstel, - nt.

twenty, num. zwanzig.

twice, adv. zweimal.

twig, n. Zweig, -e m.

twilight, n. Dämmerung, -en f., Zwielicht nt.

twin, n. Zwilling, -e m.

twine, 1. n. (thread) Zwirn, -e m.; (rope) Tau, -e nt. 2. vb. winden*.

twist, 1. n. Drehung, -en f.; (distortion) Verdre'hung, -en f. 2. vb. drehen; verdre'hen.

two, num. zwei.

type, 1. n. Typ, -en m., Typus, -pen m.; (printing) Schriftsatz, -e m.; (letter) Type, -n f. 2. vb. kennzeichnen; (write on typewriter) tippen.

typewriter, n. Schreibmaschine, -n f.

typhoid fever, n. Typhus m.

typical, *adj.* typisch.
typist, *n.* Schreibdame, -n *f.*
tyranny, *n.* Tyrannei' *f.*
tyrant, *n.* Tyrann', -en, -en *m.*

U

ugliness, *n.* Häßlichkeit *f.*
ugly, *adj.* häßlich.
ulcer, *n.* Geschwür', -e *nt.*
ulterior, *adj.* höher; weiter; **(u. motives)** Hintergedanken *pl.*
ultimate, *adj.* äußerst-.
umbrella, *n.* Regenschirm, -e *m.*
umpire, *n.* Schiedsrichter, - *m.*
un- *prefix* un-.
unable, *adj.* unfähig.
unanimous, *adj.* einstimmig.
unbecoming, *adj.* unschicklich; **(of clothes)** unkleidsam.
uncertain, *adj.* ungewiß.
uncertainty, *n.* Ungewißheit, -en *f.*
uncle, *n.* Onkel, - *m.*
unconscious, *adj.* bewußt'los; **(unaware)** unbewußt.
uncover, *vb.* auf·decken; ent·blö'ßen.
under, *prep.* unter.
underground, **1.** *n.* Untergrundbahn, -en *f.* **2.** *adj.* unter der Erde gelegen; Untergrund- **(cpds.).**
underline, *vb.* unterstrei'chen*.
underneath, **1.** *adv.* unter, drunter. **2.** *prep.* unter.
undershirt, *n.* Unterhemd, -en *nt.*
undersign, *vb.* unterzeich'nen.
understand, *vb.* verste'hen*, begri'fen*.
understanding, *n.* Verständ'nis *nt.;* **(agreement)** Einvernehmen, - *nt.*
undertake, *vb.* unterneh'men*.
undertaker, *n.* Leichenbestatter, - *m.*
underwear, *n.* Unterwäsche *f.*
underworld, *n.* Unterwelt *f.*
undo, *vb.* auf·machen, lösen; ungeschehen machen.
undress, *vb.* entklei'den, (sich) aus·ziehen*.
uneasy, *adj.* unruhig, unbehaglich.
unemployed, *adj.* arbeitslos.
unemployment, *n.* Arbeitslosigkeit *f.*
unequal, *adj.* ungleich.
uneven, *adj.* uneben; ungleich; **(numbers)** ungerade.
unexpected, *adj.* unerwartet.
unfair, *adj.* ungerecht.
unfamiliar, *adj.* unbekannt; ungeläufig.
unfavorable, *adj.* ungünstig.
unfit, *adj.* untauglich.
unfold, *vb.* entfal'ten.
unforgettable, *adj.* unvergeßlich.

unfortunate, *adj.* unglücklich; bedau'erlich.
unhappy, *adj.* unglücklich.
uniform, **1.** *n.* Uniform', -en *f.* **2.** *adj.* einheitlich.
unify, *vb.* verei'nen; verein'heitlichen.
union, *n.* Verei'nigung, -en *f.;* **(labor u.)** Gewerk'schaft, -en *f.*
unique, *adj.* einzigartig.
unisex, *adj.* unisex.
unit, *n.* Einheit, -en *f.*
unite, *vb.* verei'nigen.
United Nations, *n.* die Verein'ten Natio'nen *pl.*
United States, *n.* Die Verei'nigten Staaten *pl.*
unity, *n.* Einigkeit *f.*
universal, *adj.* universal'.
universe, *n.* Weltall *nt.*
university, *n.* Universität', -en *f.*
unjust, *adj.* ungerecht.
unknown, *adj.* unbekannt.
unleaded, *adj.* bleifrei.
unless, *conj.* wenn nicht; es sei denn, daß.
unlike, *adj.* ungleich.
unlikely, *adj.* unwahrscheinlich.
unload, *vb.* ab·laden*, aus·laden*.
unlock, *vb.* auf·schließen*.
unlucky, *adj.* **(be u.)** kein Glück haben*, Pech haben*.
unmarried, *adj.* unverheiratet.
unpack, *vb.* aus·packen.
unpleasant, *adj.* unangenehm.
unqualified, *adj.* **(unfit)** ungeeignet; **(unreserved)** uneingeschränkt.
unsettled, *adj.* unsicher, in der Schwebe.
unsteady, *adj.* unstet.
unsuccessful, *adj.* erfolg'los.
untie, *vb.* auf·knüpfen.
until, **1.** *prep.* bis; **(not u.)** erst. **2.** *conj.* bis; **(not u.)** erst wenn; erst als.
untruth, *n.* Unwahrheit, -en *f.*
untruthful, *adj.* unwahr.
unusual, *adj.* ungewöhnlich.
unwell, *adj.* unpäßlich, nicht wohl.
up, **1.** *prep.* auf. *auf.* **2.** *adv.* auf, hinauf, herauf.
upbraid, *vb.* schelten*.
uphill, **1.** *adj.* **(fig.)** mühsam. **2.** *adv.* bergan', bergauf'.
uphold, *vb.* aufrecht·erhalten*.
upholster, *vb.* bezie'hen*.
upholsterer, *n.* Tapezie'rer, - *m.*
upon, *prep.* auf.
upper, *adj.* ober-.
upright, *adj.* aufrecht.
uprising, *n.* Aufstand, ⸗e *m.*
uproot, *vb.* ausrotten.
upset, **1.** *n.* Rückschlag, ⸗e *m.;* **(stomach u.)** Magenverstimmung, -en *f.* **2.** *vb.* **(overturn)** um·werfen*; **(disturb)** über den Haufen werfen, verstim'-

men; **(discompose)** aus der Fassung bringen*.
upside down, *adv.* umgekehrt, verkehrt' herum'.
upstairs, *adv.* oben; nach oben.
uptight, *adj.* unsicher, verklemmt.
urban, *adj.* städtisch.
urge, **1.** *n.* Drang, ⸗e *m.;* **(sex)** Trieb, -e *m.* **2.** *vb.* drängen, nötigen.
urgency, *n.* Dringlichkeit *f.*
urgent, *adj.* dringend.
urinal, *n.* Harnglas, ⸗er *nt.;* **(public)** öffentliche Bedürf'nisanstalt, -en *f.*
urinate, *vb.* urinie'ren.
urine, *n.* Urin', -e *nt.*
us, *pron.* uns.
usage, *n.* Gebrauch', ⸗e *m.*
use, **1.** *n.* Gebrauch', ⸗e *m.,* Benut'zung, -en *f.* **2.** *vb.* gebrau'chen, verwen'den, benut'zen.
useful, *adj.* nützlich.
useless, *adj.* nutzlos.
user, *n.* Benut'zer, - *m.*
usher, *n.* **(theater, etc.)** Platzanweiser, - *m.;* **(wedding)** Brautführer, - *m.*
usual, *adj.* gewöhn'lich.
usury, *n.* Wucher *m.*
utensil, *n.* Gerät, -e *nt.*
uterus, *n.* Gebär'mutter, ⸗ *f.*
utility, *n.* Nutzbarkeit *f.*
utilize, *vb.* aus·nutzen.
utmost, *adj.* äusserst.
utter, **1.** *adj.* völlig. **2.** *vb.* äußern.
utterance, *n.* Äußerung, -en *f.*

V

vacancy, *n.* **(position)** freie Stellung, -en *f.;* **(hotel, etc.)** unvermietetes Zimmer, - *nt.*
vacant, *adj.* frei; **(empty)** leer.
vacate, *vb.* räumen.
vacation, *n.* Ferien *pl.*
vaccinate, *vb.* impfen.
vaccination, *n.* Impfung, -en *f.*
vaccine, *n.* Impfstoff, -e *m.*
vacuum, *n.* Vakuum, -kua *nt.*
vagrant, **1.** *n.* Landstreicher, *m.;* **(worker)** Saison'arbeiter, - *m.* **2.** *adj.* vagabundie'rend.
vague, *adj.* unbestimmt, vage.
vain, **1.** *adj.* **(conceited)** eitel; **(useless)** vergeb'lich. **2.** *n.* **(in v.)** umsonst', verge'bens.
valet, *n.* Diener, - *m.*
valiant, *adj.* tapfer.
valid, *adj.* gültig.
valise, *n.* Reisetasche, -n *f.*
valley, *n.* Tal, ⸗er *nt.*
valor, *n.* Tapferkeit *f.*
valuable, *adj.* wertvoll.
value, *n.* Wert, -e *m.*
valve, *n.* Ventil', -e *nt.;* **(med.)** Klappe, -n *f.*
van, *n.* **(delivery truck)** Lieferwagen, - *m.;* **(moving v.)** Möbelwagen, - *m.*

vandal, n. Vanda'le, -n, -n m.

vanguard, n. Vorhut f.; (person) Vorkämpfer, - m.

vanilla, n. Vanil'le f.

vanish, vb. verschwin'den*.

vanity, n. Eitelkeit f.

vanquish, vb. besie'gen.

vapor, n. Dampf, -e m.

variance, n. Widerstreit m.

variation, n. Abwechslung, -en f.; Abänderung, -en f., Variation', -en f.

varied, adj. verschie'den; mannigfaltig.

variety, n. Mannigfaltigkeit f.; (choice) Auswahl f.; (theater) Varieté nt.

various, adj. verschie'den.

varnish, 1. n. Firnis, -se m. 2. vb. firnissen.

vary, vb. variie'ren, verän'dern.

vase, n. Vase, -n f.

vasectomy, n. Vasektomie f.

vast, adj. riesig.

vat, n. Faß, ̈sser nt.

vaudeville, n. Varieté nt.

vault, n. Gewöl'be, - nt.; (burial chamber) Gruft, ̈e f.; (bank) Tresor', -e m.; (jump) Sprung, ̈e m. 2. vb. springen*.

veal, n. Kalbfleisch nt.

vegetable, n. Gemü'se, - nt.

vehement, adj. heftig.

vehicle, n. Fahrzeug, -e nt.

veil, 1. n. Schleier, - m. 2. vb. verschlei'ern.

vein, n. Vene, -n f., Ader, -n f.

velocity, n. Geschwin'digkeit, -en f.

velvet, n. Samt m.

veneer, n. Furnier', -e nt.

vengeance, n. Rache f.

venom, n. Gift, -e nt.

vent, 1. n. Öffnung, -en f.; (escape passage) Abzugsröhre, -n f. 2. vb. freien Lauf lassen*.

ventilate, vb. lüften, ventilie'ren.

ventilation, n. Lüftung f., Ventilation' f.

venture, 1. n. Wagnis, -se nt. 2. vb. wagen.

verb, n. Verb, -en nt., Zeitwort, ̈er nt.

verbal, adj. verbal'; (oral) mündlich.

verdict, n. Urteil, -e nt.

verge, 1. n. (fig.) Rand, ̈er m. 2. vb. (v. on) grenzen an.

verification, n. Bestä'tigung, -en f.

verify, vb. bestä'tigen.

vernacular, 1. n. Umgangssprache, -n f. 2. adj. umgangssprachlich.

versatile, adj. vielseitig.

verse, n. Vers, -e f.

versify, vb. in Verse bringen*.

version, n. Fassung, -en f., Version', -en f.

versus, prep. gegen.

vertebrate, 1. n. Wirbeltier, -e nt. 2. adj. Wirbel- (cpds.).

vertical, adj. senkrecht.

very, adv. sehr.

vespers, n. Vesper, -n f.

vessel, n. Schiff, -e nt.; (container) Gefäß', -e nt.

vest, n. Weste, -n f.

vestige, n. Spur, -en f.

veteran, n. Veteran', -en, -en m.

veterinary, 1. n. Tierarzt, ̈e m. 2. adj. tierärztlich.

veto, 1. n. Veto, -s nt. 2. vb. das Veto ein-legen.

vex, vb. ärgern; verblüf'fen.

via, prep. über.

viaduct, n. Viadukt', -e m.

vibrate, vb. vibrie'ren, schwingen*.

vibration, n. Vibration', -en f., Schwingung, -en f.; (tremor) Erschüt'terung, -en f.

vice, n. Laster, - nt.

vicinity, n. Nähe f., Umge'bung, -en f.

vicious, adj. gemein', heimtückisch.

victim, n. Opfer, - nt.

victor, n. Sieger, - m.

victorious, adj. siegreich.

victory, n. Sieg, -e m.

videodisc, n. Videoscheibe, -n f.

Vienna, n. Wien nt.

view, 1. n. Aussicht, -en f. 2. vb. bese'hen*, betrach'ten.

vigil, n. Nachtwache, -n f.

vigilant, adj. wachsam.

vigor, n. Kraft, ̈e f., Energie', -i'en f.

vigorous, adj. kräftig, kraftstrozend.

vile, adj. gemein', niederträchtig.

village, n. Dorf, ̈er nt.

villain, n. Bösewicht, -e m., Schurke, -n, -n m.

vindicate, vb. rechtfertigen.

vine, n. Rebstock, ̈e m.; (creeper) Ranke, -n f.

vinegar, n. Essig m.

vineyard, n. Weingarten, - m., Weinberg, -e m.

vintage, n. (gathering) Weinlese f.; (year) Jahrgang, ̈e m.

viol, viola, n. Bratsche, -n f.

violate, vb. verlet'zen; (oath) brechen*; (law, territory) übertre'ten*.

violation, n. Verlet'zung, -en f., Bruch, ̈e m.; Übertre'tung, -en f.

violator, n. Verlet'zer, - m.; Übertre'ter, - m.

violence, n. Gewalt'tätigkeit, -en f.; (vehemence) Gewalt'samkeit f., Heftigkeit f.

violent, adj. gewalt'tätig; gewalt'sam, heftig.

violet, 1. n. Veilchen, - nt. 2. adj. violett', veilchenblau.

violin, n. Geige, -n f.

virgin, n. Jungfrau, -en f.

virile, adj. männlich.

virtue, n. Tugend, -en f.

virtuous, adj. tugendhaft, tugendsam.

virus, n. Virus, -ren m.

visa, n. Visum, -sa nt.

vise, n. Schraubstock, ̈e m.

visible, adj. sichtbar.

vision, n. Sehkraft, ̈e f.; (visual image) Vision', -en f.

visit, 1. n. Besuch', -e m. 2. vb. besu'chen.

visitor, n. Besu'cher, - m.

visual, adj. visuell'.

vital, adj. (essential) wesentlich; (strong) vital'.

vitality, n. Lebenskraft f., Vitalität' f.

vitamin, n. Vitamin', -e nt.

vivacious, adj. lebhaft, temperament'voll.

vivid, adj. leben'dig, lebhaft.

vocabulary, n. Wortschatz, ̈e m.; (list of words) Wörterverzeichnis, -se nt.

vocal, adj. Stimm-, Gesang'- (cpds.); lautstark.

vogue, n. Mode, -n f.

voice, n. Stimme, - n f.

void, adj. ungültig.

volcano, n. Vulkan', -e m.

volt, n. Volt, - nt.

voltage, n. Stromspannung, -en f.

volume, n. Volu'men, - nt.; (book) Band, ̈e m.; (quantity) Umfang, ̈e m.

voluntary, adj. freiwillig.

volunteer, 1. n. Freiwillig-m.&f. 2. vb. sich freiwillig melden.

vomit, vb. erbre'chen*.

vote, 1. n. (individual ballot) Wahlstimme, -n f.; (casting) Stimmabgabe, -n f.; (v. of confidence) Vertrau'ensvotum nt. 2. vb. wählen, stimmen, ab-stimmen.

voter, n. Wähler, - m.

vouch for, vb. verbür'gen für.

vow, 1. n. Gelüb'de - nt. 2. vb. gelo'ben.

vowel, n. Vokal', -e m.

voyage, n. Reise, -n f.

vulgar, adj. vulgär', ordinär'.

vulgarity, n. Ordinär'heit, -en f.

vulnerable, adj. verletz'bar; angreifbar.

W

wad, n. Bündel, - nt.; (of cotton) Wattebausch, ̈e m.; (roll) Rolle, -n f.

wade, vb. waten.

wag, 1. n. Spaßvogel, ̈ m. 2. vb. wedeln.

wage, 1. n. Lohn, ̈e m. 2. vb. (w. war) Krieg führen.

wager, 1. n. Wette, -n f. 2. vb. wetten.

wagon, n. Wagen - m.

wail, vb. wehklagen.

waist, n. Taille, -n f.

waistcoat, *n.* Weste, -n *f.*

wait, 1. *n.* Wartezeit, -en *f.* **2.** *vb.* warten; **(w. for)** warten auf.

waiter, *n.* Kellner, - *m.*

waitress, *n.* Kellnerin, -nen *f.*

waiver, *n.* Verzicht'leistung, -en *f.*

wake, 1. *n. (vigil)* Totenwache, -n *f.; (of boat)* Kielwasser *nt.* **2.** *vb. (tr.)* wecken; *(intr.)* erwa'chen.

walk, 1. *n.* Spazier'gang, ⁼e *m.* **2.** *vb.* gehen*, laufen*.

wall, *n.* Wand, ⁼e *f.; (of stone or brick)* Mauer, -n *f.*

wallcovering, *n.* Wandverkleidung *f.*

wallet, *n.* Brieftasche, -n *f.*

wallpaper, *n.* Tape'te, -n *f.*

walnut, *n.* Walnuß, ⁼sse *f.*

walrus, *n.* Walroß, -sse *nt.*

waltz, 1. *n.* Walzer, - *m.* **2.** *vb.* Walzer tanzen.

wander, *vb.* wandern; **(w. around)** umher'wandern.

want, 1. *n.* Mangel, ⁼ *m.; (needs)* Bedarf' *m.; (poverty)* Armut *f.* **2.** *vb.* wollen, wünschen.

war, *n.* Krieg, -e *m.*

ward, *n.* Mündel, - *nt.; (city)* Bezirk', -e *m.; (hospital, prison)* Abtei'lung, -en *f.*

ware, *n.* Ware, -n *f.*

warlike, *adj.* kriegerisch.

warm, 1. *adj.* warm (⁼). **2.** *vb.* wärmen.

warmth, *n.* Wärme *f.*

warn, *vb.* warnen.

warning, *n.* Warnung, -en *f.*

warp, *vb.* krümmen; *(fig.)* Verdre'hen, entstel'len.

warrant, 1. *n. (authorization)* Vollmacht, -en *f.; (writ of arrest)* Haftbefehl, -e *m.* **2.** *vb.* gewähr'leisten, garantie'ren.

warrior, *n.* Krieger, - *m.*

warship, *n.* Kriegsschiff, -e *nt.*

wash, 1. *n.* Wäsche, -n *f.* **2.** *vb.* waschen*.

wash-basin, *n.* Waschbecken, - *nt.*

washroom, *n.* Waschraum, ⁼e *m.*

wasp, *n.* Wespe, -n *f.*

waste, 1. *n.* Abfall, ⁼e *m.* **2.** *adj. (superfluous)* überflüssig; *(bare)* öde. **3.** *vb.* verschwen'den, vergeu'den.

watch, 1. *n. (guard)* Wache, -n *f.; (timepiece)* Uhr, -en *f.; (wrist w.)* Armbanduhr, -en *f.; (pocket w.)* Taschenuhr, -en *f.* **2.** *vb. (guard)* bewa'chen, passen auf; *(observe)* beob'achten, acht·geben; **(w. out)** auf·passen; **(w. out!)** Vorsicht!

watchful, *adj.* wachsam.

watchmaker, *n.* Uhrmacher, - *m.*

water, 1. *n.* Wasser, - *nt.* **2.** *vb.* wässern, begie'ßen*.

waterbed, *n.* Matratze mit Wasser gefüllt *f.*

waterfall, *n.* Wasserfall, ⁼e *m.*

waterproof, *adj.* wasserdicht.

wave, 1. *n.* Welle, -n *f.* **2.** *vb.* wellen, wogen; *(flag)* wehen; *(hand)* winken.

waver, *vb.* schwanken.

wax, 1. *n.* Wachs, -e *nt.* **2.** *vb.* wachsen; *(moon)* zu·nehmen*.

way, *n.* Weg, -e *m.*

we, *pron.* wir.

weak, *adj.* schwach (⁼).

weaken, *vb. (tr.)* schwächen; *(intr.)* schwach werden*.

weakness, *n.* Schwäche, -n *f.*

wealth, *n.* Reichtum, ⁼er *m.; (possessions)* Vermö'gen, - *nt.; (abundance)* Fülle *f.*

wealthy, *adj.* reich, vermö'gend.

weapon, *n.* Waffe, -n *f.*

wear, *vb.* tragen*, an·haben*, *(hat)* auf·haben*; **(w. out)** ab·tragen*, *(fig.)* erschöp'fen; **(w. away)** aus·höhlen.

weary, *adj.* müde, erschöpft'.

weasel, *n.* Wiesel, - *nt.*

weather, 1. *n.* Wetter *nt.* **2.** *vb. (fig.)* durch·stehen*.

weave, *vb.* weben(*).

weaver, *n.* Weber, - *m.*

web, *n.* Netz, -e *nt.*, Gewe'be *nt.; (spider w.)* Spinnennetz, - e *nt.*, Spinngewebe *nt.*

wedding, *n.* Hochzeit, -en *f.*

wedge, 1. *n.* Keil, -e *m.* **2.** *vb.* ein·klemmen.

Wednesday, *n.* Mittwoch, -e *m.*

weed, 1. *n.* Unkraut *nt.* **2.** *vb.* jäten.

week, *n.* Woche, -n *f.*

weekday, *n.* Wochentag, -e *m.*

week end, *n.* Wochenende, -n *nt.*

weekly, 1. *n.* Wochenschrift, - en *f.* **2.** *adj.* wöchentlich.

weep, *vb.* weinen.

weigh, *vb.* wiegen*; *(ponder)* wägen.

weight, *n.* Gewicht', -e *nt.; (burden)* Last, -en *f.*

weird, *adj.* unheimlich.

welcome, 1. *n.* Willkom'men *nt.* **2.** *vb.* bewill'kommnen, begrü'ßen. **3.** *adj.* willkom'men; **(you're w.)** bitte.

welfare, *n.* Wohlergehen *nt.; (social)* Wohlfahrt *f.*

well, 1. *n.* Brunnen, - *m.* **2.** *adv.* gut; *(health)* gesund' (⁼, -), wohl.

well-known, *adj.* bekannt'.

west, 1. *n.* Westen *m.* **2.** *adj.* westlich; West- *(cpds.).*

western, *adj.* westlich.

westward, *adv.* nach Westen.

wet, 1. *adj.* naß (⁼, -). **2.** *vb.* nässen, naß machen.

whale, *n.* Walfisch, -e *m.*

what, 1. *pron.* was. **2.** *adj.* welcher, -es, -e

whatever, 1. *pron.* was . . .

wheat, *n.* Weizen *m.*

wheel, 1. *n.* Rad, ⁼er *nt.* **2.** *vb.* rollen.

when, 1. *adv. (question)* wann. **2.** *conj. (once in the past)* als; *(future; whenever)* wenn; *(indirect question)* wann.

whence, *adv.* woher', von wo.

whenever, 1. *conj.* wenn. **2.** *adv.* wann . . . auch.

where, 1. *adv. (in what place)* wo; *(to what place)* wohin'; **(w. . . .** *from)* woher'.

wherever, *adv.* wo(hin) . . . auch.

whether, *conj.* ob.

which, *pron.&adj.* welcher, -es, -e.

whichever, *pron.&adj.* welcher, -es, -e . . . auch.

while, 1. *n.* Weile *f.* **2.** *conj.* während.

whim, *n.* Laune, -n *f.*

whip, 1. *n.* Peitsche, -n *f.* **2.** *vb.* peitschen, schlagen*.

whirl, *vb.* wirbeln.

whirlpool, *n.* Strudel, - *m.*

whirlwind, *n.* Wirbelwind, -e *m.*

whisker, *n.* Barthaar, -e *nt.*

whiskey, *n.* Whisky, -s *m.*

whisper, *vb.* flüstern.

whistle, 1. *n.* Flöte, -n *f.*, Pfeife, -n *f.* **2.** *vb.* flöten, pfeifen*.

white, *adj.* weiß.

who, *pron. (interrogative)* wer; *(relative)* der, das, die.

whoever, *pron.* wer . . . auch.

whole, 1. *n.* Ganz- *nt.* **2.** *adj.* ganz; *(unbroken)* heil.

wholesale, 1. *n.* Großhandel *m.* **2.** *adv.* en gros.

wholesome, *adj.* gesund' (⁼, -)

why, *adv.* warum', wieso', deshalb.

wicked, *adj.* böse, verrucht'.

wickedness, *n.* Verrucht'heit *f.*

wide, *adj.* weit; breit.

widen, *vb.* erwei'tern.

widespread, *adj.* weit verbrei'tet.

widow, *n.* Witwe, -n *f.*

widower, *n.* Witwer, - *m.*

width, *n.* Weite, -n *f.;* Breite, -n *f.*

wield, *vb.* handhaben*; *(fig.)* aus·üben.

wife, *n.* Frau, -en *f.*

wig, *n.* Perü'cke, -n *f.*

wild, *adj.* wild.

wilderness, *n.* Wildnis, -se *f.*

wildlife, *n.* Tiere und Pflanzen in freier Natur.

wilful, *adj.* eigensinnig; *(intentional)* vorsätzlich.

will, 1. *n.* Wille(n) *m.; (testament)* Testament', -e *nt.* **2.** *vb. (future)* werden*; (want to) wollen*; *(bequeath)* verma'chen.

willing, *adj.* willig; gewillt'; **(be w.)** wollen*.

willow, *n.* Weide, -n *f.*

wilt, *vb.* welken, verwel'ken.

wilted, *adj.* welk.

win, *vb.* gewin'nen*.

wind, 1. *n.* Wind, -e *m.* **2.** *vb.* winden*, wickeln; *(watch)* auf'ziehen*.

window, *n.* Fenster, - *nt.*

windy, *adj.* windig.

wine, *n.* Wein, -e *m.*

wing, *n.* Flügel, - *m.*

wink, *vb.* blinzeln.

winner, *n.* Gewin'ner, - *m.,* Sieger, - *m.*

winter, *n.* Winter, - *m.*

wintry, *adj.* winterlich.

wipe, *vb.* wischen.

wire, 1. *n.* Draht, ⁼e *m.; (telegram)* Telegramm', -e *nt.* **2.** *vb.* telegrafie'ren.

wire recorder, *n.* Drahtaufnahmegerät, -e *nt.*

wisdom, *n.* Weisheit, -en *f.*

wise, *adj.* weise, klug (⁻).

wish, 1. *n.* Wunsch, ⁼e *m.;* **(make a w.)** sich etwas wünschen. **2.** *vb.* wünschen.

wit, *n.* Verstand' *m.; (humor)* Humor' *m.*

witch, *n.* Hexe, -n *f.*

with, *prep.* mit.

withdraw, *vb.* zurück'-ziehen*.

wither, *vb.* verdor'ren.

withhold, *vb.* zurück'-halten*; ein'behalten*.

within, 1. *adv.* drinnen. **2.** *prep.* innerhalb.

without, 1. *adv.* draußen. **2.** *prep.* ohne.

witness, 1. *n.* Zeuge, -n, -n *m.* **2.** *vb.* Zeuge sein* von.

witty, *adj.* witzig; geistreich.

woe, *n.* Leid *nt.*

wolf, *n.* Wolf, ⁼e *m.*

woman, *n.* Frau, -en *f.*

womb, *n.* Mutterleib *m.*

wonder, 1. *n.* Wunder, - *nt.* **2.** *vb.* **(I w.)** ich möchte gern wissen.

wonderful, *adj.* wunderbar, herrlich.

woo, *vb.* umwer'ben*.

wood, *n.* Holz, ⁼er *nt.; (forest)* Wald, ⁼er *m.*

wooden, *adj.* hölzern.

wool, *n.* Wolle *f.*

woolen, *adj.* wollen.

word, *n. (single)* Wort, ⁼er *nt.; (connected)* Wort, -e *nt.*

wordy, *adj.* (fig.) langatmig.

work, 1. *n. (labor)* Arbeit, -en *f.; (thing produced)* Werk, -e *nt.; (gas w.s)* Gaswerke *pl.* **2.** *vb.* arbeiten; *(function)* gehen*, funktionie'ren.

worker, *n.* Arbeiter, - *m.*

workman, *n.* Arbeiter, - *m.*

world, *n.* Welt, -en *f.*

worldly, *adj.* weltlich.

worm, *n.* Wurm, ⁼er *m.*

worn-out, *adj.* abgenutzt.

worry, 1. *n.* Sorge, -n *f.* **2.** *vb.* sich sorgen.

worse, *adj.* schlimmer, schlechter.

worship, 1. *n.* Vereh'rung, -en *f.; (church)* Gottesdienst, -e *m.* **2.** *vb.* vereh'ren, an'beten.

worst, *adj.* schlimmst-, schlechtest-.

worth, 1. *n.* Wert, -e *m.* **2.** *adj.* wert.

worthless, *adj.* wertlos.

worthy, *adj.* würdig, ehrenwert.

wound, 1. *n.* Wunde, -n *f.* **2.** *vb.* verwun'den.

wrap, 1. *n.* Umhang, ⁼e *m.* **2.** *vb.* wickeln.

wrapping, *n.* Verpa'ckung, -en *f.*

wrath, *n.* Zorn *m.*

wreath, *n.* Kranz, ⁼e *m.*

wreck, 1. *n.* Wrack, -s *nt.* **2.** *vb.* demolie'ren, kaputt'machen.

wrench, 1. *n.* Ruck *m.; (tool)* Schraubenschlüssel, - *m.* **2.** *vb.* verren'ken.

wrestle, *vb.* ringen*.

wretched, *adj.* erbärm'lich.

wring, *vb. (hands)* ringen*; *(laundry)* wringen*; *(neck)* ab'drehen.

wrinkle, 1. *n.* Falte, -n *f.,* Runzel, -n *f.* **2.** *vb.* runzeln; *(cloth)* knittern.

wrist, *n.* Handgelenk, -e *nt.*

wrist-watch, *n.* Armbanduhr, -en *f.*

write, *vb.* schreiben*.

writer, *n.* Schreiber, - *m.; (by profession)* Schriftsteller, - *m.; (author)* Verfas'ser, - *m.*

writing, *n.* Schrift, -en *f.;* **(in w.)** schriftlich.

wrong, 1. *n.* Unrécht *nt.* **2.** *adj.* falsch; unrecht; **(be w.)** unrecht haben*; sich irren. **3.** *vb.* Unrecht tun*.

X

x-ray, 1. *n.* Röntgenaufnahme, -n *f.* **2.** *vb.* röntgen.

x-rays, *n.pl.* Röntgenstrahlen *pl.*

xylophone, *n.* Xylophon', -e *nt.*

Y

yacht, *n.* Jacht, -en *f.*

yard, *n. (garden)* Garten, ⁼ *m.; (railroad)* Verschie'bebahnhof, ⁼e *m.; (measure)* Yard, -s *nt.*

yarn, *n.* Garn, -e *nt.; (story)* Geschich'te, -n *f.*

yawn, *vb.* gähnen.

year, *n.* Jahr, -e *nt.*

yearly, *adj.* jährlich.

yearn, *vb.* sich sehnen.

yell, 1. *n.* Schrei, -e *m.* **2.** *vb.* schreien*, brüllen.

yellow, *adj.* gelb.

yes, *interj.* ja.

yesterday, *adv.* gestern.

yet, 1. *adv. (still)* noch; *(already)* schon; *(not y.)* noch nicht. **2.** *conj.* doch.

yield, 1. *n.* Ertrag', ⁼e *m.* **2.** *vb.* ein'bringen*; *(cede)* nach'geben*.

yoke, *n.* Joch, -e *nt.*

yolk, *n.* Eigelb, - *nt.*

you, *pron.* du, Sie.

young, *adj.* jung (⁻).

youth, 1. *n.* junger Mann, ⁼er *m.,* Jüngling, -e *m.; (young people; time of life)* Jugend, -en *f.*

youthful, *adj.* jugendlich.

Yugoslav, *n.* Jugosla'we, -n, -n *m.*

Yugoslavia, *n.* Jugosla'wien *nt.*

Yugoslavian, 1. *n.* Jugosla'we, -n, -n *m.* **2.** *adj.* jugosla'wisch.

Z

zap, *vb. (lit.)* töten; *(slang)* fertig machen, zerschmettern.

zeal, *n.* Eifer *m.*

zebra, *n.* Zebra, -s *nt.*

zero, *n.* Null, -en *f.*

zest, *n. (zeal)* Eifer *m.; (relish)* Genuß' *m.*

zinc, *n.* Zink *nt.*

zip code, *n.* Postleitzahl, -en *f.*

zipper, *n.* Reißverschluß, ⁼sse *m.*

zone, *n.* Zone, -n *f.*

zoo, *n.* Zoo, -s *m.*

zoological, *adj.* zoolo'gisch.

zoology, *n.* Zoologie' *f.*

Authoritative Guides
to Better
Self-Expression

Call toll free 1-800-733-3000 to order by phone and use your major credit card. Or use this coupon to order by mail.

THE WORD-A-DAY VOCABULARY BUILDER,
Berger Evans with Jess Stein (Ed.)   345-30610-4   2.95
In just five minutes a day anyone can enlarge his or her vocabulary and learn to speak and write more clearly and persuasively. Never before available in mass market paperback. This is an extremely effective guide to developing a technique that is natural, practical, and habit-forming! For students, professors, business people—everyone!

1,000 MOST IMPORTANT WORDS,
Norman W. Schur   345-29863-2   3.50
Available for the first time in mass market paperback, this guide helps us unlock our "passive" vocabularies and develop a keener appreciation of the richness of our language. Fun and easy to use!

THE RANDOM HOUSE BASIC SPELLER/DIVIDER
Editor: Jess Stein   345-29255-5   3.95
More than 50,000 entries, more than any comparable book. Includes names of nations, states, famous people, lists of common abbreviations, and a Basic Manual of Style.

THE RANDOM HOUSE BASIC DICTIONARY OF SYNONYMS AND ANTONYMS, Editor: Laurence Urdang   345-29712-1   3.50
When the "nearly right" word won't do, this handy volume provides over 80,000 synonyms and antonyms, with all entries easy to locate in one alphabetical list.

Name _____

Address _____

City _____ State _____ Zip _____

Please send me the BALLANTINE BOOKS I have checked above.

I am enclosing $ _____
plus
Postage & handling* $ _____
Sales tax (where applicable) $ _____
Total amount enclosed $ _____

*Add $2 for the first book and 50¢ for each additional book.

Send check or money order (no cash or CODs) to:
Ballantine Mall Sales, 400 Hahn Road, Westminster, MD 21157.

Prices and numbers subject to change without notice.
Valid in the U.S. only.
All orders subject to availability.   REFERENCE1